Independent Central Banks and Economic Performance

The International Library of Critical Writings in Economics

Series Editor: Mark Blaug

Professor Emeritus, University of London
Professor Emeritus, University of Buckingham
Visiting Professor, University of Exeter

This series is an essential reference source for students, researchers and lecturers in economics. It presents by theme a selection of the most important articles across the entire spectrum of economics. Each volume has been prepared by a leading specialist who has written an authoritative introduction to the literature included.

A full list of published and future titles in this series is printed at the end of this volume.

Wherever possible, the articles in these volumes have been reproduced as originally published using facsimile reproduction, inclusive of footnotes and pagination to facilitate ease of reference.

For a list of all Edward Elgar published titles visit our site on the World Wide Web at
http://www.e-elgar.co.uk

Independent Central Banks and Economic Performance

Edited by

Sylvester C.W. Eijffinger

Professor of Economics at the College of Europe, Bruges, Belgium, Humboldt University of Berlin, Germany, Tilburg University, The Netherlands and Fellow of the CentER of Economic Research, Tilburg University, The Netherlands

THE INTERNATIONAL LIBRARY OF CRITICAL WRITINGS IN ECONOMICS

An Elgar Reference Collection
Cheltenham, UK • Lyme, US

Published by
Edward Elgar Publishing Limited
8 Lansdown Place
Cheltenham
Glos GL50 2HU
UK

Edward Elgar Publishing, Inc.
1 Pinnacle Hill Road
Lyme
NH 03768
US

A catalogue record for this book is available from the British Library.

Library of Congress Cataloguing-in-Publication Data
Independent central banks and economic performance / edited by
Sylvester C.W. Eijffinger.
(International library of critical writings in
financial economics : 82) (An Elgar reference collection)
Includes bibliographical references.
ISBN 1-85898-447-5
1. Banks and banking, Central. 2. Monetary policy.
I. Eijffinger, Sylvester C.W. II. Series. III. Series: An Elgar
reference collection.
HG1811.I46 1997
332.1'1—dc21 97–5354
CIP

Printed and bound in Great Britain by Bookcraft (Bath) Ltd

ISBN 1 85898 447 5

Contents

Acknowledgements

The editor and publishers wish to thank the authors and the following publishers who have kindly given permission for the use of copyright material.

American Economic Association for articles: Susanne Lohmann (1992), 'Optimal Commitment in Monetary Policy: Credibility versus Flexibility', *American Economic Review*, **82** (1), March, 273–86; Carl E. Walsh (1995), 'Optimal Contracts for Central Bankers', *American Economic Review*, **85** (1), March, 150–67.

Banca Nazionale del Lavoro Quarterly Review for articles: Jakob De Haan and Jan Egbert Sturm (1992), 'The Case for Central Bank Independence', *Banca Nazionale del Lavoro Quarterly Review*, **XLV** (182), September, 305–27; Sylvester Eijffinger and Eric Schaling (1993), 'Central Bank Independence in Twelve Industrial Countries', *Banca Nazionale del Lavoro Quarterly Review*, **XLVI** (184), March, 49–70; Sylvester Eijffinger and Martijn Van Keulen (1995), 'Central Bank Independence in Another Eleven Countries', *Banca Nazionale del Lavoro Quarterly Review*, **XLVIII** (192), March, 39–83; Thomas F. Cargill (1995), 'The Statistical Association Between Central Bank Independence and Inflation', *Banca Nazionale del Lavoro Quarterly Review*, **XLVIII** (193), June, 159–72.

Blackwell Publishers Ltd for articles: Alberto Alesina (1989), 'Politics and Business Cycles in Industrial Democracies', *Economic Policy*, **8**, April, 55–98; Vittorio Grilli, Donato Masciandaro and Guido Tabellini (1991), 'Political and Monetary Institutions and Public Financial Policies in the Industrial Countries', *Economic Policy*, **13**, October 341–92.

Cuadernos de Economía for article: Alex Cukierman (1993), 'Central Bank Independence, Political Influence and Macroeconomic Performance: A Survey of Recent Developments', *Cuadernos de Economía*, **30** (91), December, 271–91.

Guy Debelle and Stanley Fischer for their own excerpt: (1994), 'How Independent Should a Central Bank Be?', in Jeffrey C. Fuhrer (ed.), *Goals, Guidelines, and Constraints Facing Monetary Policymakers*, Federal Reserve Bank of Boston Conference Series No. 38, 195–221.

Sylvester Eijffinger and Eric Schaling for their own articles: (1993), 'Central Bank Independence: Theory and Evidence', *CentER Discussion Paper Series*, **9325**, May, 1–32; (1995), 'Optimal Commitment in an Open Economy: Credibility vs Flexibility', *Bank of England Working Paper Series*, **41**, December, 5–48.

Elsevier Science B.V. for article and excerpt: Robert J. Barro and David B. Gordon (1983), 'Rules, Discretion and Reputation in a Model of Monetary Policy', *Journal of Monetary*

Economics, **12**, 101–21; Alex Cukierman, Pantelis Kalaitzidakis, Lawrence H. Summers and Steven B. Webb (1993), 'Central Bank Independence, Growth, Investment, and Real Rates', in Allan H. Meltzer and Charles I. Plosser (eds), *Carnegie-Rochester Conference Series on Public Policy*, **39**, December, 95–140.

Kluwer Academic Publishers B.V. for articles and excerpt: Manfred J.M. Neumann (1991), 'Precommitment by Central Bank Independence', *Open Economies Review*, **2**, 95–112; Alex Cukierman (1994), 'Commitment Through Delegation, Political Influence and Central Bank Independence', in J. Onno De Beaufort Wijnholds, Sylvester C.W. Eijffinger and Lex H. Hoogduin (eds), *A Framework for Monetary Stability*, 55–74; Jakob De Haan and Gert Jan Van 't Hag (1995), 'Variation in Central Bank Independence Across Countries: Some Provisional Empirical Evidence', *Public Choice*, **85**, 335–51.

M.I.T. Press Journals and the President and Fellows of Harvard College and the Massachusetts Institute of Technology for article: Kenneth Rogoff (1985), 'The Optimal Degree of Commitment to an Intermediate Monetary Target', *Quarterly Journal of Economics*, **C**, November, 1169–89.

Ohio State University Press for article: Alberto Alesina and Lawrence H. Summers (1993), 'Central Bank Independence and Macroeconomic Performance: Some Comparative Evidence', *Journal of Money, Credit and Banking*, **25** (2), May, 151–62.

Oxford University Press for excerpt: Adam S. Posen (1993), 'Why Central Bank Independence Does Not Cause Low Inflation: There Is No Institutional Fix for Politics', in Richard O'Brien (ed.), *Finance and the International Economy: 7: The Amex Bank Review Prize Essays*, Chapter 3, 41–65.

University of Chicago Press for article: Finn E. Kydland and Edward C. Prescott (1977), 'Rules Rather than Discretion: The Inconsistency of Optimal Plans', *Journal of Political Economy*, **85** (3), June, 473–91.

World Bank for articles: Alex Cukierman, Steven B. Webb and Bilin Neyapti (1992), 'Measuring the Independence of Central Banks and its Effect on Policy Outcomes', *World Bank Economic Review*, **6** (3), September, 353–98; Alex Cukierman and Steven B. Webb (1995), 'Political Influence on the Central Bank: International Evidence', *World Bank Economic Review*, **9** (3), September, 397–423.

Every effort has been made to trace all the copyright holders but if any have been inadvertently overlooked the publishers will be pleased to make the necessary arrangement at the first opportunity.

In addition the publishers wish to thank the Library of the London School of Economics and Political Science and the Marshall Library of Economics, Cambridge University for their assistance in obtaining these articles.

Introduction

Sylvester C.W. Eijffinger

1. Central Bank Independence: Definition and Aspects

In recent years academics and policymakers have shown increasing interest in the independence of central banks with respect to the formulation of monetary policy. It is often argued that a high level of central bank independence coupled with some explicit mandate for the central bank to aim for price stability constitute important institutional devices to maintain price stability. Indeed, various countries have recently upgraded central bank independence to raise their commitment to price stability for various reasons. First, the breakdown of other institutions designed to safeguard price stability such as the Bretton Woods system and more recently the European Monetary System led countries to search for alternatives. Second, the position of the Bundesbank is often mentioned as an example par excellence that central bank independence can function as an effective device to assure price stability. The German central bank is relatively autonomous; Germany has, at the same time, one of the best post-World War II inflation records among OECD countries. Third, the Maastricht Treaty stipulates an independent central bank as a precondition for membership in the European Economic and Monetary Union (EMU). Price stability will be the major objective of the future European System of Central Banks (ESCB), which consists of the European Central Bank (ECB) and the national central banks of all Member States of the European Union. Fourth, after recent successful stabilization periods, policymakers in many Latin American countries are looking for institutional arrangements capable of reducing the likelihood of a return of high and persistent inflation. Fifth, the creation of an independent central bank in many former socialist countries is part of the more general attempt of these countries to create the institutional framework needed for the orderly functioning of a market economy.

No doubt, the numerous recent theoretical and empirical studies suggesting that inflation and central bank independence are negatively related have also been an important motivation for enhancing central bank independence.[1] It is noteworthy that most authors provide no clear definition of central bank independence. Central bank autonomy refers to a relationship between the central bank and the government, which can be compared to the relationship between the judiciary and government. The judiciary can rule only on the basis of laws provided by the legislature, and it can be forced to rule differently only through a change in the law. In fact, central bank independence refers to three areas in which the influence of government must be excluded or drastically curtailed[2]:

- independence in personnel matters;
- financial autonomy;
- policy independence.

In practice, it is not feasible to exclude government influence completely when appointments are made to such an important public institution. So *personnel independence* refers to the influence that government has in appointment procedures. It can be discerned on the basis of criteria such as governmental representation in the governing body of the central bank, appointment procedures, term of office and dismissal of the governing board of the bank.

Furthermore, the government can influence the central bank if the government is able to finance its expenditure either directly or indirectly via central bank credits. In that case there is no *financial independence*. Direct access to central bank credits implies that monetary policy is subordinated to fiscal policy. Indirect access may result if the central bank is cashier to the government or if it handles the management of government debt.

Finally, *policy independence* is related to the manœuvering room given to the central bank in the formulation and execution of monetary policy. As pointed out by Debelle and Fischer (1994) in Chapter 17, it may be useful to distinguish between goal independence and instrument independence. With respect to goal independence, two related issues are important: the scope for the central bank to exercise its own discretion, and whether the central bank has monetary stability as its primary goal. If the central bank has been assigned various goals, such as low inflation and low unemployment, it has been accorded the greatest possible scope for discretion. In that case the central bank has *goal independence* since it is free to set the final goals of monetary policy. It could, for instance, decide that price stability is less important than output stability, and act accordingly. The central bank's discretionary powers may be restricted by giving it either general or specific objectives with respect to price stability. Finally, a central bank must wield effective instruments in order to defend its objective(s). A bank that has *instrument independence* is free to choose the means by which it seeks to achieve its goals. Clearly, if government approval is required of the central bank's use of policy instruments, no instrument independence exists. Nowadays, the Reserve Bank of New Zealand, whose goal is precisely described in a contract with the government, has no goal independence; it does, however, have instrument independence, since it chooses the method by which it tries to achieve this goal.

2. Theoretical Foundations of Central Bank Independence

Many observers believe that countries with an independent central bank have lower levels of inflation than do countries with a central bank that comes under direct control of the government. Why would central bank independence, *ceteris paribus*, yield lower rates of inflation? The literature provides three answers to this question: public choice arguments, the analysis of Sargent and Wallace (1981) and arguments that are based on the time inconsistency problem of monetary policy.[3] The most prominent argument for central bank independence is based on the *time inconsistency problem* as analyzed by Kydland and Prescott (1977) and Barro and Gordon (1983) in Chapters 1 and 2, respectively. Dynamic inconsistency arises when the best plan currently made for some future period is no longer optimal when that period actually starts.

Various models have been based upon this dynamic inconsistency approach, e.g. Rogoff (1985), Neumann (1991), Lohmann (1992), and Eijffinger and Schaling (1993b) in Chapters 3, 4, 5 and 15, respectively.

Barro and Gordon (1983) conclude that the best solution for the time inconsistency problem consists of the introduction of fixed rules in monetary policy, i.e. the authorities commit themselves to certain policy rules. Once uncertainty is introduced and the level of output is affected by shocks, the case becomes one for a feedback rule, in which monetary policy optimally responds to shocks. The problem with rules, however, is the absence of some higher authority to enforce a commitment. Handing over authority to the central bank by political authorities may help here, since it can be regarded as an act of partial commitment. By delegating some of their authority to a relatively apolitical institution, politicians accept certain restrictions on their future freedom of action.

The degree of central bank independence, of course, plays a meaningful role only if the central bank puts a different emphasis on alternative policy objectives than does the government. The literature points to two main differences.[4] One relates to possible differences between the rate of time preference of political authorities and that of central banks. For various reasons, central banks are often more conservative and tend to take a longer view of the policy process than do politicians. The other difference concerns the subjective weights in the objective function of the central bank and that of the government. It is often assumed that central bankers are relatively more concerned about inflation than about other policy goals such as achieving high employment levels and adequate government revenues. If monetary policy is set at the discretion of a conservative central banker, a lower average time-consistent inflation rate will result. The foregoing analysis makes it clear that this argument for central bank independence is primarily related to policy independence.

The best way to illustrate the argument is to present a 'stripped' version of Rogoff's model. In the Rogoff (1985) model in Chapter 3, society can sometimes make itself better off by appointing a central banker who does not share the social objective function, but instead places a higher weight on price stability relative to output stabilization. In this simplified version, output is given by equation (1), in which the natural level of output is put at zero and the parameters at one.

$$y_t = \pi_t - \pi_t^e + u_t \tag{1}$$

where u_t is a random shock. The timing of events in the Rogoff model is as follows: first π_t^e is set (nominal wage contracts are signed), then the shock u_t occurs, and finally the central banker sets π_t.

Society's loss function is given by:

$$L_t = \frac{1}{2}\pi_t^2 + \frac{\chi}{2}(y_t - \hat{y}_t)^2 \tag{2}$$

where the weight on output stabilization $\chi > 0$ and $\hat{y} > 0$, so that the desired level of output, $\hat{y}$, is above the natural level. Rogoff shows that it is optimal for society to choose an independent (conservative) central banker who assigns a higher weight to price stability in his loss function:

$$I_t = \frac{1+\varepsilon}{2}\pi_t^2 + \frac{\chi}{2}(y_t - \hat{y}_t)^2 \tag{3}$$

where ε, the additional weight on the inflation goal, lies between zero and infinity ($0 < \varepsilon < \infty$).

Substituting and taking first-order conditions with respect to π_t and solving for rational expectations, we obtain:

$$\pi_t = \frac{\chi}{1+\varepsilon}\hat{y} - \frac{\chi}{1+\varepsilon+\chi}\mu_t \tag{4}$$

Policy rule (4) shows that the introduction of a conservative central banker ($\varepsilon > 0$) leads to a lower inflationary bias and a lower variance of inflation. The variance of output is, however, an increasing function of the conservativeness of the central banker. So there is a trade off between credibility and flexibility in the Rogoff model. It can be shown that the optimal value for ε, in terms of social loss function (2), is positive but finite. This implies that it is optimal for society to appoint a conservative central banker.

Rogoff (1985) makes the crucial assumption, that the central banker is completely independent and cannot be overridden *ex post*, when the inflationary expectations π_t^e have been set and the policy is to be carried out. This can lead to large losses for society when extreme productivity shocks u_t occur. Lohmann (1992) in Chapter 5 introduces the possibility to override the central banker at a strictly positive but *finite* cost. Therefore, society's loss function changes to:

$$L_t^l = \frac{1}{2}\pi_t^2 + \frac{\chi}{2}(y_t - \hat{y}_t)^2 + \delta c \tag{5}$$

where δ is a dummy that takes on the value of 1 when the central bank is overridden and 0 otherwise; and c is a cost that society incurs when the central bank is overridden. The central bank's loss function (3) stays the same.

The timing of events in the Lohmann (1992) model is as follows: in the first stage the central banker's additional weight ε on the inflation goal is chosen as well as the cost c of overriding the central banker. Then the inflation expectations are set. In the third stage the productivity shock realizes. Then the central banker sets the inflation rate, which is either accepted or not. If it is not accepted, society overrides the central banker, incurs the cost c and resets the inflation rate. Finally, inflation and output realize. In equilibrium, the central banker will not be overridden. In the case of an extreme productivity shock he will set the inflation rate so that society is indifferent between overriding or not. Rogoff's model is a special case of Lohmann's, where $c = \infty$. Lohmann shows that the optimal central bank institution is characterized by $0 < \varepsilon^* < \infty$ and $0 < c^* < \infty$.

An important result from the Rogoff model is that the reduction in the equilibrium inflation rate resulting after appointing a conservative and independent central banker generally comes at the expense of greater output variability from supply shocks, since the central banker offsets output shocks to a lesser extent than would governments. Nevertheless, gains from lower inflation exceed losses due to decreased stability. Therefore, on net, society is made better off by appointing a conservative central banker. It is, however, not optimal in the Rogoff model to appoint a central banker whose only concern is low and stable inflation.

Apart from a legislative approach to create by law an independent central bank and to mandate it, also by law, to direct its policies towards achieving price stability, other mechanisms have been suggested to overcome the incentive problems of monetary policy. This so-called contracting approach regards design of monetary institutions as one that involves structuring a contract between the central bank and the government. The optimal contract is an application of ideas from the principal-agent literature. In this application government is viewed as the principal and the central bank as the agent. The principal signs a contract with the agent according to which the bank is subject to an *ex post* penalty schedule that is linear in inflation. The nature of the contract will affect, according to Walsh (1995) in Chapter 6, the incentives facing the bank and will, thereby, affect monetary policy. Persson and Tabellini (1993) suggest a targeting approach, in which the political principals of the central bank impose an explicit inflation target and make the central bank leadership explicitly accountable for its success in meeting this target. Such a system exists since 1989 in New Zealand, where the governor of the Reserve Bank can, under certain circumstances, be dismissed if the inflation rate exceeds two percent.[5]

It is interesting to note that it follows from their analysis that the optimal contract with the central bank implies no loss in terms of stabilization policy. As pointed out above, this result contrasts with the outcomes of most models where monetary policy is delegated to an independent central bank, where credibility is increased at the expense of an optimal output stabilization policy. Walsh (1995) shows that the optimal central bank contract may serve to eliminate the inflation bias, while still preserving the advantages of stabilization. This conclusion holds even if the central bank has private information. From the foregoing analysis, it will be clear that the contracting approach is clearly related to instrument independence, but not to goal independence.

3. Measures of Central Bank Independence

It is rather difficult to measure the degree of legal independence of various central banks, let alone the degree of their actual independence of the government. Cukierman (1992) has pointed out that actual, as opposed to formal independence, hinges not only on legislation, but also on a myriad of other factors such as informal arrangements with government, the quality of the personnel of the bank, and the personal characteristics of key individuals in the bank. Obviously, these other factors are virtually impossible to quantify. Most of the existing research has, therefore, focused on legal independence and is restricted to industrial countries.

Table 1 presents four measures of central bank independence, as developed by Alesina (1989), Grilli, Masciandaro and Tabellini (1991), Cukierman, Webb and Neyapti (1992), Eijffinger and Schaling (1993a) and Eijffinger and Van Keulen (1995) in the Chapters 7, 8, 9, 10 and 12, respectively and Cukierman (1992). For the various indices the following rule applies: the higher the score, the more independent the central bank is. The measures of Alesina and Eijffinger-Schaling range from 1 to 4, and from 1 to 5, respectively. The index of Grilli, Masciandaro and Tabellini is the total of their indicators for political and economic independence (see below for further details). The lowest actual score is 3, the highest value amounts to 13. The value for their index of political independence is shown in parentheses. This measure ranges between 0 to 6. The index of Cukierman varies between 0 and 1.

Table 1. Legal indices for central bank independence

	Alesina	Grilli, Masciandaro and Tabellini[a]	Eijffinger-Schaling	Cukierman[c]
Australia	1	9 (3)	1	0.31
Austria	–	9 (3)	3[b]	0.58
Belgium	2	7 (1)	3	0.19
Canada	2	11 (4)	1	0.46
Denmark	2	8 (3)	4[b]	0.47
Finland	2	–	3[b]	0.27
France	2	7 (2)	2	0.28
Germany	4	13 (6)	5	0.66
Greece	–	4 (2)	–	0.51
Iceland	–	–	–	0.36
Ireland	–	7 (3)	–	0.39
Italy	1.5	5 (4)	2	0.22
Japan	3	6 (1)	3	0.16
Netherlands	2	10 (6)	4	0.42
New Zealand	1	3 (0)	3[b]	0.27
Norway	2	–	2[b]	0.14
Portugal	–	3 (1)	2[b]	–
Spain	1	5 (2)	3[b]	0.21
Sweden	2	–	2	0.27
Switzerland	4	12 (5)	5	0.68
United Kingdom	2	6 (1)	2	0.31
United States	3	12 (5)	3	0.51

Notes:

[a] The measure of Grilli, Masciandaro and Tabellini is the index for political and economic independence. Their index for political independence is shown in parentheses.

[b] These extensions of the Eijffinger-Schaling index are based upon Eijffinger and Van Keulen (1995). The ranking of these countries refers to relatively new central bank laws (adjusted during the last ten years), except for Denmark.

[c] The Cukierman legal index of central bank independence (LVAU) is based on Cukierman (1992) and Cukierman, Webb and Neyapti (1992).

The pioneering attempt to codify legal central bank independence of Bade and Parkin (1988) was extended by Alesina (1989) in Chapter 7.[6] This index focuses on questions such as: does the central bank have final authority over monetary policy?; are there government officials on the governing board of the bank? and are more than half of the board members appointed by government?

Grilli, Masciandaro and Tabellini (1991) in Chapter 8 present indices of political and economic independence. The first part focuses on appointment procedures for board officials, the length of their term to office and the existence of the statutory requirement to pursue monetary stability. The economic independence indicator focuses on the extent to which the central bank is free from government influence in implementing monetary policy. Generally the total score on the political and economic independence is employed as indicator for legal central bank independence.

Cukierman (1992) and Cukierman, Webb and Neyapti (1992) in Chapter 9 provide an index which is aggregated from sixteen basic legal characteristics of central bank charters which are grouped into four clusters: 1. the appointment, dismissal and legal term of office of the governor of the central bank; 2. the institutional location of the final authority for monetary policy and procedures for resolution of conflicts between the government and the bank; 3. the importance of price stability in comparison to other objectives; 4. the stringency and universality of limitations on the ability of government to borrow from the central bank.

Eijffinger and Schaling (1993) and Eijffinger and Van Keulen (1995) in Chapters 10 and 12 have constructed an index which is based on three issues: the location of the final responsibility for monetary policy, the absence or presence of a government official on the board of the central bank and the fraction of board appointees made by government. Central bank laws in which the central bank is final authority get a double score in this index.

Cukierman (1992) and Cukierman, Webb and Neyapti (1992) have also developed a yardstick for central bank autonomy based on the actual average term of office of central bank governors in different countries during the period 1950–89. This indicator is based on the presumption that, at least above some threshold, a higher turnover of central bank governors indicates a lower level of independence. The idea behind this measure is that, even if the central bank law is quite explicit, it may not be operational if a different tradition has precedence. A striking example is Argentina, where the legal term of office of the central bank governor is four years, but where there it is also an informal tradition that the governor will resign whenever there is change of government, or even a new finance minister. Consequently, the actual average term of office of the governor of the central bank amounted to only ten months during the 1980s. This example suggests that the turnover rate of central bank governors may be a good indicator for the degree of central bank autonomy. Table 2 presents the average turnover rate of central bank governors for 55 countries during the 40 years ending in 1989, for both OECD countries and some developing countries. From Table 2 two conclusions can be drawn. First, the turnover rate differs greatly across countries and varies between 0.03 (Iceland) and 0.93 (Argentina). Second, the average and standard deviation of the turnover rate in developing countries are much higher than the corresponding measures for OECD countries. The average turnover rate in the industrial countries amounts to 0.13; the average for the developing countries is 0.28. The highest turnover rate in the OECD countries (excluding Turkey) is 0.2 for Spain and Japan. So, this measure of central bank autonomy hardly discriminates between central banks of industrialized countries.

Cukierman and Webb (1995) in Chapter 22 have gone one step further. They argue that the frequency of central bank governor transfers reflect both the frequency of political change (e.g. regimes shifts, or a new head of government) and the fraction of political changes that are followed by changes of the central bank governor. They therefore develop an indicator of the *political vulnerability* of the central bank, which is defined as the fraction of political transitions that are followed promptly (i.e. within six months) by a replacement of the central bank governor. For the period 1950–89 they calculate that the average political vulnerability index amounts to 0.24. For industrial countries it is 0.10, while the index for developing countries is 0.34. Again, one should be careful in interpreting this index.

Table 2. The turnover rate of central bank governors, 1950–1989

OECD Countries:		Developing Countries:	
Belgium	0.13	Argentina	0.93
Canada	0.10	Bahamas	0.19
Denmark	0.05	Barbados	0.11
Finland	0.13	Botswana	0.41
France	0.15	Chili	0.45
Germany	0.10	Colombia	0.20
Greece	0.18	Costa Rica	0.58
Iceland	0.03	Egypt	0.31
Ireland	0.15	Ethiopia	0.20
Italy	0.08	Ghana	0.28
Japan	0.20	Honduras	0.13
Luxembourg	0.08	India	0.33
Netherlands	0.05	Israel	0.14
New Zealand	0.15	Kenya	0.17
Norway	0.08	Lebanon	0.19
Spain	0.20	Malaysia	0.13
Sweden	0.15	Malta	0.28
Switzerland	0.13	Mexico	0.15
Turkey	0.40	Nigeria	0.19
United Kingdom	0.10	Panama	0.24
United States	0.13	Peru	0.33
		Philippines	0.13
		Singapore	0.37
		South Africa	0.10
		South Korea	0.43
		Tanzania	0.13
		Thailand	0.20
		Uganda	0.34
		Uruguay	0.38
		Venezuela	0.30
		Zaire	0.23
		Zambia	0.38
		Zimbabwe	0.15
Average:	0.13	Average:	0.28
Standard deviation:	0.08	Standard deviation:	0.17

Source: Cukierman (1992) and Cukierman, Webb and Neyapti (1992); the (previously) communist countries are not included.

It follows from the foregoing analysis that existing indices of central bank independence are often incomplete and noisy indicators of actual independence. However, this does not mean that they are uninformative. It does imply that their use should be supplemented by judgement in light of the problem under consideration. In particular some indices are more appropriate for some purposes than for others. According to Cukierman (1993) in Chapter 11, legal independence measures may be a better proxy for actual independence in industrial countries than in developing countries. In some cases, various proxies may be usefully combined to get a fuller picture, since they capture different aspects of central bank independence. Legal measures of central bank independence are more likely to be exogenous with respect to the economy. However, due to little variance over time, they have poor explanatory power for developments in economic variables within countries. Therefore, most empirical studies on the consequences of central bank independence are of a cross-section nature.

4. Empirical Evidence on Central Bank Independence

The well-known inverse relationship between central bank independence and the level of inflation is supported by most empirical studies such as De Haan and Sturm (1992), Alesina and Summers (1993), and Eijffinger and Schaling (1993b) in the Chapters 13, 14 and 15, respectively. An exception is Cargill (1995) in Chapter 18, who argues that this statistical association is not robust and depends on countries and time periods included and on the regression specification. However, this argument is unconvincing, as Cargill uses only one measure of central bank independence. Furthermore, one would expect different results under fixed and under floating exchange rate regimes. Under the Bretton Woods system of fixed exchange rates, countries were committed to an exchange rate target and had little room to conduct an autonomous domestic monetary policy. Thus, the relation between central bank independence and inflation is likely to be much less straightforward before 1973. Regression analysis by Grilli, Masciandaro and Tabellini (1991), De Haan and Sturm (1992), and Eijffinger and Schaling (1993b) supports this view. Indeed, one could argue that if no evidence of a relationship between independence and inflation is found in the Bretton Woods period, while there exists such a link for the post-Bretton Woods era, this would strengthen the argument that central bank independence is a primary determinant of a country's inflation performance.

Despite the overwhelming evidence in support of a negative relationship between central bank independence and inflation, it should, however, be noted that a negative correlation does not necessarily imply causation. The correlation between both variables could be explained by a third factor, e.g. the culture and tradition of monetary stability in a country, explaining both an independent central bank and low inflation. Similarly, there may exist a two-way causality between inflation and central bank independence. It is likely that less independence contributes to higher inflation. However, high inflation may also affect independence. As will be explained in more detail in the following section, it can be argued that high inflation leads to more or less central bank independence. On the one hand, high inflation may lead to political pressure for low inflation, while on the other hand it may encourage processes that make it easier for the government to influence monetary policy, thereby reducing actual independence. Most studies do not address this issue of two-way causality.

Most empirical studies consist of simple cross-section estimates in which the average inflation rate is 'explained' by some measure of central bank independence. However, some authors include other explanatory variables as well. Grilli, Masciandaro and Tabellini (1991) in Chapter 8 and De Haan and Sturm (1992) in Chapter 13 include some indicators for political instability. This does not rob the coefficients of the central bank independence indicators of their significance.

Although many empirical studies examine the relationship between central bank independence and inflation, only two studies try to differentiate between the various aspects of central bank autonomy. Debelle and Fischer (1994) in Chapter 17 decompose the independence measure of Grilli, Masciandaro and Tabellini (1991) into goal independence, instrument independence, and personnel independence. They conclude that lack of goal independence (i.e. a mandate for price stability) and instrument independence are most closely tied to inflation performance, while personnel independence is not significantly related to inflation.

The main conclusion from empirical studies on the relationship between central bank autonomy and inflation is that central bank independence is inversely related to the level of inflation in both developed and developing countries. However, the independence measures used to reach this conclusion differ between the two groups of countries. While legal independence is a good proxy for actual autonomy in industrial countries, proxies such as the turnover rate of the central bank governor or political vulnerability of the central bank should be used for LDCs.

The foregoing analysis put forward two arguments why central bank independence may stimulate economic growth in the longer run. These arguments are (1) less uncertainty about inflation, and (2) the better functioning of the price mechanism. Empirical research by Grimes (1991) and Barro (1995) suggests that inflation reduces economic growth.[7] This may be explained by the positive correlation between the level and variability of inflation. Greater variation in the rate of inflation can imply increasing uncertainty about inflation and may, thereby, lead to lower economic growth. This relationship between inflation variability and economic growth is, however, not supported by most studies.

Various studies, like De Haan and Sturm (1992), Alesina and Summers (1993), Eijffinger and Schaling (1993b), Cukierman, Kalaitzidakis, Summers and Webb (1993) in Chapters 13, 14, 15 and 16 respectively, have examined directly whether central bank independence is related to economic growth. Despite the fact that a high degree of central bank independence is associated with lower inflation in the long run, a policy of disinflation is apparently not associated with high costs or great benefits in terms of long-run economic growth. Indeed, it is tempting to conclude that the absence of a long-run tradeoff between inflation and growth implies that the establishment of central bank independence is a free lunch. On the other hand, recall that price stability is, in general, regarded as an essential condition for sustainable economic growth and that, accordingly, central bank independence would lead to a higher level of economic growth. From this point of view, lack of a significant, positive relation between growth and independence would, therefore, be rather disappointing. There are studies, however, that report a positive relationship between central bank autonomy and economic growth. Cukierman, Kalaitzidakis, Summers and Webb (1993) in Chapter 16, find that economic growth in the industrial countries is not correlated with central bank independence, even after corrections have been made for other factors that may influence economic growth. Using the frequency of central bank president changes as a proxy for independence, they find, however, a positive relation between this variable and economic growth in developing countries.

A next question is, of course, whether a relationship exists between central bank independence and the variation of economic growth. Alesina and Summers (1993) in Chapter 14 argue that an autonomous central bank will be less inclined to conduct a 'stop-go' policy, which may limit fluctuations in economic growth. It is shown that a higher degree of central bank independence is generally not associated with greater variation of real economic growth rates.

The net effect of independence on the costs of disinflation is an empirical question. Debelle and Fischer (1994) in Chapter 17 compare the output costs of recessions in Germany and the United States. It appears that the output cost of German recessions are similar to those of US recessions. The sacrifice ratio (output lost due to the reduction of inflation) in Germany is larger than that in the US for all recent recessions, despite the widely assumed 'credibility bonus' of the Bundesbank. Debelle and Fischer also report a positive and significant relationship between the GMT index of central bank independence and output losses. As Debelle and Fischer argue, this suggests that no credibility bonus exists in the labour markets for more independent central banks: they have to prove their toughness by continually being tough.

What should we make of the preceding review of empirical studies on the relationship between central bank independence and macroeconomic variables, such as inflation and growth? Is it true, as Grilli, Masciandaro and Tabellini (1991, p. 375) claim, that 'having an independent bank is almost like having a free lunch; there are benefits but no apparent costs in terms of macroeconomic performance'? Although overwhelming evidence exists that central bank independence and inflation are negatively related, one should be careful in jumping to this conclusion. As has been pointed out, only limited support exists for the view that central bank independence stimulates economic growth, while central bank independence also does not reduce disinflation costs.

5. Determinants of Central Bank Independence

The question arises which factors ultimately determine the degree of central bank independence. It is quite remarkable that the literature dealing with this question is, so far, hardly developed. Various economic and political determinants of central bank independence have been formulated. Such determinants can be categorized as follows:

1. the equilibrium or natural rate of unemployment;
2. the stock of government debt;
3. political instability;
4. supervision of financial institutions;
5. financial opposition to inflation;
6. public opposition to inflation; and
7. other determinants.

The first determinant of central bank independence may be the average employment-motivated inflationary bias in a country. This inflationary bias can be approximated empirically by the equilibrium or natural rate of unemployment. Cukierman (1994) in Chapter 20 shows that the larger the average employment-motivated inflationary bias in a country is, the higher are the costs for the government to override the central bank and, therefore, the more independent the central bank will be. Because in the case of nominal wage contracts unexpected inflation has positive effects on the level of both production and employment, a higher equilibrium or natural rate of unemployment implies that surprise inflation is more valuable for the government.

De Haan and Van 't Hag (1995) in Chapter 21 have tested this hypothesis, using two measures of Cukierman and the index of Grilli, Masciandaro and Tabellini (GMT). Proxies for inflationary bias are the equilibrium rate of unemployment, as estimated by Layard, Nickell and Jackman (1991) for 19 OECD countries, and the difference between the actual and the equilibrium rate of unemployment during the 1980s.[8] In simple cross-country regressions with each measure of central bank independence as a dependent variable, the coefficients of both proxies proved to be insignificant. Eijffinger and Schaling (1995) in Chapter 23 employed a latent variables method in order to distinguish between the actual (legal) and optimal degree of central bank independence in these countries. As measures for actual central bank autonomy, the indices of Alesina, GMT, Eijffinger-Schaling (ES) and Cukierman (LVAU) were chosen. These authors also found an insignificant coefficient for the natural rate of unemployment. We may therefore conclude that empirical studies provide no support for any relationship between the equilibrium or natural rate of unemployment and the degree of central bank independence. The stock of government debt is another potential determinant of central bank independence. The larger the sum the government wants to borrow on the capital market, the more weight is placed on lower inflationary expectations and, thus, on lower nominal capital-market interest rates. The benefits of a once-and-for-all reduction of the real value of government debt by unexpected inflation do not outweigh (in this case) the costs of permanently higher interest payments as a consequence of lower credibility. Cukierman (1994) has argued that the larger the debt, the more politicians tend to delegate authority to the central bank and the more independent the central bank will be. This hypothesis has been empirically investigated by De Haan and Van 't Hag (1995) for several measures of independence (LVAU, SUMLV and GMT) during the period 1980–89. Using gross government debt as a percentage of GDP in their regression analysis, these authors found no significant coefficient for the debt ratio.

The influence of political instability on central bank independence is, at first sight, less obvious than the impact of the other factors discussed so far. It could be argued that when politicians in office are faced with a greater probability that they will be removed from office, they have a stronger interest in delegating authority to the central bank as an apolitical institution, in order to restrict the range of policy actions available to the opposition if the latter would come into office. This implies that greater political instability leads to a more independent central bank. Conversely, we might argue that the incumbent politicians will fortify their hold on the central bank, if there is a greater probability of government change, and will eventually overrule central bank decision making. The short-term benefits of surprise inflation can, thereby, exceed their long-term costs. It follows that greater political instability would result in a more dependent central bank.

Cukierman and Webb (1995) in Chapter 22 use a measure of political vulnerability – i.e. the fraction of times that political transition is followed by a change of central bank governor as a dependent variable and four types of political instability as explanatory variables for a mixture of developed and developing countries during the period 1950–89. Only high-level political instability (change in regime) and the dummy for developing countries proved to be significant. However, Cukierman (1994) states that the larger the political instability is, the higher the degree of central bank independence will be '... provided political polarization is sufficiently large' (p. 65). The intuition behind this proposition is that the ruling party prefers a more independent central bank, when the prospects for its re-election are slim. As the probability of re-election shrinks, benefits of central bank independence increase in terms of restricting public expenditure by the other (opposition) party. This hypothesis of Cukierman is investigated by De Haan and Van 't Hag (1995) for three different measures of central bank autonomy during the 1970s and 1980s with regression analysis based on industrial countries. These authors used the frequency of government changes, as well as the frequency of significant government changes, for example in case another party or coalition comes to office, as indices of political instability. For the first index all three measures of central bank independence showed a significant, negative relationship; the second is not significant.

We may therefore conclude that the empirical results regarding political instability are mixed, but the various studies are hard to compare properly, as they refer to different groups of countries, diverging measures of central bank independence and various proxies for political instability.

A political-economic determinant of the degree of central bank independence can also be the supervision of financial institutions ('banking supervision'). Empirical evidence on the relationship between financial supervision and central bank independence provides no uniform conclusion. De Haan and Van 't Hag (1995) find no empirical relationship between two of the three different measures of independence and an index measuring the degree of banking supervision. This index is taken from Posen (1993), Chapter 19, and includes also the central bank restrictions on lending rates and on the amount of bank credit to the private sector. Only for one measure of independence there appears a significant, negative relation with the index for the degree of banking supervision. This result also contrasts with the view put forward by Posen, to which we will now turn.

Posen (1993) advocates a new view of monetary policy and central bank independence which are, in his opinion, determined by the degree of financial opposition to inflation, and the effectiveness of the financial sector to mobilize – through the political system – its opposition to inflation. According to Posen, the causal relationship between central bank independence and low inflation is illusory. Posen maintains that central bank autonomy has no noticeable effect on cross-country differences in inflation rates. He argues that a third factor exists, which explains the negative correlation between central bank independence and the level of inflation: financial opposition to inflation (FOI) in a country. Posen asserts that monetary policy is driven by a coalition of political interests in society, because central banks will be prepared to take strong anti-inflationary actions only when there is a coalition of interests politically capable of protecting their anti-inflationary policy. In industrial countries, the financial sector represents such a (powerful) coalition of interests. Therefore, Posen developed a measure of effective financial opposition to inflation, predicting both the degree of central bank independence and the rate of inflation in the various countries. He claims to have found clear statistical evidence that supports a causal link between FOI on the one side and central bank independence (i.e. Cukierman's LVAU) and lower inflation rates on the other, for the period 1950–89. However, De Haan and Van 't Hag (1995) have tested the proposition of Posen on universal banking by means of a dummy variable for the presence (1) or not (0) of a universal banking system. Only for one of the three independence indices did they find a significant, positive relationship with the dummy for universal banking. As explained before, these authors report a similar finding with respect to the relationship between prudential supervision and central bank independence. So it seems that Posen's conclusion is sensitive with respect to the measure of central bank independence used.

Another important determinant of central bank independence is public support for the objective of price stability or, analogous to the former determinant, the public opposition to inflation. It is quite obvious that this determinant should not be analyzed apart from the financial opposition to inflation as defined by Posen (1993), but that it has a much broader meaning. The experience of the public with extremely high inflation or even hyperinflation in the past is, generally, seen as the cause of such public opposition to inflation. This implies that a two-way causal relationship can exist between central bank independence and the level of inflation: on the one hand, an independent central bank may foster low inflation in the medium and long run but, on the other hand, high inflation may result in the very long run in the creation of an autonomous central bank. There seems to be a threshold value for the level of inflation, above which public opposition to inflation in a country will be mobilized and taken into account by the politicians.

Using cross-country OLS regressions with the average level of inflation between 1900 and 1940 as an explanatory variable of three different measures of central bank independence in industrial countries, De Haan and Van 't Hag (1995) have shown that a significant positive relationship exists between very-long-term inflation and independence.

Not referring to the very long run, but to the medium and long run, Eijffinger and Schaling (1995) in Chapter 23, using their game-theoretical model, arrive at the following proposition: the stronger society's preferences for unemployment stabilization relative to inflation stabilization are, the higher the optimal degree of central bank independence will be. The underlying intuition of this proposition is as follows. If society becomes more concerned with unemployment, the time-consistent rate of inflation goes up. Therefore, society's credibility problem becomes more pressing. With an unaltered relative weight placed on inflation stabilization, the balance between credibility and flexibility needs to be adjusted in favor of an increased commitment of the authorities to fight inflation. Eijffinger and Schaling have tested this proposition with the number of years of socialist (left-wing) dominated government over the total period studied as a proxy for society's preference for unemployment versus inflation stabilization. These authors found a positive relationship between society's preferences for unemployment relative to inflation stabilization and the optimal degree of central bank independence, although it was not significant.

In general, the conclusion may be drawn that central bank independence is strongly associated with society's fundamental support for the objective of price stability. Notwithstanding the theoretical and empirical arguments for an independent central bank as discussed before, not every society and, thus, not every government will be prepared to accept such an autonomous position of its central bank.

Finally, Eijffinger and Schaling (1995) state that the steeper the slope of the Phillips curve is, the higher the optimal degree of central bank independence will be. If the slope of the Phillips curve increases, then the benefits of unanticipated inflation rise. It therefore becomes more tempting for the government to inflate the economy and, *ceteris paribus*, society's credibility problem gains in importance. With constant relative weights on inflation stabilization, the balance between credibility and flexibility needs to shift towards more commitment to fight inflation. This proposition has been tested by Eijffinger and Schaling with the compensation of employees paid by resident producers as a ratio of GDP as a proxy for the slope of the Phillips curve. Using the latent variables method, a significant positive relationship was found between the slope of the Phillips curve and the optimal degree of central bank independence for nineteen industrial countries in the period 1960–93.

6. Conclusions

An independent central bank is *not* a *sufficient* and/or a *necessary* condition for price stability. In accordance with the theoretical literature and previous empirical studies, we must conclude, however, that a country with an independent central bank, *ceteris paribus*, will have a lower rate of inflation than does a country where politicians can steer the central bank's policy. Attaining lower inflation rates bears no costs in terms of lower long-term economic growth. Although the determinants of central bank independence have only recently been investigated, current research leads to the conclusion that every society gets the central bank it deserves. This conclusion implies also that just a change of the central bank law is insufficient to guarantee structurally lower levels of inflation. Only in case of widespread and overwhelming support for anti-inflation policy by an independent central bank, will inflation effectively be reduced. The policy to give the Banque de France a more independent position, for example, is backed both by the government, as well as by the opposition parties. After the failed experiment of an expansionary policy in France at the beginning of the 1980s, governments of alternating political composition have chosen a monetary policy strongly focused on Germany. In such circumstances, the development towards an independent central bank is a logical step.

Notes

1. For a critical survey of central bank independence, see: S.C.W. Eijffinger and J. de Haan (1996), 'The Political Economy of Central-Bank Independence', *Princeton Special Papers in International Economics*, No. 19, May. Princeton: New Jersey.
2. See also: R.H. Hasse (1990), *The European Central Bank: Perspectives for the Further Development of the European Monetary System*, Gütersloh: Bertelsmann Foundation.
3. The analysis of Sargent and Wallace is also called 'some unpleasant monetarist arithmetic'. See: N.J. Sargent and N. Wallace (1981), 'Some Unpleasant Monetarist Arithmetic', *Federal Reserve Bank of Minneapolis Quarterly Review*, **5**, 1–17.
4. For an overview of this literature, see Chapter 18 of: A. Cukierman (1992), *Central Bank Strategy, Credibility, and Independence*, Cambridge: MIT Press.
5. See also: T. Persson and G. Tabellini (1993), 'Designing Institutions for Monetary Stability', *Carnegie-Rochester Conference Series on Public Policy*, **39**, 53–84.

6. See also: R. Bade and M. Parkin (1988), *Central Bank Laws and Monetary Policy*, Unpublished Manuscript, University of Western Ontario.
7. See: A. Grimes (1991), 'The Effects of Inflation on Growth: Some International Evidence', *Weltwirtschaftliches Archiv*, **127**, 631–44; and R.J. Barro (1995), 'Inflation and Economic Growth', *Bank of England Quarterly Bulletin*, **35**, May, 166–76.
8. See R. Layard, S. Nickell and R. Jackman (1991), *Unemployment, Macroeconomic Performance and the Labour Market*, Oxford: Oxford University Press.

Part I
Theoretical Foundations of Central Bank Independence

[1]

Rules Rather than Discretion: The Inconsistency of Optimal Plans

Finn E. Kydland

Norwegian School of Economics and Business Administration

Edward C. Prescott

Carnegie-Mellon University

Even if there is an agreed-upon, fixed social objective function and policymakers know the timing and magnitude of the effects of their actions, discretionary policy, namely, the selection of that decision which is best, given the current situation and a correct evaluation of the end-of-period position, does not result in the social objective function being maximized. The reason for this apparent paradox is that economic planning is not a game against nature but, rather, a game against rational economic agents. We conclude that there is *no* way control theory can be made applicable to economic planning when expectations are rational.

I. Introduction

Optimal control theory is a powerful and useful technique for analyzing dynamic systems. At each point in time, the decision selected is best, given the current situation and given that decisions will be similarly selected in the future. Many have proposed its application to dynamic economic planning. The thesis of this essay is that it is not the appropriate tool for economic planning even when there is a well-defined and agreed-upon, fixed social objective function.

We find that a discretionary policy for which policymakers select the

We would like to thank Walter Dolde, Leif Johansen, Robert E. Lucas, Jr., Christopher A. Sims, and Neil Wallace, who all provided comments on an earlier draft. We also would like to acknowledge the support of the Guggenheim Foundation, National Science Foundation, and the Bank of Norway.

[*Journal of Political Economy*, 1977, vol. 85, no. 3]

best action, given the current situation, will not typically result in the social objective function being maximized. Rather, by relying on some policy rules, economic performance can be improved. In effect this is an argument for rules rather than discretion, but, unlike Friedman's (1948) argument, it does not depend upon ignorance of the timing and magnitude of the effects of policy.

The reasons for this nonintuitive result are as follows: optimal control theory is an appropriate planning device for situations in which current outcomes and the movement of the system's state depend only upon current and past policy decisions and upon the current state. But, we argue, this is unlikely to be the case for dynamic economic systems. Current decisions of economic agents depend in part upon their expectations of future policy actions. Only if these expectations were invariant to the future policy plan selected would optimal control theory be appropriate. In situations in which the structure is well understood, agents will surely surmise the way policy will be selected in the future. Changes in the social objective function reflected in, say, a change of administration do have an immediate effect upon agents' expectations of future policies and affect their current decisions. This is inconsistent with the assumptions of optimal control theory. This is not to say that agents can forecast future policies perfectly. All that is needed for our argument is that agents have *some* knowledge of how policymakers' decisions will change as a result of changing economic conditions. For example, agents may expect tax rates to be lowered in recessions and increased in booms.

The paradox also arises in situations in which the underlying economic structure is not well understood, which is surely now the case for aggregate economic analyses. Standard practice is to estimate an econometric model and then, at least informally, to use optimal-control-theory techniques to determine policy. But as Lucas (1976) has argued, since optimal decision rules vary systematically with changes in the structure of series relevant to the decision maker, any change in policy will alter the structure of these rules. Thus changes in policy induce changes in structure, which in turn necessitate reestimation and future changes in policy, and so on. We found for some not implausible structures that this iterative procedure does not converge, and, instead, stabilization efforts have the perverse effect of contributing to economic instability. For most examples, however, it did converge, and the resulting policy was consistent but suboptimal. It was consistent in the sense that at each point in time the policy selected was best, given the current situation. In effect the policymaker is failing to take into account the effect of his policy rule upon the optimal decison rules of the economic agents.

In this paper, we first define consistent policy and explain for the two-period problem why the consistent policy is suboptimal. The implications of the analysis are then considered for patent policy and flood-control problems for which consistent policy procedures are not seriously considered. Then, for the aggregate demand management problem, it is shown that the application of optimal control theory is equally absurd, at least if expectations are rational. Doing what is best, given the current situation, results in an excessive level of inflation, but unemployment is no lower than it would be if inflation (possibly deflation or price stability) were at the socially optimal rate. Consistency for infinite-period recursive economic structures is then considered. In equilibrium, optimizing agents follow rules which specify current decisions as a function of the current state.[1] Methods are developed for computing these equilibrium decision rules for certain specialized structures. The methods are used to evaluate alternative investment-tax-credit policies designed both to stabilize and to yield optimal taxation. Among the policies evaluated is the suboptimal consistent policy. Within the class of feedback policy rules, we found that the optimal one depended upon the initial conditions. Thus it was not optimal to continue with the initial policy in subsequent periods; that is, the optimal policy was inconsistent.

II. Consistent Policy

Let $\pi = (\pi_1, \pi_2, \ldots, \pi_T)$ be a sequence of policies for periods 1 to T (which may be infinite) and $x = (x_1, x_2, \ldots, x_T)$ be the corresponding sequence for economic agents' decisions. An agreed-upon social objective function

$$S(x_1, \ldots, x_T, \pi_1, \ldots, \pi_T) \tag{1}$$

is assumed to exist.[2] Further, agents' decisions in period t depend upon all policy decisions and their past decisions as follows:

$$x_t = X_t(x_1, \ldots, x_{t-1}, \pi_1, \ldots, \pi_T), \qquad t = 1, \ldots, T. \tag{2}$$

In such a framework an optimal policy, if it exists, is that feasible π which maximizes (1) subject to constraints (2). The concept of consistency is less obvious and is defined as follows:

> *Definition:* A policy π is *consistent* if, for each time period t, π_t maximizes (1), taking as given previous decisions, $x_1, \ldots, x_{t-1}$, and that future policy decisions (π_s for $s > t$) are similarly selected.

[1] The original objective of this research was to demonstrate the applicability of optimal control methods in a rational-expectations world. We recognized the nonoptimality of the consistent solution obtained by using control-theory techniques, but initially considered this a minor problem. Further thought, in large part motivated by C. A. Sims's criticism of our initial analyses, led us to the radical conclusions of this essay.

[2] Uncertainty is not the central issue of this essay. As with Arrow-Debreu state-preference theory, one need only define the decision elements to be functions contingent upon observables to incorporate uncertainty as is done for the stabilization example in Sec. V.

The inconsistency of the optimal plan is easily demonstrated by a two-period example. For $T = 2$, π_2 is selected so as to maximize

$$S(x_1, x_2, \pi_1, \pi_2), \tag{3}$$

subject to

$$x_1 = X_1(\pi_1, \pi_2)$$

and

$$x_2 = X_2(x_1, \pi_1, \pi_2). \tag{4}$$

For a plan to be consistent, π_2 must maximize (3), given the past decisions π_1, x_1, and constraint (4). Assuming differentiability and an interior solution, then necessarily

$$\frac{\partial S}{\partial x_2}\frac{\partial X_2}{\partial \pi_2} + \frac{\partial S}{\partial \pi_2} = 0.$$

The consistent policy ignores the effects of π_2 upon x_1. For the optimal decision rule, the first-order condition is

$$\frac{\partial S}{\partial x_2}\frac{\partial X_2}{\partial \pi_2} + \frac{\partial S}{\partial \pi_2} + \frac{\partial X_1}{\partial \pi_2}\left[\frac{\partial S}{\partial x_1} + \frac{\partial S}{\partial x_2}\frac{\partial X_2}{\partial x_1}\right] = 0.$$

Only if either the effect of π_2 upon x_1 is zero (i.e., $\partial X_1/\partial \pi_2 = 0$) or the effect of changes in x_1 upon S both directly and indirectly through x_2 is zero (i.e., $[\partial S/\partial x_1 + \partial S/\partial x_2 \, \partial X_2/\partial x_1] = 0$) would the consistent policy be optimal.

Pollak (1968) resolved a planning inconsistency which arose because different generations had different preference orderings by assuming at each stage that the policy selected was best (relative to that generation's preferences), given the policies which will be followed in the future. For the T-period problem, the π_T is determined which, conditional upon previous decisions π_t and x_t, is best:

$$\pi_T = \Pi_T(\pi_1, \ldots, \pi_{T-1}, x_1, \ldots, x_{T-1}).$$

Once the functional relationship Π_T is known, the determination of the best policy rule $\pi_{T-1} = \Pi_{T-1}(\pi_1, \ldots, \pi_{T-2}, x_1, \ldots, x_{T-2})$ can be determined, and in general the consistent policy

$$\pi_t = \Pi_t(\pi_1, \ldots, \pi_{t-1}, x_1, \ldots, x_{t-1})$$

can be determined once future policy rules are known. With such a procedure, the policy decision at each stage is optimal, given the rules for future policy selection.[3] But as the simple example illustrated, this procedure is suboptimal.

Two examples follow:

The issues are obvious in many well-known problems of public policy. For example, suppose the socially desirable outcome is not to have houses built in a particular flood plain but, given that they are there, to take certain costly flood-control measures. If the government's policy were not to build the dams and levees needed for flood protection and agents knew this was the case, even if houses were built there, rational agents would not live in the flood plains. But the rational agent knows that, if he and others build houses there, the government will take the necessary flood-control measures. Consequently, in the absence of a law prohibiting the construction of houses in the flood plain, houses are built there, and the army corps of engineers subsequently builds the dams and levees.

A second example is patent policy. Given that resources have been allocated to inventive activity which resulted in a new product or process, the efficient policy is not to permit patent protection. For this example, few would seriously consider this optimal-control-theory solution as being reasonable. Rather, the question would be posed in terms of the optimal patent life (see, e.g., Nordhaus 1969), which takes into consideration both the incentive for inventive activity provided by patent protection and the loss in consumer surplus that results when someone realizes monopoly rents. In other words, economic theory is used to predict the effects of alternative policy rules, and one with good operating characteristics is selected.

III. The Inflation-Unemployment Example

The suboptimality of the consistent policy is not generally recognized for the aggregate demand management problem. The standard policy prescription is to select that policy which is best, given the current situation. This may seem reasonable, but for the structure considered, which we argue is a plausible abstraction of reality, such policy results in excessive rates of inflation without any reduction in unemployment. The policy of maintaining price stability is preferable.

[3] There are some subtle game-theoretic issues which have not been addressed here. Peleg and Yaari (1973) criticized Pollak's solution because sometimes it did not exist and proposed an alternative solution to the noncooperative intergeneration game. As explained by Kydland (1975*b*), in the language of dynamic games, Pollak used the feedback solution and Peleg and Yaari the open-loop solution. For policy selection, the policymaker is dominant, and for dominant-player games, the open-loop solution is inconsistent (see Kydland 1975*a*, 1975*b* for further details). That is why Peleg and Yaari's solution was not considered here.

The attempts of economists to rationalize the apparent trade-off between unemployment and inflation in modern theoretical terms have resulted in models with the following structure: unemployment (employment) is a decreasing (increasing) function of the discrepancy between actual and expected inflation rates. This example assumes such a relationship and that it is linear:

$$u_t = \lambda(x_t^e - x_t) + u^*, \tag{5}$$

where u_t is unemployment in period t, λ a positive constant, x_t the inflation rate, x_t^e the forecasted or expected inflation rate, and u^* the natural rate implied by these theories. As has been recently shown by Phelps and Taylor (1975), one need not rely upon imperfect information across firms about the "generality" of shock or imperfect foresight about the persistence of shock over time to obtain a similar relationship. They obtained one by assuming price rigidities, namely, that prices and wages are set prior to the realization of demand.

The crucial issue is what assumption to make concerning price expectations. The conventional approach is to assume that expectations depend in some mechanical ad hoc way upon past prices. If so, control theory would be an appropriate tool to determine the optimal path of unemployment and inflation. The policy decision in each period would consider both current outcomes and a proper evaluation of the terminal price expectations state variable. Such a treatment of expectations is difficult to justify either on a priori or empirical grounds. A change in administration which reflects a change in the relative costs society assigns to unemployment and inflation will have an immediate effect upon expectations—contrary to the implicit assumption of the proponents of control theory. Moreover, private agents or their agents have as much information about the economic structure as does the policymaker and some information concerning the implicit objective function which rationalizes policy selections. Therefore their forecasts of future policy behavior will be related to actual policy selection. This does not imply that policy is perfectly predicted, but then neither is the behavior of private agents. Just partial predictability of policy is sufficient to invalidate the use of optimal control theory.

For this example, we shall assume that the expectations are rational, so that the mathematical expectation of inflation equals the expected rate:

$$x_t^e = Ex_t.$$

Whether forecasts are rational is still open to debate. In Sargent (1973) the rational-expectations hypothesis is tested and accepted. He also explains why many other tests that rejected the hypothesis are invalid. He does not, however, comment on the Hirsch and Lovell (1969) test

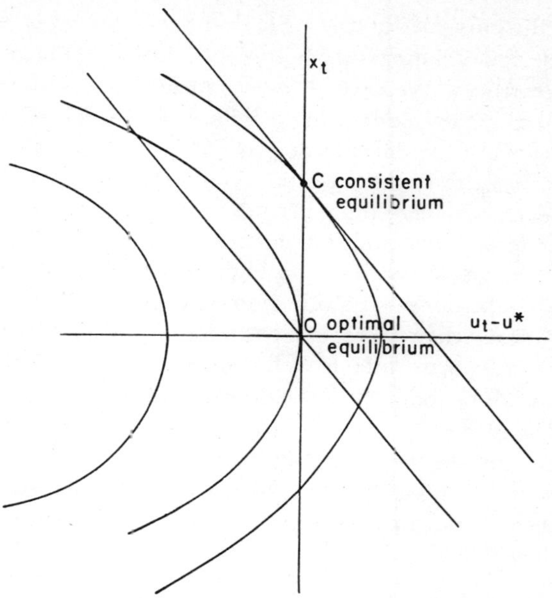

FIG. 1.—Consistent and optimal equilibrium

which used direct measures of expectations and found that forecast errors were systematically related to lagged sales, so we will do so. Responses to this finding are that there may be biases in their measurement of expectations, and these biases are related to lagged sales. This is not implausible, given the subtleness of the expectations concept and the imprecision of survey instruments. Further, even if there were a systematic forecast error in the *past*, now that the Hirsch and Lovell results are part of agents' information sets, future forecast errors should not be subject to such biases.

To complete the model, a theory of policy selection is needed. Here it is assumed that there is some social objective function which rationalizes policy choice:

$$S(x_t, u_t).$$

If the rationalization is not perfect, a random term must be introduced into the function. The consistent policy maximizes this function subject to the Phillips curve constraint (5).

Figure 1 depicts some Phillips curves and indifference curves. From (5) the Phillips curves are straight lines having slope $-\lambda^{-1}$ and intersecting the vertical axis at x_t^e. For a consistent equilibrium, the indifference curve must be tangent to a Phillips curve at a point along the vertical axis—as at point C. Only then are expectations rational and the policy selected best, given the current situation. The indifference curves imply that the socially preferred inflation rate is zero, which seems consistent with the public's preferences. We of course recognize that inflation is a tax on reserves and currency, and a more informed public might prefer some positive or negative inflation rate. If so, x_t need only be interpreted as deviation from the optimal rate. The outcome of a consistent policy selection clearly is not optimal. If the policymakers were compelled to maintain price stability and did not have discretionary powers, the resulting equilibrium would have no higher unemployment than the consistent policy. The optimal equilibrium is point O, which lies on a higher indifference curve than the consistent-equilibrium point C.

It is perhaps worthwhile to relate our analysis to that of Taylor's (1975), in which he found that the optimal monetary policy was random in a rational-expectations world. Similar results would hold for our problem if uncertainty in the social objective function had been introduced. Both for his structure and for ours, the optimal policy is inconsistent, and consequently it is not optimal for the policymaker to continue with his original policy rules.

IV. Consistent Planning for the Infinite Horizon

The method of backward induction cannot be applied to infinite-period problems to determine a consistent policy because, unlike the finite-period problem, there is no final period with which to begin the induction. For recursive structures, however, the concept of consistency can be defined in terms of policy *rules*. Suppose that the economy at time t can be described by a vector of state variables y_t, a vector of policy variables π_t, a vector of decision variables x_t for the economic agents, and a vector of random shocks ε_t which are temporally independent. The movement over time of these variables is given by the system of equations

$$y_{t+1} = F(y_t, \pi_t, x_t, \varepsilon_t).$$

Let the feedback policy rule for future periods be

$$\pi_s = \Pi^f(y_s), \qquad s > t. \tag{6}$$

For certain structures, rational economic agents will in the future follow a rule of the form

$$x_s = d^f(y_s; \Pi^f). \tag{7}$$

It is important to note that changes in policy rule Π^f change the functional form of d^f, a point convincingly made by Lucas (1976) in his critique of current econometric policy-evaluation procedures. The decisions of agents in the current period will have the form

$$x_t = d^c(y_t, \pi_t; \Pi^f).$$

Again, it is important to note that expectations of future policy affect current decisions. For example, the effect of an increase in the investment tax credit will depend upon the expected future levels of the investment tax credit.

If, in addition, the social objective function is of the form

$$\sum_{s=t}^{\infty} \beta_{\pi}^{s} q(x_s, y_s, \pi_s), \qquad 0 < \beta_{\pi} < 1,$$

and the objective is to minimize its expected value, the optimal value for π_t will depend upon both y_t and Π^f, the policy rule which will be used in the future. In other words, the best policy rule for the current period $\Pi^c(y)$ is functionally related to the policy rule used in the future $\Pi^f(y)$, say

$$\Pi^c = g(\Pi^f).$$

A stationary policy rule Π is consistent if it is a fixed point of mapping g, for then it is best to use the same policy rule as the one expected to be used in the future.[4]

Suppose policymakers and agents do not have a clear understanding of the dynamic structure of the economy. Over time, agents will grope for and most likely converge to the equilibrium rules of forms (6) and (7). Policymakers taking the decision rules of agents as given, when evaluating alternative decisions, typically would consider the trade-off of current outcomes relative to the desirability or value of the end-of-period state. Assuming that their valuation of the terminal state is approximately correct, they will be selecting the approximately consistent policy, assuming also that agents have approximately rational expectations. Thus it seems likely that the current practice of selecting that policy which is best, given the current situation, is likely to converge to the consistent but *suboptimal* policy.[5]

It is hard to fault a policymaker acting consistently. The reason that such policies are suboptimal is not due to myopia. The effect of this decision upon the entire future is taken into consideration. Rather, the suboptimality arises because there is no mechanism to induce *future* policymakers to take into consideration the effect of their policy, via the expectations mechanism, upon *current* decisions of agents.

[4] This is the solution concept used by Phelps and Pollak (1968) for an infinite-period second-best growth problem when different generations had inconsistent preferences.

[5] Optimal policy refers to the best policy, assuming it exists, within a certain class of policies. Within the class of linear feedback rules $\Pi(y_t)$, we found that the best policy rule depended upon the initial condition. The most general class of decision policies are characterized by a sequence of probability measures indexed by the history $\{\Pi_t(x^t, \pi^t, y^t)\}$, with the superscripted variables denoting all previously observed values of the variables. It was necessary to consider probability distributions because for some games a randomized strategy will be optimal and not dominated by a deterministic one. For games against nature, only deterministic strategies need be considered.

V. The Investment-Tax-Credit Example

In this section an equilibrium framework is developed for evaluating a class of investment-tax-credit policies. The assumed technological structure is similar to the one used by Jorgenson (1963), though increasing costs associated with rapid adjustment in capacity are assumed. A firm uses k_t units of capital and n_t units of labor to produce an output $Ak_t^{\alpha}n_t^{(1-\alpha)}$. Output price is p_t, and the real wage is assumed to be a constant, say 1. Investment planned in period t and carried out that period and the next, x_t, does not become productive until period $t + 2$. The relationship between current productive capital, planned investment, and future productive capital is

$$k_{t+2} = x_t + (1 - \delta)k_{t+1},$$

where δ is the constant physical rate of depreciation. Investment costs associated with x_t, the new investment plans in period t, occur in both period t and period $t + 1$. This reflects the fact that time is required to expand capacity, and investment expenditures occur over the entire time interval. The fraction of the investment effort induced by plan x_t in the current period is ϕ, and the fraction induced in the subsequent period is $1 - \phi$. The investment rate in period t is then

$$z_t = \phi x_t + (1 - \phi)x_{t-1}.$$

Following Haavelmo (1960), Eisner and Strotz (1963), Lucas (1967), Gould (1968), and Treadway (1969), we assume that the investment expenditures are an increasing convex function of the rate of capital expansion z_t. In order to insure constant returns to scale in the long run, the function is assumed to have slope equal to the price q of capital goods at $z_t = \delta k_t$. Making the quadratic approximation, the investment expenditures in period t are then

$$i_t = qz_t + \gamma(z_t - \delta k_t)^2,$$

where γ is positive. Observe that i_t depends upon investment plans in both the current and previous periods and that, if x_t is constant over time and sufficient to maintain the capital stock, $i_t = qx_t$.

The gross cash inflow during period t is

$$p_t A k_t^{\alpha} n_t^{(1-\alpha)} - p_t n_t - i_t. \tag{8}$$

In period t a tax rate θ is applied to sales less labor costs and depreciation. Letting Ψ be the fraction of the "true" depreciation being tax deductible, the tax bill is then

$$\theta(p_t A k_t^{\alpha} n_t^{(1-\alpha)} - p_t n_t - \Psi\delta k_t). \tag{9}$$

Finally, an investment tax credit is offered at the value π_t, so there will be a tax offset of

$$\pi_t z_t. \tag{10}$$

The view is that the adjustment cost term reflects costs internal to the firm and therefore not eligible for the investment tax credit.[6]

The net cash inflow in period t is (8) less (9) plus (10). The objective of the firm is to maximize the expected present value of this net cash inflow stream. Maximizing each period's cash flow over the period's n_t, the objective function to be maximized becomes

$$E \sum_{t=0}^{\infty} \beta^t[(1 - \theta)p_t \alpha\lambda k_t + \theta\Psi\delta k_t - (q - \pi_t)z_t - \gamma(z_t - \delta k_t)^2],$$

where $\lambda = [1/(1 - \alpha)][A(1 - \alpha)]^{1/\alpha}$ is output per unit of capital and β is the discount factor.

The inverse aggregate demand function is assumed to be linear. Letting capital letters denote the aggregates of the corresponding variables for the individual firms, the inverse demand function is of the form

$$p_t = a_t - b\lambda K_t,$$

where b is a positive constant, a_t is a stochastic demand shift parameter, and K_t is the aggregate capital stock for the firms. We assume that a_t is subject to the first-order autoregressive process

$$a_{t+1} = \rho a_t + \varepsilon_t, \qquad -1 < \rho < 1, \tag{11}$$

where the ε_t are positive independent random variables with mean μ and variance σ_ε^2.

For the economy to be in equilibrium, the expected and actual distribution of the random elements must be equal. Here we are assuming rational expectations of Muth (1961) and of Lucas and Prescott (1971). Brock (1972) has characterized such expectations schemes as being self-fulfilling. We are implicitly assuming that the economy is Hicksian in the sense that a single consumer could have the implicit excess demand function. For such economies wealth effects net out, and our equilibrium yields the same allocation as the Arrow-Debreu state preference equilibrium upon extension of their analysis to infinite-dimensional space.

In the Appendix we develop direct methods for computing the competitive equilibrium, given the policy rule.[7] Also discussed in the Appendix is the stability of the equilibrium.

[6] We are also implicitly assuming a per unit rather than a percentage tax credit.

[7] If policy does not depend upon agents' decisions, the competitive equilibrium is efficient and therefore maximizes the utility of the economy-wide consumer, a fact exploited in Lucas and Prescott (1971) to characterize the competitive equilibrium. For these examples, policy rules are of the feedback variety and depend upon past decisions of private economic agents. In effect this introduces an externality. Suppose, e.g., that future investment tax credits depend positively upon the magnitude of future capital stocks. If all agents invest less now, future capital stocks will be smaller and, consequently, future investment tax credits larger. Because of this externality, the competitive equilibrium will not in general maximize the utility of the economy-wide consumer, given the policy rule. This is why it was necessary to devise direct methods.

The policymakers are choosing values for π in each time period so as to minimize the value of some social preference function. We use a quadratic approximation of a function which includes the terms likely to carry any weight. The assumed form is

$$E \sum_{t=0}^{\infty} \beta_{\pi}^{t}[\omega_1(\lambda K_t - g_1)^2 + \omega_2(Z_t - g_2)^2 + \omega_3(\lambda K_t + Z_t - g_3)^2 + \omega_4(p_t - p_{t-1})^2 + \omega_5 \pi_t Z_t + \omega_6 \pi_t^2],$$

where each ω_i, $i = 1, \ldots, 6$, indicates the relative weight on each of the components. The terms g_1, g_2, and g_3 are targets for real output of the industry, for real investments, and for the total of the two, respectively. Reasons for including the tax credit in the loss function are that the amount paid may have to be collected elsewhere in the form of taxes and inefficiencies generally caused by such measures.

Our examples assume that a passive investment-tax-credit stabilization policy had been pursued in the past and that the function describing investment behavior was equilibrium, given this passive policy. They also assume that econometricians have estimated the investment relationship[8] and that the policymaker uses control theory to determine which policy rule is optimal under the incorrect assumption that the equilibrium investment function is invariant to the policy rule used. Subsequent to the implementation of this policy rule, the economy moves to the new equilibrium investment function. Econometricians revise their estimate of the investment function, arguing that there has been structural change, and the policymaker uses optimal control to determine a new policy rule. The change in policy induces still another change in the investment function, which in turn induces a change in the policy rule, once the shift in the investment function is recognized. This iterative process, we think, captures the essence of what is actually happening. We observe that econometricians are continually revising their estimates of the structure on the basis of which new policies are devised and are continually surprised to find that the structure has changed.

Our results can be summarized as follows:

Factor shares, the capital output ratio, tax rates, and capital consumption allowances were used to deduce not unreasonable values for parameters of technology and preferences with the exception of ϕ, the distributed lag coefficient of investment, and ρ, the autoregressive parameter of the

[8] We recognize that there may be problems involved in estimating the investment function because of perfect multicollinearity between π_t and the other independent variables. However, the model could be modified to permit random fluctuations in the price of capital. For estimation purposes, one would then, instead of using the investment tax credit, use the price of capital which is affected by the tax credit in a predictable way.

aggregate demand relation.[9] Only these parameters and the parameters of the objective function were subject to variation. Space constraints preclude more than a brief summary of the results.[10]

Typically the iterative process of the policy rule change inducing investment function change inducing policy rule change, etc., did converge. Given that it converges, the limiting policy rule is consistent in the sense described in Sections II and IV. In all cases for which it did converge, we searched for and found linear feedback policy rules which were superior to this consistent rule, typically by a substantial amount.

For one example ($\omega_1 = 2$, $\omega_2 = 4$, $\omega_3 = 1$, $\omega_4 = 10$, $\omega_5 = 20$, $\omega_6 = 10$, and $\rho = 0.6$), the application of optimal control initially improved the performance of the economy relative to the assumed objective function. For the first two iterations, the economy was subject to less fluctuation and fluctuated about a preferred point. After the third iteration, however, performance deteriorated, and the consistent policy to which the process converged was decidedly inferior to the passive policy for which the investment tax credit was not varied. The difference in performance corresponded roughly to the variables being 10 percent on average away from their targets.

For another example ($\omega_1 = 1$, $\omega_2 = 2$, $\omega_3 = 1$, $\omega_4 = 10$, $\omega_5 = 3$, $\omega_6 = 20$, and $\rho = -0.6$), the iterative process did not converge. Changes in the policy rule induced ever larger changes in the investment function. The variables fluctuated about their targeted values but fluctuated with increased amplitude with each iteration. This is a very disturbing result, for it indicates that current practice, if continued, could conceivably result in even greater fluctuations than are now being experienced.

There are two lessons we learned from the examples. First, the use of optimal control theory is hazardous and could very well increase economic fluctuations or even make a stable economy unstable. Second, even when it does work reasonably well, it can be improved upon by following some other simple feedback rule.

This is not an argument that economic fluctuations are either desirable or unavoidable. That our economy has experienced periods of reasonable stability is evidence that much of the fluctuation is avoidable. Rather, it is a plea for the use of economic theory to evaluate correctly the performance of a policy rule before it is implemented. We emphasize that

9 The values used for the fixed parameters were $\delta = 0.1$, $\theta = 0.5$, $A = 1.15$, $\gamma = 0.03$, $\alpha = 0.28$, $b = 0.4$, $\lambda = 0.7$, $q = 1$, $\beta = \beta_\pi = 0.9$, $\phi = 0.3$, and $\sigma_\varepsilon = 0.03$. Given ρ, the parameter μ was chosen so as to give a mean of 2.5 for a_t. For instance, if $\rho = 0.6$, as in the first example, we get $\mu = 1$. In the examples discussed, we used $g_1 = 2.008$, $g_2 = 0.2837$, and $g_3 = 2.292$, which are the stationary levels of the corresponding target variables when the passive policy of $\pi_t = 0$ is used in every period.

10 More details of the results of the numerical examples can be found in our original working paper, which is available upon request.

optimal control theory can *not* be made applicable to economic planning by taking into consideration the way changes in the policy rule change the behavioral equation of the model when expectations are rational.

VI. Discussion

The analysis has implications in other situations as well. Kydland (1975*a*) has explored the implications for a dynamic oligopoly problem with a dominant firm. Like the policymaker, the dominant firm takes into consideration the reaction of the other agents in selecting its decision. Precisely the same paradox arises.

The analysis also has implications for constitutional law. A majority group, say, the workers, who control the policy might rationally choose to have a constitution which limits their power, say, to expropriate the wealth of the capitalist class. Those with lower discount rates will save more if they know their wealth will not be expropriated in the future, thereby increasing the marginal product and therefore wage and lowering the rental price of capital, at least for most reasonable technological structures.

Still another area is the current energy situation. We suspect that rational agents are not making investments in new sources of oil in the anticipation that price controls will be instituted in the future. Currently there are those who propose to tax away "excessive" profits of the oil companies with the correct argument that this will not affect past decisions. But rational agents anticipate that such expropriations may be made in the future, and this expectation affects their current investment decisions, thereby reducing future supplies.

VII. Summary and Conclusions

We have argued that control theory is not the appropriate tool for dynamic economic planning. It is not the appropriate tool because current decisions of economic agents depend upon expected future policy, and these expectations are not invariant to the plans selected. We have shown that, if in each period the policy decision selected is the one which maximizes the sum of the value of current outcomes and the discounted valuation of the end-of-period state, the policy selected will be consistent but not optimal. This point is demonstrated for an investment-tax-credit policy example, using a rational-expectations equilibrium theory with costs of adjustment and distributed lags for expenditures. In fact, active stabilization effects did, for some distributed lag expenditure schedules, contribute to economic instability and even make a stable economy unstable.

The structures considered are far from a tested theory of economic fluctuations, something which is needed before policy evaluation is undertaken. The implication of this analysis is that, until we have such a theory, active stabilization may very well be dangerous and it is best that it not be attempted. Reliance on policies such as a constant growth in the money supply and constant tax rates constitute a safer course of action.

When we do have the prerequisite understanding of the business cycle, the implication of our analysis is that policymakers should follow rules rather than have discretion. The reason that they should not have discretion is not that they are stupid or evil but, rather, that discretion implies selecting the decision which is best, given the current situation. Such behavior either results in consistent but suboptimal planning or in economic instability.

If we are not to attempt to select policy optimally, how should it be selected? Our answer is, as Lucas (1976) proposed, that economic theory be used to evaluate alternative policy rules and that one with good operating characteristics be selected. In a democratic society, it is probably preferable that selected rules be simple and easily understood, so it is obvious when a policymaker deviates from the policy. There could be institutional arrangements which make it a difficult and time-consuming process to change the policy rules in all but emergency situations. One possible institutional arrangement is for Congress to legislate monetary and fiscal policy rules and these rules to become effective only after a 2-year delay. This would make discretionary policy all but impossible.

Appendix

Let y be the state variables and x the decision variables for the firm. There is a linear relationship between the next period's state variables, y_{t+1}, and the current x_t and y_t:

$$y_{t+1} = f(x_t, y_t). \tag{A1}$$

The movement of economy-wide state variables Y and aggregate (or per firm) decision variables X are described by the same linear function:

$$Y_{t+1} = F(X_t, Y_t). \tag{A2}$$

We also include a vector of autonomous shocks, W, which are subject to a first-order autoregressive process,

$$W_{t+1} = \Omega W_t + \eta_t, \tag{A3}$$

where Ω is a matrix of fixed coefficients and η a random vector with finite variances. In the vector W we may also include other variables on which decisions can depend and which may be common to the firm and the economy as a whole. An example would be the lagged price level of output.

The firm's objective is to maximize

$$E\left[\sum_{t=0}^{T} \beta^t R(x_t, y_t, X_t, Y_t, W_t, \pi_t)\right], \qquad 0 < \beta < 1,$$

where π_t is a vector of policy variables assumed to be given by a sequence of linear policy rules,

$$\pi_t = \Pi_t(Y_t, W_t), \quad t = 0, \ldots, T, \tag{A4}$$

which in equilibrium are correctly anticipated by the firm.

The cash-flow function R is quadratic. The decisions x_t are selected sequentially conditional on y_t, X_t, Y_t, and W_t. Let $v_t(y_t, Y_t, W_t)$ be the value of the firm at time t. The v_t functions satisfy the recursive relationship

$$v_t(y_t, Y_t, W_t) = R(x_t, y_t, X_t, Y_t, W_t, \pi_t) + \beta E[v_{t+1}(y_{t+1}, Y_{t+1}, W_{t+1})] \tag{A5}$$

subject to constraints (A1)–(A4) and one additional constraint. To explain this last constraint, note that, since x_t is chosen so as to maximize the valuation at time t, if v_t is quadratic and the right-hand side of (A5) concave in x_t, the x_t which maximizes the right-hand side of (A5), taking as given X_t, Y_t, W_t, and the motion of the economy-wide state variables, will be linearly related to y_t, X_t, Y_t, W_t, and π_t:

$$x_t = d_t(y_t, X_t, Y_t, W_t, \pi_t). \tag{A6}$$

In order for the economy to be in equilibrium, we have to impose the constraint that, when firms behave according to (A6), the aggregate or per firm X_t is indeed X_t. Therefore[11]

$$X_t = d_t(Y_t, X_t, Y_t, W_t, \pi_t),$$

which can be rewritten as

$$X_t = D_t(Y_t, W_t, \pi_t). \tag{A7}$$

As the constraints are all linear and the right-hand side of (A5) quadratic, the function v_t is quadratic, given that v_{t+1} is quadratic. The function v_{T+1} is the null function and therefore trivially quadratic, so by induction all the v_t are quadratic. The equilibrium per firm decision function for each time period t is given by (A7).

If the social objective function is quadratic of the form

$$E\left[\sum_{t=0}^{T} \beta_\pi^t S(X_t, Y_t, W_t, \pi_t)\right], \qquad 0 < \beta_\pi < 1,$$

the determination of the consistent policy is straightforward. Let

$$u_t(Y_t, W_t) = E\left[\sum_{i=t}^{T} \beta_\pi^{i-t} S(X_i, Y_i, W_i, \pi_i)\right],$$

given that policy is selected consistently and that the economy is competitive. Thus the function u_t gives the total expected value of the social objective function from period t throughout the rest of the horizon for the consistent policy. By backward induction

$$u_t(Y_t, W_t) = \min_{\pi_t} \{S(X_t, Y_t, W_t, \pi_t) + \beta_\pi E[u_{t+1}(Y_{t+1}, W_{t+1})]\},$$

11 We think of a large corporation as being the aggregate of several small firms. Therefore the effect of an investment-tax-credit policy is proportional to size.

subject to (A2), (A3), and (A7). If u_{t+1} is quadratic, a quadratic function is being minimized subject to linear constraints. Therefore u_t must be quadratic if u_{t+1} is quadratic. As $u_{T+1} = 0$ and is thus trivially quadratic, all the u_t are quadratic by backward induction, and the consistent policy is a linear function of Y and W:

$$\pi_t = \Pi_t(Y_t, W_t).$$

It is perhaps worthwhile to make the connection between the structure just analyzed and the one described in Section V. The state vector is

$$y_t = (k_t, x_{t-1})',$$

and the linear equations governing its movement over time are

$$y_{t+1} = \begin{pmatrix} 1-\delta & 1 \\ 0 & 0 \end{pmatrix} y_t + \begin{pmatrix} 0 \\ 1 \end{pmatrix} x_t.$$

The equations governing the economy-wide variables are the same. Furthermore,

$$W_{t+1} \equiv a_{t+1} = \rho a_t + \varepsilon_t \equiv \Omega W_t + \eta_t.$$

The revenue function R for the firm is

$$(1-\theta)\alpha\lambda p_t k_t + \theta\Psi\delta k_t - (q - \pi_t)z_t - \gamma(z_t - \delta k_t)^2,$$

which has the assumed form, given that

$$p_t = a_t - b\lambda K_t$$

and

$$z_t = \phi x_t + (1-\phi)x_{t-1}.$$

Finally, the social objective function S given by

$$\omega_1(\lambda K_t - g_1) + \omega_2(Z_t - g_2) + \omega_3(\lambda K_t + Z_t - g_3) + \omega_4(p_t - p_{t-1})^2 + \omega_5\pi_t Z_t + \omega_6\pi_t^2$$

also has the quadratic form, given the assumed definitions of the variables.

Computations for the Infinite-Period Problem

Equilibrium decision rules for agents were determined as the limit of first-period decision rules as the life of the economy went to infinity. There is an interesting and as yet unsolved problem as to the uniqueness of the equilibrium.[12] For these examples the equilibrium associated with a stationary policy rule did appear to be unique, for when we used the method of successive approximation in the value space (i.e., the v function in [A5]) the value function and therefore decision rules converged to the same limit for a number of initial approximations. For some unreasonable policy rules and finite T, there were no competitive equilibria.

Consistent solutions were computed in two different ways. The first determined the first-period consistent policy for T-period problems and the limit determined as T went to infinity. The second determined the nth approximation to the consistent-equilibrium investment function X^n, given the nth approximation to the consistent policy rule Π^n, using the methods described above. Optimal control theory was then used to determine the policy Π^{n+1} which would be

[12] Standard dynamic programming arguments such as those of Denardo (1967) could not be applied because there was not monotonicity of the mapping in the value space.

optimal if X^n were not to change as a result of the change in Π^n. Given initial linear feedback rule Π^0, sequences of linear rules $\{\Pi^n, X^n\}$ were obtained. When such sequences existed and converged, the limits constituted a consistent policy rule and the corresponding equilibrium investment function. In no case did we ever obtain two different consistent policies for the same structure, though both methods of successive approximations were used and a number of different starting values tried.

Stability of the Competitive Equilibrium

We also checked whether the computed competitive equilibria were stable, as follows: given the expected aggregate investment function (which implies expectations) at stage n,

$$X = G_n(y, W, \pi),$$

and given structural relations (A2) and (A3), one finds the optimal firm investment function

$$x = d_n(y, X, Y, W, \pi),$$

which in the aggregate becomes

$$X = D_n(Y, W, \pi).$$

Now let

$$G_{n+1}(Y, W, \pi) = G_n(Y, W, \pi) + \xi[D_n(Y, W, \pi) - G_n(Y, W, \pi)].$$

For the numerical examples in Section V for which we found competitive equilibria, this process converged for various initial aggregate investment functions G_0 for $\xi = 1$ and of course for smaller positive values of ξ as well.

References

Brock, W. A. "On Models of Expectations That Arise from Maximizing Behavior of Economic Agents over Time." *J. Econ. Theory* 5 (December 1972): 348–76.

Denardo, E. "Contraction Mappings in the Theory Underlying Dynamic Programming." *SIAM Review* 9 (April 1967): 165–77.

Eisner, R., and Strotz, R. "Determinants of Business Investment." In Commission on Money and Credit, *Impacts of Monetary Policy*. Englewood Cliffs, N.J.: Prentice-Hall, 1963.

Friedman, M. "A Monetary and Fiscal Framework for Economic Stabilization." *A.E.R.* 38 (June 1948): 245–64.

Gould, J. P. "Adjustment Costs in the Theory of Investment of the Firm." *Rev. Econ. Studies* 35 (January 1968): 47–55.

Haavelmo, T. *A Study of the Theory of Investment.* Chicago: Univ. Chicago Press, 1960.

Hirsch, A. A., and Lovell, M. C. *Sales Anticipations and Inventory Behavior.* New York: Wiley, 1969.

Jorgenson, D. W. "Capital Theory and Investment Behavior." *A.E.R.* (Proc.) 53 (May 1963): 247–59.

Kydland, F. "Equilibrium Solutions in Dynamic Dominant Player Models." Discussion Paper, Norwegian School of Economics and Business Administration, 1975. (*a*)

———. "Noncooperative and Dominant Player Solutions in Discrete Dynamic Games." *Internat. Econ. Rev.* 16 (June 1975): 321–35. (*b*)

Lucas, R. E., Jr. "Adjustment Costs and the Theory of Supply." *J.P.E.* 75, no. 4, pt. 1 (August 1967): 321–34.

———. "Econometric Policy Evaluation: A Critique." In *The Phillips Curve and Labor Markets*, edited by K. Brunner and A. H. Meltzer. Amsterdam: North-Holland, 1976.

Lucas, R. E., Jr., and Prescott, E. C. "Investment under Uncertainty." *Econometrica* 39 (September 1971): 659–81.

Muth, J. F. "Rational Expectations and the Theory of Price Movements." *Econometrica* 29 (July 1961): 315–35.

Nordhaus, W. D. *Invention Growth and Welfare: A Theoretical Treatment of Technological Change*. Cambridge, Mass.: M.I.T. Press, 1969.

Peleg, B., and Yaari, M. E. "On the Existence of a Consistent Course of Action When Tastes Are Changing." *Rev. Econ. Studies* 40 (July 1973): 391–401.

Phelps, E. S., and Pollak, R. A. "On Second-best National Saving and Game-Equilibrium Growth." *Rev. Econ. Studies* 35 (April 1968): 185–99.

Phelps, E. S., and Taylor, J. B. "Stabilizing Properties of Monetary Policies under Rational Price Expectations." Department of Economics Working Paper no. 75-7607, Columbia Univ., 1975.

Pollak, R. A. "Consistent Planning." *Rev. Econ. Studies* 35 (April 1968): 201–8.

Sargent, T. J. "Rational Expectations, the Real Rate of Interest, and the 'Natural' Rate of Unemployment." *Brookings Papers on Economic Activity*, no. 2 (1973), pp. 429–72.

Taylor, J. B. "Monetary Policy during a Transition to Rational Expectations." *J.P.E.* 83, no. 5 (October 1975): 1009–22.

Treadway, A. B. "On Rational Entrepreneurial Behavior and the Demand for Investment." *Rev. Econ. Studies* 36 (April 1969): 227–39.

[2]

Journal of Monetary Economics 12 (1983) 101–121. North-Holland

RULES, DISCRETION AND REPUTATION IN A MODEL OF MONETARY POLICY*

Robert J. BARRO

University of Chicago, Chicago, IL 60637, USA
NBER, Cambridge, MA 02138, USA

David B. GORDON

University of Rochester, Rochester, NY 14627, USA

In a discretionary regime the monetary authority can print more money and create more inflation than people expect. But, although these inflation surprises can have some benefits, they cannot arise systematically in equilibrium when people understand the policymaker's incentives and form their expectations accordingly. Because the policymaker has the power to create inflation shocks ex post, the equilibrium growth rates of money and prices turn out to be higher than otherwise. Therefore, enforced commitments (rules) for monetary behavior can improve matters. Given the repeated interaction between the policymaker and the private agents, it is possible that reputational forces can substitute for formal rules. Here, we develop an example of a reputational equilibrium where the outcomes turn out to be weighted averages of those from discretion and those from the ideal rule. In particular, the rates of inflation and monetary growth look more like those under discretion when the discount rate is high.

1. Introduction

In a discretionary regime the monetary authority can print more money and create more inflation than people expect. The benefits from this surprise inflation may include expansions of economic activity and reductions in the real value of the government's nominal liabilities. However, because people understand the policymaker's incentives, these types of surprises — and their resulting benefits — cannot arise systematically in equilibrium. People adjust their inflationary expectations in order to eliminate a consistent pattern of surprises. In this case the potential for creating inflation shocks, ex post, means that, in equilibrium, the average rates of inflation and monetary growth — and the corresponding costs of inflation — will be higher than otherwise. Enforced commitments on monetary behavior, as embodied in monetary or price rules, eliminate the potential for ex post surprises. Therefore, the equilibrium rates of inflation and monetary growth can be

*We have benefited from discussion at the conference and from seminars at Chicago, Northwestern and Iowa. We are particularly grateful for comments from Gary Fethke, Roger Myerson, José Scheinkman, and John Taylor. Part of this research is supported by the National Science Foundation.

lowered by shifts from monetary institutions that allow discretion to ones that enforce rules.

When monetary rules are in place, the policymaker has the temptation each period to 'cheat' in order to secure the benefits from inflation shocks. (Because of existing distortions in the economy, these benefits can accrue generally to private agents, rather than merely to the policymaker.) However, this tendency to cheat threatens the viability of the rules equilibrium and tends to move the economy toward the inferior equilibrium under discretion. Because of the repeated interactions between the policymaker and the private agents, it is possible that reputational forces can support the rule. That is, the potential loss of reputation — or credibility — motivates the policymaker to abide by the rule. Then, the policymaker foregoes the short-term benefits from inflation shocks in order to secure the gain from low average inflation over the long term.

We extend the positive theory of monetary policy from our previous paper [Barro and Gordon (1983)] to allow for reputational forces. Some monetary rules, but generally not the ideal one, can be enforced by the policymaker's potential loss of reputation. We find that the resulting equilibrium looks like a weighted average of that under discretion and that under the ideal rule. Specifically, the outcomes are superior to those under discretion — where no commitments are pertinent — but inferior to those under the ideal rule (which cannot be enforced in our model by the potential loss of reputation). The results look more like discretion when the policymaker's discount rate is high, but more like the ideal rule when the discount rate is low. Otherwise, we generate predictions about the behavior of monetary growth and inflation that resemble those from our previous analysis of discretionary policy. Namely, any change that raises the benefits of inflation shocks — such as a supply shock or a war — leads to a higher growth rate of money and prices.

2. The policymaker's objective

As in our earlier analysis, we think of the monetary authority's objective as reflecting the preferences of the 'representative' private agent. Ultimately, we express this objective as a function of actual and expected rates of inflation. Specifically, benefits derive from positive inflation shocks (at least over some range), but costs attach to higher rates of inflation.

2.1. The benefits from surprise inflation

We assume that some benefits arise when the inflation rate for period t, π_t, exceeds the anticipated amount, π_t^e. One source of benefits — discussed in Barro and Gordon (1983) and in an example from Kydland and Prescott (1977, p. 477) — derives from the expectational Phillips curve. Here, unanticipated monetary expansions, reflected in positive values for $\pi_t - \pi_t^e$, lead to increases in real economic activity. Equivalently, these nominal shocks lower the unemployment rate below the natural rate. By the natural rate, we mean here the value that would be ground out by the private sector in the absence of monetary disturbances. This natural rate can shift over time because of supply shocks, demographic changes, shifts in governmental tax and transfer programs, and so on. The natural rate also need not be optimal. In fact, the benefits from surprise inflation arise when the policymaker views the natural rate as excessive. This can occur, for example, if the distortions from income taxation, unemployment compensation, and the like make the average level of privately-chosen work and production too low. Because of the externalities from these distortions, the government (and the private agents) would value stimulative policy actions that lower the unemployment rate below its natural value.

Other sources of benefits from surprise inflation involve governmental revenues. Barro (1983) focuses on the proceeds from inflationary finance. The expectation of inflation (formed the previous period), π_t^e, determines people's holdings of real cash, M_{t-1}/P_{t-1}. Surprise inflation, $\pi_t - \pi_t^e$, depreciates the real value of these holdings, which allows the government to issue more new money in real terms, $(M_t - M_{t-1})/P_t$, as a replacement. The policymaker values this inflationary finance if alternative methods of raising revenue — such as an income tax — entail distortions. Hence, the benefit from surprise inflation depends again on some existing externality. Calvo (1978) discusses the necessity of existing distortions in this type of model.

The revenue incentive for surprise inflation relates to governmental liabilities that are fixed in nominal terms, rather than to money, *per se*. Thus, the same argument applies to nominally-denominated, interest-bearing public debt. Suppose that people held last period the real amount of government bonds, B_{t-1}/P_{t-1}. These bonds carry the nominal yield, R_{t-1}, which is satisfactory given people's inflationary expectations over the pertinent horizon, π_t^e. Surprise inflation, $\pi_t - \pi_t^e$, depreciates part of the real value of these bonds, which lowers the government's future real expenditures for interest and repayment of principal. In effect, surprise inflation is again a source of revenue to the government. Quantitatively, this channel from public debt is likely to be more significant than the usually discussed mechanism, which involves revenue from printing high-powered money. For example, the outstanding public debt for the U.S. in 1981 is around \$1 trillion.[1] Therefore, a surprise inflation of 1% lowers the real value of this debt by about \$10 billion. Hence, this channel produces an effective lump amount of revenue of about \$10 billion for each extra 1% of surprise inflation. By contrast, the entire annual flow of revenue through the Federal

[1]For this purpose we should actually look at the privately-held component of the funded national debt, which is about \$700 billion in 1981.

Reserve from the creation of high-powered money is about the same magnitude ($8 billion in 1981, $13 billion in 1980).

The attractions of generating revenue from surprise inflation are clear if we view the depreciation of real cash or real bonds as an unexpected capital levy. As with a tax on existing capital, surprise inflation provides for a method of raising funds that is essentially non-distorting, ex post. Once people have built up the capital or held the real cash or real bonds, the government can extract revenue without disincentive effects. Of course, the distortions arise — for capital, money or bonds — when people anticipate, ex ante, the possibility of these capital levies, ex post. That's why these forms of raising revenue will not end up being so desirable in a full equilibrium where people form expectations rationally. But, for the moment, we are just listing the benefits that attach, ex post, to surprise inflation.

2.2. The costs of inflation

The second major element in our model is the cost of inflation. Costs are assumed to rise, and at an increasing rate, with the realized inflation rate, π_t. Although people generally regard inflation as very costly, economists have not presented very convincing arguments to explain these costs. Further, the present type of cost refers to the actual amount of inflation for the period, rather than to the variance of inflation, which could more easily be seen as costly. Direct costs of changing prices fit reasonably well into the model, although the quantitative role of these costs is doubtful. In any event the analysis has some interesting conclusions for the case where the actual amount of inflation for each period is not perceived as costly. Then, the model predicts a lot of inflation!

3. The setup of our example

We focus our discussion on the simplest possible example, which illustrates the main points about discretion, rules and reputation. Along the way, we indicate how the results generalize beyond this example.

The policymaker's objective involves a cost for each period, z_t, which is given by

$$z_t = (a/2)(\pi_t)^2 - b_t(\pi_t - \pi_t^e) \quad \text{where} \quad a, b_t > 0. \tag{1}$$

The first term, $(a/2)(\pi_t)^2$, is the cost of inflation. Notice that our use of a quadratic form means that these costs rise at an increasing rate with the rate of inflation, π_t. The second term, $b_t(\pi_t - \pi_t^e)$, is the benefit from inflation shocks. Here, we use a linear form for convenience.[2] Given that the benefit parameter, b_t, is positive, an increase in unexpected inflation, $\pi_t - \pi_t^e$, reduces costs. We can think of these benefits as reflecting reductions in unemployment or increases in governmental revenue.

We allow the benefit parameter, b_t, to move around over time. For example, a supply shock — which raises the natural rate of unemployment — may increase the value of reducing unemployment through aggressive monetary policy. Alternatively, a sharp rise in government spending increases the incentives to raise revenue via inflationary finance. In our example, b_t is distributed randomly with a fixed mean, $\bar{b}$, and variance, σ_b^2.[3] (Hence, we neglect serial correlation in the natural unemployment rate, government expenditures, etc.)

The policymaker's objective at date t entails minimization of the expected present value of costs,

$$Z_t = E[z_t + (1/(1+r_t)) \cdot z_{t+1} + (1/(1+r_t)(1+r_{t+1}))z_{t+2} + \dots], \tag{2}$$

where r_t is the discount rate that applies between periods t and $t+1$. We assume that r_t is generated from a stationary probability distribution. (Therefore, we again neglect any serial dependence.) Also, the discount rate is generated independently of the benefit parameter, b_t. For the first period ahead, the distribution of r_t implies a distribution for the discount factor, $q_t = 1/(1+r_t)$. We denote the mean and variance for q_t by $\bar{q}$ and σ_q^2, respectively.

The policymaker controls a monetary instrument, which enables him to select the rate of inflation, π_t, in each period. The main points of our analysis do not change materially if we introduce random discrepancies between inflation and changes in the monetary instrument. For example, we could have shifts in velocity or control errors for the money supply. Also, the policymaker has no incentive to randomize choices of inflation in the model.

We begin with a symmetric case where no one knows the benefit parameter, b_t, or the discount factor for the next period, q_t, when they act for period t. Hence, the policymaker chooses the inflation rate, π_t, without observing either b_t or q_t. Similarly, people form their expectations, π_t^e, of the policymaker's choice without knowing these parameters. Later on we modify this informational structure.

[2]Our previous paper [Barro and Gordon (1983)] uses a term of the form, $[\phi_t - \lambda(\pi_t - \pi_t^e)]^2$, where $\phi_t > 0$ depends on the natural unemployment rate for the period. Then, the policymaker values inflation shocks — that is, $\pi_t > \pi_t^e$ — only over some range. But, the general nature of the results does not change if we substitute this more complicated form. Also, we could modify the cost of inflation to depend on $(\pi_t - \bar{\pi}_t)^2$, where $\bar{\pi}_t$ is the optimal inflation tax on cash balances.

[3]In some models, such as Lucas (1973) and Barro (1976), the coefficient b_t depends on the forecast variance of inflation. Most of our results would not be affected if we allowed for this type of dependence. However, this element matters when we compare across regimes that have different forecast variances for inflation.

4. Discretionary policy

Our previous paper [Barro and Gordon (1983)] discusses discretionary policy in the present context as a non-cooperative game between the policymaker and the private agents. In particular, the policymaker treats the current inflationary expectation, π_t^e, and all future expectations, π_{t+i}^e for $i>0$, as given when choosing the current inflation rate, π_t. Therefore, π_t is chosen to minimize the expected cost for the current period, Ez_t, while treating π_t^e and all future costs as fixed. Since future costs and expectations are independent of the policymaker's current actions, the discount factor does not enter into the results. The solution from minimizing Ez_t, where z_t is given in eq. (1), is

$$\hat{\pi}_t = \bar{b}/a \qquad \text{(discretion)}. \tag{3}$$

We use carets to denote the solution under discretion. (With other cost functions, π_t would depend also on π_t^e.)

Given rational expectations, people predict inflation by solving out the policymaker's optimization problem and forecasting the solution for $\hat{\pi}_t$ as well as possible. In the present case they can calculate exactly the choice of inflation from eq. (3) — hence, the expectations are

$$\pi_t^e = \hat{\pi}_t = \bar{b}/a. \tag{4}$$

Since inflation shocks are zero in equilibrium — that is, $\hat{\pi}_t - \pi_t^e = 0$ — the cost from eq. (1) ends up depending only on $\hat{\pi}_t$. In particular, the cost is

$$\hat{z}_t = (1/2)(\bar{b})^2/a \qquad \text{(discretion)}. \tag{5}$$

5. Policy under a rule

Suppose now that the policymaker can commit himself in advance to a rule for determining inflation. This rule can relate π_t to variables that the policymaker knows at date t. In the present case no one knows the parameters, b_t and q_t, at date t. But, everyone knows all previous values of these parameters. Therefore, the policymaker can condition the inflation rate, π_t, only on variables that are known also to the private agents. (The policymaker could randomize his choices, but he turns out not to have this incentive.) Therefore, the policymaker effectively chooses π_t and π_t^e together, subject to the condition that $\pi_t^e = \pi_t$. Then, the term that involves the inflation shock, $\pi_t - \pi_t^e$, drops out of the cost function in eq. (1). Given the way that we modeled the costs of inflation — namely, as $(a/2)(\pi_t)^2$ — it follows immediately that the best rule prescribes zero inflation at all dates,

$$\pi_t^* = 0 \qquad \text{(rule)}. \tag{6}$$

We use an asterisk to denote the results from a rule. Eq. (6) amounts to a constant-growth-rate-rule, where the rate of growth happens to be zero.

Finally, we can calculate the costs under a rule from eq. (1) as

$$z_t^* = 0 \qquad \text{(rule)}. \tag{7}$$

The general point is that the costs under the rule, z_t^*, are lower than those under discretion, $\hat{z}_t$ from eq. (5). The lower cost reflects the value of being able to make commitments — that is, contractual agreements between the policymaker and the private agents. Without these commitments, inflation ends up being excessive — specifically, $\hat{\pi}_t > 0$ — but, no benefits from higher inflation result.

6. Cheating and temptation

As noted by others [e.g., Taylor (1975), B. Friedman (1979)], the policymaker is tempted to renege on commitments. In particular, if people expect zero inflation — as occurs under the rule — then the policymaker would like to implement a positive inflation rate in order to secure some benefits from an inflation shock. Further, this desire does not stem from a peculiarity in the policymaker's tastes. Rather, it reflects the distortions that make inflation shocks desirable in the first place.

How much can the policymaker gain in period t by cheating? Assume that people have the inflationary expectation, $\pi_0^e = 0$, which they formed at the start of period t. If the policymaker treats this expectation as a given, the choice of π_t that minimizes z_t is the one that we found before under discretion[4] — namely,

$$\tilde{\pi}_t = \bar{b}/a \qquad \text{(cheating)}. \tag{8}$$

We use tildes to denote values associated with cheating. The expected cost follows from eq. (1) as

$$E\tilde{z}_t = -(1/2)\bar{b})^2/a \qquad \text{(cheating)}. \tag{9}$$

The general point is that this expected cost is lower than that, $z_t^* = 0$, from following the rule. We refer to the difference between these expected costs as the temptation to renege on the rule — or simply as the temptation. In the present case we have

$$\text{temptation} = E(z_t^* - \tilde{z}_t) = (1/2)(\bar{b})^2/a > 0. \tag{10}$$

[4]With a different cost function, the result for $\tilde{\pi}_t$ generally differs from that under discretion, $\hat{\pi}_t$.

At the present stage we have three types of outcomes. Ranging from low costs to high, these are

(1) cheating (with people expecting the rule), $E\tilde{z}_t = -(1/2)(\bar{b})^2/a$,
(2) rule, $z_t^* = 0$,
(3) discretion, $\hat{z}_t = (1/2)(\bar{b})^2/a$.

Discretion is worse than the rule because first, no inflation shocks arise in either case, but second, the commitment under the rule avoids excessive inflation. However, the rule is only a second-best solution. Cheating — *when people anticipate the rule* — delivers better results. That's because the inflation shock eliminates part of the existing distortion in the economy (which is worth the extra inflation). But, the cheating outcome is feasible only when people can be systematically deceived into maintaining low inflationary expectations. In our subsequent analysis this cannot happen in equilibrium. However, the incentive to cheat determines which rules are sustainable without legal or institutional mechanisms to enforce them. There is a tendency for the pursuit of the first best — that is, the cheating outcome — to generate results that are poorer than the second best (rules) and closer to the third best (discretion).

7. Enforcement of rules

Generally, a credible rule comes with some enforcement power that at least balances the temptation to cheat. We consider here only the enforcement that arises from the potential loss of reputation or credibility. This mechanism can apply here because of the repeated interaction between the policymaker and the private agents.[5] Specifically, if the policymaker engineers today a higher rate of inflation than people expect, then everyone raises their expectations of future inflation in some manner. Hence, in a general way, the cost of cheating today involves the increase in inflationary expectations for the future.

Consider a rule that specifies the inflation rate, π_t^*, for period t. The rule might prescribe $\pi_t^* = 0$, as before, or it might dictate some non-zero rate of inflation. Generally, the rule can specify some dependence of π_t^* on the realizations of all variables through date $t-1$ — that is, the values for date t are still not observed when π_t^* is set.

We postulate the following form of expectations mechanism, which we eventually show to be rational:

$$\begin{aligned} &(1) \quad \pi_t^e = \pi_t^* \quad \text{if} \quad \pi_{t-1} = \pi_{t-1}^e, \quad \text{and} \\ &(2) \quad \pi_t^e = \hat{\pi}_t \quad \text{if} \quad \pi_{t-1} \neq \pi_{t-1}^e. \end{aligned} \tag{11}$$

[5]This type of repeated game is discussed in J. Friedman (1971).

In other words if the previous inflation rate, π_{t-1}, accords with expectations, π^e_{t-1}, then people trust the government to perform in line with its announced rule for period t — that is, $\pi^e_t = \pi^*_t$. But, if the actual value departs from expectations last period, $\pi_{t-1} \neq \pi^e_{t-1}$, then people do not expect the government to follow its rule this period — hence, $\pi^e_t \neq \pi^*_t$. Rather, private agents anticipate that the policymaker will optimize subject to given expectations, which defines a discretionary situation. Hence, expectations are $\pi^e_t = \hat{\pi}_t$, where $\hat{\pi}_t$ is again the discretionary outcome.

If the government follows its rule in every period, then it also validates expectations each period. Then, the first part of eq. (11) says that the government maintains its reputation (or credibility) in each period. On the other hand, if the government cheats during period t, then the second part of eq. (11) says that the next period's expectations are the ones associated with discretion, $\hat{\pi}_{t+1}$. Then, if in period $t+1$ the government chooses the discretionary inflation rate, $\hat{\pi}_{t+1}$ (which is optimal given that expectations are $\hat{\pi}_{t+1}$), the actual and expected inflation rates coincide, although at the discretionary levels. Accordingly, the first part of eq. (11) says that people anticipate the rules outcome, π^*_{t+2}, for the following period. In other words the 'punishment' from violating the rule during period t is that the discretionary (non-cooperative) solution obtains during period $t+1$. But, credibility is restored as of period $t+2$ — that is, things carry on as of date $t+2$ as though no previous violation had occurred. Therefore, the mechanism in eq. (11) specifies only one period's worth of punishment for each 'crime'.[6] Other equilibria exist that have punishment intervals of different length, as we discuss later on.

Consider our previous rule where $\pi^*_t = 0$. Suppose that the policymaker has credibility in period t, so that $\pi^e_t = 0$. If the policymaker cheats during period t, then his best choice of inflation is $\tilde{\pi}_t = \bar{b}/a$ from eq. (8). [Note that eq. (11) says that the size and length of the punishment do not depend on the size of the crime.] Then, the policymaker gains the temptation, $E(z^*_t - \tilde{z}_t) = (1/2)(\bar{b})^2/a$, from eq. (10).

The cost of this violation is that discretion, rather than the rule, applies for period $t+1$. Hence, the policymaker realizes next period the cost, $\hat{z}_{t+1} = (1/2)(\bar{b})^2/a$, from eq. (5), rather than that, $z^*_{t+1} = 0$, from eq. (7). Since costs for period $t+1$ are discounted by the factor $q_t = 1/(1+r_t)$ in eq. (2), the expected present value of the loss is

$$\text{enforcement} = E[q_t(\hat{z}_{t+1} - z^*_{t+1})] = \bar{q} \cdot (1/2)(\bar{b})^2/a. \qquad (12)$$

We use the term, enforcement, to refer to the expected present value of the loss from transgressions.

[6]Green and Porter (1981) use an analogous model for oligopoly pricing. There, the observation of a low price triggers $(T-1)$ periods of punishment, during which firms behave in a Cournot manner.

The policymaker abides by the rule during period t — that is, sets $\pi_t = \pi_t^*$ — if the enforcement is at least as great as the temptation. Otherwise, he opts for the cheating solution, $\pi_t = \tilde{\pi}_t$ (and suffers the consequences next period). But, when forming expectations for period t, π_t^e, people know whether the policymaker will find it worthwhile to cheat. Hence, if the cheating solution is preferable to the rule, then the expectation, $\pi_t^e = \pi_t^* = 0$, is irrational. Therefore, people would not stick with the expectation mechanism from eq. (11). The rules that can apply in equilibrium are those that have enough enforcement to motivate the policymaker to abide by them, given the expectations mechanism in eq. (11). Then, the equilibrium satisfies two properties. First, the expectations are rational. In particular, each individual's projection, π_t^e, is the best possible forecast of the policymaker's actual choice, π_t, given the way the policymaker behaves and given the way others form their expectations. Second, the policymaker's choice π_t, maximizes his objective, given the way people form their expectations.[7]

In equilibrium rules satisfy the enforceability restriction,

$$\text{temptation} = E(z_t^* - \tilde{z}_t) \leqq \text{enforcement} = E[q_t(\hat{z}_{t+1} - z_{t+1}^*)]. \tag{13}$$

This condition says that the costs incurred today by following the rule, rather than cheating, are not greater than the expected value of having the cooperative (rules) outcome next period, rather than discretion. Consider now whether the proposed rule, $\pi_t^* = 0$, satisfies the enforceability restriction. From eq. (10), the temptation is $(1/2)(\bar{b})^2/a$, while from eq. (12), the enforcement is $\bar{q} \cdot (1/2)(\bar{b})^2/a$.[8] Since $\bar{q} < 1$, the temptation is strictly greater than the enforcement. Hence, the ideal rule, $\pi_t^* = 0$, is not enforceable, at least given the expectations mechanism from eq. (11). Therefore, zero inflation is not an equilibrium in our model. [With a different form of cost function, rather than eq. (1), the ideal rule may or may not be enforceable.]

8. The best enforceable rule

We look here for the best enforceable rule — that is, the one that minimizes expected costs, subject to the constraint that the enforcement be at least as great as the temptation. In the present setting, where the parameters,

[7]The expectations mechanism from eq. (11) cannot be rational if the game has a known, finite endpoint. Then, no punishment arises for crimes in the last period. Working backward, the solution unravels period by period. Our framework assumes no known termination date for the game, although the game may end probabilistically. Then, a higher probability of termination shows up as a higher discount rate — that is, as a lower mean discount factor, $\bar{q}$. For some related game-theory literature, see Selten (1978), Kreps and Wilson (1980), and Milgrom and Roberts (1980).

[8]The two terms are equal when $\bar{q} = 1$ only because of the specific cost function from eq. (1). Generally, equality would arise for a value of $\bar{q}$ that is either above or below one

b_t and q_t, are unobservable at date t, the best rule has the simple form,

$$\pi_t^* = \pi. \tag{14}$$

That is, the rule specifies constant inflation (a 'constant-growth-rate rule'). But, we already know that the ideal rule, $\pi = 0$, is not enforceable. Given this, the enforceability restriction turns out to hold with equality for the best enforceable rule.

Using the procedures described before, we can calculate the temptation and enforcement associated with the rule, $\pi_t^* = \pi$. (Note that $\pi_t^e = \pi$ also applies here.) The results are

$$\text{temptation} = E(z_t^* - \tilde{z}_t) = (a/2)(\bar{b}/a - \pi)^2, \quad \text{and} \tag{15}$$

$$\text{enforcement} = \bar{q} \cdot E(\hat{z}_{t+1} - z_{t+1}^*) = \bar{q} \cdot (a/2)[(\bar{b}/a)^2 - \pi^2]. \tag{16}$$

We graph the temptation and enforcement versus the inflation rate, π, in fig. 1. (This figure was suggested to us by John Taylor.) At $\pi = 0$, the temptation follows from eq. (10) as $(\bar{b})^2/2a$. Then, as π rises, the gain from cheating diminishes — hence, the temptation falls. Finally, when π equals the discretionary value, $\bar{b}/a$, the temptation equals zero. That's because the cheating solution and the rule prescribe the same inflation rate, $\bar{b}/a$, at this point. (As π increases further, the temptation increases, because — for given expectations — the policymaker prefers the discretionary inflation rate, $\bar{b}/a$, to higher rates of inflation.)

The enforcement equals $\bar{q}(\bar{b})^2/2a$ when $\pi = 0$, from eq. (12). Then, as π rises, the enforcement declines. That's because the cost from losing reputation becomes smaller when the rule prescribes a higher rate of inflation. As with the temptation, the enforcement equals zero when π equals the discretionary value, $\bar{b}/a$. Here, when the policymaker cheats, people expect the same rate of inflation — namely, the discretionary amount $\bar{b}/a$ — as when the policymaker abides by the rule. Consequently, there is no enforcement. (When π increases further, the enforcement becomes negative — that is, the policymaker prefers the punishment, where people anticipate the inflation rate $\bar{b}/a$, to the maintenance of the rule, where people expect an inflation rate that exceeds $\bar{b}/a$.)

Notice that fig. 1 determines a range of announced inflation rates that can be equilibria. Specifically, the enforcement is at least as large as the temptation for values of π in the interval, $(\bar{b}/a)(1-\bar{q})/(1+\bar{q}) \leqq \pi \leqq \bar{b}/a$. Among these, we focus on the value of π that delivers the best results in the sense of minimizing the expected costs from eq. (2). We can rationalize this focus on one of the possible equilibria by allowing the policymaker to choose which value of π to announce in some initial period. Then, as long as this value is

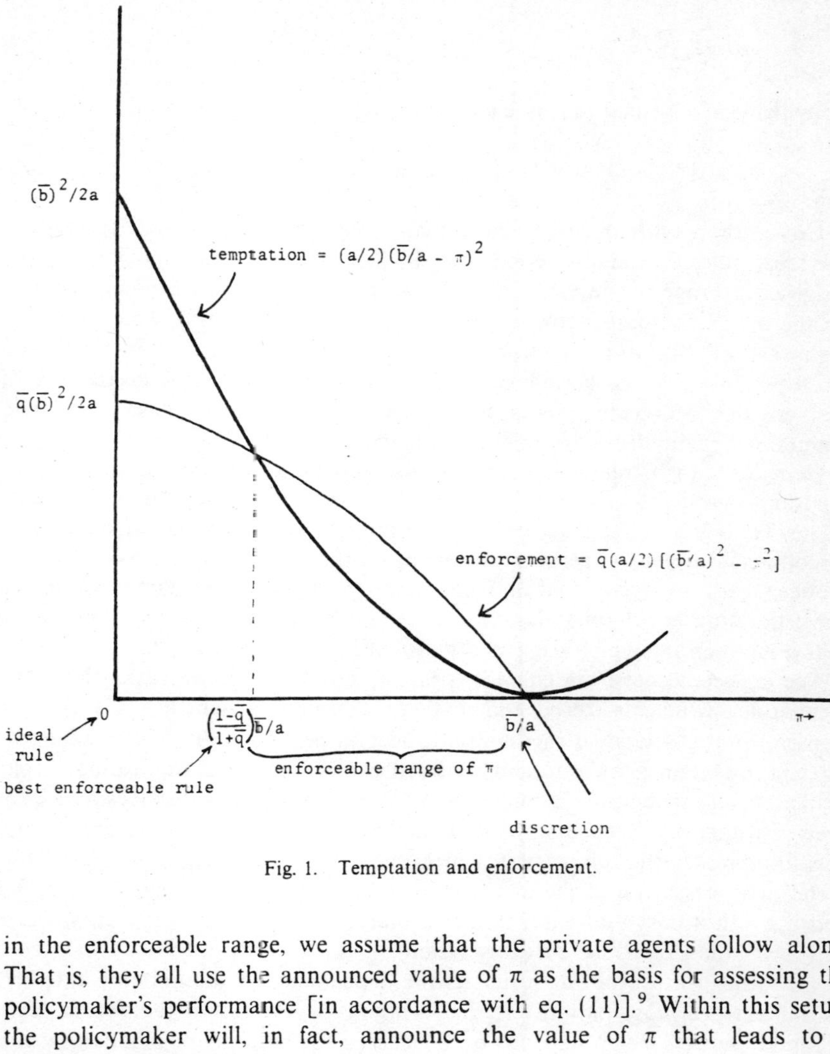

Fig. 1. Temptation and enforcement.

in the enforceable range, we assume that the private agents follow along. That is, they all use the announced value of π as the basis for assessing the policymaker's performance [in accordance with eq. (11)].[9] Within this setup, the policymaker will, in fact, announce the value of π that leads to a minimum of expected costs.

The best of the enforceable rules occurs where the curves for temptation and enforcement intersect in the interior of fig. 1. (The curves also intersect at the discretionary value, $\pi = \bar{b}/a$, but expected costs are higher at this point.)

[9]But, recall that the equilibrium is itself non-cooperative. In particular, each agent calculates the best forecast, π_t^e, of the policymaker's actions, while taking as given the way the policymaker behaves and the way other agents form their expectations.

Hence, the announced inflation rate is

$$\pi^* = (\bar{b}/a)(1-\bar{q})/(1+\bar{q}) \qquad \text{(best enforceable rule)}, \tag{17}$$

for which the expected cost in each period is

$$Ez_t^* = [(1/2)(\bar{b})^2/a] \cdot [(1-\bar{q})/(1+\bar{q})]^2. \tag{18}$$

Notice that, with $0<\bar{q}<1$, the inflation rate, π^*, is intermediate between the ideal rule, 0, and discretion, $\bar{b}/a$. In fact, the best enforceable rule is a weighted average of the ideal rule and discretion, with the weights depending on the mean discount factor, $\bar{q}$. A relatively small value of $\bar{q}$, which means a high rate of discount on future costs, implies a relatively high weight on discretion — that is, a high value of π^*. That's because a decrease in $\bar{q}$ weakens the enforcement [eq. (16)], which requires π^* to increase in order to maintain the equality between the enforcement and the temptation.

Generally, an increase in the mean discount factor, $\bar{q}$, reduces π^*, with π^* tending toward zero (the ideal rule) as $\bar{q}$ tends to one.[10] On the other hand, π^* tends to $\bar{b}/a$ — the discretionary result — as $\bar{q}$ tends to zero. (A zero discount factor means zero enforcement, so that only discretion is credible.) Notice that any force that influences the mean discount factor, $\bar{q}$, has a corresponding effect on inflation. For example, during a war we anticipate that $\bar{q}$ will be low, which triggers high inflation (via high monetary growth).

The expected cost from eq. (18) is also intermediate between that from the ideal rule, which is zero, and that for discretion, which is $(1/2)(\bar{b})^2/a$. Remember that the ideal rule is itself a second-best solution, which is inferior to cheating when people anticipate the ideal rule. But, cheating cannot occur systematically when people understand the policymaker's incentives and form their expectations accordingly. Rather, the lure of the better outcome from cheating creates the temptation, which makes the ideal rule non-enforceable. Hence, the attraction of the first best makes the second best unattainable. We end up with a cost that exceeds the second best (the ideal rule), but which is still lower than the third best (discretion).

The other feature of our results is the dependence of the inflation rate, π^*, on the ratio of cost parameters, $\bar{b}/a$. This ratio pertains to the benefit from inflation shocks, which depends on $\bar{b}$, relative to the costs of inflation, which depends on the parameter a. An increase in the ratio, $\bar{b}/a$, raises the temptation, relative to the enforcement, which requires π^* to increase. In particular, if inflation is not very costly, so that the parameter a is small, then we end up with a lot of inflation. Also, anything that raises the mean benefit attached to an inflation shock, $\bar{b}$, leads to higher inflation (but, not to

[10]This last condition depends on the specifics of our example. However, the direction of effect for $\bar{q}$ on π^* applies generally.

more benefits from inflation shocks). In our previous paper [Barro and Gordon (1983)], which focused on the results under discretion, we discussed some changes in the economy that can affect the benefits from inflation shocks. For example, the parameter $\bar{b}$ tends to be high in the following cases:

— when the natural unemployment rate is high,
— during a recession,
— during a war or other period where government expenditures rise sharply,
— when the deadweight losses from conventional taxes are high, and
— when the outstanding real stock of nominally-denominated public debt is large.

In each case we predict that the high value of $\bar{b}$ triggers a high value of π^* — that is, a high rate of monetary expansion by the policymaker. This view accounts for[11]

— a rise in the mean inflation rate along with a rise in the natural unemployment rate (as in the U.S. over the last 10–15 years),
— countercyclical response of monetary policy,
— high rates of monetary expansion during wartime,
— high rates of monetary growth in some less developed countries, and
— an inflationary effect from the outstanding real stock of public debt.

9. Contingent rules

We get some new results when we modify the informational structure in ways that motivate the policymaker to employ a contingent rule. Then, the inflation rate varies each period in accordance with the state of the economy.

Suppose that the policymaker knows the values of the benefit parameter, b_t, and the discount factor, q_t, when choosing the inflation rate, π_t. If people also condition their expectations, π_t^e, on b_t and q_t, then the results change little from those already presented. So, we focus on the case where π_t^e is still generated without knowledge of the contemporaneous variables, b_t and q_t.

One possibility is that the policymaker receives information more quickly than private agents. However, our setup does not require this informational asymmetry. For example, when setting demands for real money balances or holdings of real government bonds, people have to forecast rates of inflation. Once people hold the government's nominal liabilities, their real wealth changes when subsequent inflation shocks occur. Therefore, although the government and private agents may have the same information at any point

[11]Some of these results can also be explained by changes in the optimal tax rate on cash balances, which applies to the systematic part of inflation. For example, this effect is probably important for monetary growth during wartime and in less developed countries.

in time, the agents' decisions (on how much real money and bonds to hold) depend on expectations of inflation that were formed earlier. Therefore, we can think of π_t^e as not being conditioned on the realizations, b_t and q_t. However, these realizations can influence the actual inflation rate, π_t.

The situation is less clear for the example of the Phillips curve. In models where only unperceived nominal disturbances matter for real variables — as in Lucas (1972, 1973) and Barro (1976) — the pertinent value for π_t^e is the one based on contemporaneously available information. However, some models with long-term nominal contracting [Gray (1976), Fischer (1977), Taylor (1980)] suggest that inflationary expectations formed at earlier dates will matter for today's choices of employment, production, etc. Then, the situation resembles that from above where people choose their holdings of money and bonds based on forecasts of inflation. However, the rationality of the Gray–Fischer–Taylor contracts has been questioned [Barro (1977)].

9.1. Discretion

We find the results under discretion in the same way as before. Specifically, we get

$$\hat{\pi}_t = b_t/a. \tag{19}$$

Now, the policymaker reacts to the actual value of the benefit parameter, b_t, rather than to its mean, $\bar{b}$. However, people's expectations — not conditioned on b_t — are $\pi_t^e = \bar{b}/a$. Therefore, although $\pi_t^e = E\hat{\pi}_t$, the realizations for b_t generate departures of inflation from its expectation. Therefore, the inflation shocks — and the corresponding benefits from them — are sometimes positive and sometimes negative.

The costs under discretion are now

$$\hat{z}_t = (1/2)(b_t)^2/a - (b_t/a)(b_t - \bar{b}). \tag{20}$$

The results correspond to those from before [eq. (5)] if $b_t = \bar{b}$. Looking one period ahead, we can calculate

$$E\hat{z}_{t+1} = (1/2a)[(\bar{b})^2 - \sigma_b^2]. \tag{21}$$

The new term is the variance of the benefit parameter, σ_b^2.

9.2. The ideal contingent rule

When b_t is observed, the ideal rule no longer prescribes zero (or constant) inflation at all times. Rather, the policymaker conditions the inflation rate on the realizations for the benefit parameter. The present example is simple enough to write out the ideal contingent rule in closed form. Specifically — abstracting from enforcement problems — the best rule turns out (after a large amount of algebra) to be

$$\pi_t^* = (1/a)(b_t - \bar{b}). \tag{22}$$

As before, the prior mean of inflation, $\pi_t^e = E\pi_t^*$, is zero. But, realized inflation exceeds its expectation — and benefit from inflation shocks arise — when b_t exceeds its mean, $\bar{b}$. Conversely, inflation is below its expectation — so that costs from unexpectedly low inflation occur — when b_t is below its mean.

Note that inflationary expectations are always zero, but the policymaker creates surprisingly low inflation (i.e., deflation) when the benefits parameter takes on relatively low values. These realizations may show up as a recession or as other costs from a negative inflation shock. Yet, ex post, it would clearly be preferable to have zero, rather than negative, inflation. Then, we avoid the negative inflation shock and also have less costs due to inflation [which are $(a/2)(\pi_t)^2$]. So, the negative inflation shocks may appear pointless. Yet, the ideal rule says that the policymaker should 'bite the bullet' — that is, cause a recession through contractionary monetary policy — under some circumstances. That's because the surprisingly low rule of inflation when the benefit parameter, b_t, is low is the counterpart of the surprisingly high rate of inflation when the benefit parameter is high. Choosing zero, rather than negative, inflation for the low states means that the prior expectation of inflation is higher than otherwise. Then, the policymaker achieves lower benefits in the states where b_t is relatively high. In fact, it is worthwhile to incur some costs in the low states — namely, bite the bullet through unexpectedly low inflation — in order to 'buy' the unexpectedly high inflation and the corresponding benefits in the high states. In effect the policymaker invests in credibility when it is relatively cheap to do so — namely, when b_t is low — in order to cash in on this investment when it is most important — that is, when b_t is high.

The costs associated with the ideal rule turn out to be

$$z_t^* = -(1/2a)[(b_t)^2 - (\bar{b})^2]. \tag{23}$$

Again, we get our previous results [eq. (7)] if $b_t = \bar{b}$. Looking ahead one period, the expectation of these costs is

$$Ez_{t+1}^* = -(1/2a)\sigma_b^2 \tag{24}$$

Because the policymaker can match the variations in b_t with appropriate responses in π_t, the expected costs fall with an increase in the variance of the benefit parameter, σ_b^2.[12]

As before, we can show that the ideal rule is not enforceable in our model.[13] Therefore, we go on now to examine the best enforceable, contingent rule.

9.3. Enforceable contingent rules

We look at rules that express the inflation rate, π_t^*, as a stationary function of the state, which specifies the values of the two variables, b_t and q_t. Given that the ideal rule is unattainable, the best enforceable rule in our model turns out to equate the temptation to the enforcement *for all realizations of b_t and q_t*.[14] The temptation cannot exceed the enforcement for any of these realizations in order for the rule to be credible. Further, if the enforcement exceeds the temptation in some state, then we can do better by changing the inflation rate for that state. That is, we bear more costs than necessary by having excessive enforcement.

The present example is sufficiently simple to work out the results in closed form. The solution for inflation turns out to be a linear function of b_t and of $\sqrt{q_t}$ — that is,[15]

$$\pi_t^* = c_1 + c_2 b_t + c_3 \sqrt{q_t}, \tag{25}$$

where the c's are constants, which have to be determined. If we conjecture that the rule for inflation takes the form of eq. (25), then we can work out the temptation and enforcement as functions of the parameters, c_1, c_2, c_3, and the realizations for b_t and q. Then, we determine the value of the c-coefficients in order to equate the temptation to the enforcement for all values of (b_t, q_t). Since eq. (25) has the correct form, this operation turns out to be feasible. The results are

$$c_1 = 0, \quad c_2 = 1/a, \quad c_3 = -2(\bar{b}/a)\overline{\sqrt{q}}/(1+\bar{q}), \tag{26}$$

where $\overline{\sqrt{q}}$ is the mean of $\sqrt{q_t}$. Hence, the best enforceable contingent rule

[12] However, we did not enter the variance of inflation directly into the cost function of eq. (1). If we had, this result could change.

[13] When considering the ideal rule, the temptation and enforcement turn out to be independent of the realization for b_t. Further, the temptation exceeds the enforcement for all discount factors, q_t, that are less than one.

[14] With other cost functions, the enforcement may exceed the temptation for some realizations. In particular, we then find that the inflation rate does not react to variations in q_t in some regions.

[15] The enforcement is linear in q_t. But, the temptation involves the square of the inflation rate. Therefore, if π_t is linear in $\sqrt{q_t}$, then the temptation also involves terms that are linear in q_t.

for inflation is [16]

$$\pi_t^* = (b_t/a) - 2(\bar{b}/a)\sqrt{\bar{\bar{q}}} \cdot \sqrt{\bar{q}_t}/(1+\bar{q}). \tag{27}$$

The enforceable rule can again be viewed as a weighted average of the ideal rule — eq. (22) — and discretion — eq. (19). In particular, the mean rate of inflation is positive, but lower than that associated with discretion, which is $\bar{b}/a$. The relative weights depend on the discount factor — both on the parameters of the probability distribution for q_t and on the realized value. Given the parameters of the distribution, a higher realization for q_t means a lower inflation rate, π_t^*.[17]

Note that the realization of the discount factor does not affect current benefits and costs from inflation, but does influence the amount of enforcement. Thus, the ideal rule does not depend on q_t in eq. (22). But, for low realizations of q_t, low inflation rates are not credible, because the temptation would exceed the enforcement. Therefore, the best enforceable rule does depend on q_t in eq. (27).

The inflation rate now moves around with fluctuations in the benefit parameter, b_t, or in the discount factor, q_t. In particular, relatively high realizations for b_t and relatively low ones for q_t lead to unexpectedly high inflation. Conversely, the policymaker 'bites the bullet' — that is, creates negative inflation shocks — when the benefit parameter is lower than normal or the discount factor is higher than normal. The reasoning here is similar to that from before. It is worthwhile to suffer negative inflation shocks in some cases — that is, for low values of b_t or high values of q_t — in order to sustain low prior expectations of inflation. Then, large gains are attained in the cases where the benefit parameter, b_t, is high or the discount factor, q_t, is low. These last cases are likely to be emergencies — such as wars or other times where economic activity or government revenues are valued especially highly. In effect, the policymaker bites the bullet during the non-emergencies in order to invest in credibility — an investment that yields returns during the emergencies.

10. The length of the punishment interval

So far, our results apply when the length of the punishment interval is fixed at one period. That is, the length of time for which the discretionary outcome obtains, conditional on cheating, equals the length of time over which the policymaker can enjoy the results of his cheating. (The last interval

[16]The solution reduces to the previous one in eq. (17) if there is no random variation in b_t and q_t. Then, $b_t = \bar{b}$, $q_t = \bar{q}$, and $\sqrt{\bar{\bar{q}}} = \sqrt{\bar{\bar{q}}}$.

[17]Given the variance for $\sqrt{\bar{q}_t}$ and the realized value of $\sqrt{\bar{q}_t}$, a higher value of $\sqrt{\bar{\bar{q}}}$ also lowers π_t^*. This follows by using the formula, $\bar{q} = \mathrm{var}(\sqrt{\bar{q}_t}) + (\sqrt{\bar{\bar{q}}})^2$.

essentially defines the length of the period.) Given the length of the punishment interval, we obtained a unique reputational equilibrium by allowing the policymaker to announce the best one. But, if we look at different punishment intervals (which can be either greater or smaller than one period), then we find an array of reputational equilibria. At this point, we have no satisfactory way to resolve this problem of multiple equilibria. However, we have some observations.

First, we know that the length of the punishment interval cannot be zero. That is, the policymaker cannot instantly restore a lost reputation. If he could, there would be no enforcement, which means that the only equilibrium is the discretionary one.

We can calculate the effect of longer punishment intervals on expected costs. In the present model the punishments — that is, discretionay outcomes — never occur as part of a reputational equilibrium. Hence, we always do at least as well if we increase enforcement, which corresponds here to raising the length of the punishment interval. In particular, it always looks desirable in this model to have an infinite interval, which amounts to a form of 'capital punishment'.

We can modify the model so that punishments take place occasionally.[18] For example, suppose that inflation depends partly on the policymaker's actions and partly on uncontrollable events. Further, assume that people cannot fully sort out these two influences on inflation, even ex post. Then, people adopt a form of control rule where the policymaker loses reputation if the observed inflation rate exceeds some critical value. But, because of the uncontrollable element, this loss of reputation — and hence, the punishment — actually occur from time to time. Then, in contemplating a more severe form of punishment, we have to weigh the losses when punishments occur against the benefits from greater enforcement. Thus, it is likely that the optimal punishment interval would be finite. (However, from a positive standpoint, it does not necessarily follow that the equilibrium with this punishment interval will be selected.)

Finally, another possibility is to introduce uncertainty about the policymaker's preferences. Then, people try to learn about these preferences by observing behavior. Further, the policymaker knows that people learn from his actions, and acts accordingly. Kreps and Wilson (1980), and Milgrom and Roberts (1980), who uses this general type of model, show that unique equilibria sometimes obtain.[19] But, we have not yet pursued this route in our context, because it relies on differences in tastes among potential policymakers. Unfortunately, we have nothing interesting to say about the sources of these differences. But possibly, this idea would become meaningful

[18]Green and Porter (1981) have this feature in their model of oligopoly pricing.

[19]Also, the solution does not necessarily degenerate to the discretionary equilibrium when the game has a known, finite endpoint. See footnote 7, above.

if we identified policymakers with shifting interest groups, each of which were affected differently by variations in inflation.

11. Concluding observations

Our analysis provides an example of a reputational equilibrium for monetary policy. The results amount to a combination of the outcomes from discretion with those from the ideal rule. Previously, we analyzed discretion and rules as distinct possible equilibria. Now, the relative weights attached to the discretionary and rules solutions depend on the policymaker's discount rate and some other factors. From a predictive standpoint for monetary growth and inflation, the results modify and extend those that we discussed previously.

In some environments the rules take a contingent form, where inflation depends on the realization of the benefit parameter or the discount factor. Here, the policymaker sometimes engineers surprisingly low inflation, which is costly at a point in time. Thus, the monetary authority 'bites the bullet' and pursues a contractionary policy, given some states of the world. By acting this way, the policymaker sustains a reputation that permits surprisingly high inflation in other states of the world.

We have difficulties with multiplicity of equilibria, which show up also in the related game-theory literature. Here, the problem arises in determining how long a loss of reputation persists. In an extended version of the model, we can figure out the optimal length for this interval of punishment. But, from a positive standpoint, it is unclear which equilibrium will prevail.

References

Barro, R.J., 1976, Rational expectations and the role of monetary policy, Journal of Monetary Economics 2, Jan., 1–32.

Barro, R.J., 1977, Long-term contracts, sticky prices, and monetary policy, Journal of Monetary Economics 3, July, 305–316.

Barro, R.J., 1983, Inflationary finance under discretion and rules, Canadian Journal of Economics, Jan.

Barro, R.J. and D.B. Gordon, 1983, A positive theory of monetary policy in a natural-rate model, Journal of Political Economy 91, Aug.

Calvo, G., 1978, On the time consistency of optimal policy in a monetary economy, Econometrica 46, Nov., 1411–1428.

Fischer, S., 1977, Long-term contracts, rational expectations and the optimal money supply rule, Journal of Political Economy 85, Feb., 191–205.

Friedman, B., 1979, Optimal expectations and the extreme information assumptions of 'rational expectations' macromodels, Journal of Monetary Economics 5, Jan., 23–42.

Friedman, J.W., 1971, A non-cooperative equilibrium for supergames, Review of Economic Studies 38, Jan., 861–874.

Gray, J.A., 1976, Wage indexation: A macroeconomic approach, Journal of Monetary Economics 2, April, 221–236.

Green, E.J. and R.H. Porter, 198[illegible], Noncooperative collusion under imperfect price information, unpublished, California Institute of Technology, Pasadena, CA, Jan.

Kreps, D.M. and R. Wilson, 1980, On the chain-store paradox and predation: Reputation for toughness, unpublished, Stanford University, Stanford, CA, July.

Kydland, F.E. and E.C. Prescott, 1977, Rules rather than discretion: The inconsistency of optimal plans, Journal of Political Economy 85, June, 473–491.

Lucas, R.E., 1972, Expectations and the neutrality of money, Journal of Economic Theory 4, April, 103–124.

Lucas, R.E., 1973, Some international evidence on output-inflation tradeoffs, American Economic Review 63, June, 326–334.

Milgrom, P. and J. Roberts, 1980, Predation, reputation and entry deterrence, unpublished, Northwestern University, Evanston, IL.

Selten, R., 1978, The chain-store paradox, Theory and Decision 9, 127–159.

Taylor, J., 1975, Monetary policy during a transition to rational expectations, Journal of Political Economy 83, Oct., 1009–1022.

Taylor, J., 1980, Aggregate dynamics and staggered contracts, Journal of Political Economy 88, Jan., 1–23.

[3]

THE OPTIMAL DEGREE OF COMMITMENT TO AN INTERMEDIATE MONETARY TARGET*

KENNETH ROGOFF

Society can sometimes make itself better off by appointing a central banker who does not share the social objective function, but instead places "too large" a weight on inflation-rate stabilization relative to employment stabilization. Although having such an agent head the central bank reduces the time-consistent rate of inflation, it suboptimally raises the variance of employment when supply shocks are large. Using an envelope theorem, we show that the ideal agent places a large, but finite, weight on inflation. The analysis also provides a new framework for choosing among alternative intermediate monetary targets.

I. INTRODUCTION

It is now widely recognized that even if a country has a perfectly benevolent central bank (one that attempts to maximize the social welfare function), it may suffer from having an inflation rate which is systematically too high.[1] Suppose, for example, that a distortion (such as income taxation) causes the market rate of employment to be suboptimal. Then inflation can arise because wage setters rationally fear that the central bank will try to take advantage of short-term nominal rigidities to raise employment systematically. Only by setting high rates of wage inflation can wage setters discourage the central bank from trying to reduce the real wage below their target level.

This paper considers some institutional responses to the time-consistency problem described above. In particular, we examine the practice of appointing "conservatives" to head the central bank, or of giving the central bank concrete incentives to achieve an intermediate monetary target. Our analysis of intermediate monetary targeting is quite different from conventional analyses in which the central bank is rigidly constrained to follow a particular feedback rule. Indeed, an important conclusion is that it is not generally optimal to legally constrain the central bank to hit its intermediate target (or follow its rule) exactly, or to choose

*I am indebted to Matthew Canzoneri, David Folkerts-Landau, Maurice Obstfeld, Michael Parkin, Alessandro Penati, Franco Spinelli, Lawrence Summers, Clifford Wymer, and to three anonymous referees for helpful comments on an earlier draft.

1. See, for example, Phelps [1967], Kydland and Prescott [1977], or Barro and Gordon [1983a,b].

The Quarterly Journal of Economics, November 1985 CCC 0033-5533/85/041169-21$04.00

"too" conservative an agent to head the central bank. By appointing a conservative or by providing the central bank with incentives to hit an intermediate monetary target, it is possible to induce less inflationary wage bargains. But this comes at the cost of distorting the central bank's responses to unanticipated disturbances, especially supply shocks. This is a cost because although the central bank cannot systematically raise employment (since private agents anticipate its incentives to inflate) monetary policy can still be used to stabilize inflation and employment around their mean market-determined levels.[2] Thus, rigid targeting is appropriate only in certain very special cases. It is important to stress that, while "flexible" monetary targeting is preferable to either fully discretionary monetary policy or rigid monetary targeting, it is not necessarily the first-best solution to the problem of stagflation in this model. That depends on the source of the underlying labor market distortion which causes the market-determined level of employment to be too low. If this distortion can be removed at low social cost, then it would be possible both to raise employment and to lower inflation. A second-best solution, which does nothing to raise the mean level of employment, would be to legally impose a complete state-contingent money supply rule. As is discussed in Section III, there are a number of problems inherent in designing such a rule. But it is only when the first- and second-best solutions are too costly or unachievable that monetary targeting (or appointing a "conservative" central banker) should be used as a "third-best" solution to the problem of stagflation.

Section II of the text describes a stochastic rational expectations macroeconomic model in which, because of wage contracting, there is a well-defined role for central bank stabilization policy. Section III derives the time-consistent equilibrium under fully discretionary monetary policy. Section IV shows how society can make itself better off by appointing as head of the central bank an agent whose dislike for inflation relative to unemployment is known to be stronger than average. Section V reinterprets the formal analysis of Section IV as a model of inflation-rate targeting, and demonstrates how to extend the framework to encompass nominal GNP targeting, money supply targeting, and nominal interest rate targeting. Section VI discusses comparisons

2. This follows from the assumption that there are nominal wage contracts. See, for example, Fischer [1977].

across regimes. Which target works best depends, of course, on the structure of the economy and the nature of the underlying disturbances. (Though we demonstrate that the interest rate is generally an unsatisfactory tool for precommitment.) In Section VII, the Conclusions, we stress the envelope-theorem interpretation of the main result: society wants the central bank to place "too large" a weight on inflation-rate stabilization relative to employment stabilization, but the weight should not be infinite.

II. The Macroeconomic Model

Here we develop a stochastic rational expectations IS-LM model. Monetary policy can have short-term real effects in this model because nominal wage contracts are set a period in advance. Due to high administrative and negotiation costs, these contracts are not indexed fully against all possible disturbances.[3]

1. Aggregate Supply

Each of the large number of identical firms in the economy has a Cobb-Douglas production function. In the aggregate,

$$y_t = c_0 + \alpha\bar{k} + (1 - \alpha)n_t + z_t, \tag{1}$$

where y is output, $\bar{k}$ is the fixed capital stock, n is labor, c_0 is a constant term, and z is an aggregate productivity disturbance; $z \sim N(0,\sigma_z^2)$. Throughout, lowercase letters denote natural logarithms and subscript t denotes time. All coefficients are nonnegative. Firms hire labor until the marginal product of labor equals the real wage:

$$c_0 + \log(1 - \alpha) + \alpha\bar{k} - \alpha n_t^d + z_t = w_t - p_t, \tag{2}$$

where w is the nominal wage, p is the price level, and n^d is labor demand.

Labor supply n^s is an upward-sloping function of the real wage:

$$n_t^s = \bar{n} + \omega(w_t - p_t). \tag{3}$$

To simplify algebra without loss of generality, $\bar{n}$ is set equal to $\bar{k} + (1/\alpha)[\log(1 - \alpha) + c_0]$. As we shall later discuss, the above labor supply curve (3) is assumed to embody a distortion that

3. The aggregate demand specification is the same as in Canzoneri, Henderson, and Rogoff [1983]. The aggregate supply specification is based on Gray [1976].

raises the real wage required to induce a given level of labor supply.

The nominal wage rate for period t is negotiated (on a firm-by-firm basis) at the end of period $t - 1$. The nature of the employment contract is that laborers agree to supply whatever amount of labor is demanded by firms in period t, provided that firms pay the negotiated wage rate $\overline{w}_t$. The level of employment in period t is thus found by substituting $\overline{w}_t$ into equation (2):

$$n_t = \overline{n} + (p_t - \overline{w}_t)/\alpha + z_t/\alpha. \tag{4}$$

In choosing $\overline{w}_t$, wage setters seek to minimize $E_{t-1}(n_t - \overline{n}'_t)^2$, where E_{t-1} denotes expectations based on period $t - 1$ information and $\overline{n}'_t$ is the level of employment that would arise if contracts could be negotiated after observing the productivity disturbance z_t and all other period t information. $\overline{n}'_t$ is found using the labor supply and demand equations (2) and (3):

$$\overline{n}'_t = \overline{n} + \omega z_t/(1 + \alpha\omega). \tag{5}$$

From equations (4) and (5),

$$n_t - \overline{n}'_t = z_t/\eta + (p_t - \overline{w}_t)/\alpha, \tag{6}$$

where $\eta \equiv \alpha(1 + \alpha\omega)$. It is clear from equation (6) that $E_{t-1}(n_t - \overline{n}'_t)^2$ is minimized by setting $\overline{w}_t = E_{t-1}(p_t)$.[4] (The possibility of indexing wages to the price level will be discussed later.)

With equations (1) and (4), together with the analytically convenient normalization that $-c_0 = \alpha\overline{k} + (1 - \alpha)\overline{n}$ so that $E_{t-1}(y_t) = 0$, one can write the aggregate supply equation as

$$y^s_t = (1 - \alpha)(p_t - \overline{w}_t)/\alpha + z_t/\alpha, \tag{7}$$

It is very important to note that output and employment stabilization are not equivalent to price prediction error minimization in the presence of a productivity shock (z).

2. Aggregate Demand

Demand for the good that firms produce is a decreasing function of the real interest rate:

$$y^d_t = -\delta\{r - [E_t(p_{t+1}) - p_t]\} + u_t, \tag{8}$$

4. This is the first of many times throughout the paper where use is made of the fact that certainty equivalence holds when the loss function is quadratic; see Sargent [1979].

where r is the *level* of the nominal interest rate and $E_t(p_{t+1}) - p_t$ represents the rate of inflation expected by investors, based on complete period t information. The serially uncorrelated goods market demand disturbance is $u_t \sim N(0,\sigma_u^2)$; u may be viewed as a transitory shift in intertemporal consumption preferences.

The demand for real money balances is a decreasing function of the nominal interest rate and an increasing function of output:

$$m_t - p_t = -\lambda r_t + \phi y_t + v_t, \tag{9}$$

where m is the logarithm of the nominal money supply and v is a shift in portfolio preferences between money and bonds; $v \sim N(0,\sigma_v^2)$. To simplify exposition, the disturbances, v, u, and z, are assumed to be independent and serially uncorrelated.

3. *The Social Loss Function*

The principal differences between the present paper and previous rational expectations cum wage contracting analyses of monetary stabilization policy derive from the specification of the social objective function. Because most models embody the natural rate hypothesis, the issue of whether or not the central bank *wishes* it could lower the average level of employment is commonly ignored. But this potential source of tension is fundamental to the conduct of stabilization policy. Indeed, if there does not exist any temptation for the monetary authorities to inflate systematically, then there is no reason to consider any regime other than fully discretionary monetary policy. (Note that the central bank's incentives to inflate need not be motivated by employment considerations, but can also arise due to the presence of nominal government debt or short-term rigidities in the tax system.)

Here we shall assume that some factor such as income taxation or unemployment insurance distorts the labor-leisure decision and causes the market-determined level of employment $\bar{n}'_t$ to lie below the socially optimal level of employment $\tilde{n}'_t$ (see Barro and Gordon [1983a]). We shall further assume that $\tilde{n}'_t - \bar{n}'_t$ is constant and equal to $\tilde{n} - \bar{n}$.

The social loss function Λ depends on deviations of employment and inflation from their optimal (socially desired) levels:[5]

5. A similar social objective function is employed in Kydland and Prescott [1977] and Barro and Gordon [1983a]. Although the analysis below would have to be modified substantially if the central bank had a multiperiod objective function, the main points would still obtain.

$$\Lambda_t = (n_t - \bar{n}'_t)^2 + \chi(\pi_t - \bar{\pi})^2, \tag{10}$$

where $\pi_t \equiv p_t - p_{t-1}$, $\bar{\pi}$ is the socially desired trend inflation rate, and χ is the relative weight society places on inflation stabilization versus employment stabilization.

Motivate!

It is somewhat difficult, in the context of a rational expectations model, to argue that the level of the inflation rate has much direct weight in the social loss function.[6] (However, the analysis below does not depend on χ being particularly large.) The costs of inflation include the administrative costs of posting new prices and the costs of adjusting the tax system to be fully neutral with respect to inflation. And, of course, high rates of inflation force agents to economize on their holdings of non-interest-bearing money—the so-called "shoe leather cost of inflation." Despite the foregoing considerations, $\bar{\pi}$ may be nonzero if alternative taxes to seignorage also generate deadweight costs through distortions (see Phelps [1973]).

III. Time-Consistent Equilibrium Under Fully Discretionary Monetary Policy

Here, stochastic equilibrium is derived under the assumption that the monetary authorities attempt to minimize the social loss function Λ, given by equation (10) above.

Expectations about the future path of the money supply are not exogenously given in this model, but depend endogenously on agents' expectations about the monetary authorities' future short-run stabilization objectives. Wage setters will not believe promised future paths for the money supply that are not time-consistent. Instead, equilibrium nominal wage increases are set at a sufficiently high level so that, in the absence of disturbances, the central bank will not choose to inflate the money supply beyond the point consistent with wage setters' desired real wage. At this high level of inflation, the central bank finds that the marginal gain from trying to raise employment above the natural rate is fully offset by the marginal cost of still higher inflation. Note also, that no individual group of wage setters has any incentive to change their wage bargain in the time-consistent equilibrium. Even though individual wage setters are concerned about infla-

6. Unanticipated inflation enters *indirectly* into the social loss function (10) through its effect on employment. Fischer and Modigliani [1978] catalog the economic costs of both anticipated and unanticipated inflation.

tion, the contract at their firm has only a small impact on the aggregate inflation rate.

By substituting equation (6) into equation (10), and recalling that $\tilde{n}' - \bar{n}' = \tilde{n} - \bar{n}$, the central bank's objective function under fully discretionary monetary policy may be written as

$$D_t = \Lambda_t = [z_t/\eta + (p_t - \overline{w}_t^D)/\alpha - (\tilde{n} - \bar{n})]^2 + \chi[p_t - p_{t-1} - \tilde{\pi}]^2, \tag{11}$$

where superscript D stand for "fully discretionary regime." The central bank maximizes social welfare by choosing a level of the money supply consistent with p_t^D, the period t price level that minimizes Λ_t:[7]

$$p_t^D = \left[\frac{\overline{w}_t^D}{\alpha^2} + \frac{\tilde{n} - \bar{n} - z_t/\eta}{\alpha} + \chi(p_{t-1} + \tilde{\pi})\right] \Bigg/ \left[\chi + (1/\alpha)^2\right]. \tag{12}$$

Recall that (the logarithm of) wage setters' target real wage is zero. Thus, wage setters select $\overline{w}_t^D$ by taking expectations across (12) and setting $\overline{w}_t^D = E_{t-1}(p_t^D)$:[8]

$$\overline{w}_t^D = E_{t-1}(p_t^D) = p_{t-1} + \tilde{\pi} + (\tilde{n} - \bar{n})/\chi\alpha = p_{t-1} + \overline{\pi}^D. \tag{13}$$

By choosing $\overline{w}_t^D$ according to (13), wage setters assure themselves that the monetary authorities will not systematically drive down the real wage. Thus, as Kydland and Prescott [1977] point out, the time-consistent rate of inflation is too high when $\tilde{n} > \bar{n}$.

We are now prepared to evaluate social welfare under fully discretionary monetary policy. But to facilitate exposition in later sections, we shall first develop a notation for evaluating the expected value of the social welfare function under any arbitrary monetary policy regime "A", Λ_t^A:

7. p_t^D is found by setting $\partial D_t/\partial p_t = 0$. The second-order conditions for a minimum are met; given the quadratic form of D, the minimum is global.

8. Investors can apply the same algorithm repeatedly to derive a time-consistent path for all future prices:

$$E_{t-1}(p_{t+s}^D) = (\tilde{n} - \bar{n})(s + 1)/\chi\alpha + (s + 1)\tilde{\pi} + p_{t+1}, \quad s \geqq 0. \tag{8.1}$$

(For simplicity, we treat the monetary authorities' objective function as constant.) Note that we are treating the price level as if the monetary authorities controlled it directly, ignoring the fact that the central bank directly controls only the money supply. The anticipated future path of the money supply consistent with (8.1) may be found using the macro model of equations (7)–(9), together with the assumption of saddlepath stability. (For microeconomic justification of the saddlepath assumption in monetary models, see Obstfeld and Rogoff [1983].)

$$(14) \qquad \Lambda_t^A = (\tilde{n} - \overline{n})^2 + \chi \Pi^A + \Gamma^A,$$

where $\Pi^A \equiv (\overline{\pi}^A - \tilde{\pi})^2$ and

$$\Gamma^A \equiv E_{t-1}\{[z_t/\eta + (p_t^A - E_{t-1}(p_t^A))/\alpha]^2 + \chi[p_t^A - E_{t-1}(p_t^A)]^2\}$$

(we have made use of the fact that $E_{t-1}(p_t) = \overline{w}_t$). The first component of Λ_t^A is nonstochastic and invariant across monetary regimes. It represents the deadweight loss due to the labor market distortion. This loss cannot be reduced through monetary policy in a time-consistent rational expectations equilibrium. The second term depends on the difference between the expected rate of inflation and society's target rate. This term is also nonstochastic but does depend on the choice of monetary policy regime. The final term, Γ^A, represents the "stabilization" component of the loss function. It measures how successfully the central bank offsets disturbances to stabilize employment and inflation around their mean *market-determined* values.

We have already solved for the mean level of inflation under fully discretionary monetary policy $\overline{\pi}^D$; see equation (13). To derive Γ^D, first multiply both sides of equation (12) by $(E_t - E_{t-1})$, noting that $\overline{w}_t^D = E_{t-1}(p_t^D)$. This yields

$$(15) \quad [p_t - E_{t-1}(p_t)]^D \equiv dp_t^D = - z_t/\eta[\alpha\chi + (1/\alpha)] \equiv \rho^D z_t.$$

Note that u and v do not enter the expression for the price prediction error that the central bank allows to occur. The central bank offsets the price level effects of aggregate demand shocks to the best of its ability (here perfect, because of the complete information assumption), because offsetting these shocks is consistent with both employment stabilization and inflation-rate stabilization. By substituting (15) into (14), and simplifying, one can obtain

$$(16) \qquad \Gamma^D = (\sigma_z^2/\eta^2)[\chi/(\chi + (1/\alpha)^2)].$$

It should be observed that an individual group of wage setters has little incentive to index positively to the price level under the fully discretionary regime. The monetary authorities fully offset the effects of demand shocks, and because inflation as well as employment enters the social objective function, they do not allow the price level to move *enough* to optimally offset the employment effects of aggregate supply shocks.

Obviously, a first-best solution to the stagflation problem described above would be to remove the labor market distortion. If this cannot be achieved at low social cost, a second-best solution would be to design a permanent constitutional reform that absolutely ruled out systematic inflation, and yet left the central bank scope to respond to disturbances. However, there are some practical drawbacks with constitutionally instituting a state-contingent money supply rule. To be fully effective, a rule must be set in place in such a way that it is very difficult to change. This, in turn, raises the danger that the rule will be difficult to alter after it becomes outmoded. Such problems might well arise because it is very difficult to predict the qualitative nature of the shocks buffeting the economy decades in advance. In the sixties, for example, it might have been difficult to anticipate the supply shocks of the seventies. Other factors such as innovations in transactions technology, regulatory changes, and the evolution of financial intermediaries all complicate the problem of designing a permanent monetary rule. (We are not suggesting that these problems are necessarily insurmountable.)

IV. Social Welfare Under a "Conservative" Central Banker

Here we consider an alternative, less drastic, response to the stagflation problem posed above. We demonstrate that society can make itself better off by selecting an agent to head the independent central bank who is known to place a greater weight on inflation stabilization (relative to unemployment stabilization) than is embodied in the social loss function Λ. The term of the agent need last only one period, though in a multiperiod setting, reputational considerations will further help ameliorate the central bank's time-consistency problems.[9] However, in choosing among potential candidates, it is never optimal to choose an individual who is known to care "too little" about unemployment, in a sense that will be made precise below.

Suppose, for example, that in period $t-1$ society selects an agent to head the central bank in period t. The reputation of this individual is such that it is known that if he is appointed to head the central bank, he will maximize the following objective function (henceforth, time t subscripts are omitted where the meaning is obvious):

$$I = (n - \tilde{n}')^2 + (\chi + \varepsilon)(\pi - \tilde{\pi})^2, \qquad \chi + \varepsilon > 0. \tag{17}$$

9. See Barro and Gordon [1983b], for example.

When ε is strictly greater than zero, then this agent places a greater relative weight on inflation stabilization than society does.

The algorithm for deriving the time-consistent equilibrium is exactly the same as in the previous section. Equations (18), (19), and (20) are the "I" regime counterparts of equations (13), (15), and (16), respectively:

$$(18) \quad \Pi^I = (\overline{\pi}^I - \tilde{\pi})^2 = [(\tilde{n} - \overline{n})/\alpha(\chi + \varepsilon)]^2,$$

$$(19) \quad [p_t - E_{t-1}(p_t)]^I = dp_t^I = -z_t/\eta[(1/\alpha) + \alpha\chi + \alpha\varepsilon],$$

$$(20) \quad \Gamma^I = (\sigma_z^2/\eta^2)[(\chi + \varepsilon)^2 + (\chi/\alpha^2)]/[(1/\alpha)^2 + \chi + \varepsilon]^2.$$

Note that Γ^I is obtained by plugging dp_t^I into Γ^A, as defined in equation (14). The regime should be evaluated on the basis of the expected value of the social loss function, not the expected value of the central banker's loss function. The reader can confirm that equations (18)–(20) are the same as (13), (15), and (16) when $\varepsilon = 0$. The expected value of the social loss function under regime "I" is

$$(21) \quad \Lambda^I = (\tilde{n} - \overline{n})^2 + \chi\Pi^I + \Gamma^I.$$

To solve for the value of ε that minimizes Λ^I, differentiate (21) with respect to ε:

$$(22a) \quad \frac{\partial\Lambda^I}{\partial\varepsilon} = \chi\left(\frac{\partial\Pi^I}{\partial\varepsilon}\right) + \frac{\partial\Gamma^I}{\partial\varepsilon},$$

$$(22b) \quad \frac{\partial\Gamma^I}{\partial\varepsilon} = 2\left(\frac{\sigma_z^2}{\eta^2}\right)\left[\left(\frac{\varepsilon}{\alpha^2}\right)\Big/(\alpha^{-2} + \chi + \varepsilon)^3\right],$$

$$(22c) \quad \frac{\partial\Pi^I}{\partial\varepsilon} = -\frac{2[(\tilde{n} - \overline{n})/\alpha]^2}{(\chi + \varepsilon)^3}.$$

Define $\varepsilon^{\min}$ as the value of ε that minimizes Λ^I.[10] We are now ready to prove:

THEOREM. For $\tilde{n} > \overline{n}$, $0 < \varepsilon^{\min} < \infty$.

Proof. Note that $\varepsilon > -\chi$ by assumption. Thus, by inspection of (22c), $\partial\Pi^I/\partial\varepsilon$ is strictly negative. Note also, by inspection of (22b), that $\partial\Gamma^I/\partial\varepsilon$ is strictly negative for $-\chi < \varepsilon < 0$, zero when $\varepsilon = 0$, and positive for $\varepsilon > 0$. Therefore, $\partial\Lambda^I/\partial\varepsilon$ is strictly negative for $\varepsilon \leqq 0$. $\partial\Lambda^I/\partial\varepsilon$ must change from negative to positive at some

10. Although it is extremely difficult to write down a closed-form solution for $\varepsilon^{\min}$, one can prove that $\varepsilon^{\min}$ is the unique positive real root of $\partial\Lambda^I/\partial\varepsilon = 0$, and therefore that Λ^I is concave in ε.

sufficiently large value of ε, since as ε approaches positive infinity, $\partial\Gamma^I/\partial\varepsilon$ converges to zero at rate ε^{-2}, whereas $\partial\Pi^I/\partial\varepsilon$ converges to zero at rate ε^{-3}. Therefore, $\varepsilon^{min} < \infty$.

Q.E.D.

It follows immediately that for $\tilde{n} = \bar{n}$, $\varepsilon^{min} = 0$. The Theorem states that in the presence of a labor market distortion, it is optimal to choose an agent to head the central bank who places a greater, but not infinitely greater, weight on inflation than society does. To interpret the Theorem intuitively, consider the effects of raising ε from zero. By increasing the central bank's commitment to fighting inflation, the time-consistent average rate of wage inflation is reduced. But the relative weight the central bank places on inflation versus employment stabilization is altered, and this distorts the monetary authorities' responses to unanticipated shocks. To see why the benefit outweighs the cost at $\varepsilon = 0$, it is suggestive to expand (22a) as follows:

$$\frac{\partial\Lambda^I}{\partial\varepsilon} = \left[\frac{\partial\Lambda^I}{\partial(\bar{\pi} - \tilde{\pi})^I}\right]\left[\frac{\partial(\bar{\pi} - \tilde{\pi})^I}{\partial\varepsilon}\right] + \frac{\partial\Gamma^I}{\partial\varepsilon}. \tag{23}$$

In the neighborhood of $\varepsilon = 0$, the monetary authorities are minimizing Γ^I (they are stabilizing optimally), so that $\partial\Gamma^I/\partial\varepsilon$ is zero. But inflation is not being minimized, so that neither term in $(\bar{\pi} - \tilde{\pi})$ is zero. We can argue similarly to suggest why $\varepsilon^{min} < \infty$. As ε becomes large, $\bar{\pi}^I$ goes to $\tilde{\pi}$ and Π^I is being minimized. Thus, for large ε, the marginal inflation cost of reducing ε is small relative to the stabilization gain. Of course, when there is no labor market distortion, so that $\tilde{n} = \bar{n}$, then $\bar{\pi}^D = \tilde{\pi}$, and it does not pay to appoint a central banker who minimizes anything other than the social loss function.

We have assumed that the preferences of the agent appointed to head the central bank can be known with certainty. Clearly, many strategic problems arise when this assumption is relaxed. However, as long as there is some information on the probable preferences of alternative candidates, the basic point of the above analysis is still germane.[11] The model is certainly consistent with the fact that central bankers are typically chosen from conservative elements of the financial community. One incentive that the head of the central bank might have for holding down inflation

11. For an illustration of some issues that arise when the monetary authorities' preferences are unknown, see Backus and Driffill's [1985] interpretation of Kreps and Wilson's [1982] analysis.

is that he can thereby improve his standing in the financial community, and thus earn greater remuneration upon returning to the private sector.

V. Intermediate Monetary Targeting

In the previous section we demonstrated conditions under which society can make itself better off by appointing an individual to head the central bank who is (somewhat) more inflation-conscious than average. The same model can be employed to explain many of the measures that countries take to insulate their central banks from inflationary pressures. For example, central banks are often endowed with a significant measure of political and fiscal independence. The analysis also suggests why it would be desirable to have a central bank's operations financed in such a way that its expenditures are independent of the government's seignorage revenues. (It is interesting to observe that during the high inflation years of the late sixties and the seventies, architecturally stunning new Federal Reserve buildings sprouted up all over the United States.)

In some sense, the widespread adoption of intermediate monetary targeting during the seventies may be viewed as an institutional response to the time-consistency problem. Suppose, for example, that through a system of rewards and punishments the central bank's incentives are altered so that it places some direct weight on achieving a low rate of growth for a nominal variable such as the price level, nominal GNP, or the money supply. Although these alternative targets have different stabilization properties, credibly increasing the central bank's commitment to achieving any of them would reduce the time-consistent rate of inflation (as can be demonstrated along the lines of the Theorem in Section IV). A very direct way of making the commitment credible would be to tie the annual remuneration or budget of the monetary authorities to their success in hitting their intermediate monetary targets. This could perhaps be accomplished through a system of bonuses or by fixing their income in nominal terms. Other explicit penalties might include requiring the central bank to devote substantial resources to publicly justifying a deviation from its targets. An implicit penalty would be if the central bank's powers and independence are affected by how well it succeeds in hitting its stated targets. (Of course, if the central bank is already controlled by inflation-conscious forces, measures to reduce its independence could raise the time-consistent inflation rate.)

A. Inflation-Rate (Price Level) Targeting

Using the above interpretation of monetary targeting, we may view the analysis of Section IV as formally equivalent to an analysis of inflation-rate (price-level) targeting.[12] With this interpretation, the ε term in the central bank's objective function (17) measures the extra incentives (rewards or punishments) the central bank has for fulfilling its inflation-rate target. These incentives are additional to the fact that the inflation rate enters directly into the social objective function Λ.

In the absence of productivity disturbances, inflation-rate targeting works extremely well, since there is then no tradeoff with employment stabilization. Indeed, it would then make sense to make ε as large as possible; raising ε lowers the time-consistent inflation rate without placing any constraints on the ability of the monetary authorities to offset aggregate demand disturbances. If money supply changes transmit quickly into price level changes, then CPI targeting would be relatively easy to implement. The CPI is published monthly in many countries, and it would not be extraordinarily expensive to gather data at higher frequencies. The present model abstracts, however, from problems that arise if there are long lags in the monetary transmission mechanism.

If supply shocks are important, then it is natural to ask whether there are other intermediate targets that would allow the central bank to bring down the mean inflation rate at lower stabilization cost. We shall consider, in turn, nominal GNP targeting, money supply targeting, and interest rate targeting.

B. Nominal GNP Targeting

Because a positive supply shock tends to raise output and lower the price level, one would expect there to be some circumstances in which nominal GNP targeting is more appropriate than inflation-rate targeting. Suppose then that the central bank's target is nominal GNP so that its objective function is given by

12. Price-level targeting and inflation-rate targeting are equivalent here, since p_{t-1} is known at the time the central bank commits itself to achieving a target for $p_t - p_{t-1}$.

$$G = (n - \tilde{n}')^2 + \chi(\pi - \tilde{\pi})^2 + \tau(y_t + p_t - \bar{y} - p_{t-1} - \tilde{\pi})^2, \tag{24}$$

where G stands for "nominal GNP targeting regime," and the index parameter τ gives the weight that the central bank places on achieving its intermediate target relative to the weight it places on directly maximizing the social objective function Λ; $\bar{y}$ is the level of output corresponding to $n = \bar{n}$, and $z = 0$. The assumption that the central bank's nominal GNP target is consistent with the natural rate $\bar{n}$ rather than the socially optimal $\tilde{n}$ is nontrivial. It may be politically difficult for the central bank to commit to a nominal GNP target consistent with a level of employment lower than the socially optimal rate $\tilde{n}$. If $\bar{y}$ is replaced by $\tilde{y}$ in (24), the stabilization properties (Γ) of nominal GNP targeting would remain unchanged, but the mean inflation rate would be higher for any level of τ. In particular $\bar{\pi} - \tilde{\pi}$ will not converge to zero but to $(1 - \alpha)(\tilde{n} - \bar{n})$ as $\tau \to \infty$. This problem is not sufficient to reject nominal GNP targeting when the variance of supply shocks is large, but is an important drawback.

We can rewrite the objective function G by using equations (6) and (7):

$$G = \left[\frac{z_t}{\eta} + \frac{p_t - \overline{w}_t^G}{\alpha} - (\tilde{n} - \bar{n})\right]^2 + \chi[p_t - p_{t-1} - \tilde{\pi}]^2$$
$$+ \tau\left[\frac{z_t}{\alpha} + (1 - \alpha)\left(\frac{p_t - \overline{w}_t^G}{\alpha}\right) + p_t - p_{t-1} - \tilde{\pi}\right]^2, \tau \geqq 0. \tag{25}$$

To find the time-consistent path of the economy under nominal GNP targeting, we again follow the algorithm of Section III:

$$\Pi^G = (\bar{\pi}^G - \tilde{\pi})^2 = (\tilde{n} - \bar{n})^2/[\tau + \chi\alpha]^2, \tag{26}$$

$$dp_t^G = -z_t[(\alpha/\eta) + \tau]/[1 + \tau + \alpha^2\chi] = \rho^G z_t, \tag{27}$$

$$\Gamma^G = \frac{\sigma_z^2\{[(\chi\alpha^2/\eta) - (\tau\alpha\omega/\eta)]^2 + \chi[\alpha/\eta + \tau]^2\}}{(1 + \tau + \alpha^2\chi)^2}. \tag{28}$$

As in the case of inflation-rate targeting, one can prove that $0 < \tau^{\min} < \infty$.[13] Nominal GNP targeting and fully discretionary monetary policy always imply the same response to aggregate

13. The fact that $0 < \tau^{\min} < \infty$ may be demonstrated analogously to the Theorem in Section IV. A simpler proof makes use of the fact that Γ^A is minimized at $\rho^A = \rho^D$, and that Γ^A is strictly increasing in $|\rho^A - \rho^D|$.

demand disturbances; in both cases the central bank tries to stabilize the price level. The response to supply shocks is in general different. However, if wages are indexed to unanticipated movements in the price level (so that $w_t = \overline{w} + \beta(p_t - \overline{w}_t)$, $0 \leqq \beta \leqq 1$), then there does exist one special parameter configuration such that fixing nominal GNP is exactly what the monetary authorities would do if unconstrained. Obviously, $\tau^{min} = \infty$ in this case.[14]

C. Money-Supply Targeting

Because the formal analysis of money-supply targeting is quite similar to that of the preceding sections, we shall focus only on the special features of this case. The central bank's objective function under money-supply targeting is assumed to be given by

$$(29) \quad M = (n - \tilde{n}') + \chi(\pi - \tilde{\pi})^2 + \mu(m_t - \tilde{m}_t)^2, \qquad \mu \geqq 0,$$

where $\tilde{m}_t = \tilde{\pi} + p_{t-1} + \lambda\overline{\pi}^M$; superscript M denotes the money-supply targeting regimes. Employing the macro model of equations (7)–(9), one can demonstrate that the target level of the money supply $\tilde{m}_t$ is the level of m_t that would be consistent with society's desired inflation rate $\tilde{\pi}$ provided that (a) there are no disturbances in period t, and (b) $\overline{\pi}^M$ is the expected inflation rate between periods t and $t + 1$.

The fact that the demand for money is interest elastic creates some problems in selecting an appropriate level for $\tilde{m}_t$. In setting $\tilde{m}_t$, the central bank needs to form an estimate at time $t - 1$ of $\overline{\pi}_{t+1}$, which depends in turn on the policy regime expected to prevail in period $t + 1$. Here we have assumed that everyone expects the same money-supply targeting regime to remain in place. Because the nominal contract rigidities last only one period, this assumption is not crucial. It is crucial, however, that the central bank's money supply target be set at a level consistent with market expectations of $\overline{\pi}_{t+1}$. If the central bank were to set $\tilde{m}$ optimistically under the assumption that $E_t(\pi_{t+1}) = \tilde{\pi}$, it would overestimate the demand for real balances and choose too high a level of $\tilde{m}$. Choosing a target level for $\tilde{m}$ that is too high would not affect the stabilization properties of money-supply targeting, but would raise the time-consistent inflation rate for any level of μ. This problem with medium-term money-supply targeting is

14. $\tau^{min} = \infty$ if $(1 - \beta)^2 + \alpha^2\chi = (1 - \beta)(1 + \alpha\beta - \beta)/(\alpha\omega + 1)$. Note that if $\beta = \omega = 0$, then rigid nominal GNP targeting is equivalent to employment targeting.

quite similar to the problem with medium-term nominal GNP targeting discussed earlier.

Equation (29) can be rewritten with p_t as the central bank's control variable by using equations (7)–(9) to substitute out for m_t:

$$(30) \quad m_t = -\lambda\bar{\pi}^M + \xi p_t + (1-\xi)\overline{w}_t^M - (\lambda/\delta)u_t + (\xi - 1)z_t/(1-\alpha) + v_t,$$

where $\xi \equiv 1 + [(1-\alpha)/\alpha](\lambda/\delta + \phi)$. By substituting into equation (29) using equations (30) and (6), one obtains

$$M = \left[\frac{z_t}{\eta} + \frac{p_t - \overline{w}_t^M}{\alpha} - (\tilde{n} - \bar{n})\right]^2$$

$$(31) \quad + \chi[p_t - p_{t-1} + \bar{\pi}]^2 + \mu\left[\xi p_t + (1-\xi)\overline{w}_t^M - (\lambda/\delta)u_t + (\xi - 1)\left(\frac{z_t}{1-\alpha}\right) + v_t - p_{t-1} - \bar{\pi}\right]^2.$$

As before, one can demonstrate that $0 < \mu^{\min} < \infty$, except in the special case where there are no aggregate demand shocks ($\sigma_u^2 = \sigma_v^2 = 0$), and one special parameter configuration obtains.[15] In this special case $\rho^M = \rho^D$, and $\mu^{\min} = \infty$. (An infinite μ is equivalent to a *k* percent rule.) Monetary targeting then can lower the mean rate of inflation to its socially optimal level without any stabilization cost. The condition that the aggregate demand shocks be zero can be relaxed when the monetary authorities have incomplete contemporaneous information.[16]

D. Nominal Interest Rate Targeting

The monetary authorities cannot systematically raise or lower the mean value of the real interest rate in the rational expectations model employed in this paper. But it might seem reasonable for the central bank to try to bring down the inflation rate by committing itself to achieving a low nominal interest rate.[17] Here

15. The condition for $\mu^{\min} = \infty$ is that

$$(1 + \alpha^2\chi)(\xi^2 - \xi)(1 + \alpha\omega) = \xi^2(1 - \alpha).$$

16. An appendix to an earlier version of this paper discusses how to extend the present analysis to the case of incomplete contemporaneous information. This appendix and details of the proofs concerning $\mu^{\min}$ and $\tau^{\min}$ are available from the author on request.

17. As Canzoneri et al. [1983] demonstrate, the central bank can only literally peg the nominal interest rate if it also announces at least one point on a mutually consistent money supply path; otherwise the price level is indeterminate.

we argue that this method of intermediate monetary targeting is counterproductive.

Consider the objective function,

$$(32)\quad R = (n - \tilde{n}')^2 + \chi(\pi - \tilde{\pi})^2 + \theta(r - \tilde{r})^2, \qquad 0 \leqq \theta < \infty,$$

where $\tilde{r}$ is the nominal interest rate target. Using equations (6)–(8), we may write the objective function (32) as

$$R = \left[\frac{z_t}{\eta} + \left(\frac{p_t - \overline{w}_t^R}{\alpha}\right) - (\tilde{n} - \overline{n})\right]^2 + \chi(p_t - p_{t-1} - \tilde{\pi})^2$$

$$(33)\qquad + \theta\left[\overline{\pi}_{t+1}^A + \left(\frac{1-\alpha}{\delta\alpha}\right)(\overline{w}_t^R - p_t) + \left(\frac{u_t - z_t/\alpha}{\delta}\right) - \tilde{r}\right]^2.$$

As we shall see, the value of $\overline{\pi}_{t+1}^A \equiv E_t(p_{t+1}^A) - p_t$ is crucial to the analysis; it depends on the monetary policy regime expected to prevail in period $t + 1$. Following the algorithm of Section III for deriving the time consistent equilibrium, one obtains

$$(34)\quad \overline{\pi}^R - \tilde{\pi} = [(\tilde{n} - \overline{n}) + (\theta(1 - \alpha)/\delta)(\overline{r}_{t+1}^A - \tilde{r})]/\alpha\chi,$$

where $\overline{r}_{t+1}^A$ has been substituted in for $\overline{\pi}_{t+1}^A$. (Given the assumptions we have made about the parameters of the macro model, the mean real interest rate under any monetary regime is zero.)

A comparison of equations (13) and (33) reveals that $\overline{\pi}^R \gtreqless \overline{\pi}^D$ as $\tilde{r} \lesseqgtr \overline{r}_{t+1}^A$. In other words, suppose that an intermediate targeting regime is put in place for one period, and the central bank is given incentives to bring interest rates below their trend rate, so that $\tilde{r} < \overline{r}_{t+1}^A$. Then, instead of falling, the expected inflation rate and expected nominal interest rate rise. They rise because wage setters recognize that *once wages are set,* the central bank can lower interest rates through money growth. While it is true that the central bank could try to bring down inflation by setting $\tilde{r}$ greater than $\overline{r}_{t+1}^A$, the fact that this would indeed cause the market-determined interest rate $\overline{r}_t$ to be less than $\overline{r}_{t+1}^A$ suggests a serious credibility problem. The central bank has to target high interest rates if it wants low interest rates.

The underlying problem is that given $E_{t-1}(p_{t+1} - p_t)$, announcing a target for r_t is, in fact, tantamount to targeting the real interest rate. For the regimes analyzed earlier, targeting succeeds in at least temporarily lowering the inflation rate regardless of how long the targeting regime is expected to last. This is no longer true when the nominal interest rate is used as a target.[18] (It should be clear that a misguided attempt to target a low real interest rate will produce similar problems.)

The nominal interest rate would not appear to be a suitable instrument for precommitment. This conclusion, of course, does not imply that the interest rate should not be used as an information variable in setting monetary policy, as in Poole [1970].

VI. On Comparing Alternative Targeting Regimes

In more traditional analyses of intermediate monetary targeting, a conventional result is that the optimal target choice depends on all the parameters of the model as well as on the relative sizes of the disturbances.[19] While one must also consider strategic factors in the more general model developed here, the standard stabilization considerations are still relevant. For example, money-supply targeting makes less sense when the monetary authorities have information about how aggregate demand shocks are affecting the price level. Inflation-rate targeting works poorly when supply shocks are significant, etc. Indeed, if we were to restrict our attention to "rigid" targeting regimes (that is, if the monetary authorities are required to hit their target exactly), then (of course) the ranking of regimes depends only on these conventional stabilization considerations (see the Appendix).

Ranking the optimally flexible regimes of Section V is somewhat more difficult because they do not have tractable closed-form solutions. (For specific parameter values, numerical comparisons are easily obtained.) It is worth noting, however, that the ranking of optimally flexible regimes is not necessarily the same as the ranking of "rigid" regimes presented in the Appendix.[20] This is not surprising in view of the "second-best" nature of the rigid targeting regimes; it is almost never optimal to constrain the monetary authorities to hit their target exactly.

18. It can be shown that low nominal interest rate targeting is counterproductive when the regime is expected to last for any finite number of periods, as long as the expected inflation rate in the final period is consistent with a return to fully discretionary monetary policy. The regime fails because the central bank cannot systematically achieve a below-market real interest rate for any future period.

19. See Poole [1975], Friedman [1975], or Parkin [1978] for analyses of the stabilization properties of alternative intermediate monetary targets.

20. Numerical examples of rank reversal are presented in an earlier version of this paper, available on request. Numerical solutions for τ^{min} are easier to obtain when $\partial\Lambda^G/\partial\tau$ is strictly concave in τ. Using Descartes' Law of Signs, one can derive the sufficient condition $1/(\alpha - \alpha^2) > \chi$. Similarly, $\partial\Lambda^M/\partial\mu$ is definitely concave in μ if $[\phi + (\lambda/\delta)]/(\alpha - \alpha^2) > \chi$.

VII. Conclusions

It can be entirely rational for society to structure its central bank in such a way that the monetary authorities have an objective function very different from the social welfare function. Whenever a distortion causes the time-consistent rate of inflation to be too high, then society can be made better off by having the central bank place "too large" a weight on inflation rate stabilization. The model presented here may help explain why many countries set up an independent central bank and choose its governors from conservative elements of the financial community.

Although society does want the central bank to place a large weight on inflation rate stabilization relative to employment stabilization, society will not (in general) want the weight to be infinite. By having the central bank place an infinite weight on inflation stabilization, society could succeed in bringing inflation down to its socially optimal level. But the central bank would also end up responding very inappropriately to supply shocks, allowing them to pass entirely through to employment. By lowering the weight which the central bank places on inflation, society could achieve a first-order stabilization gain at a second-order inflation cost. However, the inflation weight should not be so low that the central bank is placing the same weight on inflation-stabilization as society does. For then the central bank would be stabilizing optimally and by raising the central bank's weight on inflation, it would be possible to achieve a first-order inflation gain at a second-order stabilization cost (by the envelope theorem).

When supply shocks are important, society may prefer to give the central bank incentives to focus on a monetary target other than the inflation rate (though again, it is not optimal to have the weight on the target be infinite). It might be expected that the best monetary target would be the one most highly correlated with the society's ultimate objective function. But while this is a useful rule of thumb, the situation is actually somewhat more complicated. If one compares how each of the targets would work if used rigidly, one does not necessarily get the same ranking as when the central bank gives its target an optimal weight relative to direct social objectives. Thus, it can be misleading to analyze separately the stabilization and credibility problems of the central bank. The model also highlights strategic problems that can arise in setting targets at a non-inflationary level. If the central bank sets its nominal GNP target consistent with the socially optimal rate of employment, rather than the lower natural rate (perhaps because of political constraints), then nominal GNP targeting will have an inflationary bias. Money supply targeting presents similar problems if the demand for money is interest elastic. The central bank will overestimate next period's demand for money if it assumes (or is constrained to assume) that *next* period's expected inflation rate will be at the socially desired rate, rather than at the higher time-consistent rate. (This problem does not arise under a permanent k percent rule.) We demonstrated that targeting low nominal interest rates is counterproductive and actually raises the time-consistent inflation rate. The problem is that once nominal wages are set, interest rates fall as money growth rises. Real interest rate targeting presents similar problems.

In order to make the macroeconomic model rich enough to do a meaningful analysis of alternative intermediate monetary targets, it was necessary to choose a rather simple game-theoretic structure. In particular, we did not allow for reputational factors that can be important in a multiperiod setting.[21] However, although reputational considerations can ameliorate the central bank's credibility problems, they do not eliminate them except in certain very special cases. Therefore, the main point of this paper should extend to a more dynamic setting.

Appendix

Equations (A1) through (A4) give the expected value of the social loss function (10) under fully discretionary monetary policy, and rigid inflation rate, nominal GNP and money-supply targeting (the common term $(\tilde{n} - \overline{n})^2$ is omitted):

$$\text{(A1)} \qquad \Lambda^D = \left(\frac{\sigma_z^2}{\eta^2}\right)\left[\frac{\alpha^2\chi}{1 + \alpha^2\chi}\right] + \chi\left[\frac{\tilde{n} - \overline{n}}{\alpha\chi}\right]^2,$$

$$\text{(A2)} \qquad \Lambda^I|_{\varepsilon=\infty} = \frac{\sigma_z^2}{\eta^2},$$

$$\text{(A3)} \qquad \Lambda^G|_{\tau=\infty} = \sigma_z^2\left[\left(\frac{1}{\eta}\right)^2 + \left(\frac{1}{\alpha}\right)^2 + \chi - \frac{2}{\alpha\eta}\right],$$

21. See Barro and Gordon [1983b], Backus and Driffill [1985], or Canzoneri [1985].

$$\text{(A4)} \qquad \Lambda^M|_{\mu=\infty} = \sigma_z^2\left[\left(\frac{1}{\eta^2}\right) + \left(\frac{1}{\alpha^2} + \chi\right)J^2 - \frac{2J}{\alpha\eta}\right] + \left[\frac{1}{\alpha^2} + \chi\right]\left[\sigma_v^2 + \left(\frac{\lambda}{\delta}\right)^2\sigma_u^2\right]\bigg/\xi^2,$$

where $J \equiv (\xi - 1)/(1 - \alpha)\xi$.

UNIVERSITY OF WISCONSIN—MADISON

REFERENCES

Backus, David, and John Driffill, "Inflation and Reputation," *American Economic Review,* LXXV (1985), 530–38.

Barro, Robert J., and David B. Gordon, "A Positive Theory of Monetary Policy in a Natural-Rate Model," *Journal of Political Economy,* XCI (Aug. 1983a), 589–610.

——, and ——, "Rules, Discretion and Reputation in a Model of Monetary Policy," *Journal of Monetary Economics,* XII (July 1983b), 101–21.

Canzoneri, Matthew B., Dale W. Henderson, and Kenneth Rogoff, "The Information Content of the Interest Rate and Optimal Monetary Policy," this *Journal,* XCVIII (Nov. 1983), 545–66.

Canzoneri, Matthew B., "Monetary Policy Games and the Role of Private Information," *American Economic Review,* LXXV (1985), forthcoming.

Fischer, Stanley, "Long-Term Contracts, Rational Expectations, and the Optimal Money Supply Rule," *Journal of Political Economy,* LXXXV (Feb. 1977), 191–206.

——, and Franco Modigliani, "Towards an Understanding of the Real Effects and Costs of Inflation," *Weltwirtschaftliches Archiv,* CXIV (1978), 810–33.

Friedman, Benjamin M., "Targets, Instruments, and Indicators of Monetary Policy," *Journal of Monetary Economics,* I (Oct. 1975), 443–73.

Gray, Jo Anna, "Wage Indexation: A Macroeconomic Approach," *Journal of Monetary Economics,* II (April 1976), 221–35.

Kreps, David, and Robert Wilson, "Reputation and Imperfect Information," *Journal of Economic Theory,* XXVII (Aug. 1982), 253–79.

Kydland, Finn E., and Edward C. Prescott, "Rules Rather than Indiscretion: The Inconsistency of Optimal Plans," *Journal of Political Economy,* LXXXV (June 1977), 473–92.

Obstfeld, Maurice, and Kenneth Rogoff, "Speculative Hyperinflations in Maximizing Models: Can We Rule Them Out?" *Journal of Political Economy,* XCI (Aug. 1983), 675–87.

Parkin, Michael, "A Comparison of Alternative Techniques of Monetary Control under Rational Expectations," *The Manchester School,* XI (Sept. 1978), 252–87.

Phelps, Edmund S., "Phillips Curves, Expectations of Inflation and Optimal Employment Over Time," *Economica,* XXXIV (Aug. 1967), 254–81.

——, "Inflation in the Theory of Public Finance," *Swedish Journal of Economics,* LXXV (March 1973), 68–82.

Poole, William, "Optimal Choice of Monetary Instruments in a Simple Stochastic Macro Model," this *Journal,* LXXXIV (May 1970), 197–216.

Sargent, Thomas J., *Macroeconomic Theory* (New York: Academic Press, 1979).

[4]

Open economies review **2**: 95—112, 1991.

Precommitment by Central Bank Independence

MANFRED J. M. NEUMANN
Universität Bonn

Key Words: central bank, precommitment, rules, price stability, EMU

Abstract

The paper addresses the issue of central bank independence. The central argument is that government can precommit to the objective of price stability by providing a constitutional status of independence to the central bank. A sufficient set of institutional elements and the problem of incentive compatibility are discussed. It is argued that the solution is superior to a constitutional money rule as no rule can take adequately into account trend changes in output or velocity.

Europe is on the verge of uniting forces and fundamentally reorganizing her internal as well as external economic and political relations. What this will eventually mean for the citizens of Europe clearly depends on which type of political and economic constitution will finally be adopted.

Among the manifold issues to be solved, an important one is designing a constitution for European monetary union (EMU). To that purpose the European Council had set up the Delors Committee, which essentially consisted of government-dependent central bank governors. Naturally, the committee settled with a solution of centralized coordination (Vaubel 1989). For the final stage of EMU it proposed to replace national currencies with a single European currency and to merge national central banks in a new European System of Central Banks (ESCB). The ESCB is seen by the Delors Committee as an 'autonomous Community institution' that is 'committed to the objective of price stability'. The emphasis put on this objective meets the rising public recognition in Europe that the primary objective of monetary policy should be achieving and preserving price stability. However, the committee has added that, subject to this objective, the ESCB shall be obliged to support the general economic policy at the Community level.

The question is: will the envisaged set-up deliver price stability or will it have a built-in bias towards inflation? If the latter is the case, what may be the necessary and sufficient institutional elements to eliminate such bias? More generally, is there a way for government to precommit to price stability, or is time consistent monetary policy, and the inflation it generates, an unavoidable fate?

In this paper, I argue that there is a solution to the precommitment problem. The solution is not to write a coercive k-percent money rule into the constitution because fixed money rules cannot cope with changes in the trends of real growth or velocity. The solution is a constitutional reform which provides the central bank with a status of full independence from government and the political process. In contrast to solemn announcements, this institutional reform provides precommitment to price stability as it effectively binds the hands of current and future governments without foregoing the flexibility of monetary adjustment in the advent of trend changes in the velocity of money or real growth.

The next section briefly reviews the fundamental problem of the suboptimality of time consistent policy. Section 2 discusses in detail a set of institutional elements which together define a sufficient status of central bank independence. Section 3 develops the main argument on the interconnection of independence and precommitment. Finally, section 4 draws major conclusions.

1. The nature of the problem

Since the invention of fiat money and the monopolization of issuing rights by government, money holders are forced to absorb a permanently inflating money supply. Government has a deeply rooted interest in creating inflation because inflation permits the flow of seigniorage (over a certain range of inflation rates) to be raised, drives private agents into higher income tax brackets, reduces the real value of outstanding government debt, and promises a transitory stimulation of the economy, hence employment.

It goes without saying that inflation is costly, as it generates a variety of welfare-reducing distortions.[1] Consequently, one can think of an optimal rate of inflation, equating social marginal revenue with social marginal cost. The point was stressed by the pure theory of optimal taxation (Phelps 1973). But it may be noted that the concept cannot be used to explain the great variety of inflation rates observed in the real world. First, the concept does not rule out that the socially optimal rate of inflation is close to zero (Garfinkel 1989). Second and more importantly, the concept neglects the phenomenon of self-interested government. From the point of view of such government, what counts is not just the perceived social cost of inflation but also the government's perception of its own private cost with regard to losing voters' support (Nordhaus 1975). While the long-run social cost may not be disregarded completely, it is likely to be heavily discounted, given the short time horizon of the average politician.

Apart from the incentives of self-interested government, the application of game theory shows that time consistent monetary policy enforces suboptimally high inflation (Kydland and Prescott 1977, Barro and Gordon 1983). The result derives from assuming that wage-setters lock themselves into fixed wage contracts which take expected inflation into account while the government tries to raise employment above the natural level by choosing an optimal inflation surprise.

Given rational expectations with full information about the government's preference function, wage setters will anticipate the government's best-response rate of inflation. Therefore, the Nash equilibrium implies that the government is forced to validate a suboptimally high inflation rate while employment remains at the natural level. As Kydland and Prescott (1977) point out, this failure of the consistent policy of selecting the best policy, given the current situation, arises because there is no mechanism to induce government to take into consideration *after* the wage agreement the effect of its policy, via the expectations mechanism, upon *previous* wage negotiations.

Is there an easy way out? Cukierman (1989) proposes that government or the government-dependent central bank, for that matter, "should irrevocably commit its policy for the period prior to the setting of the wage contract." As a result of this "precommitment", the policy announcement would be credible, hence eliminate expectations of inflation from wage contracts. But in fact, Cukierman begs the question by employing the tempting word "irrevocably".

It is important to understand why an "irrevocable" commitment by declaration is impossible or meaningless. Suppose, the government commits itself to zero inflation by a solemn announcement, before the wage contract is concluded. Suppose further that it is subjectively serious about not deceiving the private agents later on. Then the fact remains that *after* the wage agreement the government faces a different opportunity set. By setting a positive rate of inflation, it can raise employment. Failure to do so would not be rational. Consequently, even if the private agents were convinced of the government's ex-ante seriousness, they would nevertheless play non-cooperative, because they know that matters will look differently ex post.

It remains to consider the question of reputation. Given that in reality the game between the government and private agents is a repeated game, in principle, the government can try to build a reputation by initially validating its announcement of zero inflation and exploiting the resulting reputation later on. There are two main strands in the reputation literature: wage setters may have complete or incomplete information about the government's preferences.

With complete information, as in Barro and Gordon (1983), a reputational equilibrium does not exist, if the time-horizon is finite, because backward induction reduces the sequentially rational equilibrium to the equilibrium of the one-shot game. With an infinite horizon, on the other hand, a multiplicity of equilibria results and it is not clear how agents can coordinate on a 'good' rather than a 'bad' equilibrium (Rogoff 1987). As Persson and Tabellini (1989) note, the predictive content of these models is seriously reduced due to non-uniqueness.

Moreover, the concept of reputation building is somewhat at odds with the assumption of complete information. A more congenial assumption is to let private agents be uncertain about the government's preferences or type.[2] Hence agents have to draw inferences from observed behavior. For example, Backus and Driffill (1985) analyze a finitely repeated policy game where the government is either a hard-nosed, zero-inflation government or a wet government, going for additional employment with inflation. Using the sequential equilibrium concept of Kreps and Wilson (1982), Backus and Driffill show that there exists an initial equilibrium with zero inflation which extends over time with the time horizon of the finite supergame. Yet, the inflation bias remains as the government demanding additional employment will inflate with probability one in the last period.

To sum up, reputation building is a means to reduce the inflation bias, not to eliminate it.[3] Only a subgame-perfect supergame with infinite time horizon could provide an equilibrium with permanent inflation of zero under certain conditions. If the time horizon is finite and rather short and the discount factor is small, as it is the case with real-world governments, the attempt of reputation building will not provide zero inflation.

In conclusion, no government can provide precommitment to zero inflation by declaration or by temporary good conduct. The concept of precommitment has been made very precise in game theory. Precommitment presupposes an external mechanism which effectively ties the hands of the player (Schelling 1960). In finite micro economic games precommitment can be achieved by the exchange of hostages or collateral. But in macroeconomics no comparable solution has been proposed so far. Indeed, there is widespread agreement among macroeconomists that under realistic conditions governments have no device for precommitment (Persson and Tabellini 1989).

The central argument of this paper is that the provision of a constitutional status of independence to the central bank is an effective device for government to precommit to price stability over an infinite time horizon. Suppose incentives can be set such that the governing bodies of the central bank will focus on the objective of price stability and leave the employment problem to the government.[4] In this case, setting up such a bank constitutes effective precommitment by the government, as it provides an external mechanism that binds the hands of current and future governments.

2. Constitutive features of an independent central bank

This section is devoted to clarifying the status of central bank independence. It reviews and develops a sufficient set of institutional elements which together secure the full status of independence.[5]

The following elements or principles will be considered: (i) prohibition of lending to public-sector authorities, (ii) independence of instructions from governmental authorities, (iii) exchange rate sovereignty, (iv) provisions for personal independence of board and council members, (v) constitutional rank for the central bank statutes.

2.1. Prohibition of lending to public-sector authorities

There is a broad consensus that the objective of price stability requires to free monetary policy from the traditional obligation of having to finance public-sector budget deficits through central bank credit. All major inflations of this century, including Germany's hyperinflation of 1921/23, resulted from the misuse of monetary policy as a convenient, 'noiseless' means of government finance. Hence cutting the loan link between government and the central bank is essential.

However, it is not sufficient to rule out direct lending only. Outright purchase of government bills and bonds is just another way of directly contributing central bank money to the finance of government. Unlimited open market operations in government paper, even if they are conducted with the only aim of implementing a monetary target, interfere with deficit finance, facilitating it at times, hampering it at other times. Unavoidably, this link between open market operations in government paper and deficit finance provides another opportunity for political pressure on the central bank.

Note that the prohibition of buying any type of government debt serves to protect the central bank against being forced into monetizing the debt. This does not rule out that the central bank will have the means to indirectly facilitate deficit finance, should it choose so.

2.2. Independence from instructions by governmental authorities

Trivially, there is no independence if the central bank receives and has to follow instructions issued by government or other authorities. Therefore, the governing body of the central bank, the central bank council, should be explicitly provided with the undivided authority to decide on the target of monetary policy, on instruments and implementation procedures, on the bank's internal organization, and, last but not least, on the budget.[6]

Formal independence from government instructions is indispensable. But it cannot guarantee factual independence from the government's will, if the statutes of the central bank contain an obligation to support general economic policy. An explicit obligation provides government with the right to ask for a more expansionary course of monetary policy at any time, and may make it very difficult for the central bank not to comply with such demands. Of course, the legal obligation can be weakened by attaching a modifying clause. For example, the statutes of the Deutsche Bundesbank read: the bank is obliged to support the government's general economic policy 'subject to the preservation of its primary objective' of safeguarding the domestic value of the currency.

However, such a modifying clause is much too vague to shield the central bank effectively from political pressure for monetary overexpansion. An important empirical aspect to be considered in this connection is the existence of a variable time lag of monetary policy with respect to measured inflation. Typically, politicians neglect this lag and, consequently, argue at times of relatively low inflation that an increase in the rate of money growth would be welfare improving as it would not add to inflation but raise employment. Though the argument is unfounded, it may serve its purpose of pressing the central bank into adopting an easier policy stance.

The monetary history of Germany shows that even the Bundesbank was unable to resist such political pressure at times. Examples are the years 1977/78 and 1985 to 1987. In both cases the allegedly harmless money acceleration induced a resurgence of inflation later on.

In conclusion, an explicit obligation of the central bank to support general economic policy impairs the status of independence and secures government an inroad on the central bank's primary objective of price stability. A modifying clause does not make a substantial difference in this respect. Therefore, a clean solution is to avoid any explicit obligation. Indeed, there is no need for an explicit reminder or tie. An independent central bank will support general economic policy anyway, as long as this is in line with the preservation of domestic monetary stability.

2.3. Exchange rate sovereignty

The objective of permanent price stability is not necessarily in conflict with exchange rate stability. But the cumulative evidence since the early seventies indicates that safe-guarding the domestic value of the currency over longer periods of time is possible only if the external value of the currency is permitted to settle at or gradually approach its equilibrium value or path. The price stability objective implies, therefore, that the central bank should be provided with full sovereignty to decide on all exchange rate and intervention matters.

Alternatively, if the central bank were forced by government to permanently fix the exchange rate at some preset value, it would lose its ability to control the domestic price level over the medium to long run. Monetary policy would then serve to turn the targeted exchange rate into an equilibrium rate by effectively adjusting the domestic price level path to the path of foreign inflation. It is well known that fixing the exchange rate vis-à-vis a dominant currency may make an efficient monetary policy for a smaller country, provided (i) its economy responds to world market shocks in a similar fashion as the dominant economy, and (ii) the authorities of the dominant economy maintain a stable monetary path. The experiences with the Bretton-Woods system as well as with the EMS indicate, however, that an adjustment of the exchange rate parity may be necessary at times to avoid importing inflation.

In general, flexible exchange rates are to be preferred to fixed rates. But this is not to be argued here, because the decision can be left to the central bank. The point is that government should renounce its privilege to decide on exchange rate matters. The EMS is a good example that the involvement of government in exchange rate matters leaves much to be desired. For example, the timing as well as the degree of several parity adjustments has been affected by considerations other than economic stabilization. This is not surprising, given that governments are forced to pay attention to special interest groups like farmers or export industries. But, for this very reason, it is important that governments hand over to central banks the sovereignty over intervention and exchange rate matters.

2.4. Provisions for personal independence of board and council members

The three institutional elements considered so far — prohibition of lending to public-sector authorities, independence of instructions from governmental authorities, and exchange rate sovereignty — are necessary but not sufficient to constitute the full status of independence. They permit but cannot guarantee that monetary policy will be geared to safeguarding the domestic purchasing power of the currency, if the members of the central bank council lack professional competence and/or are dependent on the domestic political process.

As regards professional competence, two aspects are to be considered. First, the central banker must be sufficiently qualified to fulfill his institutional duty of controlling his own department. It goes without saying that the specific qualification necessary depends on the department to be administered, be it accounting, banking, human resources or research.

Second, and more importantly, a central banker must have a sufficient analytical understanding of macroeconomics in general and of the specifics of monetary policy in particular. Lack of macroeconomic competence results in an undesirable dependence on the judgement of other people within or outside the bank. For this reason the designs of the eligibility standard and of the selection procedure need careful evaluation.

A more fundamental issue than lack of professional competence is independence from internal domestic politics. Whether a central banker will act independently of the political process will depend to some extent on his personal characteristics and specifically on his past involvement in actual politics. It is for this reason that all over the world governments tend to implant into the governing bodies of central banks — as well as into constitutional courts — people of their own political affiliation. I know of no appointment procedure that could avoid this though it will certainly make a difference whether the government holds the exclusive right to appointment or whether the parliament is to be involved. The more checks there are, the more 'moderate' personalities are likely to be chosen.

But note that the significance of the appointment procedure with respect to partisanship must not be overestimated. Public-choice considerations suggest that actual constraints are more important for the determination of behavior than partisanship or personal loyalties. From this it follows that the people appointed to central bankers are likely to act independently rather than as partisans, provided such behavior is sufficiently rewarding, promising personal satisfaction rather than disadvantages. A necessary condition is that they cannot be removed from office under normal circumstances.[7]

However, the crucial aspect is incentive compatibility. The conditions of contract and of office would have to be set such that the appointee frees him- or herself from all former political ties or dependencies and accepts the central bank's objective of safeguarding the value of the currency as his or her professional leitmotif.[8] We may call this a 'Thomas-Becket' effect. To achieve it, incentives must be provided which make it unattractive to leave the central bank before the normal age of retirement. Two specific issues have to be considered: salaries and terms of office.

With respect to salaries, it is advisable to set them at levels comparable to those received in top positions of the banking industry. Otherwise the risks are that either highly qualified people will not be available or — as it frequently happens in the U.S. — that candidates will use the appointment only as an attractive stepping stone to a better paying position in the financial industry. In the latter case, the desired personal independence of central bankers will not be guaranteed.

Another point in this respect is the question of indexation. Suppose the salaries of board and council members were fully indexed. This would be counterproductive as it would reduce the incentive to avoid inflation. On this consideration, the proposal to fix the salaries of central bankers in nominal terms for the whole term of office has some merits. But note that this implies a fall in the relative wage rate over time, given that wages in the market place rise with productivity. Therefore, indexing to trend growth of economy-wide productivity would be appropriate.

In regard to the duration of the term of office, it seems obvious that it must be finite, in order to rule out shirking, and long enough to encourage independent behavior (O'Flaherty 1990). In order to avoid that a new administration can get a handle on majority opinion in the central bank council by making several appointments, the minimum duration of the term must exceed the normal length of the electoral cycle (of 4 or 5 years) by a safe margin. On the additional consideration that most administrations manage to become elected for a second term, it seems that the minimum length of the central bankers' terms should be set at about 10 years.[9]

Another aspect related to contract length is the practice of reappointment. This does not support independent behavior. For example, suppose a person is appointed at the age of 45 for a 10-year term. Given that most people will not wish to retire at age 55, it follows that from the very beginning the central banker will have the incentive to raise the probability of reappointment by keeping his or her political ties and by supporting a course of monetary policy which meets the interest of the administration.[10]

Therefore, independence requires ruling out reappointment by providing a sufficiently long, single term of office. An attractive approach is to permit for some flexibility by combining a variable, though not unlimited, appointment age with a uniform retirement age. For example, for a uniform retirement age of 70 years the appointment age might be set at a minimum of 45 and a maximum of 55 years. Depending on the age of the appointee the effective contract length would vary between 15 and 25 years.

The proposed procedure for appointment provides the institutional cornerstone for personal independence of council and board members. Clearly, the numbers mentioned are less important than the general structure of the solution. Its strength is to be seen in the following characteristics: (i) it eliminates the undesirable incentives associated with short-term contracts and the possibility of reappointment, (ii) it nevertheless provides the necessary flexibility for the choice of candidates by setting a reasonable time span with respect to appointment age. Note that a staggering of appointments, as it is practiced for example in Germany, would serve as a further safeguard against the import of partisanship into the central bank council (Waller 1989).

Finally, a more specific issue may be considered: the appointment of the chairman. It is common practice that government appoints the chairman by the same procedure as any ordinary member of the central bank council. This assignment is in line with the basic philosophy of existing monetary constitutions that the central bank must be subordinated to government. But under the alternative constitution of central bank independence the justification of the traditional assignment loses its force.

There are three considerations which suggest that it is preferable to have the chairman be elected by the governing body of monetary policy, i.e. by the central bank council, instead of being appointed by the government. First, while it is advantageous to provide the members of the central bank council with longer-term contracts of 15 to 25 years duration, there is no need to appoint one of them as a chairman for his whole term. Second, with regard to professional competence and reputation a preferable solution to current practice is to have a person first serve some years on the council before he or she becomes selected for chairperson. In fact, selecting a chairman from among the central bank council rules out government intervention; otherwise, council members would be induced to lobby with the government.

Third, given that they possess the expertise on monetary policy matters, enjoy personal independence and, consequently, concentrate on the task of preserving price stability, council members will tend to select as chairman the one whom they consider to be truly primus inter pares and who, therefore, in all likelihood will be the best representative. In contrast to government, the council is likely to make selections by disregarding any specific political constellation.

Providing the central bank council with the right to elect the chairman presupposes that the admissible term of chairmanship, say 5 to 10 years, is specified in the statutes of the bank. Repeated re-election would have not to be ruled out.

2.5. Constitutional rank for central bank statutes

In most, if not all countries, the central bank statutes can be changed by a simple majority in parliament. This implies that even a government which has to rely on a bare majority can threaten the central bank with a radical change of the statutes, when the bank does not comply with its demands. Actually, it does not require an explicit threat; the mere possibility may be sufficient to induce the central bank council to choose a more expansionary monetary stance than is compatible with its stability objective.

Therefore, it is advisable to put the status of central bank independence on safer footing by making changes of the central bank statutes very difficult. This suggests to either write the statutes into the country's constitution or to provide the statutes with a comparable rank. The requirement of a qualified majority in both houses, say, two thirds, to amend the statutes would be the cornerstone of central bank autonomy.

3. Precommitment

This section explains why central bank independence, as defined above, is superior to coercive monetary rules in providing effective precommitment to price stability. It is useful to clarify first the notion of price stability.

3.1. On the concept of price stability

In policy discussions it is seldom spelled out what is meant by price stability. Equating price stability with price level constancy certainly does not provide a useful standard for monetary policy.

First, the standard is not operational. Given that the price level is shocked by a variety of random disturbances which cannot be anticipated and given that the central bank cannot affect the price level immediately but only with a variable lag, the attempt at offsetting the price level effects of such shocks tends to be counterproductive. An exception are price level shocks caused by money supply surprises. It is best to avoid the unnecessary uncertainty from such surprises.

Second, the norm of price level constancy requires destabilizing action in the case of larger one-time price level shifts. Consider the famous example of an oil-price shock. A larger jump in this relative price will raise the supply price of output and reduce output and employment for unchanged aggregate demand. Undoing the induced price level increase by contracting the money supply would reduce aggregate demand, hence further contract production and employment. There are no merits in trying to offset price level effects induced directly by large real shocks. This is even more obvious in the case of purely tax-induced price level changes.

From these considerations it follows that monetary policy should be guided by a price stability norm which sets the *permanent* rate of inflation at zero and avoids unnecessary noise in the supply of base money.

3.2. Central bank independence versus coercive rules

The unfortunate state of affairs resulting from time consistent behavior under discretion induced monetarist economists to favor the subordinance of monetary policy under some coercive money supply rule. The basic idea underlying the rules debate is that the problem of permanent inflation can be eliminated by taking away from central bankers the power of discretion. Since the famous proposal of a k-percent rule by Milton Friedman (1968), several alternative monetary rules have been proposed (Meltzer 1984, McCallum 1987). All of them were designed to tie the hands of central bankers such that future monetary policy becomes predictable to private agents. Presumably, the rule would be written into the statutes of the central bank.

However, and this is crucial, none of these coercive rules guarantees an expected zero-rate of permanent inflation (Neumann 1990b). Apart from the important aspect of enforceability, no rule is capable of taking appropriate account of trend changes in the velocity of money or/and in the normal supply of output.[11] In the advent of a trend change, therefore, monetary rules would require timely amendment, in order to keep the expected rate of permanent inflation to the intended zero path. But permitting such an amendment invites political abuse, especially if a cut-back in the trend growth of output is diagnosed. The danger of any amendment is that it provides politicians with the opportunity to put the objective of price stability into the asides.

To sum up, coercive rules for monetary policy cannot satisfactorily solve the problem of precommitment to the objective of price stability. At this point, it is useful to recall what causes the suboptimality of time consistent monetary policy, hence the necessity of precommitment. It is the obligation of the government-dependent central bank to achieve two macroeconomic goals, price stability and above-normal employment, although the bank has only one instrument at its disposal, the base money stock.

Precommitment to the objective of a zero-rate of permanent inflation implies that private agents can trust that the objective will be attained over an indefinite future with a probability of (almost) one. This presupposes an institutional setting which provides central bankers with the ability as well as with the incentive not to permanently deviate from a monetary expansion path that keeps permanent inflation at the zero value. It remains to be shown that a central bank which enjoys the status of full independence vis-à-vis government will fulfill both conditions.

Consider first the question of ability. There are two aspects to this question. One is freedom of action. Given the set of institutional elements discussed above, the independent central bank will be an authority of its own. It can neither directly nor indirectly be forced to stimulate the economy at the expense of the price stability objective. The second aspect is technical ability. In contrast to the mechanics of any coercive rule, the independent central bank can readily take account of any trend change in velocity or output supply. Technical errors may be made. But corrective action will be taken the very moment errors are diagnosed, provided the set-up is incentive compatible.

There is incentive compatibility if the central bankers cannot increase their payoffs by deviating from the path of monetary stability. The payoffs consist of a pecuniary and a non-pecuniary component. The pecuniary component is the salary. Given that their salaries will not be indexed to inflation, central bankers will suffer a rising loss in personal real income, if they permit permanent inflation. Hence they will have a pecuniary disincentive to create inflation. Consequently, there is no need to provide for extra punishment though such a threat would do no harm.[12]

The non-pecuniary component of the payoff is social image and power in the domestic policy game. Both will suffer, if there is permanent inflation. The independent central banker's job is to safeguard the internal value of the currency. Not to live up to this, indicates lack of professional competence or irresponsible behavior, or both; hence, it is image reducing.

Power may be more important to central bankers than image. But, as the history of the Deutsche Bundesbank indicates, both aspects are closely interrelated. The power provided to central bankers by the status of full independence will be fully utilized and maintained only by executing the policy of price stability against the special interests of organized interest groups and government. To deviate for a relevant period of time from the stability path is power reducing, as it induces expectations of inflation which, in turn, will make it difficult to return to price stability.

In sum, the status of independence provides central bankers with the ability and the incentives to avoid permanent inflation. In comparison to any other existing or proposed institutional solution only the status of independence constitutes an incentive-compatible precommitment of government to a zero-rate of permanent inflation.

Still, it remains to consider the logical possibility of deflation. Similar to inflation, permanent deflation is welfare reducing, given that existing social institutions, like accounting rules and the tax system, are not neutral with respect to a permanent rate of price level change.[13] At the surface it may seem that independent central bankers will be tempted to create a permanent rate of deflation, in order to raise the real value of their nominally fixed, personal income. But in fact, the setting of independence does not create an incentive for central bankers to enforce deflation because that would reduce the probability of remaining in office. While inflation redistributes income from the private sector to government, a deflation generates continuous losses of government revenue by reducing the normal flow of central bank profit.[14]

For this reason, in contrast to inflation even a moderate deflation, if permanent, would immediately raise strong opposition from all factions in parliament. Rational central bankers will not ignore this. They will take into account that permanent deflation is likely to generate a qualified majority which will suspend the central bank statutes and dismiss the central bank council. Again, it seems that there is no need for a threat of additional punishment.

In sum, it is safe to conclude that the status of full independence is a solution which reliably sets the incentive to avoid inflation as well as deflation.

Finally, it may be noted that the status of full independence does not contribute to improving on X-inefficiency. On the other hand, I know of no argument that permits one to deduce that a government-dependent central bank will operate more efficiently than an independent central bank.

4. Concluding remarks

This study has tried to establish that providing a central bank with the status of complete autonomy solves the precommitment problem. Complete independence appears to be the only institutional solution to generate among citizens the necessary trust and expectation that price stability, in the sense of a zero-rate of permanent inflation, will be kept over an indefinite time horizon. The study has also discussed extensively a sufficient set of institutional elements which together define the full status of independence. Those elements are: (i) prohibition of lending to public-sector authorities, (ii) independence from instructions by governmental authorities, (iii) exchange rate sovereignty, (iv) provisions for personal independence of board and council members, (v) constitutional rank for the central bank statutes.

To be sure, the proposed setting is not likely to be embraced by all politicians. A standard objection is the lack of democratic accountability. But apart from the unquestionable aspects of orderly auditing and of regular reporting to the public in the form of monthly and annual reports, there is no need for specific institutionalized procedures of political accountability. Democratic accountability is appropriate in cases where institutions make political decisions, i.e. face a trade off with respect to conflicting objectives. But the independent central bank would be committed to only one objective, price stability. Hence the bank will not make political decisions but technical decisions with respect to policy implementation.

As the US practice indicates, where the chairman of the Federal

Reserve System has to appear in Congress on a regular basis, such accountability procedures do not further the central bank's stability performance in any significant way. On the contrary, such procedures are likely to be counter-productive by creating the incentive among politicians to regain political influence over monetary policy through the backdoor.

After all, independence is not to be equated with irresponsible behavior. The conjecture to the contrary has no empirical backing from monetary history. There is no evidence available that the more independent central banks, for example the Deutsche Bundesbank or the Schweizerische Nationalbank, have behaved in a less responsible fashion than government-dependent central banks. On the contrary, the evidence suggests that their policies of comparatively low inflation have been more conducive to stable economic growth than those of most other central banks.

Finally, it may be noted that central bank independence might be an efficient vehicle for facilitating Europe's move towards EMU (Neumann 1990a). Suppose Europe's national governments or parliaments would grant their central banks the status of full independence in the near future during the first stage of the transitional process towards EMU. By this very reform, each country would establish precommitment to the objective of price stability. Consequently, it would enable each national central bank to initiate a credible monetary path towards price stability, the precondition of entering the final stage of EMU. The parallel move of national monetary policies would be promoted by the exchange of information and by discussion in the EC Committee of Central Bank Governors. But the members of this committee would then be independent equals, instead of delegates of governments. Hence major conflicts would be unlikely and there would be no need to enforce coordination by majority vote.

Acknowledgements

Earlier versions have been presented at the EC-Workshop on EMU (Brussels, April 1990), at the 4th v. Hayek symposium on Knowledge, Evolution and Competition (Freiburg), June 1990 and at the International Macroeconomics Programme Meeting (Perugia, July 1990). The author is particularly indebted to Michele Fratianni, Michelle Garfinkel, Jürgen von Hagen, Martin Klein, Reinhard Selten, Guido Tabellini, and an anonymous referee of this journal for useful comments and suggestions. The usual disclaimer applies. Research was supported by the

Commission of the European Communities and by the Deutsche Forschungsgemeinschaft (Sonderforschungsbereich 303).

Notes

1. For a recent survey see Garfinkel (1989).
2. See the monetary policy models of Backus and Driffill (1985), Barro (1986) and Tabellini (1988). A further complication is introduced by Cukierman and Meltzer (1986) who assume that the central bank continuously changes its type through time.
3. Rogoff (1987, p. 165) notes, "It is certainly too soon to conclude that reputational constraints substantially vitiate the case for imposing legal constraints on monetary policy, as some have inferred."
4. The set-up implies to make central bankers more conservative than the 'conservative' central bankers in Rogoff (1985).
5. This section draws on Neumann (1990a).
6. However, the central bank statutes would provide for book-keeping rules and auditing procedures.
7. Impeachment by a high court under specific circumstances, such as criminal actions or insanity, would be admissable.
8. Naturally, this would not happen at once upon appointment but be a gradual process.
9. This conclusion does not depend on the specifics of the appointment procedure. It covers the European case, where the opposition party has no say with respect to appointments, as well as the US case where the opposition is involved in the confirmation procedure. Waller (1990) shows that lengthening the term of office relative to the electoral cycle will lead to more moderate appointments, if they have to be confirmed by the opposition party.
10. The alternative is to turn the first term into an effective stepping stone for a career in private industry.
11. But note that Meltzer's rule (1984), being completely retrospective, achieves an automatic trend adjustment after three years.
12. Vaubel (1989) has proposed to threaten central bankers with loss of pension in case permanent inflation exceeds a specified threshold.
13. When Friedman (1979) argued that a permanent rate of deflation, matching the real rate of interest, would be welfare improving, he considered only the welfare gain resulting from an optimal size of the quantity of money.
14. Note that the status of central bank independence is compatible with seigniorage accruing to government, provided seignorage is exclusively distributed through profit disbursement and the central bank's book-keeping rules are stated in the statutes.

References

Backus, D. and J. Driffill (1985) "Inflation and Reputation," *The American Economic Review* 3, 530—538.

Barro, R. (1986) "Reputation in a Model of Monetary Policy with Incomplete Information," *Journal of Monetary Economics* 17, 3—20.

Cukierman, A. (1989) "Discretion, Precommitments and the Prospects for a European Central Bank — Fixed Parities versus a Commonly Managed Currency," *Discussion Paper*, Jerusalem.

Cukierman, A. and A. Meltzer (1986) "The Theory of Ambiguity, Credibility, and Inflation under Discretion and Asymmetric Information," *Econometrica* 54, 1099—1128.

Friedman, M. (1968) "The Role of Monetary Policy," *American Economic Review* 58, 1—17.

Friedman, M. (1969) *The Optimum Quantity of Money*, London: Macmillan.

Garfinkel, M. (1989) "What is an 'Acceptable' Rate of Inflation?", *Federal Reserve Bank of St. Louis Review* 71(4), 3—15.

Kydland, F. E. and E. C. Prescott (1977) "Rules Rather than Discretion: The Inconsistency of Optimal Plans," *Journal of Political Economy* 85, 473—491.

Kreps, D. and R. Wilson (1982) "Sequential Equilibria," *Econometrica* 52, 863—894.

McCallum, B. (1987) "The Case for Rules in the Conduct of Monetary Policy: A Concrete Example," *Weltwirtschaftliches Archiv* 123, 415—429.

Meltzer, A. (1984) "Overview." In Federal Reserve Bank of Kansas City, *Price Stability and Public Policy*, Kansas City.

Neumann, M. J. M. (1990a) "Central Bank Independence as a Prerequisite of Price Stability," to appear in: *European Community, The Economics of European Monetary Union*, Vol. II: Contributions of Independent Economists, Brussels.

Neumann, M. J. M. (1990b) "Precommitment to Rules in Monetary Policy: A Comment." In M. T. Belongia (ed), *Monetary Policy on the Fed's 75th Anniversary*, Kluwer Academic Publishers, pp. 179—185.

Nordhaus, W. (1975) "The Political Business Cycle," *Review of Economic Studies* 42, 169—190.

O'Flaherty, B. (1990) "The Care and Handling of Monetary Authorities," *Economics and Politics* 2 (No. 1), 25—44.

Phelps, E. (1973) "Inflation in the Theory of Public Finance," *Swedish Journal of Economics*, 67—83.

Persson, T. and G. Tabellini (1989) *Macroeconomic Policy Credibility and Politics*, draft.

Rogoff, K. (1985) "The Optimal Degree of Commitment to an Intermediate Monetary Target," *The Quarterly Journal of Economics* 100, 1169—1189.

Rogoff, K. (1987) "Reputational Constraints on Monetary Policy," *Carnegie-Rochester Conference Series on Public Policy* 26, 141—182.

Schelling, T. C. (1960) *The Strategy of Conflict*, Cambridge/Mass.

Tabellini, G. (1988) "Centralized Wage Setting and Monetary Policy in a Reputational Equilibrium," *Journal of Money, Credit and Banking* 20, 102—118.

Vaubel, R. (1989) "Überholte Glaubenssätze," *Wirtschaftsdienst* 1989/VI, 276—279.

Waller, C. J. (1989) "Monetary Policy Games and Central Bank Politics," *Journal of Money, Credit and Banking* 21, 422—431.

Waller, C. J. (1990) "A Bargaining Model of Partisan Appointments to the Central Bank," *Discussion Paper*, Indiana University, Bloomington.

[5]

Optimal Commitment in Monetary Policy: Credibility versus Flexibility

By SUSANNE LOHMANN*

The classic time-consistency problem in monetary policy arises from a policymaker's futile attempt to stimulate output above the natural level, resulting in an inflationary bias to discretionary monetary policy (Finn E. Kydland and Edward C. Prescott, 1977; Robert J. Barro and David B. Gordon, 1983). The policymaker can eliminate the inflationary bias by credibly committing to a zero-inflation policy rule. Yet she would like to retain the flexibility to employ monetary instruments to stabilize employment and output. As a result, the *ex ante* optimal policy rule is contingent on the state of the world.[1]

In practice, it is infeasible for a policymaker to commit to a state-contingent policy rule: it is impossible or prohibitively costly to specify all possible contingencies in advance. The policymaker is constrained to make simple commitments, which are invariant to the state of the world. By committing to a simple central banking institution, the policymaker may be able to improve on the outcome she achieves when she sets monetary policy at her discretion or commits to a simple rule (John B. Taylor, 1983; Guido Tabellini, 1987).

This paper examines the optimal design of a central banking institution that lends credibility to a low-inflation monetary policy while allowing for a flexible policy response to unforeseen contingencies. The policymaker grants partial independence to a conservative central banker, who places a higher weight on inflation-stabilization than the policymaker. This central banker implements a lower average time-consistent inflation rate at the cost of a distorted response to output shocks (Kenneth Rogoff, 1985). The deadweight loss induced by this distortion is larger for extreme shocks. If the policymaker retains the option to override the central banker's decisions at some strictly positive but finite cost, she induces the central banker to implement a nonlinear policy rule. In normal times, the central banker sets the inflation rate independently at his discretion. In extreme situations, he implements a flexible escape clause: the larger the output shock, the more the central banker accommodates the policymaker's *ex post* demands in order to avoid being overridden.

The proposed institution dominates a number of other institutional arrangements in central banking: the discretionary regime, the regimes of full or partial commitment to the simple zero-inflation rule, and the insti-

*James and Doris McNamara Faculty Fellow 1991/92, Graduate School of Business, Stanford University, Stanford, CA 94305. This paper is based on Chapter 2 of my doctoral dissertation at Carnegie Mellon University. I thank the members of my dissertation committee, Howard Rosenthal, Alberto Alesina, and John Londregan for their guidance. Insightful comments were provided by two anonymous referees, Alex Cukierman, Allan Meltzer, Maurice Obstfeld, and participants at the meetings of the Public Choice Society in Orlando (March 1989), the Society for Economic Dynamics and Control in Minneapolis (June 1990), and the Midwestern Political Science Association in Chicago (March 1991), as well as seminar participants at Carnegie Mellon University, Harvard University, Indiana University at Bloomington, the Massachusetts Institute of Technology, Stanford University, the University of California at Irvine, the University of Rochester, the University of Washington at Seattle, and Washington University at St. Louis. Fellowship support from the Alfred P. Sloan Foundation and the John M. Olin Foundation is gratefully acknowledged.

[1]Alternatively, the need for flexibility in monetary policy could be based on Milton Friedman's (1948) idea that the policymaker is uncertain about the structure of the economy and the mapping of monetary-policy actions into policy outcomes. Even if the policymaker is following a "robust" rule of the type suggested by Friedman, she would like to retain the option to revise the policy rule in the light of new information.

tution of a fully independent conservative central banker.

Empirically, the theory is consistent with the stylized fact that the monetary policies of more independent central banks tend to be less inflationary and less activist. Moreover, it implies that policy responses vary with the size of the shocks impinging on the economy. Occasional bouts of inflation and deflation will be observed under extreme circumstances: wars, oil price shocks, stock-market crashes, and the like. Finally, the variability of inflation is predicted to increase with the average inflation rate.

The next section contains a brief literature overview. Section II characterizes the optimal central banking institution and the monetary policy implemented under this institution. The normative and empirical implications of the analysis are discussed in Section III. Conclusions are presented in Section IV.

I. Rules versus Discretion

The following macroeconomic model captures the features of monetary policy essential for the trade-off between credibility and flexibility (Stanley Fisher, 1977). The economy is characterized by the supply function

$$y = \pi - w + z \tag{1}$$

where y is output, π is the inflation rate, and w is the rate of growth of nominal wages. The output shock z is assumed to be normally distributed with zero mean and strictly positive but finite variance (σ_z^2).[2] The model is formulated in logarithms.

The wage-setters target the natural level of output in their wage contracts but cannot write state-contingent contracts. They negotiate nominal wage growth before observing π and z:

$$w = E\pi \tag{2}$$

where E is an expectations operator denoting expectations based on information available before z and π are observed.

The policymaker's preferences over policy outcomes reflect competing political pressures arising from the distributional effects of monetary policy (Christopher J. Waller, 1990). She minimizes the loss function[3]

$$L = (y - \hat{y})^2 + \chi\pi^2 + \delta c \tag{3}$$

where $\hat{y}$ is the policymaker's output bliss point, $\hat{y} > 0$; χ is the relative weight placed on the inflation and output goals, $0 < \chi < \infty$; δ is a dummy variable which takes on a value of 1 when the policymaker reneges on a commitment, and 0 otherwise; and c is a cost that the policymaker incurs when she reneges, $c \geq 0$. (The nature of this cost will be discussed later on.) The inflation rate π is the policymaker's choice variable, set after nominal wage contracts have been negotiated and the output shock z has been observed.

Given the inflationary expectations embodied in the nominal wage contracts, the policymaker can offset the output shock z by adjusting inflation to affect the real wage, employment, and output. The concave formulation of the policymaker's loss function implies that the policymaker desires to stabilize output to some extent, at the cost of destabilizing inflation.

Because of distortions in the labor markets, it is reasonable to assume that the policymaker's output bliss point $\hat{y}$ is strictly greater than zero, the normalized logarithm of the natural level of output (Barro and Gordon, 1983). As a consequence, the policymaker faces a time-consistency problem when she sets monetary policy at her discretion. The wage-setters know that the policymaker has an incentive to stimulate employment and output above the natural level by

[2]One can also interpret z as an "unforeseen" contingency or as new information about the mapping of monetary-policy actions into output outcomes.

[3]Due to the lack of micro foundations for the private-sector behavior in the Fisher model, welfare comparisons across monetary regimes characterized by different levels of inflation and different variability of inflation and real output may not be very meaningful.

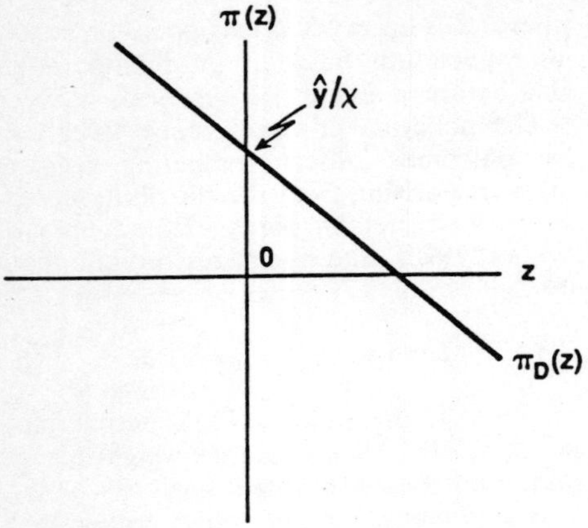

FIGURE 1. REACTION FUNCTION UNDER THE DISCRETIONARY REGIME

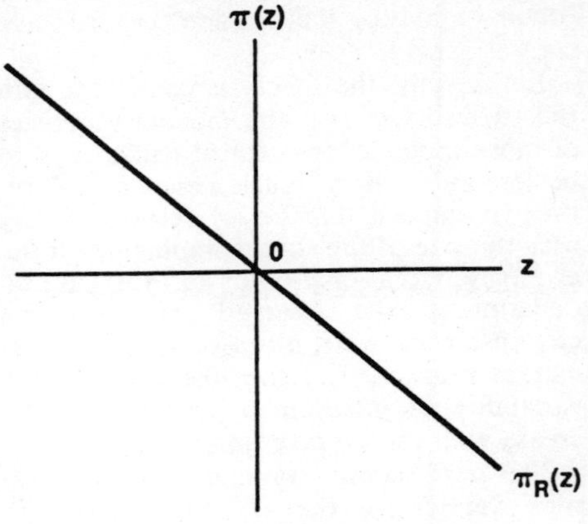

FIGURE 2. REACTION FUNCTION UNDER THE REGIME OF FULL COMMITMENT TO THE OPTIMAL STATE-CONTINGENT RULE

inflating. They write an inflationary markup into their wage contracts that is sufficiently high to give the inflation-averse policymaker a disincentive to stimulate output. As a result, the policymaker achieves the natural level of output on average, while the inflation rate exhibits the inflationary bias $\hat{y}/\chi$:[4]

$$\pi_D = -\frac{z}{1+\chi} + \frac{\hat{y}}{\chi} \tag{4}$$

where the subscript D stands for discretion. Figure 1 graphs the inflation rate set under the discretionary regime.

The policymaker, who has a zero inflation bliss point, would be better off if she could credibly commit to the *ex ante* optimal policy rule. This rule proscribes zero inflation on average but allows for a flexible policy response to shocks:

$$\pi_R = -\frac{z}{1+\chi} \tag{5}$$

where the subscript R stands for rule. The inflation rate set under the *ex ante* optimal state-contingent rule is graphed in Figure 2.

In practice, it is impossible for the policymaker to legislate a fully state-contingent rule. The policymaker may be unable to foresee all possible contingencies. Alternatively, the existence of transaction costs may make it prohibitively costly for the policymaker to specify the inflation rate to be set in the event of every possible contingency. As a consequence, the policymaker can make simple commitments only, which are invariant to the state of the world.

The *ex ante* optimal simple policy rule eliminates the inflationary bias at the cost of admitting a higher variance in real output:[5]

$$\pi_S = 0 \tag{6}$$

where the subscript S stands for simple rule. Figure 3 graphs the inflation rate set under the optimal simple rule (6).

Rogoff (1985) proposes a modification to the discretionary regime to reduce the in-

[4]Substituting (1) and (2) into (3), taking the first derivative of the resulting expression with respect to π, and substituting the expected value of the first-order condition into the first-order condition yields (4).

[5]Equation (6) is established by substituting equations (1), (2), and $\pi = E\pi = k$ into (3) and taking the first derivative of the resulting expression with respect to k.

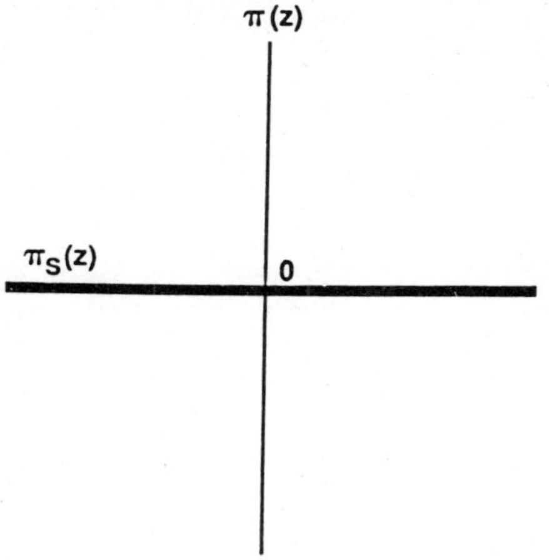

FIGURE 3. REACTION FUNCTION UNDER THE REGIME OF FULL COMMITMENT TO THE OPTIMAL SIMPLE RULE

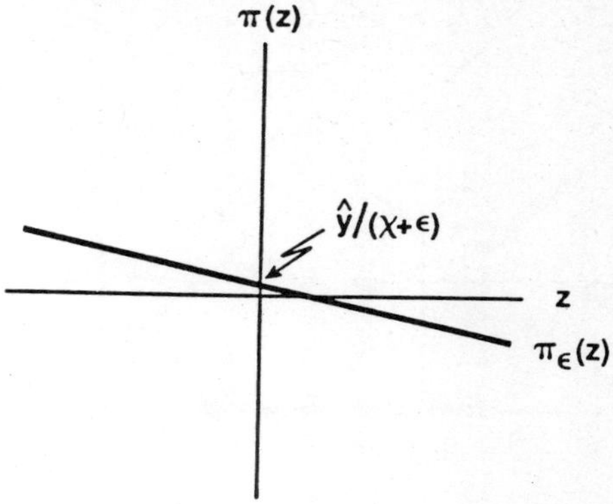

FIGURE 4. REACTION FUNCTION OF A FULLY INDEPENDENT CONSERVATIVE CENTRAL BANKER (ROGOFF)

flationary bias. In Rogoff's model, monetary policy is set at the discretion of a conservative central banker, who places a higher weight on inflation stabilization than does the policymaker. A central banker of type ε, $0<\varepsilon<\infty$, minimizes the loss function

$$L^{\varepsilon}=(y-\hat{y})^{2}+(\chi+\varepsilon)\pi^{2} \tag{7}$$

where $\chi+\varepsilon$ is type ε's relative weight on inflation stabilization. Compared to the policymaker, a central banker characterized by a strictly positive ε is more averse to stimulating and stabilizing output at the cost of destabilizing inflation. Empirically, the appointment of a central banker with a strictly positive ε might correspond to selecting a central banker from the conservative banking sector or deliberately allowing the central banker to be captured by the financial community.[6]

When setting monetary policy at his discretion, the central banker generates a lower average time-consistent inflation rate and offsets output shocks to a lesser extent than would the policymaker:[7]

$$\pi_{\varepsilon}=-\frac{z}{1+\chi+\varepsilon}+\frac{\hat{y}}{\chi+\varepsilon}. \tag{8}$$

The time-consistency problem is alleviated at the cost of a distorted response to output shocks. Figure 4 graphs the central banker's reaction function, which has a lower intercept and a flatter slope than the policymaker's discretionary reaction function.

Robert P. Flood and Peter Isard (1988) propose that the monetary authority be mo-

[6]The nature of the institutional arrangements by which an anti-inflationary bias is built into a central bank's discretionary decision-making differs across countries. In the United States, the private status of the district banks in the Federal Reserve System implies that the presidents of the district banks, who serve on the Federal Reserve Board, are appointed by boards dominated by members of regional financial and business communities. Between 20 percent and 40 percent of district-bank presidents and staff eventually hold full-time positions in the financial sector (John T. Woolley, 1984 p. 65). Susan Belden (1989) and Woolley (1984 p. 64) present some empirical evidence that the district-bank presidents tend to support tighter monetary policies than the political appointees on the Federal Reserve Board. Even these political appointees are likely to be more conservative than the President, who is constrained by the need to maintain the confidence of the financial markets when making Federal Reserve appointments.

[7]Equation (8) is established by substituting $\chi+\varepsilon$ for χ in (4).

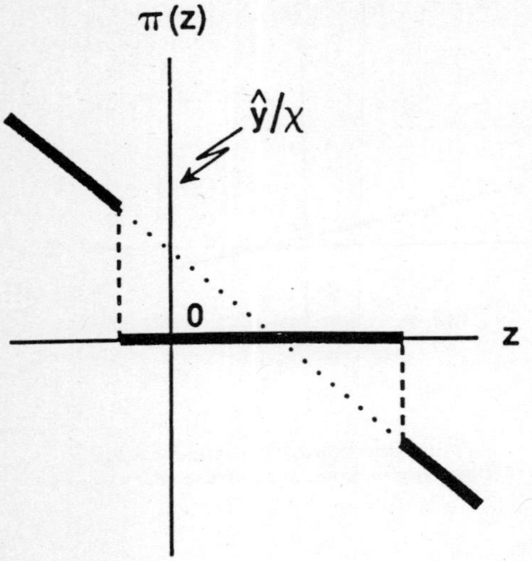

FIGURE 5. REACTION FUNCTION UNDER THE SIMPLE ZERO-INFLATION RULE SUPPLEMENTED BY AN ESCAPE CLAUSE (FLOOD AND ISARD)

tivated to follow the simple zero-inflation rule in "normal" times and to deviate from the rule when large output shocks are realized. This arrangement mitigates the deadweight loss arising from the lack of a response to output shocks, at the cost of reintroducing an inflationary bias into monetary policy. Flood and Isard's proposal is implemented if the policymaker commits to the simple rule (6) and incurs a strictly positive but finite cost if she reneges on the rule. Figure 5 graphs the policymaker's discontinuous, linear reaction function under this arrangement.[8]

II. Partial Commitment to a Conservative Central Banker

This section examines the optimal design of a central banking institution and characterizes the monetary policy implemented under this institution. Following Rogoff (1985), I assume that the policymaker delegates monetary policy to a central banker chosen from a heterogeneous population, whose members differ in the relative weight $(\chi + \varepsilon)$ they place on inflation stabilization; equivalently, the policymaker sets the parameter ε in the central banker's loss function (7).

In addition, the policymaker's commitment to the central banker is explicitly formalized by the introduction of the additive cost term into the policymaker's loss function (3). I assume that the policymaker can choose a cost c, which she incurs when she *ex post* overrides the central banker's monetary policy decisions.

The nature of this cost is determined by the political institutions in the society. Some institutional features of central banks (such as their budgetary autonomy, their penchant for complex and secretive procedures, and the long tenure of central-bank appointees) might institutionally reflect the size of the cost incurred by policymakers when they override the decisions made by their central banks. Alternatively, the "policymaker" might be thought of as a heterogeneous policymaking body (cf. Lohmann and Sharyn O'Halloran, 1991). The members of this body can set majority rules and other procedural rules which make it difficult (costly) to change a legislated law or override the decisions of a political appointee (Stanley Bach, 1989).[9]

[8] As a function of w and z, the policymaker's incentive to renege on the simple zero-inflation rule is: $I_S(w,z) = (-z + \hat{y} + w)^2 \chi/(1+\chi) - c$. For $0 < c < \infty$, it holds that $I_S < 0$ for a strict and nonempty subset of $\{z | z \in \Re\}$. In equilibrium, w is lower than under the discretionary regime, since the zero-inflation rule is partially adhered to. It follows that the reaction function is discontinuous and symmetric around a strictly positive constant and that the discretionary segments have the same slope as the discretionary reaction function in Figure 1 but are shifted downward (cf. Lohmann, 1990).

[9] The institutional arrangements that make it costly for politicians to interfere with their central bank's monetary-policy decisions differ across countries. The Dutch model is described in *The Economist* (1990 pp. 10–11): "Normally the [Netherlands] Bank conducts its own monetary policy. But the Dutch government can override it. If the Bank then objects, the government can have its way only if it publishes the Bank's case alongside its own reasons for ignoring it. This would lead to a parliamentary motion of no confidence in the

The set of feasible central banking institutions is characterized by two variables: the central banker's additional weight ε on inflation stabilization, $\varepsilon \in \mathbb{R}$, and the cost c incurred by the policymaker when overriding the central banker, $c \in [0, \infty)$. The model of delegation consists of three stages:

Stage 1.—The policymaker chooses the central banker's additional weight ε on the inflation goal and sets the cost c of overriding the central banker.

Stage 2.—The wage-setters set nominal wage growth w.

Stage 3.—(i) The output shock z is realized. (ii) The central banker sets the inflation rate. (iii) Either the policymaker accepts the inflation rate set by the central banker; or she pays the cost c of overriding the central banker and resets the inflation rate. (iv) Inflation π and output y are realized.

In the institutional-design stage, the policymaker commits to a central banking institution (ε, c). The wage-setters, the policymaker, and the central banker play a noncooperative game in the second and third stages. The players' equilibrium strategies are a function of the institutional parameters ε and c. Under the optimal institutional arrangement, the noncooperative game played is that in which the equilibrium outcome minimizes the policymaker's expected loss, evaluated at the institutional design stage. The model is solved by backwards induction.

Proposition 1 characterizes the equilibrium of the two-stage noncooperative game.[10]

PROPOSITION 1: *For given ε and c, the sequentially rational equilibrium is defined by the following set of strategies:*

1. *The central banker's announcement and inflation-setting best response is given by*

$$\pi_{\varepsilon,c}(z) = \begin{cases} \pi_{\mathrm{I}}(z) & \text{if } z \in \mathrm{I} \\ \phi(z)\pi_{\mathrm{A}}(z) + [1-\phi(z)]\pi_{\mathrm{I}}(z) & \text{otherwise.} \end{cases}$$

2. *The policymaker's overriding and inflation-resetting best response is given by*

$$\delta(z) = \begin{cases} 0 & \text{if } \dfrac{(-z+\hat{y}+w)^2\varepsilon^2[1-\phi(z)]^2}{(1+\chi)(1+\chi+\varepsilon)^2} - c \le 0 \\ 1 \text{ and } \pi_{\mathrm{A}}(z) = \dfrac{-z+\hat{y}+w}{1+\chi} & \text{otherwise.} \end{cases}$$

3. *The wage-setters' best response is given by*

$$w = \frac{-q\phi^e z_{\mathrm{A}}^e \varepsilon + \hat{y}[1+\chi+q\phi^e\varepsilon]}{(1+\chi)(\chi+\varepsilon) - q\phi^e\varepsilon}$$

where

$$\pi_{\mathrm{A}}(z) = \frac{-z+\hat{y}+w}{1+\chi}$$

$$\pi_{\mathrm{I}}(z) = \frac{-z+\hat{y}+w}{1+\chi+\varepsilon}$$

$$\mathrm{I} = \left\{ z \,\middle|\, \frac{(-z+\hat{y}+w)^2\varepsilon^2}{(1+\chi)(1+\chi+\varepsilon)^2} - c \le 0 \right\}$$

$$\mathrm{A} = \mathbb{R}\backslash\mathrm{I}$$

$$q = \Pr\{z | z \in \mathrm{A}\}$$

$$\phi(z) = \begin{cases} 1 - \dfrac{[c(1+\chi)]^{1/2}(1+\chi+\varepsilon)}{\varepsilon(\hat{y}+w-z)} & \text{if } z \in \mathrm{A} \\ 0 & \text{otherwise} \end{cases}$$

$$\phi^e \equiv E[\phi(z)]$$

$$z_{\mathrm{A}}^e \equiv E[z | z \in \mathrm{A}].$$

(See Appendix for the proof.)[11]

government: in due course, either the government or the central bank's board would resign."

[10]Torsten Persson and Tabellini (1990) explain why the concept of sequentially rational equilibrium (and not that of subgame-perfect equilibrium) is the appropriate equilibrium concept for the games of the type analyzed here.

[11]The proof of existence is standard.

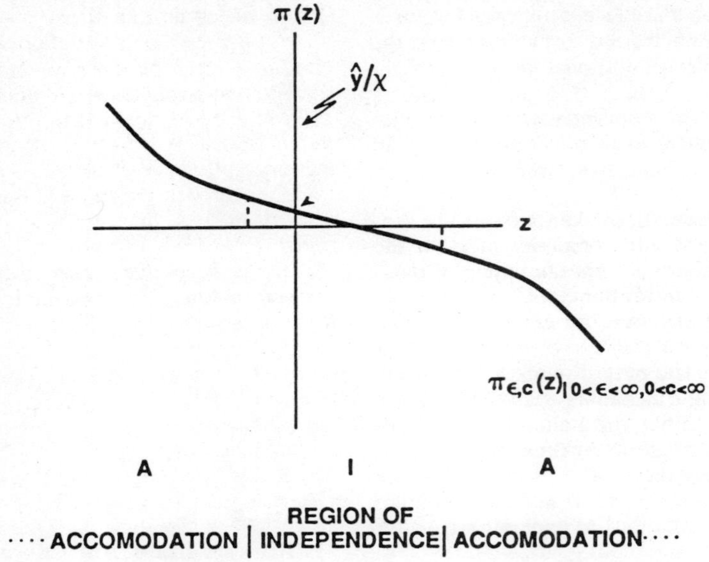

FIGURE 6. REACTION FUNCTION OF A PARTIALLY INDEPENDENT CONSERVATIVE CENTRAL BANKER

First, the strategic interaction between the policymaker and thc central banker in the last stage of the game is examined with reference to Figure 6, which graphs the nonlinear central-bank reaction function induced by one particular combination of strictly positive but finite ε and c. Then, the wage-setters' strategies in the second stage are analyzed.

In the last stage of the game, the central banker announces the inflation rate $\pi_{\mathrm{I}}(z)$ for shock realizations in the region of independence, I. A central banker characterized by a strictly positive ε sets a lower inflation on average and offsets the output shock to a lesser extent than would the policymaker. If the policymaker were to override the central banker, she would achieve a positive output-stimulation effect and avoid the central banker's distortionary response to the output shock, at the price of paying the cost c of overriding the central banker. For shock realizations in region I, the cost c dominates the gains achieved by overriding the central banker.

For the policymaker, the deadweight loss arising from the central banker's distortionary response to output shocks is larger for extreme shocks. For shock realizations in the region of accommodation, A, the announcement of the inflation rate $\pi_{\mathrm{I}}(z)$ would trigger the central banker's decision being overridden. The policy-motivated central banker is better off if he avoids being overridden by announcing the linear combination $\phi(z)\pi_{\mathrm{A}}(z)+[1-\phi(z)]\pi_{\mathrm{I}}(z)$, which drives the policymaker to the point of indifference between overriding the central banker and not doing so. The larger the shock, the more the central banker is forced to accommodate; that is, the higher is the weight $\phi(z)$ placed on $\pi_{\mathrm{A}}(z)$. The central banker is never overridden in equilibrium.

In the second stage of the game, the wage-setters form their inflationary expectations, rationally taking into account the institutional parameters ε and c, as well as the induced central-bank reaction function. The growth rate of nominal wages is set equal to the expected inflation rate.

So far, the equilibrium strategies and outcome induced by a given choice of ε and c have been presented. The following proposition presents the optimal central banking institution (ε^*, c^*) which minimizes the policymaker's expected loss, evaluated at the institutional design stage.

PROPOSITION 2: *The optimal central banking institution is characterized by* $0 < \varepsilon^* < \infty$; $0 < c^* < \infty$.

(See Appendix for the proof.)

The policymaker appoints a central banker who places a higher but finite weight on inflation stabilization, and she retains the option to override the central banker's decisions at some strictly positive but finite cost. This arrangement minimizes the deadweight loss induced by the inflationary bias and the distortionary response to the output shock.[12] The intuition underlying Proposition 2 is as follows.

An increase in the cost c decreases the policymaker's incentive to override the central banker. The resulting increase in the size of the region of independence, I, leads to a reduction in the time-consistent average inflation rate, at the price of an aggravated distortionary response to the output shock. This effect is reinforced by the fact that the central banker accommodates to a lesser extent for each shock realization in the region of accommodation, A.

If the cost c is close to zero, the region of independence, I, is small. An increase in c reduces the inflationary bias by a substantial amount, since the probability density is high for the shock realizations in the increment to region I. These shock realizations are low in absolute value so that the increase in the distortion to the stabilization problem is negligible. On the other hand, as the cost c goes to infinity, an increase in c leads to a small reduction in the inflationary bias at the price of a large increase in the distortionary response to the output shock. The assumption that the density function of the shocks has infinite support and is quasiconvex in the tails is crucial for this argument.

The first-order effect of an increase in the central banker's additional weight on inflation stabilization ε is to reduce the time-consistent average inflation rate and aggravate the distortionary response to the output shock. In addition, an increase in ε increases the policymaker's incentive to override the central banker, which leads to a second-order effect in the opposite direction.

If the central banker's additional weight ε is close to zero, the first-order effect of an increase in ε on the inflationary bias dominates all other effects. As ε goes to infinity, the second-order effect outweighs the first-order effect. If, instead of increasing ε, the policymaker increased the cost c by an appropriately chosen amount, the resulting decrease in the inflationary bias is bought at a lower price in terms of aggravating the distortionary response to output shocks.[13]

III. Discussion

Proposition 2 implies that the institution of a partially independent conservative central banker dominates a number of other arrangements which are contained in the set of feasible central banking institutions: discretion ($\varepsilon = 0$ or $c = 0$), full commitment to the simple zero-inflation rule ($\varepsilon = \infty$ and $c = \infty$), commitment to the simple rule supplemented by an escape clause ($\varepsilon = \infty$ and $0 < c < \infty$), and the institution of a fully independent conservative central banker ($0 < \varepsilon < \infty$ and $c = \infty$).

Rogoff's model corresponds to the case in which the policymaker faces an infinite cost of overriding a political appointee. Since the deadweight loss incurred under this arrangement is larger for extreme shocks, the policymaker is better off if she forces the

[12] The policymaker does not incur any deadweight loss due to the cost of overriding the central banker, since this cost is never realized in equilibrium.

[13] Moreover, the results stated in Propositions 1 and 2 continue to hold even if the central banker has an incentive to avoid being overridden due to a cost he privately incurs when he is overridden. The addition of a cost term to the central banker's loss function given in equation (7) does not change the policymaker's incentives to override the central banker. As a consequence, the equilibrium strategies followed in the second and third stages and the central banking institution set in the first stage of the game are not affected.

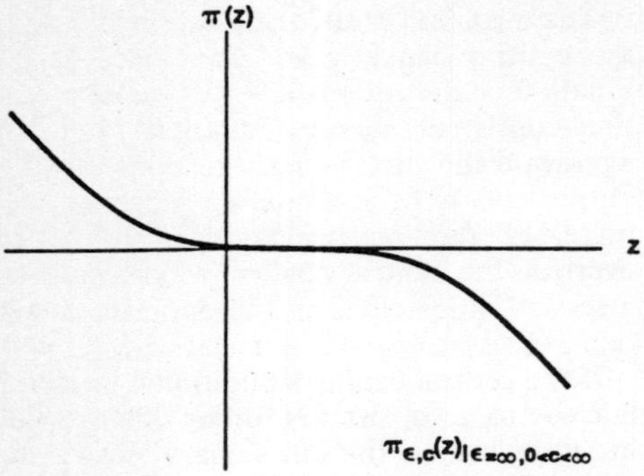

FIGURE 7. REACTION FUNCTION UNDER THE SIMPLE ZERO-INFLATION RULE SUPPLEMENTED BY AN ESCAPE CLAUSE

central banker to partially accommodate her *ex post* demands when large output shocks are realized. Empirically, Matthew B. Canzoneri (1985) points out that Rogoff's arrangement is too stable to explain episodic bouts of inflationary breakdown.

The institutional arrangement proposed by Flood and Isard allows for an escape clause under extreme circumstances. If their proposal were implemented in practice, zero inflation would be observed in normal times, and inflationary or deflationary breakdown would occur in extreme situations, while moderate inflation would never be observed (see Fig. 5). In contrast, the institution of a simple rule with an escape clause gives rise to a continuous, segmentwise linear and nonlinear reaction function in the present model (see Fig. 7).

The reputational models developed by Tabellini (1985, 1988), Canzoneri (1985), Barro (1986), and others imply occasional inflationary breakdown. The Tabellini and Barro models predict that inflationary breakdown is more likely to be observed as the monetary authority's term in office comes to an end; if inflationary breakdown occurs before the last period, it affects the monetary authority's credibility in later periods. Canzoneri's model predicts inflationary breakdown when high money-demand shocks are realized.

In my model, the implication of episodic inflationary and deflationary breakdown is driven by the assumption that the policymaker's cost of dismissing the central banker is constant, while the deadweight loss induced by the central banker's distortionary response to shocks is larger for extreme shock realizations. Inflationary and deflationary breakdown is predicted to occur under extreme circumstances: wars, oil-price shocks, stock-market crashes, and the like. Inflationary bouts are more likely to be observed than deflationary bouts, since the central banker's reaction function is symmetric around a strictly positive constant, while the shocks are symmetrically distributed around zero (see Fig. 6). The central banking institution is deliberately designed to implement a flexible escape clause in extreme situations. As a consequence, the policymaker does not lose credibility when breakdown occurs.

An outside observer who is unaware of my theory might analyze the behavior of the central bank in terms of stochastic process switching: Flood and Peter M. Garber (1983) argue that monetary-policy authorities tend to follow a particular policy rule as long as some important variables remain within certain bounds, yet switch to another policy rule when the variables cross these bounds. My theory implies that policy responses that vary with the size of shocks are consistent with rational, utility-maximizing behavior on the part of the monetary-policy authority.

The segmentwise linear and nonlinear policy rule implemented by the partially independent central banker is consistent with Dennis E. Logue and Thomas D. Willett's (1976) finding that the variability of inflation increases with the average inflation rate, above a threshold level of inflation.

In a cross-country comparison, Robin Bade and Michael Parkin (1985) establish the existence of an inverse relationship between the average inflation rate in a country and the degree of central-bank independence. King Banaian et al. (1986) come to the same conclusion and find that more independent central banks have a lower propensity to accommodate real shocks. My theory provides a foundation for these empirical results.

Moreover, these authors classify the Federal Reserve as a fairly independent central bank. My theory reconciles this classification with Kevin B. Grier's (1991) rejection of the hypothesis of Federal Reserve independence, which is based on his empirical finding of a link between the monetary growth rate in the United States and changes in the leadership of the Senate Banking Committee.

IV. Conclusion

This paper proposes that monetary policy be delegated to a partially independent conservative central banker. A number of other institutional arrangements which have played a prominent role in the debate on rules versus discretion in monetary policy are dominated by the proposed arrangement. Empirically, this arrangement and the policy implemented under this arrangement correspond closely to some features of central banking that are observed in practice. The analysis might be extended to a multiperiod setting with private information, to examine how reputational forces and institutional design play complementary roles in solving time-consistency problems.

Another task for future research is to model explicitly the "technology" by which a sovereign, heterogeneous policy-making body commits to an institution. Ultimately, the characteristics of a society and its political institutions are related to constraints on the commitment ability of its policymakers and induce restrictions on the set of implementable policies. By analyzing the connection between political institutions and economic performance, one may come to a better understanding of why some countries cope very well with time-consistency problems, others very poorly.

Appendix

PROOF OF PROPOSITION 1:[14]

First, $\delta(z)$ is shown to uniquely minimize L given $\pi_{\varepsilon,c}(z)$ and w. To begin, $\pi_A(z)$ uniquely minimizes L conditional on $\delta(z)=1$ (see footnote 4). Moreover,

$$\text{(A1)}\quad L(\pi_{\varepsilon,c}(z))|_{\delta=0} - L(\pi_A(z))|_{\delta=1} = \frac{(-z+\hat{y}+w)^2\varepsilon^2[1-\phi(z)]^2}{(1+\chi)(1+\chi+\varepsilon)^2} - c.$$

This expression is strictly negative for $z \in \mathrm{I} \setminus \mathrm{Bd(I)}$ and zero for $z \in \mathrm{Bd(I)} \cup \mathrm{A}$ by definition of $\phi(z)$ and set I, where Bd(I) is the set of boundary points of set I. Thus, in equilibrium, $\delta(z)=0$ uniquely minimizes L for all z, given $\pi_{\varepsilon,c}(z)$ and w.[15]

Then, $\pi_{\varepsilon,c}(z)$ is shown to uniquely minimize L^{ε}, given $\delta(z)$ and w. If the central banker announces an inflation rate that triggers $\delta(z)=1$, the policymaker sets the inflation rate $\pi_A(z)$. On the other hand, if the announcement of $\pi_{\varepsilon,c}(z)$ induces $\delta(z)=0$, then $\pi_{\varepsilon,c}(z)$ is set. Since the following expression is strictly positive for all z, the central banker is strictly better off under the latter outcome:

$$\text{(A2)}\quad L^{\varepsilon}(\pi_A(z)) - L^{\varepsilon}(\pi_{\varepsilon,c}(z)) = \frac{(-z+\hat{y}+w)^2\varepsilon^2\left[1-\phi(z)^2\right]}{(1+\chi)^2(1+\chi+\varepsilon)}.$$

Next, it is known that $\pi_1(z)$ uniquely minimizes L^{ε} conditional on $\delta(z)=0$ (see footnote 4). For $z \in \mathrm{I}$, the announcement of $\pi_1(z)$ that induces $\delta(z)=0$ uniquely minimizes L^{ε}.

For $z \in \mathrm{A}$, four cases must be examined. The central banker can announce $\gamma\pi_1(z)$,

[14]The proof deals with the case of $\varepsilon \neq 0$. The case of $\varepsilon = 0$ is trivial.

[15]In equilibrium, the policymaker overrides the central banker with probability zero if she is indifferent between overriding him and not doing so. If the central banker were overridden with some strictly positive probability in this case, he would have the incentive to avoid being overridden by setting an inflation rate that differs by an arbitrary small amount from the one that drives the policymaker to the point of indifference between overriding the central banker and not doing so. For any inflation rate arbitrarily close to the latter inflation rate, there exists an inflation rate that is even closer and induces a lower loss for the central banker. Thus, an equilibrium of this kind does not exist.

$\gamma < 1$; $\varphi\pi_A(z)+(1-\varphi)\pi_I(z)$, $0<\varphi<\phi(z) \le 1$; $\eta\pi_A(z)+(1-\eta)\pi_I(z)$, $0<\phi(z)<\eta \le 1$; or $\xi\pi_A(z)$, $\xi > 1$. For $z \in \text{A}$, the expression in (A1) is equal to zero by definition of $\phi(z)$, which implies that

$$\text{(A3)} \quad L(\gamma\pi_I(z))|_{\delta=0} - L(\pi_A(z))|_{\delta=1}$$
$$= \frac{(-z+\hat{y}+w)^2[(1+\chi+\varepsilon)-\gamma(1+\chi)]^2}{(1+\chi)(1+\chi+\varepsilon)^2} - c$$
$$> 0$$

$$\text{(A4)} \quad L(\varphi\pi_A(z)+(1-\varphi)\pi_I(z))|_{\delta=0}$$
$$- L(\pi_A(z))|_{\delta=1}$$
$$= \frac{(-z+\hat{y}+w)^2\varepsilon^2(1-\varphi)^2}{(1+\chi)(1+\chi+\varepsilon)^2} - c > 0.$$

Thus, $\delta(z)=1$ uniquely maximizes L if the central banker announces $\gamma\pi_I(z)$ or $\varphi\pi_A(z)+(1-\varphi)\pi_I(z)$; and (A2) implies that the central banker is strictly better off announcing $\pi_{\varepsilon,c}(z)$.

In the remaining two cases, if an announcement induces $\delta(z)=1$, then (A2) implies that the central banker is strictly better off announcing $\pi_{\varepsilon,c}(z)$; if the announcement induces $\delta(z)=0$, then the central banker strictly prefers announcing $\pi_{\varepsilon,c}(z)$, since the following expressions are strictly positive:

$$\text{(A5)} \quad L^{\varepsilon}(\eta\pi_A(z)+(1-\eta)\pi_I(z))$$
$$- L^{\varepsilon}(\pi_{\varepsilon,c}(z))$$
$$= \frac{(-z+\hat{y}+w)^2\varepsilon^2[\eta^2-\phi(z)^2]}{(1+\chi)^2(1+\chi+\varepsilon)}$$

$$\text{(A6)} \quad L^{\varepsilon}(\xi\pi_A(z)) - L^{\varepsilon}(\pi_{\varepsilon,c}(z))$$
$$= (-z+\hat{y}+w)^2$$
$$\times \frac{[\xi(1+\chi+\varepsilon)-(1+\chi)]^2 - \phi(z)^2\varepsilon^2}{(1+\chi)^2(1+\chi+\varepsilon)}.$$

Finally, w is established to be equal to $E\pi$, given $\pi_{\varepsilon,c}(z)$ and $\delta(z)$. This is done by solving the following expression for w:

$$\text{(A7)} \quad w = E\pi = qE[\pi_{\varepsilon,c}(z)|z \in \text{A}]$$
$$+(1-q)E[\pi_{\varepsilon,c}(z)|z \in \text{I}]$$
$$= qE\left[\frac{\phi(z)(-z+\hat{y}+w)}{1+\chi}\right.$$
$$\left. + \frac{[1-\phi(z)](-z+\hat{y}+w)}{1+\chi+\varepsilon}\right| z \in \text{A}\Bigg]$$
$$+(1-q)E\left[\frac{(-z+\hat{y}+w)}{1+\chi+\varepsilon}\right| z \in \text{I}\Bigg].$$

PROOF OF PROPOSITION 2:

Given $\delta(z)=0$ for all z, in equilibrium, the policymaker's expected loss can be written as

$$\text{(A8)} \quad \text{EL}(\varepsilon,c)$$
$$= q\,\text{EL}[\pi_{\varepsilon,c}(z)|z \in \text{A}]$$
$$+(1-q)\text{EL}[\pi_{\varepsilon,c}(z)|z \in \text{I}]$$
$$= [\sigma_z^2 + (\hat{y}+w)^2]$$
$$\times \left[\frac{\chi}{1+\chi} + \frac{\varepsilon^2}{(1+\chi)(1+\chi+\varepsilon)^2}\right]$$
$$- \frac{q\varepsilon^2(-z_A^e+\hat{y}+w)^2\phi^e(2-\phi^e)}{(1+\chi)(1+\chi+\varepsilon)^2}.$$

To prove that ε^* and c^* are strictly positive but finite, it is sufficient to show that Lemmas 1–5 hold:

LEMMA 1:

$$\text{EL}|_{\varepsilon=0;\,0\le c\le\infty} = \text{EL}_D.$$

LEMMA 2:

$$\text{EL}|_{\varepsilon\in\mathbb{R};\,c=0} = \text{EL}_D.$$

LEMMA 3:

$$(\partial\,\text{EL}/\partial\varepsilon)|_{\varepsilon=0;\,0<c\le\infty} < 0.$$

LEMMA 4:

$$\mathrm{EL}|_{0<\varepsilon'\leq\infty;\, c'=\infty} > \mathrm{EL}|_{\text{some } \varepsilon'',\, 0<\varepsilon''\leq\infty;\ \text{some } c'',\, 0<c''<\infty}$$

where ε', ε'', c', and c'' solve $w|_{\varepsilon',c'} = w|_{\varepsilon'',c''}$.

LEMMA 5:

$$\mathrm{EL}|_{\varepsilon'''=\infty;\, 0<c'''<\infty} > \mathrm{EL}|_{\text{some } \varepsilon'''',\, 0<\varepsilon''''<\infty;\ \text{some } c'''',\, 0<c''''<\infty}$$

where ε''', ε'''', c''', and c'''' solve $w|_{\varepsilon''',c'''} = w|_{\varepsilon'''',c''''}$.

Under $\varepsilon = 0$ or $c = 0$, the policymaker achieves EL_D, the expected loss level under the discretionary regime (Lemmas 1 and 2). Lemmas 2 and 3 imply that the policymaker can strictly decrease her expected loss by picking some strictly positive c and ε. Thus, ε^* and c^* must be strictly positive. Lemma 4 implies that if c were infinite and ε strictly positive, the policymaker could reduce her expected loss by setting some combination of strictly positive ε and strictly positive but finite c that induces the wage-setters to set the same nominal wage growth. Lemma 5 implies that, if ε were infinite and c strictly positive but finite, the policymaker could reduce her expected loss by setting some combination of strictly positive but finite ε and c that induces the wage-setters to set the same nominal wage growth. Thus, ε^* and c^* must be finite.

The expression in (A1), that is, the policymaker's incentive to override the central banker after ε, c, and w have been set and z is realized, contains information that is utilized in the proofs of Lemmas 1–5. Evaluated at $\varepsilon = 0$ and $c \geq 0$, this incentive is negative, and the derivative of this incentive with respect to ε is zero, for all $z \in \mathbb{R}$. Thus, $q = \phi^e = q\sigma_A^2 = qz_A = 0$ and $(\partial q/\partial\varepsilon) = (\partial\phi^e/\partial\varepsilon) = (\partial z_A^e/\partial\varepsilon) = 0$ if $\varepsilon = 0$ and $c \geq 0$, where $\sigma_A^2 \equiv E[z^2|z \in A]$. Evaluated at $\varepsilon \neq 0$ and $c = 0$, this incentive is strictly positive for all $z \in \mathbb{R}\backslash\{\hat{y} + w\}$. This implies that $q = \phi^e = 1$, $\sigma_A^2 = \sigma_z^2$, and $z_A^e = 0$ if $\varepsilon \neq 0$ and $c = 0$. It immediately follows that $\mathrm{EL}|_{\varepsilon=0;\, 0\leq c\leq\infty}$ and $\mathrm{EL}|_{\varepsilon\in\mathbb{R};\, c=0}$ simplify to EL_D and that $(\partial\,\mathrm{EL}/\partial\varepsilon)|_{\varepsilon=0;\,0<c\leq\infty}$ simplifies to $-2\hat{y}^2/\chi^2 < 0$. This establishes that Lemmas 1–3 hold.

Evaluated at any $\varepsilon \in \mathbb{R}$ and $c = \infty$, the expression in (A1) is negative for all $z \in \mathbb{R}$. This implies that $q = \phi^e = q\sigma_A^2 = qz_A^e = 0$ if $c = \infty$. Thus, the inequality in Lemma 4 can be written as

$$\text{(A9)}\quad [\sigma_z^2 + (\hat{y} + w')^2] \times \{1 - \varepsilon'^2(1+\chi+\varepsilon'')^2[\varepsilon''^2(1+\chi+\varepsilon')^2]\} < q''(-z_A^{e''} + \hat{y} + w')^2\phi^{e''}(2 - \phi^{e''})$$

where the variables indexed by one prime are evaluated under ε' and c', while the variables indexed by two primes are evaluated under ε'' and c''. (Note that $q' = \phi^{e'} = z_A^{e'} = 0$.) By $(\partial w/\partial c) = 0$ and definitions of ε', c', ε'', and c'', it holds that

$$\text{(A10)}\quad dw = [(\partial w/\partial\varepsilon)d\varepsilon + (\partial w/\partial q)\,dq + (\partial w/\partial\phi^e)\,d\phi^e + (\partial w/\partial z_A^e)\,dz_A^e]|_{0<\varepsilon'\leq\infty;\, c'=\infty} = 0.$$

The information contained in (A1) implies that $(\partial w/\partial\varepsilon)|_{0<\varepsilon\leq\infty;c=\infty} = -\hat{y}/(\chi+\varepsilon)^2$. Due to the convexity of the normal distribution in the tails, it holds that $(\partial q/\partial c) = (\partial\phi^e/\partial c) = (\partial z_A^e/\partial c) = 0$ if $0 < \varepsilon \leq \infty$ and $c = \infty$. This implies that

$$(\partial w/\partial q)|_{0<\varepsilon\leq\infty;\, c=\infty} = (\partial w/\partial\phi^e)|_{0<\varepsilon\leq\infty;\, c=\infty} = (\partial w/\partial z_A^e)|_{0<\varepsilon\leq\infty;\, c=\infty} = 0.$$

As ε goes to infinity, $(\partial w/\partial\varepsilon)|_{c=\infty}$ goes to zero at a slower rate than $(\partial w/\partial q)|_{c=\infty}$, $(\partial w/\partial\phi^e)|_{c=\infty}$, and $(\partial w/\partial z_A^e)|_{c=\infty}$. Consequently, (A10) holds only if dq, $d\phi^e$, and $d(-z_A^e + \hat{y} + w')^2$ strictly dominate $d\varepsilon$. It follows that the inequality in (A9) holds. This establishes that Lemma 4 holds.

The inequality in Lemma 5 can be written as

$$\text{(A11)}\quad [\sigma_z^2+(\hat{y}+w''')^2][(1+\chi+\varepsilon'''')^2-\varepsilon''''^2]$$
$$>q'''(-z_\Lambda^{c'''}+\hat{y}+w''')^2$$
$$\times\phi^{c'''}(2-\phi^{c'''})(1+\chi+\varepsilon''')$$
$$-q''''(-z_\Lambda^{c''''}+\hat{y}+w''')^2$$
$$\times\phi^{c''''}(2-\phi^{c''''})\varepsilon''''^2$$

where the variables indexed by three primes are evaluated under ε''' and c''', while the variables indexed by four primes are evaluated under ε'''' and c''''. By $(\partial w/\partial c)=0$, $(\partial w/\partial\varepsilon)|_{\varepsilon=\infty;\ 0<c<\infty}=0$, and definitions of ε', c', ε'', and c'', it holds that

$$\text{(A12)}\quad dw=\big[(\partial w/\partial q)\,dq+(\partial w/\partial\phi^c)\,d\phi^c$$
$$+(\partial w/\partial z_\Lambda^c)\,dz_\Lambda^c\big]\big|_{\varepsilon'''=\infty;\ 0<c'''<\infty}=0.$$

The expression in (A1), evaluated at $\varepsilon=\infty$ and $0<c<\infty$, is strictly greater than zero for a nonempty and strict subset of $\{z|z\in\mathbb{R}\}$. This implies that $0<q<1$, $0<\phi^c<1$, and $-\infty<z_\Lambda^c<0$ if $\varepsilon=\infty$ and $0<c<\infty$. It follows that

$$(\partial w/\partial q)|_{\varepsilon=\infty;\ 0<c<\infty},\ (\partial w/\partial\phi^c)|_{\varepsilon=\infty;\ 0<c<\infty}$$

and

$$(\partial w/\partial z_\Lambda^c)|_{\varepsilon=\infty;\ 0<c<\infty}$$

are nonzero. Consequently, (A12) holds only if dq, $d\phi^c$, and dz_Λ^c are approximately zero. This implies that the inequality in (A11) holds if the following inequality holds:

$$\text{(A13)}\quad \big[\sigma_z^2+(\hat{y}+w''')^2\big]$$
$$>q'''(-z_\Lambda^{c'''}+\hat{y}+w''')^2\phi^{c'''}(2-\phi^{c'''}).$$

Since

$$\big[\sigma_z^2+(\hat{y}+w''')^2\big]>q'''(-z_\Lambda^{c'''}+\hat{y}+w''')^2$$

and $\phi^{c'''}(2-\phi^{c'''})<1$, the inequality in (A13) holds. This establishes that Lemma 5 holds.

REFERENCES

Bach, Stanley, "The Nature of Congressional Rules," *Journal of Law and Politics*, Summer 1989, *5*, 725–57.

Bade, Robin and Parkin, Michael, "Central Bank Laws and Monetary Policy," mimeo, University of Western Ontario, October 1985.

Banaian, King, Laney, Leroy O. and Willett, Thomas D., "Central Bank Independence: An International Comparison," in Eugenia F. Toma and Mark Toma, eds., *Central Bankers, Bureaucratic Incentives, and Monetary Policy*, Dordrecht: Martinus Nijhoff, 1986, pp. 199–217.

Barro, Robert J., "Reputation in a Model of Monetary Policy with Incomplete Information," *Journal of Monetary Economics*, February 1986, *17*, 3–20.

______ **and Gordon, David B.,** "Rules, Discretion and Reputation in a Model of Monetary Policy," *Journal of Monetary Economics*, July 1983, *12*, 101–21.

Belden, Susan, "Policy Preferences of FOMC Members as Revealed by Dissenting Votes," *Journal of Money, Credit, and Banking*, November 1989, *21*, 432–41.

Canzoneri, Matthew B., "Monetary Policy Games and the Role of Private Information," *American Economic Review*, December 1985, *75*, 1056–70.

Fisher, Stanley, "Long-Term Contracts, Rational Expectations, and the Optimal Money Supply Rule," *Journal of Political Economy*, February 1977, *85*, 191–206.

Flood, Robert P. and Garber, Peter M., "A Model of Stochastic Process Switching," *Econometrica*, May 1983, *51*, 537–51.

______ **and Isard, Peter,** "Monetary Policy Strategies," NBER (Cambridge, MA) Working Paper No. 2770, November 1988.

Friedman, Milton, "A Monetary and Fiscal Framework for Economic Stability," *American Economic Review*, June 1948, *38*, 245–64.

Grier, Kevin B., "Congressional Influence on U.S. Monetary Policy: An Empirical Test," *Journal of Monetary Economics*,

October 1991, *28*, 201–20.

Kydland, Finn E. and Prescott, Edward C., "Rules Rather than Discretion: The Inconsistency of Optimal Plans," *Journal of Political Economy*, June 1977, *85*, 473–91.

Logue, Dennis E. and Willett, Thomas D., "A Note on the Relation between the Rate and Variability of Inflation," *Economica*, May 1976, *43*, 151–8.

Lohmann, Susanne, "Monetary Policy Strategies—A Correction: Comment on Flood and Isard," *International Monetary Fund Staff Papers*, June 1990, *37*, 440–5.

______ **and O'Halloran, Sharyn,** "Delegation and Accommodation in U.S. Trade Policy," mimeo, Stanford University, November 1991.

Persson, Torsten and Tabellini, Guido, *Macroeconomic Policy, Credibility and Politics*, Chur, Switzerland: Harwood, 1990.

Rogoff, Kenneth, "The Optimal Degree of Commitment to an Intermediate Monetary Target," *Quarterly Journal of Economics*, November 1985, *100*, 1169–89.

Tabellini, Guido, "Accommodative Monetary Policy and Central Bank Reputation," *Giornale degli Economisti e Annali di Economia*, August 1985, *44*, 389–425.

______, "Reputational Constraints on Monetary Policy: A Comment," *Carnegie-Rochester Conference Series on Public Policy*, Spring 1987, *26*, 183–90.

______, "Centralized Wage Setting and Monetary Policy in a Reputational Equilibrium," *Journal of Money, Credit, and Banking*, February 1988, *20*, 102–18.

Taylor, John B., "Comments on 'Rules, Discretion and Reputation in a Model of Monetary Policy,'' *Journal of Monetary Economics*, July 1983, *12*, 123–5.

Waller, Christopher J., "A Bargaining Model of Partisan Appointments to the Central Bank," mimeo, Indiana University, September 1990.

Woolley, John T., *Monetary Politics: The Federal Reserve and the Politics of Monetary Policy*, Cambridge: Cambridge University Press, 1984.

The Economist, "What Kind of EMU? The Only Good Central Bank Is One That Can Say No to Politicians," 10 February 1990, pp. 10–11.

[6]

Optimal Contracts for Central Bankers

By CARL E. WALSH*

This paper adopts a principal–agent framework to determine how a central banker's incentives should be structured to induce the socially optimal policy. In contrast to previous findings using ad hoc targeting rules, the inflation bias of discretionary policy is eliminated and an optimal response to shocks is achieved by the optimal incentive contract, even in the presence of private central-bank information. In the one-period model that has formed the basis for much of the literature on discretionary monetary policy, it is shown that the optimal contract ties the rewards of the central banker to realized inflation. (*JEL* E52, E58)

Finn Kydland and Edward Prescott (1977) and Robert Barro and David Gordon (1983) have shown that, if the monetary authority faces an incentive to expand output above its equilibrium level, discretionary policy has an inflationary bias. At a zero rate of inflation, the marginal benefit of an expansion induced by surprise inflation exceeds the marginal cost of the resulting inflation. When the central bank chooses the rate of inflation to equate marginal costs and benefits, and the public understands that it will do so, the central bank's announcement of a zero-inflation policy will not be credible. The public will expect a positive rate of inflation, and the central bank can do no better than to fulfill those expectations.

A key insight that has motivated the large literature expanding on this analysis is the recognition that central banks respond to the incentives they face.[1] Most existing work has viewed the incentive problem as one involving many principals (the individuals in the economy) and one agent (the central banker). In this framework, the principals may select the agent, but they are unable to specify the objective function of the agent.[2] However, in no country is the institutional framework such that the actual agents in charge of monetary policy are directly chosen by the individual citizens. Instead, citizens in democracies choose a government, and the central-bank head is chosen by the government. Thus, monetary policy involves a multilevel principal–agent problem. Kenneth Rogoff (1985), Susanne Lohmann (1992), and Christopher Waller (1992) focus on the government's choice of

*Department of Economics, University of California, Santa Cruz, CA 95064, and Economic Research, Federal Reserve Bank of San Francisco, P.O. Box 7702, San Francisco, CA 94120. I thank Ramon Moreno, David VanHoose, and two anonymous referees for helpful comments. This research was partially supported by grants from the Center for German and European Studies at UC Berkeley, the Division of Social Sciences at UC Santa Cruz, and the National Science Foundation. Any opinions expressed are those of the author and not necessarily those of the Federal Reserve Bank of San Francisco or the Federal Reserve System.

[1]This literature has analyzed the conduct of monetary policy under such different central-bank objective functions as a social loss function, partisan political preferences, personal preferences of the central-bank head, and targeting rules imposed by (in the context of the United States) Congress or the President. As Torsten Persson and Guido Tabellini (1990 p. 2) describe this recent literature, "From a positive point of view, the theory describes the policymaker's behavior under alternative incentive constraints. From a normative point of view, it suggests how to embed desirable incentive constraints in the existing political and economic institutions, through appropriate institutional reform."

[2]Although see Brendan O'Flaherty (1990).

a central-banker, viewing the government as choosing from a population of potential bankers with differing preferences over inflation and output fluctuations. The government picks the banker whose preferences are such that the resulting conduct of monetary policy maximizes the government's expected utility. In particular, the inflationary bias of discretionary policy can be reduced, at the cost of suboptimal policy responses to aggregate supply shocks, if the central banker minimizes a loss function that puts less weight on output fluctuations than the principal's loss function does

However, in dealing with a central-bank head, a government can directly affect the central banker's objective function and incentives in many ways. Lohmann (1992) considers the case in which the central banker knows she will be overridden by the government if the economy is subject to a disturbance that is "too" big, and Rogoff (1985 p. 1180) argues that targeting rules might be enforced by making the monetary authority's budget depend on adherence to the rule. Similarly, Michelle Garfinkle and Seonghwan Oh (1993) suggest that a targeting rule might be enforced by legislation punishing the monetary authority if it fails to achieve the target. Such institutional aspects of the central bank's structure and its relationship with the government can be thought of as representing a "contract" between the government and the monetary authority. The conduct of monetary policy is then affected by the contract the government offers to the central bank.

This point of view raises the question of whether there is an optimal contract the government should offer to the central banker. That is, if central banks respond to the incentives they face, with what incentives should they be faced? This is exactly the type of question addressed in the principal–agent literature. In a standard principal–agent problem, one would think of the principal offering to her agent a contract that is designed to affect the agent's choice of action. The principal might structure a contract so that the agent's income depends on the agent's actions, thereby affecting the incentives the agent faces. In the monetary-policy context, the institutional design of the central bank can influence the incentives the bank faces in its conduct of policy. For example, incentives are affected by such facets of design as the appointment and reappointment procedures for members of the policy-making committee, the existence of reporting requirements, and the presence of legislated policy goals. The determination of these aspects of the contract would constitute what Lohmann (1992) has described as the institutional design stage or would correspond to the legislative approach suggested by Matthew Canzoneri (1985) and Garfinkle and Oh (1993) for establishing targeting rules. The institutional structure of the central bank also includes the budgetary procedures that determine how central-bank operations are financed, and Rogoff (1985) has suggested that a government might make the central bank's budget or the income of the head of the central bank contingent on the state of the economy, thereby influencing the incentives the central banker faces in choosing the rate of inflation. As part of its central-bank reform, the New Zealand government actually considered including a financial incentive in the contract for the head of their central bank that would have resulted in a bonus payment if the bank's inflation target were achieved.[3] Legislated aspects of the central bank's structure are costly and time-consuming to change. Governments can plausibly commit to an institutional structure more easily than they can commit to a specific monetary-policy action.

The objective of this paper is to determine how the rewards to the central bank should be structured in order to induce the socially optimal policy (as defined below). That is, the optimal incentive structure is derived directly. This seems a necessary first step in any analysis of policy design, one that must be taken before the issue of implementing optimal policy design can be

[3]As ultimately passed by New Zealand's Parliament, the Reserve Bank Act of 1989 did not include such an incentive (see Walsh, 1994).

usefully addressed. In order to focus on the nature of the incentives with which the central bank should be faced, I assume that both the government and the individuals who might head the bank share the same preferences over inflation and output fluctuations. This could be taken to reflect the outcome of some (unmodeled) appointment process that ensures a similarity of views between the central-bank head and the government. As in the standard model of time-inconsistent monetary policy, both the government and the central bank would like to be able to commit to a low-inflation policy, but both face incentives to support inflationary policies once private agents have entered into wage and price contracts. I examine the incentives the government would like to establish for the central bank at the institutional-design stage in order to eliminate the inflation bias of discretionary policy while still preserving the ability of the central bank to respond with discretion to new information. Thus, the focus is similar to that of the literature on targeting rules in which the government attempts to impose some limits on the central bank's independence in order to reduce a bias toward inflation.[4]

To determine the optimal incentive structure for the central bank, I assume that the government can offer the central-bank head a state-contingent wage contract. Such a contract allows one to derive explicitly the manner in which the bank's incentives should be dependent on the state of the economy. While there are numerous reasons to question the effectiveness and implementability of such employment contracts in the context of monetary-policy determination, a (possibly) state-contingent wage contract for the central banker represents a useful fiction for deriving the optimal incentive structure with which the central bank should be faced and provides a convenient starting point for the analysis of optimal central-bank incentives.[5]

While the use of a state-contingent wage contract is convenient for determining the optimal incentive structure, the specific institutional structure that might implement these incentives is only briefly touched upon in this paper. However, viewing the contract only in the sense of a wage contract is an unnecessarily narrow interpretation of the contract between the government and the central bank. The incentives implied by the optimal contract might be implemented by more traditional institutional structures. For example, the optimal contract is shown to

[4]Implicit in this and other analyses of central-bank design is the assumption that the specialized knowledge required to manage the day-to-day conduct of monetary policy requires the delegation of responsibility to a separate agency, a central bank, equipped with the ability to respond flexibly to new information. Much of the focus associated with the design of a common central bank for Europe and the reform of the Reserve Bank of New Zealand has been on limiting the government's ability to interfere with the conduct of monetary policy. However, in the United States, congressionally imposed targeting and reporting requirements arose from a desire to limit inflationary monetary policy. I assume that *ex ante* the government and the central bank share a desire for a low-inflation policy. Consequently, the government sets an incentive structure for the central bank to ensure that, *ex post*, the central bank still prefers low inflation. The government, *ex post*, prefers higher inflation; therefore, it is desirable to limit the government's influence over the conduct of policy. Thus, the optimal contract derived in Section I allows the central bank complete discretion in the actual determination of policy.

[5]As noted in footnote 4, the government's preferences *ex post* will differ from those of the central bank under a state-contingent contract. If the transfer payment to the central bank represents the employment contract of the central banker, then the legal enforceability of contracts might ensure that the government could credibly commit to the transfer scheme. However, one referee has raised the concern that a government could always make side-payments to undo any incentives created by a legislated wage contract. While there are agencies of government that are designed to make such circumventions more difficult (such as the GAO in the United States), the feasibility of implementing any incentive contract is problematic. This does not reduce the usefulness of determining the optimal incentive structure. In Walsh (1993b), a simple dismissal rule (i.e., fire the central banker if inflation exceeds a critical value) is shown to sustain the optimal policy when the government's ability to offer a state-contingent wage contract is limited. A dismissal threat is credible when the government can choose from a supply of identical potential central bankers.

resemble an inflation-targeting rule, and Rogoff (1985), Canzoneri (1985), and Garfinkle and Oh (1993), have suggested that central banks could be punished for deviating from legislative targeting rules. Walsh (1993b) demonstrates that, in some circumstances, a dismissal rule can substitute for a state-contingent wage contract. Legislated budget procedures, targeting rules, or publicly announced conditions under which the central banker will be fired can be costly to change.[6] Thus, while the formal analysis treats contracts in a fairly narrow sense, a broader interpretation is often possible.

The existing literature on monetary-policy design has not adopted as its starting point the consideration of optimal incentive structures. Instead, the traditional approach has normally analyzed the effects on policy of ad hoc incentive structures, such as targeting rules, imposed on the central bank. As a result, it is never clear to what extent the economic outcomes and policy trade-offs that arise are inherent in the policy problem or simply arise from the suboptimality of the targeting rules chosen for analysis. For example, by deriving the optimal contract, I show that the trade-off between inflationary bias and suboptimal stabilization in Rogoff (1985), Garfinkle and Oh (1993), and others arises because these authors place arbitrary restrictions on the targeting rules they consider. This trade-off disappears under the optimal contract; full credibility and flexibility are simultaneously achieved. By determining whether trade-offs arise from the nature of the model or are artifacts of the targeting rules, the optimal contract provides insight into how the targeting rules might be respecified or how the limitations of the model might appear to make the policy choice too easy by neglecting important aspects of actual policy problems.

In this paper, I consider the optimal contract for the policymaker to offer the central banker in the one-period model that has formed the basis for much of the literature on discretionary monetary policy. It is shown that a contract exists that eliminates the inflation bias of discretionary policy while still ensuring that inflation responds optimally to aggregate supply shocks. In the standard strategic-policy model of Barro and Gordon (1983), a contract that makes the payment to the central banker depend only on inflation eliminates the inflationary bias and leads to an optimal policy in the presence of aggregate demand and supply shocks if the central banker also shares the government's preferences over output and inflation. The intuition is straightforward. In the standard monetary-policy game, the inflationary bias is constant across states of nature; a contract therefore only needs to raise the marginal cost of inflation to the central banker by a constant amount, leaving the central banker free to respond with discretion to economic disturbances. Such a contract can be interpreted as a type of inflation-targeting rule; such rules are normally thought to be suboptimal in the presence of supply shocks.

The impact of imperfect information on the optimal contract is also examined. Canzoneri (1985) has argued that reputational solutions to the time-inconsistency problem will be difficult to sustain if the central bank has private information. I show that central-bank private information of the type considered by Canzoneri is, in fact, irrelevant. Optimal stabilization policy with no inflationary bias can be achieved by a contract that depends only on publicly observable variables. The optimal contract is simple in the sense that it depends only on the actual rate of money growth or inflation. Canzoneri (1985) and Garfinkle and Oh (1993) have emphasized that the presence of information that is private to the central bank makes it difficult to determine whether the central bank is cheating or deviating from the optimal policy, and this leads them to consider various forms of targeting rules. These problems are avoided under the optimal contract.

Optimal contracts are derived when the central bank has private information on a

[6]Under New Zealand's 1989 central-banking law, changes in the target rate of inflation must be published and tabled in Parliament.

forecast of an aggregate supply shock, when the government can only observe a broad monetary aggregate that reflects both central-bank actions and control errors, and when central bankers differ in their ability and can choose among alternative operating procedures that affect the informational content of observable signals of economic disturbances. In all cases, contracts exist that eliminate average inflation while still achieving an optimal policy response to shocks.

I. A Contract Solution to Inflation Bias and Suboptimal Stabilization

Rogoff (1985), Lohmann (1992), and Waller (1992) have studied models of discretionary monetary policy in which the inflationary bias is reduced by appointing as head of the central bank an individual who dislikes inflation more than society does as a whole. From society's point of view, the cost of giving control of monetary policy to such a "conservative" central banker is the lower priority placed on employment or output stabilization by the central bank. In the face of an adverse aggregate supply shock, for instance, the central banker is willing to trade off too much employment reduction to prevent inflation from rising than would be optimal from the perspective of the social welfare function.

Instead of viewing the central bank as headed by a "conservative" whose welfare function differs from that of society, one can interpret Rogoff's (1985) framework as modeling the situation in which the central bank maximizes its budgetary transfer from the government, where this transfer depends on inflation and employment. The problem for the government is to set the optimal weight on inflation relative to employment in this transfer function. Rogoff, in fact, offers this interpretation of his results. In this section, I show that the conflict that arises between inflationary bias and suboptimal stabilization results from the restrictive set of central-bank contracts previously considered.

Rogoff (1985) and Lohmann (1992) carry out their analysis using a framework that is by now standard in this literature. Suppose the government's objective is to minimize a quadratic cost function that depends on the rate of inflation, π, and deviations of real output around a target level, $y - y^*$:

$$V = (y - y^*)^2 + \beta\pi^2. \tag{1}$$

Since I am focusing on the principal–agent relationship between the government and the central banker, and not on that between the public and the government, equation (1) will be viewed interchangeably as reflecting both the government's and society's preferences.[7]

The presence of nominal contracts set at the start of the period leads to an aggregate relationship between output and unexpected inflation of the form

$$y = y^c + \alpha(\pi - \pi^e) + \varepsilon \tag{2}$$

where ε is a mean-zero, serially uncorrelated real aggregate supply shock, π^e is the public's expectation of inflation, and y^c is the equilibrium level of output in the absence of supply shocks or unanticipated inflation. It is assumed that expectations are formed (i.e., nominal wage contracts signed) before ε can be observed but that the monetary authority can set its policy instrument after observing a signal θ about ε. The signal will be taken to be the private information of the central bank and is equal to ε plus a measurement error term ϕ: $\theta = \varepsilon + \phi$, where ε and ϕ are mutually uncorrelated, normally distributed, white-noise processes. The expectation of ε, conditional on observing θ is $s\theta$, where $s = \sigma_\varepsilon^2/(\sigma_\varepsilon^2 + \sigma_\phi^2)$, $0 < s \le 1$.[8]

[7] In keeping with the Barro and Gordon framework used by Rogoff (1985) and others, it will be assumed that the social welfare function is well defined and represents the preferences of a homogeneous population. When the economy is not characterized by homogeneous preferences, Waller (1992) shows that it may not always be optimal to appoint a conservative central banker.

[8] If one prefers to think of θ as a rational forecast of ε, then s can be set equal to 1 in the subsequent analysis of this and the following section. The measurement-error specification is adopted here because in Section III I will assume that the quality of the signal is affected by the central bank's competency and its choice of operating procedure.

In order to provide an incentive for the policymaker to attempt to create inflation surprises, it must be the case that

$$(3) \qquad k \equiv y^* - y^c > 0.$$

It is standard in this type of model to treat inflation as the central bank's policy instrument. However, since I will later wish to examine contracts that attempt to influence the central bank's choice of operating procedures, it will be useful to distinguish between inflation and the central bank's policy instrument, the latter taken to be the rate of growth of a monetary aggregate directly controlled by the central bank (the monetary base, for example). Denoting this growth rate by m, the inflation rate is given by

$$(4) \qquad \pi = m + v - \gamma\varepsilon$$

where v is interpreted as either a control error or a velocity shock, and the term $\gamma\varepsilon$ allows aggregate supply shocks to have a direct negative impact on inflation. The stochastic shock v is taken to be an exogenous white-noise process whose realization occurs after m is set.

Using (1)–(4), the optimal policy that minimizes expected social loss conditional on θ and subject to the constraint that average inflation be zero is given by

$$(5) \qquad m(\theta) = \left(\gamma - \frac{\alpha}{\alpha^2 + \beta}\right) s\theta \equiv \delta s\theta.$$

The optimal response of the money supply is proportional to the forecast of ε, $s\theta$. If the direct effect of aggregate supply shocks on inflation is zero ($\gamma \equiv 0$), the factor of proportionality is negative; a positive aggregate supply shock raises output, and to stabilize output, the money supply should be reduced. Since this leads to fluctuations in the rate of inflation, the response of money is smaller, in absolute value, the larger is the weight placed on inflation stability in the government's objective function (β). If $\gamma > 0$, a positive aggregate supply shock acts directly to reduce the rate of inflation. If γ is sufficiently large, the desire to stabilize inflation around zero can produce a positive monetary response to the aggregate supply shock.

As is well known, the policy given by equation (5) is time-inconsistent and therefore not credible if implemented either directly by the government or by a central bank whose objective function is given by equation (1). Suppose, however that monetary policy is conducted by an independent central bank, one who shares the government's preferences as in (1), but who also receives a monetary transfer payment from the government. This payment could be thought of either as the direct income of the central banker or as the budget of the central bank. Alternatively, the transfer payment can be viewed more broadly as reflecting legislated performance objectives for the central bank. Let t represent the contract transfer to the central bank, and assume that the central bank's utility is given by

$$(6) \qquad U = t - V.$$

That is, the central bank cares about both the transfer it receives and the social loss generated by inflation and output fluctuations.[9] Equation (6) will arise if the central

[9]This assumption affects the form of the optimal contract but not the set of policies that can be implemented: if a transfer function $t^*(\cdot)$ implements the policy $m^*(\cdot)$ when the central bank's preferences are given by (6), then the transfer function $\tau^* = t^* - V$ implements m^* if the central bank cares only about its transfer. Most central banks seem concerned with the same macroeconomic outcomes that concern politicians, so equation (6) is the most natural assumption. One advantage of the specification in (6) is that the transfer function directly indicates how the government would like the central bank's objectives to differ from its own. In Sections II and III, it will be assumed that the central bank is interested solely in its transfer. As one referee points out, V might be huge compared to any feasible transfer to the central banker. However, if the objective of the government is expressed in terms of the utility of a representative agent, V would be a per capita measure and not the aggregate social loss. While these considerations are critical for analyzing the implementability of an optimal contract, they are not directly relevant at this stage, when the objective is to determine the optimal incentives with which the central banker should be faced.

banker's preferences are separable in social loss and income and the banker is risk-neutral. The central bank sets m to maximize the expected value of U, conditional on the realization of θ. The problem faced by the government (the principal) is to design a transfer function t that induces the central bank to choose $m = m(\theta)$, subject to the requirement that $E(t - V) \geq U_0 = 0$, where U_0 is the central banker's reservation level of utility, normalized to 0 for convenience.[10]

If the government can verify θ *ex post*, there are clearly many contracts that would achieve the desired result. For example, any contract that imposes a large penalty on the central bank if m deviates from $m(\theta)$ will ensure that $m(\theta)$ is chosen. Such knife-edge, or forcing, solutions are of little practical interest as they require that the government specify a complete contingent contract that mandates a value of m for each realization of θ. While the standard Barro-Gordon framework offers no reasons to explain why such contracts might not be feasible, it is generally agreed that the actual difficulty of determining both the possible states of nature *ex ante* and the actual realization of shocks *ex post* make such contracts infeasible to write and impossible to enforce. A major argument, in fact, for the existence of specialized institutions for the conduct of monetary policy must rest on the difficulty of specifying a complete set of rules to follow under all contingencies.

In the present model, the informational structure precludes contracts that are contingent on θ since the signal realization is assumed to be the private information of the central bank. The contract payment to the central bank must depend, therefore, only on the observable variables m, π, and y. As I will show, taking the transfer to be a function solely of either m or π is not restrictive in that the optimal policy can still be supported.

Consider then a transfer function $t(m)$ that makes the government's payment to the central bank contingent on the observed rate of money growth. The transfer function $t(m)$ implements the optimal policy $m(\theta)$ if $m(\theta)$ maximizes $E_\theta(t(m) - V)$ for all θ where E_θ denotes the central bank's expectation conditional on θ. That is, $t(m)$ implements $m(\theta)$ if $m(\theta)$ is the solution to the central banker's problem of maximizing her expected utility.

The first-order condition for the central banker's problem can be solved for $m^{CB}(\theta)$, the optimal discretionary policy:[11]

$$(7)\quad m^{CB}(\theta) = \frac{\alpha k}{\beta} + \left(\frac{1}{2\beta}\right) E_\theta(\partial t/\partial m) + \frac{\alpha^2}{2(\alpha^2+\beta)\beta}[E(\partial t/\partial m) - E_\theta(\partial t/\partial m)] + \delta s \theta$$

where $E(\cdot)$ denotes the public's expectations. Note that in the absence of the terms involving the transfer function, m^{CB} exhibits the standard inflation bias, $\alpha k/\beta$. The last term in (7) shows that the optimal discretionary policy response to the signal θ is equal to the response under the optimal commitment policy (5). This is important since it implies that the government's objective will be to design a contract that eliminates the inflationary bias while leaving the central bank free to respond with discretion to θ. Setting $m^{CB}(\theta)$ equal to $m(\theta)$ for all θ

[10]An alternative approach would assume that the government's objective is to minimize the expected loss plus the transfer to the central banker. However, in the present context, the government will always be able to offer a minimum-cost contract. Therefore, assuming that the government minimizes $E(V)$ instead of $E(V+t)$ involves no loss of generality. In Section III, however, central bankers may potentially earn rents, so it will be important to account for the cost of the contract the government offers.

[11]It is well known in the principal–agent literature that the first-order approach adopted here may be inappropriate. However, the first-order conditions are both necessary and sufficient as long as $t(\cdot) - V$ is continuous and concave, which will be the case here. For a recent discussion of the first-order approach, see Ian Jewitt (1988).

requires that $t(m)$ satisfy

$$(8)\quad \tfrac{1}{2}E_\theta(\partial t/\partial m) + \frac{\alpha^2}{2(\alpha^2+\beta)\beta}[E(\partial t/\partial m) - E_\theta(\partial t/\partial m)] = -\alpha k \leq 0.$$

The optimal commitment policy $m(\theta)$ can be implemented, therefore, by the transfer function

$$(9)\qquad t(m) = t_0 - 2\alpha k m$$

with the constant t_0 set to ensure $E(t - V) = 0$. Note that the transfer is based solely on the observed value of m, the central bank's instrument. Presenting the central banker with the incentive contract (9) achieves the dual objectives of eliminating the inflationary bias while still ensuring optimal stabilization policy in response to the central bank's private information about the aggregate supply shock.

If the government's loss function in (1) took the form $(y - y^*)^2 + \beta(\pi - \pi^*)^2$ where π^* is a target rate of inflation [implicitly equal to zero in (1)], then the transfer function would take the form

$$t = t_0 - 2\alpha k(m - m^*)$$

where $m^* = \pi^*$. In this form, it looks like a targeting rule in which the central bank is penalized for deviations of actual money growth above m^* and rewarded for money growth rates below m^*. Because the penalty is linear in money growth, it raises the marginal cost of monetary expansion by the same amount for all realizations of θ. This does not distort the central bank's response to supply shocks, but it reduces the average rate of money growth under discretion to m^*.

Optimal policy can also be implemented through the use of a transfer function of the form $t_0 - 2\alpha k\pi$ based directly on the realized rate of inflation. Even though the expected rate of inflation conditional on θ will differ from m when $\theta \neq 0$, $E_\theta d\pi/dm = 1$. Consequently, the linear transfer function based on inflation has the same effect on the marginal cost of money growth as does the function based directly on m. The same policy can be achieved regardless of whether the central bank's transfer is based on a money target or an inflation target.

The contract in (9) implements the optimal policy despite the fact that the policy depends on the central bank's private, unverifiable information on θ. It has often been suggested that reputational equilibria might serve to substitute for commitment and act to reduce the resulting inflationary bias. However, Canzoneri (1985) has argued that this would be difficult to enforce If the central bank has private information. The central bank, for example, might justify faster than expected money growth by claiming its private forecast revealed an upward shift in money demand; the public may be unable to determine whether money demand has in fact increased or the central bank is simply attempting to produce a surprise expansion.[12] If the central bank's objective is to minimize the expected social loss function (1), conditional on the observation of θ, and if the public believes that the central bank will follow the optimal rule given by (5), the central bank would actually like to set m equal to $\delta s\theta + \alpha k/(\alpha^2 + \beta)$. To implement such a policy, while attempting to maintain a reputation for following the rule in (5), the central bank will announce that θ is equal to θ^a, where $\theta^a = \theta + \alpha k/\delta s(\alpha^2 + \beta)$. In other words, the central bank has an incentive to misrepresent its observation on θ.

Under the optimal contract, however, this problem does not arise. Since the policy $m(\theta)$ can be implemented by a transfer function based solely on the realized rate of money growth, the government does not need to know θ; the fact that the central bank has private information on its forecast of ε is irrelevant. The reason for this result is straightforward. In Canzoneri's (1985) model, as in all basic versions of the generic

[12] In Canzoneri's (1985) model, the central bank has private information about a shock to money demand, as opposed to the aggregate supply considered here. The same issues, however, arise in either case.

monetary-policy model studied by Barro and Gordon (1983), Rogoff (1985), and others, the inflationary bias of policy is a constant, independent of the realization of θ. The optimal incentive contract acts to raise the marginal cost of inflation to the central bank by the same amount across all states of nature. It is thus independent of θ, and the government gains nothing from either observing θ or from inducing the central bank to reveal θ.

Equation (9) was derived under the assumption that the control error v was realized after the central bank had set m. Since v can also be interpreted as a velocity shock, it is interesting to note that the contract in (9) continues to support the optimal policy if the central bank (but not the public) can observe v before choosing m or if the central bank observes a private signal on v before setting m. The reason is that the central bank will, under discretion, optimally respond to its information about v. Again, the contract only needs to raise the marginal cost of money growth by a constant, independent of the state of nature. The central bank can then be allowed to engage in stabilization based on its private information.

While (9) implements $m(\theta)$ when the central bank cares about the social loss function V, this same outcome is equivalent to the situation in which the central banker is risk-neutral and cares only about the monetary transfer she receives from the government, and the transfer function is $t_0 - 2\alpha k\pi - (y - y^*)^2 - \beta\pi^2$. Rogoff (1985) implicity consider a government that offers the central bank a contract of the form $t' = t_0 - (y - y^*)^2 - b\pi^2$ with b chosen to minimize the government's objective function (1). Since the set of contracts of the form t' is more restrictive in that it imposes the constraint that no linear term in inflation appears, the resulting monetary policy fails to eliminate completely the inflationary bias or to achieve optimal stabilization. By parameterizing contracts solely in terms of the weight placed on the quadratic inflation term, the marginal cost of inflation can be raised to reduce the inflationary bias, but the impact on the marginal cost is made to depend on the level of the rate of inflation, unlike the contract in (9). This distorts the central bank's response to θ and leads to the trade-off emphasized by Rogoff (1985) and Lohmann (1992).[13]

In the standard monetary-policy framework, the inflationary bias of discretionary policy can be eliminated while still achieving an optimal policy response to economic disturbances through the use of a contract between the government and the central bank based only on the observed rate of money growth. The contract resembles a targeting rule. The apparent trade-off between stabilization policy and price stability suggested by previous work arises only when the contract offered to the central banker is arbitrarily restricted.

II. Contracts Based on Performance Measures

The previous section has assumed that the central bank shares the same preferences over inflation and output fluctuations as the government. If monetary policy is implemented by an agent who cares only about her transfer income from the government, the optimal contract based on *ex post* inflation and output is not unique.[14] The previous section showed that the optimal policy could be implemented if the central bank acted to maximize the expected value of $t - V$, where t was given by equation (9). If the central bank cares only about its

[13]The trade-off studied by Garfinkel and Oh (1993) also arises from the form of the targeting rules they consider. That is, the trade-off is due to the nature of the targeting rules analyzed, and not to the fundamental nature of the policy problem.

[14]When the agent cares only about her monetary transfer, it might be thought that the time-inconsistency problem would disappear, since such an agent could be paid a fixed amount to "just follow instructions" and would have no incentive to reoptimize after private agents have entered into wage contracts. However, the assumption that θ is private information to the central banker implies that the government would be unable to verify whether the instructions had in fact been followed. More importantly, this informational structure captures the notion that it is not possible to provide a complete set of contingent instructions to the central banker; some discretion is unavoidable.

expected transfer, then the transfer function $\tau(\pi, y) = t(\pi) - V$, t given by (9), will clearly lead the central bank to choose $m = \delta s\theta$. Because of the time-inconsistency problem, this differs from the standard result in the principal–agent literature with risk-neutrality in which the agent should receive $t_0 - V$, where t_0 is a constant determined by the individual rationality constraint.

The transfer function $\tau(\pi,y)$ can be thought of as a performance-based incentive mechanism; the central banker's reward is based on the realization of output and inflation. To demonstrate that τ does in fact lead to the optimal policy, consider the general quadratic performance contract based on inflation and output:

$$(10) \quad \tau(\pi, y) = b_0 + b_1\pi + b_2\pi^2 + b_3(y - y^*) + b_4(y - y^*)^2 + b_5\pi(y - y^*).$$

Using equations (2)–(4) and denoting the public's expectations of m by $E(m)$, the first-order condition for the maximization of $E_\theta\tau(\pi, y)$ can be written as

$$(11) \quad (b_1 + b_3\alpha) + 2(b_2 + \alpha^2 b_4 + \alpha b_5)(m - \gamma s\theta) + (2\alpha b_4 + b_5)[s\theta - k + \alpha E(m)] = 0.$$

Solving for m under the assumption of rational expectations yields

$$(12) \quad m^* = \frac{-(b_1 + \alpha b_3) + (2\alpha b_4 + b_5)k}{2b_2 + \alpha b_5} - \frac{(2\alpha b_4 + b_5)s\theta}{2(b_2 + \alpha^2 b_4 + \alpha b_5)} + \gamma s\theta.$$

Now, m^* will equal $m(\theta) = \delta s\theta$ if and only if the parameters of the contract jointly satisfy

$$(13) \quad \frac{\alpha b_4 + 0.5b_5}{b_2 + \alpha^2 b_4 + \alpha b_5} = \frac{\alpha}{\alpha^2 + \beta}$$

$$(14) \quad -(b_1 + \alpha b_3) + (2\alpha b_4 + b_5)k = 0.$$

It is clear that the transfer function contains redundant parameters. Since the first-order condition is unaffected by arbitrary normalization, one can set $b_4 = -1$. Setting $b_3 = b_5 \equiv 0$, the optimal values for the remaining parameters are

$$(15) \quad b_1 = 2\alpha b_4 k = -2\alpha k$$

$$(16) \quad b^2 = \beta b_4 = -\beta.$$

Thus,

$$(17) \quad \tau(\pi,y) = b_0 - 2\alpha k\pi - \beta\pi^2 - (y - y^*)^2 = t(\pi) - V$$

which verifies the claim that $t(\pi) - V$ supports the optimal policy.

Equations (13) and (14) imply that the transfer function that achieves the optimal money-supply rule is not unique. For example, a rule based on $(y - y^*)$, $(y - y^*)^2$, and $\pi(y - y^*)$ with coefficients $-2\alpha^2 k/(\alpha^2 - \beta)$, -1, and $-2\alpha\beta/(\alpha^2 - \beta)$ will also implement $m = \delta s\theta$. In all cases, the optimal performance contract must involve output; a contract expressed solely in terms of inflation fails to achieve the optimal policy.[15]

The transfer function (17) makes the central banker's payoff a function of both inflation and output. Most recent discussions of central-bank design have focused on the establishment of monetary-policy goals expressed solely in terms of the rate of inflation. For example, New Zealand's Reserve Bank Act of 1989 makes inflation control

[15]That is, stabilizing the rate of inflation in the face of aggregate supply shocks is suboptimal when preferences are given by (1), as is well known.

the sole objective of the central bank.[16] Price stability is also the only macroeconomic goal proposed for the new European Central Bank. Such contracts are socially optimal only if the central banker's utility is also made to reflect society's preference over output fluctuations, either because the central banker directly cares about V or because her contract depends on output.

Contracts based on (17) may be difficult to implement because they depend on y^*, the government's target level of real output. This may be private information to the government, and therefore it may not be feasible to condition the transfer to the central banker on y^*. Suppose then that the transfer function is based only on the realized rate of inflation and takes the form

$$(18) \qquad \tau(\pi, y) = b_0 + b_1\pi + b_2\pi^2.$$

The central bank will maximize the expected value of (18) by setting $m = \gamma s\theta - b_1/2b_2$. The deflationary bias is eliminated if $b_1 = 0$. In this case, $m = \gamma s\theta \neq \delta s\theta$ unless there are no supply shocks ($\varepsilon \equiv \theta \equiv 0$), money has no effect on real output ($\alpha \equiv 0$), or the government places no weight on output stabilization ($\beta = \infty$). Otherwise, inflation-targeting rules lead to suboptimal policy (see Rogoff, 1985).

III. Imperfect Monitoring, Competency, and Effort by the Central Bank[17]

The preceding sections have ignored two aspects of monetary-policy implementation that are critically important in considering the design of the incentives the central bank should face. First, most central banks have a variety of policy instruments available to them. The Federal Reserve, for example, uses open-market operations, the discount rate, nonprice administration of the discount window, reserve requirements, and other tools to affect the economy. The multidimensionality of the set of policy instruments makes it difficult to develop unambiguous indicators of the stance of monetary policy.[18] Even if θ were observable by the government, it may be impossible for the government to specify a policy action in response to each realization of θ and then to verify that the central bank has actually implemented that policy. Second, the informational content of financial-market and macroeconomic variables can depend on the actions of the central bank. For example, the central bank's choice of operating procedure can affect the information about future policy contained in interest-rate movements (Michael Dotsey and Robert King, 1983; V. Vance Roley and Walsh, 1985). More generally, the optimal response to the signal θ will depend on the "quality" of the signal, and that can depend on the central bank's conduct of policy in the sense of its choice of operating procedure and the efficiency with which it carries out its policy.

To capture these considerations, two changes to the basic model can be made. First, in contrast to the previous two sections, assume that the signal θ is publicly observable, but the central bank's setting of its instrument is not. Specifically, the government can observe $\mu \equiv m + v$; consequently, the government cannot separate the central bank's setting of its instrument m from the random control error v. The signal θ might correspond to a variable such as a short-term interest rate; m to the central bank's policy stance reflected in open-market operations, reserve-requirement setting, and discount-rate policy; and μ to a broad monetary aggregate like M2.

Second, it is assumed that candidates to head the central bank differ in their competency and that the distribution of the measurement error ϕ is affected both by the

[16] The Act also requires the Governor of the Reserve Bank to sign an agreement with the government establishing a target rate of inflation (currently 0–2 percent) and a date on which the target rate will be achieved. Failure to meet this target can then provide grounds for the government to dismiss the Reserve Bank Governor.

[17] The model of this section draws heavily on Jean-Jacques Laffont and Jean Tirole (1986).

[18] For recent examples of the difficulty of developing indicators of monetary policy, see Ben Bernanke and Alan Blinder (1992) and Lawrence Christiano et al. (1993).

central bank's competency and by its implementation of policy. Measurement errors might be affected by the central bank's choice of operating procedures (which could affect the information content of financial variables as in Dotsey and King [1983]), by its ability to forecast, or by its management of other policy instruments (such as reserve requirements, discount-window borrowing, regulatory oversight, etc.). Improving policy implementation, while raising the quality of the signal, imposes resource costs on the central bank. These costs might arise from increased data-collection requirements, more intensive monitoring of financial-market developments, or greater staff resources devoted to forecasting.[19]

A central banker of type a who makes effort e is assumed to experience a measurement error of $\phi = (a-e)\omega$, where ω is an exogenous, mean-zero serially uncorrelated disturbance with variance σ_ω^2, $a \in [\underline{a}, \bar{a}]$, $e \in [\underline{e}, \bar{e}]$ and $\underline{a} \geq \bar{e}$ so that $a - e \geq 0$ for all a and e. Neither the central banker's competency nor her "effort" in reducing control errors will be assumed to be observable by the government. In this framework, central bankers with low a's are "better."[20] For a given signal realization θ, the optimal setting of the money supply is still given by $\delta s \theta$, but s is now a decreasing function of $a - e$:[21]

$$s = \sigma_\varepsilon^2 / (\sigma_\varepsilon^2 + \sigma_\phi^2)$$

$$= \sigma_\varepsilon^2 / \left[\sigma_\varepsilon^2 + (a-e)^2 \sigma_\omega^2\right].$$

It will be assumed that σ_ε^2 and σ_ω^2 are known to the government. The expected value of the social loss function V will depend on σ_ϕ^2; a reduction in σ_ϕ^2, that is, an improvement in the quality of the signal θ, will reduce the expected social loss: $\partial E(V)/\partial \sigma_\phi^2 \equiv V_\phi \geq 0$.

Higher effort imposes costs on the central bank. These may be pecuniary (larger staffs, more frequent data collection) or measured directly in terms of utility (greater time invested in monitoring financial markets). Costs are assumed to be quadratic in e, so that the *ex post* utility of the central banker is $t - C(e) = t - \eta(e - \underline{e})^2$. Note that I have now assumed that the central banker's utility does not depend directly on social welfare.[22] Unlike the situations considered in previous sections, the government can no longer guarantee that contract costs will be minimized. Instead, "better" central bankers will earn rents. Thus, the objective of the principal will be to offer a contract to the central banker that minimizes expected social loss plus transfer, $E(V + t)$.

A. *Perfect Information on a*

Consider first the case in which there is no uncertainty about the central banker's type: a is known. In this case, the sequence of events evolves according to the following pattern. The government offers a contract to the central banker, after which the central banker chooses an effort level e while the public forms expectations about the rate of inflation and enters into wage contracts. The signal θ on the aggregate supply shock is then observed, after which m is set. Finally, the control error v is realized, and output and actual inflation are determined.

In this environment, the government's problem is to minimize $E(V + t)$ subject to $E(m) = 0$ and the individual rationality constraint $E(t - C(e)) \geq 0$, where the expectations are taken over the joint distribution of ε, θ, and v.[23] The optimal rule for m is again given by $m(\theta) = \delta s \theta$, although s is

[19]For an analysis of the effects of costs on the choice of operating procedure, see David VanHoose (1992).

[20]That is, the expected utility of both the government and the central banker can be shown to be decreasing in a, so central bankers with low a's earn higher expected utility and are preferred by the government.

[21]That is, once a and e are set and θ is then observed, the policy problem is exactly that posed in Section I, so that $m = \delta s \theta$ is the optimal response.

[22]This assumption is not restrictive since the case analyzed is equivalent to one in which the central banker maximizes $T - V - C(e)$ for $T = t + V$.

[23]I continue to assume that the central banker's alternative utility level is normalized to 0 so that the participation constraint takes the form $E(t - C(e)) \geq 0$.

now a function of $a-e$. Substituting $m(\theta)$ into the definition of V, the first-order condition for the optimal level of effort can be written

$$(19) \quad -V_{\phi}(a-e)\sigma_{\omega}^{2}+\eta(e-\underline{e})=0.$$

Solving for the optimal e when central-bank type is known yields

$$(20) \qquad e^{*}(a)=\psi a+(1-\psi)\underline{e}$$

$$\psi=\frac{V_{\phi}\sigma_{\omega}^{2}}{V_{\phi}\sigma_{\omega}^{2}+\eta}.$$

From (20) it follows that $0 \le \partial e^{*}(a)/\partial a \le 1$, so $(a-e)$ is increasing in a. It is optimal to have central bankers with less ability exert more effort, but not enough to completely compensate for their lower ability. As a result, social welfare is decreasing in a.

B. *Imperfect Information on the Central Banker's Type*

Now suppose that neither the government nor the public can observe the central banker's type. I restrict consideration to truthful mechanisms under which the central bank reveals its type, chooses an effort level, observes the signal θ, and sets m. It receives a transfer $\tau(a,\theta,\pi)$ and utility $\tau(a,\theta,\pi)-C(e)$. Denote by $e(a)$ the effort level the government wishes to induce from a central banker of type a, and let $s(a)=\sigma_{\varepsilon}^{2}/\{\sigma_{\varepsilon}^{2}+[a-e(a)]^{2}\sigma_{\omega}^{2}\}$ be the value of s if the central banker of type a chooses $e(a)$. As before, the socially optimal value of m, conditional on θ, equals $m(a,\theta)=\delta s(a)\theta$. I restrict attention to subgame-perfect equilibria.

Let a^{a} denote the central bank's announced type and let $e(a,a^{\mathrm{a}})$ be the effort level that maximizes the expected utility of a central banker of type a who announces her type as a^{a}. In equilibrium $a^{\mathrm{a}}=a$, and $e=e(a,a^{\mathrm{a}})$ must maximize $E(\tau(a^{\mathrm{a}},\theta,\pi)-C(e))$ for a central banker of type a.

The properties of the optimal transfer function can be derived following the analysis of Laffont and Tirole (1986); details are contained in an earlier version of the present paper and are available upon request. The requirement that the transfer function must induce truthful revelation of the central banker's type imposes restrictions on the effort levels the government will be able to elicit. In particular, the first-order condition needed to ensure that $a^{\mathrm{a}}=a$ maximizes the central banker's utility can be shown to require that

$$E(\tau_{a}(a,\theta,\pi)-C'(e(a))e'(a)) = -C'(e(a))=-2\eta[e(a)-\underline{e}]$$

while the second-order condition is satisfied if and only if $e'(a)\equiv \partial e(a)/\partial a \le 1$. This second-order condition implies that any implementable effort function must ensure that $a-e$ is increasing in a; therefore, the measurement-error variance $(a-e)^{2}\sigma_{\omega}^{2}$ increases with a. Better central bankers (i.e., those with lower a's) produce smaller forecast errors. Otherwise, a "good" central banker could mimic a "poor" central banker at a lower disutility of effort. Since $s(a)$ is decreasing in $a-e$, "better" central bankers respond more to a given signal than do "poor" central bankers. It can also be shown that central-bank utility is decreasing in a; better central bankers gain higher expected utility.

The government's objective is to minimize expected loss plus transfer. Assuming that the government has a uniform prior over central-bank types, and using the fact that the expected transfer equals $E(\tau(a,\theta,\pi))=u+C(e)$ where u is the central banker's utility, the government's problem can be expressed as

$$(21) \qquad \min E\int_{\underline{a}}^{\bar{a}}(V+u+C)\,da$$

subject to

$$E(m)=0 \qquad u\ge 0$$

$$u_{a}=-2\eta[e(a)-\underline{e}] \qquad e'(a)\le 1.$$

The expectations are taken with respect to the distributions of ε and v.

The effort level that it is optimal for the government to induce, $e(a)$, is given as the solution to

$$(22)\quad \eta(e-\underline{e}) = V_{\phi}(a-e)\sigma_{\omega}^{2} + \eta(\underline{a}-a).$$

The level of effort that solves (22) satisfies the second-order condition for a minimum of the government's objective function. In this case, (22) implies that $e'(a) \leq 1$, so that the second-order condition for the central bank's decision problem is also satisfied.

Recall that $e^{*}(a)$ given by (20) is the optimal effort level when central-banker type is known. Equations (20) and (22) can be used to show that

$$(23)\quad e(a) - e^{*}(a) = \frac{-\eta(a-\underline{a})}{V_{\phi}\sigma_{\omega}^{2}+\eta} \leq 0.$$

Therefore, $e(a) \leq e^{*}(a)$ for all a. Less investment in improving forecasts is induced when the central banker's ability is private information. Since $e(a) \leq e^{*}(a)$, $a - e(a) \geq a - e^{*}(a)$, so for $a > \underline{a}$, s is smaller when a cannot be observed. As a result, the optimal response to a given signal is smaller because the quality of the signal is lower. However, for the best central banker, the one for whom $a = \underline{a}$, $e(\underline{a}) = e^{*}(\underline{a})$. The least efficient central banker (the $\bar{a}$ banker) receives an expected transfer of $C(e(\bar{a}))$ that just compensates her for the cost of choosing an effort level of $e(\bar{a})$. More efficient central bankers earn rents.

The solution to the government's problem is given by $\{e(a), m(a,\theta)\}$ where $e(a)$ is the solution to (22) and $m(a,\theta) = \delta s(a)\theta$ for δ defined in (5). Of more interest is the form of the transfer function $\tau(a,\theta,\pi)$ that will implement this policy. The transfer function must be such that a central banker of type a finds it optimal to choose $e(a)$ and, observing θ, to set m equal to $\delta s(a)\theta$. The Appendix proves that $\{e(a), m(a,\theta)\}$ is implemented by the transfer function given by

$$(24)\quad \tau(a,\theta,\pi) = A(a) - K(a)[\pi - \pi(a,\theta)]^{2}$$

where $\pi(a,\theta) = m(a,\theta) - \gamma s(a)\theta$. A and K depend on the central banker's announced type but not on θ, and their values are given in the Appendix.

The government can implement the effort level $e(a)$ and induce the optimal setting for the monetary aggregate, $m(\theta)$, by making the central banker's transfer payment depend on the realized rate of inflation. Equation (24) is similar to an inflation-targeting rule for the central bank of the type often analyzed, with the exception that the parameters of the rule (A and K) are chosen based on the central bank's announcement. The transfer is based on a comparison of the actual rate of inflation with $\pi(a,\theta)$, the expected rate of inflation based on the central bank's announced type and the signal on the aggregate supply shock. Equation (24) then is actually an inflation-targeting rule with a reporting requirement. The central bank is penalized for (squared) deviations of actual inflation relative to the inflation rate expected on the basis of the signal θ. Using the definition of $A(a)$ given in the Appendix, the transfer can be shown to depend on

$$-K(a)\left\{[\pi - \pi(a,\theta)]^{2} - \gamma^{2}s(a)[a-e(a)]^{2}\sigma_{\omega}^{2} - \sigma_{v}^{2}\right\}.$$

The actual squared deviation of π from $\pi(a,\theta)$ is compared to its expectation under the optimal policy $\gamma^{2}s(a)[a-e(a)]^{2}\sigma_{\omega}^{2} + \sigma_{v}^{2}$. It is interesting to note that the weight given to squared inflation deviations is independent of the signal θ. The parameter $K(a)$ only affects the effort level chosen by the central bank, not its implementation of stabilization policy. The value of θ does play a role, however, in determining the target rate of inflation π.

Rogoff (1985), Canzoneri (1985), and Garfinkel and Oh (1993) find that inflation targeting results in a trade-off between reducing the inflationary bias of discretionary policy and responding optimally to aggregate supply shocks. No such trade-off is faced with the transfer function in (24) even though it closely resembles an inflation-targeting rule.[24] The difference is due to the fact that in the present framework, and unlike the framework utilized by Rogoff (1985), the government is able to implement its desired money rule $\delta s \theta$ once the signal θ is observed. Thus, (24) really incorporates both inflation targeting and a contingent money rule, and the optimal policy can be implemented even when the government is unable to determine whether movements in the monetary aggregate it observes are due to movements in the central bank's instrument or to random control errors.

The optimal contract given by (24) looks like an inflation-targeting rule with a reporting requirement. Such rules are often proposed as solutions to the inflationary-bias problem associated with discretionary monetary policy. Equation (24) and the expressions for $A(a)$ and $K(a)$ given in the Appendix suggest, however, that the informational requirements of the optimal rule may be severe.

IV. Summary

The approach adopted in this paper differs from that normally used in analyzing the design of monetary policy. Here, the central bank is viewed as the agent of the government, one who attempts to maximize an objective function that depends, in part, on contingent transfers from the government. The optimal transfer function from the government's perspective has been derived for a version of the standard Barro-Gordon model of discretionary policy in which the central bank has private information and for a version in which central bankers differ in their abilities and in the effort they devote to implementing policy.

When the central bank cares about its transfer income and about social welfare, the optimal contract resembles an inflation-targeting rule, even though such rules are generally suboptimal in the presence of supply shocks. More generally, when the central bank cares only about its transfer income, the optimal contract takes the form of a contingent inflation-targeting rule in which the target is contingent on the observed signal on aggregate supply disturbances. The contracting approach suggests that targeting rules of the type often observed may serve to eliminate inflation bias while still preserving the advantages of discretion.[25]

While the focus in this paper has been normative, it is natural to ask why state-contingent wage contracts do not appear to be observed in practice if they solve the problem of time-inconsistent optimal monetary policy. Since a wage contract was used as a tool for deriving incentives, one needs to examine existing central-banking structures to see if they give rise to incentives that mimic the effects of the optimal contracts derived here. The optimal transfer function of Section III, for example, resembles an inflation-targeting rule with a reporting requirement, suggesting that such rules may generate the appropriate incentives for the central bank. Making the central banker's employment contingent on achieving prespecified inflation targets, as is the case under the New Zealand Reserve Bank Act of 1989, may serve the same purpose. An interesting line of future research will be to determine the ways in which specific institutional structures observed in practice affect the incentives facing the makers of monetary policy.

The type of state-contingent wages studied here serves as a useful means by which to determine the nature of the incentives with which the central bank should be faced. In contrast with the traditional approach in which the central bank is subject to an ad hoc targeting rule, the contrasting approach more clearly highlights the nature of the policy problems and associated trade-offs that are inherent in the environment of the

[24] Stabilization policy is optimal, given s. However, when a and e are private information, the central bank's choice leads to a value of $a - e$ that is too large and a signal that is too noisy.

[25] Persson and Tabellini (1993) build on an earlier version of this paper to extend the contracting approach to central-bank design in a number of interesting directions. See also Walsh (1993a, b).

model, as opposed to those that arise from the use of suboptimal targeting rules. By deriving the optimal contract, I have shown that the difficulties of achieving both optimal policy responses to new information and zero average inflation, particularly in the presence of private central-bank information, are not inherent in the basic framework employed in much of the recent literature on strategic monetary policy. Instead, apparent trade-offs among price stability and stabilization, flexibility, and credibility, may simply reflect the suboptimal incentives the central bank faces under ad hoc targeting rules.

APPENDIX

This appendix shows that the transfer function given by equation (24) implements the effort function $e(a)$ and the money supply rule $m(a,\theta)$ when both a and m are private information to the central bank. A and K in (24) depend on the central banker's announced type, but not on θ, and their values are given by

$$\text{(A1)} \quad A(a) = B(a) + K(a)(\sigma_\upsilon^2 + \gamma^2 s(a)[a - e(a)]^2 \sigma_\omega^2)$$

$$\text{(A2)} \quad K(a) = \frac{C'(e(a))}{2\gamma^2 s(a)[a - e(a)]\sigma_\omega^2} = \frac{\eta[e(a) - \underline{e}]}{2\gamma^2 s(a)[a - e(a)]\sigma_\omega^2}$$

and

$$\text{(A3)} \quad B(a) = \int_a^{\bar{a}} C'(e(z))[1 - e'(z)]dz \geq 0$$

so that $B(\bar{a}) = 0$; the least-efficient central banker earns no rent.[26]

The decisions faced by the central banker form a two-stage process. In the first stage, the central banker announces her type and chooses an effort level. Effort is chosen prior to obtaining any information on the current realizations of the random disturbances (θ, ε, ω, and υ). In the second stage, the central banker observes the signal θ and sets the money supply. If m cannot be observed by the government, the central bank's contract cannot specify actions contingent on θ unless those actions are utility-maximizing for the central bank.

Consider the bank's problem once a^a has been announced, the value of e has been determined, and θ has been observed. The central banker's decision variable is the setting for m. The value of m solves[27]

$$\text{(A4)} \quad \max_m E_\theta \tau(a, \theta, \pi).$$

Using (24), the first-order condition is

$$\text{(A5)} \quad -2K(a^a)E_\theta[\pi - \pi(a^a, \theta)] = 0$$

or $E_\theta \pi = \pi(a^a, \theta)$. Using equation (4) and the definition of $\pi(a^a, \theta)$, it follows that

$$\text{(A6)} \quad m = \delta s(a^a)\theta - \gamma[s(a^a) - s(a)]\theta$$

so that $m = m(a, \theta) = \delta s(a)\theta$ if the central bank announced its type truthfully.

In the first stage, the central bank of type a announces that it is of type a^a and chooses an effort level e. Consider $\{a^a, e\}$ in the concealment set $\{a^a, e(a, a^a)\}$ where $e(a, a^a) = e(a^a) + a - a^a$.[28] Using equation (24) and (A1), the central banker's expected utility from choosing a member of this set can be written as

$$\text{(A7)} \quad B(a^a) - \gamma^2 K(a^a)\{s(a - e)^2 - s(a^a)[a^a - e(a^a)]^2\}\sigma_\omega^2 - C(e).$$

[26] If the central banker's reservation level of utility is $U_0 > 0$, then $B(\bar{a}) = U_0$.

[27] Central-bank utility is $\tau - C(e)$, but since e is a fixed parameter when the decision to set m is made, this last term is dropped for convenience.

[28] If the central bank chooses to announce a^a and undertake effort $e(a, a^a)$, such a deviation cannot be detected by the government (see Laffont and Tirole, 1986).

$$(A9) \quad B'(a^a) - K'(a^a)\gamma^2\big(s(a)(a-e)^2 - s(a^a)[a^a - e(a^a)]^2\big)\sigma_\omega^2$$
$$-2K(a^a)\gamma^2\{[a - e(a,a^a)]s(a)[1 - e'(a^a)]$$
$$-[a - e(a,a^a)]^2[\partial s/\partial(a-e)][e'(a^a) - 1]\}\sigma_\omega^2$$
$$+2K(a^a)\gamma^2\{[a^a - e(a^a)]s(a^a)[1 - e'(a^a)]$$
$$-[a^a - e(a^a)]^2[\partial s/\partial(a-e)][e'(a^a) - 1]\}\sigma_\omega^2$$
$$-C'(e(a,a^a))[e'(a^a) - 1] = 0$$

Maximizing with respect to e, the first-order condition is $2\gamma^2K(a^a)s^2(a-e)\sigma_\omega^2 - C'(e) = 0$, which implies, using the definition of $K(a^a)$ from equation (A2),

$$(A8) \quad \frac{e(a^a) - \underline{e}}{s(a^a)[a^a - e(a^a)]}s(a)(a-e) = (e - \underline{e}).$$

Maximizing (A7) with respect to a^a and using the definition of $e(a, a^a)$ yields equation (A9), above. However, (A9) is satisfied for $a^a = a$ as long as

$$B'(a) = C'(e(a))[e'(a) - 1]$$

which just defines $B(a)$. Thus, if this condition holds, (24) induces the truthful revelation of a. Substituting $a^a = a$ into (A8) yields

$$(A10) \quad \frac{e(a) - \underline{e}}{a - e(a)} = \frac{e - \underline{e}}{a - e}.$$

The right side of (A10) is monotonically increasing in e, while the left side is constant (given a). Therefore, $e = e(a)$ is the unique solution to (A10).[29] Since $a^a = a$, equation (A6) implies that $m = \delta s(a)\theta$.

[29]This would hold for any convex cost function $C(e)$.

REFERENCES

Barro, Robert J. and Gordon, David B. "A Positive Theory of Monetary Policy in a Natural Rate Model." *Journal of Political Economy*, August 1983, *91*(4), pp. 589–610.

Bernanke, Ben and Blinder, Alan. "The Federal Funds Rate and the Channels of Monetary Transmission." *American Economic Review*, September 1992, *82*(4), pp. 901–21.

Canzoneri, Matthew B. "Monetary Policy Games and the Role of Private Information." *American Economic Review*, December 1985, *75*(5), pp. 1056–70.

Christiano, Lawrence; Eichenbaum, Martin and Evans, Charles. "The Effects of Monetary Policy Shocks: Evidence from the Flow of Funds." Unpublished manuscript presented at the Canadian Macroeconomics Study Group Meeting, Victoria, BC, November 1993.

Dotsey, Michael and King, Robert G. "Monetary Instruments and Policy Rules in a Rational Expectations Environment." *Journal of Monetary Economics*, September 1983, *12*(3), pp. 357–82.

Garfinkel, Michelle R. and Oh, Seonghwan. "Stategic Discipline in Monetary Policy with Private Information: Optimal Targeting Horizons." *American Economic Review*, March 1993, *83*(1), pp. 99–117.

Jewitt, Ian. "Justifying the First-Order Approach to Principal–Agent Problems." *Econometrica*, September 1988, *55*(5), pp. 1177–90.

Kydland, Finn E. and Prescott, Edward C. "Rules Rather Than Discretion: The Inconsistency of Optimal Plans." *Journal of Political Economy*, June 1977, *85*(3), pp. 473–91.

Laffont, Jean-Jacques and Tirole, Jean. "Using Cost Observation to Regulate Firms." *Journal of Political Economy*, June 1986, *94*(3) pp. 614–41.

Lohmann, Susanne. "Optimal Commitment in Monetary Policy: Credibility versus Flexibility." *American Economic Review*, March 1992, *82*(1), pp. 273–86.

O'Flaherty, Brendan. "The Care and Handling of Monetary Authorities." *Economics and Politics*, March 1990, *2*(1), pp. 25–44.

Persson, Torsten and Tabellini, Guido. *Macroeconomic policy, credibility and politics*. Chur: Harwood, 1990.

______. "Designing Institutions for Monetary Stability." *Carnegie-Rochester Conference Series on Public Policy*, December 1993, *39*, pp. 53–84.

Rogoff, Kenneth. "The Optimal Degree of Commitment to an Intermediate Monetary Target." *Quarterly Journal of Economics*, November 1985, *100*(4), pp. 1169–89.

Roley, V. Vance and Walsh, Carl E. "Monetary Policy Regimes, Expected Inflation, and the Response of Interest Rates to Money Announcements." *Quarterly Journal of Economics*, Supplement 1985, *100*, pp. 1011–39.

VanHoose, David D. "Optimal Choice of Monetary Policy Instruments When Policymaking Is Costly." Mimeo, University of Alabama, June 1992.

Waller, Christopher J. "The Choice of a Conservative Central Banker in a Multisector Economy." *American Economic Review*, September 1992, *82*(4), pp. 1006–12.

Walsh, Carl E. "Optimal Contracts for Independent Central Banks: Private Information, Performance Measures and Reappointment." Paper prepared for the CEPR/FRBSF Conference on Macroeconomic Stabilization Policy: Lessons for the Future, Stanford, CA, March 1993a.

______. "When Should Central Bankers Be Fired?" Mimeo, University of California, Santa Cruz, September 1993b.

______. "Is New Zealand's Reserve Bank Act of 1989 an Optimal Central Bank Contract?" Mimeo, University of California, Santa Cruz, January 1994.

Part II
Measures of Central Bank Independence

[7]

Economic Policy April 1989 Printed in Great Britain

Politics

Alberto Alesina

Summary

Influences from political competition on macroeconomic policy are often thought to be a source of economic fluctuations. Politicians are described as being driven by two, not mutually exclusive, main motivations: they want to be reelected and they harbour political, or ideological, biases. When such theories are confronted with actual cycles in a number of industrial countries, the pattern of inflation, unemployment, output, and budget deficits indicates that partisan policy making is a fairly widespread phenomenon, with more limited evidence that electoral preoccupations result in major fluctuations. The combination of partisanship and electoral cycles may easily result in socially undesirable outcomes. In particular the degree of politico-institutional stability and the independence of the Central Bank have a bearing on macroeconomic outcomes. These observations raise a number of important questions about the design of political institutions.

The median voter in practice

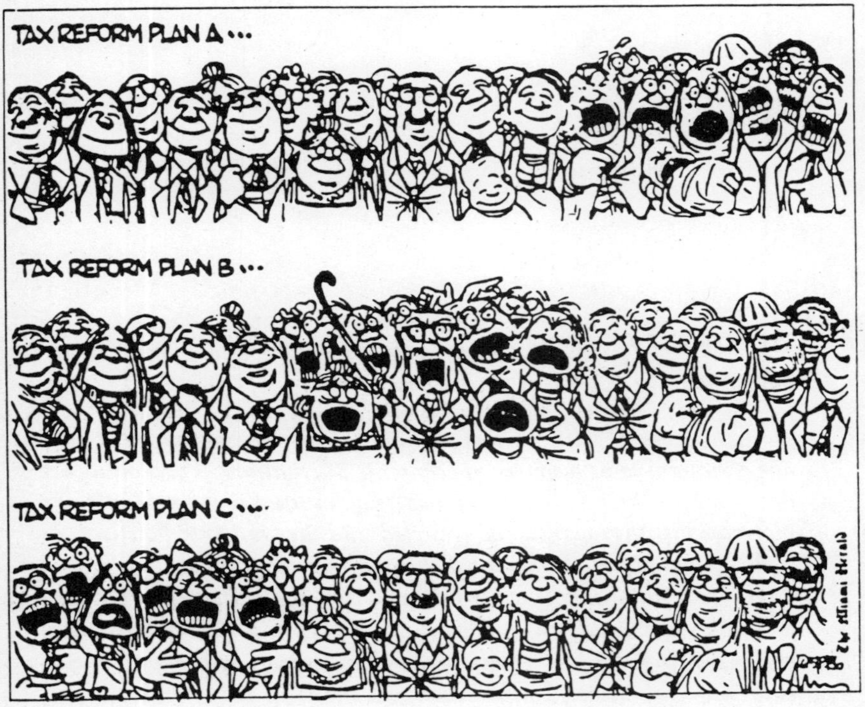

The Economist, August 1st, 1987. Copyright © 1986 *The Miami Herald*, Reprinted with permission.

Politics and business cycles in industrial democracies

Alberto Alesina
Harvard University, NBER and CEPR

1. Introduction

Macroeconomics and politics are deeply interconnected. Elections are won or lost as a result of economic conditions. However, ideological and electoral incentives influence politicians' choices of macroeconomic policies. This paper investigates how the level of inflation, unemployment, and economic growth is influenced by political forces in several industrial economies, with particular emphasis on Western Europe. It is probably fair to view politicians as mainly driven by two fundamental motivations. First, they strive to remain in office as long as possible. Second, they are partisan and wish to deliver benefits to their constituencies. Clearly, the influence of politics on macroeconomic policy depends upon the predominant motivation of politicians. Exclusive emphasis on electoral motivations characterizes the 'political business cycle' theory (henceforth, PBC) popularized by Nordhaus (1975). According to this view, politicians attempt to create the most desirable economic conditions immediately before elections, even though their policies may require costly adjustments after the elections. In particular, the economy is overstimulated before the elections with expansionary policies. Short-sighted voters reward the incumbent government, without realizing that a recession will be needed after the election to reduce inflation. Thus, the political cycle generates sub-optimal and unnecessary economic cycles, since the timing of macroeconomic policy is artificially affected by the timing of elections. There exist a number of well known instances when this appealingly simple story has occurred.

I would like to thank my discussants, Jim Mirrlees and Manfred Neumann, members of the *Economic Policy* Panel, John Black and especially Charles Wyplosz for many useful comments on the first draft; Jim Alt, Nouriel Roubini, and Guido Tabellini for several helpful conversations; and Suzanne Lohmann and Joy Beatty for excellent research assistance.

For example, a few weeks before the November 1972 election, President Nixon increased social security benefits by about 20% and indexed them to inflation, while money supply grew by more than 8% over 1972 as compared to about 4% in the preceding and following three years. However, the empirical work that has followed Nordhaus' insight has not been overly supportive of the PBC hypothesis.

Emphasizing the partisan behaviour of politicians in his 'partisan theory' (henceforth, PT), Hibbs (1977) has argued that political parties have different preferences over the trade-off between inflation and unemployment because macroeconomic outcomes have important redistributive consequences. As a low unemployment/high inflation outcome is favourable to the lower middle class, while the upper middle class benefits from the opposite combination, left-wing parties choose points on the Phillips curve with higher inflation and lower unemployment. Indeed, in the 1960s, countries with predominantly Socialist governments had a lower average unemployment and a higher average inflation than countries with predominantly non-Socialist governments. This view raises the possibility of a second political cycle and of a second type of inefficiency as the partisan behaviour of politicians may generate excessive economic fluctuations. Socialist parties underestimate the cost of inflation and overstimulate the economy; Conservative parties are too callous with respect to unemployment, when they fight inflation. Quite clearly, and this has been pointed out by Frey and Schneider (1978), the PBC and PT approaches are not necessarily mutually exclusive.

In the mid-1970s, both the occurrence of stagflation and the 'rational expectations revolution' questioned the existence of an exploitable Phillips curve, with two important implications for political business cycle theories. First, according to the new approach policymakers cannot engineer the kind of carefully timed expansions and recessions predicted by the PBC and, anyway, rational voters should not be easily 'fooled' by well timed pre-electoral expansions. Second, since employment remains unaffected beyond the short run by aggregate demand policies, identifying partisan governments should be harder beyond the short run. These 'rational' criticisms of the PBC and PT have been incorporated in the recent works of Cukierman and Meltzer (1986), Rogoff and Sibert (1988), and Rogoff (1987) based on Nordhaus' insights while Alesina (1987) has focused on the partisan theory. Once they incorporate rational expectations, the new approaches have different empirical implications from the original Nordhaus' and Hibbs' contributions. Thus, empirical support for the new partisan theory has been provided by Alesina and Sachs (1988) and Alesina (1988a) in the case of the US. Evidence regarding several industrial democracies in the

1970s and 1980s is presented in the present paper and suggests three main results.

First, partisan effects are significant. The pattern of unemployment, output growth and inflation tends to be systematically related to the political orientation of governments. However, this systematic difference is typically short-lived and occurs primarily in a short period after a change of government. On the contrary, the evidence of a systematic cycle on output and unemployment predicted by the PBC is rather inconclusive. If politicians try to expand the economy before elections they are not often successful. Another possible interpretation is that different governments are fighting different problems when elections are approaching: Conservative governments are often fighting unemployment after an early recession, and Socialist parties are trying to control inflation which resulted from their expansionary policies. Both types of government are trying to appear 'moderate' to win the support of the voters, but in order to appeal to the 'middle of the road voters' they have to follow different, often opposite policies. Second, there is a correlation between politico-institutional stability and economic performance: more polarized and unstable political systems have been associated with poorer economic performance as measured in terms of inflation and unemployment. Third, the results have a number of normative implications about the desirability of policy rules versus discretion, of institutional reforms, of an independent Central Bank, and of economic policy coordination. In particular, a better understanding of the political economy of macroeconomic policy is a crucial prerequisite for the design of efficient institutions.

The rest of the paper is divided into three sections. Section 2 reviews alternative politico-economic theories of inflation and unemployment and identifies the empirical implications which are examined in Section 3 for several industrial countries. Section 4 explores the relationship between political and economic stability. Section 5 considers several normative issues. The last section summarizes the main results of the paper.

2. Political theories of inflation and unemployment

The traditional view about politicians' behaviour is that they are self-interested individuals, maximizing their individual 'rents'. Since political 'rents' are associated with being in office, politicians simply maximize their popularity to increase the probability of reappointment (Downs, 1957). An implication is that one should presumably observe some policy convergence in a two party system: both parties seek to pursue the policy most desired by the median voter. Still, politicians might have different strategic motives, so that the convergence of policy is not robust; more importantly this result does not always fit with the empirical evidence. Lack of policy convergence, that is the fact that different parties follow different policies when in office, is quite widespread. This lack of policy convergence can be explained in several ways. For example, a self-interested politician in the US, in order to become President, needs to win the nomination in the primaries. Thus, he has to adopt a policy position close to the median voter of one of the two parties. Since the platform adopted in the primary is a constraint (for credibility reasons) on the choice of a platform for the presidential elections, even self-interested politicians may have to choose polarized policies. Other considerations, such as the threat of entry of a third candidate (Palfrey, 1984), or abstentions of voters with extreme preferences because of alienation, may destroy the result of policy convergence even in a world of purely office-motivated politicians. In multi-party systems, focus on the median voter will not be the rule, and very little is known about the optimal location of parties in this system (see Shepsle and Cohen, 1988 for a survey). There is no presumption that in a multi-party system with self-interested politicians one should observe policy convergence.

A different approach to politicians' behaviour has been suggested by Wittman (1977) and developed by Calvert (1985) and Alesina (1988b). Politicians not only care about winning elections but also act as if they had preferences defined over policy issues. Individual politicians are self-interested and represent the 'ideology' of their party or constituency. According to this 'partisan' view, different constituencies, social and/or ethnic groups support different parties, which, in turn, follow different policies in order to retain this support. In particular, different constituencies would support policies which imply income redistribution in their favour. Clearly, elections have to be won in order to implement the desired policies. However, even when partisan politicians want to win, this approach does not predict fully policy convergence aimed at the median voter's preferences.

2.1. Partisan theories of macroeconomic policy

Hibbs' (1977) hypothesis (PT) is based upon the belief that left-wing parties prefer, on average, higher inflation and lower unemployment than right-wing parties. The basic idea is that politics is about income distribution. Macroeconomic outcomes have important redistributional consequences; indeed, the lower middle class, which mostly supports the left, tends to suffer during recessions relatively more than the upper middle class. Yet, it is rather difficult to isolate the effect of macroeconomic policies on income distribution. The available evidence gathered by Hibbs (1987) for the US is unambiguous concerning the effect of unemployment: when unemployment rises the income shares of the two poorest quintiles decrease and the shares of the two richest quintiles increase while the middle quintile is essentially unaffected. However, these redistributive flows while substantial are not dramatic: a one-year increase in the rate of unemployment from 6 to 10% would shift 0.95 percentage points of income from the bottom two-fifths to the upper two-fifths of the income distribution.

The redistributive effects of inflation are less clear cut. In principle several channels are possible: the income tax brackets if they are not adjusted for inflation; the interaction between the tax structure and a firm's financial structure; the effect of inflation on the real value of nominally denominated assets; and changes in the relative prices of the baskets of goods purchased by different income groups. Hibbs' (1987) conclusion is that if inflation has had any overall effect on income distribution in the US, it has been from the rich to the poor. Minford (1985) suggests a similar effect for the UK and argues that the right is relatively more averse to inflation than the left because the right is more concerned with defending the real value of nominally denominated assets which are held in greater proportion by the upper middle class relative to the lower class. In summary, the evidence, though limited, provides some support for the view that redistributional considerations provide an incentive for the left to be expansionary and unemployment-fighting and for the right to be inflation-fighting and less concerned about unemployment.

Hence, if there is an exploitable Phillips-like trade-off, the left should opt for lower unemployment and higher inflation than the right. These systematic differences in economic activity should be relatively persistent and should be observed for the entire term of office of the various governments. This theory is inconsistent with the 'rational expectations' critique which suggests that expansionary policies result in higher inflation with very little benefit in terms of real economic activity beyond the short run. A 'rational partisan theory' (henceforth, RPT) has been proposed by Alesina (1987) and Alesina and Sachs (1988).[1] In a world of partisan politicians, electoral uncertainty generates uncertain expectations. Suppose that a recently elected right-wing government implements an anti-inflationary policy. If the public had accounted for the possibility that the left (less anti-inflationary) could have won the

[1] A 'rational politico-macro model' was also proposed in an insightful early paper by Minford and Peel (1982). The emphasis and modelling strategy of that paper is, however, different from the present paper.

election it must have (rationally) assumed an average inflation rate above actual inflation. In the presence of nominal rigidities (such as non-indexed labour contracts), economic decisions taken before the election (and based upon rational expectations), cannot be immediately readjusted after the regime change. This implies some real effects in output and employment and the magnitude of these effects is positively related to the difference between the policies expected from the rival parties. This argument is strengthened if there is a backward-looking component in expectations formation (for instance if not everybody is rational or aware of the policy change).[2] Once expectations have caught up with the new regime the level of economic activity returns to its natural level. Inflation remains low if the government is from the right and has chosen an anti-inflation stance. With a left-wing government, new expansionary policies create a temporary increase in the level of economic activity above its natural level and once expectations have adjusted, inflation remains high. One reason is the problem of 'time-inconsistency' described by Kydland and Prescott (1977) and Barro and Gordon (1983); the problem is that, since left-wing governments have a reputation for fighting unemployment, the public expects high inflation from them. In fact, a low inflation policy announced by a government concerned with unemployment would not be credible; indeed, if expected inflation was 'low', this government would create an inflation surprise in order to reduce unemployment. Instead, the public expects high inflation and the government's best course of action is to 'accommodate' those expectations to avoid a recession. As a result, the economy is 'trapped' into a high-inflation equilibrium. An expansionary government may thus produce rising inflation and unemployment in the latter part of its term of office.

The RPT differs in an important way from Hibbs' approach. In the latter, differences in output and unemployment persist and actually increase throughout the entire term of office of different governments. In contrast, the RPT predicts that such differences are transitory and should occur immediately after the change of government. Both views do, however, share an emphasis on the difference between left-wing expansionary parties and right-wing anti-inflationary parties. The partisan theory, and in particular the RPT does not rely upon voters' shortsightedness. On the contrary, it is consistent with the view that intelligent voters correctly understand the difference between parties and vote accordingly. The uncertainty about the electoral results is due

[2] In addition, imperfect information about the preferences of a newly elected policymaker can prolong the adjustment if the public has to learn the preferences of the new policymaker (see Barro, 1986).

to changes in voters' preferences, which are not perfectly predictable. Interestingly, voters' preferences may also change as a result of economic outcomes; for instance, a period of high inflation may increase the degree of inflation-aversion in the public and generate a movement toward the right. Arguably several countries have experienced such changes of opinion in the late 1970s or early 1980s.

2.2. Political business cycles

The PBC approach of Nordhaus (1975) emphasizes exclusively the electoral motivations of policymakers. All politicians simply maximize their chances of remaining in office and subsequently follow identical policies. Nordhaus' PBC is based upon two crucial assumptions. First, the voters are backward-looking and short-sighted; they vote for the incumbent if the economy is 'doing well' (low unemployment, high growth, low inflation) immediately before the elections. They forget quickly about the past and do not understand the economic relationship between inflation and unemployment. Second, the economy is characterized by a Phillips curve which is easily exploitable because of backward-looking expectations. In this context, every incumbent stimulates aggregate demand before elections. In addition, given that the inflationary consequences of an expansion are normally lagged, the stimulus can be timed in such a way that inflation will only appear after the election. At that time inflation is brought under control by a demand-induced recession, which voters soon forget in time to be fooled again before the following election.

Recent work by Cukierman and Meltzer (1986), Rogoff (1987), and Rogoff and Sibert (1988) builds a 'rational political business cycle' theory (henceforth, RPBC). They show that Nordhaus' (1975) insights may survive even when voters are not myopic and gullible as long as they are imperfectly informed about some characteristics of the environment, the policymaker's objectives, or his ability to manage the economy. For instance, immediately before elections, incumbents may want to appear as 'efficient' as possible in providing new public goods, services, or transfers. By 'hiding' or delaying the budgetary consequences, the incumbents may succeed in creating a temporary illusion of prosperity, before the voters realize that they will have to pay for it with post-election taxes. The budgetary process is sufficiently complicated, that even relatively informed and attentive voters may be 'fooled' at least temporarily. This analysis thus predicts a pre- and post-electoral manipulation of policy instruments. However, it is difficult to obtain regular and predictable four–five years' fluctuations of output and unemployment in this rational framework, since it is unrealistic to imagine that imperfect information on policy choices can last for several years. The RPBC theory is thus compatible with relatively short-run cycles of budget deficits, transfers, and money supply growth around the election date but it does not have clear implications for a longer cycle of output and unemployment.

2.3. Summing up

Four politico-economic views of the inflation-unemployment tradeoff have been presented. The first approach, the PBC, is based upon non-ideological politicians and myopic voters. It implies a recession at the beginning of every government's term of office and an expansion immediately before new elections, with no partisan differences. The second approach, the RPBC, allows for both non-ideological politicians and rational voters. This cycle has implications similar to that of the PBC on certain policy instruments (budget deficits, money supply), but has no clear implications for a several-year cycle on output and unemployment. The third approach, the PT, is based upon partisan politicians and an exploitable Phillips curve. This approach predicts a low unemployment–high inflation outcome for the entire term of office of left-wing governments and the opposite combination for right-wing governments. The fourth and last approach, the RPT, includes both ideological politicians and rational voters. It predicts an expansion at the beginning of a left-wing government and a recession at the beginning of a right-wing government. In the latter part of the term of office, output and unemployment should be indistinguishable between governments, while inflation may remain higher during left-wing administrations.

3. Empirical evidence on politico-economic cycles

Most of the available empirical work on politically induced business cycles has been performed on US data, and, to a lesser extent, on British data. The reason is presumably that such cycles are more difficult to study in European democracies; first of all, economic fluctuations in small open economies are deeply linked to the condition of world demand. Thus, politically induced 'recessions' or 'expansions' should be defined relative to the world economy. In addition, international monetary agreements such as the EMS have constrained European monetary policies relatively more than in the US. Second, European unemployment shows signs of strong persistence, due to various characteristics of the labour market (see Blanchard and Summers, 1986, and the references quoted therein). As a consequence demand policies are hardly the only determinant of unemployment. Several other difficulties relate to the politico-institutional structure. For instance, it is sometimes difficult clearly to identify changes of political regimes. Realignments of coalitions and government crises with changes of personnel occur rather frequently in several countries and often not as a result of general elections. In addition, it is sometimes hard to place coalition governments in the right–left dimension because the relative weights of the various members of a coalition may vary over time, even though the parties forming the coalition remain unchanged. More generally, coalition governments may behave rather differently from single party governments. Hence, the structure and cohesiveness of coalitions is an important matter to consider on the top of the left–right distinction. Furthermore, the timing of elections is often endogenous so that policy makers can call elections in 'good times' rather than create good times when elections are approaching. Finally, any attempt to establish general patterns and correlations between politics and economic variables for a large sample of countries implies that country-specific institutions, events or personal characteristics of individual politicians have to be assumed away.

It is quite clear that one has to make rather strong assumptions to provide statistical tests or even simply to organize the data. In an insightful paper, Alt (1985) identifies these problems and deals with some of them. His empirical evidence from several European countries favours the partisan theory of unemployment. However, he does not consider output growth and inflation, he does not confront directly the PBC and the PT, nor does he consider the RPT as a possible explanation of the empirical evidence.

3.1. Tests of partisan theories

Table 1, based upon Alt (1985) and Banks (1987), identifies all the changes of regimes in the sample period 1968–86. Note that this table considers only *changes of* governments. It does not indicate when a party or coalition is reelected. In addition to the western European countries, the US and Australia are also included to enlarge the sample. Not included in the table are: Switzerland, due to the lack of any political change; Italy, because of its chaotic electoral history; Ireland, for data problems; and Portugal, Spain and Greece because of their recent transitions from dictatorships to democracies, a major change of political regime hardly comparable to the other changes of governments included in the table. These countries are, however, considered in Section 3.3, where some international comparisons are attempted.

Table 1. Changes of political orientation of governments (1968–86)

Country and date	Direction of movement	Explanation	Country and date	Direction of movement	Explanation
Australia			Germany		
12–72	Left	Labour-single-party	09–69	Left	SPD-FDP coalition
11–75	Right	Liberal	12–72	Right	FDP gains econ. min.
03–83	Left	Labour	10–82	Right	CDU/CSU–FDP coalition
Austria			Netherlands		
04–70	Left	Socialist	05–73	Left	Labour coalition
04–83	Right	SP-FP coalition	05–77	Right	Right coalition
			09–81	Left	Labour coalition
			11–82	Right	Right coalition
Belgium			Norway		
06–68	Left	CSP-socialist	10–71	Left	Socialist
01–73	Right	CSP-Soc-lib	10–72	Right	Nonsocialist coalition
03–77	Left	CSP-Soc-minor parties	10–73	Left	Socialist
12–81	Right	Nonsocialist coalition	10–81	Right	Conservative
10–85	Left	Socialist coalition	10–85	Right	Socialist

Denmark (a)		
10–71	Left	Socialist
12–73	Right	Lib-democrat
02–75	Left	Socialist
09–82	Right	4-Party conservative coalition
Finland (b)		
11–75	Right	Centre coalition
05–77	Left	Centre/left coalition
France		
05–81	Left	Socialist
Sweden		
10–76	Right	Right coalition
10–82	Left	Left coalition
UK		
06–70	Right	Conservative
02–74	Left	Labour
06–79	Right	Conservative
US		
11–68	Right	Republican pres.
11–76	Left	Democratic pres.
11–80	Right	Republican pres.

Source: Alt (1985) and Banks (1987).
Notes: (a) A short lived Social Democrat-Liberal coalition government (8–78/10–79) is not considered a significant change of regime from the previous government. For the same reason Alt (1985) excludes this government from his analysis; (b) short-lived changes in coalition governments in the period 3–70/10–71 are ignored.

Three economic indicators are considered: real output growth, unemployment and inflation. Since the world level of economic activity affects each country's economic conditions, we consider for all countries the deviation of these variables from their average over eighteen industrialized economies.[3] Henceforth, the terms 'inflation', 'unemployment' and 'output growth' will be used to indicate deviations from the average of the corresponding variables. The following indices are defined:

I_1 = (average output growth in the first two years after a change of regime) minus (average output growth in the preceding two years).

I_2 = (average output growth in the first two years after a change of regime) minus (average output growth for the entire term of office of the new regime).[4]

The RPT predicts that I_1 and I_2 will be positive for a left-wing regime and negative for a right-wing regime. In particular, a positive value of I_2 (not to be expected with Hibbs' PT) would suggest that the real effects of aggregate demand stimulation are stronger at the outset of the new term of office.

In principle, one would want to construct indices for unemployment analogous to I_1 and I_2. However, as pointed out by Blanchard and Summers (1986), European unemployment shows a very high degree of persistence which reflects a variety of supply-side phenomena. Thus, rather than working with the actual data, we isolate 'shocks' or innovation in the behaviour of unemployment which may be caused by shifts in aggregate demand[5] and use these measures to construct the two indicators, I_3 and I_4, otherwise defined exactly as I_1 and I_2. The signs predicted by the RPT for I_3 and I_4 are opposite to those of I_1 and I_2, that is, negative for left-wing governments and positive for right-wing governments. The strict and simple version of the RPT as formulated in Alesina (1987) and Alesina and Sachs (1988) would imply that these indicators (I_1 to I_4) may be different from zero even after the reappointment of the same government because of electoral uncertainty. Quite clearly real effects of demand policies are stronger when, in addition

[3] The results do not change qualitatively if other 'reasonable' sets of countries are chosen to construct these indices. For instance, analogous results are obtained by considering the three indicators as deviation from the average of five major economies (US, Japan, Germany, France, and UK).

[4] The first year of a government is considered to be the calendar year following the year in which the change of regime occurred. The last year of a government includes the year in which the change of regime occurred. This choice is reasonable because it allows for a time lag between the change of government and the observable effects of new policies.

[5] Innovations are computed as the residuals of a first order regressive process. For every country a second lag is (with one exception) insignificant. The results of these regressions are available from the author.

to electoral uncertainty, the policy actually changes. Furthermore, in several cases of reappointment of the same government, the electoral uncertainty was very low as the likelihood of reappointment of the incumbent was very high. Some indirect evidence favourable to the more restrictive version of the RPT is presented in Section 3.2.

With respect to inflation, both the PT and the RPT predict that left-wing regimes should exhibit higher inflation than right-wing regimes. Since inflation is also highly persistent in the countries under review, inflation data were adjusted using the same procedure as the one for unemployment. The following index was constructed:

I_5 = (average inflation rate per year in one regime) minus (average inflation rate in preceding regime).

The partisan theory predicts that I_5 should be positive (negative) for left- (right-)wing governments.[6]

Table 2 reports these five indicators for all the changes of regimes described in Table 1. A yes (*Y*) stands for a sign of the indicator consistent with the RPT; a no (*N*), for a sign which is *not* consistent. The actual values of the indicators are reported in Table A1 in the Appendix. Table 2, with more than 70% of yes, provides some support for the RPT. The Netherlands is the only country which clearly does not exhibit the pattern predicted by the theory, particularly on unemployment. Excluding the Netherlands, out of the 33 regime changes listed in Table 1 only two are characterized by indicators inconsistent with the RPT (Norway in 1981 and Australia in 1972); in one case we also find an equal number of correct and incorrect signs (Germany in 1969). In all the other cases, the majority of the indicators have the sign predicted by the theory. For 22 changes of regime there are either zero or one sign not consistent with the RPT. Furthermore the indicators with the incorrect sign tend to be smaller in absolute value than the indicators with the correct sign: Table 3 shows that the indicators with the correct sign are on average larger in absolute value than the corresponding indicators with the incorrect sign, except I_4 for which there is a tie (see Table A1 for details). The difference in the averages for the output indicators is rather striking and it is relatively smaller for I_5 because of two 'large' incorrect signs (Belgium and Finland).

Several changes of regime in the late 1970s and early 1980s fit the RPT: France (1981), Sweden (1982), UK (1979), and the US (1980).

[6] The indicator I_5 is not defined on the first change of regime in the sample, since the average of the regime before the first change is not well defined. Also, we have not computed the index for the two regime changes occurring in 1985 (Belgium and Norway), since only one observation for the new regime is included in the sample.

Table 2. Test of partisan theories

Indicators:	Output growth				Unemployment				Inflation		Total	
	I_1 After minus before		I_2 First 2 years minus whole term		I_3 After minus before		I_4 First 2 years minus whole term		I_5 After minus before			
Theory prediction:												
Left	+		+		–		–		+			
Right	–		–		+		+		–			
Conformity outcome	*Y*	*N*	*Y*	*N*	*Y*	*N*	*Y*	*N*	*Y*	*N*	*Y*	*N*
Australia	2	1	2	1	1	2	3	0	2	0	10	4
Austria	2	0	2	0	2	0	1	1	0	1	7	2
Belgium	4	1	1	3	5	0	3	1	1	2	14	7
Denmark	4	0	2	0	3	1	1	1	3	0	13	2
Finland	2	0	1	0	2	0	0	1	0	1	5	2
France	1	0	1	0	1	0	1	0	NA	NA	4	0
Germany	1	2	3	0	2	1	3	0	1	1	10	4
Netherlands	2	2	0	3	0	4	1	2	3	0	6	11
Norway	3	2	2	0	3	2	1	1	2	1	11	6
Sweden	2	0	2	0	1	1	2	0	1	0	8	1
UK	2	1	3	0	2	1	2	1	2	0	11	3
US	2	1	3	0	2	1	3	0	2	0	12	2
Total	27	10	22	7	24	13	21	8	17	6	111	44
% of Yes	73		76		65		72		74		72	

Sources: Output is GNP or GDP, inflation is CPI growth rate, both from *IFS*, IMF. Unemployment rate: *Main Economic Indicators*, OECD.
Notes: Indicators are defined in the text. All variables are relative to the average of 18 countries: Australia, Austria, Belgium, Canada, Denmark, Finland, France, Germany, Greece, Italy, Japan, Netherlands, Norway, Portugal, Spain, Sweden, UK and US. Because of data problems, the unemployment average is constructed using 14 of these countries, excluding Australia, Denmark, Greece, and the Netherlands.

Table 3. Average absolute values of the indicators of Table 2

	I_1	I_2	I_3	I_4	I_5
Y	1.86	1.03	0.84	0.37	1.23
N	0.70	0.29	0.53	0.37	1.07

Notes: Computations based upon Table A1 in Appendix.

The case of the French Socialists is particularly suggestive of the RPT. In a period of world recession (1981–83), the French government pursued expansionary policies, keeping French economic growth positive, while many other major industrial economies were in a recession (see Sachs and Wyplosz, 1985, for a detailed analysis of this period). These recent examples are perhaps better known, but several other changes of regime are consistent with the theory. For example, in the mid-1970s, the Carter administration in the US and the Swedish Conservatives (1976) offer a particularly good fit. In Sweden, the output growth indicator fell from an average of about zero in 1975–76 to almost −4 in 1977, and almost −1 in 1978; in the US, from an average of −0.1 in 1973–76 to an average of more than 2 in 1977–78 (dropping to −1 in 1979–80). The unemployment and inflation indicators also conform with the RPT.[7]

Table 4 provides some additional evidence regarding the effects of regime changes on cyclical fluctuations. It shows the correlation between the output or unemployment indicators and the changes in political orientation of governments. To do so a variable 'left' is defined as follows:

$$\text{Left} = \begin{cases} +1 & \text{in two years after a change of regime toward the left} \\ -1 & \text{in two years after a change of regime toward the right} \\ 0 & \text{otherwise.} \end{cases}$$

Of course we could equally call this variable 'right' by changing its sign: the variable simply captures a change in orientation and has no particular 'partisan' implication. Table 4 displays the coefficients on the variable 'left' along with their *t*-statistics. Except for two instances where they are statistically insignificant (unemployment in the Netherlands and Norway), all the coefficients have the expected sign. More than half of them (13) are either strongly or marginally significant (they have a *t*-statistic above 1.5 in absolute value); four of the remaining

[7] The results on the UK and the US confirm earlier related results favourable to the partisan theory. For the US, see, for instance, Alesina and Sachs (1988), Alesina (1988a) and the references quoted therein. For the UK, see Hibbs (1977), Minford and Peel (1982), Borooah and Van der Ploeg (1983), Minford (1985), and Alt (1985).

Table 4. Correlation with changes to the left (1966–86)

Countries	Output	Unemployment	Countries	Output	Unemployment
Australia	0.87	−0.29 (a)	Germany	0.39	0.50
	(1.38)	(−1.08)		(0.78)	(−2.31)
Austria	1.04	−0.24	Netherlands	0.67	0.36
	(1.89)	(−1.64)		(0.78)	(0.40)
Belgium	0.21	−0.53	Norway	1.04	0.01
	(0.40)	(−2.26)		(1.51)	(0.14)
Denmark	0.67	−0.42	Sweden	1.44	−0.16
	(1.35)	(−1.28)		(2.00)	(−0.69)
Finland	2.32	−1.00 (b)	UK	1.51	−0.42
	(2.47)	(−2.77)		(1.55)	(−1.56)
France	0.31	−0.67	US	2.51	−0.66
	(0.14)	(−2.42)		(3.73)	(−1.80)

Notes: The variable 'left' is defined in the text; the regressors are a constant and the variable left; *t*-statistics are given in parentheses; (a) 1968–86; (b) the unemployment regression for Finland is the only one which exhibits first order autocorrelation of the residual, thus, a lagged dependent variable is used as an additional regressor.

coefficients have a *t*-statistic above 1. In every country except for the Netherlands and Australia, at least one of the two coefficients is statistically significant.

The results on I_2 and I_4 and Table 3 support the RPT rather than the PT, by indicating that the effects of changes in regime on output and unemployment seem to be transitory. Note, however, that there is a slighly different way of formulating a partisan theory with transitory effects. For instance, Alt (1985), and informally Cohen (1988), suggest that these real effects may be transitory not only because of expectation adjustments which shift the Phillips curve, but because economic policies change and become more cautious in the second part of governments' terms of office. Left-wing governments may turn to less expansionary policies, for instance, if the early expansion has created problems of external balance and/or if inflation is growing too fast. In other words, left-wing governments in the latter part of their terms of office often face an economy with high inflation and growing unemployment. They are thus forced to fight inflation, even though new elections may be approaching, and the more so if opinion polls show the public's concern with inflation. In some sense, left-wing governments end up following a pattern of policies opposite to the prediction of the PBC theory. The policies of the Carter administration and of President Mitterrand are perhaps the two clearest examples.

As argued in Section 2.1, the different preferences for macroeconomic policies of left and right-wing parties are due to divergent

Table 5. Changes in real disposable under Reagan and Thatcher

Change in average household real personal disposable income:	Reagan 1980–84	Thatcher 1978–79 to 1981–82
Top 20%	+8.7	+4.7
Next 20%	+3.4	−4.3
Middle 20%	+0.9	−6.4
Next 20%	−0.7	−1.1
Lowest 20%	−7.6	−9.7
Total	+3.5	−1.1

Household share of real personal disposable income:	Reagan		Thatcher			
	Post-tax		Post-tax		Pre-tax	
	1980	1984	1978–79	1981–82	1978–79	1981–82
Top 20%	37.0	38.9	39.7	42.0	42.6	45.0
Next 20%	24.5	24.5	24.8	24.0	24.7	23.9
Middle 20%	18.5	18.1	17.0	16.1	16.5	15.6
Next 20%	13.2	12.5	11.5	11.5	10.3	10.2
Lowest 20%	6.8	6.1	7.0	6.4	5.9	5.5

Source: Alt (1988).

goals regarding distributional matters. A relevant question is, then, whether the left and the right have succeeded in achieving the desired redistributions. The answer to this question for the US and the UK appears to be affirmative. For the US, Hibbs (1987) show than an index of income inequality tends to fall when a Democratic President is in office and *vice versa*. This is partly because recessions occurred primarily under Republican Presidents and, as pointed out in Section 2.1, recessions tend to increase income inequality. An additional factor is the composition of government expenditure and transfer programmes. A similar picture applies to the UK: during the 1960s and 1970s the proportion of taxable personal income received by the top half of income taxpayers has a negative trend, indicating an increase in equality during this period (Rose, 1980). The pattern of income distribution in these two countries in recent years during the 'conservative' policies of President Reagan and Prime Minister Thatcher is particularly 'partisan'. Table 5, borrowed from Alt (1988), shows that the top 20% of British taxpayers gained almost 5% of real disposable income in a three-year period in which the total disposable income fell more than 1%. During the first Reagan administration, the lowest quintile lost almost 8% despite a 3.5% overall growth.

3.2. Political business cycles

The PBC theory predicts a recession at the beginning of each new term of office and an expansion immediately before the new election, with no partisan distinctions. The implications for inflation are less clear cut and depend upon how quickly the inflation rate adjusts to the pre-electoral expansionary policies: one may observe inflation starting to increase before or after the election. Because the implications of the PBC on inflation are not clear cut this variable will not be considered as a test of the PBC. Previous empirical research has provided support to the PBC. Even though a few episodes seem to fit the PBC rather well (e.g. Nixon in 1972), when many elections are considered the predicted systematic cycle can hardly be identified; for the US this conclusion is reached by Alesina (1988a) who presents a survey of the literature. Much fewer results are available for the other countries, but they also provide a rather weak support for the PBC. For instance, Paldam (1978) concludes very cautiously that, overall, only very weak signs of PBC, if any at all, can be found in European democracies.

In order to design a test for the PBC hypothesis, one should take into account the fact that the PBC and the RPT have similar empirical implications for right-wing governments since both theories predict a recession at the beginning of these governments. Consider, for instance, the first Reagan administration. In 1981–82, the US economy was in a sharp recession, while in 1983–84 it was recovering: this observation cannot indicate if the Reagan administration was mainly driven by electoral or partisan motivations, or indeed by both at the same time. On the contrary, because the PBC and the RPT have opposite predictions for the pattern of output and unemployment during the terms of left-wing governments, these governments provide excellent observations to compare the two hypotheses. For the countries included in Table 1, Table 6 considers all the periods during which left-wing governments have been in office for at least three years. Four indicators are considered:

I_6 = (rate of growth of output in the election year) minus (average rate of growth of output for the entire term of office).

I_7 = (average rate of growth of output in the election year and the preceding year) minus (average rate of growth of output for the entire term of office).[8]

[8] The 'election year' is defined as the year in which elections are held, if the election date is after June 1. In the few cases in which elections are held before June 1, we considered the preceding year as the election year. The first year of a term of office is defined as the first year after the year in which election took place, for an election date after June 1, and the election year for elections occurring before June 1. Note that Table 6 includes both the cases in which an incumbent left-wing government has been or has not been reappointed.

Table 6. Test for 'Political Business Cycles' (1969–86)

	Output growth		Unemployment		
	I_6 Election year minus whole term	I_7 Election and previous year minus whole term	I_8 Election year minus whole term	I_9 Election and previous year minus whole term	Total
Theory prediction	+	+	–	–	
Austria					
10–71/10–85	*Y*	*N*	*Y*	*Y*	
10–75/05–79	*N*	*N*	*N*	*N*	
05–79/04–83	*N*	*N*	*Y*	*N*	
Belgium					
12–78/09–81	*N*	*Y*	*N*	*N*	
Denmark					
02–77/12–79	*Y*	*Y*	*Y*	*Y*	
Finland					
01–72/09–75	*N*	*N*	*Y*	*Y*	
03–79/03–83	*N*	*N*	*N*	*N*	
France					
05–81/09–86	*Y*	*N*	*N*	*N*	
Germany					
09–69/11–72	*N*	*N*	*N*	*N*	
11–72/10–76	*Y*	*Y*	*Y*	*Y*	
10–76/10–80	*N*	*N*	*Y*	*Y*	
Norway					
11–73/11–77	*N*	*N*	*N*	*N*	
11–77/11–81	*N*	*N*	*Y*	*Y*	
Sweden					
10–70/10–73	*Y*	*Y*	*Y*	*Y*	
10–73/10–76	*N*	*N*	*N*	*Y*	
10–82/10-85	*N*	*N*	*N*	*N*	
UK					
02–74/06–79	*N*	*Y*	*Y*	*Y*	
US					
11–76/11–80	*N*	*N*	*N*	*N*	
Total	5*Y* 13*N*	5*Y* 13*N*	9*Y* 9*N*	9*Y* 9*N*	28*Y* 44*N*
% of Yes	28	28	50	50	39

The indicators for unemployment, I_8 and I_9, are defined like I_6 and I_7, respectively, using the same unemployment innovations as in Table 2. An entry *Y* in Table 4 indicates a sign of the indicator consistent with the PBC (i.e., positive for I_6 and I_7 and negative for I_8 and I_9). An entry *N* indicates a sign not consistent with the PBC.

Overall, Table 6 shows that left-wing governments do not systematically follow a PBC pattern. More than 60% of the indicators have a sign inconsistent with the PBC. In only five of the 14 cases considered are

Table 7. The budget and the political business cycle theories

	I_{10} election year minus preceding year		I_{11} election year minus following year		Total	
Theory prediction: Conformity of outcome?	*Y*	*N*	*Y*	*N*	*Y*	*N*
Australia	3	2	1	3		
Austria	1	2	0	3		
Belgium	4	0	3	1		
Denmark	3	1	2	2		
Finland	3	0	1	2		
France	2	1	0	3		
Germany	0	4	4	0		
Netherlands	2	1	2	1		
Norway	1	2	1	2		
Sweden	2	2	2	2		
UK	2	1	3	0		
US	2	2	3	0		
Total	25	14	18	18	43	32
% of Yes	64		50		57	

Source: Mueller and Price (1985) for cyclically adjusted, inflation adjusted budget balance.
Notes: This table includes all the general elections in the sample period, but excludes elections which took place with less than a two-year interval. Election years are: Australia: 5–74, 12–75, 12–77, 10–80, 12–84; Austria: 10–75, 5–79, 4–83; Belgium: 3–74, 4–77, 12–78, 11–81; Denmark: 2–77, 10–79, 12–81, 1–84; Finland: 9–75, 3–79, 3–83; France: 9–74, 9–77, 5–81; Germany: 11–72, 10–76, 10–80, 3–83; Netherlands: 5–77, 7–80, 9–83; Norway: 10–73, 10–77, 10–81; Sweden: 10–73, 10–76, 10–79; 10–82; UK: 2–74, 6–79, 6–83; US: 11–72, 11–76, 11–80, 11–84.

the majority of the indicators consistent with the theory, and in one case out of two, there is either one indicator with a consistent sign, or none. The lack of evidence in favour of the PBC is particularly clear on output growth. The cases of the Mitterrand's government (1981–86), the Carter administration (1976–80), the German Social Democrats (1976–80), and the Swedish Social Democrats (1983–85) show a pattern opposite to the one prescribed by the PBC, while consistent with the RPT. These economies were doing much better in terms of growth and unemployment in the early parts of the terms in office than in the subsequent parts.

Even though this evidence is not overly supportive of a PBC on unemployment, pre-electoral manipulation of policy instruments such as the government budget might nevertheless occur. As noted above, recent developments in the Nordhaus tradition have emphasized 'political *budget* cycles' rather than unemployment cycles. In fact, a 10–18 month cycle in budget deficits and money supply, around election time, would be consistent with the absence of a cycle in output and unemployment, particularly with rational expectations. Table 7 considers the inflation adjusted, cyclically adjusted budget balances computed by the OECD (Mueller and Price, 1985). In order to check whether indeed fiscal policy is loose in election years, we consider two indicators:

I_{10} = (budget balance in election year) minus (budget balance in the preceding year).

I_{11} = (budget balance in election year) minus (budget balance in the following year).

The election years are defined as in Table 6. The electoral budget cycle predicts that I_{10} and I_{11} should be negative, implying that deficits increase, or that surpluses are reduced in election years. Table 6 reports the results for the period 1972–84 over which the budget data are available. In the majority (almost 65%) of the cases considered, the budget deteriorated in the election year relative to the preceding year. Additional evidence of a political cycle, on personal transfers in the US, is also provided in Tufte (1978) and Alesina (1988a).

3.3. Summing up

The stylized facts described in the preceding two sections suggest the following picture. When conservative governments are elected, they fight inflation, and they tend to create a recession, particularly if they inherited a high inflation rate. After the disinflation is over, and once inflation expectations have adjusted to the new regime, the economy grows at about the natural rate and inflation remains low. When left-wing governments are elected, they attempt to expand the economy to reduce unemployment which is their main concern. They usually succeed in the short term, but then inflation expectations catch up and the economy is locked into a high-inflation equilibrium. A few years after the election of a left-wing government, the economy may show decreasing growth and increasing inflation. The reduction in real growth is even sharper if the government attempts to fight inflation in the second part of the term. Left-wing governments thus often face new elections with decreasing real growth; this has been the case for President Carter (1980), the German Social Democrats (1980), Mitterrand (1986), and the Swedish Social Democrats (1985). On the contrary, conservative governments reach new elections with an economy recovering from an early recession; this occurred with President Reagan (1984), Margaret Thatcher (1983), and the Swedish conservatives (1979). Note that if conservative and socialist governments want to 'put the house in order' before new elections, and compete for the 'middle of the road' voters, they often need to fight opposite problems: the conservatives need to speed up the recovery, the socialists need to fight inflation. In addition, and consistent with the PBC general hypothesis, both types of government may try to avoid so-called 'unpopular' fiscal measures in election years. Indeed there is some evidence that the budget balance tends to deteriorate in election years.

Finally, one may ask how the voters react to all of this. One view, which is compatible with the PBC approach, sees the voters as rather naive and easily gullible. A well-timed short-run expansion is sufficient to increase significantly the incumbent's chances of re-election. Empirical evidence in support of this view in the US is presented by Kramer (1971), Fair (1978), and others. Another view is that voters are well informed and understand the differences between parties. Thus, they turn to the left when they want to see unemployment reduced, and to the right when they are more concerned with inflation. Evidence in support of this latter view is presented, for the US, by Kiewiet (1983) and Alesina and Rosenthal (1989).

4. Political stability and economic stability

The preceding sections have focused on the pattern *over time* of inflation, output, and unemployment in several economies. Political variables can also explain differences *across countries.* This is what Hibbs (1977) found for the inflation rate in the 1960s. Hansson (1987) convincingly argues that this pattern persists in the 1970s and 1980s if one accounts for other economic and institutional differences between countries; relevant considerations would include the degree of unionization and of wage indexation, differences in the effects of oil shocks and the degree of Central Bank independence. The recent politico-macroeconomic literature suggests that the degree of political instability is an additional explanation for cross-country differences in economic outcomes. Two arguments have been presented to explain why politically unstable and polarized countries should exhibit relatively 'poor' economic outcomes. The first one is directly related to the 'partisan theory' and suggests that, in highly polarized countries, 'partisan' governments follow divergent policies. Economic uncertainty is thus increased and expectations are destabilized. Excessive instability and polarization of economic policies can generate sub-optimal outcomes.

This point is implicit in the RPT of inflation and unemployment and made more explicit in the context of fiscal policy by Alesina and Tabellini (1987), Tabellini and Alesina (1988), and Persson and Svensson (1987). Furthermore, if a government is unlikely to be reelected, it has an incentive to follow particularly shortsighted policies, since it is not concerned with a future in which it is likely to be out of office. The second argument emphasizes the effects of unstable coalition governments. Roubini and Sachs (1988) argue that for large and fragile coalitions it may be difficult to implement 'tough' economic policies when needed, either because they have a short horizon or because of political deadlocks due to disagreements between members.

Table 8 shows that the degree of political instability may be associated with poor economic performance as measured in terms of inflation and unemployment. In this table, and in the related discussion, inflation and unemployment should be interpreted as the actual variables (not as the deviation of innovations from a multi-country average). An index of political stability ranging from 1, the most stable, to 4, the least stable, is compared to the average level of inflation and unemployment (1973–86) in 20 countries. This stability index is a summary of several politico-institutional characteristics of each country which accounts for: the political cohesion of governments, using an index proposed by Roubini and Sachs (1988); the occurrence of major institutional changes, such as the transition from dictatorships to democracies; the existence of politically relevant extreme parties; the frequency of early elections; and the presence of regional/ethnic/linguistic conflicts. The construction of this index is described in the Appendix.

The positive correlation between instability, as measured by the index of Table 8, and Okun's misery index (the sum of inflation and unemployment) is quite strong. With only one exception (still the Netherlands), none of the least stable countries – those with an index of stability of 3 and 4 – are in the bottom half of the 18 countries for which the misery index is available. Systematically the countries with an index of 4 have the highest misery index and the highest inflation rates. The two countries with an index of 1 have two of the three lowest misery indexes. In addition, Spain and Greece show the worst economic performance (particularly in terms of inflation) in the transition period from dictatorship to democracy, therefore in the period of the highest political instability and uncertainty. The economic outlook has substantially improved when more stable democratic institutions have been established in these countries. The UK represents an interesting outlier, combining a rather high misery index with a quite stable political index (2). This country has a 'textbook' style, institutionally robust two-party system. However, most observers would agree that British politics is

Table 8. Inflation, unemployment and political stability (1973–86)

	Average inflation (rank) (a)	Average unemployment (rank) (b)	Misery index (rank) (a) + (b)	Index of political stability
Portugal	19.0 (1)	NA	NA	4
Greece	17.2 (2)	NA	NA	4
Spain	13.6 (4)	11.3 (2)	24.9 (1)	4
Italy	13.7 (3)	8.1 (4)	21.8 (2)	4
Belgium	6.9 (14)	11.9 (1)	18.8 (3)	3
UK	10.7 (6)	8.1 (4)	18.8 (3)	2
Canada	7.8 (13)	8.5 (3)	16.3 (5)	2
Denmark	8.8 (10)	7.2 (6)	16.0 (6)	3
Australia	9.7 (8)	6.2 (8)	15.9 (7)	2
France	9.2 (9)	6.5 (7)	15.7 (8)	3
Finland	9.8 (7)	4.8 (10)	14.6 (9)	2
New Zealand	12.0 (5)	2.2 (13)	14.2 (10)	2
US	6.9 (14)	7.2 (6)	14.1 (11)	2
Netherlands	5.5 (17)	7.8 (5)	13.3 (12)	3
Sweden	8.7 (11)	2.4 (12)	11.1 (13)	2
Norway	8.4 (12)	1.7 (15)	10.1 (14)	2
Germany	4.1 (19)	5.7 (9)	9.8 (15)	2
Japan	6.4 (16)	2.1 (14)	8.5 (16)	1
Austria	5.4 (18)	2.9 (11)	8.3 (17)	2
Switzerland	4.1 (19)	0.5 (16)	4.6 (18)	1

Sources: Inflation and unemployment: see footnote 10; Index of political stability see the Appendix.

rather polarized: the Labour and Conservative parties are probably more differentiated ideologically than, say, the Democratic and Republican parties in the US, which is another two-party system with the same index of stability as the UK, and a much lower misery index. This example is a useful reminder that it is quite difficult to account for ideological distances between parties in different countries and the proposed index suffers from this defect.

What Table 8 shows is that there exists an association between economic outcomes and political stability, but it does not establish any direction of causality. However, we have suggested, implicitly at least, an interpretation which asserts causality running primarily from political stability to economic stability. The reasons are the same as those advanced by Roubini and Sachs (1988), and reproduced here almost literally: first, the regime character crucially depends upon its institutional process (for instance, voting rules); and, second, the regime character is rather stable over time. Needless to say, these arguments do not exclude some role for a reverse causality, or some interplay between the two.

Table 9. Inflation and Central Bank independence (1973–86)

	Average inflation	Index of Central Bank independence
Italy	13.7	1/2
Spain	13.6	1
New Zealand	12.0	1
UK	10.7	2
Finland	9.8	2
Australia	9.7	1
France	9.2	2
Denmark	8.8	2
Sweden	8.7	2
Norway	8.4	2
Canada	7.8	2
Belgium	6.9	2
US	6.9	3
Japan	6.4	3
Netherlands	5.5	2
Switzerland	4.1	4
Germany	4.1	4

Sources: Inflation: see footnote 6; index of Central Bank independence: see the text and Alesina (1988a) for more details.

Finally, Table 9, based upon a similar table in Alesina (1988a), shows a positive relationship between an index measuring how independent is the Central Bank from the Executive branch and the inflation rate. (A model consistent with this regularity is presented in Rogoff, 1985a). Central Banks are classified in four groups from the least independent (1) to the most independent (4). This classification, based on Bade and Parkin (1985) and Masciandaro and Tabellini (1988), accounts for several institutional characteristics of different central banks, such as: the formal institutional relationship between the Central Bank and the Executive (for instance who appoints the head of the central bank, and how often, the presence of government officials on the executive boards of the Central Bank, and so on); the extent of informal contacts between the Executive and the Central Bank; and the existence of rules forcing the Central Bank to automatically accommodate fiscal policy. Table 9 shows that the four most independent Central Banks (Japan, US, and especially, Germany and Switzerland) have been associated with four of the five lowest inflation rates. Much as in the case of political stability, this association does not necessarily imply a causality link. However, it may suggest that countries with a preference for low inflation prefer to set up independent Central Banks as the most effective means of achieving this goal.

5. Policy Implications

5.1. Rules, discretion and institutions

The politico-economic approach brings new arguments to the debate on policy rules versus discretion. For some time now this debate has been profoundly influenced by the important contributions of Kydland and Prescott (1977) and Barro and Gordon (1983). They have strengthened the traditional case for monetary policy rules, based on the view that governments have an inherent tendency to misuse or overuse the instruments at their disposal. Starting from the same premise that discretionary policymakers face an incentive to inflate the economy to achieve short-run reductions in unemployment, the more recent contributions further note that the repeated use of this policy instrument raises inflationary expectations with the result that, in the end, unemployment is unaffected and inflation remains too high. The politico-economic approach shows that the partisan behaviour of different successive governments may well produce magnified economic fluctuations: partisan behaviour may have a destabilizing effect on the economy because of an excessive variability in policymaking. An implication is that an agreement of all political parties on a set of policy rules, by reducing each government's discretionary power, may be beneficial if it reduces excessive variability of partisan policies and/or an electoral use of macroeconomic policy. In other words, commonly agreed policy rules, such as a monetary rule and/or a budget balance rule, can bring about some degree of 'intertemporal policy coordination' between governments in office at different times in a particular country. In order to reduce excessive volatility through intertemporal cooperation, for the current government to follow an agreed-upon rule, it must believe that preceding governments have done the same, and that future governments will continue to do so. Policy rules of this type need an enforcement mechanism; otherwise each government, when in office, would abandon the rule and follow its own partisan policies.

One institutional mechanism to enforce policy rules could be provided by independent agencies (such as Central Banks) not subject to each government's discretion. The issue of Central Bank independence has been extensively discussed. The 'conventional wisdom' is that independent Central Banks are desirable, because they are less subject to political pressure. There are, however, three difficulties with this view. The first is that it is very difficult, if not impossible, completely to eliminate indirect and informal political pressure over Central Bankers. For instance, Woolley (1984) provides several convincing examples of the influence of American Presidents over the relatively independent Federal Reserve. The second argument against independence is that it may create problems of monetary and fiscal policy coordination. A conflict of goals between the fiscal and the monetary authorities may lead to a sub-optimal choice of uncoordinated policy instruments. The third argument is simply that one may not want to give up democratic control over monetary policy. Indeed, society may want to make sure that the goals of an independent agency, such as a Central Bank, do not deviate from the social objectives. Thus, it may be impossible or even undesirable to set up a completely independent Central Bank. The question then is which is the more desirable form of political control over monetary policy. The preceding sections suggest that it may be desirable to isolate monetary policy from direct influence of 'partisan' executives. Consider, instead, the following institutional set up. The general rules governing monetary policy are chosen by the legislature, with a qualified majority. The requirement of a qualified majority would ensure that each government with a simple majority in the legislature could not abrogate the rule. The Central Bank would then implement the rule. The existence of the rule would make it difficult for the executive to influence the Central Bank, which would be responsible to the legislature for the implementation of the rule. This arrangement ensures democratic control over monetary policy, limiting the effects of excessive partisan volatility and of an electoral use of this instrument. Related arguments in support of a legislative control of monetary policy are also suggested in Monti (1985).

It should be emphasized at this point that nothing in the arguments provided so far suggests which is the 'best' rule. In particular, there is no presumption that a monetarist fixed growth rate is the optimal rule. The optimal rule may, in fact leave some role to stabilization policy by specifying under what circumstances which policy action ought to be taken. However, it is well known that the more complicated is the rule, the harder it is to monitor its implementation. Thus relatively simple rules should be designed. Since simple rules may perform rather poorly under exceptional circumstances, one may want to leave a certain degree of discretionality in policymaking to avoid the risk of being institutionally locked into a monetary rule which becomes highly inefficient in a particularly exceptional time. In summary, the institutional design sketched above should target the optimal point on the tradeoff between rigid rules and discretion.

5.2. International economic policy coordination

The problem of intertemporal policy coordination between governments in office at different times is closely connected with the issue of economic policy coordination between countries at a given point in time. Several authors have emphasized the potential benefits of international economic policy coordination (a survey is provided by Fischer, 1987). Policy coordination is always beneficial if policymakers are 'benevolent social planners' following the optimal policy.[9] In practice international agreements are not set up by 'social planners,' but by real world politicians. Putnam and Bayne (1987) document the connections between domestic political incentives and the outcome of international summit meetings of the Seven Powers. Lohmann (1987) and Tabellini (1987) formalize the interaction between international and intertemporal problems of policy coordination. The basic message is the need to distinguish between two types of international policy coordination.

The first type is one in which coordinated discretionary policy decisions are taken by each government in office at a particular point in time: countries coordinate with each other but political parties do not. This type of international policy coordination can easily be counterproductive because two cooperating 'partisan' governments may well team up and reduce the overall social welfare as they strive to make their respective constituencies better off. The second type of international policy coordination implies simultaneously solving the domestic intertemporal coordination problem: political parties in each country agree to cooperate through policy rules which are also internationally coordinated.

An international agreement to adopt some specific discretionary policy decisions at some point in time may easily fall in the first category. Putnam and Bayne (1987) argue, for instance, that at the 1978 Summit, the coordination of three major 'left-wing' governments (US, West Germany, and UK) led to an 'overestimation' of the world economy which, coupled with the second oil shock, led to the high inflation of the late 1970s and early 1980s. Similarly, in the early 1980s the almost contemporaneous turn to anti-inflation policies by the conservatives in the same three countries may have magnified the dimensions of the world recession. In contrast, the international agreement which led to the creation of the EMS can be interpreted as a policy coordination of the second type, since it is an agreement on a policy rule, rather than on a specific, discretionary action at one particular point in time.

[9] For an example of counterproductive policy coordination with social planners having domestic time consistency problems, see Rogoff (1985b).

5.3. Are democratic institutions 'bad' for the economy?

All the politico-economic theories of the inflation-unemployment trade-off examined above, have in common the implication that elections may have costs for the economy. However, there are at least two reasons why elections can have *economic* benefits.[10] The first one is an argument of efficiency. Elections can be a device for distinguishing the competent policymakers from incompetent ones. Rogoff (1987) and Rogoff and Sibert (1988) show that politicians may bend backward before elections and adopt sub-optimal policies in order to successfully make voters believe that they are very 'competent'. Then, if elected to long terms of office, 'incompetent' policymakers could remain in office for a long time. As a result, frequent elections may have the costs of frequent sub-optimal cycles but the benefits of avoiding long terms of office of incompetent policymakers. Second, elections can serve the purpose of signalling (possibly evolving) social preferences in a world of partisan politicians. Even if different parties agree to some form of intertemporal policy coordination and 'cooperate' over time with each other, electoral results change the relative size of the parties. As a result, elections influence the parties' bargaining power and therefore the choice of which cooperative agreement is reached. This argument of political bargaining is formalized in Alesina (1987 and 1988b).

These considerations inevitably bring to the forefront the question of the optimal frequency of elections and of the optimality of having exogenous timing of elections. Is it preferable (from an economic perspective) to have fixed election dates or to leave open the possibility of calling early elections? In the latter case, early elections may be strategically called by an incumbent government to take advantage of particularly favourable economic conditions. This may distort the policymakers' incentives and generate suboptimal economic outcomes. On the other hand, early elections may solve political deadlocks and the lack of action associated with them. One has to trade-off costs and benefits of the two alternatives and the evaluation of this trade-off may be related to the structure of the party system. For instance, in multi-party systems with large coalition governments, the possibility of costly political deadlocks is higher than in two-party systems so that endogenous election timing may be beneficial. Perhaps the optimal arrangement would be to make it difficult, but not impossible, to call early elections by clearly identifying the cases in which this option is available.

[10] There is no need to emphasize the obvious non-economic benefits of democratic institutions.

This point leads to an even more fundamental question: what is the 'optimal number' of parties? The number of parties can obviously be influenced by institutional design, such as voting rules. The recent results by Roubini and Sachs (1988) and those presented here in Section 3.3 suggest, at least tentatively, that multiparty systems with large coalition governments, *ceteris paribus*, exhibit relatively high budget deficits and high 'misery indexes' (inflation and unemployment). However, these results have to be taken cautiously since it is hard to establish precise causality links.

6. Conclusions

The 'partisan theory' of economic policy, emphasizing systematic differences between political parties, appears to be supported by the evidence of several industrial economies over the last 20 years. The difference in real economic outcomes under different governments is for the most part transitory and concentrated at the beginning of the terms of office. Thus Conservative parties often start their terms in office with below-average growth, an increase in cyclical unemployment, and a reduction of inflation. The opposite outcome often occurs at the beginning of left-wing governments. In the latter part of the terms in office, the difference in real economic outcomes tends to disappear, even though inflation may remain (on average) higher with left-wing governments. The evidence in favour of the 'political business cycles' theory is more problematic. Several conservative governments show a pattern of growth and unemployment which is consistent with this view. However, this pattern – recession at the beginning, recovery toward the end of the term of office – is also consistent with the partisan theory, with transitory effects. On the contrary, there is very little, if any, evidence that left-wing governments have usually followed this pattern.

The empirical results adduced in the present study suggest the following stylized facts. Once in office, conservative governments tend to fight inflation, particularly if they inherited a high inflation rate. This causes an early recession; once the economy adjusts, a recovery occurs usually in time before next elections and conservative governments certainly do not fight the pre-electoral recovery if inflation remains low. Particularly good examples of this view are the first Reagan term, the first term of the Swedish conservatives, the first government of Thatcher, and, perhaps, the Kohl government. On the other hand, when left-wing governments are elected, they fight unemployment and achieve an economic expansion early in their terms. Once inflation catches up, they allow the rate of growth to fall, even in preelectoral periods as inflation may actually be perceived as the main economic problem. In such circumstances the pattern of output growth and unemployment is the opposite of the one predicted by Nordhaus (1975). Particularly good examples are President Carter (1976–80), President Mitterrand (1981–86), the German Social Democrats (1976–80), and the Swedish Social Democrats (1983–85). Finally, a closer and more specific look at fiscal policy may suggest that, consistent with the spirit of the 'political business cycle' approach, fiscal policy is rarely tightened immediately before elections, regardless of the ideological orientation of the government.

Economic stability and political stability may be highly correlated. Countries with relatively stable and less polarized political systems and political histories, show superior economic outcomes. Even though it is generally difficult to establish causality links in this context, a number of arguments indicate that the causality goes from political stability to economic stability. Finally, the explicit consideration of the interaction between politics and economics has important normative implications for institutional design. Several normative issues such as the desirability of policy rules, Central Bank independence, and international economic policy coordination cannot be usefully addressed without an explicit consideration of the political factors affecting economic policy.

Discussion

James Mirrlees
Nuffield College, Oxford

Alberto Alesina has drawn together recent work on the impact of politics upon the economy, and most valuably confronted theory with data for many countries. It is a stimulating paper. He supports one particular theory, the rational partisan theory, a theory that combines Hibbs' earlier partisan theory with rational-expectations macroeconomic theory.

The rational partisan theory has many elements. It is based on the hypothesis that different political parties have distinctly different positions, particularly different distributional values. This is plausible, but different from the Hotelling–Downs theory that predicted parties would come to essentially similar positions, in the game of trying to capture as many voters from the other side as possible. Alesina has indicated some of the reasons that make one doubt the validity of the Hotelling theory; for example, the two-stage American presidential election. Money clearly matters in politics, more in some countries than others, and in itself provides reasons for parties to differ distinctly. If they were the same, there would be little to pay for. The existence of third parties also makes a difference. All of these considerations vary so much from country to country that one may wonder whether it is reasonable to expect the same theory to hold for many different countries. Sadly, it must be virtually impossible to test the theory statistically for any single country.

Other elements of the theory are less attractive. It is assumed that governments always have the same theory of the economy, and always use the same policy instruments. In Alesina's model, no government doubts the natural rate of unemployment theory, and no government considers using price and income controls, or international capital controls.

Alesina tests his theory alongside the political business cycle theory, which he does not favour. In the political business cycle theory, any party adopts expansionary policies as an election approaches, after a period of contraction in the earlier part of its term of office. In the partisan theory, left wing parties (giving greater weight to high employment and less to low inflation than parties of the right) adopt expansionary policies after they have won an election, whereas right-wing parties adopt deflationary policies. In each case, according to the theory, employment returns to its natural rate, and the inflation rate to a constant value.

These theories could be interpreted in an exclusive sense: the first, that governments are motivated only by continuing power; the second, that governments are motivated only by the distributional preferences they represent. It is more natural to interpret them as potentially both true, in some degree. Whichever view one takes, the method of testing used by Alesina is unsatisfactory. First he compares the RPT with an (implicit) alternative null hypothesis, in which neither right nor left parties bring in changed policies just after a change in regime. This alternative is implausible. Alesina claims that the data supports the RPT over the null. I think he overstates his claim, for the data in Table 2 could have occurred at random without excessive deviations from the mean outcomes expected under the null hypothesis. But between these two alternatives, one should accept the RPT, though not with perfect confidence.

Alesina then sets up a competition between theories that are not mutually exclusive. He compares the RPT with the PBC, restricting attention to left-wing governments, on the grounds that the theories make the same predictions for right-wing governments (which is not quite true, since timing during the electoral cycle is somewhat different under the two pure theories). His Table 6 actually shows that there is no association between the (adjusted) level of unemployment and the period of the government's life; and that there is a pronounced tendency for growth to be lower just before an election. In effect he claims that, if one must choose between the RPT and PBC, one should accept the RPT because the observations are more probable given RPT than they are given PBC. But one does not have to choose between RPT and PBC.

It is conceivable that both influences are at work: possibly left-wing governments use expansionary policies when they follow right-wing governments, because they have different distributional values, and then use expansionary policies again when an election approaches. That would be consistent with the observations about unemployment. The observed tendency in this small and heterogeneous sample for growth to be lower towards the end of a term of office may just be due to falling growth rates in other industrial countries. In general, if both prudential and ideological considerations may potentially govern economic policy, their relative importance can be assessed only by examining the whole pattern of employment, output and inflation, throughout the period between elections. But this period is often quite short, and the available data insufficient to allow us to judge confidently the relative strength of these influences, far less to warrant estimating either influence as zero.

In the concluding part of his paper, Alesina discusses the desirability of economic agencies that are non-political, or at least much less sensitive to changes in governments than policies currently are. If successive governments do indeed follow the rational partisan theory, how could institutions be set up to smooth macroeconomic policy? There must be some substantial gain from their existence if the many reasons for reluctance to reduce the scope of politics are to be overcome. The gain is supposed to be a reduction in uncertainty: can it be large enough, I wonder?

An economic agency could achieve substantial continuity without being confined to simple, checkable rules. What would it do? If the government of the day were to set rates of taxation and levels of public expenditure, the agency would be left to determine the financing of the deficit: it would be a central bank. Is the conclusion then simply that the central bank should be less responsive to current government preferences? I think not. The argument from which we started is really one for reducing fluctuations in the distributional structure of public policy. The argument applies as much to the structure of taxation (including social security and other public expenditures), as to the inflation 'tax' and the form of the national debt. We are led to consider an institution for economic management that encompasses the full range of economic policies. In British terms, that would mean independence for the Treasury. I do not draw this conclusion as a *reductio ad absurdum*, though it would be widely so regarded. It is a possibility to be taken seriously. It poses the challenge of adequately expressing the compromise distributional judgements that should govern the institution, in other words of determining the social welfare function.

Manfred J. M. Neumann
University of Bonn

Let me begin by discussing some analytical issues. The starting point of the political business cycle theory (PBC) is the deliberately restrictive assumption that politicians, whether called left or right, all behave as rational 'homines oeconomici' who maximise their own preferences – instead of just the 'social good'. This yields the strong implication that incumbents try to deceive voters about their level of competence by a suitable pre-electoral manipulation of policy instruments, in order to raise the probability of re-election. For this to be possible requires a second assumption that voters suffer from some informational disadvantage.

This second assumption is not too demanding (though Alesina is right that the early literature's voter myopia was too crude an assumption). So it is hardly surprising that cross-country observations on cycles in output, unemployment or inflation, do not allow us to reject the null hypothesis of pure random walks. A more relevant test of the PBC refers to short cycles in policy instruments. Alesina's Table 6, showing the budget balance in 12 countries, indicates that in 64% of cases the deficit was increased in election years. This observation is suggestive but inconclusive.

The PBC is a theory about the incumbent's behaviour, with implications for certain economic variables. In contrast, the 'rational partisan theory' (RPT), espoused by Alesina and others, does not explain the behaviour of the ruling party. It simply assumes that left-wing parties prefer a higher rate of expansion than right-wing parties. It uses this assumption to explain the effect of elections on macroeconomic variables. To do this it relies on election-induced uncertainty. If agents write contracts before an election, these contracts will be based on the probability-weighted expectation about the post-election rate of inflation. The actual rate of inflation will be either higher or lower than this expectation, depending on whether the left or the right-wing party takes office. So there will be a transitory expansion or contraction in real economic activity after each election.

I have two major reservations. First, why do rational agents not make contracts conditional on the result of the election, or simply time them to expire on election day? Doing one or the other would eliminate election-induced real effects. Second, why should voters wish to vote for a party that can achieve real economic effects only by surprising – that is by deceiving – its own voters? Overall, the voter of the RPT-approach is no more shrewd than the voter of the traditional PBC-approach.

Alesina investigates a rich collection of data on inflation, real growth, and unemployment from 12 countries. Each of the five indicators he presents in Tables 2 and A1 appears to be consistent with the RPT. If the political regime shifts are independent events, we may use the binomial distribution to test the RPT against the null hypothesis that the observations were generated by random policies. Consider first the inflation indicator I_5. Excluding the German case of 1972 – which was not a regime shift – we observe that in 73% of the regime shifts sampled (16 out of 22) the average rate of inflation corroborates the prediction of the RPT. The null hypothesis is rejected at the 5% significance level.

The output and employment indicators are harder to interpret. A strong test is to stick to the sample of 22 regime shifts for which indicator I_5 is computable, and to examine Alesina's indicators I_1 to I_4 for this sample. Beginning with output indicator I_1 we find that only in 13 cases (59%) did post-election output behave as predicted by RPT. And the remaining indicators I_2 to I_4 do so in less than 50% of cases (respectively 10, 8 and 9 cases out of 22). The null hypothesis can certainly not be rejected. A weaker test is to include in the sample also those cases for which inflation indicator I_5 is not computable. The null hypothesis can then be rejected at the 5% level for the output indicators I_1 and I_2, but not for the unemployment indicators I_3 and I_4. Alesina also presents regressions of output growth and of unemployment on a regime change dummy (Table 4). While the parameter estimates have the sign predicted by RPT, most are not significantly different from zero.

In sum, we may tentatively conclude that there is weak evidence in support of the RPT. But there are further qualifications. First, the evidence has no direct bearing on the validity of the competing PBC-hypothesis: the theories make different predictions only when there are leftward shifts of regime. Second, for good reasons Alesina has not worked with the original country data but has tried approximately to eliminate the impact of the world level of economic activity. But in contrast to previous work, Alesina does not apply country weights in computing for inflation, output growth, or unemployment the world averages which are then subtracted from the raw data. The procedure introduces bias, and it is impossible to tell to what extent this might have affected the results.

In the last sections of his paper Alesina discusses the impact of political instability on economic performance. It is an important question which institutions can best preserve continuity of policy. In principle it might seem to make no difference to the risk of inflation whether (as Alesina proposes) parliament sets a monetary rule that the central bank must obey, or instead establishes an independent central bank. After all, parliament can change its mind in either event. But in practice, as the experiences of Switzerland and Germany indicate, once enough time has gone by, parliaments no longer dare to disturb the independent status of the central bank which therefore provides a more credible insurance against inflation.

General discussion

The panel members discussed theoretical aspects of the connection between politics and macroeconomic policy, as well as the problems of measurement encountered in assessing those theories.

On the theory side, David Begg explained that he was not bothered as much as Manfred Neumann about the apparent lack of justification for the difference in objectives among governments in the partisan theory. In his opinion, a difference in the objectives of left- and right-wing governments might simply stem from a different perception of the constraints in economic policy. Left-wing governments would thus see the world as more Keynesian than right-wing governments. Still discussing the partisan theories, some panel members insisted that it was not rational for workers to enter into wage contracts covering an election period. Contracts contingent on the election results could be written. Alesina acknowledged this point but argued that the absence of such contracts, presumably difficult to set up, was a common assumption. Charles Wyplosz was concerned about the shortsightedness of both partisan and political business cycle theories. Indeed, governments in those models only consider one election at a time. It would seem more realistic to have a model where governments have long-term objectives covering several elections. In this respect, it is puzzling that in the context of partisan theories, left-wing governments should not be in office too often; indeed, the partisan theory suggest that left-wing governments will end up their term of office with higher inflation than right-wing governments, whereas unemployment is similar under the two regimes. This should not help the re-election of left-wing governments.

Following the comments of Mirrlees, there was a discussion as to whether partisan and political business cycle approaches should be seen as competing theories. Alesina pointed out that even though these approaches were complements rather than substitutes in terms of explanations, yet they had sometimes opposite implications with regard to the evolution of inflation and unemployment. Assessing those implications could still indicate that one theory was more relevant than the other.

On the side of measurement, Jean-Pierre Danthine suggested that the reaction of the financial markets could be used to assess the validity of the partisan theory. Indeed, one would expect the financial markets to react differently according to whether a right-wing or a left-wing government is elected. Jeffrey Sachs indicated that in the US exchange-rate movements could well be related to election results along the lines of the partisan theory. Alesina acknowledged that a similar analysis should be performed for Europe. Sachs suggested that assessment of inflation surprises should not be limited to the year following an election. Governments could indeed use the exchange rate at the time of a fiscal expansion in order to postpone inflation. As a result, one should look at changes in inflation over a longer period of time.

Wyplosz suggested that maybe too much emphasis was put on macroeconomic variables to identify different policies. In his opinion, more attention should be given to changes in income distribution. He indicated that French governments were particularly creative in this respect.

Appendix

A1. Table A1: data for Table 2

This table reports the values of the five indicators in Tables 2 and 3 for every change of regime. Changes of regime toward the left (right) are identified by L(R). The definition of the indices is given in the text.

A2. Construction of the index of political stability used in Table 7

This index is constructed by summing seven indicators, displayed in Table A2, below.

Column 1 of Table A2 is based upon the index of Roubini and Sachs (1988) (R–S). This column reports the sum of the R–S yearly index for the period 1973–86. The R–S index assumes, in every year, these values:

- 0 for one-party majority parliamentary governments; or presidential governments with the same party with the majority in the executive and legislative branch;
- 1 coalition parliamentary governments with 2 coalition partners; or presidential governments, with different parties in control of the executive and legislative branches;

Table A1. Indicator values

		I_1	I_2	I_3	I_4	I_5
Australia						
12/72	L	−0.64	−0.85	0.05	0.35	NA
11/75	R	−1.60	−0.72	−0.29	0.01	−0.62
3/83	L	3.18	1.13	−1.21	−0.07	0.35
Austria						
4/70	L	1.11	1.03	−0.44	−0.14	NA
4/83	R	−1.05	−0.05	0.20	−0.09	0.87
Belgium						
6/68	L	2.15	1.00	−1.18	−0.41	NA
1/73	R	−0.10	0.25	0.76	−0.11	−0.02
3/71	L	−0.52	−0.19	−0.66	−0.26	−0.90
12/81	R	−0.23	0.35	0.21	0.76	1.67
10/85	L	1.62	NA	−0.63	NA	NA
Denmark						
10/71	L	1.76	NA	−0.41	NA	NA
12/73	R	−1.91	NA	2.22	NA	−1.43
2/75	L	2.73	1.02	−0.70	0.41	1.64
9/82	R	−0.30	−0.10	−0.36	0.52	−1.00
Finland						
11/75	R	−3.80	NA	2.01	NA	NA
5/77	L	4.63	0.68	−1.17	0.70	−1.48
France						
5/81	L	0.50	1.00	−0.46	−0.72	NA
Germany						
9/69	L	−0.17	0.15	0.31	−0.03	NA
12/72	R	−0.64	−0.98	0.91	0.50	−1.52
10/82	R	0.81	−0.05	0.07	0.15	0.35
Netherlands						
5/73	L	1.34	−0.08	0.31	0.32	NA
5/77	R	−1.50	0.24	−0.05	−0.72	−0.28
3/81	L	−0.64	NA	1.69	NA	0.90
11/82	R	1.14	0.07	−1.44	0.51	−0.76
Norway						
10/71	L	1.22	NA	−0.01	NA	NA
10/72	R	−1.68	NA	0.40	NA	−2.05
10/73	L	4.80	1.47	−0.52	−0.17	0.58
10/81	R	0.07	−2.34	−0.22	−0.03	1.17
10/85	L	−0.43	NA	0.62	NA	NA
Sweden						
10/76	R	−2.30	−1.05	1.00	0.26	NA
10/82	L	0.86	0.67	0.30	−0.17	0.43
UK						
6/70	R	2.02	−0.58	0.15	0.42	NA
2/74	L	0.12	0.01	1.01	0.56	2.04
6/79	R	−3.08	−2.49	2.18	1.13	−3.17
US						
11/68	R	−3.54	−2.81	1.14	0.29	NA
11/76	L	2.53	1.96	−1.55	−0.71	1.89
11/80	R	0.56	−1.37	−0.23	0.70	−2.22

Table A2. Construction of an index of political stability

	1 (R–S)	2 Dictatorship	3 Exogenous elections	4 Communist party	5 Extreme right	6 Conflict	7 No change	Total
Australia	0	0	0	0	0	0	0	0
Austria	−1	0	0	0	0	0	0	−1
Belgium	2	0	0	0	0	1	0	3
Canada	−1	0	0	0	0	1	0	0
Denmark	2	0	0	0	0	0	0	2
France	0	0	0	1	1	0	0	2
Germany	0	0	0	0	0	0	0	0
Finland	0	0	0	0	0	0	0	0
Greece	0	3	0	1	1	1	0	6
Italy	2	0	0	1	1	0	0	4
Japan	−2	0	0	0	0	0	−1	−3
Netherlands	2	0	0	0	0	0	0	2
New Zealand	0	0	0	0	0	0	0	0
Norway	0	0	−1	0	0	0	0	−1
Portugal	0	3	0	1	1	0	0	5
Spain	0	3	0	1	1	1	0	6
Sweden	1	0	−1	0	0	0	0	0
Switzerland	−2	0	−1	0	0	0	−1	−4
UK	−2	0	0	0	0	1	0	−1
US	−1	0	−1	0	0	0	0	−2

2 coalition parliamentary governments with 3 or more coalition partners;
3 minority parliamentary governments; (more details can be found in R–S, 1988).

The index of the first column of Table A2 assumes the following values:

−2 for countries with a R–S cumulative index of zero;
−1 for countries with a R–S cumulative index from 1 to 10;
0 for countries with a R–S cumulative index from 11 to 15;
1 for countries with a R–S cumulative index 16 to 20;
2 for countries with a R–S cumulative index above 20.

Roubini and Sachs' (1988) sample of countries has been extended using Banks (1987).

Column 2 of Table A2 shows an index of major political change from dictatorship to democracy. This index assumes the values of:

3 for countries which experienced at least one change of regime from dictatorship to democracy (or vice versa);
0 otherwise.

The countries with an index of 3 in this column have an arbitrarily assigned zero index in column 1. Columns 1 and 2 viewed together, imply that country with a dictatorship-democracy transition are considered slightly more unstable than the more unstable democracies, according to R–S index.

Column 3 is an index of exogenous/endogenous elections. This column assumes the value of:

−1 for countries with exogenously given timing of elections or countries which did not have any early election in the sample period;
0 otherwise.

Column 4 captures the existence of a significant communist party. This index assumes the values of:

1 in countries with one or more politically significant (according to Banks, 1987) communist parties;
0 otherwise.

Column 5 captures the existence of significant extreme right-wing parties. This index assumes the values of:

1 in countries with one or more politically significant (according to Banks, 1987) extreme right-wing party;
0 otherwise.

Column 6 captures the existence of regional/ethnic conflict. This index assumes the values of:

1 in countries with ethnic/regional conflicts;
0 otherwise.

Column 7 identifies the countries with no change of political orientation of the government in the sample period. This index assumes the value of:

−1 in countries with no changes in the political orientation of the government;
0 otherwise.

The total index of stability (last column of Table A2) is increasing in the degree of political instability. Given the qualitative nature of this index, rather than a complete ranking of these countries, four groups are formed based upon the Total:

group 1	Total ≤ -3
group 2	$0 \geq$ Total ≥ -2
group 3	$3 \geq$ Total ≥ 1
group 4	Total ≥ 4

References

Alesina, A. (1987). 'Macroeconomic Policy in a Two-Party System as a Repeated Game', *Quarterly Journal of Economics.*

—— (1988a). 'Macroeconomics and Politics', *NBER Macroeconomic Annual 1988*, MIT Press, Cambridge, Mass.

—— (1988b). 'Credibility and Policy Convergence in a Two-Party System With Rational Voters', *American Economic Review.*

Alesina, A. and H. Rosenthal (1989). 'Ideological Cycles in Congressional Elections and the Macroeconomy', *American Political Science Review.*

Alesina, A. and J. Sachs (1988). 'Political Parties and the Business Cycle in the United States, 1948–1984', *Journal of Money Credit and Banking.*

Alesina, A. and G. Tabellini (1987). 'A Political Theory of Fiscal Deficits and Government Debt in a Democracy', NBER Working Paper No. 2308.

Alt, J. (1985). 'Political Parties, World Demand and Unemployment: Domestic and International Sources of Economic Activity', *American Political Science Review.*

—— (1988). 'New Wine in Old Bottles: Thatcher's Conservative Economic Policy', in F. Cooper, A. Kornberg and W. Mishler (eds.) *The Resurgence of Conservatism in Anglo-American Democracies*, Duke University Press, Durham.

Bade, R. and M. Parkin (1985). 'Central Bank Laws and Monetary Policy', unpublished.

Banks, A. (1987). *Political Handbook of the World.*

Barro, R. (1986). 'Reputation in a Model of Monetary Policy with Incomplete Information', *Journal of Monetary Economics.*

Barro, R. and D. Gordon (1983). 'Rules, Discretion and Reputation in a Model of Monetary Policy', *Journal of Monetary Economics.*

Blanchard, O. and L. Summers (1986).'Hysteresis and the European Unemployment Problem', *NBER Macroeconomic Annual*, MIT Press, Cambridge, Mass.

Borooah, V. and F. Van der Ploeg (1983). *Political Aspects of the Economy*, Cambridge University Press, Cambridge.

Calvert, R. (1985). 'Robustness of the Multidimensional Voting, Candidate Motivations, Uncertainty and Convergence', *American Journal of Political Science.*

Cohen, D. (1988). 'What Caused the Rise of Conservatism: A French View', *Economic Policy.*

Cukierman, A. and A. H. Meltzer (1986). 'A Positive Theory of Discretionary Policy, the Cost of a Democratic Government, and the Benefits of a Constitution', *Economic Inquiry.*

Downs, A. (1957). *An Economic Theory of Democracy.* Harper and Row, New York.

Fair, R. (1978). 'The Effects of Economic Events on Votes for Presidents', *The Review of Economic and Statistics.*

Fischer, S. (1987). 'International Macroeconomic Policy Coordination', NBER Working Paper No. 2244.

Frey, B. and F. Schneider (1978). 'An Empirical Study of Politico-Economic Interaction in the United States', *The Review of Economics and Statistics.*

Hansson, A. (1987). 'Politics, Institutions and Cross-Country Inflation Differentials', unpublished.

Hibbs, D. (1977). 'Political Parties and Macroeconomic Policy, *The American Political Science Review.*

—— (1987). *The American Political Economy,* Harvard University Press, Cambridge, Mass.

Kiewiet, R. (1983). *Macroeconomics and Micropolitics,* University of Chicago Press, Chicago.

Kramer, J. (1971). 'Short Term Fluctuations in U.S. Voting Behaviour, 1896–1964, *American Political Science Review.*

Kydland, F. and E. Prescott (1977). 'Rules Rather than Discretion: The Inconsistency of Optimal Plans', *Journal of Political Economy.*

Lohmann, S. (1987). 'Domestic Political Competition and International Policy Coordination', unpublished.

Masciandaro, D. and G. Tabellini (1988). 'Fiscal Deficits and Monetary Institutions: A Comparative analysis', in H. Cheng, (ed.) *Challenges to Monetary Policy in the Pacific Basin Countries,* Kluwar Publishers.

Minford, P. (1985). 'Interest Rates and Bond Financed Deficits in a Ricardian Two-Party Democracy', CEPR Discussion Paper No. 79.

Minford, P. and D. Peel (1982). 'The Political Theory of the Business Cycle', *European Economic Review.*

Monti, M. (1985). 'Politica Monetaria Disinflazionistica E Assetto Istituzionale', *Rivista Mensile Di Economia.*

Mueller, P. and R. Price (1985). 'Structural Budget Indicators and the Interpretation of Fiscal Policy Stance in OECD Economies', OECD Working Paper.

Neumann, M. J. M. and S. Lohmann (1987). 'Political Business Cycles in Industrialized Democratic Countries: A Comment', *Kylos.*

Nordhaus, W. (1975). 'The Political Business Cycle', *Review of Economic Studies.*

Paldam, M. (1978). 'Is There an Electoral Cycle? A Comparative Study of National Accounts', *Scandinavian Journal of Economics.*

Palfrey, T. (1984). 'Spatial Equilibrium with Entry', *Review of Economic Studies.*

Persson, T. and L. Svensson (1987). 'Checks and Balances on the Government Budget', unpublished.

Putnam, R. and N. Bayne (1987). *Hanging Together: Cooperation and Conflicts in the Seven Powers summits,* Harvard University Press, Cambridge, Mass.

Rogoff, K. (1985a). 'The Optimal Degree of Commitment to an Intermediate Monetary Target', *Quarterly Journal of Economics.*

—— (1985b). 'Can International Policy Cooperation be Counter-productive?', *Journal of International Economics.*

—— (1987). 'Equilibrium Political Budget cycles', NBER Working Paper No. 2428.

Rogoff, K. and A. Sibert (1988). 'Equilibrium Political Business cycles', *Review of Economic Studies.*

Rose, R. (1980). *Do Parties Make A Difference?*, Chatham House, New York.

Roubini, N. and J. Sachs (1988). 'Political and Economic Determinants of Budget Deficits in the Industrial Democracies', NBER Working Paper No. 2628.

Sachs, J. and C. Wyplosz (1985). 'The Economic Consequences of President Mitterrand', *Economic Policy.*

Schumpeter, J. A. (1942). *Capitalism, Socialism, and Democracy,* New York.

Shepsle, K. and R. Cohen (1988). 'Multiparty Competition, Entry and Entry Deterrence in Spatial Models of Elections', unpublished.

Tabellini, G. (1987). 'Domestic Politics and the International Coordination of Fiscal Policies', CEPR Working Paper.

Tabellini, G. and A. Alesina (1988). 'Voting on the Budget Deficit', CEPR Working Paper.

Tufte, E. (1978). *Political Control of the Economy,* Princeton University Press, Princeton.

Wittman, D. (1977). 'Candidates with Policy Preferences: A Dynamic Model', *Journal of Economic Theory.*

Woolley, J. (1984). *Monetary Politics,* Cambridge University Press, Cambridge.

[8]

Economic Policy October 1991 Printed in Great Britain

Institutions and policies

Vittorio Grilli, Donato Masciandaro
and Guido Tabellini

Summary

Why do countries as similar as the industrialized OECD countries go through such different experience in terms of public deficits and debts or in terms of inflation? The answer cannot come from macroeconomic policy responses to different disturbances, nor from the principles of optimal taxation, but rather from politics. This article focuses on the role that particular institutions exert in providing constraints and incentives which shape the actions of policy-makers. The electoral process and political traditions affect the ability of governments to deal with deficits and mounting debts. What seems to matter most, it is found, is the effect of the durability of governments. Governments with short horizons act myopically and never quite tackle the hard choices. Such governments typically exist in countries with an electoral system favouring many small political parties. Central bank independence promotes low inflation with no apparent costs in terms of real economic performance, irrespective of the political institutions. In fact there is no link between monetary and fiscal discipline. These findings carry powerful implications for countries facing high indebtedness or stubborn inflation, but also for the construction of the European Economic and Monetary Union.

Political and monetary institutions and public financial policies in the industrial countries

Vittorio Grilli
Birkbeck College, London
Donato Masciandaro
Centre for Financial and Monetary Economics, Università Bocconi
Guido Tabellini
Università di Cagliari, University of California, Los Angeles and Innocenzo Gasparini Institute for Economic Research

1. Introduction

The post-war experience of industrialized countries features striking differences in public debt policies. Table 1 reports data on the accumulation of net public debt in 18 OECD countries. At the end of the 1980s, the debt to GNP ratio in these countries ranged from about 10% in Switzerland to over 100% in Belgium and Ireland.

What are the reasons for these differences? Normative macroeconomic theory stresses the 'shock absorber' and 'distortion smoothing' role of budget deficits and prescribes that government debt should be adjusted over time to respond to exogenous shocks. According to this view, public debts differ because the various national economies have undergone different shocks. This is quite unconvincing for the OECD countries which are quite similar and highly interconnected. In addition, the positive trend displayed by government debt in many countries after World War II is difficult to reconcile with the view that budget deficits were only smoothing the effects of temporary shocks. This is why we

We wish to thank, without implicating, Charlie Bean, Jeff Frieden, David Gowland, Edmond Malinvaud, Marco Pagano, Luigi Spaventa, Charles Wyplosz and the participants in the *Economic Policy* panel, as well as in workshops at the Bank of Italy, the Bank of Portugal and the Universities of Cagliari, Campbasso and Milan for several helpful comments on an earlier draft. Charles Wyplosz deserves particular gratitude. His comments and help throughout the editorial process were essential for us. We also thank G. Albrecht, A. Grimes, H. Jepsen, J. Larsen, I. L. Macfarlane, K. Rohl and G. Spencer for providing us with information about the monetary institutions of various countries and Cindy Miller for editorial assistance. Vincenzo Galasso provided excellent research assistance. Guido Tabellini gratefully acknowledges financial support from the NSF grant SES-8909 and from the UC Center for Pacific Rim Studies.

Table 1. Government net debt (% of GNP)

	1960	1970	1980	1989
Australia	na	40.1	24.9	16.5
Austria	na	19.4	37.2	57.8
Belgium	82.3	52.6	69.3	122.4
Canada	27.5	11.6	13.0	38.0
Denmark	na	−2.8	4.3	23.1
France	na	9.7	14.3	25.4
Germany	na	−8.1	14.3	21.9
Greece	9.2	21.3	27.8	79.0
Ireland	na	35.7	78.0	122.6
Italy	25.2	36.8	54.0	94.3
Japan	−4.4	−6.5	17.3	14.1
Netherlands	na	29.9	24.9	57.2
New Zealand	na	na	na	74.7
Portugal (a)	23.0	24.0	40.0	71.8
Spain	na	na	7.9	29.3
Switzerland	na	na	na	10.4
UK	123.2	79.2	47.3	30.3
US	45.0	27.8	18.8	29.2

Sources: *OECD Economic Outlook* and Bank of Portugal.
Note: (a) Only data for gross debt are available.

focus instead on those political and institutional aspects which may affect the process of policy formation, and ask whether constitutional differences among the various democratic regimes have any bearing on debt policy decisions. For example, does the level of government debt depend on electoral and representational systems?

Public debt is not the only dimension along which countries differ. In Table 2 we observe that, in the 1980s, average inflation was 3% in Japan and 21% in Greece. In the current debate over the European monetary union, an important issue is whether such divergences in inflation are related to the differences in fiscal policies described above. Are large deficits associated with inflation? Is there any connection between the political system and inflation? If this were the case the creation of a monetary union among countries with dissimilar fiscal policies could be problematic.

To explain international differences in monetary stability, we extend the institutional analysis beyond the general characteristics of political systems to include regulations which are specific to the activity of national central banks such as their degree of independence. In the current debate over monetary and political union in Europe one of the crucial issues is whether a complete convergence in monetary and fiscal policy should be achieved before the monetary union. If it can be established that the institutional and political systems have a significant

Table 2. Inflation rate (%)

	1950–59	1960–69	1970–79	1980–89
US	1.8	2.3	7.1	5.6
UK	3.5	3.6	12.6	7.4
Austria	6.8	3.3	6.1	4.0
Belgium	1.9	2.7	7.1	5.1
Denmark	3.8	5.3	9.3	7.1
France	6.2	3.8	8.9	7.8
Germany	1.1	2.4	4.9	2.9
Italy	2.9	3.4	12.5	11.8
Netherlands	3.8	4.2	7.1	3.1
Switzerland	1.1	3.1	5.0	3.3
Canada	2.4	2.5	7.4	6.7
Japan	3.1	5.4	9.1	2.5
Greece	6.5	2.0	12.3	20.1
Ireland	3.9	4.0	12.7	9.9
Portugal	0.7	4.0	17.1	18.2
Spain	6.2	5.8	14.1	10.6
Australia	6.5	2.5	9.8	7.6
New Zealand	5.0	3.2	11.4	12.5
Mean	3.7	3.5	9.7	8.1
Standard deviation	1.99	1.08	3.28	5.04

Source: International Monetary Fund, *International Financial Statistics.*
Note: Inflation is based on the GNP deflator.

and independent effect on the choice of economic policy, then waiting for further convergence would be inappropriate. Complete convergence, in fact, could only be achieved by a political and monetary union.

Our investigation is also motivated by the recent positive theories of economic policy. This literature studies the incentives brought on policy-makers by political and monetary institutions. So far, though, there exist very few empirical studies which attempt to explore the implications and hypotheses of these recent theories. An important forerunner of this paper is the work of Roubini and Sachs (1988, 1989) who also relate observed fiscal policies to political institutions in the industrial countries. Some of our results confirm their previous findings, but our paper is based on a more detailed description of the institutional environment, and bears a closer tie to the theoretical debate. In addition, we study monetary policy and monetary institutions, which were absent from their research.[1] The recent literature, pioneered by Rogoff

[1] Empirical evidence similar to that of Roubini and Sachs (1988) and to the evidence of this paper is presented, for developing countries, in Edwards and Tabellini (1990, 1991).

(1985), showed that the design of the monetary regime can be a fundamental determinant of public financial policies and more generally of macroeconomic performance. Our paper investigates the empirical validity of this approach, providing an accurate definition of central bank independence.

A preliminary caveat is in order. When trying to establish a link between institutional structure and economic policy decisions, one has to keep in mind that the terms of the contract establishing a central bank and even the constitutional structure of a country evolve and change over time. Institutional arrangements are possibly affected by economic performance. These types of feedback, however, occur over long periods of time, and thus we take institutional arrangements as given over the relatively short horizon which is the focus of our analysis. When we take into account institutional changes we ignore the possibility that they may have been induced by current economic performance.

The paper's outline is as follows. In Section 2 we analyse the determinants of debt policies and ask whether observed fiscal decisions are consistent with 'shock absorber' behaviour, as predicted by the theory of optimal taxation. For many countries they are definitely not. In fact, in a number of countries, public debt is on an explosive path: this will require major changes in future spending and tax policies. In Section 3, we ask whether the political system has any effect on public deficits. A comparison of political systems of the 18 OECD countries shows that, in almost all instances, explosive debts are found in countries governed by highly proportional electoral systems, with short-lived coalition or minority governments. In Sections 4 and 5 we turn to monetary policies. The recent literature on seigniorage (e.g. Mankiw, 1987) stresses that inflation is a source of revenue and should be considered a part of the global budgetary policy. There is little evidence that this is a fruitful way of looking at monetary policies. Moreover, contrary to popular opinion, we find no evidence that budget deficits lead to lax monetary policies. If for some countries seigniorage is indeed an important source of government revenue, for most countries seigniorage has actually declined in the 1980s when the budget deficits were largest. Next, in Section 5, we compare the monetary regimes of the 18 countries. While lower and less variable inflation is associated with central bank independence, there is no indication that the monetary regime matters for real economic performance (growth or unemployment) or for budgetary choices. Thus, fiscal discipline and monetary discipline seem to be unrelated, being determined by respectively the political and the monetary institutions. Section 6 concludes and summarizes the main findings.

2. The evolution of public debt

2.1. Sustainable paths for public debt

Governments, like private economic agents, face budget constraints. However, unlike private agents, governments do not always bear the burden of servicing the debt that they have issued; the burden can be pushed onto future governments or future generations of tax payers. What determines whether governments pay attention to their budget constraints? In particular, what determines the division between taxes and deficits? According to the theory of optimal taxation, public deficits should be designed to minimize the distortionary effects (the so-called excess burden) of taxation, given a politically desired path of public spending. The government should equate the marginal distortions associated with the last dollar of revenue collected on all tax bases at all points in time. The role of public debt should be to 'smooth' tax distortions over time. Temporary expenditures or temporary shortfalls in revenue should thus be financed by issuing debt, whereas tax rates should be changed right away in the face of permanent shocks. In particular, government debt should not be used to postpone unavoidable tax increases, since doing so would simply result in larger tax distortions when the debt eventually has to be serviced.[2]

Without knowing the exact nature of the economic shocks, this normative theory is difficult to test. There are, however, certain minimal conditions that an efficient debt policy should satisfy, irrespective of the particular shocks which affect the economy. In particular, the government should not allow the debt to become unsustainable. More precisely government debt (as a percentage of GNP) cannot forever grow faster than the excess of its rate of return over the growth rate of the economy.[3] Only then is the stock of debt outstanding at any

[2] The 'tax smoothing' principle of debt policy was first applied by Barro (1979, 1986) to explain the debt policies of the US and the UK.

[3] Consider the government budget constraint (all variables are expressed as a percentage of GNP):

$$b_t \geq R_t b_{t-1} + d_t \tag{1}$$

where b is public debt, R is one plus the rate of return divided by one plus the growth rate of real GNP, and d is the primary deficit. By recursive forward substitution, Equation (11) can be rewritten as:

$$b_{t-1} \leq \sum_{i=0}^{N-1} q_{t+i} d_{t+i} + q_{t+N} b_{t+N} \tag{2}$$

where:

$$q_{t+i} = \prod_{k=0}^{i} R_{t+k}$$

Since the market will not allow public debt to grow in excess of the government capacity to service it,

$$\lim_{N \to \infty} q_{t+N} b_{t+N} = 0 \tag{3}$$

Table 3. Government surplus (% of GNP)

	Primary				Total			
	1950–59	1960–69	1970–79	1980–89	1950–59	1960–69	1970–79	1980–89
US	1.3	0.9	−0.3	−1.5	−0.2	−0.6	−2.1	−3.9
UK	2.6	2.2	−0.5	0.0	−1.1	−0.9	−3.7	−3.7
Austria	−2.1	−1.2	−2.0	−2.2	−2.4	−1.8	−2.5	−4.7
Belgium	−2.0	−0.1	−1.6	na	−4.1	−2.6	−4.5	−11.3
Denmark	1.8	1.5	1.5	−0.7	−0.1	1.0	0.8	−4.9
France	−2.7	−0.2	0.1	−1.0	−4.4	−1.0	−0.6	−2.4
Germany	−0.6	−0.1	−0.5	−0.6	−0.8	−0.5	−0.9	−1.6
Italy	−1.5	−1.4	−6.9	−5.0	−3.2	−2.7	−9.8	−13.5
Netherlands	1.2	0.0	−0.5	−3.1	1.2	−1.3	−1.9	−5.3
Switzerland	1.3	0.7	−0.3	0.2	0.4	0.2	−0.7	−0.03
Canada	2.2	0.8	−1.1	−4.5	0.4	−1.0	−2.7	−4.4
Japan	na	na	na	na	na	na	na	na
Greece	−1.1	−1.1	−1.6	−2.9	−1.2	−1.6	−3.0	−9.4
Ireland	−0.5	−2.3	−5.2	−5.8	−4.8	−5.4	−9.6	−12.5
Portugal	na	na	na	na	na	na	−5.8	−10.8
Spain	na	na	na	na	na	−1.5	−1.5	−6.2
Australia	na	na	na	na	1.5	−1.8	−1.9	−2.0
New Zealand	na	na	na	na	−2.7	−3.0	−4.9	−6.1
Mean	−0.01	−0.02	−1.45	−2.53	−1.43	−1.53	−3.25	−6.04
Standard deviation	1.74	1.21	2.16	2.46	1.98	1.42	2.86	4.04

Source: International Monetary Fund, *International Financial Statistics.*

point in time equal to the present discounted value of all future surpluses.

2.2. The evidence

Several pieces of evidence suggest that, in many countries, the debt path is unsustainable. Table 3 presents 10-year averages of primary (i.e. exclusive of interest payments) and total surpluses in the post-war period (both measures disregard seigniorage revenues). The pattern of the two variables is similar. We observe an increase over time in both the size and the cross-country dispersion of deficits. In the 1960s and especially in the 1950s surpluses were as common as deficits. A number of countries – Austria, Belgium, Italy, Greece, Ireland (and possibly Portugal and Spain for which we lack data) – have kept running primary deficits throughout the period. The consecutive build-up of debt and debt service explains why their total budget deficits far exceed those of the remaining countries. These five, possibly seven, countries are thus the most likely to have an unsustainable debt path. These conclusions are confirmed by the examination of Figure 1 where we present the evolution of net debt to GNP ratios in the OECD area. The countries

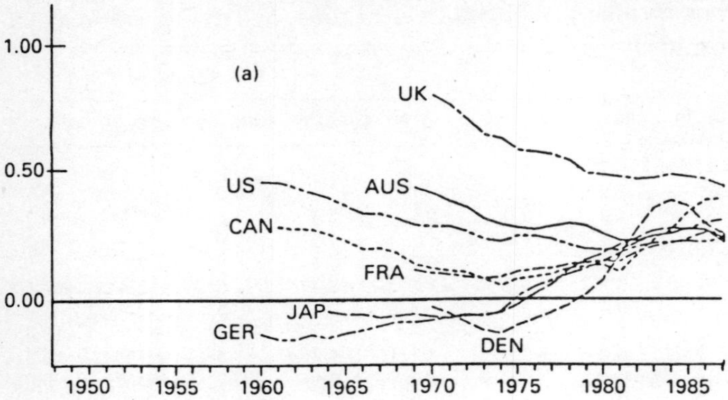

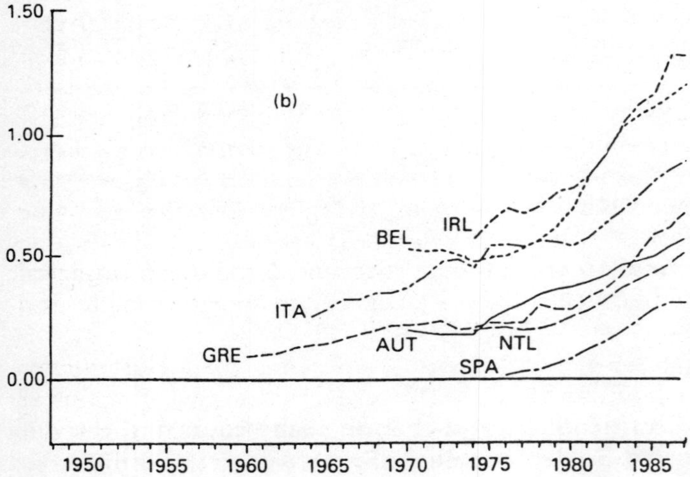

Figure 1. Net debt to GNP ratios

Source: *OECD Economic Outlook.*

can be divided into two groups. In the first group (Panel a) the debt to GNP ratio is stable or converges toward moderate levels of about 35%. In the second group (Panel b) the debt to GNP ratio has a clearly explosive pattern. In this group we find Austria, Belgium, Italy, Greece, Ireland, Portugal, Spain, as before, and the Netherlands.

A more formal approach is presented in Appendix A and provides indications of debt unsustainability for the same seven countries: Austria, Belgium, Italy, Greece, Ireland, Portugal and Spain. The consistency in the results makes it difficult to accept the view that public debt accumulation in those countries was the optimal response to temporary economic shocks.

3. Political institutions and fiscal policy

3.1. Political theories of government debt

Can international differences in debt accumulation be due to differences in the political incentives faced by the governments? We attempt to answer this question by comparing the domestic political institutions of the OECD countries. The recent literature on the theory of economic policy pays considerable attention to how political institutions shape the policy-makers' incentives. (For a survey, see Persson and Tabellini, 1990). A first approach (pioneered by Alesina and Tabellini, 1990; Persson and Svensson, 1989; and Tabellini and Alesina, 1990) investigates how the political system affects over time the behaviour of governments with different ideological preferences which alternate in office. The central result concerns how policy-makers weigh the future (their rate of time discount). Two features of the political system matter: instability (i.e. how likely it is that the current government or legislative majority will be thrown out of office) and polarization (i.e. how strong is the disagreement between the alternating policy-makers). More unstable and polarized political systems behave more myopically, i.e. they discount the future more. This approach yields the sharp empirical prediction that public debts should be larger in more unstable and polarized societies.

The second theoretical approach also focuses on disagreement between different political actors but focuses on the role of different decision-makers (such as different cabinet ministers or different levels of government). The greater is the conflict between these different decision-makers, the more difficult it is to change the status quo or to enact controversial policies. (This idea has been applied to the coordination of monetary and fiscal policies by Tabellini, 1986; to the choice of stabilization programmes by Alesina and Drazen, 1989; to the inflation tax by Aizenman, 1989 and Drazen and Grilli, 1990; and to budget decficits by Sanguinetti, 1990). Disagreement results in the postponement of unpopular policies. Thus, here too, collective decisions are short-sighted and political conflict is associated with the accumulation of public debt, the more so the more difficult is the resolution of the political conflict.

There is an important conceptual difference between the first and the second explanation of why political institutions can induce collective myopia. The second approach stresses *government weakness* so that the postponement of unpopular decisions is not a deliberate policy choice. Rather, it reflects a sequence of disparate and unrelated spending and taxing decisions, accompanied by the inability to change the status quo. The first approach, on the other hand, emphasizes *political stability* to explain how the electorate ends up favouring budget deficits because their future costs are not fully recognized. This distinction is important, because it leads to different policy implications. According to the second approach, what matters is the support that governments enjoy in the legislature and among the voters at large. According to the first line of thought, instead, collective myopia is not caused by the weakness of the executive, but rather by its instability. In the empirical analysis, we attempt to discriminate between these two alternative hypotheses.

3.2. The political institutions

The countries that we study were democracies throughout the postwar period, except for Greece, Portugal and Spain, and all of them have been democracies since the second half of the 1970s. We describe three main features of these democracies: (a) their broad constitutional rules; (b) their party systems; and (c) the attributes of their governments. Except for France and for the countries that became democracies, the constitutions did not significantly change during the post-war period, at least along the dimensions considered in this section. Hence the features described under (a) are independent of economic policies in general, and of the evolution of public debts in particular. While the political indicators examined below can in principle be influenced by economic events and by previous economic policy decisions, these indicators are quite stable over time. In fact, they can be classified quite precisely according to the constitutional rules and the properties of the party system. This suggests that, even for the features described under (c), the main direction of causation runs from the political system to economic policies, and not vice versa.

3.2.1. The political constitution. The first distinction (column 1 in Table 4) is between presidential and parliamentary democracies. In the former, the president is voted directly into office and has significant independent authority. In the latter, the prime minister is accountable to the legislature. Even though there are some mixed arrangements (Switzerland can almost be considered a multiperson presidential system, and since 1958 France combines elements of both systems), most countries are parliamentary democracies. Parliamentary systems in turn differ by the degree of proportionality of the electroral laws. We follow Bingham Powell (1982) in identifying the degree of proportionality with the

Table 4. Political fractionalization

Country	Democracy (a)	Representatives (b)	Fractionalization (c)		
			1960–64	1965–76	1980–90
Australia	Pa-M	1	0.63	0.61	0.59
Austria	Pa-R	6	0.54	0.54	0.59
Belgium	Pa-R	7	0.63	0.76	0.86
Canada	Pa-M	1	0.62	0.63	0.52
Denmark	Pa-R	10	0.72	0.79	0.81
France	Pr	1	0.69	0.71	0.68
Germany	Pa-M	2	0.58	0.57	0.66
Greece	Pa-R	6	0.59	0.68	0.55
Ireland	Pa-M	4	0.62	0.61	0.64
Italy	Pa-R	19	0.73	0.73	0.75
Japan	Pa-M	4	0.54	0.60	0.63
Netherlands	Pa-R	150	0.77	0.84	0.73
New Zealand	Pa-M	1	0.51	0.49	0.49
Portugal	Pr	14 (d)	na	0.68 (d)	0.66
Spain	Pa-R	7 (d)	na	0.76 (d)	0.62
Switzerland	Pa-M	na	0.79	0.81	0.82
UK	Pa-M	1	0.50	0.48	0.53
US	Pr	1	0.44	0.61	0.48

Sources: Bingham Powell (1982), Banks (1987) and various other years, Keasing archives, various years.
Notes: (a) Pr = Presidential Democracy, Pa-M = Majoritarian Parliamentary Democracy, Pa-R = Representational Parliamentary Democracy; (b) Representatives per district, defined as the number of legislators in the popular house of the legislature, divided by the number of electoral districts. The numbers refer to the late 1960s. In 1971 Austria decreased the number of districts, increasing the number of representatives per district to nearly 20; (c) Fractionalization Index, defined as the probability that two legislators chosen at random belong to different parties. The second column is computed from elections in the 1966–76 period, and refers to the average votes taken by each party. The other two columns refer instead to the average number of seats in the lower house taken by each party in elections held during the specified periods; (d) Years 1975 and 1976 only (dictatorship prior to then).

number of representatives per district (column 2 of Table 4). Systems with less than five representatives per district are classified as majoritarian, with five or more as representational. Naturally, electoral laws differ in several other dimensions, which can reinforce or weaken the degree of proportionality of a political system.[4]

All the countries that seem to have an unsustainable debt, except Ireland and Portugal, are governed by representational systems. Conversely, all representational democracies except Denmark have unsustainable fiscal policies. This finding is strikingly illustrated in Figure 2

[4] In particular, Germany, Ireland and Japan also have less representational features in their electoral laws.

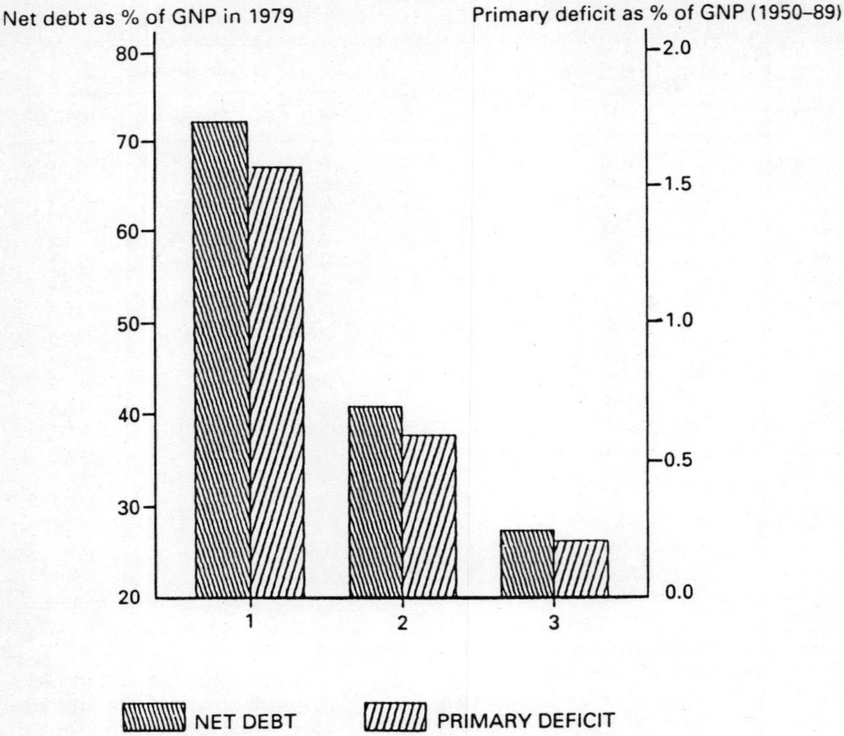

Figure 2. Net debt and primary deficits

Notes: Group 1: Representational Parliamentary Democracies (Austria, Belgium, Denmark, Greece, Italy, the Netherlands, Spain); Group 2: Majoritarian Parliamentary Democracies (Australia, Canada, Germany, Ireland, Japan, New Zealand, Switzerland, UK); Group 3: Presidental Democracies (France, US). France 1950–58 is included in Group 1. Only the years of democratic regime for Greece and Spain are included. Data for Portugal are missing.

which displays for three country groupings the average net debt in 1989 and the average primary deficit between 1950 and 1989, both as percentage of GNP. Group 1 consists of all representational democracies, group 2 is made up of majoritarian parliamentary systems and group 3 of presidential democracies (except Portugal, for which data are missing).[5] Clearly, net debts and primary deficits are much larger in the representational democracies.

[5] France is included in the second group, but its primary deficit is only averaged between 1960 and 1989, since before 1959 it was a representative democracy. The primary deficit of France in 1950–59 is instead included in group 1.

This strong association between representational political systems and lack of fiscal discipline is also evident from particular episodes of constitutional reform. In 1958, France reformed its electoral law and enacted a number of constitutional changes. The constitutional role of the president was strengthened relative to the parliament and the government, while the government in turn was strengthened relative to the parliament. The electoral law was changed from proportional to majoritarian. As can be seen from Table 3, the size of fiscal deficits changed dramatically. While in the 1950s France had an average primary deficit of 2.7% of GNP (the largest of all countries in the sample), its average primary deficit from 1960–89 was 0.4% of GNP, one of the smallest in the sample.

3.2.2. The party system. The electoral laws, and in particular their degree of proportionality, influence two central features of a party system: the number of parties, and the extent to which minority interests are represented in the legislature. With a high degree of proportionality, several parties are likely to coexist; moreover, extremist parties that represent the interests of minorities are more likely to survive. These two features determine the kind of government (coalition, majority government or minority government) that is likely to be formed, as well as its durability, thereby indirectly shaping the policy-making process.

The last three columns of Table 4 present an indicator of fractionalization of the party system over three sub-periods. We follow the literature in defining fractionalization as the probability that two legislators chosen at random belong to different parties.[6] This index ranges between 0 and 1. A value of 0.5 is associated with a perfectly balanced two-party system. A value larger than 0.5 is generally associated with more than two parties.The larger the index, the greater is the number of parties in the legislature. The lowest values of this index are found in two-party systems, such as the US, the UK and New Zealand. Countries with several parties, such as Italy, Denmark, Switzerland or the Netherlands, have the highest values. The fractionalization index is quite stable over time, and it is highly positively correlated with the index of proportionality of the electoral system. This confirms that proportionality of the electoral laws leads to fractionalization.

The relative importance of extremist parties (measured by their percentage of votes in the elections) is reported in Table 5. These parties

[6] This definition is based on Rae (1967); it is $(1-\sum_{i=1}^{N} T_i^2)$, where N is the number of parties and T is the ith party's decimal share of the vote in the legislature. See also Bingham Powell (1982, p. 233).

Table 5. Political extremism

Country	1960–64	1965–75	1980–90
Australia	0	0	2
Austria	0	1	2
Belgium	6	21	15
Canada	0	0	0
Denmark	10	18	20
France	22	25	12
Germany	0	3	4
Greece	7	11	5
Ireland	2	0	0
Italy	32	37	38
Japan	4	16	14
Netherlands	5	13	4
New Zealand	0	1	0
Portugal	na	20	15
Spain	na	7	12
Switzerland	2	8	5
UK	0	3	3
US	0	0	0

Sources: Bingham Powell (1982) and *Europe World Yearbook* Various years.
Notes: The first and last columns refer to the average number of seats in the Lower House taken by extremist parties, whereas the second column refers to their average votes.

promise radical changes of the status quo and represent either stable constituencies or temporary dissatisfaction with the existing political apparatus. The classification is due to Bingham Powell (1982). He defines a party as extremist if it is associated with any of the following characteristics: (a) a well developed non-democratic ideology; (b) a proposal to change the boundaries of the nation; (c) diffuse alienation and distrust of the existing political system. The communist parties in France and Italy, or the linguistic parties in Belgium are examples of extremist parties. Like fractionalization, extremism is stable over time and is more prevalent under highly proportional electoral systems. Naturally, historical events beside electoral laws are important determinants of the size of extremist parties.

Tables 4 and 5 show that unsustainable fiscal policies are prevalent in countries with fractionalized party systems and where there are large extremist parties. To further understand this finding, we now turn to a description of the types of government that are generally formed in each country.

3.2.3. The government. The political theories of public debt summarized in Subsection 3.1 have different predictions regarding which government attributes create the incentives to borrow. Government weakness means that public debt is a residual source of finance which simply reflects government inability to cut expenditures or raise taxes. The political stability interpretation instead views public debt as a legacy deliberately left by a government to its successors. The borrowing government doesn't expect to inherit tomorrow the debt issued today, because it doesn't expect to be reappointed in office. The less likely is the reappointment, the higher is the amount borrowed. This second approach thus predicts that public debt is larger in countries with more frequent government changes from one party or leading group to another, i.e. in more politically unstable environments.

Government weakness is a rather vague concept which is difficult to quantify. A first possibility is to consider government support in the legislature. We distinguish between three kinds of government: majority, coalition and minority governments. A majority government is supported by a single party that has a majority in the legislature. A coalition government is supported by a coalition of parties, that together reach a legislative majority. A minority government is supported by a single party or by a coalition without a legislative majority. Clearly, decision-making capacity is greatest in majority governments and lowest in minority governments. The first three columns of Table 6 describe the fraction of time between 1950 and 1989 for which the government was of each of these three types. A second measure of government weakness is average durability, defined as the average number of years between one government change and the next. A short-lived government is also likely to be weak, and frequent government crises are a symptom of a divided executive with weak support in the legislature. Average government durability between 1950 and 1989 is displayed in the fourth column of Table 6.

A change in government does not result in a significant change in political leadership if the new government is still supported by the same political parties and/or it is made up by the same group of individuals as the previous one. Thus it would be wrong to use government durability as an index of political stability. To construct an index of political stability, we compute the average number of years between significant government changes, those which result in a transfer of power from one leading group or party to another. We define a government change to be significant if the following conditions are met: for a majoritarian parliamentary system, there is a change in the party of the prime minister; for a representational parliamentary system, there is a change in both the prime minster party *and* the coalition of parties supporting the government; and for a presidential system, there is a change in the party of either the prime minister or the president (except for the US,

Table 6. Government attributes

Country	Government type (a) Maj.	Coa.	Min.	Government durability (b)	Political stability (c)
Australia	26.8	73.3	0.0	4.44	10
Austria	39.0	58.5	2.4	2.67	40
Belgium	9.8	90.2	0.0	1.43	10
Canada	80.5	0.0	19.5	4.00	8
Denmark	0.0	34.1	65.9	2.11	5.7
France	41.5	39.0	19.5	1.29	2.5
Germany	9.6	90.0	0.0	2.00	20
Greece (d)	91.2	5.9	2.9	0.97	4
Ireland	65.9	24.4	9.8	1.90	5
Italy	0.0	95.1	4.9	0.95	10
Japan	80.5	12.2	7.3	1.67	40
Netherlands	0.0	100.0	0.0	3.33	6.7
New Zealand	100.0	0.0	0.0	4.44	8
Portugal (e)	26.7	53.3	20.0	1.48	5
Spain (f)	50.0	35.7	14.3	2.00	20
Switzerland	0.0	100.0	0.0	1.60	20
UK	92.7	0.0	7.3	4.00	8
US	41.5	0.0	58.5	5.00	8

Sources: Banks (1987) various volumes, Taylor and Jodice (1983), Keasing Archives, various years.
Notes: (a) Maj. = single party majority, Coa. = coalition majority, Min. = Minority (coalition or single party). The number in each column refers to the percentage of years in which the government was of each of the three types, out of the years of democratic regime between 1950 and 1990. The type is defined with reference to the popular chamber; (b) Durability of the executive between 1950 and 1990 (average number of years); (c) Average number of years between 'significant' government changes in the period 1950–89. See the text for more details; (d) Dictatorship between 1967 and 1973; (e) Dictatorship until 1973. New democratic constitution in 1976; (f) Dictatorship until 1974. First democratic election in 1977.

where the president is also prime minister). Naturally, any change from a democracy to a dictatorship or vice versa is recorded as a significant change. The resulting political stability variable is shown in the last column of Table 6 for the period 1950–89.

Table 6 shows that representational democracies tend to have shorter-lived governments and more coalition or minority governments than the other two political regimes. Average government durability is 1.9 years in representational democracies, three years in majoritarian democracies and 3.2 years in presidential democracies. The percentage of governments supported by a single party majority is 23.3%, 57.0% and 49.1% in representational, majoritarian and parliamentary

Table 7. Debt accumulation and government attributes

	Correlation matrix		
	MAJORITY	*DURABILITY*	*STABILITY*
DEBT	−0.298	−0.713	−0.061
MAJORITY		0.332	−0.044
DURABILITY			0.295

Regression

$$\underset{(0.904)}{DEBT = 3.732^{**}} - \underset{(0.011)}{0.002}\ MAJORITY - \underset{(0.304)}{0.981^{**}}\ DURABILITY + \underset{(0.066)}{0.048}\ STABILITY$$

$\bar{R}^2 = 0.408$ $SE = 1.409$ Number of observations = 15
(0.066)

Note: Debt is the change in net debt to GNP ratio between 1970 and 1989. The remaining variables are as defined in Table 6, and also refer to 1970–89. Standard errors are in parenthesis. A* (**) denotes significance at the 5% (1%) level.

democracies, respectively.[7] These government attributes reflect the greater fractionalization and strength of extremist parties in representational democracies. On the other hand, there is no significant difference in the political stability index across the three kinds of constitutional regimes. Note that the three government attributes measures in Table 6 are not correlated with each other in our sample of 18 countries. The correlation coefficients are: 0.02 between political stability and single party majority; 0.12 between political stability and government durability; and 0.31 between durability and single party majority.

3.3. Government attributes and public debt

How do these three government attributes relate to the accumulation of public debt? Table 7, which performs cross-country comparisons, provides a very clear answer. The first part of the table reports correlations between the change in net debt (as percentage of GNP) from 1970 to 1989 (*DEBT*) and the following variables, also measured in the period 1970–89 in a sample of 15 countries:[8] the percentage of governments supported by a single party majority (*MAJORITY*), average government durability (*DURABILITY*) and the political stability index

[7] In computing these numbers, France was considered a representational democracy in 1950–58, and a presidential democracy in 1959–89. Only the years of democratic regime in Spain, Greece and Portugal were included.

[8] Net debt data are missing for Spain, Switzerland and New Zealand. For Portugal the data refer to gross public debt.

(*STABILITY*). Debt accumulation is strongly negatively correlated to average government durability, while it is not correlated with either of the other two variables. The same results are obtained when we regress debt accumulation on all three variables (plus an intercept). The results are displayed in the second part of Table 7: only durability has a negative and significant coefficient. The overall fit of the regression is remarkably good (government attributes explain over 50% of the variance in public debts), and the impact of durability is also quantitatively significant.

More information can be obtained from cross-country differences by separating the whole period 1950–89 into four decades. Since in 1950 many countries had large stocks of debt inherited from the war, it is preferable to consider primary deficits (as percentage of GNP), dropping the years of non-democratic regime in Spain and Portugal. To avoid truncation problems at the start and end of each decade, we replaced the variables *DURABILITY* and *STABILITY* with the frequency of government changes (*FREQUENCY*) and of significant government changes (*SIGNIFICANT*) within each decade (the data used to construct these indices are shown in Appendix B). The regressions results in Table 8 confirm the previous findings.[9] The frequency of government changes always leads to higher deficits and the effect is significant in three out of four decades. The estimated coefficients for the other two variables are generally of the wrong sign and are never significantly different from zero.

These findings are partly consistent with the view that budget deficits are a residual source of finance, used by a weak government that does not have any politically viable alternative. However, it is surprising that budget deficits are not systematically related to the extent of government support in the legislature. On the other hand the results are inconsistent with the view that political instability is a cause of budget deficits. Budget deficits are related to the frequency of *any* government change, not only to changes which transfer power from one leading group to another one, as the theory predicts. Could it be that the results are sensitive to the definition of what represents a 'significant' change in government? To explore this possibility, the definition is weakened by considering that more changes in government are 'significant'. This provides mixed results. First, the effects of any government change in general (i.e. the variables *DURABILITY* and *FREQUENCY*), reported in Tables 7 and 8, are confirmed. Second, the variables *STABILITY* and *SIGNIFICANT* that only refer to significant government changes now are

[9] Regressions performed using the method of seemingly unrelated regressions.

Table 8. Primary budget deficits and government attributes (Dependent variable: primary budget deficit/GNP)

Explanatory variables	1950–59	1960–69	1970–79	1980–89
FREQUENCY	2.868*	1.902*	4.925**	4.460
	(0.944)	(0.765)	(1.256)	(2.604)
SIGNIFICANT	−1.361	−2.205	−4.123	1.566
	(1.721)	(2.148)	(2.657)	(6.110)
MAJORITY	−0.008	0.006	0.007	0.011
	(0.007)	(0.007)	(0.008)	(0.011)
$\bar{R}^2$	0.242	−0.066	0.386	0.458
SE	1.578	1.298	1.763	1.893
Number of observations	13	13	13	12

Notes: Intercept not reported. Standard errors in parenthesis. A* (**) denotes significance at the 5% (1%) level. The system is estimated by seemingly unrelated regressions.

correlated with budget deficits, *but only if the other measures of government change are excluded.* Thus the modified variable *STABILITY* has a high and negative simple correlation coefficient with the change in net debt between 1970 and 1989. Similarly the variable *SIGNIFICANT* has a significant and positive effect on the budget deficit if the variable *FREQUENCY* is omitted from the specification, but it is generally insignificant and of the wrong sign otherwise.

These findings strongly indicate that high government turnover plays a crucial role in explaining public borrowing. Yet they do not convincingly discriminate between the two competing views: that short government durability is a symptom of a weak executive, or that it is an indication of political instability. Moreover, other plausible indicators of government weakness (such as government support in the legislature) are not systematically related to government borrowing. Naturally, there may be other explanations, beside these two, of why short government durability creates incentives to borrow.

Summarizing, our analysis of political institutions in the OECD countries suggests the following ‘stylized facts’. First, lack of fiscal discipline is almost exclusively found in countries governed by representational democracies and, conversely, there are very few examples of representational democracies that do not have a high public debt problem. Second, the one feature of representational democracies that seems responsible for the lack of fiscal discipline is short government durability. Exactly why that is so remains an issue open for further research.

Table 9. Government fiscal aggregates (% of GNP)

	1950–59			1960–69			1970–79			1980–87		
	Public spending	Tax revenue	Seign.	Public spending	Tax revenue	Seign.	Public spending	Tax revenue	Seign.	Public spending	Tax revenue	Seign.
US	18	18	0.2	18	18	0.3	20	18	0.5	24	20	0.4
UK	27	29	0.5	28	31	0.4	35	34	0.8	40	37	0.1
Austria	21	18	1.6	21	20	1.1	33	31	1.0	39	35	0.4
Belgium	23	18	0.8	24	21	0.9	43	38	0.9	54	45	0.2
Denmark	14	16	0.3	21	23	0.6	34	34	0.2	43	40	0.3
France,	na	20	1.5	na	22	1.1	35	32	0.7	43	41	0.5
Germany	15	14	1.1	14	13	0.6	27	26	1.0	31	29	0.3
Italy	17	16	1.9	17	16	1.6	26	19	3.2	37	27	1.8
Netherlands	24	25	0.7	25	25	0.7	42	41	0.5	57	51	0.4
Switzerland	9	9	0.9	8	8	1.9	9	8	1.5	9	9	0.3
Canada	16	17	0.3	16	16	0.4	20	20	0.7	24	20	0.2
Japan	14	14	0.7	13	12	1.2	12	9	1.3	na	na	0.6
Greece	17	16	1.7	18	17	1.8	22	19	2.6	32	23	3.7
Ireland	26	21	0.6	29	24	1.7	40	31	2.2	55	41	0.9
Portugal	na	na	1.4	na	na	1.7	25	21	4.1	44	35	3.3
Spain	na	na	1.4	12	12	1.5	21	21	2.2	31	26	3.2
Australia	23	25	0.1	23	21	0.4	22	23	0.7	28	26	0.6
New Zealand	32	29	0.3	28	27	−0.1	32	31	0.7	42	38	0.2
Mean	19.7	19.1	0.9	19.7	19.2	1.0	27.7	25.3	1.4	37.2	31.9	1.0
Standard deviation	0.06	0.05	0.006	0.06	0.06	0.006	0.09	0.09	0.010	0.12	0.10	0.012

Source: International Monetary Fund, *International Financial Statistics* and *Government Finance Statistics*.

4. Evidence on inflation and seigniorage

Turning to the analysis of cross-country differences in monetary policies and inflation, the first question is whether there exists a relationship between fiscal and monetary policies and, in particular, whether budget deficits affect the rate of inflation. The potential existence of a link between fiscal policy and inflation is stressed by the public finance approach to monetary policy. This approach considers inflation as just one form of taxation, and as such, it is viewed a source of distortion like any other tax. The principle of optimal taxation asserts that taxes should be set in such a way that the last amount collected with each tax be equally distortionary. Hence, if taxes need to be changed, all of them should be changed in the same direction. In particular, the rate of inflation should be positively corrected with all other tax rates.[10]

4.1. The cross-country evidence

In Table 9, government revenues are broken down in two broad categories: (i) tax revenues, which include all forms of 'explicit' taxation, like income taxes, sales taxes, VAT etc. and (ii) seigniorage, i.e. revenues from monetization (defined as the change in base money). For all countries tax revenues reach their *highest* post-war levels in the 1980s, while in the majority of countries (10 out of 18) this is the decade where seigniorage is *lowest*, and in only two countries (Greece and Spain) is seigniorage higher in the 1980s than in the 1970s. The 1980s is also the period of largest budget deficits. This fact alone should cast serious doubts on the popular opinion that budget deficits are a cause of inflation.

On the other hand, seigniorage is on average higher in the countries that have an unsustainable debt path. This is particularly true for Spain, Greece, Portugal and Italy. In the 1980s the average level of seigniorage for these four countries was 3% of GNP, against less than 0.4% elsewhere. The other three countries on an unsustainable debt path (Austria, Belgium and Ireland) do not have seigniorage levels significantly higher than the rest of the sample. Thus across countries there is some evidence of a link between budget deficits and seigniorage, but not so over time.

[10] The fiscal approach to inflation has been developed by Phelps (1973) (see also Mankiw, 1987). Faig (1988) and Kimbrough (1986) show that since money performs the role of an intermediate input, it should not be taxed. However, as shown by Aizenman (1987), this conclusion does not apply in the presence of tax evasion or tax collection costs.

Table 10. Inflation and taxes (partial correlation)

Australia	0.882* (0.377)	Italy	−0.059** (0.019)
Austria	1.278 (0.721)	Japan	0.937 (0.797)
Belgium	0.573 (0.472)	Netherlands	−0.806 (0.537)
Canada	1.075** (0.366)	New Zealand	0.268 (0.296)
Denmark	0.325 (0.460)	Portugal	−0.324 (1.334)
France	1.034 (0.472)	Spain	1.133 (1.174)
Germany	0.518 (0.408)	Switzerland	−0.923* (0.373)
Greece	0.381 (0.420)	UK	−0.330 (0.361)
Ireland	0.500 (0.321)	US	0.330 (0.361)

Notes: Partial coefficient of correlation from regressions of inflation on taxes in first differences. The estimation period is 1950–87 or a fraction of it, according to the availability of data. Standard errors in parenthesis. A* (**) denotes significance at the 5% (1%) level. The system is estimated by OLS.

4.2. The time series evidence

To check whether the inflation tax is correlated over time with other distorting tax rates, as predicted by the theory of optimal taxation, we approximate the tax rate on seigniorage by the inflation rate.[11] The non-inflation tax rate is measured as the ratio of tax revenue to GNP. For each country, we regress the change in the rate of inflation on the change in the tax rate. The results, reported in Table 10 show that there is no systematic relationship between tax rates and inflation. For all countries but three (Australia, Canada and France), the link is insignificantly different from zero, and sometimes it has the wrong (negative) sign. Table 11 further shows that in most countries the change in government spending is strongly positively correlated with the change in the tax rate (the estimated coefficient on the tax rate is always positive and generally highly significant), while there is no evidence of a positive correlation between changes in spending and inflation.[12] Thus while

[11] This is standard practice in the literature. Using the rate of money growth instead leads to the same results, while data on the nominal interest rate are not available for all countries over long enough periods of time.

[12] The same results are obtained if the inflation regressions are estimated with instrumental variables, with lagged variables as instruments.

Table 11. Inflation, taxes and government expenditure (partial correlation)

	Inflation and government expenditure	Taxes and government expenditure
Australia	0.295	0.755**
	(0.455)	(0.149)
Austria	1.152	0.436**
	(0.519)	(0.100)
Belgium	−0.074	0.210
	(0.236)	(0.087)
Canada	0.475	0.225
	(0.377)	(0.156)
Denmark	0.288	0.122
	(0.315)	(0.116)
France	0.514	0.339*
	(0.390)	(0.146)
Germany	−0.235	0.087**
	(0.147)	(0.064)
Greece	−0.589	0.684**
	(0.369)	(0.101)
Ireland	0.520**	0.458**
	(0.190)	(0.072)
Italy	−0.025**	0.329**
	(0.009)	(0.056)
Japan	−0.821	0.259
	(0.888)	(0.233)
Netherlands	0.614	0.383**
	(0.328)	(0.085)
New Zealand	−0.23	0.490**
	(0.319)	(0.175)
Portugal	−0.956	0.169
	(0.763)	(0.168)
Spain	0.078	0.459**
	(0.875)	(0.129)
Switzerland	−0.045	0.522**
	(0.435)	(0.157)
UK	0.607	0.570**
	(0.380)	(0.154)
US	−0.313	0.208
	(0.348)	(0.158)

Notes: Coefficients from regressions of inflation or taxes on government, expenditures in first differences. The estimation period is 1950–87 or a fraction of it, according to the availability of data. Standard errors in parenthesis. A* (**) denotes significance at the 5% (1%) level. The system is estimated by OLS.

the tax rate seems to respond to spending changes, inflation does not and this is the reason for the lack of complementarity between taxes and inflation.

It might be that the monetary authorities disregard in the short run the budgetary consequences of their actions. Could the principle of optimal taxation be relevant only in the long run? A way to test this hypothesis is to look for a positive long-run relationship between the average tax rate and the rate of inflation (technically we conduct cointegration tests, not reported).[13] There is no evidence of such a long-term relationship (except for Switzerland where anyway the correlation is negative in contradiction to the theoretical prediction). This accords with the earlier observation that, in the 1980s, tax rates were increasing while seigniorage revenues were declining in most countries.

These results could still be reconciled with the principle of optimal taxation if the velocity of circulation of money is continuously increasing over time. Then the general tax base (income) grows relatively to the base of the inflation tax (money), and it becomes optimal to rely increasingly more on general taxation than on inflation. In this case, Poterba and Rotemberg (1989) and Trehan and Walsh (1989) show that we should expect a long-run relationship between three variables: the tax rate, inflation and velocity. When this is tested (and not reported here) evidence of a positive comovement between inflation and other taxes is found only for the US and UK but not for the remaining 16 countries.

4.3. Summary

First, we have found that the countries that rely most on seigniorage typically have unsustainable debt paths, but the converse is not true: some countries with unsustainable debt paths have managed to maintain low inflation. Second, for most countries regular taxes and inflation are not 'complementary' sources of revenues: these rates do not vary together as predicted by the theory of optimal taxation. Third, inflation does not vary systematically with expenditures, either in the short or

[13] Two non-stationary (i.e. with no stable mean) series are said to be cointegrated if there exists a linear combination of them which is stationary. Cointegration tests are common in the empirical literature on optimal taxation – see Grilli (1989), Trehan and Walsh (1989), among others. However, they raise a problem. The prediction that 'optimal' tax rates are non-stationary is derived from models which neglect the constraint that the rates are bounded between 0 and 1. Proper microfoundations, such as in Lucas and Stokey (1983), imply that the optimal tax rate is stationary, in which case the notion of cointegration does not apply. We reject non-stationarity of the tax rate for the US, the UK, Austria, Denmark, Switzerland, Greece and Ireland. For the inflation rate, non-stationarity is rejected in Austria, Belgium, Denmark, France, Germany, the Netherlands, Switzerland and Japan. Hence, the cointegration tests reported in the text should be taken with a grain of salt.

in the long run, and not even across countries. The conclusion is that for most OECD countries fiscal policy has not been a major determinant of monetary stability in the post-war period. Rather, the evidence suggests that the often observed combination of large seigniorage and high public debt may reflect some other fundamental determinant, possibly linked to monetary institutions.

5. Monetary institutions, credibility and economic policy

The principle of optimal taxation completely overlooks the fact that policy-makers face political constraints and incentives. In the case of monetary policy, credibility has long been known to be of fundamental importance. The reason is that the monetary authorities have an incentive to collect the inflation tax by surprising the private sector with unexpected monetary expansions. Indeed, unexpected inflation acts as a non-distortionary tax precisely because, being unanticipated, it does not affect private behaviour, at least *ex ante*. However, once this is understood, private agents are likely to raise their inflation expectations accordingly. If they cannot convince the private sector that they do not intend to engineer such surprises, the monetary authorities may be forced to accommodate these expectations, with the consequence that inflation will be higher than desired. Lack of credibility, therefore, results in an excessive reliance on seigniorage revenues.

This credibility problem can be overcome by delegating monetary policy to an independent central bank, committed to the goal of low inflation. Having a credible monetary policy may matter not only for the price and wage decisions of the private sector, but also for the budgetary decisions of the public sector. In particular a credible commitment not to inflate away the debt and not to provide monetary financing of the fiscal deficit may strengthen the government incentive to balance its budget. Hence low inflation as well as a more disciplined fiscal policy are more likely to be observed in countries with a more independent central bank.[14] Naturally, having an independent central bank committed to low inflation has its cost too: monetary policy is less likely to respond optimally to unexpected shocks and may tolerate excessive output fluctuations. Similarly, an independent central bank may pay too little attention to the budgetary consequences of its actions. This is why the design of the monetary regime should be an important determinant of public financial policies and, more generally, of

[14] This point is shown in Rogoff (1985). Tabellini (1987a, b) analyses the connection between central bank independence and budget deficits.

macroeconomic performance. In particular, we expect central bank independence to be associated with low inflation and smaller budget deficits, but also with larger output fluctuation and greater deviations from the predictions of the theory of optimal taxation.

5.1. The monetary institutions

To compare the monetary regimes we focus exclusively on institutional features, disregarding behavioural indicators such as the average rate of growth of the money supply or the level and variability of interest rates. There is no doubt that such behavioural indicators shape expectations and thus contribute to identify a monetary regime. The independence of the Bundesbank is the result of specific central bank laws but also of its reputation and a tradition of monetary discipline. Hence, by neglecting behavioural indicators we miss an important dimension of monetary regimes. Our attitude can be justified on the following grounds. First, to assess the effect of institutional design on policy performance we need to keep institutions and behaviour as distinct as possible. Second, behavioural indicators have often varied over time (e.g. with the personalities in charge of monetary policy) whereas monetary institutions have generally been more invariant and, to the extent that there have been institutional reforms, they are more clearly identifiable.

Monetary institutions can be characterized by the political and economic independence of the central bank. Political independence is the capacity to choose the *final goal* of monetary policy, such as inflation or the level of economic activity. Economic independence is the capacity to choose *the instruments* with which to pursue these goals. The few studies which compare monetary regimes in a large number of countries are not consistently linked to the theoretical debate and their classifications are based on somewhat arbitrary criteria. The most comprehensive studies of the political dimension of central bank independence are Fair (1978) and Bade and Parkin (1982). The economic dimension has recently been stressed by Masciandaro and Tabellini (1988), who compare the central banks of the US, Canada, Australia, New Zealand and Japan, by Tabellini (1987b) in a study of Italy, and by Masciandaro (1990).

5.1.1. Political independence of the central bank. The capacity of the monetary authorities to choose the final goals of policy is primarily determined by three aspects of a monetary regime; (i) the procedure for appointing the members of the central bank governing bodies; (ii) the relationship between these bodies and the government; and (iii) the formal responsibilities of the central bank. In principle, independence to choose the final goals can be defined without reference to the contents of such goals. In practice, however, the main virtue of having an independent central bank is that it can provide credibility. This is why we identify independence with autonomy to pursue the goal of low inflation. Any institutional feature that enhances the central bank capacity to pursue this goal will, on our definition, increase central bank independence.

Table 12 contrasts these three aspects of the monetary regimes in the 18 countries. Each column refers to a different attribute. A star indicates that the country in question possesses that attribute. Appendix C provides more information on each column. The first four columns describe the rules for appointing the governor and the board of the central bank. The political independence of the central bank is clearly higher if the appointments are not under the control of the government (but are determined by representatives of the bank, like in Italy or in Canada), and if they are for a long and predetermined period of time. Columns 5 and 6 summarize the relationship between the central bank governing bodies and the government. The political independence of the central bank is greater if there is no mandatory participation of a government representative in the board and if prior government approval of monetary policy is not legally required.[15] Finally (columns 7 and 8) the central bank's constitutional position is clearly strengthened if its role in preserving monetary stability is explicitly stated in the constitution, and if there are explicit legal directives that, in case of conflict between the bank and the government, describe a transparent procedure for how the conflict is to be resolved. In other words, both attributes enhance the 'gate keeping' power of the monetary regime: they make it less likely that, in case of conflict, the bank's position will be overruled by the government.

The overall degree of central bank political independence is determined by a combination of these attributes. Combining them is unavoidably arbitrary so we adopt the simplest procedure of adding them up. The result, shown in the last column of Table 12, is our synthetic indicator of the political independence of the central bank. Switzerland,

[15] In some countries – e.g. Italy – the requirement that monetary policy be approved by the government is a mere formality that has never resulted in the approval being denied or even threatened with denial. Nevertheless, we classify these countries as requiring government approval for two reasons. First, as stated in the text, we want to be consistent in classifying institutions rather than behaviour. Second, just observing that approval is never denied is no proof that the formal requirement is not binding: a rational and fully informed central bank would never pursue a policy that would not be approved by the government, even in the case of a strong disagreement.

Table 12. Political independence of central banks

	Appointments				Relationship with government		Constitution		Index of political independence
Countries	(1)	(2)	(3)	(4)	(5)	(6)	(7)	(8)	(9)
Australia		*					*	*	3
Austria						*	*	*	3
Belgium				*					1
Canada	*	*					*	*	4
Denmark		*				*	*		3
France		*		*					2
Germany		*		*	*	*	*	*	6
Greece			*					*	2
Ireland		*				*	*		3
Italy	*	*	*		*				4
Japan							*		1
Netherlands		*		*	*	*	*	*	6
New Zealand									0
Portugal					*				1
Spain				*	*				2
Switzerland		*			*	*	*	*	5
UK					*				1
US				*	*	*	*	*	5

Sources: See Appendix C.
Notes: (1) Governor *not* appointed by government; (2) Governor appointed for >5 years; (3) *All* the Board *not* appointed by government; (4) Board appointed for >5 years; (5) No mandatory participation of government representative in the Board; (6) No government approval of monetary policy formulation is required; (7) Statutory requirements that central bank pursues monetary stability amongst its goals; (8) Legal provisions that strengthen the central bank's position in conflicts with the government are present; (9) Overall index of political independence, constructed as the sum of the asterisks in each row. See Appendix C for more details.

West Germany and the US, but also the Netherlands, Canada and Italy, enjoy the highest degree of political independence. At the other end are Austria, New Zealand, the UK, Belgium and Portugal, and not far above Greece, Spain and France.[16]

5.1.2. Economic independence of the central bank. The autonomy of a central bank in choosing the instruments of monetary policy is described by: (i) the influence of the government in determining how much to borrow from the central bank; and (ii) the nature of the monetary instruments under the control of the central bank. If the government can influence

[16] Towards the late 1980s New Zealand reformed its monetary system and now has perhaps the most independent central bank of all OECD countries. Its new central bank law even contains an explicit clause stating that the governor can be dismissed if the inflation target is exceeded. Our rankings are based on the older law.

Table 13. Economic independence of central banks

Countries	Monetary financing of budget deficit					Monetary instruments		Index of economic independence
	(1)	(2)	(3)	(4)	(5)	(6)	(7)	(8)
Australia	*	*	*	*	*	*		6
Austria			*	*	*	*	**	6
Belgium		*		*	*	*	**	6
Canada	*	*	*	*		*	**	7
Denmark		*			*	*	**	5
France				*	*	*	**	5
Germany	*	*	*	*	*	*	*	7
Greece				*		*		2
Ireland		*	*	*		*		4
Italy				*				1
Japan	*		*		*	*	*	5
Netherlands			*	*	*	*		4
New Zealand			*	*		*		3
Portugal				*		*		2
Spain			*	*			*	3
Switzerland		*	*	*	*	*	**	7
UK	*	*	*	*		*		5
US	*	*	*	*	*	*	*	7

Sources: See Appendix C.
Notes: (1) Direct credit facility: not automatic; (2) Direct credit facility: market interest rate; (3) Direct credit facility: temporary; (4) Direct credit facility: limited amount; (5) Central bank does not participate in primary market for public debt; (6) Discount rate set by central bank; (7) Banking supervision *not* entrusted to the central bank (**) or not entrusted to the central bank alone (*); (8) Overall index of economic independence (being the sum of the asterisks in columns 1–7). See Appendix C for more detailed information.

the quantity and the conditions on which it borrows from the central bank, it also influences the creation of monetary base and lessens the economic independence of the central bank. The first five columns of Table 13 summarize the government's ease of access to central bank credit. This can be done in two ways: through direct credit facilities (columns 1–4), and by purchasing government securities in the primary market (column 5: a star indicates that the central bank does not participate as a buyer in this market and is more free from implicit or explicit pressures to lend to the government). Economic independence of the central bank is greater if direct credit to the government is: non-automatic (column 1), at a market interest rate (column 2), explicitly stated as temporary (column 3), and in a limited amount (column 4).

The second aspect, the nature of the monetary instruments under the control of the central bank, is described in the next two columns of Table 13. If the central bank does not have control of the discount rate, its ability to determine the general level of interest rates is severely impaired. Column 6 reveals that most, but not all, central banks are responsible for setting the discount rate. Column 7 is concerned with banking supervision, in particular administrative instruments such as portfolio constraints on bank intermediaries or ceilings to private bank loans. Such instruments facilitate the financing of government borrowing by administratively increasing the private demand for government securities. They can weaken central bank independence by removing part of monetary control from the market. In column 7 we classify as most independent (denoted with two stars) a bank that has no responsibility for bank supervision, as relatively independent (denoted with one star) a bank that is sharing responsibility for bank supervision with some other institution, and as least independent (no asterisk) a bank which is the only institution in charge of bank supervision.

As before, to determine the overall degree of economic independence of the central bank, we add up the attributes. The resulting indicator appears in the last column of Table 13. Economic independence of the central bank is high in West Germany, Switzerland, the US, but also in Austria and Belgium. Conversely, central banks in Italy, New Zealand, Portugal, Greece and Spain have very little economic independence. Interestingly, political and economic independence are not always positively correlated. Thus a ranking that pays attention to only one of the two dimensions can give rise to very misleading international comparisons.

5.1.3. Central bank independence and seigniorage. Figure 3 summarizes Tables 12 and 13 showing the overall degree of economic and political independence of the 18 countries under consideration. Four groups of countries are identifiable. Those in the upper-right portion of the diagram have the most independent central banks, those which enjoy both political and economic independence. The countries on the lower-left portion have the least independent central banks, both economically and politically. The remaining two groups of countries are in between, with monetary institutions independent in only one of the two dimensions.

It is instructive to compare Figure 3 with Figure 1 and Table 9. Of the four countries with highly dependent central banks (Greece, New Zealand, Portugal and Spain), three (Greece, Portugal and Spain) also have highly unstable political systems and unsustainable debt paths. These are the three countries with the highest level of seigniorage. Other politically unstable countries also have unsustainable debt policies (Austria, Belgium, Ireland, Italy and the Netherlands), but they have relatively independent central banks, at least on one dimension. These

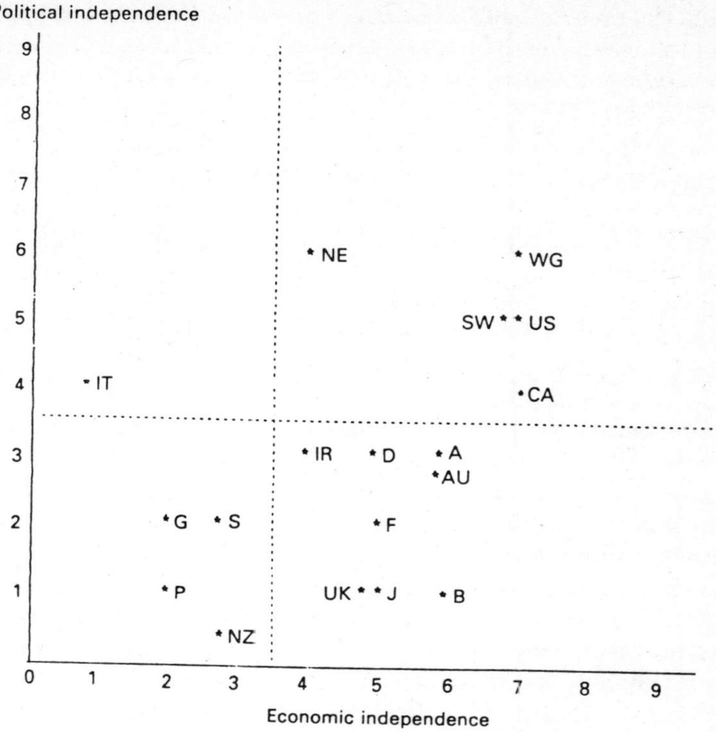

A = Australia
AU = Austria
B = Belgium
CA = Canada
D = Denmark
F = France
WG = West Germany
G = Greece
IR = Ireland
IT = Italy
J = Japan
NE = Netherlands
NZ = New Zealand
P = Portugal
S = Spain
SW = Switzerland
UK = United Kingdom
US = United States

Figure 3. Political and economic independence of central banks
Source: As Tables 12 and 13.

other countries (with the exception of Italy and possibly Ireland) collect much smaller seigniorage revenues. These facts suggest that central bank independence may bring about monetary stability and low inflation even if there are political incentives towards lax budgetary policies. It also means that a European monetary union among countries with very different debt policies is feasible provided that the monetary authorities face adequate incentives and independence.

5.2. Central bank independence and economic performance

To find out whether inflation is related to central bank independence, we divide the period 1950–89 into four decades and measure the effect

Table 14. Inflation and central bank independence (Dependent variable: inflation)

Explanatory variables	1950–59	1960–69	1970–79	1980–89	1950–89
Intercept	5.288**	4.457**	17.183**	18.670**	11.637**
	(1.252)	(0.679)	(1.108)	(1.934)	(0.148)
Economic independence	−0.167	−0.135	−1.211**	−1.913**	−0.897**
	(0.261)	(0.142)	(0.231)	(0.402)	(0.148)
Political independence	−0.266	−0.101	−0.611*	−0.429	−0.0277
	(0.275)	(0.149)	(0.243)	(0.431)	(0.0163)
EMS	—	—	—	−0.685	−0.854
	—	—	—	(0.927)	(0.541)
$\bar{R}^2$	0.109	0.111	0.745	0.658	0.782
SE	2.061	1.118	1.825	3.249	1.039

Notes: Standard errors in parenthesis. A* (**) denotes significance at the 5% (1%) level. The system is estimated by seemingly unrelated regressions, except for the last column, which is estimated by OLS.

of the indicators presented in the previous section on cross-country differences in inflation rates (using seemingly unrelated regressions). An interesting question is the role played by the EMS. For high inflation countries like Italy, participation in the EMS may have strengthened the independence of the central bank *vis-a-vis* the national government because it has increased its commitment to price stability. This argument does not necessarily hold for low inflation countries, like West Germany, since the EMS has transformed a technical issue (exchange rate management) into a major political issue (whether or not to realign the EMS parities) on which the government may have more to say than the central bank. For this reason, we treat EMS participation as a separate dimension of the regime, not included in the ranking of central bank independence. This is done by including a dummy variable that takes a value of 1 for the EMS countries and 0 otherwise in the regressions for the 1980s.

Table 14 reports the estimated effects on inflation of the indicators of economic and political central bank independence plus the EMS dummy for the last decade. The indicators of central bank independence always have the expected (negative) sign. The indicator of economic independence is significant in the periods of high inflation, while the indicator of political independence is significant only in the 1970s. On the other hand, the estimated coefficient of the EMS dummy is not significantly different from zero. The results also hold for the average inflation rate throughout the whole period 1950–89, as shown in the last column. So monetary institutions matter, indirectly, through their effects on credibility, and directly, by shaping the central bank incentives. Our results also confirm previous findings obtained by other authors for a different sample of countries and a slightly different

Table 15. Inflation, political instability and central bank independence (Dependent variable: inflation)

Explanatory variables	1950–69	1960–69	1970–79	1980–89	1950–89
Intercept	8.419**	4.329**	6.76*	16.653**	10.343**
	(1.716)	(1.040)	(3.186)	(2.941)	(1.454)
FREQUENCY	1.661	−0.363	5.944**	6.008*	0.076
	(0.103)	(0.705)	(1.838)	(0.678)	(1.295)
SIGNIFICANT	4.037	−0.084	6.785*	24.592**	7.423
	(2.185)	(2.222)	(2.895)	(4.714)	(3.471)
MAJORITY	−0.018	−0.002	0.020	−0.012	−0.008
	(0.009)	(0.006)	(0.013)	(0.019)	(0.009)
Independence	−0.453**	−0.087	−0.327	−1.093**	−0.559**
	(0.146)	(0.088)	(0.208)	(0.226)	(0.108)
EMS	—	—		−1.112	−1.126
				(1.204)	(0.675)
$\bar{R}^2$	0.206	−0.186	0.796	0.760	0.748
SE	1.720	1.101	1.533	2.473	1.117

Notes: Standard errors in parenthesis. A* (**) denotes significance at the 5% (1%) level. Columns (1)–(4) are estimated by seemingly unrelated regressions. Column 5 is estimated by ordinary least squares.

ranking of independence (see Bade and Parkin, 1982 and Alesina, 1989).

Central bank independence might conceivably be related to the broad political characteristics used in the analysis of budget deficits. To check whether this is the case, we have included the variables *FREQUENCY*, *SIGNIFICANT* and *MAJORITY* as additional regressors. To save on degrees of freedom, we sum together the two measures of central bank independence to obtain a single indicator.[17] The results which appear in Table 15, show that central bank independence always has a negative estimated effect on inflation, and that is is significant half of the time. The political variables also play a role, but their coefficient is often not of the expected sign. Estimates over the whole period (last column) confirms the greater importance of central bank independence as compared to political variables.

One of the alleged benefits of an independent central bank is that it is more credible in its resolve not to engage in public financing. This may affect the Treasury's behaviour, reducing the likelihood of unsustainable debt policies (see, for instance, Tabellini, 1987a). This hypothesis

[17] The same results are obtained if we use instead a ranking of 1 to 4, corresponding to the four quadrants of Figure 3, or if we use the two indicators separately, again with economic independence being more important than political independence. Finally, similar results are obtained if some of the political variables are omitted.

Table 16. Central bank independence and real macroeconomic performance

Dependent variables/ explanatory variables	Output growth	Standard error of output growth
Intercept	0.042**	0.071*
	(0.008)	(0.025)
Economic independence	−0.0009	−0.005
	(0.001)	(0.005)
Political independence	0.002	−0.001
	(0.001)	(0.005)
EMS	−0.007	0.013
	(0.006)	(0.018)
$\bar{R}^2$	−0.070	−0.013
SE	0.012	0.035

Notes: Standard errors in parenthesis. A *(**) denotes significance at the 5% (1%) level. Each equation is separately estimated by OLS. Each observation is the average over the 1950–87 period.

receives no support from the data. In a regression of the primary deficit on the political variables *FREQUENCY, SIGNIFICANT* and *MAJORITY*, and the overall indicator of central bank independence, *INDEP*, the latter variable is always insignificant (though generally with a negative estimated coefficient). The coefficient of the political variables, on the other hand, are not very different from those reported in the previous section. Similar results are obtained if the primary deficit is replaced by net debt accumulation.

Finally, does central bank independence come with a cost in overall macroeconomic performance? For the whole period, we find no systematic effect of the two indicators of central bank independence on the real growth rate of real output. In Table 16, even though central bank independence seems to be associated with lower output growth, the estimated effect is generally insignificant. The same results are obtained if the regressions are estimated by averaging the data over the four decades, if the political variables are added as regressors, or if we replace the growth rate with the rate of unemployment (in this last case, the EMS dummy has a positive and significant estimated coefficient).[18] Hence, it does not seem that there is a sharp tradeoff in the design of monetary institutions. A more independent central bank brings

[18] Alesina and Summers (1990) independently obtained similar results based on a different sample of countries and a central bank ranking analogous to our political independence index.

about low inflation, but not necessarily worse real macroeconomic performance.

6. Summary and conclusions

The striking differences in the public financial policies of the industrialized countries throughout the post-war period cannot be explained as the optimal government response to different shocks or to different initial conditions. A more convicing explanation is that the governments of these countries were subject to different political or economic incentives, and as a result they enacted different policies. Four main results emerge.

First, the accumulation of large public debts is concentrated among countries characterized by (i) representational democracies (as opposed to majoritarian parliamentary democracies and presidential democracies); and (ii) fractionalized party systems. These institutional features induce budget deficits because they lead to short-lived governments.

Second, while countries that extensively rely on seigniorage also have high public debt, the converse is not true. In some high debt countries seigniorage is a trivial source of revenue. These countries share the characteristic of having an independent central bank. In general, central bank independence leads to low inflation, irrespective of political institutions and budgetary problems. At the same time, monetary independence does not discourage budget deficits. Monetary and fiscal discipline thus seem to be orthogonal to each other: a country can have either, both or neither of them, depending on its monetary and political institutions.

Third, if central bank independence is on average associated with lower inflation, there is no systematic impact on real output growth, nor on its variability. Thus having an independent central bank is almost like having a free lunch; there are benefits but no apparent costs in terms of macroeconomic performance.

Fourth, there is very little evidence that over time the inflation tax is caused by lax budgetary policies or that it is used efficiently. Few countries use seigniorage and regular taxes as complementary sources of revenues. And in most countries changes in government spending are absorbed by changes in regular taxes rather than by changes in the inflation tax.

These findings have some important implications for the ongoing debate over the feasibility and appropriate sequencing of the European monetary integration. On the one hand, they suggest that there is no need to subordinate monetary integration to having first achieved fiscal convergence. The future European Central Bank has been designed to be very independent from the national governments and from the European Commission. On our criteria, it would be one of the most – if not the most – independent of all OECD central banks. Our results suggest that this should be sufficient to insulate the common European monetary policy from the accommodating pressure coming from the budget deficits of some countries.

On the other hand, there is a case for accompanying monetary integration with some budgetary rules binding on the national governments. Such rules may be in the interest of the high debt countries. Because debt accumulation in the representational democracies is probably due to some domestic political distortion, binding external rules – such as a balanced budget on current expenditures and revenues – may act as an offsetting force and hence be welfare improving. As for monetary policy, one of the advantages of joining an international ageement may consist in 'tying one's hands', in this case, the hands of the fiscal authorities.

There is one additional, historical, argument in favour of fiscal rules in a new European monetary constitution. Our finding that the lack of fiscal discipline does not necessarily lead to monetary instability only relates to the post-war period. This period, however, may be too short and, as recently argued by Giovannini and Spaventa (1991), the real challenges for the European monetary union are more likely to come from the management of the high stocks of public debt. Furthermore, the pre-war experience indicates that fiscal crises and public debt runs did occur, and were often accompanied by monetary instability. For this reason, the credibility of a unified European monetary system would be enhanced by fiscal rules that guaranteed the long-run solvency of the high debt countries.

Discussion

Edmond Malinvaud
College de France

Since it is well recognized that the institutions of a country play a role in the choice and efficiency of its economic policy, one can only be pleased when witnessing the recent trend toward serious studies of this role. The present paper adds to the flow of such studies, to which the authors have already contributed on other occasions.

Before addressing the paper itself, I shall make a general comment. When discussing the politics or the institutional conditions of economic policy, we are entering a field in which scientific experience is definitely still less advanced than in economics *stricto sensu*. We must then be particularly careful not to rush too quickly to the type of supposedly hard theory and econometrics that our professional journals like; there is a serious danger that the hypotheses of our theories and econometric tests miss important points. I cannot help remembering in this respect what Sir John Hicks used to say, namely that economists should pay more attention to history. Indeed, historical research shows that the relevant aspects of institutions are multifarious; moreover a knowledge of history is required for the proper identification of institutional changes.

The challenge to research workers is all the greater as the most relevant empirical proofs about the role of institutions in the modern world will come from intercountry comparisons. If they are to be at all rigorous, these comparisons require good data bases, which moreover have to include a large number of countries so as to reduce the risk of inferring unwarranted conclusions from particular cases. But new research hardly ever finds available the reliable data base it needs; some work has to be devoted to data collection. A difficulty then comes from the fact that one cannot expect any author, or even any team of authors, to know all the historical circumstances that mattered for each of the countries considered. This is why attention should be devoted to improving the data bases and to put on record any hidden national specificity that may exist or have occurred.

The article contains very interesting new material on the institutions of the industrialized OECD countries. In Tables 4 to 6 and Appendix B the authors have collected a quantity of data concerning the political conditions of budgetary policy decisions. Similarly Tables 12 and 13, supported by Appendix C, present indicators of central bank independence. Motivated by the above considerations and of course not meaning to downgrade the usefulness of the material, I carefully looked at the part concerning my country about which my life gave me opportunities to be directly informed. Here is what I find worth reporting.

I am surprised to see in Table B1 three 'significant government changes' in the decade 1960–69, while de Gaulle had consistently strong power up to the spring of 1969 (a change of the party of the prime minister had really no significant consequence). But my main comment is for saying that the Banque de France is given a higher degree of independence than it really has. In particular one reads in Table C1 that the term of the governor is 'indefinite' and this gives a star to France in column 2 of Table 12; the adjective 'indefinite' is confusing since in fact the governor can be removed any time by decision of the French President: governor Wormser was immediately dismissed in 1974 after an article he had published in a widely read daily newspaper and governor de la Geniere was replaced in 1984 exactly five years after his appointment; in neither case was the political decision welcomed by the outgoing governor. Similarly, the double star granted to France in column 7 of Table 13 is explained in Table C4 by the fact that banking supervision is not entrusted to the central bank but to the 'Banking Commission'; everybody in France considers this commission, chaired by the governor, as belonging to Banque de France where it has its quarters.

I repeat: these comments should not be seen as negative but as constructive. They are meant to induce others to check how the particular features of their own countries are translated into simple numerical scores. The translation has to be made in order to serve as input for international comparison; but a margin of more or less subjective appreciation cannot be avoided and should be as enlightened as possible.

This also means an additional source of possible inaccuracy in the cross-section regressions from which conclusions are drawn. International cross-sections are notoriously exposed to errors due to omission of variables that have not been identified as potential explanatory factors (and there are many). Measurement fuzziness on the variables taken as regressors uncomfortably adds to the problem.

The authors convincingly argue when they identify five to seven countries 'that are most likely to be on an unsustainable debt path' if no major step is taken for jumping out of this path. The conclusion naturally emerges from Table 3 and Figure 1. Footnote 3 and Appendix A are meant to support the conclusion; but the support is weak both because of the overly simple nature of the intertemporal model in which the question is being placed and because of the still uncertain validity of the econometric technique.

Experts in econometric methodology have not yet reached the point where they will agree as to the proper way of selecting between two models for the representation of a given time series: a model involving a deterministic trend perturbed by a stationary shock process and a model in which the shock process would have a unit root. (The now standard theory of testing for unit root applies when the maintained hypothesis is a pure autoregressive process.) One thing is sure, however: the procedure that will eventually be recommended will have poor power unless the autoregressive representation of the underlying stochastic process involves only few important coefficients, these coefficients concerning small lags. Power and robustness will *a fortiori* be weak when similar but more complex tests are generally accepted for dealing with such questions as the long-run sustainability of public finance patterns.

Part 3 of the article studies whether different political incentives provide the proper explanation for different public finance patterns. It indeed finds that high public deficits occur in representational democracies and are the direct consequence of the weakness of the executive or of government instability. This looks like a sensible conclusion, which many people had accepted before, General de Gaulle being one notable example: his 1959 constitution was aimed at eradicating political instability from France; for so doing it replaced a representational democracy by a strong presidential democratic regime. But one may be pleased to see that what may have looked to be a purely intuitive idea now passes the test of scientific examination.

In this respect the paper, however, leaves us with a puzzle. The regressions tell us that the frequency of any kind of government change is what really matters: significant government changes do not emerge as playing a significantly higher role than insignificant ones. Since the conclusion is hard to fit within any sensible prior set of ideas, I am tempted to be a Bayesian econometrican on this occasion and to say that this particular conclusion does not appear in my posterior for beliefs.

Finally, the authors identify as an important finding of their article that the inflation tax (seigniorage) and regular taxes do not appear as being complementary sources of government revenues. This finding seems to bother them because it is hard to reconcile with the principle of optimal taxation. Is there anyone seriously claiming that optimal taxation theory can explain everything? Can it explain inflation in particular? For accepting the idea one has to assume first that the government decides the speed of inflation and second that it chooses it such as to generate the proper amount of seigniorage. Each one of these two assumptions appears so unrealistic that a formal test on their joint result has little interest. It could hardly change the views of those who believe that regular distorting taxes tend to be positively correlated, as predicted by optimal taxation theory. It teaches us nothing about actual monetary policy.

All in all, it is refreshing to read an article showing that General de Gaulle was right and that scholastic applications of optimal taxation theory are wrong.

Marco Pagano
Università de Napoli

Grilli, Masciandaro and Tabellini have provided an original and valuable contribution to the fast-growing literature on politics and macroeconomic policy. Fairness requires that I dwell first on the numerous merits of their paper, and leave my few complaints to the end.

One virtue of this paper is that, being an empirical study, it goes some way towards filling a vacuum in the political economy literature, that has so far produced a wealth of theoretical models, but few tests of their predictions. After reading this paper, even the skeptical reader is left with the impression that this literature can provide important insights into the actual determinants of policy-making, and in some cases may help in predicting future policy choices.

A second merit of this paper is its wide scope. The predictions subjected to scrutiny concern the choice between debt and taxes as well as that between taxes and seigniorage, and relate each of these choices to several features of political and monetary institutions, for as many as 18 OECD countries.

Thirdly, the authors are to be praised for the impressive data-gathering effort that is behind their empirical work. I know of no previous study that assembles and exploits such a vest array of data and indicators on political and monetary institutions for so many countries. I expect the data appendices of this paper to make as lasting a contribution to future research as the work reported in the rest of the study.

Fourthly, as one would expect from successful applied work, the paper does indeed reject some models in favour of others, and points to useful directions for further theoretical research, especially in the area of fiscal policy. This 'weeding out' exercise is especially important in an area that has witnessed a proliferation of theoretical models in recent years.

The most interesting empirical result in this sense is that over-accumulation of public debt is associated not with political instability and polarization (as in the models of Alesina and Tabellini, 1990, Persson and Sevensson, 1989 and Tabellini and Alesina, 1990) but rather with frequent changes of government, irrespective of whether they involve significant changes in political leadership or not. To understand the importance of this distinction, consider the case of Italy: the Italian political leadership has been extraordinarily stable in the post-war period, while the average life span of governments in Rome has been less than a year – shorter than in any other country analysed in this study. More generally, the distinction between instability and frequency of government changes is important in all the countries typically ruled by coalition governments, where changes of government are rarely due to a total breakdown of the underlying coalition.

Insofar as frequent changes of government simply reflect conflict between different power groups within the ruling coalition, its association with over-accumulation of debt can be read as providing support for another group of models that attribute postponement of unpopular choices to the 'war of attrition' between policy-makers (Tabellini, 1986, Alesina and Drazen, 1989, Drazen and Grilli, 1990 and Sanguinetti, 1990). In this view, governments are 'weak' because they are torn by internal conflict. To my knowledge, however, a model showing explicitly that power struggles within ruling coalitions lead both to frequent government changes and to over-accumulation of debt has not yet been proposed in the literature. Such a model would be a good description of Italian politics, where each coalition member constantly attempts to extend its power base at the expense of the others, by channeling public spending towards its own constitutency or by preserving the latter's 'de facto' tax privileges. This competition leads on the one hand to frequent government break-ups, and on the other to a bias towards deficit financing to pay for the fiscal privileges of special interest groups.

Apart from its descriptive value (which would go well beyond the case of Italy), such a model could perhaps tell us when to expect this disruptive rivalry between ruling parties to arise. It could, for instance, explain whether it is made more likely by the fractionalization of the party system or by the absence of alternative coalitions (whereby some of the ruling parties could be replaced by opposition parties).

Before concluding, I want to mention a couple of aspects of the paper that I find questionable. One relates to the criterion used to select the countries that place 'excessive' reliance on debt as a source of financing. The authors use 'solvency tests' to identify these countries. They argue that a government whose current policies are not sustainable is not using debt efficiently, since it will eventually have to increase taxes – and tax distortions – by more than if it had pursued sustainable policies from the start. However, leaving aside the many criticisms that could be levelled against solvency tests (some of which are acknowledged by the authors), in the present context they are simply unnecessary: the analysis conducted in the rest of the paper purports to show that some institutional features are more conductive to a greater bias towards deficit financing than others, but not that they necessarily lead to insolvency. Another objectionable aspect of the paper is the authors' disregard for non-political factors in shaping choices about fiscal or monetary policy. In their effort to make a case for the importance of political factors, the authors neglect other likely sources of international differences in debt accumulation and inflation rates. Even granting that the 18 OECD countries they examine have been hit by the same exogenous shocks in the post-war period, structural differences among these economies can go a long way towards explaining different responses to these shocks. For instance, the cross-country variation in inflation rates may be explained by international differences in labour relations systems, wage indexation mechanisms, degree of vulnerability to oil or materials price shocks and preferences for inflation versus unemployment. The role played by these factors can be as important as that played by the political and economic independence of the central bank.

General discussion

A number of panel members wondered about theoretical underpinnings to the presumption that government weakness could be captured by attributes such as single party majority, durability and stability. Damien Neven argued that counter-examples could certainly be found to the presumption that large coalitions are weaker than smaller ones; in Belgium, coalitions which include: a large number of members tend to be rather more stable and durable than small ones. Some more refined measure of the power enjoyed by any particular party, like its Shapley value, might therefore prove useful in the analysis.

John Vickers felt that a better theory of government would be useful to explore the link between deficits and government weakness, however measured. He suggested that the theory of delegation, developed in industrial organization, could find a useful application in this regard. There is indeed a parallel between the principles which guide the choice of a manager by shareholders and the choice and representatives by the electorate. Paul Seabright added that the well known problem of aggregating the diversity of people's political preferences should be carefully considered. When these problems are severe, a sequence of seemingly irrational decions can result from independently rational moves.

Sweder van Wijnbergen indicated that the authors should not be apologetic regarding their inability to distinguish between current and capital expenditure in testing for the sustainability of debt accumulation. given that government investments have by and large fallen over the last decade, the authors' results would probably be strengthened if a proper distinction could be made.

Richard Baldwin suggested that the cross-section evidence presented by the authors could be supplemented by careful case studies of regime changes. For example, a study of France, Spain and Portugal could provide useful insights.

Axel Weber finally noticed that the lack of economic independence of the central bank took a particular form in Germany, which is not captured by the data. The Bundesbank's profits, which are substantial, accrue to the treasury; the treasury anticipates this income from the bank in budget planning and the Bundesbank is under pressure to distribute its profits even though such distribution might conflict with its primary objectives insofar as it has inflationary consequences.

Appendix A. Tests of debt sustainability

There is a large literature on how to test Equation (3) in footnote 3. The literature originates with Hamilton and Flavin (1986) with more recent contributions from Wilcox (1989), Trehan and Walsh (1988) and Grilli (1989). A problem with all of this literature, which is present also in our paper, is the failure to distinguish between current and capital public expenditure, for lack of consistent data. This distinction matters because capital expenditures are presumably self-financing, since they generate future revenues. Hence treating all expenditures as current amounts to underestimating future revenues. On the other hand, the probability of a war – and high military spending – is positive even during peacetime, so there is a risk that future expenditures are likely to exceed actually observed expenditures. These two effects tend to offset each other.

The idea is to check for the stationarity of the (appropriately discounted) debt or of the total (i.e. inclusive of interest payments) deficit. One critical problem of this approach is that the appropriate discount factor, q, is not observable. Bohn (1990) shows that the discount factor varies across states of nature and time, depending on the stochastic properties of output and government spending, and does not necessarily bear any relationship with the expected or realized rate of return on government debt. These tests, therefore, are really joint tests of the stationarity hypothesis and of the assumption made about q. Here we present results obtained using the technique suggested by Trehan and Walsh (1988). Their method tests Equation (3) under the assumption that q, even if not observable, is approximately constant over time.[19] Trehan and Walsh (1988) show that, under this assumption, and if the underlying expenditure and revenue series are stationary in first differences, a necessary and sufficient condition for (3) to hold is that the deficit inclusive of interest (as a percentage of GNP) is a stationary variable with zero drift.[20] To test the null hypothesis that the deficit is non-stationary, we proceed as follows (see also Perron, 1988). First we test the existence of a unit root against the more general alternative of a stationary autoregressive model with drift and time trend. This is the $Z(\tau\tau)$ test. If rejection of the unit root is not possible, we test the existence

[19] We also tried other tests of (3), along the lines of Wilcox (1989). But they were unable to discriminate across countries; we could not reject the hypothesis that all countries were on an unsustainable path. This test presupposes that the correct rate of return with which to discount the budget constraint coincides with the realized real rate on government debt. As noted by Bohn (1990), however, this presumption is very likely to be incorrect.

[20] Since we did not subtract seigniorage from the deficit, we are not consolidating the balance sheets of the Treasury and the central bank together. Thus our test of the transversality condition (3) applies to the sum of the debt held by the private sector and by the central bank.

Table A1. Unit root tests (total deficit/GNP)

	$Z(\tau\tau)$	$Z(\Phi_2)$	$Z(\tau\mu)$	$Z(\tau)$
US	99%			
UK	—	—	—	—
Austria	—	—	—	—
Belgium	—	—	—	—
Denmark	—	—	—	97.5%
France	—	—	—	95%
Germany	99%			
Italy	—	—	—	—
Netherlands	90%			
Switzerland	99%			
Canada	99%			
Japan	na	na	na	na
Greece	—	—	—	—
Ireland	—	—	—	—
Portugal	—	—	—	—
Spain	—	—	—	—
Australia	—	—	—	90%
New Zealand	95%			

Notes: $Z(\tau\tau)$ – H1: autoregressive model with drift and time trend; $Z(\Phi_2)$ – joint hypothesis of unit root and no drift; $Z(\tau\mu)$ – H1: autoregressive model with drift; $Z(\tau)$ – H1: pure autoregressive model; x% = confidence level for rejection of unit root; — = rejection of unit root is not possible at conventional confidence levels.

Table B1. Government instability and political instability

	Frequency				Significant			
Country	1950–59	1960–69	1970–79	1980–89	1950–59	1960–69	1970–79	1980–89
Australia	0	3	5	1	1	0	2	1
Austria	5	5	3	2	0	0	1	0
Belgium	8	4	8	8	2	0	2	0
Canada	1	3	3	3	1	1	1	2
Denmark	4	5	6	4	2	1	3	1
France	15	5	5	6	9	3	1	3
Germany	5	9	3	3	0	1	0	1
Greece	15	16	7	3	3	4	1	2
Ireland	5	2	8	6	3	0	2	3
Italy	8	10	11	13	0	0	0	4
Japan	8	4	5	7	1	0	0	0
Netherlands	2	4	3	3	1	2	3	0
New Zealand	2	1	5	1	1	1	2	1
Portugal	3	1	15	8	0	0	4	4
Spain	0	2	12	6	0	0	1	1
Switzerland	10	8	6	1	2	0	0	0
UK	4	2	4	0	1	1	3	0
US	1	3	2	2	1	2	1	1

Sources: Jodice and Taylor (1982), Banks (1987), Keasing Archives, various years.
Notes: Frequency = Number of government changes for the decade; Significant = Number of 'significant' government changes for the decade.

Table C1. Central bank governor

Country	Governor appointed by	Term (years)	Reappointability
Belgium	Sovereign (i.e. Government)	Five	Yes
Denmark	Sovereign	Indefinite	—
France	President	Indefinite	—
Germany	President proposal of the Government	Eight	—
Greece	Government proposal of the bank	Four	Yes
Ireland	President proposal of the Government	Seven	Yes
Italy	Bank Board approval of the Government	Indefinite	—
Netherlands	Sovereign (i.e. Government) proposal of the bank	Seven	Yes
Portugal	Government	Five	Yes
UK	Sovereign proposal of the Government	Five	Yes
Spain	Sovereign proposal of the Government	Four	Yes
Switzerland	Government	Six	Yes
Australia	Government	Seven	Yes
Canada	Board	Seven	Yes
Japan	Government	Five	Yes
New Zealand	Government	Five	Yes
US	President	Four	Yes
Austria	President	Five	Yes

Sources: Aufricht (1967) and national legislation.

of the unit root against more restrictive alternatives i.e. a stationary autoregression model with drift ($Z(\tau\mu)$) and a pure autoregressive model ($Z(\tau)$). However, in order to be able to apply these two tests, we first check for the existence of drift which is done by testing the joint hypothesis of unit root and no drift ($Z(\Phi_2)$). If the hypothesis of no drift is rejected, in fact, the more specialized tests cannot be used. The results are shown in Table A1. Note that for the UK the evidence of non-stationarity is clearly due to the implosive path of the debt to GNP ratio, and hence it cannot be taken as evidence of unsustainability.

Appendix B. Indicators of government attributes

The political event data used to construct the variables *FREQUENCY* and *SIGNIFICANT* of Table 8 are reported in Table B1.

Appendix C. Indicators of central bank independence

The institutional information used to construct our indicators of central bank independence is summarized in Tables C1–C4.

Table C2. Central bank board

Country	Board appointed by	Members (*)	Term (years)	Reappointment	Government inst. representatives
Belgium	Sovereign (i.e. Government)	3–6	Six	Yes	Yes Government Commissioner (advisory/suspensive rights)
Denmark	Parliament (8); Trade Min. (2); Bank Board (15)	25	Five	Yes	Yes Minister of Trade (supervisory right)
France	Minister of Finance (9) Bank (1)	10	Six	Yes	Yes Director Minister of Finance (advisory/suspensive right)
Germany	President proposal Government	8	Eight	—	No
Greece	Shareholders General Meeting	9	Three	Yes	Yes Government Commissioner (suspensive right)

Table C2—continued

Country	Board appointed by	Members (*)	Term (years)	Reappointment	Government inst. representatives
Ireland	Government	3–8	Five	—	Yes Permanent Secretary Minister of Finance ?
Italy	Shareholders Regional Meetings	13	Three	Yes	No
Netherlands	Sovereign (i.e. Government)	3–5	Seven	Yes	No (yes in the Bank Council: Royal Commissioner)
Portugal	Government	7–9	Five	Yes	No (yes in the General Council)
UK	Sovereign (i.e. Government)	16	Four	—	No
Spain	Government (6); Min. Fin. (2) Governor (1–4); Bank (1)	10–14	Two	—	No
Switzerland	Government (25) Bank (15)	40	Four	Yes	No
Australia	Government	7	Five	Yes	Yes Secretary of Treasury (voting right)
Canada	Government	12	Three	Yes	Yes Deputy Minister of Finance (advisory right)
Japan	Government (4); Econ. Ag. & Min. Fin. (2)	6	Four	Yes	Yes Representatives Min. of Finance Min. Ec. Planning (advisory right)
New Zealand	Government	5	Five	Yes	Yes Secretary of the Treasury (casting vote)
US	President	5	Fourteen	No	No
Austria	Government (5) Sh. Gen. Meeting (6)	11	Five	Yes	Yes Government Commissioner (advisory and suspensive right)

Source: Aufricht (1967) and national legislation.
Note: (*) except Governor and Vice-Governor(s), government representative(s).

Table C3. Government financing accommodation: monetary and regulatory framework

	Monetary framework		Regulatory framework		
Country	Direct Cred. (characters)	Primary Issue	Central Bank	Other institutions	Government
Belgium	OVERDRAFT * limited * automatic * disc. rate * no terms	No	—	Banking Commission	—
Denmark	OVERDRAFT * unlimited * automatic * disc. rate * no terms	No	—	Supervisor of Comm. Banks & Savings Bank	—
France	OVERDRAFT * limited * automatic * no rate * no terms	No	—	Banking commission	—
Germany	ADVANCES * limited * discretion * disc. rate * terms (3 m)	No	Yes	Federal Banking Supervisory Office	—
Greece	ADVANCES * limited * automatic * symbolic rate * terms	Yes	Yes	—	—
Ireland	OVERDRAFT * limited * automatic * terms (m) * market rate	Yes	Yes	—	—
Italy	OVERDRAFT * limited * automatic * symbolic rate * no terms	Yes	Yes	—	—
Netherlands	OVERDRAFT * limited * automatic * no rate * terms	No	Yes	—	—
Portugal	OVERDRAFT * limited * automatic *no rate * terms (1 y)	Yes	Yes	—	—
UK	No	Yes	Yes	—	—

Table C3—continued

Country	Monetary framework: Direct Cred. (characters)	Monetary framework: Primary Issue	Regulatory framework: Central Bank	Regulatory framework: Other institutions	Regulatory framework: Government
Spain	OVERDRAFT * limited * automatic * no rate *terms (1 y)	Yes	Yes	—	Ministry of finance
Switzerland	OVERDRAFT * limited * automatic * market rate * terms (m)	No	—	Federal Banking Commission	—
Australia	OVERDRAFT * limited * discretion * m. rate * terms	No	Yes	—	—
Canada	ADVANCES * limited * discretion * bank rate * terms	Yes	—	General Inspector of Banks	—
Japan	ADVANCES * limited * discretion * no m. rate * terms	No	Yes	—	Ministry of Finance
US	No	No	Yes	Comptroller of the Currency FDIC FHLB	
Austria	Advances * limited * automatic * no m. rate * terms (d)	No	—	—	Ministry of Finance

Sources: Aufricht (1967) and national legislation.

Table C4. Central bank, government and accountability

Country	Relation with Government	Relation with Parliament	Monetary stability objective	Provisions in case of disagreement Central Bank-Gov't
Belgium	Approval	Through Government	No	Yes Government directives
Denmark	Consultation	Annual report	Yes	No
France	Approval	Through Government	No	No
Germany	Consultation	Not accountable	Yes	Yes temporary post-position
Greece	Consultation		No	Yes Arbitration Commission
Ireland	Consultation	Annual report	Yes	No
Italy	Approval	On Call	No	Yes Government directives
Netherlands	Consultation	Through Government	Yes	Yes Government directives
Portugal	Approval	Through Government	No	Yes Government directives
UK	Approval	Through Government Annual report	No	No
Spain	Approval	Through Government	Yes	No
Switzerland	Consultation	Annual report	Yes	No (independence guarantee)
Australia	Approval	Annual report	Yes	Yes Government directives informing Parliament
Canada	Approval	On call	Yes	Yes Government directives informing Parliament
Japan	Approval	Approval	Yes	No
New Zealand	Approval	Annual report	No	No
US	Consultation	Approval	Yes	Yes Parliament directives
Austria	Consultation	Not accountable	Yes	Yes Arbitration tribunal

Source: Aufricht (1967) and national legislation.

References

Aizenman, J. (1987). 'Inflation, Tariffs and Tax Enforcement Costs', *Journal of International Economic Integration.*

—— (1989). 'Competitive Externalities and the Optimal Seigniorage', mimeo, NBER Working Paper No. 2937.

Alesina, A. (1989). 'Inflation, Unemployment and Politics in Industrial Democracies', *Economic Policy.*

Alesina, A. and A. Drazen (1989). 'Why are Stabilizations Delayed?', mimeo, Harvard University.

Alesina, A. and L. Summers (1990). 'Central Bank Independence and Macroeconomic Performance: Some Comparative Evidence', mimeo, Harvard University.

Alesina, A. and G. Tabellini (1990). 'A Political Theory of Fiscal Deficits and Government Debt in a Democracy', *The Review of Economic Studies.*

Aufricht, H. (1967). *Central Banking Legislation*, International Monetary Fund Monograph Series, Washington D.C.

Bade, R. and M. Parkin (1982). 'Central Bank Laws and Inflation – A Comparative Analysis', mimeo, University of Western Ontario.

Banks, A. (1987). *The Political Handbook of the World.*

Barro, R. (1979). 'On the Determination of Public Debt', *Journal of Political Economy.*

—— (1986). 'The Behavior of US Deficits' in R. Gordon (ed.) *The American Business Cycle*, The University of Chicago Press, Chicago.

Bingham Powell, A. (1982). *Contemporary Democracies – Participation, Stability and Violence*, Harvard University Press, Cambridge.

Bohn, H. (1990), 'The Sustainability of Budget Deficits in a Stochastic Economy', mimeo, The Wharton School.

Drazen, A. and V. Grilli (1990). 'The Benefit of Crisis for Economic Reform', mimeo, Birkbeck College.

Edwards, S. and G. Tabellini (1990). 'Explaining Fiscal Policies and Inflation in Developing Countries', NBER Working Paper No. 3493.

—— (1991). 'Political Instability, Political Weakness and Inflation – An Empirical Analysis', mimeo, UCLA.

Faig, M. (1988). 'Characterization of the Optimal Tax on Money when it Functions as a Medium of Exchange', *Journal of Monetary Economics.*

Fair, D. (1978). 'Relationships between Central Banks and Governments in the Determination of Monetary Policy', SUERF Working Paper.

Giovannini, A. and L. Spaventa (1991). 'Fiscal Rules in the European Monetary Union: A No-entry Clause', CEPR Discussion Paper Nr. 516.

Grilli, V. (1989). 'Seigniorage in Europe', in M. De Cecco and A. Giovannini (eds.) *A European Central Bank?*, Cambridge University Press, London.

Hamilton, J. and M. Flavin (1986). 'On the Limitations of Government Borrowing: A Framework for Empirical Testing', *American Economic Review.*

Kimbrough, K. (1986). 'The Optimal Quantity of Money Rule in the Theory of Public Finance', *Journal of Monetary Economics.*

Lucas, R. and N. Stokey (1983). 'Optimal Fiscal and Monetary Policies in an Economy without Capital', *Journal of Monetary Economics.*

Mankiw, G. (1987). 'The Optimal Collection of Seignorage: Theory and Evidence', *Journal of Monetary Economics.*

Masciandaro, D. (1990). 'Central Bank Independence, Macroeconomic Models and Monetary Regimes', mimeo, Centre For Monetary and Financial Economics, Bocconi University.

Masciandaro, D. and G. Tabellini (1988). 'Monetary Regimes and Fiscal Deficits – A Comparative Analysis' in H. S. Cheng (ed.) *Monetary Policy in Pacific Basin Countries*, Kluwer Academic Publishers, Dordrecht.

Perron, P. (1988). 'Trend and Random Walks in Macroeconomic Time Series', *Journal of Economic Dynamics and Control.*

Persson, T. and L. Svensson (1989). 'Why a Stubborn Conservative Would Run a Deficit: Policy with Time Inconsistent Preferences', *Quarterly Journal of Economics.*

Persson, T. and G. Tabellini (1990). *Macroeconomic Policy Credibility and Politics*, London: Harwood Academic Publishers.

Phelps, E. (1973). 'Inflation in the Theory of Public Finance', *Swedish Journal of Economics.*

Poterba, J. and J. Rotemberg (1989). 'Inflation and Taxation with Optimizing Governments', *Journal of Money, Credit and Banking.*

Rae, D. (1967). *The Political Consequences of Electoral Laws*, Yale University Press, New Haven.

Rogoff, K. (1985). 'The Optimal Degree of Commitment to an Intermediate Monetary Target', *Quarterly Journal of Economics.*

Roubini, N. and J. Sachs (1988). 'Political and Economic Determinants of Budget Deficits in the Industrial Democracies', *European Economic Review.*

—— (1989). 'Government Spending and Budget Deficits in the Industrialized Countries', *Economic Policy.*

Sanguinetti, P. (1990). 'Fiscal Deficits and Federal Government', mimeo, UCLA.

Tabellini, G. (1986). 'Money, Debt and Deficits in a Dynamic Game', *Journal of Economic Dynamics and Control.*

Tabellini, G. (1987a). 'Central Bank Reputation and the Monetization of Budget Deficits', *Economic Inquiry.*

—— (1987b). 'Monetary and Fiscal Policy Coordination with a High Public Debt', in F. Giavazzi and L. Spaventa (eds.) *Surviving with a High Public Debt: Lessons from the Italian Experience*, Cambridge University Press, London.

Tabellini, G. and A. Alesina (1990). 'Voting on the Budget Deficit', *American Economic Review.*

Taylor, C. and D. Jodice (1983). *World Handbook of Political and Social Indicators*, Third Edition, Yale University Press, New Haven.

Trehan, B. and C. Walsh (1988). 'Common Trends, the Government Budget Constraint and Revenue Smoothing', *Journal of Economic Dynamics and Control.*

—— (1989). 'Seignorage and Tax Smoothing in the United States: 1914–1986', mimeo, UC Santa Cruz.

Wilcox, D. (1989). 'The Sustainability of Government Deficits: Implications of the Government Borrowing Constraint', *Journal of Money, Credit and Banking.*

[9]

THE WORLD BANK ECONOMIC REVIEW, VOL. 6, NO. 3: 353-398

Measuring the Independence of Central Banks and Its Effect on Policy Outcomes

Alex Cukierman, Steven B. Webb, and Bilin Neyapti

Making the central bank an agency with the mandate and reputation for maintaining price stability is a means by which a government can choose the strength of its commitment to price stability. This article develops four measures of central bank independence and explores their relation with inflation outcomes. An aggregate legal index is developed for four decades in 72 countries. Three indicators of actual independence are developed: the rate of turnover of central bank governors, an index based on a questionnaire answered by specialists in 23 countries, and an aggregation of the legal index and the rate of turnover.

Legal independence is inversely related to inflation in industrial, but not in developing, countries. In developing countries the actual frequency of change of the chief executive officer of the bank is a better proxy for central bank independence. An inflation-based index of overall central bank independence contributes significantly to explaining cross-country variations in the rate of inflation.

"*Willpower is trying hard* not *to do something that you really want to do,*" *said Frog.*

"*You mean like trying* not *to eat all these cookies,*" *asked Toad.*

"*Right,*" *said Frog. He put the cookies in a box.* "*There, now we will not eat any more cookies.*"

"*But we can open the box,*" *said Toad.*

"*That is true,*" *said Frog. He tied some string around the box. He got a ladder and put the box up on a high shelf.* "*There, now we will not eat any more cookies.*"

"*But we can climb the ladder . . . .*" (Lobel 1972)

Institutions cannot absolutely prevent an undesirable outcome, nor ensure a desirable one, but the way that they allocate decisionmaking authority within the public sector makes some policy outcomes more probable and others less likely. An important example of this principle concerns the balance of authority between the central bank and the executive and legislative branches of government. Economists and practitioners in the area of monetary policy generally

Alex Cukierman is with the Department of Economics, Tel Aviv University; Steven B. Webb is with the Country Economics Department at the World Bank; and Bilin Neyapti is with the Country Economics Department at the World Bank and the Economics Department, University of Maryland.

believe that the degree of independence of the central bank from other parts of government affects the rates of expansion of money and credit and, through them, important macroeconomic variables, such as inflation and the size of the budget deficit.

Ultimately, the central bank's authority and scope of action depends on the government. But governments often pass laws and follow customs that grant their central banks authority and autonomy to pursue price stability, even when it conflicts with other government objectives. Making the central bank an agency with the mandate and reputation for maintaining price stability benefits the economy and the government itself in various ways. Central bank independence is one of the means by which a government can choose the strength of its commitment to price stability (Cukierman 1992a, chap. 23, and 1992b; Lohmann 1992). A vast literature discusses the costs of inflation (see Fischer [1986] for a survey); the central bank's pursuit of price stability can help reduce these costs. Price stability is also necessary, although far from sufficient, for developing a local capital market where both government and businesses can borrow more conveniently and cheaply in the long run. International financing, such as for the countries recovering from hyperinflation in the 1920s, has often been conditional on the central bank's mandate and authority to pursue the stability of prices and exchange rates.

Pursuing price stability necessarily competes at least some of the time with other tasks that central banks can and often do perform—such as managing the government's financial transactions, financing the government's deficits with money issue, financing development projects, and bailing out insolvent businesses, including banks and publicly owned enterprises. Although most governments recognize the long-run benefit of price stability, other goals often loom larger in the short run. Assuring price stability, therefore, usually requires ensuring that the central bank is not forced to perform these functions, at least not when they would cause inflation. Sometimes the government or the treasury takes direct responsibility for limiting the demands on a subservient central bank. Even in these cases, but especially in the more typical case where the government has strong tendencies to focus on issues other than price stability, central bank independence and an explicit mandate to pursue price stability are generally regarded as important institutional devices for ensuring price stability.

This belief has eluded comprehensive verification in the past because of the difficulties in measuring the autonomy of central banks independently from

Many individuals helped assemble the data for this study. Particular thanks are due to Walter Wasserfallen, Herman-Josef Dudler, John Flemming, D. Hiss, Wolfgang Schill, Marc-Olivier Strauss-Kahn, Ann Johannessen, and those who answered the questionnaire. The authors also received useful comments from James Alt, Tomas Balino, Edgardo Barandiaran, Paul Beckerman, Mario Blejer, Michael Bruno, Gerald Caprio, Max Corden, Andrew Crockett, Jose de Gregorio, Patrick Downes, Robert Effros, Valeriano Garcia, Sergio Pereiro Leite, Alfredo Leone, Klaus Richel, Lawrence Summers, V. Sundararajan, Mark Swinburne, Richard Webb, Eduardo Wiesner, and participants at the November 1991 NBER Conference on Political Economics.

observation of the inflation outcomes. Actual, as opposed to formal, central bank independence depends not only on the law, but also on many other less-structured factors, such as informal arrangements between the bank and other parts of government, the quality of the bank's research department, and the personality of key individuals in the bank and the (rest of the) government. Because of the difficulty in quantifying such features in an impartial manner, previous studies developed indexes of central bank independence based mostly on legal independence—and only for the industrial countries at that. The multi-country studies that attempt to rank independence for a cross-section of countries include Bade and Parkin (1980), Skanland (1984), Parkin (1987), Alesina (1988), Masciandaro and Tabellini (1988), Bodart (1990), Swinburne and Castello-Branco (1991), and Grilli, Masciandaro, and Tabellini (1991), plus Leone's (1991) study of limits on lending in several industrial and developing countries. There is also a large literature of single- or multicountry case studies, which includes Mittra (1977), Schokker (1980), Eizenga (1983), Kearney (1984), Dotsey (1986), Epstein and Schor (1986), Bordes and Strauss-Kahn (1987), Bordo and Redish (1987), Eizenga (1987), Keenan and Mayes (1987), Suzuki (1987), Goodhart (1988), Holtfrerich (1988), Willett (1988), Fazio (1991), Cargill and Hutchison (1990), Mayer (1990), Meltzer (1991), Maxfield (1992), and Volcker, Mancera, and Godeaux (1991).

Indicators based only on the law have two problems. First, the laws are incomplete in that they cannot specify explicitly the limits of authority between the central bank and the political authorities under all contingencies. These voids are filled by tradition at best and by power politics at worst. Second, even when the law is quite explicit, actual practice may deviate from it.

This article develops unified and broadly based measures of central bank independence, uses them to rank central banks by their degree of independence, and explores the relation between their independence and inflation outcomes. The study goes beyond previous work in three dimensions. First, the set of countries is wider, including up to 72 countries (21 industrial countries and 51 developing countries). The wider sample makes it possible to examine whether there are systematic differences in central bank independence between industrial and developing countries. Second, the coverage in time goes back to the 1950s, if the bank existed then. Third, the study uses a wider range of information on central bank independence. The spirit of the law and its application in practice are generally more important than the letter of the law. In addition to coding characteristics of the central bank law, the study looks at the actual frequency of turnover of central bank governors and at the questionnaire responses from specialists on monetary policy in a subsample of 23 countries. The questionnaire was designed to identify divergences between the central bank's charter and actual practice. We use several different indicators of independence because, in addition to the noise that they contain, each indicator captures a somewhat different aspect of independence.

Examining the relation of inflation to alternate indicators for independence reveals that legal independence is an important determinant of inflation in the industrial countries. In developing countries, by contrast, governors' turnover is strongly and positively associated with inflation. This finding suggests that there are larger divergences between actual practice and the law in developing than in industrial countries (see, for example, Bodart 1990 and Leone 1991).

I. Measures of the Legal Independence of Central Banks

Legal independence is, of course, an essential component of actual independence, but it is also of interest for several other reasons. First, it indicates what is the degree of independence that legislators meant to confer on the central bank. Second, practically all existing attempts at systematically characterizing central bank independence rely solely on legal aspects of independence (Bade and Parkin 1980; Banaian, Laney, and Willett 1983; Skanland 1984; Parkin 1987; Alesina 1988; Masciandaro and Tabellini 1988; Grilli, Masciandaro, and Tabellini 1991). Establishing comparability with previous studies requires an index of legal independence for our sample of countries.

The laws of central banks differ in their focus, scope, and degree of detail. Many provisions in central bank charters have no direct bearing on the issue of central bank independence. Ranking central bank charters by their degree of legal independence is therefore difficult and inevitably requires subjective judgment.

Coding Legal Independence

Our coding of the legal central bank independence followed two principles. First, we coded only a few narrow but relatively precise legal characteristics. Second, we used only the written information from the charters. Additional information on how the law is applied was deliberately left out, since it is reflected by separate indexes that are discussed in section II. These principles make it possible to rank central banks by their degree of independence in various legal dimensions with relatively few subjective judgments and to focus on concrete details of the law rather than on a broader but more impressionistic view of it.

The legal characteristics of the central bank as stated in its charter are grouped into four clusters of issues:

- The appointment, dismissal, and term of office of the chief executive officer of the bank—usually the governor
- The policy formulation cluster, which concerns the resolution of conflicts between the executive branch and the central bank over monetary policy and the participation of the central bank in the budget process
- The objectives of the central bank
- Limitations on the ability of the central bank to lend to the public sector; such restrictions limit the volume, maturity, interest rates, and conditions

for direct advances and securitized lending from the central bank to the public sector.

The clusters were built up from 16 different legal variables, each coded on a scale of 0 (lowest level of independence) to 1 (highest level of independence). The detailed classification and codings appear in table 1. The codes are set so that a higher number indicates what we expected would lead to a stronger mandate and greater autonomy for the central bank to pursue price stability.

In coding various central banks by the degree of independence within each group of characteristics, the following criteria were used. Central banks in which the legal term of office of the chief executive officer (CEO) is longer and in which the executive branch has little legal authority in appointing or dismissing the governor are classified as more independent in the CEO dimension. By the same logic, central banks with wider authority to formulate monetary policy and to resist the executive branch in cases of conflict are classified as more independent in the policy formulation dimension.

For the objective of the central bank, there are six possible ratings, according to the prominence given to price stability compared with other stated objectives that might conflict with price stability. For instance, when the charter specifies price stability as the main or only goal, the bank is classified as being more independent in this dimension than a central bank with objectives in addition to, but not inconsistent with, price stability, such as stable banking. These banks are, in turn, classified as more independent than banks whose objectives include things like full employment, which might conflict with price stability. The objectives variable is designed to capture the legal mandate of the bank to single-mindedly pursue the objective of price stability. Only the central banks in the Federal Republic of Germany and the Philippines have unequivocal legal mandates for price stability. The objectives variable does not, therefore, reflect the general level of independence from government, in contrast to the CEO and policy formulation variables. In Rogoff's (1985) terminology, the objectives variable measures the strength of the "conservative bias" of the bank's charter.

Similarly, we classify a central bank with tighter limits on its lending to the public sector as more independent to pursue the objective of price stability. These limitations encompass a number of more detailed variables, such as separate limitations on advances and securitized lending and restrictions on maturities and on interest rates. The stricter the limitation, the higher the independence coding given to the bank in that dimension. The comparability of various types of limitations is complicated because the limitations are specified in different ways in different countries. In a few countries limitations on lending are specified in absolute cash amounts and in others as a percentage of central bank liabilities. The limitation is formulated in most cases as a percentage of government's revenues from taxes but in a minority of cases as a percentage of government's expenditures. The "bite" of these limitations obviously depends on the magnitudes of the reference variables. Other things being equal, however, abso-

Table 1. *Variables for Legal Central Bank Independence*

Variable number	*Description of variable*	*Weight*	*Numerical coding*
1	Chief executive officer (CEO)	0.20	
	a. Term of office		
	Over 8 years		1.00
	6 to 8 years		0.75
	5 years		0.50
	4 years		0.25
	Under 4 years or at the discretion of appointer		0.00
	b. Who appoints CEO?		
	Board of central bank		1.00
	A council of the central bank board, executive branch, and legislative branch		0.75
	Legislature		0.50
	Executive collectively (e.g. council of ministers)		0.25
	One or two members of the executive branch		0.00
	c. Dismissal		
	No provision for dismissal		1.00
	Only for reasons not related to policy		0.83
	At the discretion of central bank board		0.67
	At legislature's discretion		0.50
	Unconditional dismissal possible by legislature		0.33
	At executive's discretion		0.17
	Unconditional dismissal possible by executive		0.00
	d. May CEO hold other offices in government?		
	No		1.00
	Only with permission of the executive branch		0.50
	No rule against CEO holding another office		0.00
2	Policy formulation	0.15	
	a. Who formulates monetary policy?		
	Bank alone		1.00
	Bank participates, but has little influence		0.67
	Bank only advises government		0.33
	Bank has no say		0.00
	b. Who has final word in resolution of conflict?[a]		
	The bank, on issues clearly defined in the law as its objectives		1.00
	Government, on policy issues not clearly defined as the bank's goals or in case of conflict within the bank		0.80
	A council of the central bank, executive branch, and legislative branch		0.60
	The legislature, on policy issues		0.40
	The executive branch on policy issues, subject to due process and possible protest by the bank		0.20
	The executive branch has unconditional priority		0.00
	c. Role in the government's budgetary process		
	Central bank active		1.00
	Central bank has no influence		0.00
3	Objectives	0.15	
	Price stability is the major or only objective in the charter, and the central bank has the final word in case of conflict with other government objectives		1.00
	Price stability is the only objective		0.80
	Price stability is one goal, with other compatible objectives, such as a stable banking system		0.60
	Price stability is one goal, with potentially conflicting objectives, such as full employment		0.40

Table 1. *(continued)*

Variable number	*Description of variable*	*Weight*	*Numerical coding*
	No objectives stated in the bank charter		0.20
	Stated objectives do not include price stability		0.00
4	Limitations on lending to the government		
	a. Advances (limitation on nonsecuritized lending)	0.15	
	No advances permitted		1.00
	Advances permitted, but with strict limits (e.g., up to 15 percent of government revenue)		0.67
	Advances permitted, and the limits are loose (e.g., over 15 percent of government revenue)		0.33
	No legal limits on lending		0.00
	b. Securitized lending	0.10	
	Not permitted		1.00
	Permitted, but with strict limits (e.g., up to 15 percent of government revenue)		0.67
	Permitted, and the limits are loose (e.g., over 15 percent of government revenue)		0.33
	No legal limits on lending		0.00
	c. Terms of lending (maturity, interest, amount)	0.10	
	Controlled by the bank		1.00
	Specified by the bank charter		0.67
	Agreed between the central bank and executive		0.33
	Decided by the executive branch alone		0.00
	d. Potential borrowers from the bank	0.05	
	Only the central government		1.00
	All levels of government (state as well as central)		0.67
	Those mentioned above and public enterprises		0.33
	Public and private sector		0.00
	e. Limits on central bank lending defined in	0.025	
	Currency amounts		1.00
	Shares of central bank demand liabilities or capital		0.67
	Shares of government revenue		0.33
	Shares of government expenditures		0.00
	f. Maturity of loans	0.025	
	Within 6 months		1.00
	Within 1 year		0.67
	More than 1 year		0.33
	No mention of maturity in the law		0.00
	g. Interest rates on loans must be	0.025	
	Above minimum rates		1.00
	At market rates		0.75
	Below maximum rates		0.50
	Interest rate is not mentioned		0.25
	No interest on government borrowing from the central bank		0.00
	h. Central bank prohibited from buying or selling government securities in the primary market?	0.025	
	Yes		1.00
	No		0.00

Note: The ranking under each criteria indicates the degree of independence of central banks—the higher the code, the more independent the central bank.

a. Often the law does not contain a separate provision on the resolution of conflict. In those cases, the variable was coded on the basis of the impression from reading the law in its entirety. If the law gives the impression that the government formulates policy guidelines that the bank simply follows, then the ranking is low.

Source: Various central bank laws, Aufricht (1961, 1967); Bank for International Settlements (1963); Effros (1982); and the IMF's computerized files on central bank laws.

lute cash limits are more binding than limits in terms of central bank liabilities, which, in turn, are more binding than limits in terms of government's revenues. The most accommodative limits are those which are specified in terms of government's expenditures. These considerations were embodied in a "type-of-limit" variable and also influenced the classification of the variables for limitations on lending via advances and for limitations on lending via securities. Table 1 shows the details of the several variables for limitations on lending.

Limitations on lending are also classified as stricter the nearer are the rates paid by government to market rates and the shorter are the maturities of the loans from the central bank to the public sector. They are also stricter the narrower the circle of institutions that is allowed to borrow from the central bank and the smaller the discretion of the executive branch to decide to whom and how much the central bank will lend. In addition, central bank laws that prohibit the central bank from buying government securities on the primary market are considered, all things being equal, stricter than laws that do not contain such a prohibition.

The period considered covers the four decades from 1950 to 1989. It is divided into four subperiods: 1950–59, 1960–71, 1972–79, and 1980–89, which we refer to according to the decades in which they are centered. They correspond, respectively, to the gold-dollar standard period before most currencies had convertibility, the period of convertibility with the dollar, the period of the two oil shocks after the end of the Bretton Woods currency system, and the period of disinflation and the debt crisis. Legal variables were coded separately for each decade. Since central bank legislation changes relatively slowly, the codes are, in many cases, identical across subperiods. Nonetheless this procedure captures important legislative changes for some countries. Only one code per decade was assigned for each country for each legal variable. Whenever a change occurred within a decade, the classification was done in line with the legislation that was in effect during at least half of that decade. When a central bank was founded within a decade, its legal variables were coded only if it existed for at least three years during the decade. The coded variables appear in Table A-1 following the concluding section.

Aggregating the Legal Variables

The individual components of legal independence are aggregated in two steps to yield a hierarchy of indexes. Later in the article we investigate the association of those indexes with other variables, such as other indicators of central bank independence and inflation. The basic data on the 16 legal variables described in table 1 were aggregated into eight legal variables as follows. The four variables concerning the appointment and term of office of the governor of the central bank were aggregated into a single variable labeled CEO, equal to the mean of the four components. The three variables under policy formulation were aggregated into a single variable by computing a weighted mean of the variables in that group, with weights of 0.5 for the resolution of conflict, 0.25 for who formulates monetary policy, and 0.25 for active role of the central bank in formulating the government budget. The objectives variable was treated separately. The first four variables for limits on lending were treated separately; the last four variables in the group were averaged with equal weights into a single variable. This aggregation procedure produces one summary legal variable for each of the first three groups in table 1, and five legal variables for the limitations on lending group. When an entry is not available (—) for one or more variables within a subgroup, only the variables with meaningful entries are aggregated. In such cases the weights of the missing variables are allocated proportionally to the remaining variables within the subgroup.

When the legal variables appear at a high level of disaggregation (as in table 1), a missing observation on at least one variable precludes the use of that country or decade. Partial aggregation alleviates this problem by reducing the number of observations with entries that are not available. In addition, multicollinearity among the 16 legal variables reduces the precision of the estimated effect of each of them on inflation. Partial aggregation alleviates this problem, too.

The eight legal variables from the first round of aggregation were aggregated further into a single index for each country and decade, using weights that we considered most plausible. The weights are indicated in table 1. When a component is missing, the weights of those remaining are expanded proportionately to sum to 1.0. For all the observations, the weights of the component variables summed to at least 0.7. The variable for the legal central bank independence aggregated in this way is similar to a variable aggregated with equal weights; the two are highly correlated.

Table 2 ranks industrial and developing countries according to their aggregate variable for legal central bank independence for 1980–89 and also provides their average inflation rates in the 1980s. Countries classified by the World Bank as low- or middle-income, on the basis of 1985 incomes, are classified as developing; the others are referred to as industrial. Observations for each country and decade are given in appendix table A-1. Austria, Germany, and Switzerland—all industrial countries—have the highest legal independence, while Morocco and Poland—both developing countries—have the lowest. Otherwise the two country groups have very similar distributions of aggregate legal independence. The medians are virtually identical—0.33 and 0.34.

II. Informal Indicators of Actual Independence

The legal status of a central bank is only one of several elements that determine its actual independence. Many central bank laws are highly incomplete and leave a lot of room for interpretation. As a result, factors such as tradition or the personalities of the governor and other high officials of the bank at least partially shape the actual level of central bank independence. Even when the law is

Table 2. *Legal Central Bank Independence and Average Annual Inflation, 1980–89*

Industrial economy			*Developing economy*					
Economy	*Legal central bank independence*[a] *(index)*	*Average annual rate of inflation*[b] *(percent)*	*Economy*	*Legal central bank independence*[a] *(index)*	*Average annual rate of inflation*[b] *(percent)*	*Economy*	*Legal central bank independence*[a] *(index)*	*Average annual rate of inflation*[b] *(percent)*
Germany, Fed. Rep. of	0.69	3	Greece	0.55	18	Botswana	0.33	10
Switzerland	0.64	3	Egypt	0.49	16	Zambia	0.33	25
Austria	0.61	4	Costa Rica	0.47	23	Ghana	0.31	37
Denmark	0.50	7	Chile	0.46	19	Romania	0.30	4
United States	0.48	5	Turkey	0.46	41	Bolivia	0.30	119
Canada	0.45	6	Nicaragua	0.45	128	Western Samoa	0.30	12
Ireland	0.44	9	Malta	0.44	3	China	0.29	8
Netherlands	0.42	3	Tanzania	0.44	27	Singapore	0.29	3
Australia	0.36	8	Kenya	0.44	10	Korea, Republic of	0.27	8
Iceland	0.34	32	Philippines	0.43	13	Indonesia	0.27	9
Luxembourg	0.33	5	Zaire	0.43	45	Colombia	0.27	21
Sweden	0.29	8	Peru	0.43	108	Thailand	0.27	6
Finland	0.28	7	Honduras	0.43	7	South Africa	0.25	14
United Kingdom	0.27	7	Venezuela	0.43	19	Hungary	0.24	9
Italy	0.25	11	Bahamas, The	0.41	6	Uruguay	0.24	45
New Zealand	0.24	12	Portugal	0.41	16	Panama	0.22	3
France	0.24	7	Argentina	0.40	143	Pakistan	0.21	7
Spain	0.23	10	Ethiopia	0.40	4	Brazil	0.21	119
Japan	0.18	3	Lebanon	0.40	—	Taiwan	0.21	5
Norway	0.17	8	Israel	0.39	72	Zimbabwe	0.20	12
Belgium	0.17	5	Barbados	0.38	7	Qatar	0.20	4
			Uganda	0.38	72	Nepal	0.18	10
			Nigeria	0.37	18	Yugoslavia	0.17	73
			Malaysia	0.36	4	Morocco	0.14	7
			Mexico	0.34	50	Poland	0.10	36
			India	0.34	9			

— Not available.
a. The potential range of the index for legal central bank independence is from zero (minimal independence) to one (maximum independence).
b. Inflation is computed in logs.

quite explicit, reality may be very different. For example, in Argentina the legal term of office of the governor is four years, but there is also a tradition that the governor of the central bank offers to resign whenever the government, or even the finance minister, changes. Argentine governors have invariably adhered to this tradition. As a consequence, the average actual term of office of the governor was about one year from 1950 to 1989. Obviously the actual independence of the Argentine central bank is substantially lower than the legal indicators imply. It is hard to find systematic indicators of actual independence when it diverges from legal independence, and we do not pretend to resolve this measurement issue fully. Here we develop two indicators of actual, as opposed to legal, central bank independence from the actual frequency of change of the governor and from responses to a questionnaire sent to experts on each country.

Turnover of Central Bank Governors

This indicator is based on the presumption that, at least above some threshold, more rapid turnover of central bank governors indicates a lower level of independence. Indeed, more rapid turnover presumably creates dependence. If the political authorities frequently take the opportunity to choose a new governor, they will at least have the opportunity to pick those who will do their will. Frequent turnover may reflect the firing of those who choose to challenge the government. A government would even have some incentive to appoint a governor with a reputation for some independence, thereby gaining a temporary increase in the potential for stimulating output or collecting resources through seigniorage, and then use up his reputation, as happened with Arthur Burns at the Federal Reserve Bank of the United States in the 1970s.

For high turnover rates, the tenure of the central bank governor is shorter than that of the executive branch. This makes the central bank governor susceptible to influence by the executive branch and discourages the governor from trying to implement longer-term policies, especially those that would extend beyond the election cycle. Because in most countries the electoral cycle is at least four years, it is likely that the threshold turnover, above which independence declines seriously, is somewhere between 0.2 and 0.25 changes a year (for an average tenure of four to five years). One would expect that turnovers at the central bank that occur simultaneously with or shortly after changes in the government would indicate lower independence than turnovers that occur at other times. Further work will investigate this issue.

If, however, a governor stays on for several years and perhaps outlasts several heads of government, thus presiding over price stability, the governor's reputation can become strong enough to resist considerable pressure. The government's desire to preserve financial stability can deter it from challenging a well-established central bank governor.

A low turnover does not necessarily imply a high level of central bank independence, however, because a relatively subservient governor may stay in office

Table 3. *Turnover Rates of the Central Bank Governor, 1950–89*
(average number of changes a year)

Economy	*1950–89*	*1950–59*	*1960–71*	*1972–79*	*1980–89*
Industrial economy					
Iceland	0.03	—	0.09	0.00	0.00
Netherlands	0.05	0.00	0.08	0.00	0.10
Denmark	0.05	0.10	0.08	0.00	0.00
Luxembourg	0.08	0.10	0.08	0.13	0.00
Norway	0.08	0.10	0.08	0.00	0.10
Italy	0.08	0.00	0.08	0.25	0.00
United Kingdom	0.10	0.00	0.17	0.13	0.10
Canada	0.10	0.10	0.08	0.13	0.10
Germany, Fed. Rep. of	0.10	0.10	0.08	0.13	0.10
Australia	0.10	0.00	0.08	0.13	0.20
Finland	0.13	0.20	0.08	0.00	0.20
Switzerland	0.13	0.10	0.08	0.13	0.20
Belgium	0.13	0.10	0.08	0.13	0.20
United States	0.13	0.10	0.08	0.25	0.10
Ireland	0.15	0.10	0.17	0.13	0.20
France	0.15	0.00	0.17	0.25	0.20
Sweden	0.15	0.20	0.00	0.38	0.10
New Zealand	0.15	0.00	0.17	0.13	0.30
Austria	0.15	0.10	0.17	0.25	0.10
Japan	0.20	0.20	0.17	0.13	0.30
Spain	0.20	0.20	0.25	0.25	0.10
Developing economy					
Qatar	0.06	—	—	0.14	0.00
South Africa	0.10	0.00	0.17	0.00	0.20
Barbados	0.11	—	—	0.13	0.10
Taiwan	0.13	0.10	0.17	0.00	0.20
Philippines	0.13	0.00	0.25	0.00	0.20
Honduras	0.13	0.11	0.00	0.38	0.10
Tanzania	0.13	—	0.18	0.13	0.10
Malaysia	0.13	—	0.08	0.00	0.20
Israel	0.14	0.20	0.08	0.13	0.20
Zimbabwe	0.15	0.27	0.17	0.13	0.10
Mexico	0.15	0.10	0.08	0.13	0.30
Kenya	0.17	—	0.36	0.00	0.20
Greece	0.18	0.10	0.08	0.38	0.20
Hungary	0.18	0.38	0.17	0.13	0.10
Lebanon	0.19	—	0.24	0.25	0.10

a long time. This is probably true for countries with exceptionally low turnover rates, such as Iceland, Denmark, Norway, and the United Kingdom.

Table 3 presents the average annual turnover rates in the sample countries for 1950–89 and for each decade within that period. These rates are presented separately for developing and industrial countries. Average turnover rates for 1950–89 range from a minimum of 0.034 (one change in 29 years) in Iceland to a maximum of 0.93 (average tenure of about 13 months) in Argentina. Turnover rates in developing countries extend into a range considerably above the highest rates in the industrial countries. The highest average turnover among the indus-

Table 3. *(continued)*

Economy	*1950–89*	*1950–59*	*1960–71*	*1972–79*	*1980–89*
Developing economy (continued)					
Nigeria	0.19	—	0.17	0.25	0.10
Bahamas, The	0.19	—	—	0.18	0.20
Morocco	0.20	—	0.25	0.00	0.20
Ethiopia	0.20	—	0.00	0.50	0.10
Colombia	0.20	0.20	0.25	0.13	0.20
Romania	0.20	0.40	0.08	0.13	0.20
Portugal	0.20	0.20	0.08	0.25	0.30
Thailand	0.20	0.40	0.08	0.25	0.10
Yugoslavia	0.23	0.30	0.17	0.25	0.20
Indonesia	0.23	0.20	0.33	0.13	0.20
Zaire	0.23	—	0.26	0.25	0.20
Nepal	0.24	0.27	0.33	0.25	0.10
Panama	0.24	—	0.56	0.00	0.20
Pakistan	0.25	0.10	0.33	0.25	0.30
Poland	0.28	0.20	0.25	0.13	0.50
Malta	0.28	—	0.27	0.38	0.20
Ghana	0.28	—	0.33	0.25	0.20
Venezuela	0.30	0.20	0.25	0.25	0.50
Egypt	0.31	0.46	0.33	0.13	0.30
India	0.33	0.20	0.33	0.50	0.30
Peru	0.33	0.30	0.33	0.38	0.30
China	0.34	—	—	—	0.30
Uganda	0.34	—	0.36	0.50	0.20
Nicaragua	0.35	—	0.29	0.38	0.40
Singapore	0.37	—	—	0.00	0.60
Zambia	0.38	—	0.38	0.25	0.50
Turkey	0.40	0.30	0.50	0.38	0.40
Botswana	0.41	—	—	0.44	0.40
Korea, Republic of	0.43	0.31	0.67	0.13	0.50
Chile	0.45	0.20	0.33	0.50	0.80
Uruguay	0.48	—	1.03	0.38	0.30
Western Samoa	0.56	—	—	—	0.56
Costa Rica	0.58	0.20	0.83	0.88	0.40
Brazil	0.68	1.01	0.50	0.38	0.80
Argentina	0.93	0.71	1.08	0.88	1.00

— Not available.

Note: Turnover rates were calculated if at least three years of data were available for the decade.

Source: Correspondence with central banks.

trial countries for 1950–89 is 0.2 (or an average tenure of five years) for Spain. More than half of the developing countries have turnover rates exceeding this maximum.

Because average turnover rates for all industrial countries for 1950–89 are less than 0.2, these rates probably do not reveal much about the variations of independence within that group. But because turnover rates vary widely among the developing countries, however, they seem more likely to reveal variations in the independence of those governors.

A governor's legal term of office does not seem to have much effect on the

Table 4. *Questionnarie Variables, Weights, and Numerical Coding*

Variable number	*Variable description*	*Weight*	*Numerical coding*
1	Tenure of central bank CEO overlap with political authorities	0.10	
	Little overlap		1.0
	Some overlap		0.5
	Substantial overlap		0.0
2	Limitations on lending in practice	0.20	
	Tight		1.00
	Moderately tight		0.66
	Moderately loose		0.33
	Loose or nonexistent		0.00
3	Resolution of conflict	0.10	
	Some clear cases of resolution in favor of bank		1.0
	Resolution in favor of government in all cases		0.0
	All other cases		0.5
4	Financial independence	0.10	
	a. Determination of the central bank's budget		
	Mostly central bank		1.0
	Mixture of bank and executive or legislative branches		0.5
	Mostly executive or legislative branches		0.0
	b. Determination of the salaries of high bank officials and the allocation of bank profits		
	Mostly by bank or fixed by law		1.0
	Mixture of bank and executive or legislative branches		0.5
	Mostly executive or legislative branches		0.0
5	Intermediate policy targets	0.15	
	a. Quantitative monetary stock target		
	Such targets exist; good adherence		1.00
	Such targets exist; mixed adherence		0.66
	Such targets exist; poor adherence		0.33
	No stock targets		0.00
	b. Formal or informal interest rate targets		
	No		1
	Yes		0
6	Actual priority given to price stability	0.15	
	First priority		1.00
	First priority assigned to a fixed exchange rate		0.66
	Price or exchange rate stability are among the bank's objectives, but not first priority		0.33
	No mention of price or exchange rate objectives		0.00
7	Function as a development bank, granting credit at subsidy rates?	0.20	
	No		1.00
	To some extent		0.66
	Yes		0.33
	The central bank heavily involved in granting subsidized credits		0.00

actual turnover. To explore this issue, we regressed actual turnover rates in the four subperiods on the legal terms of office and on decade dummies to control for possible period-specific effects on turnover. The coefficient of the legal term-of-office variable was negative and statistically significant, but the adjusted R^2 was low (0.07), thus indicating that actual turnover is affected by many other factors besides the legal term of office.

Questionnaire on Central Bank Independence

The other group of indicators of central bank independence is based on responses to a questionnaire that was sent to a nonrandom sample of specialists on monetary policy in various central banks. Some questions involve the same issues that underlie the legal variables, but they focus on the practice rather than the law—for example, central bank objectives, their importance in practice, and the strictness of limitations on lending in practice. Some questions refer to additional issues, such as subsidized credits from the bank to the private sector, quantitative targets for the money stock, the determination of the bank budget, and the degree of actual tenure overlap between the governor and high officials in the executive branch. Although the judgments of those responding to the questionnaire are subjective and not entirely uniform, the responses help to identify divergence between actual and legal independence, particularly when the divergence is large.

Answers to the questionnaire sufficed for coding most of the nine questionnaire variables described in table 4 in 23 countries (The codings for each country are given in appendix table A-2). We coded only the parts of the questionnaires that could be translated into clear rankings and for which an adequate share of the questionnaires had responses. Since the questionnaire was worded in the present tense and since policymakers' thinking is dominated by the recent past, the responses are taken to refer to the 1980s.

Variable 1 is designed to reflect the extent to which the terms of office of the governor and of the board of directors are likely to be independent from government. The more the turnover at the central bank coincides with turnover in the government, the less independent the bank is likely to be, and vice versa. Variable 2 reflects the actual limitations on lending in practice and is coded by applying criteria similar to those used to classify the legal limitations on lending described earlier. The lowest level of independence is assigned if there are no limitations on lending or if the government can adjust the limits very easily.

Variable 3 reflects the extent to which conflicts between the government and the central bank are resolved in favor of the latter. Variable 4 captures two aspects of the financial independence of the bank: the determination of its budget and the setting of salaries of its top officials. It is calculated as a simple average of the variables 4a and 4b. The two parts of variable 5 reflect the relative importance of targets for the monetary stock or interest rates—these targets being precommitments agreed to by the bank and government. Money stock targets would enhance the pursuit of price stability, because the bank could adhere to them in the face of pressure from the government. A target for the nominal interest rate, however, would typically work to limit the ability of the bank to respond to upsurges of inflation. Variable 5 is calculated as a simple average of the variables 5a and 5b. Variable 6 captures more directly the priority assigned to price stability, and variable 7 reflects the extent to which the central bank has the competing objective of providing subsidized credits to encourage development. Further details appear in chapter 19 of Cukierman (1992a).

Aggregating the seven variables gives the results in table 5. The weights used in the aggregation are based on our priors and are shown in table 4; using equal weights gave an almost identical ranking. The indexes are reported only for countries in which the weights of the responses sum up to at least 0.7. Because it is based on subjective evaluations, the questionnaire-based index probably contains more noise than the index of legal central bank independence, but it also probably contains additional pertinent information about actual independence. The main limit of the questionnaire is the small number of countries with responses, but we hope to expand this in the future.

Table 5. *The Questionnaire-based Index of Central Bank Independence and Average Annual Inflation*

Country	*Questionnaire-based index of central bank independence*	*Average annual rate of inflation,*[a] *1980–89 (percent)*
Germany, Fed. Rep. of	1.00	3
Costa Rica	0.81	23
Finland	0.78	7
Australia	0.76	8
Italy	0.73	11
Denmark	0.73	7
Bahamas, The	0.71	6
Luxembourg	0.66	5
France	0.65	7
United Kingdom	0.64	7
South Africa	0.64	14
Zaire	0.61	45
Lebanon	0.59	—
Ireland	0.57	9
Barbados	0.54	7
Uganda	0.53	72
Uruguay	0.49	45
Belgium	0.47	5
Turkey	0.44	41
Tanzania	0.38	27
Peru	0.22	108
Yugoslavia	0.17	73
Ethiopia	0.13	4

— Not available.

a. Inflation is computed in logs.

Table 6. *Rank Correlations between Indexes of Legal Central Bank Independence*

	Country sample		
Correlation pair	*All*	*Industrial*	*Developing*
Legal index and rate of turnover			
1950–89	0.000	0.018	0.011
1980–89	0.000	0.065	0.015
Legal and questionnaire-based indexes[a]	0.041	0.334*	0.056
Questionnaire-based index and rate of turnover[a]	0.068	0.050	0.031

* Significant at 10 percent level.
a. Covers 1980–89.

The questionnaires clearly indicate that central banks in developing countries are less independent than those in industrial countries. Only two industrial countries—Ireland and Belgium—are below the median of 0.60, and only four developing countries—The Bahamas, Costa Rica, South Africa, and Zaire—are above it. This contrasts with the findings for legal independence, where the two country groups do not differ widely, but is similar to the finding for turnover.

Relationships between Indexes of Independence

Table 6 shows the rank correlations between indexes of central bank independence: the legal index, the turnover rate, and the questionnaire-based index. None of the various indexes of central bank independence are closely correlated. Only the correlation between the legal independence index and the questionnaire-based index of independence for the industrial countries is even marginally significant, which suggests that the law is a more important determinant of actual independence in the industrial countries. Since the correlation across these indexes is not high, they can be usefully combined to obtain a better measure of overall central bank independence, which is done toward the end of the article.

III. Inflation and Central Bank Independence

Do countries with more independent central banks have lower rates of inflation? The hypothesis that inflation should be negatively related to the legal and questionnaire variables has two bases. (Recall that for both variables a higher code in the range between 0 and 1 reflects a higher level of independence.) First, there is a presumption that central banks are more concerned about price stability than the political authorities (see Rogoff [1985], for instance). Because actual policy is normally the outcome of a compromise between the central bank and the executive branch, a more independent central bank will have a stronger impact on actual policy, and therefore average inflation will be lower (Alesina and Tabellini 1987; Cukierman 1992a, chap. 18). Second, the legal independence variable is intentionally structured to reflect, among other things, the extent to which the central bank has an explicit mandate to pursue price stability at the expense of other objectives. For a given level of independence from the political authorities, a more focused legal mandate to pursue price stability is expected to result in a lower rate of inflation.

The legal independence of the central bank is neither a necessary nor a sufficient condition for low inflation, although, other things being equal, less legal independence contributes to higher inflation. Some of the countries with the highest average rates of inflation, such as Argentina, Peru, and Nicaragua, have rankings of legal independence above the median. However, countries such as Belgium, Japan, Morocco, and Qatar, with very low rates of inflation, are ranked in the lowest quartile of legal central bank independence.

To investigate systematically the relation between central bank independence and inflation, we regressed inflation on the various indexes of central bank independence. Because a higher numerical code assigned to the legal and questionnaire variables indicates a higher level of independence, the hypothesis implies that the effect of each of these variables on inflation is negative. The effect of the turnover of central bank governors, at least above some threshold, is predicted to be positive.

The inflation variable was transformed in order to reduce heteroskedasticity of the error and thus improve the efficiency of the estimate. Most countries had average inflation rates of 20 percent or less, but a few had three-digit inflation rates in some decades. Using the straight inflation rate would give undue weight to these outlier observations. So we transformed each year's inflation rate into inflation divided by one plus the inflation rate and then took the geometric average for the decade. This variable represents the annual real depreciation of a given amount of money; we call it D:

$$D = \pi/(1 + \pi) \tag{1}$$

where π is the inflation rate and D (hence, the transformed inflation rate) takes a value from 0 to 1.0. When inflation is 100 percent a year, D is 0.5.

Table 7 presents regressions of the transformed inflation rate (D) on disaggregated indexes of legal central bank independence, along with the governor's turnover variable. Each observation pertains to one decade in one country. Not all countries have observations for all four decades, because some countries or central banks start after 1950. Inflation was counted only for years when the central bank existed, if it started late in the decade. The results show the importance of the turnover rate for explaining variations of inflation in the whole sample and among the developing countries. None of the disaggregated legal variables has a significant coefficient (at the 5 percent level), and an F-test reveals that the variables as a group are not quite significant at the 10 percent level even within the group of industrial countries.

To overcome the collinearity among the disaggregated legal variables, we ran the regressions with the aggregate index of legal independence. Table 8 reports

Table 7. *The Transformed Inflation Rate, Disaggregated Variables of Legal Central Bank Independence, and the Turnover Rate, 1950–89*

Explanatory variable	*All countries*	*Industrial countries*	*Developing countries*
Intercept	0.09**	0.09***	0.09*
	(2.47)	(3.50)	(1.71)
CEO	−0.00	0.02	0.01
	(−0.10)	(0.54)	(0.18)
Policy formulation	0.05	−0.02	0.09
	(0.90)	(−0.54)	(1.08)
Central bank objectives	−0.04	0.01	−0.08
	(−1.29)	(0.42)	(−1.61)
Limitations on lending			
a. Advances	−0.04	−0.02	−0.04
	(−1.11)	(−0.88)	(−0.72)
b. Securitized lending	0.03	−0.01	0.04
	(0.73)	(−0.13)	(0.69)
c. Terms of lending	0.06	0.01	0.08
	(1.27)	(0.42)	(1.15)
d. Potential borrowers	0.02	0.00	0.03
	(1.15)	(0.33)	(0.90)
e. Others	−0.07	−0.06*	−0.05
	(−1.14)	(−1.79)	(−0.57)
Rate of turnover of central bank governor	0.30***	−0.07	0.30***
	(5.99)	(−1.13)	(4.47)
Dummy: 1950–59	−0.08***	−0.03**	−0.10**
	(−2.92)	(−2.05)	(−2.14)
Dummy: 1960–71	−0.09***	−0.02	−0.12***
	(−4.04)	(−1.48)	(−3.57)
Dummy: 1972–79	−0.02	0.03**	−0.03
	(−1.10)	(2.10)	(−1.18)
R^2	0.29	0.29	0.27
F-statistic for legal variables[a]	1.24	1.62	1.20
	(0.28)	(0.15)	(0.30)
Number of observations	177	60	117

Note: The dependent variable is the transformed inflation rate, *D*. The *t*-statistics are reported in parentheses under estimated coefficients. * indicates significance at the 10 percent level, ** at the 5 percent level, and *** at the 1 percent level.

a. The significance levels are in parentheses.

the results. (We used the index based on our priors for weights. Using the index with equal weights produced similar results.) The key results come out when we split the sample into industrial and developing countries.

For the industrial countries, the aggregate legal variable has a statistically significant coefficient with the predicted negative sign. Laws do make a difference. The turnover rate, always low in any case for this subsample, has a negative sign, contrary to our prediction; the *t*-statistic indicates marginal statistical significance. The most anomalous case is Iceland, with the highest inflation rate and lowest turnover among industrial countries. Dropping Iceland from the industrial country subsample makes the estimated coefficient on the turnover rate slightly positive and totally insignificant. The coefficient on the aggregate index of legal central bank independence becomes more significant (the *t*-statis-

Table 8. *The Transformed Inflation Rate, Aggregate Index of Legal Central Bank Independence, and the Turnover Rate, 1950–89*

Explanatory variable	*All countries*	*Industrial countries*	*Developing countries*	*All countries with decomposed turnover variable*
Intercept	0.09***	0.09***	0.11**	0.10***
	(3.55)	(7.17)	(2.51)	(3.54)
Legal central bank independence (aggregate index)	−0.02	−0.06**	0.01	−0.03
	(−0.39)	(−2.54)	(0.11)	(−0.45)
Rate of turnover of central bank governor	0.28***	−0.08*	0.28***	
	(6.64)	(−1.81)	(4.80)	
Decomposed turnover[a]				
High turnover range				0.27***
				(6.27)
Low turnover range				0.20*
				(1.86)
Dummy: 1950–59	−0.08***	−0.03***	−0.11***	−0.08***
	(−3.31)	(−2.94)	(−2.62)	(−3.33)
Dummy: 1960–71	−0.09***	−0.02**	−0.13***	−0.09***
	(−4.45)	(−2.11)	(−4.14)	(−4.47)
Dummy: 1972–79	−0.02	0.03***	−0.04	−0.02
	(−0.88)	(2.90)	(−1.28)	(−0.86)
$\bar{R}^2$	0.26	0.34	0.23	0.25
Number of observations	214	79	135	214

Note: The dependent variable is the transformed inflation rate, *D*. The *t*-statistics are reported in parentheses under estimated coefficients. * indicates significance at the 10 percent level, ** at the 5 percent level, and *** at the 1 percent level.

a. The rate of turnover is in the high range if there are 0.25 or more turnovers per year; it is in the low range if there are fewer than 0.25.

tic is −4.32), and the adjusted R^2 increases to 0.61. Italy also has low turnover rates but high inflation, while Japan has high turnover compared with other industrial countries but low inflation. In Japan, the Ministry of Finance has an unusually strong anti-inflation attitude, as well as strong influence over the central bank.

To explore further the composition of the legal variable, we made an index—the lending-limit index—from only the five components pertaining to limits on lending. These components drive the result for the industrial countries. The *t*-statistic for the lending-limit index is about the same as for the whole composite legal variable. The other components of the legal independence variable—CEO, policy formation, and objectives—do not make any significant contribution to explaining inflation. The lending-limit index is not significant for the developing countries.

For the developing countries, the turnover rate is highly significant with the predicted positive coefficient. But the aggregate legal variable remains insignificant. This is not to deny that the legal charter has helped ensure the central bank's independence and commitment to price stability in some developing countries. But statistical evidence for developing countries does not reveal that the central bank laws contribute to explaining the variation of inflation across periods and between countries.

What is the relation between the results for the whole sample and the results for the two subsamples (industrial and developing countries)? In particular, why does the result of the importance of the legal variable for the industrial countries not show up in the whole sample, while the result of the importance of the turnover variable for the developing countries does show up for the entire sample? Figure 1 illustrates these relations.

The left panel in figure 1 shows the partial relation of the aggregate index of legal central bank independence with the transformed inflation rate (*D*). The downward-sloping line shows the significance of the aggregate index of legal central bank independence for industrial countries. The horizontal line shows that the index does not on average affect inflation (*D*) in developing countries. Combining the two samples masks the effect of legal central bank independence on inflation in industrial countries, because including the developing countries raises the average inflation rate (*D*) across the whole range of values for the aggregate index of legal central bank independence.

The right panel shows the partial relation between the rate of turnover of the central bank governor and inflation (*D*). The upward-sloping line shows that the increasing rate of turnover leads to increased inflation in developing countries. The short and low horizontal line shows that the rate of turnover and inflation are both generally lower in the industrial countries. The overall regressions on the rate of turnover reveal a stronger effect of turnover on real depreciation of money in the entire sample than in the developing-country subsample, because

Figure 1. *Partial Relation of Inflation to the Legal Independence and to the Turnover Rate of Governors of Central Banks in Industrial and Developing Countries*

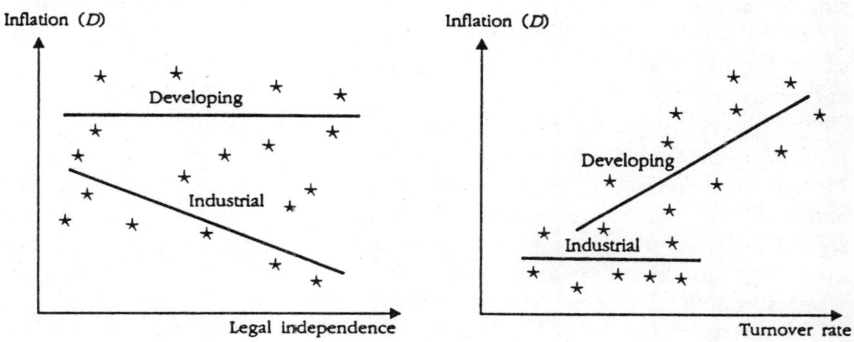

the overall regression also reflects differences between industrial and developing countries in the general levels of D and of turnover rates.

To explore further the possibility that variations in the rate of turnover of the central bank governor at high rates of turnover might have a stronger effect on inflation than variations at low levels, the regression in the fourth column of table 8 decomposes the turnover variable into high and low turnover ranges. The cutoff of 0.25 turnovers a year or an average tenure of four years seems reasonable, in view of the typical length of electoral cycles. The coefficient on turnover for the high range is very significant, although it is significant for the low range at only the 10 percent level. This result is consistent with the view that turnover is more negatively associated with actual central bank independence in the high range for turnovers.

Although the observations of the questionnaire results (and inflation) were available for a much smaller sample—only 22 countries and one period, the 1980s—than the sample for the turnover and aggregate legal central bank independence variables, we combined it into the regression reported in column 1 of table 8 and obtained the following results:

$$D = 0.27 + 0.16\ \text{Legal-CBI} + 0.57\ \text{TOR} - 0.46\ \text{Question-CBI} \qquad (2)$$
$$\qquad\qquad (0.62) \qquad\qquad (2.22)^{**} \qquad (-2.97)^{***}$$

adjusted $R^2 = 0.38$, $N = 22$

where ** and *** indicate significance at the 0.05 and 0.01 levels, respectively, Legal-CBI is the index of aggregate legal central bank independence, TOR is the rate of turnover of the central bank governor, and Question-CBI is the aggregate questionnaire-based index computed with the weights listed in table 4. The questionnaire variable has the predicted sign and is very significant statistically. The turnover variable also remains significant, which suggests that it reveals information about actual central bank independence that is not captured by the questionnaire. (The coefficient on the turnover variable may also reflect some simultaneity with the inflation variable, which is discussed below.)

To test the robustness of our results, we tried several variants of the regressions in table 8. Using regular inflation rates instead of the transformed version (D) as the dependent variable yields qualitatively similar results. Using versions of the legal central bank independence and questionnaire variables that were aggregated using equal weights on the component variables did not substantially change the results. We also tried aggregating legal variables with weights derived from principal components analysis. For the industrial-country subsample, the first principal component gave results very similar to those with equal weights and with the weights we selected. The aggregations with weights from the second and third principal components did not have significant coefficients. For the overall sample and the developing-country subsample, the aggregation with weights from the first principal component was not statistically significant.

The turnover rate also reflects the extent to which the government complies with the law's specification of the governor's term of office. To address this issue more directly, we generated a variable (the compliance variable) equal to the ratio of the actual average term in office to the legal term of office in each country and decade. In most countries and decades, actual average terms in office (including reappointments) are shorter than the legal term. Our hypothesis is that the lower the actual tenure compared with the one in the law, the lower the actual independence of the central bank and the higher the inflation rate (*D*). When the compliance variable is entered instead of the turnover variable, it gives qualitatively similar results to those with the turnover variable—significant coefficients for the overall sample and the developing countries but not in the group of industrial countries. When the compliance and turnover variables are entered together on the right-hand side, however, the compliance variable loses all significance, while the coefficient on the turnover variable remains positive and significant. In other words, it seems to be turnover itself that affects the ability and will to control inflation, rather than the relation of actual to legally stipulated turnover.

We also explored whether the low turnover would identify a subset of developing countries where the degree of legal independence did contribute to explaining inflation. An interaction term of the aggregate index of legal independence times a dummy for low turnover (0.25 or below) was not significant, however, for the whole sample or for the developing countries. Thus low turnover does not seem to be sufficient to reveal or engender a systematic respect for the legal stipulations of independence.

Previous work on inflation and central bank independence is based only on legal data and, in some cases, refers to a subset of the developed countries (Alesina 1988; Grilli, Masciandaro, and Tabellini 1991). These analyses find a significant negative relationship between some of their indexes of central bank independence and average inflation in some periods. Because the indexes of independence used here differ from those used in the previous studies, it is instructive to reexamine their samples with our indexes. We did this with the country subsamples from the earlier studies, and our variables give a better fit with the country subsamples from the previous studies than with the whole industrial-country subsample. The Grilli and others (1991) sample includes Greece and Portugal, which are in our developing-country subsample. (Further details appear in Cukierman [1992a], chap. 20.)

The same degree of central bank independence may be associated with different rates of inflation when there are different economic shocks. It is also possible that the degree of independence affects the response of policy to shocks. A more dependent central bank, for example, may inflate at a higher rate in response to a slowdown in economic activity. The investigation of such interactions is beyond the scope of this article, but it represents an intriguing avenue for future empirical research.

In summary, legal independence is systematically and inversely related to inflation in industrial, but not in developing, countries. In the latter group the actual frequency of change of the CEO of the bank is a better proxy for central bank independence. The divergence between the letter of the law and actual practice seems substantially higher in developing than in industrial countries. This may be due to a general norm of more adherence to the law in industrial countries.

Two-Way Causality between Inflation and Central Bank Independence

There may be two-way causality between inflation and the actual degree of central bank independence. As shown above, less independence contributes to higher inflation. However, high inflation is likely to result, at least after a while, in less independence. High inflation encourages processes that make it easier for the government to influence monetary policy even if the bank charter does not change. Most central bank laws are highly incomplete contracts that do not fully delimit the areas of responsibility of the bank and of the executive branch. In times of high inflation it is harder for the bank to closely control the money supply. In addition, high inflation is partly blamed on the bank, which tarnishes its public image and thus reduces its authority in relation to the treasury, even if this contradicts the charter. Argentina is a dramatic example. If inflation affects actual independence, we expect it also affects the rate of turnover of governors. Therefore, at least part of the positive relation found between inflation and turnover may reflect the effect of inflation on the independence of central banks and therefore on the turnover rate of their CEOs. The legal charters change infrequently and do not seem likely to be simultaneously determined with inflation outcomes.

To examine the possibility that the results for the turnover variable in tables 7 and 8 result from a simultaneity bias, we reestimated the regressions using two-stage least squares and introduced an instrumental variable for the rate of turnover of the central bank governor. The instruments used are transformed inflation (D) and the turnover variable in the previous decade, legal central bank independence, the legal term of office, and the decade dummies. Because periods are about a decade each, the previous observation is about 10 years away from the center of the current one—enough to be predetermined. The use of lagged values of D and turnover as instruments cuts the number of observations used in the equation by about a quarter, to 142. The coefficient of turnover remains positive, actually increases, and remains highly significant (its t-statistic is 6.98). Qualitatively similar results were also obtained with the developing-country subsample.

To investigate further the causality between inflation and the turnover of central bank governors, we did a simple Granger causality test by estimating the bivariate autoregressive processes for inflation and turnover. The periods are the four approximate decades used throughout the article. The long periods seem appropriate for slow-moving processes such as the erosion or the buildup of central bank independence and its interaction with inflation. The estimated processes for transformed inflation (D) and turnover (TOR) are given in equations 3 and 4 with t-statistics in parentheses under the coefficients.

$$D = 0.02 + \underset{(7.54)^{***}}{0.79\, D_{-1}} + \underset{(3.53)^{***}}{0.17\, \text{TOR}_{-1}} \tag{3}$$

$$\text{TOR} = 0.09 + \underset{(3.41)^{***}}{0.54\, D_{-1}} + \underset{(5.93)^{***}}{0.43\, \text{TOR}_{-1}}. \tag{4}$$

The coefficient of lagged turnover in the inflation equation is highly significant, as is the coefficient of lagged inflation in the turnover equation. A similar picture emerges when the straight inflation rate is substituted for D. The pattern also holds up for the developing-country subsample, but not for the industrial-country subsample, as the earlier results would lead one to expect.

These results imply that there is a vicious circle between inflation and low levels of central bank independence. When sufficiently sustained, inflation erodes central bank independence. Then low independence contributes to higher inflation. Although central bank independence and price stability reinforce each other, the significant coefficients for the turnover variable reported in tables 7 and 8 do seem to reflect a true effect of central bank independence on inflation, and not just simultaneity.

Central Bank Independence and the Variability of Inflation

Variability of inflation imposes economic costs. Indeed, many of the costs of high inflation arise because it is usually more variable and uncertain when the average is high (Cukierman 1984, chap. 3–6). Furthermore, theory implies that inflation will be more variable when the central bank is less independent (Cukierman 1992a, chap. 18). Thus it is important to investigate whether our proxies for central bank independence actually affect the variability of inflation. As a measure of inflation variability, we take the standard deviation of D.

The proxies for central bank independence explain inflation variability to about the same extent that they explain inflation levels (table 9). Turnover contributes significantly to explaining the variance of D in the overall sample and in the developing countries, but the variable for legal independence does not. For the industrial-country sample, the legal variable is significant at the 10 percent level. Again, with Iceland removed from the industrial subsample, the coefficient on turnover is much smaller and more insignificant, and the coefficient for legal central bank independence is significant at the 5 percent level.

The conceptual framework in chapter 18 of Cukierman (1992a) implies that the mean level of inflation and its standard deviation are both negatively related to the degree of independence of central banks across countries. As a consequence the mean level of inflation and its standard deviation are positively related to each other. There is empirical evidence that the variation in the independence of central banks explains some of the correlation between the average level of inflation rates and their variance (Cukierman 1992a, chap. 22).

Table 9. *The Standard Deviation of Transformed Inflation, Aggregate Index of Legal Central Bank Independence, and the Turnover Rate, 1950–89*

Explanatory variable	*All countries*	*Industrial countries*	*Developing countries*	*All countries with decomposed turnover variable*
Intercept	0.04***	0.04***	0.05***	0.04***
	(4.16)	(7.42)	(2.88)	(3.96)
Legal central bank independence (aggregate index)	−0.00	−0.02*	0.02	−0.01
	(−0.20)	(−1.77)	(0.40)	(−0.23)
Rate of turnover of central bank governor	0.10***	−0.02	0.09***	
	(6.23)	(−1.28)	(4.05)	
Decomposed turnover[a]				
High turnover range				0.10***
				(5.92)
Low turnover range				0.08**
				(1.95)
Dummy: 1950–59	−0.01	0.00	−0.03	−0.01
	(−1.46)	(0.80)	(−1.52)	(−1.48)
Dummy: 1960–71	−0.03***	−0.01***	−0.04***	−0.03***
	(−3.87)	(−3.14)	(−3.22)	(−3.88)
Dummy: 1972–79	−0.01	−0.00	−0.01	−0.01
	(−1.29)	(−0.77)	(−1.13)	(−1.27)
$\bar{R}^2$	0.19	0.18	0.15	0.19
Number of observations	215	79	136	215

Note: The dependent variable is the standard deviation of transformed inflation (*D*). The *t*-statistics are reported in parentheses under estimated coefficients. * indicates significance at the 10 percent level, ** at the 5 percent level, and *** at the 1 percent level.

a. The rate of turnover is in the high range if there are 0.25 or more turnovers per year; it is in the low range if there are fewer than 0.25.

Central Bank Independence and the Growth of Credit to the Government

Providing credit to the government would seem to be the most important channel through which the lack of central bank independence leads to inflation because the issue of how to finance its budget deficit is immediately relevant to the government. Providing credit to private and publicly owned business also contributes to inflation, however, as do problems with managing exchange rates. Political authorities are very concerned with these issues as they affect unemployment, bankruptcy rates, export incentives, and the domestic currency cost of imports. Although a systematic evaluation of these considerations lies beyond the scope of this article, we can at least examine the relation between central bank independence and its extension of credit to the government.

Regressing the rate of growth of credit from the bank to the public sector on the two main indicators of central bank independence—the legal independence of the central bank and turnover variables—reveals a pattern similar to, but generally less strong than, what was found with the regressions for the transformed inflation rate (table 10). The aggregate index of legal variables was not significant at all, even in the industrial-country subsample. Turnover of the central bank governor contributes significantly to explaining credit growth to the public sector, although variation of turnover at low rates does not matter much. Within the subsamples of country groups, the coefficients are not statistically significant. Yet they are consistent with the following two hypotheses. The first is that among industrial countries more legal independence limits credit expansion to the public sector, whereas the turnover rate is too low to matter much. The second is that among developing countries higher turnover reflects lower independence, which contributes to faster credit expansion, but the law does not matter much.

That the results for the growth of central bank credit are weaker than the results for inflation suggests that issues other than deficit financing are more important than we had originally thought.

An Overall Index of Inflation-Based Central Bank Independence

Legal independence and turnover capture different dimensions of central bank independence, and each seems to be important for a different subset of countries. This section combines the indicators with a weighting scheme in order to obtain an overall measure of central bank independence. Such weighting is perforce arbitrary, but we reduce the arbitrariness by setting the weights equal to the coefficients from the regressions in which they are used to explain the variation in the transformed inflation variable (D). In this sense, the resulting index of overall independence is based on inflation.

Different regressions for the industrial and developing countries generate the measures of overall central bank independence for members of each group. For

Table 10. *The Rate of Growth of Central Bank Credit to the Public Sector, 1950–89*

Explanatory variable	*All countries*	*Industrial countries*	*Developing countries*	*All countries with decomposed turnover variable*
Intercept	0.22***	0.14**	0.27**	0.22***
	(3.06)	(2.15)	(2.34)	(2.71)
Legal central bank independence (aggregate index)	−0.05	−0.13	0.20	−0.05
	(−0.33)	(−1.21)	(0.67)	(−0.33)
Rate of turnover of central bank governor	0.46***	−0.06	0.27	
	(3.48)	(−0.27)	(1.52)	
Decomposed turnover[a]				
High turnover range				0.46***
				(3.38)
Low turnover range				0.45
				(1.46)
Dummy: 1950–59	−0.19***	−0.09*	−0.20*	−0.19***
	(−2.80)	(−1.67)	(−1.79)	(−2.79)
Dummy: 1960–71	−0.15***	−0.01	−0.22***	−0.15***
	(−2.73)	(−0.28)	(−2.66)	(−2.71)
Dummy: 1972–79	−0.01	0.10**	−0.06	−0.01
	(−0.16)	(2.12)	(−0.83)	(−0.16)
$\bar{R}^2$	0.13	0.14	0.06	0.12
Number of observations	175	68	107	175

Note: The dependent variable is the rate of growth of central bank credit to the public sector. The t-statistics are reported in parentheses under estimated coefficients. * indicates significance at the 10 percent level, ** at the 5 percent level, and *** at the 1 percent level.

a. The rate of turnover is in the high range if there are 0.25 or more turnovers per year; it is in the low range if there are fewer than 0.25.

the industrial countries, the equation has only the aggregate index of legal independence, because the coefficient on turnover in tables 7 and 8 had a sign contrary to the prediction and because virtually all the observations from the industrial countries had turnover rates below the relevant threshold. For developing countries, the equation has both turnover and the index of legal independence. The two equations have the same left-side variable, *D*, and so the predicted values of *D* offer an inflation-based indicator or index of central bank independence that is comparable across the two subsamples. We estimated the equations across all periods. Table 11 shows the countries ranked by their

Table 11. *Ranking of Central Banks by an Overall Index of Independence during the 1980s*

	Transformed inflation rate (D)			
Economy	*Fitted*	*Actual*	*Legal central bank independence (aggregate index)*	*Rate of turnover of central bank governor*
Germany, Fed. Rep. of	0.04	0.02	0.69	n.a.
Switzerland	0.05	0.03	0.64	n.a.
Austria	0.05	0.03	0.61	n.a.
Denmark	0.05	0.05	0.50	n.a.
United States	0.05	0.04	0.48	n.a.
Canada	0.06	0.05	0.45	n.a.
Ireland	0.06	0.07	0.44	n.a.
Netherlands	0.06	0.02	0.42	n.a.
Australia	0.06	0.07	0.36	n.a.
Iceland	0.06	0.24	0.34	n.a.
Luxembourg	0.06	0.04	0.33	n.a.
Sweden	0.06	0.06	0.29	n.a.
Finland	0.07	0.06	0.28	n.a.
United Kingdom	0.07	0.05	0.27	n.a.
Italy	0.07	0.08	0.25	n.a.
New Zealand	0.07	0.09	0.24	n.a.
France	0.07	0.06	0.24	n.a.
Spain	0.07	0.08	0.23	n.a.
Japan	0.07	0.02	0.18	n.a.
Norway	0.07	0.07	0.17	n.a.
Belgium	0.07	0.04	0.17	n.a.
Qatar	0.11	0.03	0.20	0.00
Nepal	0.14	0.08	0.18	0.10
Zimbabwe	0.14	0.11	0.20	0.10
Hungary	0.14	0.07	0.24	0.10
Thailand	0.14	0.04	0.27	0.10
Nigeria	0.14	0.16	0.37	0.10
Barbados	0.14	0.05	0.38	0.10
Lebanon	0.14	—	0.40	0.10
Ethiopia	0.14	0.04	0.40	0.10
Honduras	0.14	0.05	0.43	0.10
Tanzania	0.14	0.21	0.44	0.10
Morocco	0.16	0.06	0.14	0.20
Yugoslavia	0.17	0.51	0.17	0.20
Taiwan	0.17	0.03	0.21	0.20

indexes of central bank independence during the 1980s. The actual values of D in the 1980s are presented too, for comparison, along with the legal independence variable for all countries and the turnover variable for the developing countries.

The overall index usually classifies extreme cases in the expected ranges. Thus Germany and the United States are classified near the top and Argentina, Brazil, and Venezuela toward the bottom. For 24 out of the 71 countries (with inflation data) in table 11, the distance between the actual and the predicted transformed inflation rate (D) is less than or equal to 0.03.

Table 11. *(continued)*

	Transformed inflation rate (D)			
Economy	*Fitted*	*Actual*	*Legal central bank independence (aggregate index)*	*Rate of turnover of central bank governor*
Panama	0.17	0.02	0.22	0.20
South Africa	0.17	0.12	0.25	0.20
Colombia	0.17	0.17	0.27	0.20
Indonesia	0.17	0.07	0.27	0.20
Romania	0.17	—	0.30	0.20
Ghana	0.17	0.28	0.31	0.20
Malaysia	0.17	0.03	0.36	0.20
Uganda	0.17	0.47	0.38	0.20
Israel	0.17	0.47	0.39	0.20
Bahamas, The	0.17	0.05	0.41	0.20
Zaire	0.17	0.34	0.43	0.20
Philippines	0.17	0.11	0.43	0.20
Kenya	0.17	0.09	0.44	0.20
Malta	0.17	0.02	0.44	0.20
Greece	0.17	0.14	0.55	0.20
Pakistan	0.19	0.06	0.21	0.30
Uruguay	0.19	0.33	0.24	0.30
China	0.19	0.07	0.29	0.30
India	0.19	0.07	0.34	0.30
Mexico	0.19	0.38	0.34	0.30
Portugal	0.20	0.14	0.41	0.30
Peru	0.20	0.64	0.43	0.30
Egypt	0.20	0.13	0.49	0.30
Botswana	0.22	0.09	0.33	0.40
Nicaragua	0.22	0.67	0.45	0.40
Turkey	0.22	0.28	0.46	0.40
Costa Rica	0.22	0.19	0.47	0.40
Poland	0.25	0.29	0.10	0.50
Korea, Republic of	0.25	0.05	0.27	0.50
Zambia	0.25	0.25	0.33	0.50
Venezuela	0.25	0.16	0.43	0.50
Western Samoa	0.27	0.05	0.30	0.56
Singapore	0.28	0.02	0.29	0.60
Brazil	0.33	0.68	0.21	0.80
Chile	0.33	0.15	0.46	0.80
Argentina	0.39	0.74	0.40	1.00

— Not available.
n.a. Not applicable.

The coefficient of rank correlation between the actual and predicted real depreciation of money is 0.25 for the countries in table 11, which indicates that the combination of variables for turnover and legal central bank independence can predict a reasonable amount of the cross-country variation in inflation in the 1980s. Using only the legal variable (and country group dummies), the coefficient of rank correlation is merely 0.19. The inclusion of turnover in the construction of an index of central bank independence improves the ability of this index to predict cross-country variations in inflation. Argentina and Brazil would have been ranked as 55th and 29th from the top in legal independence alone, instead of 71st and 69th in the overall index of independence. The large change of rankings reflects the effect of the turnover variable, which is very high for Argentina and Brazil. In most other cases, where including the turnover variable substantially improved the prediction of a country's inflation, low turnover brought the prediction down closer to the actual.

All the industrial countries are above the median of overall independence (*D* predicted 0.17), and most of the developing countries are below it. Among the countries with overall independence above the median—*D* estimated below the median—only two (Iceland and Tanzania) have actual *D* values above 0.17. This indicates that a reasonably high overall independence is highly likely to prevent high inflation. All of the countries with inflation above 50 percent (*D* 0.33) have less than median central bank independence. For 11 countries, however, the actual *D* is less than 0.17, even though they have lower-than-median overall central bank independence (estimated *D* above 0.17). In other words, lower-than-median levels of overall central bank independence do not necessarily lead to high inflation.

These findings are consistent with the view that below-median independence by itself does not necessarily result in high inflation. When there are adverse shocks, however, countries with independence levels within the low range are more likely to develop high and even exceptionally high rates of inflation.

Austria, The Bahamas, Belgium, Luxembourg, Netherlands, and Panama have lower inflation in the 1980s than their central bank independence would indicate, because their monetary policy is dominated by a policy rule fixing their exchange rate to a relatively stable currency. Korea and Japan have lower inflation than their indicators of central bank independence predict, probably because the governments, to which their central banks are subservient, have their own commitment to price stability. These examples demonstrate that high central bank independence is not necessary for price stability.

IV. Conclusions

The notion of central bank independence underlying this study is not unconditional independence from government, but rather the independence to pursue the objective of price stability, even at the cost of other objectives that may be more important to the political authorities. Thus, our measures of independence include indexes of institutional independence such as appointment procedures, as well as measures of the relative importance attached to price stability in the central bank law and in practice.

Unavoidably, there were subjective or arbitrary decisions in coding, classifying, and weighing legal information and responses to questionnaires. Results of sensitivity analysis offer some reassurance that the main results are robust, but questions about various details may remain. This study aims to contribute to the systematization of future work by committing to a systematic and documented way of characterizing central bank independence.

The study produces four different rankings of independence of central banks. The first is by legal independence, and the second is by governors' turnover rates. The third ranking utilizes responses of specialists to a questionnaire on central bank independence. The fourth ranking is based on an aggregation of the first two.

Legal independence is an important and statistically significant determinant of price stability among industrial countries, but not among developing countries. Within the latter group, some countries have elaborately locked cookie boxes, to borrow a metaphor from the beginning of the article, but some of them either break or undo the lock when they are hungry. An important step in creating an independent central bank, therefore, must involve establishing respect for the central bank charter and management, even when they are not ideal. The rate of turnover of the governors contributes significantly to explaining inflation, and it is even more important in explaining variations in inflation across the overall sample of countries. An inflation-based index of overall central bank independence—combining legal and turnover information—contributes significantly to explaining cross-country variations in the rate of inflation. These results seem robust to possible biases due to reverse causality. The results imply that the discrepancies between actual and legal independence are wider on average in developing countries than in the industrial countries. The turnover rate was not significant in explaining variations of inflation within the industrial group.

Preliminary evidence from the 1980s suggests that when questionnaire variables are used to explain variations in inflation, there is some additional information in the rate of governors' turnover but not in the legal variables.

There seems to be a vicious circle between inflation and the lack of central bank independence, which deserves fuller investigation. Preliminary results here indicate a two-way (positive in both directions) causality between inflation and turnover of central bank governors, a proxy for lack of independence. Lower independence induces higher future inflation, which, in turn, reduces the subsequent actual level of central bank independence, and so on. Success in controlling inflation, however, seems to enhance the independence of central banks.

Finally, central bank independence is only one of several institutional devices for ensuring price stability. Some of the structural and political determinants of central bank independence are discussed in Cukierman (1992a, chap. 23, and 1992b).

Table A-1. *Disaggregated and Aggregated Legal Central Bank Independence Variables, by Country and Decade*

	Disaggregated legal variables																	
	CEO variables				Policy formulation variables			Central bank	Limitations on lending variables								Aggregate legal
Economy and decade	Term of office (1a)	Who appoints (1b)	Dis-missal (1c)	Other offices (1d)	Who formu-lates (2a)	Final authority (2b)	Role in budget (2c)	objectives variable (3)	Advances (4a)	Securitized lending (4b)	Terms of lending (4c)	Potential borrowers (4d)	Type of limit (4e)	Maturity of loans (4f)	Interest rates (4g)	Primary market (4h)	central bank independence variable
Argentina																	
1972–79	0.25	0.25	0.83	1.00	0.33	0.00	0.00	0.40	0.33	0.33	0.33	1.00	0.33	1.00	0.50	0.00	0.40
1980–89	0.25	0.25	0.83	1.00	0.33	0.00	0.00	0.40	0.33	0.33	0.33	1.00	0.33	1.00	0.50	0.00	0.40
Australia																	
1960–71	0.75	0.00	0.83	1.00	0.33	0.20	0.00	0.40	0.33	0.00	0.33	0.00	—	0.67	1.00	0.00	0.36
1972–79	0.75	0.00	0.83	1.00	0.33	0.20	0.00	0.40	0.33	0.00	0.33	0.00	—	0.67	1.00	0.00	0.36
1980–89	0.75	0.00	0.83	1.00	0.33	0.20	0.00	0.40	0.33	0.00	0.33	0.00	—	0.67	1.00	0.00	0.36
Austria																	
1950–59	0.50	0.00	0.83	1.00	0.67	0.60	0.00	0.60	1.00	0.67	0.33	1.00	1.00	1.00	1.00	0.00	0.65
1960–71	0.50	0.00	0.83	1.00	0.67	0.60	0.00	0.60	1.00	0.67	0.33	1.00	1.00	1.00	1.00	0.00	0.65
1972–79	0.50	0.00	0.83	1.00	1.00	0.60	0.00	0.60	1.00	0.67	0.33	0.33	0.33	1.00	1.00	0.00	0.61
1980–89	0.50	0.00	0.83	1.00	1.00	0.60	0.00	0.60	1.00	0.67	0.33	0.33	0.33	1.00	1.00	0.00	0.61
Bahamas, The																	
1972–79	0.50	0.00	0.83	0.50	0.33	—	0.00	0.60	0.33	0.33	0.33	1.00	0.33	1.00	0.25	0.00	0.41
1980–89	0.50	0.00	0.83	0.50	0.33	—	0.00	0.60	0.33	0.33	0.33	1.00	0.33	1.00	0.25	0.00	0.41
Barbados																	
1972–79	0.50	0.00	0.83	0.00	0.33	0.20	0.00	0.80	0.33	0.33	0.33	0.67	—	0.33	0.25	0.00	0.38
1980–89	0.50	0.00	0.83	0.00	0.33	0.20	0.00	0.80	0.33	0.33	0.33	0.67	—	0.33	0.25	0.00	0.38
Belgium																	
1950–59	0.50	0.00	0.00	0.50	0.00	0.00	0.00	0.00	0.00	0.00	0.33	0.33	—	1.00	0.50	0.00	0.15
1960–71	0.50	0.00	0.00	0.50	0.00	0.00	0.00	0.00	0.00	0.00	0.33	0.33	—	1.00	0.50	0.00	0.15
1972–79	0.50	0.00	0.00	0.50	0.00	0.20	0.00	0.00	0.00	0.00	0.33	0.33	—	1.00	0.50	0.00	0.17
1980–89	0.50	0.00	0.00	0.50	0.00	0.20	0.00	0.00	0.00	0.00	0.33	0.33	—	1.00	0.50	0.00	0.17
Bolivia																	
1950–59	0.00	0.00	0.83	1.00	0.67	0.20	0.00	0.60	0.33	0.00	0.00	0.00	0.00	1.00	0.25	0.00	0.30
1960–71	0.00	0.00	0.83	1.00	0.67	0.20	0.00	0.60	0.33	0.00	0.00	0.00	0.00	1.00	0.25	0.00	0.30
1972–79	0.00	0.00	0.83	1.00	0.67	0.20	0.00	0.60	0.33	0.00	0.00	0.00	0.00	1.00	0.25	0.00	0.30
1980–89	0.00	0.00	0.83	1.00	0.67	0.20	0.00	0.60	0.33	0.00	0.00	0.00	0.00	1.00	0.25	0.00	0.30

Botswana																	
1972–79	0.50	0.00	0.83	0.50	—	0.00	0.00	0.20	0.33	0.67	0.33	0.67	0.33	0.33	0.25	0.00	0.33
1980–89	0.50	0.00	0.83	0.50	—	0.00	0.00	0.20	0.33	0.67	0.33	0.67	0.33	0.33	0.25	0.00	0.33
Brazil																	
1960–71	0.00	0.50	0.00	0.00	0.33	—	0.00	0.00	0.67	0.00	0.00	1.00	—	0.00	0.25	0.00	0.21
1972–79	0.00	0.50	0.00	0.00	0.33	—	0.00	0.00	0.67	0.00	0.00	1.00	—	0.00	0.25	0.00	0.21
1980–89	0.00	0.50	0.00	0.00	0.33	—	0.00	0.00	0.67	0.00	0.00	1.00	—	0.00	0.25	0.00	0.21
Canada																	
1950–59	0.75	0.75	0.83	1.00	0.33	0.20	0.00	0.20	0.33	0.67	0.44	0.67	0.33	0.67	0.75	0.00	0.45
1960–71	0.75	0.75	0.83	1.00	0.33	0.20	0.00	0.20	0.33	0.33	0.67	0.67	0.33	0.67	0.75	0.00	0.45
1972–79	0.75	0.75	0.83	1.00	0.33	0.20	0.00	0.20	0.33	0.33	0.67	0.67	0.33	0.67	0.75	0.00	0.45
1980–89	0.75	0.75	0.83	1.00	0.33	0.20	0.00	0.20	0.33	0.33	0.67	0.67	0.33	0.67	0.75	0.00	0.45
Chile																	
1950–59	0.00	1.00	1.00	0.50	0.67	0.00	0.00	0.20	0.00	0.00	0.67	0.00	—	0.00	0.25	0.00	0.26
1960–71	0.00	1.00	1.00	0.50	0.67	0.00	0.00	0.20	0.00	0.00	0.67	0.00	—	0.00	0.25	0.00	0.26
1972–79	0.50	0.00	0.83	0.50	0.67	0.20	0.00	0.80	0.33	0.33	0.67	1.00	—	0.00	0.25	0.00	0.46
1980–89	0.50	0.00	0.83	0.50	0.67	0.20	0.00	0.80	0.33	0.33	0.67	1.00	—	0.00	0.25	0.00	0.46
China																	
1950–59	0.50	—	—	0.00	—	0.80	0.00	0.20	—	0.33	0.00	—	—	0.00	0.25	1.00	0.29
1960–71	0.50	—	—	0.00	—	0.80	0.00	0.20	—	0.33	0.00	—	—	0.00	0.25	1.00	0.29
1972–79	0.50	—	—	0.00	—	0.80	0.00	0.20	—	0.33	0.00	—	—	0.00	0.25	1.00	0.29
1980–89	0.50	—	—	0.00	—	0.80	0.00	0.20	—	0.33	0.00	—	—	0.00	0.25	1.00	0.29
Colombia																	
1960–71	0.00	0.75	0.83	0.00	0.00	0.20	0.00	0.00	0.67	0.00	0.33	0.00	0.67	0.67	0.25	0.00	0.27
1972–79	0.00	0.75	0.83	0.00	0.00	0.20	0.00	0.00	0.67	0.00	0.33	0.00	0.67	0.67	0.25	0.00	0.27
1980–89	0.00	0.75	0.83	0.00	0.00	0.20	0.00	0.00	0.67	0.00	0.33	0.00	0.67	0.67	0.25	0.00	0.27
Costa Rica																	
1960–71	—	1.00	0.67	1.00	—	—	0.00	0.60	0.67	0.33	0.33	0.33	0.00	0.67	0.25	0.00	0.47
1972–79	—	1.00	0.67	1.00	—	—	0.00	0.60	0.67	0.33	0.33	0.33	0.00	0.67	0.25	0.00	0.47
1980–89	—	1.00	0.67	1.00	—	—	0.00	0.60	0.67	0.33	0.33	0.33	0.00	0.67	0.25	0.00	0.47
Denmark																	
1950–59	0.00	0.00	0.33	0.00	—	1.00	0.00	0.60	1.00	0.33	0.67	0.00	—	1.00	0.25	0.00	0.50
1960–71	0.00	0.00	0.33	0.00	—	1.00	0.00	0.60	1.00	0.33	0.67	0.00	—	1.00	0.25	0.00	0.50
1972–79	0.00	0.00	0.33	0.00	—	1.00	0.00	0.60	1.00	0.33	0.67	0.00	—	1.00	0.25	0.00	0.50
1980–89	0.00	0.00	0.33	0.00	—	1.00	0.00	0.60	1.00	0.33	0.67	0.00	—	1.00	0.25	0.00	0.50

(Table continues on the following page.)

Table A-1. *(continued)*

Economy and decade	Term of office (1a)	Who appoints (1b)	Dis-missal (1c)	Other offices (1d)	Who formu-lates (2a)	Final authority (2b)	Role in budget (2c)	Central bank objectives variable (3)	Advances (4a)	Securitized lending (4b)	Terms of lending (4c)	Potential borrowers (4d)	Type of limit (4e)	Maturity of loans (4f)	Interest rates (4g)	Primary market (4h)	Aggregate legal central bank independence variable
	Disaggregated legal variables																
	CEO variables				*Policy formulation variables*				*Limitations on lending variables*								
Egypt																	
1950–59	0.50	0.50	1.00	1.00	0.33	0.00	0.00	0.60	0.67	0.67	0.33	1.00	0.33	0.00	0.25	0.00	0.52
1960–71	0.50	0.50	1.00	1.00	0.33	0.00	0.00	0.60	0.67	0.67	0.33	1.00	0.33	0.00	0.25	0.00	0.52
1972–79	0.50	0.50	1.00	0.00	0.33	0.00	0.00	0.60	0.67	0.67	0.33	1.00	0.67	0.67	0.25	0.00	0.49
1980–89	0.50	0.50	1.00	0.00	0.33	0.00	0.00	0.60	0.67	0.67	0.33	1.00	0.67	0.67	0.25	0.00	0.49
Ethiopia																	
1960–71	0.50	0.25	0.00	0.00	—	—	—	0.60	—	—	—	—	—	0.00	0.25	0.00	—
1972–79	0.00	0.25	0.00	0.00	—	1.00	1.00	0.00	0.33	0.33	0.67	1.00	0.33	0.67	0.50	0.00	0.40
1980–89	0.00	0.25	0.00	0.00	—	1.00	1.00	0.00	0.33	0.33	0.67	1.00	0.33	0.67	0.50	0.00	0.40
Finland																	
1950–59	1.00	0.00	—	0.00	—	0.00	0.00	0.80	0.00	0.00	0.67	—	—	0.00	0.25	0.00	0.28
1960–71	1.00	0.00	—	0.00	—	0.00	0.00	0.80	0.00	0.00	0.67	—	—	0.00	0.25	0.00	0.28
1972–79	1.00	0.00	—	0.00	—	0.00	0.00	0.80	0.00	0.00	0.67	—	—	0.00	0.25	0.00	0.28
1980–89	1.00	0.00	—	0.00	—	0.00	0.00	0.80	0.00	0.00	0.67	—	—	0.00	0.25	0.00	0.28
France																	
1950–59	0.00	0.25	1.00	0.50	0.33	0.60	0.00	0.20	0.33	0.00	0.33	0.00	1.00	0.00	0.00	0.00	0.28
1960–71	0.00	0.25	1.00	0.50	0.33	0.60	0.00	0.20	0.33	0.00	0.33	1.00	1.00	1.00	0.00	0.00	0.36
1972–79	0.00	0.25	1.00	0.50	0.67	0.60	0.00	0.00	0.00	0.00	0.33	1.00	—	—	—	0.00	0.24
1980–89	0.00	0.25	1.00	0.50	0.67	0.60	0.00	0.00	0.00	0.00	0.33	1.00	—	—	—	0.00	0.24
Germany, Fed. Rep. of																	
1950–59	1.00	0.75	1.00	0.00	0.67	1.00	0.00	1.00	0.67	0.67	0.67	0.33	1.00	1.00	0.25	0.00	0.69
1960–71	1.00	0.75	1.00	0.00	0.67	1.00	0.00	1.00	0.67	0.67	0.67	0.33	1.00	1.00	0.25	0.00	0.69
1972–79	1.00	0.75	1.00	0.00	0.67	1.00	0.00	1.00	0.67	0.67	0.67	0.33	1.00	1.00	0.25	0.00	0.69
1980–89	1.00	0.75	1.00	0.00	0.67	1.00	0.00	1.00	0.67	0.67	0.67	0.33	1.00	1.00	0.25	0.00	0.69

Ghana																	
1950–59	0.50	0.00	0.83	0.50	0.33	0.00	0.00	0.60	0.67	0.67	0.33	1.00	0.33	0.67	0.75	0.00	0.49
1960–71	0.50	0.00	0.83	0.50	0.33	0.00	0.00	0.60	0.00	0.33	0.33	0.00	0.33	1.00	0.50	0.00	0.31
1972–79	0.50	0.00	0.83	0.50	0.33	0.00	0.00	0.60	0.00	0.33	0.33	0.00	0.33	1.00	0.50	0.00	0.31
1980–89	0.50	0.00	0.83	0.50	0.33	0.00	0.00	0.60	0.00	0.33	0.33	0.00	0.33	1.00	0.50	0.00	0.31
Greece																	
1950–59	0.25	0.75	0.67	0.50	0.33	0.60	0.00	0.80	0.67	0.67	0.33	0.33	1.00	0.67	0.75	0.00	0.56
1960–71	0.25	0.75	0.67	0.50	0.33	0.60	0.00	0.80	0.33	0.67	0.33	0.33	1.00	0.67	0.75	0.00	0.51
1972–79	0.25	0.75	0.67	0.50	0.33	0.60	0.00	0.80	0.67	0.67	0.33	0.00	1.00	1.00	0.75	0.00	0.55
1980–89	0.25	0.75	0.67	0.50	0.33	0.60	0.00	0.80	0.67	0.67	0.33	0.00	1.00	1.00	0.75	0.00	0.55
Honduras																	
1950–59	0.75	0.00	0.83	1.00	0.33	1.00	0.00	0.00	—	0.33	0.67	0.33	0.33	0.67	0.25	0.00	0.43
1960–71	0.75	0.00	0.83	1.00	0.33	1.00	0.00	0.00	—	0.33	0.67	0.33	0.33	0.67	0.25	0.00	0.43
1972–79	0.75	0.00	0.83	1.00	0.33	1.00	0.00	0.00	—	0.33	0.67	0.33	0.33	0.67	0.25	0.00	0.43
1980–89	0.75	0.00	0.83	1.00	0.33	1.00	0.00	0.00	—	0.33	0.67	0.33	0.33	0.67	0.25	0.00	0.43
Hungary																	
1950–59	0.50	0.25	1.00	0.00	0.33	0.00	0.00	0.40	0.00	0.00	0.00	0.33	1.00	0.67	1.00	0.00	0.24
1960–71	0.50	0.25	1.00	0.00	0.33	0.00	0.00	0.40	0.00	0.00	0.00	0.33	1.00	0.67	1.00	0.00	0.24
1972–79	0.50	0.25	1.00	0.00	0.33	0.00	0.00	0.40	0.00	0.00	0.00	0.33	1.00	0.67	1.00	0.00	0.24
1980–89	0.50	0.25	1.00	0.00	0.33	0.00	0.00	0.40	0.00	0.00	0.00	0.33	1.00	0.67	1.00	0.00	0.24
Iceland																	
1950–59	1.00	—	—	—	—	—	—	—	—	—	—	—	—	—	—	—	—
1960–71	1.00	0.75	0.83	0.50	0.33	0.20	0.00	0.40	0.00	0.00	0.33	1.00	—	0.33	0.25	0.00	0.34
1972–79	1.00	0.75	0.83	0.50	0.33	0.20	0.00	0.40	0.00	0.00	0.33	1.00	—	0.33	0.25	0.00	0.34
1980–89	1.00	0.75	0.83	0.50	0.33	0.20	0.00	0.40	0.00	0.00	0.33	1.00	—	0.33	0.25	0.00	0.34
India																	
1950–59	0.50	0.25	0.83	0.50	—	0.00	0.00	0.40	0.00	0.00	0.33	0.33	1.00	0.33	0.25	0.00	0.25
1960–71	0.50	0.25	0.83	0.50	—	0.00	0.00	0.40	0.33	0.00	0.67	0.33	1.00	0.33	0.25	0.00	0.34
1972–79	0.50	0.25	0.83	0.50	—	0.00	0.00	0.40	0.33	0.00	0.67	0.33	1.00	0.33	0.25	0.00	0.34
1980–89	0.50	0.25	0.83	0.50	—	0.00	0.00	0.40	0.33	0.00	0.67	0.33	1.00	0.33	0.25	0.00	0.34
Indonesia																	
1950–59	0.50	0.25	0.00	0.50	0.67	0.00	0.00	0.00	0.33	0.33	0.00	1.00	0.33	0.00	0.25	0.00	0.24
1960–71	0.50	0.25	0.00	0.50	0.67	0.00	0.00	0.40	0.33	0.33	0.00	1.00	0.33	0.00	0.25	0.00	0.30
1972–79	0.50	0.25	0.00	0.50	0.67	0.20	0.00	0.40	0.00	0.00	0.33	1.00	0.33	0.33	0.25	0.00	0.27
1980–89	0.50	0.25	0.00	0.50	0.67	0.20	0.00	0.40	0.00	0.00	0.33	1.00	0.33	0.33	0.25	0.00	0.27

(*Table continues on the following page.*)

Table A-1. *(continued)*

	Disaggregated legal variables																
	CEO variables				Policy formulation variables			Central bank objectives variable	Limitations on lending variables								Aggregate legal central bank independence variable
Economy and decade	Term of office (1a)	Who appoints (1b)	Dis-missal (1c)	Other offices (1d)	Who formu-lates (2a)	Final authority (2b)	Role in budget (2c)	(3)	Advances (4a)	Securitized lending (4b)	Terms of lending (4c)	Potential borrowers (4d)	Type of limit (4e)	Maturity of loans (4f)	Interest rates (4g)	Primary market (4h)	
Ireland																	
1950–59	0.75	0.50	0.83	1.00	—	—	0.00	0.80	—	0.00	0.33	0.33	—	0.67	0.75	0.00	0.44
1960–71	0.75	0.50	0.83	1.00	—	—	0.00	0.80	—	0.00	0.33	0.33	—	0.67	0.75	0.00	0.44
1972–79	0.75	0.50	0.83	1.00	—	—	0.00	0.80	—	0.00	0.33	0.33	—	0.67	0.75	0.00	0.44
1980–89	0.75	0.50	0.83	1.00	—	—	0.00	0.80	—	0.00	0.33	0.33	—	0.67	0.75	0.00	0.44
Israel																	
1950–59	0.50	0.50	0.50	0.50	0.67	0.20	0.00	0.40	0.33	0.00	0.67	1.00	0.00	0.67	0.25	0.00	0.39
1960–71	0.50	0.50	0.50	0.50	0.67	0.20	0.00	0.40	0.33	0.00	0.67	1.00	0.00	0.67	0.25	0.00	0.39
1972–79	0.50	0.50	0.50	0.50	0.67	0.20	0.00	0.40	0.33	0.00	0.67	1.00	0.00	0.67	0.25	0.00	0.39
1980–89	0.50	0.50	0.50	0.50	0.67	0.20	0.00	0.40	0.33	0.00	0.67	1.00	0.00	0.67	0.25	0.00	0.39
Italy																	
1950–59	0.00	0.75	0.67	1.00	—	—	0.00	0.20	0.33	0.00	0.33	—	0.00	0.00	0.25	0.00	0.25
1960–71	0.00	0.75	0.67	1.00	—	—	0.00	0.20	0.33	0.00	0.33	—	0.00	0.00	0.25	0.00	0.25
1972–79	0.00	0.75	0.67	1.00	—	—	0.00	0.20	0.33	0.00	0.33	—	0.00	0.00	0.25	0.00	0.25
1980–89	0.00	0.75	0.67	1.00	—	—	0.00	0.20	0.33	0.00	0.33	—	0.00	0.00	0.25	0.00	0.25
Japan																	
1950–59	0.50	0.25	0.83	0.50	0.67	0.00	0.00	0.00	0.00	0.00	0.33	—	—	0.00	0.25	0.00	0.18
1960–71	0.50	0.25	0.83	0.50	0.67	0.00	0.00	0.00	0.00	0.00	0.33	—	—	0.00	0.25	0.00	0.18
1972–79	0.50	0.25	0.83	0.50	0.67	0.00	0.00	0.00	0.00	0.00	0.33	—	—	0.00	0.25	0.00	0.18
1980–89	0.50	0.25	0.83	0.50	0.67	0.00	0.00	0.00	0.00	0.00	0.33	—	—	0.00	0.25	0.00	0.18
Kenya																	
1960–71	0.25	0.00	0.83	0.50	—	0.20	0.00	0.40	0.67	0.67	0.33	0.33	1.00	0.67	0.75	0.00	0.44
1972–79	0.25	0.00	0.83	0.50	—	0.20	0.00	0.40	0.67	0.67	0.33	0.33	1.00	0.67	0.75	0.00	0.44
1980–89	0.25	0.00	0.83	0.50	—	0.20	0.00	0.40	0.67	0.67	0.33	0.33	1.00	0.67	0.75	0.00	0.44

Korea, Republic of																	
1950–59	0.25	0.25	0.83	0.00	0.33	—	0.00	0.60	0.33	0.00	0.33	0.00	—	0.67	0.25	0.00	0.30
1960–71	0.25	0.25	0.83	0.00	0.33	—	0.00	0.60	0.33	0.00	0.33	0.00	—	0.67	0.25	0.00	0.30
1972–79	0.25	0.25	0.83	0.50	0.33	—	0.00	0.60	0.33	0.00	0.33	0.00	—	0.67	0.25	0.00	0.32
1980–89	0.25	0.25	0.83	0.50	0.33	—	0.00	0.60	0.00	0.00	0.33	0.00	—	0.67	0.25	0.00	0.27
Lebanon																	
1950–59	0.75	0.25	0.83	1.00	0.67	—	0.00	0.00	0.67	0.00	0.33	0.33	0.33	1.00	1.00	0.00	0.40
1960–71	0.75	0.25	0.83	1.00	0.67	—	0.00	0.00	0.67	0.00	0.33	0.33	0.33	1.00	1.00	0.00	0.40
1972–79	0.75	0.25	0.83	1.00	0.67	—	0.00	0.00	0.67	0.00	0.33	0.33	0.33	1.00	1.00	0.00	0.40
1980–89	0.75	0.25	0.83	1.00	0.67	—	0.00	0.00	0.67	0.00	0.33	0.33	0.33	1.00	1.00	0.00	0.40
Luxembourg																	
1980–89	0.75	0.25	0.83	0.00	0.33	—	0.00	0.60	0.00	0.00	0.33	1.00	—	1.00	0.25	0.00	0.33
Malaysia																	
1960–71	0.50	0.00	0.83	0.00	0.00	0.20	0.00	0.60	0.33	—	0.67	0.00	0.33	0.67	0.25	0.00	0.36
1972–79	0.50	0.00	0.83	0.00	0.00	0.20	0.00	0.60	0.33	—	0.67	0.00	0.33	0.67	0.25	0.00	0.36
1980–89	0.50	0.00	0.83	0.00	0.00	0.20	0.00	0.60	0.33	—	0.67	0.00	0.33	0.67	0.25	0.00	0.36
Malta																	
1960–71	0.50	0.50	0.83	1.00	0.00	0.20	0.00	0.40	0.67	0.00	0.33	1.00	0.33	1.00	0.25	0.00	0.44
1972–79	0.50	0.50	0.83	1.00	0.00	0.20	0.00	0.40	0.67	0.00	0.33	1.00	0.33	1.00	0.25	0.00	0.44
1980–89	0.50	0.50	0.83	1.00	0.00	0.20	0.00	0.40	0.67	0.00	0.33	1.00	0.33	1.00	0.25	0.00	0.44
Mexico																	
1950–59	—	0.00	0.83	1.00	0.00	0.20	0.00	0.00	0.00	0.00	0.33	1.00	—	0.67	0.25	0.00	0.25
1960–71	—	1.00	0.83	1.00	0.67	0.20	0.00	0.00	0.00	0.00	0.33	1.00	—	0.67	0.25	0.00	0.34
1972–79	—	1.00	0.83	1.00	0.67	0.20	0.00	0.00	0.00	0.00	0.33	1.00	—	0.67	0.25	0.00	0.34
1980–89	—	1.00	0.83	1.00	0.67	0.20	0.00	0.00	0.00	0.00	0.33	1.00	—	0.67	0.25	0.00	0.34
Morocco																	
1960–71	—	0.25	0.00	0.00	—	—	0.00	0.20	0.33	0.00	0.00	0.33	0.33	0.67	0.25	0.00	0.14
1972–79	—	0.25	0.00	0.00	—	—	0.00	0.20	0.33	0.00	0.00	0.33	0.33	0.67	0.25	0.00	0.14
1980–89	—	0.25	0.00	0.00	—	—	0.00	0.20	0.33	0.00	0.00	0.33	0.33	0.67	0.25	0.00	0.14
Nepal																	
1950–59	0.50	0.25	0.00	0.00	—	0.00	0.00	0.20	0.00	0.00	0.33	1.00	—	0.67	0.25	0.00	0.18
1960–71	0.50	0.25	0.00	0.00	—	0.00	0.00	0.20	0.00	0.00	0.33	1.00	—	0.67	0.25	0.00	0.18
1972–79	0.50	0.25	0.00	0.00	—	0.00	0.00	0.20	0.00	0.00	0.33	1.00	—	0.67	0.25	0.00	0.18
1980–89	0.50	0.25	0.00	0.00	—	0.00	0.00	0.20	0.00	0.00	0.33	1.00	—	0.67	0.25	0.00	0.18

(*Table continues on the following page.*)

Table A-1. *(continued)*

	Disaggregated legal variables																	
	CEO variables				Policy formulation variables			Central bank	Limitations on lending variables									Aggregate legal
Economy and decade	Term of office (1a)	Who appoints (1b)	Dis-missal (1c)	Other offices (1d)	Who formu-lates (2a)	Final authority (2b)	Role in budget (2c)	objectives variable (3)	Advances (4a)	Securitized lending (4b)	Terms of lending (4c)	Potential borrowers (4d)	Type of limit (4e)	Maturity of loans (4f)	Interest rates (4g)	Primary market (4h)	central bank independence variable
Netherlands																	
1950–59	0.75	0.00	0.17	1.00	0.33	0.20	0.00	0.80	0.67	0.00	0.00	1.00	1.00	0.00	0.00	0.00	0.42
1960–71	0.75	0.00	0.17	1.00	0.33	0.20	0.00	0.80	0.67	0.00	0.00	1.00	1.00	0.00	0.00	0.00	0.42
1972–79	0.75	0.00	0.17	1.00	0.33	0.20	0.00	0.80	0.67	0.00	0.00	1.00	1.00	0.00	0.00	0.00	0.42
1980–89	0.75	0.00	0.17	1.00	0.33	0.20	0.00	0.80	0.67	0.00	0.00	1.00	1.00	0.00	0.00	0.00	0.42
New Zealand																	
1950–59	0.50	0.00	0.83	0.00	0.00	0.00	0.00	0.00	—	—	0.00	0.33	0.33	1.00	0.75	0.00	0.18
1960–71	0.50	0.00	0.83	1.00	0.00	0.00	0.00	0.40	0.00	0.00	0.00	1.00	—	0.00	0.50	0.00	0.24
1972–79	0.50	0.00	0.83	1.00	0.00	0.00	0.00	0.40	0.00	0.00	0.00	1.00	—	0.00	0.50	0.00	0.24
1980–89	0.50	0.00	0.83	1.00	0.00	0.00	0.00	0.40	0.00	0.00	0.00	1.00	—	0.00	0.50	0.00	0.24
Nicaragua																	
1960–71	0.00	0.00	0.83	1.00	1.00	—	0.00	0.00	1.00	0.33	0.67	0.00	0.33	0.67	0.50	0.00	0.45
1972–79	0.00	0.00	0.83	1.00	1.00	—	0.00	0.00	1.00	0.33	0.67	0.00	0.33	0.67	0.50	0.00	0.45
1980–89	0.00	0.00	0.83	1.00	1.00	—	0.00	0.00	1.00	0.33	0.67	0.00	0.33	0.67	0.50	0.00	0.45
Nigeria																	
1960–71	0.50	0.00	0.83	0.50	0.33	0.20	0.00	0.60	0.33	0.33	0.33	0.00	0.33	0.67	0.75	0.00	0.37
1972–79	0.50	0.00	0.83	0.50	0.33	0.20	0.00	0.60	0.33	0.33	0.33	0.00	0.33	0.67	0.75	0.00	0.37
1980–89	0.50	0.00	0.83	0.50	0.33	0.20	0.00	0.60	0.33	0.33	0.33	0.00	0.33	0.67	0.75	0.00	0.37
Norway																	
1950–59	0.75	0.00	0.33	1.00	0.00	0.20	0.00	0.00	—	—	0.00	0.00	—	0.67	0.25	0.00	0.20
1960–71	0.75	0.00	0.33	1.00	0.00	0.20	0.00	0.00	0.00	0.00	0.00	0.00	—	0.67	0.25	0.00	0.15
1972–79	0.75	0.00	0.33	1.00	0.33	0.20	0.00	0.00	0.00	0.00	0.00	0.00	—	0.67	0.50	0.00	0.17
1980–89	0.75	0.00	0.33	1.00	0.33	0.20	0.00	0.00	0.00	0.00	0.00	0.00	—	0.67	0.50	0.00	0.17
Pakistan																	
1950–59	0.50	0.25	0.83	0.50	0.00	0.00	0.00	0.40	0.00	0.00	0.00	0.33	—	0.67	0.25	0.00	0.21
1960–71	0.50	0.25	0.83	0.50	0.00	0.00	0.00	0.40	0.00	0.00	0.00	0.33	—	0.67	0.25	0.00	0.21
1972–79	0.50	0.25	0.83	0.50	0.00	0.00	0.00	0.40	0.00	0.00	0.00	0.33	—	0.67	0.25	0.00	0.21
1980–89	0.50	0.25	0.83	0.50	0.00	0.00	0.00	0.40	0.00	0.00	0.00	0.33	—	0.67	0.25	0.00	0.21

Panama																	
1950–59	—	0.25	0.83	1.00	0.33	0.00	0.00	0.40	0.00	0.00	0.00	0.33	—	0.00	0.25	0.00	0.24
1960–71	—	0.25	0.83	1.00	0.33	0.00	0.00	0.40	0.00	0.00	0.00	0.33	—	0.00	0.25	0.00	0.24
1972–79	—	0.25	0.83	1.00	0.33	0.00	0.00	0.40	0.00	0.00	0.00	0.00	—	0.00	0.25	0.00	0.22
1980–89	—	0.25	0.83	1.00	0.33	0.00	0.00	0.40	0.00	0.00	0.00	0.00	—	0.00	0.25	0.00	0.22
Peru																	
1960–71	0.00	1.00	0.83	1.00	0.67	0.20	0.00	0.40	0.00	0.67	0.67	0.33	0.33	1.00	0.25	0.00	0.43
1972–79	0.00	1.00	0.83	1.00	0.67	0.20	0.00	0.40	0.00	0.67	0.67	0.33	0.33	1.00	0.25	0.00	0.43
1980–89	0.00	1.00	0.83	1.00	0.67	0.20	0.00	0.40	0.00	0.67	0.67	0.33	0.33	1.00	0.25	0.00	0.43
Philippines																	
1950–59	0.75	0.00	0.83	0.50	0.67	0.20	0.00	1.00	0.33	0.00	0.33	0.67	0.33	0.33	0.25	0.00	0.43
1960–71	0.75	0.00	0.83	0.50	0.67	0.20	0.00	1.00	0.33	0.00	0.33	0.67	0.33	0.33	0.25	0.00	0.43
1972–79	0.75	0.00	0.83	0.50	0.67	0.20	0.00	1.00	0.33	0.00	0.33	0.67	0.33	0.33	0.25	0.00	0.43
1980–89	0.75	0.00	0.83	0.50	0.67	0.20	0.00	1.00	0.33	0.00	0.33	0.67	0.33	0.33	0.25	0.00	0.43
Poland																	
1950–59	0.50	0.25	0.00	0.50	0.33	0.00	0.00	0.00	0.00	0.00	0.33	0.00	—	0.67	0.25	0.00	0.14
1960–71	0.50	0.25	0.00	0.50	0.33	0.00	0.00	0.00	0.00	0.00	0.33	0.00	—	0.67	0.25	0.00	0.14
1972–79	0.50	0.25	0.00	0.00	0.67	0.00	0.00	0.00	0.00	0.00	0.33	0.00	—	0.00	0.25	0.00	0.10
1980–89	0.50	0.25	0.00	0.00	0.67	0.00	0.00	0.00	0.00	0.00	0.33	0.00	—	0.00	0.25	0.00	0.10
Portugal																	
1972–79	0.50	0.25	1.00	1.00	0.33	0.40	0.00	0.60	0.33	0.33	0.67	0.67	0.00	0.67	0.25	0.00	0.48
1980–89	0.00	0.25	1.00	0.00	0.33	0.60	0.00	0.00	0.67	0.67	0.67	0.00	1.00	1.00	0.25	0.00	0.41
Qatar																	
1972–79	0.50	0.25	0.83	0.50	0.33	0.00	0.00	0.40	0.00	0.00	0.00	0.33	—	0.00	0.25	0.00	0.20
1980–89	0.50	0.25	0.83	0.50	0.33	0.00	0.00	0.40	0.00	0.00	0.00	0.33	—	0.00	0.25	0.00	0.20
Romania																	
1950–59	0.50	0.25	1.00	1.00	0.67	0.60	0.00	0.60	0.67	0.33	0.67	0.00	0.67	0.67	0.00	0.00	0.53
1960–71	0.50	0.25	1.00	1.00	0.67	0.60	0.00	0.60	0.67	0.33	0.67	0.00	0.67	0.67	0.00	0.00	0.53
1972–79	—	0.25	—	0.00	1.00	0.80	0.00	0.20	—	—	0.67	0.00	—	0.00	0.25	0.00	0.30
1980–89	—	0.25	—	0.00	1.00	0.80	0.00	0.20	—	—	0.67	0.00	—	0.00	0.25	0.00	0.30
Singapore																	
1972–79	0.25	0.00	0.83	0.00	—	—	0.00	0.60	—	—	0.33	0.00	—	1.00	0.25	0.00	0.29
1980–89	0.25	0.00	0.83	0.00	—	—	0.00	0.60	—	—	0.33	0.00	—	1.00	0.25	0.00	0.29

(*Table continues on the following page.*)

Table A-1. *(continued)*

Economy and decade	*Disaggregated legal variables*																Aggregate legal central bank independence variable
	CEO variables				Policy formulation variables			Central bank objectives variable	Limitations on lending variables								
	Term of office (1a)	Who appoints (1b)	Dis-missal (1c)	Other offices (1d)	Who formu-lates (2a)	Final authority (2b)	Role in budget (2c)	(3)	Advances (4a)	Securitized lending (4b)	Terms of lending (4c)	Potential borrowers (4d)	Type of limit (4e)	Maturity of loans (4f)	Interest rates (4g)	Primary market (4h)	
South Africa																	
1950–59	0.50	0.00	0.83	0.50	—	—	0.00	0.20	0.00	0.00	0.33	1.00	—	1.00	0.25	0.00	0.25
1960–71	0.50	0.00	0.83	0.50	—	—	0.00	0.20	0.00	0.00	0.33	1.00	—	1.00	0.25	0.00	0.25
1972–79	0.50	0.00	0.83	0.50	—	—	0.00	0.20	0.00	0.00	0.33	1.00	—	1.00	0.25	0.00	0.25
1980–89	0.50	0.00	0.83	0.50	—	—	0.00	0.20	0.00	0.00	0.33	1.00	—	1.00	0.25	0.00	0.25
Spain																	
1950–59	0.00	0.25	0.00	0.50	0.33	0.00	0.00	0.00	0.33	0.00	0.33	0.00	0.00	0.00	0.00	0.00	0.13
1960–71	0.00	0.25	0.00	0.00	0.33	0.00	0.00	0.00	0.33	0.00	0.00	0.33	0.00	0.00	0.00	0.00	0.09
1972–79	0.00	0.25	0.00	0.00	0.33	0.00	0.00	0.00	0.33	0.00	0.00	0.33	0.00	0.00	0.00	0.00	0.09
1980–89	0.25	0.00	0.00	1.00	0.33	0.00	0.00	0.60	0.33	0.00	0.00	0.33	0.00	0.00	0.00	0.00	0.23
Sweden																	
1950–59	0.00	1.00	—	0.50	—	—	0.00	0.20	0.33	0.00	0.67	0.00	1.00	0.67	0.25	0.00	0.29
1960–71	0.00	1.00	—	0.50	—	—	0.00	0.20	0.33	0.00	0.67	0.00	1.00	0.67	0.25	0.00	0.29
1972–79	0.00	1.00	—	0.50	—	—	0.00	0.20	0.33	0.00	0.67	0.00	1.00	0.67	0.25	0.00	0.29
1980–89	0.00	1.00	—	0.50	—	—	0.00	0.20	0.33	0.00	0.67	0.00	1.00	0.67	0.25	0.00	0.29
Switzerland																	
1950–59	0.75	0.25	—	1.00	—	1.00	0.00	0.00	0.67	0.33	0.67	1.00	—	1.00	0.25	0.00	0.53
1960–71	0.75	0.25	—	1.00	—	1.00	0.00	0.00	0.67	0.33	0.67	1.00	—	1.00	0.25	0.00	0.53
1972–79	0.75	0.25	—	1.00	—	1.00	0.00	0.00	0.67	0.33	0.67	1.00	—	1.00	0.25	0.00	0.53
1980–89	0.75	0.25	—	1.00	—	1.00	0.00	0.00	1.00	—	1.00	1.00	—	1.00	0.25	0.00	0.64
Taiwan																	
1980–89	0.50	0.50	1.00	0.00	0.00	0.00	0.00	0.60	0.00	0.00	0.00	0.33	0.00	0.00	0.00	0.00	0.21
Tanzania																	
1960–71	0.25	0.00	0.83	0.50	0.67	0.20	0.00	0.40	0.67	0.33	0.33	1.00	0.33	0.67	0.75	0.00	0.44
1972–79	0.25	0.00	0.83	0.50	0.67	0.20	0.00	0.40	0.67	0.33	0.33	1.00	0.33	0.67	0.75	0.00	0.44
1980–89	0.25	0.00	0.83	0.50	0.67	0.20	0.00	0.40	0.67	0.33	0.33	1.00	0.33	0.67	0.75	0.00	0.44

Thailand																	
1950–59	0.25	0.50	0.00	0.00	0.00	0.20	0.00	0.60	0.33	0.00	0.33	0.33	0.00	0.67	0.25	0.00	0.27
1960–71	0.25	0.50	0.00	0.00	0.00	0.20	0.00	0.60	0.33	0.00	0.33	0.33	0.00	0.67	0.25	0.00	0.27
1972–79	0.25	0.50	0.00	0.00	0.00	0.20	0.00	0.60	0.33	0.00	0.33	0.33	0.00	0.67	0.25	0.00	0.27
1980–89	0.25	0.50	0.00	0.00	0.00	0.20	0.00	0.60	0.33	0.00	0.33	0.33	0.00	0.67	0.25	0.00	0.27
Turkey																	
1950–59	0.50	0.75	1.00	1.00	0.67	0.20	0.00	0.40	0.33	0.00	0.33	0.00	0.67	1.00	0.25	0.00	0.39
1960–71	0.50	0.75	1.00	1.00	0.67	0.20	0.00	0.40	0.33	0.00	0.33	0.00	0.67	1.00	0.25	0.00	0.39
1972–79	0.50	0.75	0.83	0.00	0.33	0.80	0.00	0.60	0.33	0.67	0.33	0.33	0.00	0.67	0.25	0.00	0.46
1980–89	0.50	0.75	0.83	0.00	0.33	0.80	0.00	0.60	0.33	0.67	0.33	0.33	0.00	0.67	0.25	0.00	0.46
Uganda																	
1960–71	0.50	0.50	0.83	0.50	0.00	0.20	0.00	0.40	0.33	—	0.33	0.33	0.33	1.00	0.75	0.00	0.38
1972–79	0.50	0.50	0.83	0.50	0.00	0.20	0.00	0.40	0.33	—	0.33	0.33	0.33	1.00	0.75	0.00	0.38
1980–89	0.50	0.50	0.83	0.50	0.00	0.20	0.00	0.40	0.33	—	0.33	0.33	0.33	1.00	0.75	0.00	0.38
United Kingdom																	
1950–59	0.50	0.00	0.83	1.00	0.00	0.00	0.00	0.20	0.00	0.00	0.00	1.00	—	0.00	0.25	0.00	0.21
1960–71	0.50	0.00	0.83	1.00	0.00	0.00	0.00	0.20	0.67	0.67	0.00	1.00	1.00	1.00	0.75	0.00	0.43
1972–79	0.50	0.00	0.83	1.00	0.00	0.00	0.00	0.20	0.00	0.00	0.00	1.00	1.00	1.00	0.75	0.00	0.27
1980–89	0.50	0.00	0.83	1.00	0.00	0.00	0.00	0.20	0.00	0.00	0.00	1.00	1.00	1.00	0.75	0.00	0.27
United States																	
1950–59	0.25	0.50	0.00	1.00	—	0.20	0.00	0.40	1.00	0.33	0.33	1.00	—	1.00	0.25	0.00	0.48
1960–71	0.25	0.50	0.00	1.00	—	0.20	0.00	0.40	1.00	0.33	0.33	1.00	—	1.00	0.25	0.00	0.48
1972–79	0.25	0.50	0.00	1.00	—	0.20	0.00	0.40	1.00	0.33	0.33	1.00	—	1.00	0.25	0.00	0.48
1980–89	0.25	0.50	0.00	1.00	—	0.20	0.00	0.40	1.00	0.33	0.33	1.00	—	1.00	0.25	0.00	0.48
Uruguay																	
1950–59	0.25	0.00	—	0.50	0.67	0.00	0.00	0.20	—	—	0.33	0.33	—	0.00	0.25	0.00	0.22
1960–71	0.25	0.00	—	0.50	0.67	0.00	0.00	0.20	—	—	0.33	0.33	—	0.00	0.25	0.00	0.22
1972–79	0.25	0.25	0.83	0.00	0.67	0.20	0.00	0.40	0.00	0.00	0.67	0.00	—	0.00	0.25	0.00	0.24
1980–89	0.25	0.25	0.83	0.00	0.67	0.20	0.00	0.40	0.00	0.00	0.67	0.00	—	0.00	0.25	0.00	0.24
Venezuela																	
1950–59	0.50	0.00	—	0.00	0.00	—	0.00	0.20	—	—	0.67	1.00	—	0.67	0.25	0.00	0.28
1960–71	0.50	0.00	—	0.00	0.00	—	0.00	0.20	—	—	0.67	1.00	—	0.67	0.25	0.00	0.28
1972–79	0.50	0.00	0.83	0.50	0.33	1.00	0.00	0.40	0.67	0.00	0.67	0.00	0.33	0.00	0.50	0.00	0.43
1980–89	0.50	0.00	0.83	0.50	0.33	1.00	0.00	0.40	0.67	0.00	0.67	0.00	0.33	0.00	0.50	0.00	0.43

(*Table continues on the following page.*)

Table A-1. *(continued)*

	Disaggregated legal variables																
	CEO variables				Policy formulation variables			Central bank	Limitations on lending variables								Aggregate legal
Economy and decade	Term of office (1a)	Who appoints (1b)	Dis-missal (1c)	Other offices (1d)	Who formu-lates (2a)	Final authority (2b)	Role in budget (2c)	objectives variable (3)	Advances (4a)	Securitized lending (4b)	Terms of lending (4c)	Potential borrowers (4d)	Type of limit (4e)	Maturity of loans (4f)	Interest rates (4g)	Primary market (4h)	central bank independence variable
Western Samoa																	
1980–89	0.25	0.25	0.83	0.00	0.00	0.20	0.00	0.40	0.33	0.33	0.33	0.00	0.33	1.00	0.25	0.00	0.30
Yugoslavia																	
1960–71	0.25	0.25	0.83	0.00	0.00	0.20	0.00	0.40	0.00	—	0.00	0.00	—	0.00	0.25	0.00	0.17
1972–79	0.25	0.25	0.83	0.00	0.00	0.20	0.00	0.40	0.00	—	0.00	0.00	—	0.00	0.25	0.00	0.17
1980–89	0.25	0.25	0.83	0.00	0.00	0.20	0.00	0.40	0.00	—	0.00	0.00	—	0.00	0.25	0.00	0.17
Zaire																	
1972–79	0.50	0.00	1.00	0.00	0.67	0.20	0.00	0.60	—	0.00	0.33	0.33	0.33	0.67	0.75	0.00	0.35
1980–89	0.50	0.00	1.00	1.00	0.67	0.60	0.00	0.40	0.33	0.33	0.33	0.33	0.33	0.67	0.75	0.00	0.43
Zambia																	
1960–71	0.50	0.25	0.83	1.00	0.00	0.20	0.00	0.80	0.33	0.33	0.00	0.33	0.33	0.33	0.75	0.00	0.40
1972–79	0.50	0.25	0.83	1.00	0.00	0.20	0.00	0.80	0.33	0.33	0.00	0.33	0.33	0.33	0.75	0.00	0.40
1980–89	0.50	0.25	0.83	0.50	0.33	0.20	0.00	0.40	0.33	0.33	0.00	0.33	0.33	0.33	0.75	0.00	0.33
Zimbabwe																	
1950–59	0.75	0.00	0.00	1.00	0.00	0.00	0.00	0.00	0.33	0.33	0.00	0.67	0.33	0.33	0.25	0.00	0.23
1960–71	0.75	0.00	0.00	0.50	0.00	0.00	0.00	0.00	0.33	0.33	0.00	0.67	0.33	0.33	0.25	0.00	0.20
1972–79	0.75	0.00	0.00	0.50	0.00	0.00	0.00	0.00	0.33	0.33	0.00	0.67	0.33	0.33	0.25	0.00	0.20
1980–89	0.75	0.00	0.00	0.50	0.00	0.00	0.00	0.00	0.33	0.33	0.00	0.67	0.33	0.33	0.25	0.00	0.20

— Not available.

Table A-2. *Country Codes for the Questionnaire Variables and the Questionnaire-based Index of Central Bank Independence*

Country	Tenure overlap (1)	Limitations on lending (2)	Resolution of conflict (3)	Financial independence: Budget (4a)	Financial independence: Salaries and profits (4b)	Policy targets: Monetary stock (5a)	Policy targets: Interest rate (5b)	Priority of price stability (6)	Function as development bank (7)	Questionnaire-based index of central bank independence
Australia	1.00	0.67	0.00	1.00	0.50	0.33	1.00	1.00	1.00	0.76
Bahamas, The	0.50	0.67	0.50	1.00	1.00	0.00	1.00	0.67	1.00	0.71
Barbados	0.50	0.67	0.00	1.00	0.50	0.00	0.00	1.00	0.67	0.54
Belgium	1.00	0.00	0.00	1.00	1.00	0.00	1.00	0.67	—	0.47
Costa Rica	0.50	0.67	0.50	1.00	1.00	0.67	1.00	1.00	1.00	0.81
Denmark	1.00	1.00	0.50	0.50	1.00	0.00	0.00	0.67	1.00	0.73
Ethiopia	0.00	0.00	0.00	0.00	0.00	0.00	1.00	0.33	0.00	0.13
Finland	1.00	1.00	1.00	0.50	0.00	0.00	—	1.00	1.00	0.78
France	0.50	0.33	0.50	0.50	1.00	0.67	1.00	1.00	0.67	0.65
Ireland	0.50	0.33	0.00	0.50	0.00	0.00	1.00	1.00	1.00	0.57
Italy	1.00	0.00	0.50	1.00	1.00	0.67	1.00	1.00	1.00	0.73
Lebanon	0.50	0.33	0.50	1.00	1.00	0.00	1.00	0.33	1.00	0.59
Luxembourg	0.50	0.33	—	1.00	1.00	0.00	1.00	0.67	1.00	0.66
Peru	0.00	0.00	0.00	1.00	0.50	0.33	0.00	0.33	0.33	0.22
South Africa	0.50	0.33	0.50	1.00	0.00	0.67	1.00	—	1.00	0.64
Tanzania	0.50	0.33	0.50	1.00	0.00	0.33	1.00	0.00	0.33	0.38
Turkey	0.50	0.00	0.00	1.00	1.00	0.00	1.00	1.00	0.33	0.44
Uganda	0.50	0.33	0.50	1.00	1.00	0.33	—	1.00	0.33	0.53
Uruguay	0.50	0.33	0.50	1.00	0.50	0.00	—	0.33	1.00	0.49
United Kingdom	0.50	0.33	0.00	0.50	—	0.67	1.00	1.00	1.00	0.64
Germany, Fed. Rep. of	1.00	1.00	1.00	1.00	1.00	1.00	1.00	1.00	1.00	1.00
Yugoslavia	—	0.00	0.00	0.50	0.00	0.33	1.00	—	0.00	0.17
Zaire	0.50	0.33	0.50	1.00	1.00	0.67	1.00	1.00	0.33	0.61

— Not available.

Note: Numbers in parentheses in the column headings correspond to variable numbers in table 4.

REFERENCES

The word "processed" describes informally reproduced works that may not be commonly available through libraries.

Alesina, Alberto. 1988. "Macroeconomics and Politics." NBER *Macro-economics Annual* 3: 13–52.

Alesina, Alberto, and Guido Tabellini. 1987. "Rules and Discretion with Noncoordinated Monetary and Fiscal Policies." *Economic Inquiry* 25: 619–30.

Aufricht, Hans. 1961. *Central Banking Legislation*. Washington, D.C.: IMF.

———. 1967. *Central Banking Legislation*. Vol. II, *Europe*. Washington, D.C.: IMF.

Bade, Robin, and Michael Parkin. 1980. "Central Bank Laws and Monetary Policy." University of Western Ontario, Department of Economics, London, Ontario. Processed.

Banaian, King, Leroy Laney, and Thomas Willett. 1983. "Central Bank Independence: An International Comparison." *Economic Review: Federal Reserve Bank of Dallas* (March): 1–13.

Bank for International Settlements. 1963. *Eight European Central Banks*. New York: Praeger under the auspices of the BIS.

Bodart, Vincent. 1990. "Central Bank Independence and the Effectiveness of Monetary Policy: A Comparative Analysis." IMF, Central Banking Department, Washington, D.C. Processed.

Bordes, Christian, and M. O. Strauss-Kahn. 1987. "1977–86: Dix ans de Politique D'objectifs en France ou le 'Targeting' a la Francaise." SUERF (Societe Universitaire Europeene de Recherches Financiers) papers on Monetary Policy and Financial Systems 4, Tilburg. Processed.

Bordo, Michael, and Angela Redish. 1987. "Why Did the Bank of Canada Emerge in 1935?" *Journal of Economic History* 47 (June): 405–17.

Cargill, Thomas, and Michael Hutchison. 1990. "Monetary Policy and Political Economy: The Federal Reserve and the Bank of Japan." In Thomas Mayer, ed., *The Political Economy of American Monetary Policy*. New York: Cambridge University Press.

Cukierman, Alex. 1984. *Inflation, Stagflation, Relative Prices, and Imperfect Information*. Cambridge: Cambridge University Press.

———. 1992a. *Central Bank Strategy, Credibility, and Independence: Theory and Evidence*. Cambridge, Mass.: MIT Press.

———. 1992b. "Commitment through Delegation and Its Effect on Policy: The Case of Central Bank Independence." Paper presented at the Conference on Coalitions and Bargaining, Tel Aviv University, Department of Economics. Processed.

Dotsey, Michael. 1986. "Japanese Monetary Policy: A Comparative Analysis." *Economic Review: Federal Reserve Bank of Richmond* 72 (November/December): 12–24.

Effros, Robert, ed. 1982. *Emerging Financial Centers: Legal and Institutional Framework*. Washington, D.C.: IMF.

Eizenga, Weitze. 1983. "The Independence of the Federal Reserve System and of the Netherlands Bank." SUERF (Societe Universitaire Europeene de Recherches Financiers) Series 41A, Tilburg. Processed.

———. 1987. "The Independence of the Deutsche Bundesbank and the Nederlandsche Bank with Regard to Monetary Policy: A Comparative Study." SUERF (Societe Universitaire Europeene de Recherches Financiers) papers on Monetary Policy and Financial Systems 2, Tilburg. Processed.

Epstein, Gerald, and Juliet Schor. 1986. "The Divorce of the Banca d'Italia and the Italian Treasury: A Case Study of Central Bank Independence." Harvard Institute of Economic Research, Discussion Paper Series 1269. Cambridge, Mass. Processed.

Fazio, Antonio. 1991. "Role and Independence of Central Banks." In Patrick Downes and Reza Vaez-Zadeh, eds., *The Evolving Role of Central Banks*. Washington, D.C.: IMF.

Fischer, Stanley. 1986. *Indexing, Inflation, and Economic Policy*. Cambridge, Mass.: MIT Press.

Goodhart, Charles. 1988. *The Evolution of Central Banks*. Cambridge, Mass.: MIT Press.

Grilli, Vittorio, Donato Masciandaro, and Guido Tabellini. 1991. "Political and Monetary Institutions and Public Financial Policies in the Industrial Countries." *Economic Policy* 13: 341–92.

Holtfrerich, Carl-Ludwig. 1988. "Relations between Monetary Authorities and Governmental Institutions: The Case of Germany from the 19th Century to the Present." In Gianni Toniolo, ed., *Central Bank Independence in Historical Perspective*. Berlin: Walter de Gruyter.

Kearney, Colm. 1984. "The British Anti-Inflation Strategy: Implementing Monetarism or Turning to Radcliffe?" SUERF Series 44A. Tilburg. Processed.

Keenan, Peter, and David Mayes. 1987. "Monetary Targets and Monetary Management: The New Zealand Experience." SUERF (Societe Universitaire Europeene de Recherches Financiers) Papers on Monetary Policy and Financial Systems 3, Tilburg. Processed.

Leone, Alfredo. 1991. "Effectiveness and Implications of Limits on Central Bank Credit to the Government." In Patrick Downes and Reza Vaez-Zadeh, eds., *The Evolving Role of Central Banks*. Washington, D.C.: IMF.

Lobel, Arnold. 1972. *Frog and Toad Together*. New York: Harper and Row.

Lohmann, Susanne. 1992. "Optimal Commitment in Monetary Policy: Credibility versus Flexibility." *American Economic Review*. 82 (March): 273–86.

Masciandaro, Donato, and Guido Tabellini. 1988. "Monetary Regimes and Fiscal Deficits: A Comparative Analysis." In H. S. Cheng, ed., *Monetary Policy in Pacific Basin Countries*. Dordrecht: Kluwer Academic Publishers.

Maxfield, Sylvia. 1992. "Private Constituencies and the Power of State Monetary Authorities in Newly Industrializing Countries." Yale University, Department of Political Science, New Haven, Conn. Processed.

Mayer, Thomas, ed. 1990. *The Political Economy of American Monetary Policy*. New York: Cambridge University Press.

Meltzer, Allan. 1991. "U.S. Policy in the Bretton Woods Era." The 1991 Homer Jones Lecture. St. Louis, Mo.

Mittra, Sid. 1977. *Central Bank versus Treasury: An International Study*. Lanham, Md.: University Press of America.

Parkin, Michael. 1986. "Domestic Monetary Institutions and Deficits." In J. M. Buchanan, C. K. Rowley, and R. D. Tollison, eds., *Deficits*. New York: Basil Blackwell.

Rogoff, Kenneth. 1985. "The Optimal Degree of Commitment to an Intermediate Monetary Target." *Quarterly Journal of Economics* 100 (November): 1169–90.

Schokker, E. 1980. "The Central Bank and the State in the Light of European Integration." SUERF (Societe Universitaire Europeene de Recherches Financiers) Series 34A, Tilburg. Processed.

Skanland, Hermod. 1984. *The Central Bank and Political Authorities in Some Industrial Countries*. Oslo: Norges Bank.

Suzuki, Yoshio. 1987. *The Japanese Financial System*. Oxford: Clarendon.

Swinburne, Mark, and Marta Castello-Branco. 1991. "Central Bank Independence and Central Bank Functions." In Patrick Downes and Reza Vaez-Zadeh, eds., *The Evolving Role of Central Banks*. Washington, D.C.: IMF.

Volcker, Paul, Miguel Mancera, and Jean Godeaux. 1991. *Perspectives on the Role of a Central Bank*. Proceedings of a conference held in Beijing, China, January 5–7, 1990. Beijing: Peoples' Bank of China.

Willett, Thomas, ed. 1988. *Political Business Cycles: The Political Economy of Money, Inflation, and Unemployment*. Durham, N.C.: Duke University Press.

[10]

Central Bank Independence in Twelve Industrial Countries*

SYLVESTER EIJFFINGER and ERIC SCHALING

1. Introduction

Recently there has been worldwide interest in examining the scope for greater monetary policy autonomy for the central bank. At the EC-summit in Maastricht in December 1991 a Treaty on European Economic and Monetary Union (EMU) was agreed upon. According to this treaty, in the final stage of EMU – *i.e.* by 1997 or later – the European Central Bank is supposed to assume almost unlimited responsibility for monetary policy. Broadly speaking, according to Alesina and Grilli (1991), the accepted Statute[1] guarantees a central bank as independent from national and European political institutions as the Deutsche Bundesbank. Furthermore, in the Pacific Basin Countries the same tendency can be discerned. Since the end of 1989 governor Mieno strengthened the position of the Bank of Japan with respect to the Ministry of Finance, while New Zealand enacted legislation in February 1990 that increased the independence of its Reserve Bank. Finally, in Eastern Europe, Hungary, the Czech republic and Poland have been considering proposals concerning central bank independence.[2]

□ Tilburg University, Department of Economics, Tilburg (The Netherlands).

* The authors thank Professors Onno de Beaufort Wijnholds, Hans Bosman, Wietze Eizenga, Mervyn King, Tommaso Padoa-Schioppa, Hans Tietmeyer, Yves Ullmo, Nout Wellink and two anonymous referees for valuable comments on an earlier version. Of course, the usual disclaimer applies. Eric Schaling wishes to thank the Netherlands Organization for Scientific Research (NWO) for financial support.

[1] See Committee of Governors (1991).

[2] For an interesting survey of central banking in emerging market-oriented economies see Federal Reserve Bank of Kansas City (1990).

BNL Quarterly Review, no. 184, March 1993.

The theoretical rationale for central bank independence finds its origin in the ongoing 'Rules versus Discretion' debate. Authors like Barro and Gordon (1983) and Rogoff (1985) argue that governments and central banks are tempted to impart an inflationary bias to the economy thereby sacrificing long-term welfare to short-run political gains. The associated time-consistency problem can be overcome by legislative rules and by setting up politically independent central banks. Hence one would expect countries with independent central banks to have a lower sustainable rate of inflation.

Unlike the well-developed theoretical literature,[3] there are only a few studies that compare actual monetary regimes between a large number of countries.[4] The most comprehensive studies are Fair (1980), Bade and Parkin (1988), Alesina (1988, 1989), Alesina and Summers (1990) and Grilli, Masciandaro and Tabellini (1991). Focusing on more recent studies, it is striking that the conclusions of the latter are less clear-cut than the theoretical literature. For instance, contrary to Alesina and Summers, Bade and Parkin find no correlation between central bank independence and the variability of inflation. Next, unlike the prediction of the Barro-Gordon framework,[5] both Alesina and Summers and Grilli, Masciandaro and Tabellini find no association between central bank independence and (the variability of) real output growth.

A recent study by the International Monetary Fund (Swinburne and Castello-Branco, 1991), questions the reliability of these empirical conclusions. This is because nearly all of them are stated in terms of correlations between indices of central bank independence and macro-variables (output, inflation).[6] Therefore, these results – *e.g.* the well-known inverse relationship between independence and the level of inflation found by Alesina (1988, 1989) – are particularly sensitive to the numerical values of indices.[7] These values are dependent on *(i)* criteria used in the examination of central bank laws (statutes), *(ii)* the interpretation of the relevant statute as to whether a central bank meets this criterion, *i.e.* possesses a certain attribute, and *(iii)* the way these attributes are aggregated to a composite index of central bank independence.

---

[3] For a survey of the 'state of the art' see Cukierman (1993).

[4] Case studies are Eizenga (1987, 1990, 1991) and Eijffinger (1991, 1993).

[5] This framework is summarized in Persson and Tabellini (1990) and Alesina and Grilli (1991).

[6] Exceptions are Bade and Parkin (1988), pp. 21-23, and Schaling (1991).

[7] Since in the 1980s the establishment of the EMS made central banks more dependent on external constraints, for this period one would expect this relationship to be affected. We leave this as an item for further research.

Of course there is no non-arbitrary way of choosing criteria. Also the interpretation of the relevant statute is a delicate matter because one has to make a distinction between purely formal or legal issues, and more substantive issues regarding the conduct of monetary policy. Again, in making this distinction there is an unavoidable arbitrariness. For each economist when building an index of this kind is somewhat biased in favour of his/her own country, because the greater acquaintance with the case brings recognition of the greater freedom of behaviour acquired in current practice by the national central bank compared to the formal rule. Finally, as pointed out by Grilli, Masciandaro and Tabellini (1991, p. 31), there is no non-arbitrary way of aggregating these criteria or attributes to a composite index. Hence, there are unavoidable subjective elements in the construction of indices of central bank independence.

In order to view these elements in a broader perspective this paper compares the major indices of central bank independence as presented in Bade and Parkin (1988), Alesina (1988, 1989) and Grilli, Masciandaro and Tabellini (1991). Such a comparison does not yet exist in the literature. We focus on three aspects: *(a)* is the index based on the best possible interpretation of the central bank law within the context of monetary policy making?[8] *(b)* is the index consistent in using all relevant criteria in determining the independence of each central bank? *(c)* are the indices of the various authors different or not?

In order to answer the questions mentioned above, the paper is organized as follows. We analyse the competence of central banks on the base of central bank laws within the context of monetary policy making. Twelve industrial countries are examined: Australia, Belgium, Canada, France, Germany, Italy, Japan, the Netherlands, the United Kingdom, the United States, Sweden and Switzerland. We describe the central bank laws of these countries focusing on three areas: *(i)* relationships between central banks and government in the formulation of monetary policy, *(ii)* procedures for appointing the board of the central bank, and *(iii)* formal responsibilities (objectives) of the central bank with respect to monetary policy. This description can be found in the Appendix. After a critical examination of the existing indices in Section 2, in Section 3 we construct our 'own' index of central bank independence. This index is used to reach a critical perspective of other indices. For instance,

[8] We focus on internal monetary policy, *i.e.* we take no account of the relations of governments and central banks in the conduct of exchange rate policy. We leave this for further research.

according to this index we qualify the Bank of Japan as less independent than Alesina (1988, 1989), while for the Nederlandsche Bank the reverse applies. Finally, our conclusions can be found in Section 4.

2. Indices of Central Bank Independence

2.1 *Bade and Parkin's Courageous Attempt*

A seminal paper concerning indices of central bank independence is Bade and Parkin (1988) (BP). The paper investigates the cross-country relationship between monetary policies and the laws which establish and delimit the powers of central banks. The study is empirical and deals with the experience of twelve industrial countries (Australia, Belgium, Canada, France, Germany, Italy, Japan, the Netherlands the United Kingdom, the United States, Sweden and Switzerland) during the floating exchange rate years 1972 to 1986.[9]

They describe the central bank laws of the twelve countries focusing on three features: *(i)* The relationship between central banks and government in the formulation of monetary policy, *(ii)* the procedures for appointing the board of the central bank, and *(iii)* the financial and budgetary relations between the central bank and the government.

On the basis of features *(i)* and *(ii)* BP classify the twelve central banks according to their degrees of policy independence. On the basis of feature *(iii)* they identify the degree of financial independence from government. In this paper we focus on features *(i)* and *(ii)*. BP's description of financial and budgetary relations is discussed in Eijffinger and Schaling (1992). BP conclude that central banks which are independent both in policy-making and in the appointment of directors deliver a lower rate of inflation than other central bank types.

On the basis of feature *(i)* the relationship between central banks and government in the formulation of monetary policy[10] and feature

---

[9] Bade and Parkin (1988, p. 18) point out that a commitment to a fixed exchange rate leaves monetary policy with the task of determining the stock of foreign reserves. Therefore, they think it pointless to look to the effects of central bank laws on monetary policy in a fixed exchange rate era. Empirical support for this view can be found in de Haan and Sturm (1992), p. 308.

[10] BP's results concerning both the relationship between the central bank and the government in monetary policy making and the procedures for appointing and removing central bank directors are extensively discussed in Eijffinger and Schaling (1992), pp. 18-20.

(ii) the procedures for appointing and removing central bank directors, BP construct their index of policy independence. The degree of policy independence is determined using three criteria:

1. Is the bank the final policy authority?

2. Is there no government official (with or without voting power) on the bank board?

3. Are more than half of the board appointments made independent of the government?

Since each criterion can be met or not, eight potential policy types can be distinguished. This is summarized in Table 1.

TABLE 1

CENTRAL BANK LAWS: POLICY TYPES

Bank is final policy authority 1	No government official on bank board 2	Some board appointments independent of government [1] 3	Potential bank type [2]	Central bank type does exist	Policy type
–	–	*	(a)	no	–
–	*	*	(b)	no	–
*	–	*	(c)	no	–
*	–	–	(d)	no	–
–	–	–	(e)	yes	1
–	*	–	(f)	yes	2
*	*	–	(g)	yes	3
*	*	*	(h)	yes	4

[1] Operationalized as proportion of members *not* appointed directly or indirectly by the government. ≥ 11/21.

[2] It should be noted that the letters have nothing to do with similar symbols used in other tables.

However, BP find that in all cases where the government is responsible for the formulation of monetary policy, it also appoints over 12/14 of the policy board. That is, there is no central bank which makes some board appointments independent of the government, although it is not in charge of monetary policy. Therefore, types *(a)* and *(b)* do not exist. Moreover, a central bank being itself in charge of monetary policy and also having a government official on its board (types *(c)* and *(d)*) does not exist.[11] Therefore, the potential policy types *(a)*-*(d)* do not occur in reality. This means that no actual

[11] Of course, in this case the presence of a government official without voting power on the policy board would not make much sense.

central bank corresponds to the first four configurations of institutional features.

So, only the bottom half of Table 1 is relevant for the construction of the BP index of policy independence. The overall degree of policy independence is determined by a combination of attributes 1-3. It should be noticed that there is no non-arbitrary way of aggregating them. However, from Table 1 it can be easily seen that BP choose the simplest one: they simply summed the attributes possessed by the central bank, meaning that each attribute is weighted equally. Thus, the four remaining (existing) central bank types are ranked from 1 (least independent) to 4 (most independent) depending on the number of asterisks. For instance, the least independent central bank (zero asterisks) is not in charge of monetary policy, has a government official on the board, and does not make any board appointments independent of government.

BP's ranking of the twelve central banks can be found in the first column of table 2.

BP now turn to an investigation of the relationship between central bank types and monetary policy. In their analysis of monetary

TABLE 2

AVERAGE INFLATION AND ITS VARIABILITY GROUPED ACCORDING TO CENTRAL BANK POLICY TYPE: FLEXIBLE EXCHANGE RATE PERIOD 1972-1986

		Inflation rate		Policy variability	
Country	Type	Percent	Rank	Standard deviation	Rank
Australia	1	9.9	(10)	3.2	(7)
Belgium	2	7.1	(6)	3.0	(5)
Canada		7.9	(7)	2.8	(3)
France		9.5	(9)	3.2	(7)
Italy		14.0	(12)	4.6	(10)
Netherlands		5.8	(3)	3.0	(5)
Sweden		8.9	(8)	2.5	(2)
United Kingdom		11.2	(11)	6.0	(11)
Japan	3	6.6	(4)	6.1	(12)
United States		6.9	(5)	3.5	(9)
Germany	4	4.3	(1)	2.0	(1)
Switzerland		4.4	(2)	2.8	(3)

policy they focus on two aspects its inflationary stance (level) and the variability (variance) of inflation. The inflationary stance is measured by the average rate of change of consumer prices (CPI).

Concerning policy variability, what is of interest is the variability of inflation as well as output and employment. However, BP point out that if they were to measure variability of policy by examining both nominal and real variability, inevitably conflicting rankings would result from cross-country differences in slopes of short-run trade-offs between output and inflation.[12] Regarding these trade-offs well outside the scope of their study, they examine only the variability of inflation.[13]

Furthermore, consider Table 2 which permits a direct examination of the relationship between policy independence and monetary policy. From Table 2 it appears that there is no association between any of the policy types and the measure of variability of policy presented.

Moreover, consider the association between categories of central bank independence and the inflation performance. From Table 1 it is clear that the first category (policy type 1) differs from the second only in the presence of a government official on the bank board. According to BP it is immediately apparent that there are no discernible differences in inflation rates between the first two groups. The third and fourth groups (Japan, United States, Germany and Switzerland) are the independent central banks. BP think it striking that the two most independent central banks, those of Germany and Switzerland, have delivered a lower inflation rate than the intermediate central banks of Japan and the United States. Also, BP point out that the mean inflation rate of the eight government dominated central banks (policy types 1 and 2) is in excess of ten percent; thus, although the U.S. and Japanese inflation rates are well within two

---

[12] For an examination of aggregate demand policy and exchange rate policy rules in a multi-country Phillips-curve framework see Taylor (1982).

[13] Even though interest rates are the proximate instruments of monetary policy, according to Bade and Parkin (1988, p. 19) there is no inherent inconsistency in using the variability of inflation as the appropriate measure of the variability of policy. Short-term intetest rates are typically manipulated with a view to achieving a particular behaviour for the growth rate of various monetary aggregates, and these aggregates are further regarded as appropriate intermediate targets in achieving predictable and less variable inflation. A diagrammatic presentation of this line of reasoning is given in Eijffinger and Gerards (1990), p. 13.

standard deviations of that mean, those of Switzerland and Germany are signficantly below the mean.

On the basis of these facts BP conclude that there is an association between the degree of central bank policy independence and the average rate of inflation. By and large, the more independent the central bank, the lower the inflation rate.[14]

2.2 *Alesina's Popularization*

Bade and Parkin's work has been integrated in the positive theory of economic policy[15] by Alesina (1988, 1989). Alesina uses the BP index of policy independence to illustrate the relationship between the degree of politico-institutional stability and economic performance. Alesina extends BP's sample of industrial countries to include New Zealand, Spain, Denmark, Norway and Finland, by using institutional information provided by Masciandaro and Tabellini (1988) and Fair (1980), respectively.

Alesina likewise concludes that there is an inverse relationship between the degree of independence of central banks and the average inflation rate (Alesina, 1988, p. 41).[16] Alesina's results can be summarized in Table 3.[17]

As can be easily seen from this Table, the numerical values of the 'Alesina index of central bank independence' are identical to those of the BP index of policy independence, except for the case of Italy. Alesina has the following argument for classifying Italy as 1.5 rather than 2, as in BP:

> "Bade and Parkin's classifications disregard institutional changes in the period considered. The Italian Central Bank obtained more

[14] This tentative conclusion is given formal content by estimating first order autoregressions for inflation (were all the coefficients on lagged inflation were restricted to be equal) with inclusion of a dummy variable for the German and Swiss central bank type, see Bade and Parkin (1988), pp. 21-23.

[15] Alesina supports the rational partisan theory, a theory that combines Hibbs' (1977) partisan theory with rational expectations macroeconomic theory.

[16] This research was also published in the Report by the European Commission "One market, one money". See Commission of the European Communities (1990), pp. 97-98.

[17] For ease of comparison we focus on the BP sample, skipping New Zealand, Spain, Denmark, Norway and Finland.

TABLE 3

INFLATION AND CENTRAL BANK INDEPENDENCE (1973-1986)

Country	Average inflation	Alesina index of central bank independence	Bade-Parkin index of central bank independence
Italy	13.7	1/2	2
UK	10.7	2	2
Australia	9.7	1	1
France	9.2	2	2
Sweden	8.7	2	2
Canada	7.8	2	2
Belgium	6.9	2	2
US	6.9	3	3
Japan	6.4	3	3
Netherlands	5.5	2	2
Switzerland	4.1	4	4
Germany	4.1	4	4

economic independence in 1982 [...]. Given this change we classified Italy as 1.5 rather than 2, as in Bade-Parkin".[18]

Therefore, Alesina's argument contains two major elements:

1. Criticism of BP for their disregard of institutional changes;

2. the identification of institutional changes with changes in economic independence.

The first element of Alesina's criticism has implications for the way of aggregating the attributes which make up his index. We will return to this issue later.

The second element is based on Tabellini's (1988) account of the divorce ('divorzio') between the Treasury and the Italian Central Bank in 1981. After divorce the CICR[19] no longer obliged the Banca d'Italia to absorb all excess supply of short-term Treasury bills. This step decreased the scope for accommodating monetary policy by monetary financing of government deficits and increased the independence of Banca d'Italia.

[18] See Alesina (1988), p. 42. However, Tabellini (1988), p. 96 states this change to have taken place in the summer of 1981.

[19] See Section 2.

In the preceding sub-section we saw that the BP index of policy independence is determined by the total number of statutory attributes ('asterisks') concerning policy making and the appointment of directors (BP 1-3). If the Alesina index is an extension of the BP policy index, in the sense that it is 'richer' and more informative, it must follow that:

1. Alesina implicitly uses a fourth criterium, say A4:

Is the central bank not required to absorb excess supply of short-term Treasury bills?

2. The Alesina indicator of central bank independence is determined by a combination of BP attributes (1-3) and A4.

Having four BP policy types combined with criterion A4 yields 4 × 2 = 8 potential policy-economic types.

TABLE 4

ALESINA TYPES AND CENTRAL BANK LAWS

BP policy type	Criterion A4 met?	Potential central bank type	Central bank type does exist[a]	Alesina type[a]
1	*	(a)	no	–
3	*	(b)	no	–
4	*	(c)	no	–
1	–	(d)	yes	1
2	*	(e)	yes	1.5
2	–	(f)	yes	2
3	–	(g)	yes	3
4	–	(h)	yes	4

[a] See Table 3.

From this table it can be seen that, according to Alesina, only five central bank types can be discerned among the twelve industrial countries. These existing central bank types can be found in the bottom half of Table 4.

Again, there is no non-arbitrary way to aggregate attributes BP 1-3 and A4, *i.e.* to rank these types from least independent to most independent. However, from Table 4 it can be easily seen that Alesina did not follow BP in summing the attributes possessed by the central bank. For if he had, Banca d'Italia would have been qualified as type 3 (upgrade) rather than type 1.5 (downgrade).[20]

Therefore, if the Alesina index is internally consistent, it can be considered asymmetrical in the sense that attributes are not weighted equally.

From Table 4, reflecting our assumption that criterion A4 was applied to all the twelve industrial countries, it follows that:

(1) All central banks, except Banca d'Italia, are forced to accommodate fiscal policy with monetary policy.[21]

(2) Notwithstanding the former the Banca d'Italia, being Alesina type 1.5, is less independent than the central banks of France, Sweden, Belgium, Canada, the Netherlands and the United Kingdom. All of them are of the type 2 category.

Since (1) is obviously counterfactual it follows that the Alesina (1988, 1989) synthetic indicator of central bank independence is internally inconsistent (*reductio ad absurdum*).

However, if the Alesina index is internally inconsistent, *i.e.* it is not the case that in determining the independence of each central bank all relevant criteria are used, the numerical values in Table 4 cannot be compared and therefore do not qualify as 'indices' of central bank independence.

2.3 *The Broad Index of Grilli, Masciandaro and Tabellini*

A recent index of central bank independence is that of Grilli, Masciandaro and Tabellini (1991) (GMT). They compare the monetary regimes of eighteen industrial countries (Australia, Austria, Belgium, Canada, Denmark, France, Germany, Greece, Ireland, Italy, Japan, the Netherlands, New Zealand, Portugal, Spain, Switzerland, the United Kingdom and the United States) during the post-war period (1950-1989) by focusing on political and economic indepen-

---

[20] Correspondence with Alesina did not clarify the weighting procedure of Alesina (1988, 1989).

[21] Note that this assertion follows from our (counterfactual) hypothesis that the Alesina index is internally consistent.

dence of the central bank.[22] Like BP and Alesina, they find that in countries with more politically independent central banks inflation is on average lower and less variable. On the other hand, GMT find no indication that the monetary regime matters for real economic performance.

According to GMT, political independence is the capacity to choose the final goal of monetary policy, such as inflation or the level of economic activity. The latter capacity is primarily determined by the following features:

(i) Relationships between central banks and government in the formulation of monetary policy;

(ii) procedures for appointing the board of the central bank;

(iii) formal responsibilities (policy goals) of the central bank with respect to monetary policy.

On the basis of features *(i)*-*(iii)* GMT construct their index of policy independence. The degree of policy independence is determined using eight criteria:[23]

1. Is the governor not appointed by the government?

2. Is the governor appointed for more than five years?

3. Are all board members not appointed by the government? (Compare with BP *3*: are some board appointments made independent of the government?)

4. Is the board appointed for more than five years?

5. Is there no mandatory participation of a government representative in the board? (Compare with BP *2*: is there no government official on the bank board?)

6. Is there no government approval of monetary policy required? (Compare with BP *1*: is the bank the final policy authority?)

7. Are there statutory requirements that the bank pursues monetary stability among its goals?

8. Are there legal provisions that strengthen the bank's position in case of conflicts with the government?

---

[22] According to Grilli, Masciandaro and Tabellini, economic independence is the capacity to choose the instruments of monetary policy. Their treatment of economic independence is extensively discussed in Eijffinger and Schaling (1992).

[23] To facilitate comparison corresponding BP criteria are given in italics.

The overall index of policy independence is determined by a combination of the attributes 1-8. Again, there is no non-arbitrary way of aggregating them. Like Bade and Parkin, GMT choose the simplest one: they simply summed the attributes possessed by the central bank. Thus, each attribute is weighted equally. The eighteen central banks are ranked from 1 (least independent) to 6 (most independent). GMT's results can be summarized in Table 5.[24]

TABLE 5

POLITICAL INDEPENDENCE OF CENTRAL BANKS

Country	Appointments				Relationship with Government		Constitution		Index of Political Independence
	1	2	3	4	5	6	7	8	9
Australia		*					*	*	3
Belgium				*					1
Canada	*	*					*	*	4
France		*		*					2
Germany		*		*	*	*	*	*	6
Italy	*	*	*		*				4
Japan							*		1
Netherlands		*		*	*	*	*	*	6
Switzerland		*			*	*	*	*	5
U.K.					*				1
U.S.				*	*	*	*	*	5
Sweden	–	–	–	–	–	–		–	–

Notes:
1 = Governor *not* appointed by government.
2 = Governor appointed for > 5 years.
3 = *All* the Board *not* appointed by government.
4 = Board appointed for > 5 years.
5 = No mandatory participation of government representative in the Board.
6 = No government approval of monetary policy formulation is required.
7 = Statutory requirements that central bank pursues monetary stability among its goals.
8 = Legal provisions that strengthened the central bank position in conflicts with the government are present.
9 = Overall index of political independence, constructed as the sum of the asterisks in each row.

From this Table it can be seen that the GMT policy index is richer, *i.e.* more informative, than the BP index of political independence. The GMT policy index is more informative because more

[24] Again, for ease of comparison we focus on the BP sample, skipping Austria, Denmark, Greece, Ireland, New Zealand, Portugal and Spain.

criteria are taken into account. BP use only three criteria, whilst GMT consider eight attributes. It can be easily seen that GMT criteria 5 and 6 are identical to BP criteria 2 and 1. One is tempted to make a similar inference concerning GMT criterion 3. However, concerning the appointment of directors GMT require all board members not to be appointed by the government, whilst BP require only ≥ 11/21[25] of board members not to be appointed by the government. Therefore, GMT's criterion 3 is more strict than BP's criterion 3.

2.4 *Grilli, Masciandaro and Tabellini versus Bade and Parkin*

In order to compare GMT's findings with these of BP, we restrict attention to attributes 3, 5, and 6 of GMT. Since aggregation procedures are identical, differences in numerical values of the BP and GMT indices are dependent on:

(a) differerences in the interpretation of the central bank laws with respect to GMT attributes 5 and 6 (or BP attributes 1 and 2);

(b) the difference between GMT attribute 3 and BP attribute 3.

We label differences *(a)* and *(b)* respectively interpretation effect and criterion effect. Thus numerical differences depend on both these effects. The total effect is decomposed in Table 6.

With respect to the interpretation effect, from Table 6 it can be seen that GMT and BP differ in their interpretations of the central bank laws of Canada, France, Belgium, Japan, and the Netherlands. Canada, France, and Belgium are downgraded (−1), because contrary to BP GMT believe a government representative to be present on the central bank boards. The Nederlandsche Bank is upgraded (+1), because unlike BP, GMT consider the central bank to be the final authority in policy making. The differences are most striking in the case of Japan. The Bank of Japan is severely downgraded (−2), because GMT believe that the government has an official on the bank board, while according to BP there is no official. GMT are also of the opinion that the government is the final authority in policy making, contradicting BP. We will return to these differences in Section 4.

[25] The threshold for meeting BP's criterion 3 is the composition of the Central Bank Council of the Bundesbank.

TABLE 6

GRILLI-MASCIANDARO-TABELLINI VS BADE-PARKIN

Country	GMT policy type[a]	BP policy type[b]	Interpretation effect[c]	Criterion effect[d]	Difference[e]
Australia	1	1			
Belgium	1	2	−1		−1
Canada	1	2	−1		−1
France	1	2	−1		−1
Germany	3	4		−1	−1
Italy	3	2		+1	+1
Japan	1	3	−2		−2
Netherlands	3	2	+1		+1
Switzerland	3	4		−1	−1
UK	2	2			
US	3	3			
Sweden	–	2			

[a] (Number of asterisks in columns 3, 5 and 6 of Table 5) + 1.
[b] See Table 2.
[c] (Number of asterisks in columns 5 and 6 of Table 5 + number of asterisks in column 3 of Table 1) + 1 – BP Policy Type.
[d] (Number of asterisks in columns 1 and 2 of Table 1 + number of asterisks in column 3 of Table 5) + 1 – BP Policy Type.
[e] c + d = total difference between GMT and BP.

With respect to the criterion effect, by using a stricter version of BP 3, GMT change the ranking of the Bundesbank, Banca d'Italia and the Schweizerische Nationalbank *vis-à-vis* BP. Both the Bundesbank and the Schweizerische Nationalbank are downgraded (−1), whilst Banca d'Italia is upgraded (+1). It should be noticed that because the BP type 4 banks (Germany and Switzerland) do not meet GMT criterion 3, they become intermediate banks. That is, in terms of political independence, they get the same status as the Federal Reserve (BP type 3). This is intuitively not very appealing. Neither is the fact that Banca d'Italia is the only central bank that meets GMT criterion 3. Therefore, we conclude that by introducing a very strict criterion concerning the appointment of directors, GMT severely bias the ranking of the central banks of Germany, Switzerland and Italy.

3. Towards a New Index of Policy Independence

3.1 *A New Index of Policy Independence*

Following GMT, we identify policy independence with the capacity of the central banks to choose the final goals of monetary policy. This capacity is primarily determined by the following features:

(i) The procedures for appointing the board of the central bank;

(ii) the relationship between central banks and government in the formulation of monetary policy;

(iii) formal responsibilities (policy goals) of the central bank with respect to monetary policy.

On the basis of features *(i)*-*(iii)* we construct our own index, which is called the Eijffinger-Schaling (ES) index of policy independence. The degree of policy independence is determined using three criteria:

1. Is the bank the sole final policy authority *(b)*, is this authority not entrusted to the central bank alone *(b/g)*, or is it entrusted completely to the government *(g)*?

2. Is there no government official (with or without voting power) on the bank board?

3. Are more than half of the board appointments made independent of the government?[26]

Now we can distinguish $3 \times 2 \times 2 = 12$ potential policy types. This is summarized in Table 7.

The first four types are the BP potential types *(a)*-*(d)*. In Section 3 it was shown that these types do not exist. For sake of convenience we repeat the argument. A central bank being itself in charge of monetary policy and also having a government official on its board

---

[26] Following BP this criterion is operationalized as: proportion of members *not* appointed directly or indirectly by the government $\geq 11/21$.

TABLE 7

EIJFFINGER-SCHALING POLICY TYPES

Bank is final policy authority 1	No government official on bank board 2	Some board appointments independent of government 3	Potential central bank type	Central bank type does exist	Policy type
–(g)	–	*	(a)	no	–
–(g)	*	*	(b)	no	–
**(b)	–	*	(c)	no	–
**(b)	–	–	(d)	no	–
*(b/g)	–	–	(e)	no	–
*(b/g)	*	*	(f)	no	–
*(b/g)	–	*	(g)	no	–
–(g)	–	–	(h)	yes	1
–(g)	*	–	(i)	yes	2
*(b/g)	*	–	(j)	yes	3
**(b)	*	–	(k)	yes	4
**(b)	*	*	(l)	yes	5

(types *(c)* and *(d)*) does not occur in reality. Besides, there is no central bank that in spite of its not being in charge of monetary policy, makes some board appointments independent of the government. Therefore, types *(a)* and *(b)* do not exist.

From our examination of central bank laws in the Appendix, it follows that this argument includes the 'twin-authority' central banks, *i.e.* the central banks which have some but incomplete policy authority *(b/g)*. That is, a 'twin-authority' central bank that has a government official on its board (type *e*) does not exist. Finally, there is no twin-authority bank that makes some board appointments independent of the government. Consequently potential types *(f)* and *(g)* do not exist either. So, only the bottom part of Table 7 is relevant for the ES index of policy independence. The overall degree of policy independence is determined by a combination of attributes ES 1-3.

Contrary to BP and GMT, we do not weigh each attribute equally. This becomes clear if we take a look at ES 1. If policy making is exclusively entrusted to the central bank a country gets two asterisks. If it is not exclusively entrusted to the central it gets one asterisk. Finally, if the government is the sole authority in policy making it gets zero asterisks. Therefore, regarding our first criterion the maximum amount of asterisks is higher (two) than that with respect to criteria ES 2 and 3 (one). This means that criterion 1 has a weight of 2/4, two times the weight of the other criteria (1/4). Hence, our index is asymmetrical in the sense that attributes are not weighted equally.

We have the following argument in favour of asymmetrical weighting. Like GMT, the ES index of policy independence is based on:

(i) The relationship between central banks and government in the formulation of monetary policy;

(ii) the procedures for appointing the board of the central bank;

(iii) formal responsibilities (policy goals) of the central bank with respect to monetary policy.

However, GMT separately assess features *(i)* and *(iii)*. For example, the following conclusions can be drawn considering the Reserve Bank of Australia. From Table 5 it follows that according to GMT the Reserve Bank Act of 1959 contains provisions that the central bank pursues monetary stability (GMT 7) among its goals. On the other hand, according to Table 5, the government is the final policy authority (GMT 3). Therefore, GMT assess the contents of the final goals of monetary policy (GMT 7) irrespective of the capacity to choose these goals (GMT 6). By their separate assessment GMT allow for a one for one trade-off between the capacity to pursue a monetary policy goal and the contents of such a goal. That is, restricting attention to GMT 6 and 7, a subservient central bank with provisions for monetary stability is as independent as an autonomous central bank without these provisions. Of course, this trade-off is a natural consequence of symmetrical weighting.

Like GMT, the ES index of policy independence is based on features *(i)*-*(iii)*. However, we want to avoid the mentioned trade-off phenomenon. Therefore, feature *(i)*, the final authority in policy making, is assessed in conjunction with feature *(iii)*, the policy goals of monetary policy. That is, the extent to which a central bank is regarded to be the sole policy authority (ES 1), also depends on the presence of statutory requirements concerning monetary stability. Hence, we think a double weight (2/4 vs 1/4) with respect to ES 1 can be justified.

3.2 *Comparison with the Literature*

The five remaining (existing) central bank types are ranked from 1 (least independent) to 5 (most independent) according to the number of asterisks. Our findings are summarized in Table 8. In order to facilitate comparison with the literature we include BP's results.

TABLE 8

EIJFFINGER-SCHALING VS BADE-PARKIN

Country	ES policy type[a]	BP policy type[b]	BP asymmetrical policy type[c]	Interpretation effect[d]	Criterion effect[e]	Difference ES-BP[f]
Australia	1	1	1	0	0	0
Belgium	3	2	2	+1	0	+1
Canada	1	2	2	−1	0	−1
France	2	2	2	0	0	0
Germany	5	4	5	0	+1	+1
Italy	2	2	2	0	0	0
Japan	3	3	4	−1	+1	0
Netherlands	4	2	2	+2	0	+2
Switzerland	5	4	5	0	+1	+1
UK	2	2	2	0	0	0
US	3	3	4	−1	+1	0
Sweden	2	2	2	0	0	0

[a] (Number of asterisks in columns 1, 2 and 3 of Table 7) + 1.
[b] See Table 2.
[c] BP Asymmetrical Policy Types; BP types if BP 1 has two times the weight of BP 2 and 3. (b = **.)
[d] ES -/- BPA.
[e] BPA. -/- BP.
[f] d + e.

Again, differences in numerical values are dependent on both interpretation and criterion effects. In order to isolate the criterion effect we construct 'BP Asymmetrical Policy Types' (BPA). The latter types result when BP outcomes are entered into our (asymmetrical) aggregation procedure. For instance, consider Japan. According to BP the bank is the final policy authority. In terms of our aggregation procedure this means two asterisks, rather than one. Therefore as a consequence of the higher relative weight attached to this criterion the Bank of Japan becomes BP (asymmetrical) type 4. Now the total difference between ES and BP can be decomposed according to the following formula:

$$(1) \qquad ES - BP = (ES - BPA) + (BPA - BP)$$

where the first term on the right hand side is the interpretation effect and the second term is the criterion effect. From Table 8 it follows that the interpretation effects (see column *(d)*) concern Belgium, Canada, Japan, The Netherlands and the United States.

The National Bank of Belgium is upgraded (+1), because we regard it a twin-authority *(b/g)* rather than a government dominated institution *(g)*. This is because the bank gained more independence by the reform of the money market and monetary instruments in January 1991 (see Section 1). The Bank of Canada is downgraded (−1) because, contrary to BP, we find a government official on the board, namely the Deputy Minister of Finance (without voting power).

The Bank of Japan is downgraded (−1) because unlike BP we consider it to be a twin-authority *(b/g)* rather than a bank dominated *(b)* institution. The Nederlandsche Bank is upgraded (+2), because we consider it independent in policy making *(b)* rather than dependent *(g)* as a consequence of the only formal right of the Minister of Finance to give directions to the Bank. Finally, the Federal Reserve System is downgraded because unlike BP *(b)*, we consider it a twin-authority institution *(b/g)*.

In Table 9 our findings are confronted with GMT's.

Also, the total difference between ES and GMT may be decomposed, taking the following formula:

$$(2) \qquad ES - GMT = (ES - BP) + (BP - GMT)$$

where the first term on the right hand side is decomposed in Table 9 and the second term is decomposed in Table 6.

4. Conclusions

The theoretical rationale for central bank independence finds its origin in the ongoing 'Rules versus Discretion Debate'. A recent kind of analysis employed in this longstanding debate is to assess central

TABLE 9

EIJFFINGER-SCHALING VS GRILLI-MASCIANDARO-TABELLINI

Country	ES policy type	GMT policy type[a]	ES-BP[b]	BP-GMT[c]	Difference ES-GMT[d]
Australia	1	1	0	0	0
Belgium	3	1	+1	+1	+2
Canada	1	1	−1	+1	0
France	2	1	0	+1	+1
Germany	5	3	+1	+1	+2
Italy	2	3	0	−1	−1
Japan	3	1	0	+2	+2
Netherlands	4	3	+2	−1	+1
Switzerland	5	3	+1	+1	+2
UK	2	2	0	0	0
US	3	3	0	0	0
Sweden	2	–	0	–	–

[a] See Table 6.
[b] See column (f) Table 8.
[c] See column (e) Table 6 (signs must be reversed).
[d] b + c.

bank independence by means of the tools of quantitative indices. Numerical values of these indices are dependent on *(i)* criteria used in the examination of central bank laws (statutes), *(ii)* the interpretation of the relevant statute as to whether a central bank meets this criterion, *i.e.* possesses a certain attribute, and *(iii)* the way these attributes are aggregated to a composite index of central bank independence. Since in principle features *(i)-(iii)* are arbitrary there are unavoidable subjective elements in the construction of indices of this kind.

In order to view these elements in a broader perspective we compare the major indices of central bank independence as presented in Bade and Parkin (1988) (BP), Alesina (1988, 1989) and Grilli, Masciandaro and Tabellini (1991) (GMT). Also we construct our 'own' index of central bank independence. This index is then used to reach a critical perspective of the mentioned indices and to re-assess central bank independence in twelve industrial countries.

Our findings regarding the existing indices can be summarized as follows. Alesina (1988, 1989) made some serious mistakes in updating Bade and Parkin (1988). Hence, the Alesina revision of the position of the Banca d'Italia implies counterfactual statements concerning *e.g.* monetary accommodation of government deficits. Therefore, the Alesina revision is *ad hoc* and his index inconsistent. Furthermore, GMT and BP differ in their interpretations of the central bank laws of Canada, France, Belgium, Japan, and the Netherlands. These differences refer to both the presence of government officials on the bank board, and the final authority in policy making. Also, by using a very strict criterion with respect to the appointment of directors GMT change the ranking of the Bundesbank, Banca d'Italia and the Schweizerische Nationalbank *vis-à-vis* that by BP.

Finally, in re-assessing central bank independence in twelve industrial countries we qualify Banca d'Italia as less independent than GMT, while for the Nationale Bank van België, the Banque de France, the Bundesbank, the Bank of Japan, the Nederlandsche Bank and the Schweizerische Nationalbank the reverse applies.

[11]

Cuadernos de Economía, Año 30, N° 91, pp. 271-291 (diciembre 1993)

CENTRAL BANK INDEPENDENCE, POLITICAL INFLUENCE AND MACROECONOMIC PERFORMANCE: A SURVEY OF RECENT DEVELOPMENTS

ALEX CUKIERMAN*

ABSTRACT

Monetary policy usually enables policymakers to quickly but temporarily, achieve various real goals like high employment, financing of the budget deficit, attainment of balance of payments objectives and low interest rates. In the process, high powered money is increased fueling inflation. To offset this policy bias, various institutional mechanisms that reduce the ability of governments to freely expand the money supply have been tried. Among them, an important device, which is gaining popularity recently, is the granting of sufficient independence to the Central Bank in conjunction with an unequivocal mandate to focus on the attainment of price stability.

This paper surveys several alternative ways to characterize independence and also can be considered as validating the more general proposition that the design of policymaking institution matters.

1. INTRODUCTION

Monetary policy usually enables policymakers to quickly but temporarily, achieve various real goals like high employment, financing of the budget deficit, attainment of balance of payment objectives and low interest rates. In the process, high powered money is increased fueling inflation and inflationary expectation and creating an inflationary bias which persists long after the desirable effects of monetary expansion have vanished[1]. To offset this policy bias, various institutional mechanisms that reduce the ability of governments to freely expand the money supply have been tried. Among these are the gold standard and, various

* Tel-Aviv University. This survey is an expanded version of an invited lecture presented to the Twelfth Latin American Meeting of the Econometric Society, August 1993, Tucuman, Argentina.

1 A non technical introduction to the various mechanisms that induce the inflationary bias appear in chapter 2 of Cukierman (1992).

forms of partial commitments to fixed exchange rates like the Bretton Woods system and the European Monetary System.

Another device, which is gaining popularity recently, is the granting of sufficient independence to the Central Bank (CB) in conjunction with an unequivocal mandate to focus on the attainment of price stability. Countries like New Zealand and Chile have recently expanded the autonomy of their central banks[2] and other countries like Mexico, France and the United Kingdom are seriously considering various reforms of their central bank laws that would make them more independent of government. A likely reason for this trend is the success of the Bundesbank (Germany's CB) in maintaining one of the lowest rates of inflation for several decades. The Bundesbank is one of the most independent central banks in the world. It also is directed by its charter to elevate the objective of price stability above all other objectives. The law does specify that the Bundesbank should support the general economic policy of government, but hastens to add that in case of conflict between this goal and the Bundesbank's primary objective (i.e. stability of the currency) the bank's main responsibility is to its primary objective.

How does the degree of central bank independence (CBI) affect price stability, growth and other important macroeconomic variables? These are questions to which any country considering institutional reform of the CB should pay serious attention. In particular, how effective is CBI in achieving price stability? Do more independent central banks reduce the long run rate of growth of the economy by being less activist? Until very recently there were no systematic answers to such questions due to the absence of measures of CBI.

This paper is a survey of recent advances and ongoing work in the systematic characterization of the degree of CBI and of the effects of independence on macroeconomic performance. Granting more or less independence to the CB is a way to organize the institutions that (at least partially) decide on, and implement monetary policy. Does the structure of these institutions matter for the choice of policy and economic performance? The broad answer of this survey is; for many issues it does. This paper can, therefore, be considered as validating (in one area) the more general proposition that the design of policymaking institution matters.

The paper surveys several alternative ways to characterize independence. One measure is the degree of independence granted by law. There often are serious graps, particularly in LDCs, between the letter of the law and its application. Indices that reflect some of these gaps are the actual (as opposed to the legal) term of office of the CB governor and responses of experts on monetary institutions to a questionnaire on CBI. Independence often has many dimensions, some of which are not easily quantified. Nonetheless, the combination of these measures for different groups of countries provides, I believe, a lot of pertinent information.

Even the most independent CB is subject to political influence. But this influence varies from subtle and largely hazy influence like in the U.S.[3] to gross and obvious political influence in which new political masters routinely replace the head of the CB as in some Latin American countries. The paper briefly surveys recent advances in the measurement of gross political influence on the CB and in the identification of the effect of such influence on macroeconomic performance.

The paper is organized as follows. Section 2 describes existing measures of legal end of actual independence. Section 3 relates these measure to inflation performance in both

2 Details appear in Swinburne and Castello-Branco (1991).

3 A recent description of these channels appears in Havrilesky (1992).

developed and less developed economies. A subsection provides theoretical underpinnings for the finding that, past a certain threshold, inflation is higher the lower the probability that the chief executive officer of the CB will remain in office. Section 4 discusses recent advances in the measurement of gross political influence over the CB. Section 5 reports cross country and over time evidence on the relationship between CBI, on one hand, and growth and investment on the other in both developed and less developed economies. Section 6 briefly discusses the empirical interconnections between the intra-country variability of growth, CBI, and the level of development. The relationships between CBI and the distribution of interest rates are discussed in section 7. This is followed by concluding remarks.

Except for one subsection in Section 3, the paper's focus is empirical. To facilitate the life of quick readers major empirical regularities are highlighted in a series of "conclusions" throughout the paper.

2. Recent Developments in the Measurement of Central Bank Independence (CBI)

Central bank independence is believed to be an important determinant of policy choices, and through them - of economic performance. This belief has eluded systematic verification due to the absence of obvious quantitative measures of CBI. The first attempt to quantify CBI is due to Bade and Parkin (1980 who used a number of *legal* attributes from Central Bank charters to create measures of economic and of financial independence for a subset of industrial countries. Subsequent attempts to quantify independence extended those measures to more countries and proposed alternative ways of aggregating specific *legal* features of the law. But they followed in a similar mold by focussing on legal independence *within industrialized* economies[4]. Broadly based measures of legal independence for over sixty countries have recently been developed in Cukierman (1992) and Cukierman, Webb and Neyapti (1992).

Legal proxies for independence have two problems. First, the laws are incomplete in the sense that they do not specify explicitly the limits of authority between the central bank (CB) and the political authorities under all contingencies. These voids are filled by tradition or by power politics. Second, even when the law is quite explicit, actual practice may deviate from it. To address these problems more behaviorally, oriented proxies for actual independence have recently been developed. One is the actual (as opposed to the legally prescribed) turnover of CB governors. This proxy is available for over sixty countries including all industrial countries and over forty LDCs. A second proxy is derived by aggregating the responses of experts on monetary policy to a questionnaire on CBI. This proxy is available for a group of over twenty countries.

This section briefly surveys the procedures used to characterize legal independence as well as the other two, more behaviorally oriented, proxies of independence. It draws on materials from chapter 19 of Cukierman (1992) and Cukierman, Webb and Neyapti (1992).

4 Among these are Skanland (1984), Parking (1987), Alesina (1988, 1989) Swinburne and Catello-Branco (1991), Grilli, Masciandaro and Tabellini (1991), and Eijffinger and Schaling (1993). In addition, Leone (1991) presents information on legal limitations on lending by the central bank to government for an extensive sample of industrial and less develped countries.

a. Legal independence

Legal independence is one, but certainly not the sole, determinant of CBI. It also suggests the degree of independence that legislators meant to confer to the CB.

The specific features of legal independence, used to obtain an aggregate index of legal independence, are constructed in the following manner: A code of independence is assigned to each central bank for each characteristic based on a limited number of narrow but relatively precise legal characteristics. Only the written information from the charters is used. Additional information on how the law is applied in practice is deliberately left out because it is reflected by the other behavioral indices.

The coded legal characteristics or "variables" can be divided into four groups: (1) variables concerning the appointment, dismissal, and term of office of the chief executive officer (CEO) of the bank (usually the governor); (2) variables concerning the resolution of conflicts between the executive branch and the CB and the degree of participation of the CB in the formulation of monetary policy and in the budgetary process; (3) final objectives of the CB as stated in its charter; and (4) legal restrictions on the ability of the public sector to borrow from the CB. Such restrictions take the form of various limitations on the volume, maturity, rates, and width of direct advances and of securitized lending from the CB to the public sector.

In coding various central banks by the degree of independence within each group of characteristics, the following criteria are used: central banks in which the legal term of office of the CEO is longer and in which the executive branch has little legal authority in the appointment or dismissal of the governor are classified as more independent on the CEO dimension. By the same logic, central banks with wider authority to formulate monetary policy and to resist the executive branch in cases of conflict are classified as more independent on the policy formulation dimension.

Central banks in which the only or main objective of policy (as specified in the character) is price stability are classified as being more independent in this dimension than central banks with a number of objectives in addition to price stability. These banks are, in turn, classified as being more independent than banks with a large number of objectives or banks in whose charter price stability is not mentioned as an objective at all. This classification of the "objectives" variables is designed to capture the legal mandate of the bank to single-mindedly pursue the objective of price stability. (One of the few central banks in which such an unequivocal legal mandate exists is the Bundesbank). It does not, therefore, reflect (as the previous two groups of variables) the general level of independence from government. It indicates, instead, the legal mandate of the CB to elevate the target of price stability above other objectives. In Rogoffs's (1985) terminology, it measures how strong is the "conservative bias" of the CB as embodied in the law.

Similarly banks in which the limitations on lending from the CB to the public sector are stricter, are classified as more independent to pursue the objective of price stability. These limitations encompass a number of more detailed variables such as separate limitations on advances and securitized lending and restrictions on maturities and on interest rates. Generally, the stricter the limitation, the higher is the independence coding given to the bank on that dimension. The comparability of various types of limitations is complicated because different countries specify limitations in terms of different reference variables. A few countries specify limitations in absolute cash amounts, and other use a percentage of CB liabilities. The most prevalent type of limitation is formulated as a percentage of revenues, and in a minority of cases as a percentage of government expenditures. The "bite" of these limitations obviously depends on the magnitudes of the reference variables. Other things the same, however, absolute cash limits are more binding than limits in terms of government revenues. The most accommodative limits are those specified in terms of government expenditures. These considerations are embodied in a "type of limit" variable and also influence the coding of the severity of limitations on loans to government via advances and securitized lending.

Limitations on lending are also classified as stricter, the nearer the rates paid by government to market rates and the shorter the maturities of the loans from the CB to the public sector. They are also stricter, the narrower the circle of institutions that are allowed to borrow from the CB and the smaller the discretion of the executive branch in deciding to whom the CB will lend and how much. In addition, central bank laws that prohibit the CB from buying government securities on the primary market are considered, ceteris paribus, stricter than laws that do not contain such a prohibition.

Altogether, sixteen different legal variables are coded using a scale ranging between 0 (smallest level of independence) to 1 (highest level of independence). The number of independence levels generally varies across legal variables depending on the fineness of data on alternative legal characteristics. Using a two-step procedure, the sixteen legal variables are aggregated into a single overall measure of legal independence. This overall index is basically a weighted average of the sixteen legal variables. It varies during the 1980s, between a maximum of 0.69 (for Germany) and a minimum of 0.10 (for Poland). The median level of legal independence is about the same in developed countries and in LDCs. further details on the coding of the legal variables appear in Table 19.1 of Cukierman (1992) or in Table 1 of Cukierman, Webb, and Neyapti (1992).

b. The turnover rate of central bank governors as a proxy of actual independence

As most practitioners in the area of monetary policymaking are well aware, the legal status of a central bank is only one of several elements that determines its actual independence. Although there are important variations in the degree of completeness of different CB laws, many are highly incomplete and leave a lot of room for interpretation. As a result, factors such as tradition or the personalities of the governor and other high officials of the bank at least partially shape the actual level of CB independence. Even when the law is quite explicit, it may not be operational if there is a tradition or an understanding within government that things should be done in a different way. A striking example is Argentina, in which the legal term of office of the governor is four years. But there was also an informal tradition that the governor of the CB offers his resignation to the executive whenever there is a change of government or even of the finance minister. Argentinean governors invariably adhered to this tradition. As a consequence, the average actual term of office of the governor in Argentina during the 1980s was about ten months. Obviously, the actual degree of independence of the Argentinean CB was substantially lower than the one implied by measures of legal independence including, in particular, the four-year legal term of office.

There are no obvious indicators of actual, as opposed to legal, CB independence. This is not because the matter is not important, but because it is hard to find systematic indicators of actual independence when it diverges from legal independence. The extreme case of Argentina, though, suggests that at least above some threshold the turnover rate of central bank governors is a proxy of (lack of) actual independence. The average yearly turnover rate between 1950 and 1989 ranges from a minimum of 0.03 (average tenure of 33 years) in Iceland to a maximum of 0.93 (average tenure of about thirteen months in Argentina). Turnover rates in LDCs tend to spread into a range that has not been experienced in the developed countries (DC). The highest turnover among the DC is 0.2 (average tenure of five years) for Spain and Japan. More than half of the LDCs have turnover rates exceeding this. Table 1 presents turnover rates for selected LDCs during the 1980s.

Low turnover does not necessarily imply a high level of CB independence -a relatively subservient governor may stay in office longer precisely because he does not stand up to the executive branch. This may be true for countries with exceptionally low turnover rate such as Iceland, Denmark, Britain, and the United States. In such countries, turnover is probably unrelated to independence. On the other hand, it is very likely that above some critical turnover rate CB independence is lower the higher the turnover rate of CB governors. One reason is that for sufficiently high turnover rates the tenure of the CB governor is shorter than that of the executive branch. This makes the governor more susceptible to influence by the executive branch and discourages him or her from trying to implement longer-term policies the lower the expected tenure. Since in most countries the electoral cycle is at least four years, it is likely that the threshold turnover is somewhere between 0.2 and 0.25 (average tenure of four to five years). In addition, for very short terms of office such as three years or less (turnover rates of 0.33 or larger), it is generally more difficult to implement long-term policies for any electoral cycle. It is therefore likely, a priori, that turnover is a proxy for (lack of) independence in LDCs but that it is largely unrelated to it within industrial countries. The evidence reviewed in the next section is consistent with this conjecture.

TABLE 1: TURNOVER RATES OF THE CENTRAL BANK GOVERNOR
1980-1989
(Average number of changes a year)

Country	Turnover
Thailand	0.10
Hungary	0.10
Honduras	0.10
South Africa	0.20
Philippines	0.20
Israel	0.20
Greece	0.20
India	0.30
Uruguay	0.30
Portugal	0.30
Pakistan	0.30
Turkey	0.40
Nicaragua	0.40
Poland	0.50
Venezuela	0.50
Singapore	0.60
Chile	0.80
Brazil	0.80
Argentina	1.00

SOURCE: Adapted from Table 3 of Cukierman, Webb, and Neyapti (1992).

c. Questionnaire on central bank independence during the 1980s

The other groups of indicators of central bank independence is based on responses to a questionnaire that was sent to a non-random sample of specialists on monetary policy in various central banks. Some questions involve the same issues that underlie the legal variables, but they focus on the practice rather than the law -for example, central bank objectives, their importance in practice, and the strictness of limitations on lending in practice. Some questions refer to additional issues, such as subsidized credits from the bank to the private sector, quantitative targets for the money stock, the determination of the bank budget, and the degree of actual tenure overlap between the governor and high officials in the executive branch. One question focuses on the actual practice followed in the resolution of conflicts between government and the CB.

Although the judgments of those responding to the questionnaire are subjective and not entirely uniform, the responses help to identify divergence between actual and legal independence, particularly when the divergence is large.

Answers to the questionnaire sufficed for coding nine questionnaires variables for 23 countries. As with the legal variables, the range of codes is in the zero-one interval with one standing for the highest level of independence and zero for the lowest level. Aggregation of the questionnaire variables indicates that central banks in developing countries are less independent than those in industrial countries. Only two industrial countries -Ireland and Belgium- are below the median of 0.60, and only four developing countries- The Bahamas, Costa Rica, South Africa, and Zaire- are above it. This contrasts with the findings for legal independence, where the two country groups do not differ widely, but it is similar to the finding for turnover. Further detail appears in chapter 19 of Cukierman (1992) and in Cukierman, Webb, and Neyapti (1992).

d. Relationship between indices of independence

The correlations between legal independence, the turnover rate, and the questionnaire based index are low which suggests that each of them contains information about different aspects of CBI.

Only the correlation between the legal independence index and the questionnaire-based index of independence for the industrial countries is even marginally significant, which suggests that the law is a more important determinant of actual independence in the industrial countries. Since the correlation across these indexes is not high, they can be usefully combined to obtain a better measure of overall central bank independence. Such a measure is described in the next section.

3. Inflation and Central Bank Independence

Conventional wisdom is that, by insulating the CB from short run political pressures, independence enables the central bank to put a stronger emphasis on price stability and to achieve, therefore, a lower rate of inflation. For industrial economies, this hypothesis is, by now, supported by evidence from a number of studies. In particular, it is found that for those economies, there is a negative association between inflation and legal independence [Alesina (1988), Grilli Masciandaro and Tabellini (1991), Cukierman, Webb, and Neyapti (1992), Eijffinger and Schaling (1993b) and Alesina and Summers (1993)].

No similar relationship between inflation and legal independence emerges in LDCs. But there is a strong positive between inflation and the turnover rate of CB governors. Interestingly, no such association between turnover and inflation is found for industrial economies. These and other findings lead to the conclusion that legal independence is a more appropriate proxy for actual independence within industrial economies and that turnover is a more appropriate proxy for actual independence within LDCs. This conclusion is supported by two additional considerations: First, when both groups of countries are lumped together and the turnover variable broken down into a high and a low range, only the former is found to be significantly related to inflation. It will be recalled from the previous section that turnover within industrial countries is usually in the low range. Second, legal independence is more likely to reflect actual independence within industrial countries than in LDCs since there is more respect for the law in the first group[5]. Further detail and discussion appear in chapter 19 of Cukierman (1993) and in Cukierman, Webb, and Neyapti (1992). The main conclusions are summarized in what follows;

Conclusion 1: **Within industrial economies inflation is negatively related to legal independence and unrelated to CB governors turnover.**

Conclusion 2: **Within LDCs there is no relation between inflation and legal independence. But there is a strong positive association between inflation and CB governors turnover.**

a. Inflation and the questionnaire based index of central bank independence

For the sample of twenty-three countries for which a questionnaire based index of CBI is available there is a significant negative relationships between inflation and the questionnaire based proxy of independence[6].

b. Governor's turnover and inflation - some theoretical underpinnings

A higher average turnover rate of CB governors is equivalent to the probability of replacement of the governor being higher. This subsection briefly describes a conceptual framework in which the policy chosen by the CB governor is more inflationary, the higher the probability that he is removed from office. The intuition underlying this result is that a positive inflationary surprise produces immediate benefits like (temporarily) higher employment and lower interest rates. But the full costs of this policy (in terms of lower credibility and higher inflation) appear later. Central bank governors with shorter horizons in office are therefore more likely to succumb to inflationary temptations. Hence, there should be a positive association, at least above some threshold, between inflation and turnover. Similarly, once high inflation has been unleashed the benefits of a stabilization accrue only after a while whereas its employment and high-interest rates costs occur upfront.

5 There is evidence that the relationship between the legal and the actual term in office of the CB governor is stronger for industrial countries than for LDCs [(Pal 1993)].

6 The countries are (in decreasing order of their questionnaire based index of independence); Germany, Costa Rica, Finland, Austria, Italy, Denmark, the Bahamas, Luxemburg, France, the United Kingdom, South Africa, Zaire, Lebanon, Ireland, Barbados, Uganda, Uruguay, Belgium, Turkey, Tanzania, Peru, Yugoslavia and Ethiopia.

The formal model is an extension of the model of a policymaker with an (extended) information advantage from chapter 10 of Cukierman (1992). As long as he is in office, the governor possesses an objective function with a changing but persistent relative emphasis on the creation of surprises versus price stability. In the present context, this shifting weight can be thought of as originating in changes in the extent of political pressures on the CB. The public never gets to observe these pressures directly but can draw noisy inferences about their current and future state from past inflation rates. These inferences are noisy because the CB does not have perfect control over the rate of inflation.

Let s be the probability of survival of the governor in office in period t given that he has remained in office until period t-1[7]. In states of nature in which he is not in office, the governor does not care about either price stability or surprise creation[8]. The relevant part of the governor's objective function is

$$E_0\left\{\left[\Pi_0-\Pi_0^e\right]x_0-\frac{\Pi_0^2}{2}+\sum_{i=1}^{\infty}(s\beta)^i\left[\left(\Pi_i-\Pi_i^e\right)x_i-\frac{\Pi_i^2}{2}\right]\right\}+\sum_{i=1}^{\infty}s^{i-s}(1-s)K \qquad (1)$$

where $x_i = A + p_i$, $p_i = \rho p_{i-1} + v_i$, $A > 0$ and $0 < \rho < 1$. v_i is a normal varite with zero mean and variance σ_v^2. Here Π_i is actual inflation in period i and Π_i^e the rate of inflation expected for that period at the beginning of the period. β is the discount factor and x_i is a stochastic variable whose realizations are restricted to the positive orthant. It reflects the potency of political pressures on the CB. The larger x_i the stronger are the pressures of the political establishment on the governor to expand the money supply. x_i is private information. Its positive serial correlation reflects the presumption that when pressures are above their mean level, they tend to remain above it for some time. K is the *constant* level of utility experienced by the governor when not in office. s^i is the probability that the governor survives in office until the end of period i and s^{i-1} (1-s) is the probability that he terminates at the beginning of that period after having survived until the end of the previous period. Equilibrium is of the Nash variety; taking the (rational) process of expectation formation by the public as given, the governor plans rates of monetary expansion and inflation so as to maximize the objective function in equation (1); taking the behavioral rule of the governor as given, the public forms expectations so as to minimize the mean (square) forecast error.

Application of the results in chapter 10 of Cukierman (1992) to this case reveals that equilibrium inflation is given by

$$\Pi_i = \frac{1-s\beta\rho}{1-s\beta\lambda}A + \frac{1-s\beta\rho^2}{1-s\beta\rho\lambda}p_i + \psi_i \qquad (2)$$

Where ψ_i is a normal variate with zero mean and variance σ_ψ^2. ψ_i characterizes the (lack of) precision of monetary policy in controlling inflation. λ is function of ρ, σ_v^2 and σ_ψ^2 and satisfies the inequality $\lambda \leq \rho$.

7 I assume for simplicity that this probability is constant and independent from events in other periods.

8 This somewhat extreme assumption is used for simplicity. The main result would go through even if he cared but less than in periods in which he is in office.

Note that since s, β, ρ and λ are all smaller than one, the coefficients of A and of p_i are positive. How does an increase in the governor's survival probability affect equilibrium inflation? The following proposition provides an answer to this question.

Proposition 1: For any given realization of the political pressure shock (p_i) and of the control error (ψ_i) the rate of inflation is higher the lower is the survival probability, s, of the central bank governor.

Proposition 1 provides precise underpinnings for the intuitively plausible notion that a governor with a low probability of survival in office will inflate at a higher rate than a governor with a higher probability of survival. The reason is that part of the cost of *currently* more expansionary monetary policy takes de form of higher *future* inflationary expectations. A governor who is less sure of being in office in the future is obviously less sensitive to this cost. He, therefore, inflates, at a higher rate.

Two facts are worth noting. First, due to the dynamic nature of his optimization problem, the governor's policy while in office is influenced by what he perceives to be his future survival probability. Second, a lower survival probability raises the CB inflationary response to any given level of political pressure.

c. Two-way causality between inflation and governor's turnover

The previous subsection shows that there are theoretical reasons to believe that a lower survival probability of the CB governor induces him to follow more inflationary policies. This is consistent with the empirical positive association between turnover and inflation reported earlier in this section. But this association may also be due to reverse causality from inflation to turnover. High inflation is partly blamed on the CB, which tarnishes the bank's public images and makes it more likely that the governor will not persist in office. By the same token, the successful stabilization of inflation is often followed by an increase in the prestige of the CB which may reduce the likelihood of instability at the bank.

The possibility of reverse causality raises the issue of potential simultaneity bias in the estimated relationship between inflation and turnover. But reestimation of this relation using instrumental variables supports the view that at least part of the significant association between inflation and turnover (in LDC-s) is indeed due to causality running from the latter to inflation.

A related issue concerns the causality, in the Granger sense between turnover and inflation. Estimation of bivariate autoregressive processes for inflation and turnover in broad periods (decades) shows that (Granger) causality operates in both directions. More precisely, lagged turnover affects current inflation and lagged inflation affects current turnover. Further detail appears in subsection 6 and 7 of chapter 20 in Cukierman (1992).

4. Measures of Political Influence on the Central Bank

All central banks are probably subject to some degree of political influence. This influence may be subtle and covert or blunt and quite obvious. The first type of influence is typical of countries like the U.S. in which the CB enjoys a relatively high degree of legal independence. Havrilesky (1992) has recently described some of these channels of influence. Among those are public signalling from the administration to the CB about the "desirable" path of interest rates, the power of appointment and periodic proposals by Congress to enact legislation that would limit the Fed's authority in various ways. Those pressures are only partially successful probably because the law and the way it is implemented sufficiently shield the Fed's high officials from direct retribution when they resist pressures. U.S. presidents usually appoint Board members which they believe will support the economic orientation of the administration. But the long and secure term in office of a Board member (fourteen years) gives him a lot of leeway. The fact that the tenure of a Board member usually spans that of several administrations also increases his freedom of action.

At the other end of the spectrum, we find gross political influence, which like in Argentina or Brazil, results in the removal from office of the CB governor following a change of regime or even of prime minister. This section describes a test for the existence of gross political influence of this type as well as measures of political influence that are based on the extent to which the term in office of the CB governor depends on political changes.

a. A test for the existence of gross political influence on the CB

The test is based on a comparison of the frequency of governor changes shortly after political transitions with the same frequency in other "non political" periods. In the absence of gross political influence, we should expect those frequencies to be similar magnitudes. On the other hand, a significantly higher frequency shortly after political transitions would point to the existence of political influence. Cukierman and Webb (1993) have performed such a test for a sample of 64 countries during the 1950-89 period[9].

In order to compare the frequencies of governor changes between political and non political periods, it is necessary to find how long is the time lag following a political transition within which a governor change is identified as political. The cutoff lag is estimated in two steps. First, the first nine months following all political transitions are divided into a number of short (two or three months) intervals and the frequency of changes at the CB is calculated within each such interval as well as in the "ten months or more" interval[10]. The cutoff between political and non political periods is then found by taking the largest lag interval for which: 1) There is a significant difference between the frequency of changes at the CB within this interval and the frequency of such changes at lags of ten or more months and; 2) the frequencies in all intervals beyond this one do not significantly differ from the frequency in the ten-or-more months interval. The demarcation line between political and non political periods is then estimated to be at the upper bound of this lag interval.

Cukierman and Webb (op.cit.) find that the probability of a CB governor turnover is highest in the first lag interval and that it decays gradually as the time elapsed since the latest political transition increases. The main conclusions reached are summarized in what follows:

9 The data start later for countries that achieved political independence or established a CB after 1950.

10 This interval is considered a priori as non political.

Conclusion 3: (i) There is strong evidence of gross political influence on the CB during the 1950-1989 period.

(ii) The cutoff between political and non political period is at six months following a political transition for the entire sample.

(iii) The probability of a CB governor turnover within six months of a political transition is 3 times larger than the same probability in non political periods (seven or more months) after a political transition.

When the sample is broken down into industrial and developing countries, the same qualitative results obtain within each subgroup. Interestingly, there is evidence of gross political influence on the CB even within industrial countries. But the probability of a political turnover within that group of countries is substantially smaller than this probability in LDCs.

Within LDCs the probability of a political turnover at the CB within the same or one month following a political transition is highest in countries that have switched between a democratic and an authoritarian regime (mixed regime), second highest in countries which had only authoritarian regimes and lowest in countries which were democratic throughout the period of the sample. Further detail appears in Cukierman and Webb (1993).

b. The political vulnerability of the central bank and related measures of dependence

A central bank whose chief executive officer is frequently replaced following political transitions is likely to be more dependent on the political authorities than a central bank in which the governor outlives most political changes. This notion is captured by using an index of political vulnerability of the central bank. The index is defined as the fraction of times that a political transition is followed within 6 months by a replacement of the central bank governor. The index ranges between a minimum of zero for a number of countries (including the United States, Canada, and Austria) and a maximum of 1.375 (for Argentina).

Central Bank vulnerability is generally lower in developed economies than in LDCs. Within LDCs, it is highest in countries that alternate between democratic and authoritarian regimes and lowest in countries with authoritarian regimes. It also tends to increase in periods characterized by a change of regime, i.e., replacement of a democratic regime by an authoritarian one or vice versa.

Given the time profile of political transitions, it is possible to decompose governor's turnover into political and non political turnover. The latter is defined as CB governor's changes which occur in periods that are seven or more months following a political transition. Political turnover at the CB and vulnerability are largely substitute indices of independence. But non political turnover and CB vulnerability are probably complementary indices of CB independence. The first is a measure of general instability at the CB whereas the second is a measure of vulnerability of the governor's office to political change.

c. Inflation, political instability and instability at the central bank

Political instability and inflation tend to be positively related (see for example Cukierman, Edwards, and Tabellini (1992) or chapter 4 of Cukierman (1992)). An important question is how much of this relation is due to a direct effect from political instability to inflation and how much to (political induced and non politically induced) instability at the CB. Cukierman and Webb (1993) examine this question and find that both types of instability have positive effects on inflation. In particular, inflation is higher, the higher CB vulnerability, and the higher non political CB turnover. But it is also higher *ceteris paribus*, the higher the frequency of high and low level political changes[11]. This leads to the following conclusions.

Conclusion 4: **(i) High level political instability raises inflation directly as well as by raising the political vulnerability of the CB.**

(ii) Non political turnover at the CB has an additional positive effect on inflation.

It is well known that inflation and its variance display a strong cross sectional positive relationship. Cukierman (1992, ch. 18) proposes a causal theory in which those two variables are linked because of their common link to CBI. By using CB vulnerability and non political turnover as measures of CB dependence, it is possible to examine how much of the positive relation between inflation and its variance is due to their common relation with CBI. Cukierman and Webb (1993) find that about one third of the association between inflation and its variability is due to their common association with CBI.

5. Central Bank Independence, Growth, Investment and Productivity Growth

A priori considerations do not produce a clear cut hypothesis about the relationship between CBI and growth. On one hand, by reducing inflation and the associated nominal uncertainty, CBI may enhance the efficiency of resource allocation and encourage investment. We would, therefore, expect more CBI to lead to higher growth on average. But, by reducing the scope for policies to maintain full employment and to encourage investment directly, more independence of the central bank may reduce the average performance of the economy and the long-run rate of growth[12]. Thus it is ambiguous a priori which way central bank independence will affect real growth.

The first attempt to examine the relation between CBI and growth is due to Grilli, Masciandaro, and Tabellini (1991). They examined the cross sectional relation between average growth and legal independence in a sample of industrial countries and found no association between the two. Using a slightly different coverage of (industrial) countries and another index of legal independence Alesina and Summers (1993) reach a similar conclusion.

11 A high level political changes is a change in regime. A low level political change is a change of head of government only.

12 Those who advocate such policies probably believe that nominal contracts and/or informational asymmetries produce sufficiently long-lasting effects of money on the economy.

Since these studies do not control for other determinant of growth, this finding may reflect an omitted variables bias rather than a lack of association between growth and CBI. But for the industrial countries, this lack of association persists even after controlling for other determinants of growth like initial GDP and the initial levels of primary and of secondary education [Cukierman, Kalaitzidakis, Summers, and Webb (1993)].

Conclusion 5: Average real growth is unrelated to (legal) CBI within industrial economies.

When similar experiments are repeated for LDCs, again, no association is found between *legal* independence and growth. But this may well be due to the low association between actual and legal independence in LDCs rather than o the lack of association between growth and CBI. To handle this problem, Cukierman *et al.* (*op.cit.*) have used several *behavioral* measures of CBI like governor's turnover and the index of CB political vulnerability as proxies for CBI in LDCs. Barro (1991) has recently uncovered a number of cross sectional determinants of growth like initial levels of GDP and initial primary and secondary education levels. Using pooled cross-section time series[13] and controlling for those cross sectional determinants of growth as well as for decade effects and terms of trade shocks, Cukierman *et al.* find a *ceteris paribus* positive association between growth and CBI. In summary,

Conclusion 6: After controlling for other determinants of growth (like initial GDP and terms of trade shocks) CBI is found to have a positive effect on growth in LDCs.

The coefficient of turnover is -3.58. This implies that a 0.1 increase in turnover (one more per decade) reduces the average rate of growth, other things the same, by about 0.36 percent per year. To illustrate the orders of magnitude involved, consider Chile with an average yearly turnover of 0.54 and Indonesia with a turnover of about 0.22 over the 1960-89 period. Taken literally, this implies that about 1.15 percentage points of the difference in average yearly growth rates between these two countries is attributable to the difference in turnover.

One should not interpret this to imply that a reduction of 0.1 in turnover *without any other change* will raise average yearly growth by 0.36 percent, but it is usually the case that a lower turnover of Central Bank Governors is associated with a more stable macroeconomic policy environment. When this, and other related factors, change in conjunction with the lower turnover, it seems reasonable to expect an increase in the average rate of growth of the order of magnitude implied by the regression results. A parable may sharpen the argument. Measuring turnover is analogous to taking the temperature of a sick patient. A high temperature is a signal that something is wrong. This does not mean that a reduction of temperature by means of aspirin without taking care of the root cause is going to cure the patient. However, after treatment of the root cause, a reduction in temperature is usually taken as a genuine signal of recovery. Similarly, the reduction of turnover at the central bank without doing anything else is tantamount to the treatment of a symptom only. However, when the central bank is given more authority to pursue stable policies, this is

13 The data consists (at most) of three decade wide observations (1960s, 1970s, and 1980s) on each variable in each country.

normally accompanied by a reduction in turnover. In such cases, turnover is a good proxy for the quality of policymaking institutions.

When growth equations using turnover as a *proxy* for (lack of) independence are reestimated for the combined sample of industrial and of developing countries, the coefficient of turnover is again negative, quite significant and even larger than the corresponding coefficient for LDCs alone. This suggests that, controlling for other variables, turnover may also capture differences in growth between the two groups of countries. This conjecture is also supported by the fact that CBI is substantially higher in developed than in developing countries and that the variability of independence within the second group is much higher (see section 3). The conjunction of these findings is consistent with the hypothesis that low independence retards growth in *all* countries but that this effect is not detected within industrial countries because of the smaller variability of CBI and the smaller number of countries in that group. Another possibility is that independence has a detectable effect on growth only above a sufficiently high threshold[14].

a. Inflation as a proxy for unstable macroeconomic policies in growth equations

The commonly held view of policy-oriented economists -that unstable macroeconomic policies retard growth- evolved from the experience of high-inflation Latin American economies, and is kept alive by recent developments in some Eastern European economies and the former Soviet Union. This view has been tested by adding inflation or its variability as regressors to growth equations. When this is done, inflation and its variability are found to have a significant negative impact on growth. See for example equation (7) in Fischer (1991) and the literature quoted therein. One problem with this way of testing for the effect of unstable macroeconomic policies is that inflation itself is an endogenous variable. It is affected by monetary policy but is also influenced by other nonpolicy variables. In particular, a negative supply shock will lower the rate of growth and, given policy, raise the measured rate of inflation. Hence, the negative coefficient of inflation in the growth equation may be at least partly due to reverse causality-from growth to inflation.

To address this problem, Cukierman, Kalaitzidakis, Summers and Webb (1993) have reestimated growth equations with inflation as a regressor by means of instrumental variables. The political vulnerability of the CB and non political turnover are used (alternatively) as instruments. Since they represent long run institutional features of a country, those variables are unlikely to be directly affected by growth. We also saw in section 4 that both of them do affect inflation. They qualify, therefore, as good instruments for inflation in growth equations. The basic result is that, although, its effect is less significant, inflation still has a *ceteris paribus* negative effect on growth.

When political vulnerability of the central bank is used as a measure of unstable macroeconomic policies *instead* of inflation, it also has a negative partial effect on growth. In summary,

Conclusion 7: Unstable macroeconomic policies as proxied by instrumented inflation or central bank vulnerability have a ceteris paribus negative effect on growth.

14 Within industrial countries alone turnover is insignificant. It is possible that this insignificant effect also reflects the lack of association of turnover with actual independence in that group of countries.

b. Central bank independence, private investment and productivity growth

One of the channels through which the positive association between growth and CBI may arise is that macroeconomic instability, which is caused by or reflected through low CBI, deters private investment. Cukierman, *et. al.* (*op.cit.*) test that possibility by estimating investment equations for developing countries between 1970 and 1990. After controlling for some of the same variables that appear in the growth equations, they find that central bank turnover has a significant negative impact on private investment as a share of GDP. So does the political vulnerability of the central bank. When the Barro-Wolf proxies for political instability[15] are added as regressors, the significance of turnover and vulnerability is reduced but their effects remain negative.

The summary conclusion is:

Conclusion 8: Less CBI as proxied by a higher governor's turnover or by more political vulnerability at the central bank has a negative impact on the share of private investment in LDCs. This effect weakens but does not totally disappear in the presence of proxies for political instability.

Another channel through which CBI could affect growth is productivity growth. Cukierman *et.al.* find a weak partial negative association between productivity growth and central bank independence as proxied by turnover in LDCs. But this effect vanishes in the presence of measures of political instability.

6. THE INTRA-COUNTRY VARIABILITY OF GROWTH, CBI, AND THE LEVEL OF DEVELOPMENT

Countries with more dependent central banks normally conduct more activist monetary policies in order to affect aggregate demand. It is an open issue, though, whether such activism actually dampens or increases the amplitude of business cycles. Political authorities are more likely than the central bank to pursue a variety of objectives besides dampening of the cycle. For instance, they might produce a political cycle [for a recent empirical survey see Alesina, Cohen, and Roubini (1992)]. Even when they aim to dampen the cycle, politicians may exacerbate it, along the lines of Friedman's long and variables lags argument [see also Meltzer (1987)]. Hence, there are conflicting theoretical predictions about the relationship between a country's growth-rate variability and the independence of its central bank[16]. The type of relationship, if any, between the variability of growth and the level of CBI is, therefore, an empirical matter.

Cukierman *et al.* (*op.cit.*) find, after controlling for the effect of terms of trade shocks, that there is a negative relationship between the variability of growth within a country and CBI as proxied by turnover. But when one controls for initial GDO, this variable turns out to have a significant negative impact on the variability of growth and turnover becomes insignificant. Hence,

15 Those variables are counts of political assassinations, revolutions and coups.

16 But theory *does* imply that, other things the same, policy is more activits the more dependent is the central bank (Cukierman 1992) p. 355).

Conclusion 9: The over time variability of growth within a country is negatively related to its level of development and unrelated to the independence of its central bank as proxied by turnover.

7. CBI and Interest Rates

The first attempt to investigate the relationship between the distribution of interest rates and CBI is in Alesina and Summers (1993). Their results pertain to a sample of 18 industrialized countries. Using the Alesina (1988) legal measure of CBI, they find that: (1) There is no (cross-country) association between the level of export real rates and CBI; (2) the (intra-country) variability of real rates is inversely related to CBI. The attribute this finding to the negative association between the variability of inflation and CBI.

Using their own measure of legal independence, Cukierman, Kalaitzidakis, Summers, and Webb (1993) replicate the second result and find no association between the variability of export real rates and legal independence in LDCs. On the other hand, they find a strong positive association between this variability and central bank turnover in LDCs. These results are consistent with the view that legal independence is an appropriate proxy for actual independence in industrial countries and that turnover is the appropriate proxy in LDCs.

They also find that there is a negative relationship between CBI and the variability of nominal rates but no similar relationship between CBI and the variability of long-term nominal rates. In summary,

Conclusion 10: (i) The variabilities of export real rates and short term nominal rates are negatively related to (the appropriate respective measures of) CBI in both develped and less developed economies.

(ii) There is no relation between the variability of nominal long-term rates and CBI.

Contrary to Alesina and Summers, Cukierman, *et al.* find a positive relationship between the level of the expost real return to savers in industrial economies and legal independence.

A similar qualititative result emerges for LDCs when Argentina is included in the sample. More precisely, there is a significant negative association between the average real return to short term financial savings and turnover. When Argentina is excluded, the coefficient of turnover becomes insignificant but remains negative. In summary,

Conclusion 11: (i) The expost average real return to deposits is positive associated with legal independence in industrial economies.

(ii) The expost average real return to deposits in LDCs is negatively associated with the turnover of CB

governors. But when Argentina is excluded from the sample, this effect becomes insignificant[17]**.**

A likely explanation for the positive association between the real deposit rate and CBI is that in most countries the real return to savers in short-term financial assets is below its competitive equilibrium level because of government regulation and periodic inflationary surprises. As a consequence, the quantity of short-term financial savings is supply constrained. The lower the degree of CBI, the farther below its equilibrium value is the real return to savers because of higher interference with the short-term return to nominal savings through regulation and inflationary surprises. This view is consistent with the McKinnon and Shaw notion of financial repression [McKinnon (1973)].

In addition, conclusion 11 implies that the level of financial repression is higher, the lower CBI. This view is further supported by the observation that the real return to savers in LDCs is substantially lower than in industrial countries in conjunction with the fact (section 3) that overall independence in the second group is higher on average.

8. Concluding Remarks

The evidence surveyed in this paper leads to the conclusion that, over the long term, CBI and the absence of gross political influence on the central bank improve, or at least do not reduce macroeconomic performance. Higher levels of independence are associated with lower inflation without discernible effects on growth and its variability in developed economies. In LDCs, higher CBI and lower levels of (gross) political influence are associated with lower inflation, more growth, and more private investment without any discernible effect on the variability of growth. In addition, higher levels of independence are associated with higher returns to financial savings, less variability of these returns and most likely a more efficient allocation of financial capital.

Central bank independence (CBI) is one of several ways to *partially* commit politicians to pay relatively more attention to price stability. In the absence of *some* commitment device adverse shocks to the economy or to the political system may induce a policy response that allows the development of high inflation. CBI should be viewed mostly as a *preventive* rather than a remedial device. Once high inflation has been allowed to develop independence alone does not suffice to eradicate it.

As many recent successful stabilizations have clearly demonstrated, an ongoing inflation can be stabilized only with the full and determined participation of the highest levels of government. But one price stability has been restored, CBI can play a useful, long term, preventive role. The recent tendencies toward granting more independence to the central bank in countries like Chile, Mexico, and Argentina are, therefore, pointed in the right direction.

But an important lesson from the findings reported here is that more legal independence *alone* does not suffice. When actual practice is allowed to substantially depart from the written law, even a highly independent charter does not function as an effective commitment device. The experiences of Argentina and Chile in previous decades are living proof of this principle. A general climate of respect for the rule of law, of the kind found in

17 Further detail appears in Cukierman *et al.* (*op.cit.*).

some developed democracies, enhances the effectiveness of legal independence as a commitment device.

It seems that having an independent central bank is particularly important in situations in which the authority for deciding on fiscal expenditures is relatively decentralized as is the case in Brazil, the former Socialist Republics and may be the case in Western Europe if and when a European monetary union comes into being. As the number of players that have the authority to commit government spending increases each player pays less attention to the effect of the expenditures he advocates on the general rate of inflation. As a result, the rate of inflation increases[18]. Effective constraints on the ability of politicians to tamper with the money supply seem particularly important in such cases.

APPENDIX

1. Proof of Proposition 1: Totally differentiating equation (2) with respect to s and rearranging

$$\frac{d\Pi_i}{ds} \equiv - K \left[(1 - s\beta\lambda\rho)^2 A + (1 - s\beta\lambda)^2 \rho p_i \right] \tag{A1}$$

where

$$K \equiv \frac{\beta (\rho - \lambda)}{(1-s\beta\lambda)^2 (1-s\beta\lambda\rho)^2} \tag{A2}$$

Since $\rho - 1 > 0$, K is positive. Since $A \geq p_i$ and $(1-s\beta\lambda\rho)^2 > (1 - s\beta\lambda)^2 \rho$ it follows that the expression in square brackets on the right hand side of (A1) is positive. Hence

$$\frac{d\Pi_i}{ds} < 0$$

Which establishes Proposition 1.

18 A recent analytical formulation of this idea appears in Aizenman (1992).

REFERENCES

Aizenman, J. (1992), "Competitive Externalities and the Optimal Seigniorage", *Journal of Money, Credit and Banking*, 24: 61-71.

Alesina, A. (1988), "Macroeconomics and Politics", in Stanley Fischer (ed.), *NBER Macroeconomics Annual*. Cambridge: MIT Press.

Alesina, A. (1989), "Politics and Business Cycles in Industrial Democracies". *Economic Policy*, 8:57-98.

Alesina, A., G. D. Cohen, and N. Roubini (1992), "Macroeconomic Policy and Elections in OECD Democracies". In Alex Cukierman, Zvi Hercowitz, and Leonardo Leiderman (eds.) *Political Economy, Growth and Business Cycles*, Cambridge: MIT Press.

Alesina, A. and Lawrence, H. Summers (1993), "Central Bank Independence and Macroeconomic Performance: Some Comparative Evidence", *Journal of Money Credit and Banking*, 25: 151-162.

Bade, Robin and Michael Parkin (1980), "Central bank laws and monetary policy". Manuscript. Department of Economics, University of Western Ontario.

Barro, R. J. (1991), "Economic Growth in a Cross Section of Countries", *Quarterly Journal of Economics*, 106: 407-443.

Cukierman, A. (1992), *Central Bank Strategy, Credibility, and Independence: Theory and Evidence*, The MIT Press, Cambridge, Massachusetss.

Cukierman, A., S.B. Webb, and B. Neyapti (1992), "Measuring the Independence of Central Banks and Its Effect on Policy Outcomes". *The World Bank Economic Review*, 6, 353-398.

Cukierman, A. and S.B. Webb (1993), "Political Influence on the Central Bank - International Evidence" Manuscript, Tel-Aviv University, May.

Cukierman, A., P. Kalaitzidakis, L. H. Summers and S.B. Webb (1993), "Central Bank Independence, Growth, Investment, and Real Rates". *Carnegie-Rochester Conference Series on Public Policy*, Autumn.

Eijffinger, S. and E. Schaling (1993a), "Central Bank Independence in Twelve Industrial Countries", *Banca Nazionale del Lavoro Quarterly Review*, 184: 49-89.

Eijffinger S. and E. Schaling (1993b), "Central Bank Independence: Theory and Evidence", D.P. Nº 9325, Center for Econmic Research, Tilhurg University, May.

Fischer, S. (1991), "Growth, Macroeconomics and Development", *NBER Macroeconomics Annual*, 329-379.

Grilli, V., D. Masciandaro, and G. Tabellini (1991), Political and Monetary Institutions and Public Financial Policies in the Industrial Countries" *Economic Policy* 13: 341-392.

Havrilesky, T. (1992), *The Pressures on American Monetary Policy*, Kluwer Academic Publishers, Norwell, MA.

Leone, A. (1991), "Effectiveness and Implications of Limits on Central Bank Credit to the Government", In Patrick Downes and Reza Vaez-Zadeh (eds.). *The Evolving Role of Central Banks*, Washington: IMF, 363-413.

McKinnon, R.I. (1973), *Money and Capital in Economic Development*, the Brookings Institutions, Washington, D.C.

Meltzer, A. (1987), "Limits of Short-Run Stabilizaton Policy", *Economic Inquiry*, 25:1-14.

Pal Noga (1993), "The Effect of Statutory Laws on Turnover at the Central Bank", Graduate Term Paper, Dep. of Economics, Tel-Aviv University.

Parkin, Michael (1987), "Domestic Monetary Institutions and Deficits", in James M. Buchanan *et al.* (eds.) *Deficits*, Oxford: Basil Blackwell, 310-337.

Rogoff, Kenneth (1985) "The Optimal Degree of Commitment to an Intermediate Monetary Target". *Quarterly Journal of Economics* 100:1169-1190.

Skanland, H. (1984), *The Central Bank and Political Authorities in Some Industrial Countries.* Oslo: Norges Bank.

Swinburne, M. and M. Castello-Branco (1991), "Central Bank Independence and Cental Bank Functions". In Patrick Downes and Reza Vaez-Zadeh (eds.). *The Evolving Role of Central Banks.* Washington: IMF, pp. 414-444.

[12]

Central Bank Independence in Another Eleven Countries *

SYLVESTER EIJFFINGER and MARTIJN VAN KEULEN

1. Introduction

In recent years, there has been a growing interest in the independence of central banks. This can be explained by the institution of the European Central Bank in the context of the European Economic and Monetary Union, especially after the Treaty of Maastricht in December 1991.

The rationale for the independence of central banks is the so-called Rules versus Discretion debate. This is in favour of monetary policy rules since governments are thought to manipulate policy instruments in a discretionary way to stimulate economic growth and employment in the short run. To prevent governments from doing so, this view argues for explicit monetary legislation in order to make central banks independent of governments, and/or for fixed monetary policy rules. A central bank can only fight inflation in the long run if it is not influenced by directives of the government. A credible and steady declared monetary policy generates a better pay-off in terms of inflation and unemployment than a discretionary policy, when macroeconomic outcomes are dependent on the expectations with regard to future monetary policy.

□ Tilburg University, CentER for Economic Research, Tilburg, and College of Europe (The Netherlands)
University of South Carolina (Usa).

* The authors thank David Archer, Forrest Capie, Alex Cukierman, Lex Hoogduin, Eric Schaling, Jerzy Stopyra and two anonymous referees for valuable comments on an earlier version. The usual disclaimer applies.

BNL Quarterly Review, no. 192, March 1995.

On the basis of this debate, one would expect that countries with independent central banks would also have lower levels of inflation.

In the literature, several authors have written about the institution of an independent central bank. Bade and Parkin (1988), Alesina (1988, 1989), Grilli, Masciandaro and Tabellini (1991), Cukierman (1992) and Eijffinger and Schaling (1992, 1993) constructed indices to compare the degree of independence of central banks in various countries. Of course, the limits of the index approach are quite evident: e.g. the Czech central bank is found to be legally very independent but not necessarily independent in practice. Actual independence implies not only legal independence but also a tradition and culture of monetary stability.

Alesina and Summers (1993), de Haan and Sturm (1992), Cukierman (1992) and Eijffinger and Schaling (1993, 1995) also examined the empirical relationship between the degree of central bank independence and (the variability of) inflation and economic growth.

In this study, the respective indices of Bade and Parkin, Alesina, Grilli, Masciandaro and Tabellini and Eijffinger and Schaling are put together and applied to a group of eleven countries (Austria, Denmark, Finland, Hungary, Luxembourg, New Zealand, Norway, Poland, Portugal, Spain and the Czech Republic). However, the legal indices for central bank independence of Cukierman are not included because of a lack of sufficiently detailed information on most countries, especially regarding the limitations on lending. Then, we investigate the empirical relationship between independence and inflation.

This study is made up as follows. In Section 2 the indices of central bank independence are described and applied to the group of eleven countries. The results for every index are compared with the inflation rates and differences between the indices are explained. Section 3 contains an empirical study of significant relationships, first, between average inflation and central bank independence and, second, between inflation variability and central bank independence.

2. Four indices of central bank independence

2.1. *The Bade and Parkin index (1988)*[1]

In their study, Bade and Parkin (BP) investigate the cross-country relationships between monetary policy and central bank legislation. They describe the central bank law on the basis of three characteristics:

(i) the relationship between central banks and governments with respect to the formulation of monetary policy;

(ii) the procedures for appointment and dismissal from office of the directors of central banks;

(iii) the financial and budgetary relationships between central banks and governments.

Features (i) and (ii) are used by BP to classify the central banks according to their degree of policy independence; feature (iii) is used for the classification of their degree of financial independence. In this study we do not include (iii) since it is less comparable with the features used in the other indices. The BP degree of policy independence is defined by three criteria:

(1) Is the central bank the final monetary policy authority?
(2) Is a government official on the bank board?
(3) Are some board appointments outside government control?

After having studied the central bank laws of the eleven countries it can be concluded that the central banks of Luxembourg (−1994), New Zealand, Norway, Poland, Portugal and Spain (1994) are dependent on their respective governments with respect to monetary policy. Those of Austria, Denmark, Finland, Hungary, Luxembourg (+1994), Spain (+1994) and the Czech Republic are independent. However, legal independence does not necessarily imply actual independence. These results are summarized in Table 1, showing whether a central bank is independent on the basis of the articles of the respective central bank laws.

[1] Bade and Parkin 1988.

TABLE 1

CENTRAL BANK LAWS: MONETARY POLICY

Country	Central bank law	Article(s)	Final authority
Austria	National Bank Act 1984	4	b
Denmark	National Bank of Denmark Act 1936	1, 25 (by-laws)	b
Finland	Regulations for the Bank of Finland 1925	2, 16, 17	b
Hungary	Act LX of 1991 on the National Bank of Hungary	6	b
Luxembourg	Loi du 20 mai 1983 portant création d'un Institut Monétaire Luxembourgeois	12(3), 28	g
	Loi relative à l'Institut Monétaire Luxembourgeois du 22 octobre 1993	2	b
New Zealand	Reserve Bank of New Zealand Act 1989	8	g
Norway	Act of 24 May 1985 relating to Norges Bank and the Monetary System	2	g
Poland	Act on Narodowy Bank Polski 1989	6.2.2	g[1]
Portugal	Organic Law 1990	3	g
Spain	Law 30, 'Regulan los órganos rectores del Banco de España', 21 June 1980	3	g
	Law of 1 February 1993, 'Proyecto de Ley Autonomia del Banco de España'	2	b
Czech Republic	Act on the Czech National Bank of 17 December 1992	5.1	b

b = bank; g = government

[1] The Polish Parliament has monetary policy authority.

Table 2 gives information about the number of government officials on the bank board and the proportion of board members appointed by the government.

TABLE 2

CENTRAL BANK LAWS: APPOINTMENTS OF BANK BOARDS

Country	Central bank law	Article	Government officials on policy board[a]	Proportion of policy board appointed by government[b]
Austria	National Bank Act 1984	22-25, 45	1	8/14
Denmark	National Bank Act 1936	8 (by-law)	0	1/3
Finland	Parliament Act 1919	83	0	1
Hungary	Act LX of 1991 on the NBH	57	1	1
Luxembourg	Loi du 20 mai 1983 Loi du 22 octobre 1993	12 12	0 0	1
New Zealand	Reserve Bank Act 1989	40	0	1
Norway	Act of 24 May 1985	5, 6	0	1
Poland	Act on NBP 1989	49, 51	0	<1/2
Portugal	Organic Law 1990	38	0	1
Spain	Law 30 of 21 June 1980 Law of 1 February 1993	5, 8, 10 13, 14, 15	2 1	8/15 6/8
Czech Republic	Act of 17 December 1992	6	0	0

[a] Number of Ministers (or their representatives) who have a place in the policy board.
[b] Proportion of members appointed directly or indirectly by government or parliament.

The results of Table 1 and Table 2 can now be used to construct the BP index of policy independence. Each of the criteria may or may not appear, so eight possible policy types can be distinguished, as summarized in Table 3.

TABLE 3

CENTRAL BANK LAWS: POLICY TYPES

Bank is final policy authority 1	No government official on bank board 2	Some board appointments independent of government 3	Potential central bank type	Central bank type does exist	Policy type
–	–	*	(a)	no	–
*	–	*	(b)	no	–
–	–	–	(c)	yes	1
–	*	–	(d)	yes	2
–	*	*	(e)	yes	3
*	–	–	(f)	yes	4
*	*	*	(g)	yes	5
*	*	*	(h)	yes	6

In column 3 appointments are independent of the government if less then half of the policy board members is appointed by government or parliament.

By applying the three criteria for policy independence to every country, it can be shown that policy types (a) and (b) do not exist: only types (c)-(h) in Table 3 matter for the BP index of policy independence. BP find the overall degree of policy independence by a simple equally weighted average of the criteria. In other words, the six remaining central bank types are ranked from 1 (least independent) to 4 (most independent) on the basis of the number of asterisks in Table 3. The BP ranking for the eleven central banks is shown in the "policy type" column of Table 4.

Next, Bade and Parkin focus on the relationship between central bank laws and monetary policy, looking at two features of monetary policy: the level of inflation as measured by the change in consumer prices (CPI) and the variability of policy as measured by the dispersion (standard deviation) of the inflation level. The results are given in Table 4.

TABLE 4

BADE-PARKIN: AVERAGE INFLATION AND ITS VARIABILITY GROUPED ACCORDING TO CENTRAL BANK POLICY TYPE, 1969-1992[1]

		Inflation		Policy variability	
Country	Policy type	Percent	Rank	Standard deviation	Rank
Spain (–1994)[a]	1	8.8	(7)	3.5	(7)
Austria[°b]	2	3.0	(1)	1.3	(1)
Hungary[°c]		18.5	(9)	–	–
Luxembourg (–1994)[d]		3.4	(3)	2.6	(4)
New Zealand[e]		3.2	(2)	2.6	(5)
Norway[f]		5.3	(4)	2.3	(3)
Portugal[g]		10.2	(8)	1.8	(2)
Spain (+1994)[°]		–	–	–	–
Finland[°]	3	7.7	(6)	4.1	(8)
Luxembourg (+1994)[°]		–	–	–	–
Poland[h]		237.6	(11)	249.9	(10)
Denmark	4	7.0	(5)	3.3	(6)
Czech Republic[i]		26.2	(10)	27.3	(9)

Countries marked ° have policy independent central banks.
[a] 1981-1992; [b] 1984-1992; [c] only data available for 1992; [d] 1983-1992; [e] 1989-1992; [f] 1986-1992; [g] 1991-1992; [h] 1989-1992; [i] 1990-1992.
[1] Consumer prices, on an annual basis, *IMF International Financial Statistics Yearbook*, 1993, pp. 104-107.

In Table 4 sample periods of longer than 30 years are used only for Denmark and Finland. The other countries have had new central bank laws in the period 1963-1992 so adjusted sample periods have been used. On the basis of Table 4 no association can be discerned between policy independence and the two features of monetary policy, inflation level and variability, regarding the BP index.

It should be noted that most of the central bank laws in this study are relatively recent and, therefore, cannot be examined empirically. If only the central bank laws which have been in force more than five years are examined, the results do not change. Also for this group of countries (Spain (–1994), Austria, Luxembourg (–1994), Norway, Finland and Denmark) no relationship can be found between policy independence and inflation level or variability.

2.2. *The Alesina index (1988, 1989)*[2]

Alesina includes macroeconomic relationships such as monetary financing rules, thus enlarging the BP index of policy independence with a fourth criterion:

(4) Is the central bank obliged to buy short-term Treasury paper?

Alesina uses (4) because he sees this criterion as an additional measure of the independence of central banks, since a monetary financing obligation can seriously harm the independent position of a central bank with respect to monetary policy making.

Table 5 shows that, according to this criterion, only the central banks of Denmark, Portugal, Poland, Hungary, Spain (+1994) and Luxembourg (+1994) have no obligation to finance their respective governments.

TABLE 5

ALESINA: IS THE CENTRAL BANK REQUIRED TO ABSORB EXCESS SUPPLY OF SHORT-TERM TREASURY BILLS?

BP policy type	No[a]	Yes
1		Spain (–1994)
2	Portugal,[b] Spain (+1994), Hungary	Austria, Luxembourg (–1994), New Zealand, Norway
3	Poland, Luxembourg (+1994)	Finland
4	Denmark[c]	Czech Republic

[a] i.e. a central bank cannot be forced by government or parliament to buy short-term Treasury paper.

[b] After the coming into force of the second stage of the EMU on January 1, 1994, monetary financing is no longer allowed in EU member states.

[c] Denmark will not participate in the third stage of the EMU; with respect to the second stage it holds that "All of these prohibitions against monetary financing are already in accordance with existing practice in Denmark". See Danmarks Nationalbank, *Annual Report 1992*, pp. 20-22.

According to the Alesina index for policy independence, there are seven different types of central banks in the group of eleven countries. The independence classification of these types in comparison with Bade Parkin is shown in Table 6.

[2] Alesina 1988, pp. 13-52 and 1989, pp. 55-98.

TABLE 6

ALESINA TYPES AND CENTRAL BANK INDEPENDENCE

BP policy type	Criterion (4) met?[a]	Potential central bank type[b]	Does central bank type exist?	Alesina type exist?
1	*	(a)	no	–
1	–	(b)	yes	0/1
2	–	(c)	yes	1/2
2	*	(d)	yes	2
3	–	(e)	yes	2/3
3	*	(f)	yes	3
4	–	(g)	yes	3/4
4	–	(h)	yes	4

Notes: [a] see Table 4.
[b] see Table 5.

Taking a central bank that is not obliged to finance its respective government as being more independent than one which does, we determine the independence classification of central banks according to the Alesina index of policy independence. Table 7 gives every Alesina-type country with its corresponding level and variability of inflation.

TABLE 7

AVERAGE INFLATION AND ITS VARIANCE,
ACCORDING TO ALESINA CENTRAL BANK POLICY TYPE, 1963-1992

	Inflation rate			Policy variability	
Country	Policy type	Percent	Rank	Standard deviation	Rank
Spain (–1994)	0.5	8.8	(7)	3.5	(7)
Austria	1.5	3.0	(1)	1.3	(1)
Luxembourg (–1994)		3.4	(3)	2.6	(4)
New Zealand		3.2	(2)	2.6	(5)
Norway		5.3	(4)	2.3	(3)
Hungary	2	18.5	(9)	–	–
Portugal		10.2	(8)	1.8	(2)
Spain (+1994)		–	–	–	–
Finland	2.5	7.7	(6)	4.1	(8)
Luxembourg (+1994)	3	–	–	–	–
Poland		237.6	(11)	249.9	(10)
Czech Republic	3.5	26.2	(10)	27.3	(9)
Denmark	4	7.0	(5)	3.3	(6)

On the basis of the Alesina index, no association can be discerned between average inflation and the degree of central bank independence for the countries in Table 7. This result also applies to the relationship between central bank independence and inflation variability.

If we only look at the countries with a central bank law which is more than five years old (Spain (–1994), Luxembourg (–1994), Austria, Norway, Finland and Denmark), the same conclusions can be drawn.

2.3. *The Grilli, Masciandaro and Tabellini index (1991)*[3]

Grilli, Masciandaro and Tabellini (GMT) published a study on the independence of central banks and the indices used to measure this independence, in which they distinguish two forms of independence: political and economic.[4] Because the index of political independence corresponds best with the other three indices used in this study, only this will be treated in this subsection.

GMT define political independence as the capacity (of a central bank) to choose the final goal of monetary policy, such as the inflation level or the level of economic activity. According to GMT, this capacity depends on three features:

(i) appointment procedures for the members of the policy body of a central bank;

(ii) the relationship between this body and the government;[5]

(iii) the formal responsibilities of a central bank.

these features are then used to construct their index of policy independence. To measure the level of independence, GMT use eight criteria:

(1) Is the governor appointed by parliament?

(2) Is he appointed for more than five years?

---

[3] Grilli, Masciandaro and Tabellini 1991, pp. 366-375.

[4] GMT define economic independence as the capacity of a central bank to choose instruments with which to pursue goals of monetary policy.

[5] In the GMT study, government signifies just that, whereas in the BP paper it also includes parliament.

(3) Is the whole policy board appointed by the government?
(Compare with BP (3): Are some board appointments made independently of the government?)

(4) Is the term for the policy board members longer than five years?

(5) Is there a mandatory participation of a government representative in the board?
(Compare with BP (2): Is there a government official on the bank board?)

(6) Is government approval of monetary policy required?
(Compare with BP (1): Is the central bank the final monetary policy authority?)

(7) Are there legal obligations on the central bank to pursue monetary stability among other objectives?

(8) Are there legal provisions that strengthen the bank's position in case of conflict with the government?

GMT measure the degree of independence of a central bank by simply adding up the eight (equally weighted) criteria. This is shown in Table 8, column 9, where the total number of asterisks determines the level of independence of each of the eleven countries. On this basis we conclude that the Czech Republic has the most independent central bank. However, it is questionable to what degree this legal independence also implies actual independence.

In Table 9 the GMT policy types are compared with inflation levels and inflation variability. The same inflation data and sample periods are used as for BP and Alesina. Again, no clear association can be discerned between central bank independence and inflation performance. The results also hold for the countries with a central bank statute that has been in force for more than five years.

TABLE 8

GRILLI-MASCIANDARO-TABELLINI:
MONETARY POLICY INDEPENDENCE OF CENTRAL BANKS

Countries	Appointments				Relationship with government		Statute		Index of political independence
	1	2	3	4	5	6	7	8	9
Austria	–	–	–	–	–	*	*	*	3
Denmark	–	*	–	*	*	*	*	–	5
Finland	–	–	*	–	*	*	*	–	4
Hungary	–	*	–	–	–	*	*	–	3
Luxembourg (–1994)	–	*	–	*	*	–	*	–	4
Luxembourg (+1994)	–	*	–	*	*	*	*	–	5
New Zealand	–	–	–	–	*	–	*	–	2
Norway	–	*	–	–	*	–	*	–	2
Poland	–	*	–	[1]	*	–	*	–	3
Portugal	–	–	–	–	*	–	*	–	2
Spain (–1994)	–	–	–	–	–	–	–	–	0
Spain (+1994)	–	*	–	*	–	*	*	*	5
Czech Republic	*	*	*	*	*	*	*	–	7

[1] Not to be deduced from the Polish central bank law.

TABLE 9

GRILLI-MASCIANDARO-TABELLINI:
AVERAGE INFLATION AND ITS VARIABILITY GROUPED
ACCORDING TO CENTRAL BANK POLICY TYPE, 1963-1992

	Inflation rate			Policy variability	
Country	Policy type	Percent	Rank	Standard deviation	Rank
Spain (–1994)	1	8.8	(7)	3.5	(7)
New Zealand	2	3.2	(2)	2.6	(5)
Norway		5.3	(4)	2.3	(3)
Portugal		10.2	(8)	1.8	(2)
Hungary	3	18.5	(9)	–	–
Austria		3.0	(1)	1.3	(1)
Poland		237.6	(11)	249.9	(10)
Finland	4	7.7	(6)	4.1	(8)
Denmark	5	7.0	(5)	3.3	(6)
Luxembourg (+1994)		–	–	–	–
Spain (+1994)		–	–	–	–
Czech Republic	6	26.2	(10)	27.5	(9)

2.4. *The Eijffinger and Schaling index (1992, 1993)*[6]

Eijffinger and Schaling (ES) describe policy independence, like GMT, as the capacity of central banks to choose the final goals of monetary policy, determined by:

(i) formal responsibility of central banks with regard to monetary policy;

(ii) the relationship between the central bank and government/parliament in the formulation of monetary policy;

(iii) the procedures for the appointment of the board of a central bank.

On the grounds of these features, Eijffinger and Schaling construct their (asymmetrical) index for policy independence. The level of such independence depends on three criteria:

(1) Is the central bank alone responsible for monetary policy (b), does it share this responsibility (b/g) or does it have no influence on monetary policy (g)?

(2) Is a government representative appointed (with or without voting power) on the bank board?

(3) Are more than half the board members appointed independently of the government?[7]

Because criterion (1) has three solutions, there are 3x2x2 possible ES policy types.

Table 10 gives five different ES policy types for the group of eleven countries: classification is determined by summing up the number of asterisks plus one.

When inflation performance is set out against the ES policy types, again no association can be found between inflation level and central bank independence or between inflation variability and central bank independence. If we look at the group of countries with older central bank laws (Spain (–1994), Luxembourg (–1994), Norway, Austria, Finland and Denmark), the same conclusions can be drawn: see Table 11.

---

[6] Eijffinger and Schaling 1992, pp. 34-37 and 1993, pp. 64-68.

[7] In this subsection parliament is included under government.

TABLE 10

EIJFFINGER-SCHALING: POLICY TYPES

Bank is final policy authority 1	No government official on bank board 2	Some board appointments independent of government 3	Potential central bank type	Central bank type does exist	Policy type
–(g)	–	*	(a)	no	–
*(b/g)	–	*	(b)	no	–
*(b/g)	–	–	(c)	no	–
**(b)	–	*	(d)	no	–
–(g)	–	–	(e)	yes	1
–(g)	*	–	(f)	yes	2
–(g)	*	*	(g)	yes	3
*(b/g)	*	–	(h)	yes	3
*(b/g)	*	*	(i)	yes	4
**(b)	–	–	(j)	yes	3
**(b)	*	–	(k)	yes	4
**(b)	*	*	(l)	yes	5

TABLE 11

EIJFFINGER-SCHALING: AVERAGE INFLATION AND ITS VARIABILITY GROUPED ACCORDING TO CENTRAL BANK POLICY TYPE, 1963-1992

	Inflation rate			Policy variability	
Country	Policy type	Percent	Rank	Standard deviation	Rank
Spain (–1994)	1	8.8	(7)	3.5	(7)
Luxembourg (–1994)	2	3.4	(3)	2.6	(4)
Norway	2	5.3	(4)	2.3	(3)
Portugal	2	10.2	(8)	1.8	(2)
Hungary	3	18.5	(9)	–	–
Austria	3	3.0	(1)	1.3	(1)
Poland	3	237.6	(11)	249.9	(10)
New Zealand	3	3.2	(2)	2.6	(5)
Finland	3	7.7	(6)	4.1	(8)
Spain (+1994)	3	–	–	–	–
Denmark	4	7.0	(5)	3.3	(6)
Luxembourg (+1994)	4	–	–	–	–
Czech Republic	5	26.2	(10)	27.3	(9)

2.5. *The four indices compared*

2.5.1. *Bade-Parkin versus Alesina*

Differences between both indices can be explained by the simple fact that the Alesina index has one more criterion than the BP index. In this subsection the other two indices will only be compared to the BP index, as those three indices match best. The Alesina index is harder to compare with GMT and ES because of the fourth criterion regarding monetary financing and, therefore, omitted.

2.5.2. *Bade-Parkin versus Grilli-Masciandaro-Tabellini*

To be able to compare GMT with BP we have to focus on GMT criteria (3), (5) and (6). If we aggregate them, the outcome will not be the same as in Table 9. However, only these three criteria are really comparable with BP.

Differences between both indices are caused by interpretation effects and criterion effects. The former arise because of differences in interpretation of central bank laws [GMT (5) and (6) versus BP (1) and (2)]. The latter arise because of differences between criteria [GMT (3) versus BP (3)]. See Table 12 for a decomposition of the differences between both indices into interpretation and criterion effects.

Table 12 shows that there are no interpretation effects between BP and GMT. This can be explained by the fact that the BP criteria (1), (2) and (3) are almost the same as the GMT criteria (3), (5) and (6) and all these criteria are judged in this study on the basis of the same information. Criterion effects exist for Denmark, Finland and Poland. BP classify Denmark and Poland one policy type higher as their criterion (3) is less strict than GMT criterion (3). GMT ask if the entire policy board is appointed by the government, while BP look at what proportion of the policy board is appointed by the government. If less than half of the members are appointed by the government it is sufficient for BP, but not for GMT. The difference for Finland can be explained by the fact that for GMT the political authority is the government alone, while for BP this comprises both government and parliament.

TABLE 12

BADE-PARKIN VS. GRILLI-MASCIANDARO-TABELLINI

Country	GMT policy type[a]	BP policy type[b]	Interpre-tation[c]	Criterion effect[d]	Difference GMT – BP[e]
Austria	2	2	0	0	0
Denmark	3	4	0	–1	–1
Finland	4	3	0	1	1
Hungary	2	2	0	0	0
Luxembourg (–1994)	2	2	0	0	0
Luxembourg (+1994)	3	3	0	0	0
New Zealand	2	2	0	0	0
Norway	2	2	0	0	0
Poland	2	3	0	–1	–1
Portugal	2	2	0	0	0
Spain (–1994)	1	1	0	0	0
Spain (+1994)	2	2	0	0	0
Czech Republic	4	4	0	0	0

[a] (Number of asterisks in columns 3, 5 and 6 of Table 8) + 1.
[b] See Table 4.
[c] (Number of asterisks in columns 5 and 6 of Table 8 + number of asterisks in column 3 of Table 3) + 1 – BP policy type.
[d] (Number of asterisks in columns 1 and 2 of Table 3 + number of asterisks in column 3 of Table 8) + 1 – BP policy type.
[e] difference = total difference between GMT and BP; columns (c) and (d).

2.5.3. *Bade-Parkin versus Eijffinger-Schaling*

In comparing BP with ES, we have to take account of the fact that ES criterion (1) has twice the weight of BP criteria (2) and (3), and thus adjust the BP index for this asymmetry in order to be able to compare the two indices.

After adjustment of the BP index to the ES index, differences between the two indices consist also of interpretation and criterion effects. See Table 13 for a decomposition of these differences.

Interpretation effects occur for Denmark, Finland and New Zealand. Denmark and Finland have a lower ES classification because, in practice, their monetary policy is determined by both the central bank and government. New Zealand goes from BP (g) to ES (b/g) as its government has the final say over monetary policy, although it requires a complicated procedure to override the central bank.

TABLE 13

BADE-PARKIN VS. EIJFFINGER-SCHALING

Country	ES policy type[a]	BP policy type[b]	BP adjusted policy type[c]	Interpretation[d]	Criterion effect[e]	Difference GMT – BP[f]
Austria	3	2	3	0	1	1
Denmark	4	4	5	–1	1	0
Finland	3	3	4	–1	1	0
Hungary	3	2	3	0	1	1
Luxembourg (–1994)	2	2	2	0	0	0
Luxembourg (+1994)	4	3	4	0	1	1
New Zealand	3	2	2	1	0	1
Norway	2	2	2	0	0	0
Poland	3	3	3	0	0	0
Portugal	2	2	2	0	0	0
Spain (–1994)	1	1	1	0	0	0
Spain (+1994)	3	2	3	0	1	1
Czech Republic	5	4	5	0	1	1

[a] See Table 10.
[b] See Table 4.
[c] BP asymmetrical policy types: BP types if BP 1 has two times the weight of BP 2 and 3 (b=**).
[d] ES – BPA (BP adjusted).
[e] BPA – BP.
[f] (d) + (e).

Austria, Denmark, Finland, Hungary, Luxembourg (+1994), Spain (+1994) and the Czech Republic all have a positive criterion effect because BP-adjusted policy types have two asterisks instead of one for the unadjusted type.

2.5.4. *Eijffinger-Schaling versus Grilli-Masciandaro-Tabellini*

For the comparison of the GMT index with the ES index we have to remember that we can only look at GMT criteria (3), (5) and (6) and that the ES index is asymmetrical. Keeping this in mind, interpretation and criterion effects will appear. See Table 14 for a decomposition of both effects.

Austria, Hungary, Luxembourg (+1994), New Zealand, Spain (+1994) and the Czech Republic have positive interpretation effects, explained in Table 13. The positive criterion effects for Denmark and Poland and the negative criterion effect for Finland were explained in Table 12.

TABLE 14

EIJFFINGER-SCHALING VS. GRILLI-MASCIANDARO-TABELLINI

Country	ES policy type[a]	GMT policy type[b]	Interpretation[c]	Criterion effect[d]	Difference GMT - BP[e]
Austria	3	2	1	0	1
Denmark	4	3	0	1	1
Finland	3	4	0	−1	−1
Hungary	3	2	1	0	1
Luxembourg (−1994)	2	2	0	0	0
Luxembourg (+1994)	4	3	1	0	1
New Zealand	3	2	1	0	1
Norway	2	2	0	0	0
Poland	3	2	0	1	1
Portugal	2	2	0	0	0
Spain (−1994)	1	1	0	0	0
Spain (+1994)	3	2	1	0	1
Czech Republic	5	4	1	0	1

[a] See Table 11.
[b] See Table 12.
[c] ES - BP: see column (f) of Table 13.
[d] BP - GMT: see column (e) of Table 12 (signs must be reversed).
[e] (c) + (d).

3. Empirical analysis

In this section we check whether a negative empirical relationship can be found between central bank independence and inflation performance. We have used regression analysis (OLS method) with the different indices of central bank independence as explanatory variables of average monthly inflation (CPI) and the variance of monthly inflation. The sample period of the regression analysis is from January 1982 to December 1993. This period was chosen because the start of the stage of consolidation within the EMS was in 1982,[8] and because most of the countries in this study had new central bank laws at the beginning of the 1980s.

[8] Ungerer 1990, pp. 329-362.

To investigate the relationship between central bank independence and average monthly inflation, we regressed (OLS method) the following equation:

$$\text{(4.1) average monthly inflation} = \alpha_0 + \overset{(-)}{\alpha_1^*} \text{ central bank independence} + \varepsilon_t$$

In Table 15 the estimations are given for the BP, Alesina, GMT and ES indices for central bank independence. T-values of constant and the coefficient for the different indices are in parentheses. Moreover, we considered the group of countries where the central bank laws are more than five years old (Austria, Denmark, Finland, Luxembourg (–1994), Norway and Spain (–1994). One should note, however, that all results in this table must be carefully interpreted as the number of degrees of freedom is limited (respectively 9 and 4)

Table 15

INFLATION LEVEL AND THE INDICES OF CENTRAL BANK INDEPENDENCE

Explanatory variables	1982-1993	1982-1993 Central bank law in force > five years
Constant	–0.00053 (–0.023)	0.005226 (3.900)
Bade and Parkin (BP)	0.006339 (0.677)	–0.00058 (–1.091)
R^2	0.054232	0.229335
Constant	–0.0005 (–0.029)	0.004768 (4.630)
Alesina	0.007275 (0.940)	–0.00047 (–1.004)
R^2	0.099511	0.201235
Constant	0.018072 (0.879)	0.005834 (5.820)
Grilli-Masciandaro-Tabellini (GMT)	–0.00139 (–0.210)	–0.00062 (–2.128)*
R^2	0.00548	0.531005
Constant	0.002195 (0.087)	0.005879 (4.978)
Eijffinger and Schaling (ES)	0.004561 (0.493)	–0.0008 (–1.817)*
R^2	0.029452	0.452329

t-values are in parentheses. One asterisk indicates that the coefficient is significantly different from zero at a 90% confidence level and two asterisks indicate that the coefficient is significant at a 95% confidence level.

Source: Datastream, monthly consumer prices 1/1982-12/1993. For New Zealand only, quarterly data were available; for Poland, inflation data started in 1/1988.

From the second column of Table 15, it can be concluded that there is no significant negative relationship between central bank independence and average inflation. For BP, Alesina and ES there is even a positive α_1 coefficient, although it is not significant.

This does not correspond with the empirical results found in studies for other countries. de Haan and Sturm (1992), Cukierman (1992), Alesina and Summers (1993) and Eijffinger and Schaling (1995)[9] all discover a significant negative relationship between average inflation and central bank independence.

The results in the second column correspond with the results in Section 2, where no clear association could be discerned between average inflation and central bank independence.[10]

The third column of Table 15 gives the empirical results for the countries with older central bank laws. For this group of countries, the t-values of the α_1 coefficient for GMT and ES are significantly different from zero at a 90% confidence level. Thus, the inverse relationship between central bank independence and level of inflation is not strongly confirmed. The difference between BP/Alesina and GMT/ES can perhaps be explained by the fact that the latter indices are more precise in the determination of central bank independence.

Figures 1-4 show a negative relationship between inflation level and central bank independence for the countries with a central bank law in force for more than five years, despite some positive outliers (Spain for BP, Alesina, GMT and ES; Finland for GMT) and some negative outliers for BP, Alesina and ES (Austria and Luxembourg) and for GMT (Austria).

This cannot be used to explain the difference in significance for this group of six countries and does not correspond to the results in Section 2. However, this can be explained by the fact that in Section 2

---

[9] de Haan and Sturm 1992, pp. 305-327; Alesina and Summers 1993, pp. 151-162; Eijffinger and Schaling 1995.

[10] We did not include statistical estimates in our empirical analysis for both this "new" group of 11 countries and the "old" group of 12 countries from Eijffinger and Schaling (1992 and 1993) because the empirical results proved to be not very different from Table 15. For the combined group of 23 countries we found insignificant coefficients for the various indices of central bank independence.

FIGURE 1

THE BADE-PARKIN INDEX
AND THE LEVEL OF INFLATION

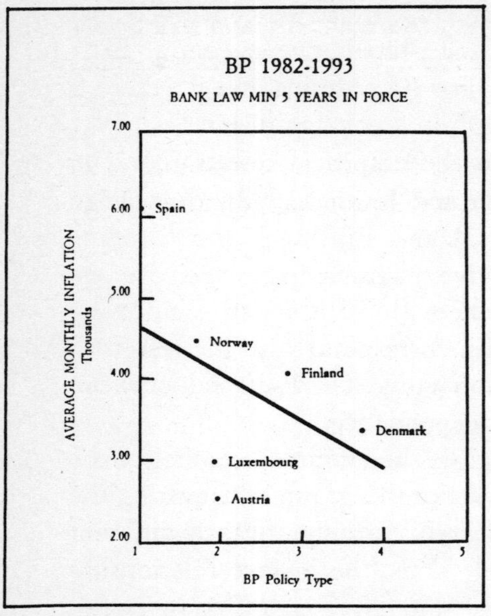

Average monthly inflation = 0.005226 − 0.00058 * BP
(3.900) (−1.191)

FIGURE 2

THE ALESINA INDEX
AND THE LEVEL OF INFLATION

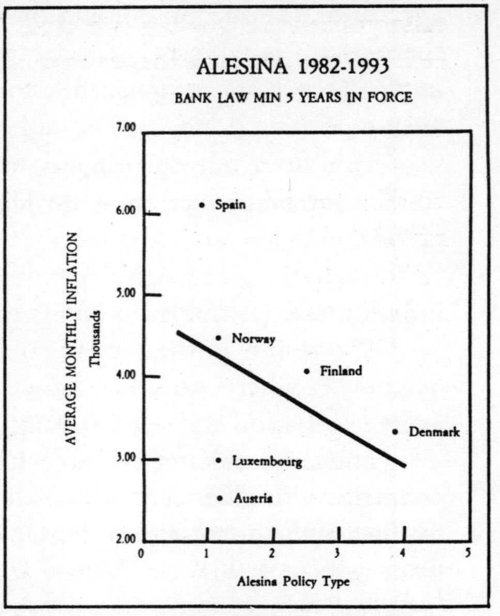

Average monthly inflation = 0.004768 − 0.00047 * Alesina
(4.630) (−1.004)

FIGURE 3

THE GRILLI-MASCIANDARO-TABELLINI
INDEX AND THE LEVEL OF INFLATION

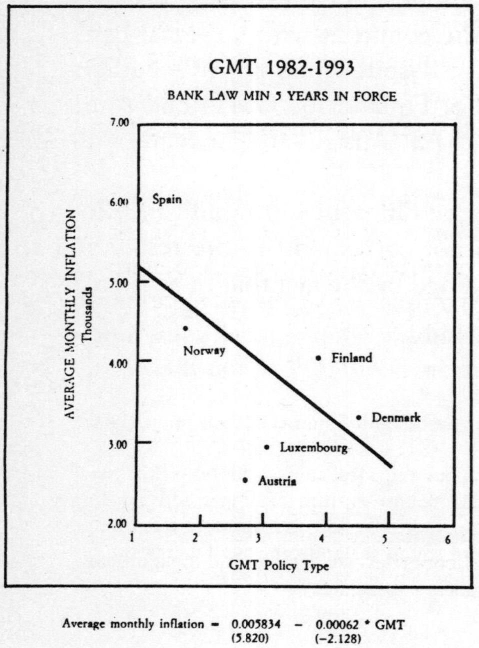

Average monthly inflation = 0.005834 − 0.00062 * GMT
(5.820) (−2.128)

FIGURE 4

THE EIJFFINGER-SCHALING INDEX
AND THE LEVEL OF INFLATION

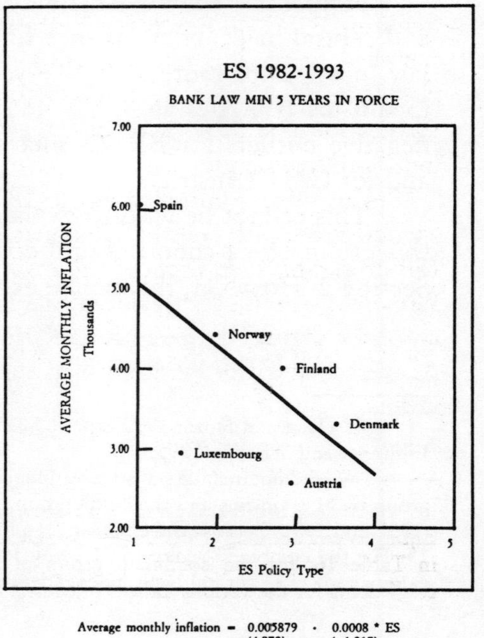

Average monthly inflation = 0.005879 · 0.0008 * ES
(4.978) (−1.817)

different sample periods are used. For Denmark, Finland and Spain (−1994) the period is longer than the 1982-1993 period in this section, while for Austria, Luxembourg (−1994) and Norway the opposite holds.

For the relationship between central bank independence and inflation variability we have estimated the following equation (OLS method):

$$\text{(4.2) monthly inflation variance} = \beta_0 + \overset{(-)}{\beta_1^*} \text{ central bank independence} + \delta_t$$

In Table 16, second column, estimations for β_0 and β_1 are given for the indices of BP, Alesina, GMT and ES. The third column gives the empirical results if we only take account of the countries with central bank laws in force for more than five years. Again, we note that the results of this table must be interpreted carefully, as the degrees of liberty are limited (respectively 9 and 4). From the second column, no clear association can be seen between central bank independence and inflation variability. On the contrary, all the four indices have a positive β_1 coefficient, although it is never significant.[11]

This result does not support de Haan and Sturm (1992) and Alesina and Summers (1993), but is compatible with Eijffinger and Schaling (1995), neither of whom find an empirical relationship between central bank independence and inflation variability. The results in the second column match those in Section 2, where no clear association could be discerned between inflation variance and central bank independence.

The third column of Table 16 gives the OLS regressions for the six countries with central bank laws in force for more than five years. It can be clearly seen that for those six countries β_1 t-values are negative. However, the GMT t-value alone is significantly different from zero. In other words, the negative relationship between central bank independence and the variability of inflation is only clear for the GMT index.

[11] Pooling this "new" group of 11 countries and the "old" group of 12 countries from Eijffinger and Schaling (1993 and 1995) gave more or less similar empirical results to those in Table 16: for the combined group of 23 countries we also found insignificant coefficients for the various indices of central bank independence.

Figures 5-8 show negative associations between inflation variability and central bank independence with positive outliers for Denmark and Spain and a negative one for Luxembourg. The fact that the latter has a high ranking in the GMT index may be the reason that the GMT index differs from the other three indices.

The results of the figures do not correspond with the results in Section 2 because in Section 2 data on an annual basis are used with different periods than in this analysis. The results of the empirical studies of de Haan and Sturm (1992), Alesina and Summers (1993) and Eijffinger and Schaling (1995) do not always agree with the results in this section. These authors find a significant negative relationship

Table 16

INFLATION VARIABILITY AND THE INDICES OF CENTRAL BANK INDEPENDENCE

Explanatory variables	1982-1993	1982-1993 Central bank law in force > five years
Constant	−0.00222 (−0.482)	0.0000228 (4.330)
Bade-Parkin (BP)	0.001649 (0.868)	−0.0000013 (−0.644)
R^2	0.086051	0.09293
Constant	−0.00186 (−0.538)	0.0000214 (5.285)
Alesina	0.001715 (1.092)	−0.0000009 (−0.498)
R^2	0.129661	0.057382
Constant	0.001298 (0.305)	0.0000258 (6.292)
Grilli-Masciandaro-Tabellini (GMT)	0.0000933 (0.068)	−0.0000019 (−1.636)*
R^2	0.000582	0.397472
Constant	−0.00092 (−0.177)	0.0000226 (4.055)
Eijffinger-Schaling (ES)	0.000957 (0.501)	−0.0000012 (−0.566)
R^2	0.030434	0.073168

Source: Datastream, monthly consumer prices 1/1982-12/1993. For New Zealand only, quarterly data were available; for Poland, inflation data started from 1/1988.

FIGURE 5

THE BADE-PARKIN INDEX
AND THE VARIABILITY OF INFLATION

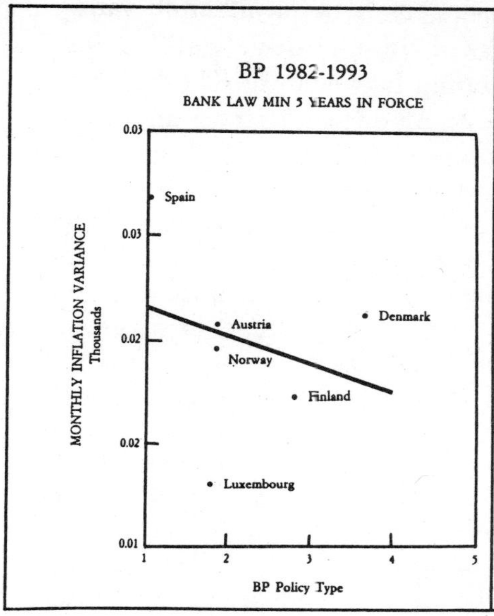

Monthly inflation variance = 0.0000228 − 0.0000013 * BP
(4.330) (−0.644)

FIGURE 6

THE ALESINA INDEX
AND THE VARIABILITY OF INFLATION

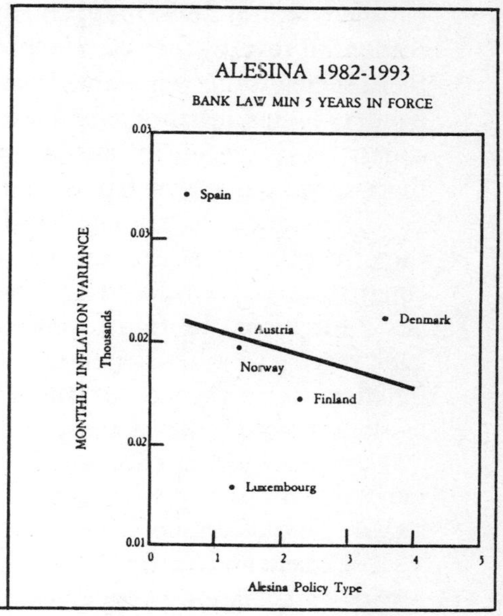

Monthly inflation variance = 0.0000214 − 0.0000009 * Alesina
(5.285) (−0.498)

FIGURE 7

THE GRILLI-MASCIANDARO-TABELLINI
INDEX AND THE VARIABILITY OF INFLATION

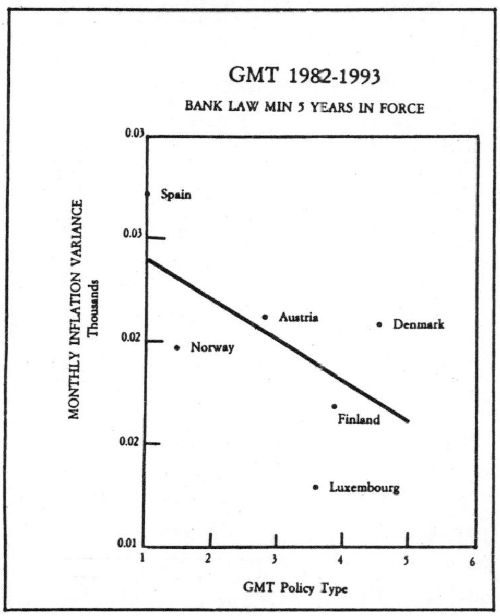

Monthly inflation variance = 0.0000258 − 0.00000196 * GMT
(6.292) (−1.636)

FIGURE 8

THE EIJFFINGER-SCHALING INDEX
AND THE VARIABILITY OF INFLATION

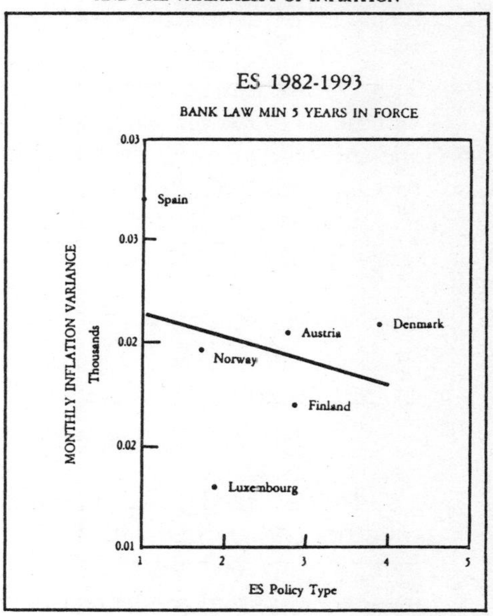

Monthly inflation variance = 0.0000226 − 0.0000012 * ES
(4.055) (−0.566)

between central bank independence and inflation level, while in this section no relationship can be discerned. On the basis of these results, there seems to be a positive relationship between central bank independence and inflation level for BP, Alesina and ES in all eleven countries. However, in the six countries with older central bank laws there seems to be a negative relationship.

Differences in the empirical results between this study and the three mentioned above are due to the fact that nine of the eleven countries have introduced new central bank legislation in the past ten years: for them, the transformation process from a dependent central bank regime to a less dependent one is still going on. In other words, inflation performances of the old regimes are still persistent and working through the new systems.

Another explanation could be the fact that inflation rates over a sample period of twelve years are used in this section, while longer sample periods are used in the other empirical studies.

de Haan and Sturm (1992) and Alesina and Summers (1993) find a negative association between central bank independence and inflation variability, while Eijffinger and Schaling (1995) find no association at all. They come to the same conclusion as this section: there is apparently no significant negative association between central bank independence and inflation variability. For all eleven countries there seems to be a positive association, while for the six countries there seems to be a negative association, according to our study.

Differences between de Haan and Sturm (1992) and Alesina and Summers (1993) on the one hand, and Eijffinger and Schaling (1995) and this study on the other can be explained by the fact that the first two use inflation data on an annual basis and the last two use that on a monthly basis. Moreover, the sample periods of the first two studies are longer than those of the latter.

4. Conclusion

In this study the independence of central banks in eleven countries is examined with four indices. Furthermore, we have tried to find an empirical relationship between the degree of central bank independence and the level and variability of inflation respectively. In

Section 2, no association could be discerned between independence and level or variability of inflation. Those results are confirmed by the regression analysis in Section 3. The fact that we also consider the group of countries with central bank laws which are more than five years old does not alter the results in Section 2. In Section 3 for this group of six countries the negative relationship between central bank independence and the level and variability of inflation respectively cannot be confirmed. Thus, the well-known negative relationship between central bank independence and inflation performance cannot be confirmed for our group of countries. However, the results in Section 3 for the group of six countries show that an empirical relationship does exist.

Bade and Parkin (1988), Alesina (1988, 1989), Grilli, Masciandaro and Tabellini (1991), Cukierman (1992) and Eijffinger and Schaling (1993 and 1995) find a negative association between central bank independence and level of inflation. However, they find no relationship between central bank independence and variability of inflation.

Empirical studies by de Haan and Sturm (1992) and Alesina and Summers (1993) find a negative relationship between central bank independence and the level and variability of inflation respectively. Eijffinger and Schaling (1995) also find a negative relationship between independence and the level of inflation, but none for independence and inflation variability.

Differences between the (empirical) literature and this study can be explained by: (i) in this study, a new group of countries is examined; (ii) nine of the eleven countries in this study have had new central bank laws in the past ten years; and (iii) the time periods examined in our study are shorter than those in the other studies. As stressed in the introduction, the limits of the index approach are quite evident. Legal independence of the central bank is a necessary but not a sufficient condition for actual independence, which also implies a tradition and culture of monetary stability with the policy makers.

Central bank laws

Austria:	National Bank Act 1984.
Denmark:	The National Bank of Denmark Act, 1937, The National Bank of Denmark By-Laws, 1937.
Finland:	Regulations for the Bank of Finland, 1925, Parliament Act, 13 January 1919, Decision of the Council of State on the External Value of the Markka, 7 June 1991.
Hungary:	Act LX of 1991 on the National Bank of Hungary.
Luxembourg:	Loi du 15 mars relative au statut monétaire du Grand-Duché de Luxembourg, Loi du 20 mai 1983 portant création d'un Institut Monétaire Luxembourgeois, Loi du 22 octobre 1993 relative à l'Institut Monétaire Luxembourgeois.
New-Zealand:	Reserve Bank of New Zealand Act 1989.
Norway:	Act of 24 May 1985 relating to Norges Bank and the Monetary System.
Poland:	Act on Narodowy Bank Polski, 1989.
Portugal:	Organic Law of the Banco de Portugal, Approved by Decree-Law No. 337/90 of October 1990.
Spain:	Ley 30 Banco de España, Organos Rectores, 21 June 1980. Ley de Autonomía del Banco de España, 1 February 1993.
Czech Republic:	Act on the Czech National Bank, 17 December 1992.

Additional literature on the central bank laws

Committee of Governors of the Central Banks of the Member States of the European Community, *Annual Report 1992*, April 1993.

Austria: "Money and the central bank", Austrian National Bank, Vienna, 1992.

Denmark: "Danmarks Nationalbank, central-bank responsibilities and tasks", Danmarks Nationalbank, Copenhagen, 1991.

Annual Report 1992, Danmarks Nationalbank, Copenhagen, 1993.

Finland: "The Bank of Finland", Suomen Pankki/Finlands Bank, Helsinki, 1993,
Rolf Kullberg: "A brief history of the Bank of Finland", Bank of Finland, *Working Paper*, 18 February 1992,
The Finnish Bankers' Association: "The Finnish banking system", 1989.

Hungary: National Bank of Hungary: "The Law on the Central Bank", *Market Letter* NBH, 10-11/1991.

Luxembourg: Institut Monétaire Luxembourgeois: "Le statut et l'organisation monétaires actuels du Grand-Duché de Luxembourg", *Etudes*, numéro 1, juin 1987.

New Zealand: Frank W. Holmes: "Money, finance and the economy, an introduction to the New Zealand financial system, Auckland, 1972,
Michele Lloyd: "The New Zealand approach to central bank autonomy", *Reserve Bank Bulletin*, vol. 55, no. 3, 1992.

Poland: OECD Economic Surveys: "Poland 1992", 1993.

Spain: Miguel Pellicer: "Functions of the Banco de España: a historical perspective", Banco de España, *Working Paper* 9330, 1993,
G. Ganzalo: "Functions of the Bank of Spain", Banco de España, *Working Paper* 8704, 1987,
"Note on the Draft-Law of Autonomy for the Bank of Spain", Banco de España, 29 January 1993.

Czech Republic: "Background to the Act on the State Bank of Czechoslovakia", State Bank of Czechoslovakia, 1990.

APPENDIX

Central bank laws in eleven countries

A.1. Austria

The first Austrian central bank, Privilegierte österreichische National-Bank, dates from 1816. In 1878, it became the Austro-Hungarian Bank. After the First World War, this ceased to exist and was succeeded by *Österreichische Nationalbank*. Austria was annexed by Nazi Germany in 1939 and the Bank was dismantled but this process was not completed before the end of the Second World War. To support Austrian independence, the Austrian National Bank resumed its activities in 1945. New statutes were adopted in 1955. The current central bank law came in force into 1984 and was based on the 1955 law.

The Austrian National Bank is a joint stock company. Tasks and organisation are described in the statute of 1984. The primary objective of the bank is price stability, viz. article 2(3); "It [the Austrian National Bank] shall ensure with all means at its disposal that the value of the Austrian currency is maintained with regard both to its domestic purchasing power and to its relationship with stable foreign currencies".

"In determining the general lines of monetary and credit policy to be followed by the Austrian National Bank in this field for the purpose of performing the functions incumbent upon it, due regard shall be paid to the economic policy of the Federal Government",[1] i.e. the government has no right to give instructions to the bank. This is confirmed in article 41(2): the Federal Republic is not allowed to take measures that could hinder the central bank in the execution of its legal objectives.

The bank is independent of the government but, in practice, takes an active part in the development of economic policy and co-operates closely with the government. Other tasks of the bank are regulating the circulation of money and attending to the settlement of payments with foreign countries; according to the Foreign Exchange Act, the bank is the Austrian foreign exchange authority.

The governing bodies of the bank are the General Meeting, the Governing Board and the Board of Executive Directors. The General Meeting elects six members of the Governing Board. "For the purpose of the election of six members of the Governing Board by the General Meeting, shareholders other than the Federal Republic may propose one person for each 12.5 million schillings of capital represented by the shareholders. If such proposals are not made, the right of proposal shall rest with the Federal Republic".[2]

---

[1] National Bank Act 1984, art. 4.

[2] Ibidem, art. 18(1).

The Governing Board is in charge of the overall direction and supervision of all the bank's actions. The Board has many tasks, such as "laying down the general directives of monetary and credit policy and giving its opinion on draft legislation in so far as the latter concerns important questions of monetary and credit policy",[3] fixing the discount and lombard rates and determining the open market policy. So the Board can independently make its own monetary policy and has a free choice of monetary instruments. The Governing Board consists of the Governor of the bank, two Deputy Governors and eleven ordinary members. The Governor is appointed by the President for a five-year term. He acts as chairman at all meetings of the Board and sees that decisions of the Board are properly executed.

The First and Second Deputy Governor are appointed by the government for five years, as well as five of the other members of the Governing Board. The Board of Executive Directors is in charge of the daily management of the bank. Because Austria has linked its currency to that of Germany, the Executive Directors' main occupation is the stabilisation of the schilling versus the mark. The Board of Executive Directors is mainly an executive body but "shall take decisions independently on all matters concerning the running of the Bank and the conduct of the business that are not reserved for decision by the Governing Board".[4]

The Federal Minister of Finance ensures that the bank acts legally and, for this, appoints a State Commissioner, who may attend the meetings of the Governing Board in an advisory capacity and is entitled to total co-operation and information from the bank. Through the State Commissioner, the government can influence on policy of the bank since he can "raise objections to decisions of the Governing Board if he considers any such decision to be in conflict with existing legislation".[5]

The bank cannot finance the government, but the Federal Minister of Finance can request it to buy short-term Federal Treasury certificates. The total amount, however, may not exceed five percent of the yearly federal tax revenues.

A.2. Denmark

Nationalbanken i Kjobenhavn was created in 1818 to assure monetary stability and had the right to issue notes. The bank became the sole banker of the Danish State in 1914 and in 1936, with the National Bank of Denmark Act, the National Bank in Copenhagen was transformed into *Danmarks Nationalbank*, the current central bank.[6]

---

[3] Ibidem, art. 20.

[4] Ibidem, art. 21.

[5] Ibidem, art. 45-46.

[6] "Danmarks Nationalbank, central bank responsibilities and tasks", Danmarks Nationalbank, Copenhagen, 1991, pp. 7, 8.

The objective of the bank is described in article 1 of the central bank law: "Danmarks Nationalbank [...] shall as the central bank of this country [...] maintain a safe and secure currency system in this country, and facilitate and regulate the traffic of money and the extension of credit". In other words, it has to stabilize purchasing power and at the same time to keep up with economic developments, so price stability is its main objective.

In order to do so, the bank makes its own monetary policy and is responsible for the management of foreign currencies. Exchange rate policy is in the hands of the government but is carried out by the bank. Banking supervision is not carried out by the bank, but by the Danish Financial Supervisory Authority.

The bank is ruled by the Committee of Directors, the Board of Directors, the Board of Governors and the Royal Bank Commissioner. The Board of Governors has three members: the chairman is appointed by the King, i.e. the government. The other two are appointed by the Board of Directors, but the Parliament has a major influence on those two appointments. The board members are appointed for life but can be relieved from their office by the King or the Board of Directors.[7] Until now this has never occurred and dismissal of a board member would be the ultimate step in case of a serious conflict between the Board of Governors and the government.

The Board of Directors consists of 25 members, of whom eight are elected by Parliament, 15 by the Board and two by the Minister of Economic Affairs. The Board of Directors has administrative and advisory capacities. The Committee of Directors has seven members; two are appointed by the Minister of Economic Affairs and five elected from the Board of Directors by the Board itself. The Committee has an intermediate position between the Board of Governors and the Board of Directors.

The Minister of Trade, Industry and Shipping, in his capacity of Royal Bank Commissioner, ensures that the bank carries out its duties. He presides over meetings of the Board of Directors and attends those of the Board of Governors. The Commissioner is the formal contact between the government and the bank.

The Board of Governors is responsible for monetary policy making, as clearly stated in the central bank law; "The Board of Governors shall fix the rate of discount and the rate of interest for advances".[8] In changing those rates, the Governors have to inform the Royal Bank Commissioner and the Minister of Finance, but the final decision rests with them.

In practice, monetary policy is formulated on the basis of co-operation between the government and the Board of Governors: the government cannot

[7] National Bank of Denmark Act, 1937; By-Laws on the National Bank of Denmark, 1937.

[8] By-Laws on the National Bank of Denmark, 1937, art. 25.

give instructions to the Board. Exchange rate policy is also determined by mutual co-operation, although it is formally a government issue.

The bank can give the government credit against "satisfactory security and normally for 1-3 months not exceeding 6 months".[9] However the government does not use this credit facility because of the co-operation in the field of monetary and exchange rate policy making. Instead, it finances its deficits by selling government paper on the capital market.

A.3. Finland

The central bank of Finland, *Suomen Pankki*, was created in 1811 and is one of the oldest in the world. Until 1868, it was under the control of the Senate; after this date the bank had to justify its actions to Staten, the Parliament. In 1875 the main objective of the bank was to maintain a stable and balanced monetary system and to stimulate money circulation. Eleven years later, it also received the sole right to issue money.

Finland became an independent state in 1917 and, according to the constitution of 1919, article 73, the bank was "under the guarantee and care of Parliament and under the surveillance of the Parliamentary Supervisory Board appointed by Parliament". At the end of 1925, the Regulations for the Bank of Finland came into force. In spite of several adjustments, they still form the central bank law of Finland.[10]

Its main objective is clearly stated in article 1 of the central bank law: "The object of the Bank of Finland is to maintain a stable and secure monetary system and to assist and facilitate the circulation of money in Finland". This means that the bank does not have price stability as its main objective.

According to article 2 of the Currency Act of 1962, it is responsible for maintaining the external value of the markka, the Finnish currency. In case of shocks in the foreign exchange market, the bank can deviate from the fluctuation margins of the markka. However, the government can revoke this right, after consultation with the bank. The government has a right of say on the external value of the markka, but co-operation in this area is stipulated by law.

There are no formal provisions which prevent the government from borrowing from the bank but normally only in exceptional circumstances does the bank give credit. The government has no power to give the bank instructions because the bank is under control of the Parliament. This can be concluded from article 2 of the Regulations for the Bank of Finland: "The Bank carries its business

[9] National Bank of Denmark Act, 1937, art. 15.

[10] "The Bank of Finland", Suomen Pankki/Finlands Bank, Helsinki, 1993, p. 4. Rolf Kulberg: "A brief history of the Bank of Finland", Bank of Finland, *Working Paper*, 18 February 1992.

under the guarantee and supervision of the Diet [Parliament]". In practice the bank is monetarily independent of the government but works together with it – in particular the Minister of Finance – to better co-ordinate economic policy.

The policy board of the bank, the Parliamentary Supervisory Board, consists of nine members, all appointed by Parliament for the whole parliamentary term (four years). A Supervisor can be a member of Parliament. The most important task of the Supervisors is to "fix the base rate of the Bank and other rates of interest applied by the Bank and limits thereon",[11] i.e. the bank is independent in monetary policy making.

Three Supervisors are appointed by Parliament as members of the Executive Committee of the Parliamentary Supervisory Board. The Executive Committee has to take care of matters not reserved for the Parliamentary Supervisory Board and to prepare decisions for the Board. "The administration of the Bank of Finland and management of the affairs are entrusted to the Board of Management, except in the case of those duties that are reserved in these regulations for the Bank Supervisors".[12] The Board of Management must always ensure that the markka keeps its legally established value, as fixed by the government. Furthermore, the Board of Management gives support to the Supervisors. The board members are appointed by the President of the Republic on the proposal of the Supervisory Board.

A.4. Hungary

The Institute of Budapest of the Austro-Hungarian Bank had the function of central bank in Hungary until the end of the First World War. In 1924 the Hungarian Parliament established the National Bank of Hungary. After the Second World War, all Hungarian banks were nationalised and from then on, the *National Bank of Hungary* was the only bank in the Hungarian financial system, apart from some specialized financial institutions. On January 1, 1987, the separation between central bank and commercial bank was re-established. All commercial activities of the Hungarian Central Bank have now been transferred to the commercial banking system.[13]

These changes in the financial system required a new central bank law, adjusted for a market economy and with an obvious place for monetary policy within economic policy. On November 16, 1991 the new central bank law came in force: its main objective is to strengthen the stability of the Hungarian currency, the forint. Thus the bank has to pursue price stability as primary objective. In doing so, "the National Bank of Hungary (NBH) develops its

---

[11] Regulations for the Bank of Finland, Helsinki, 21 December 1925, art. 17(1).
[12] Ibidem, art. 16.
[13] National Bank of Hungary: "The Law on the Central Bank", *Market Letter NBH*, 10-11/1991.

monetary policy as well as the instruments serving its implementation in an autonomous way in the framework of this act".[14] The government cannot influence the monetary policy of the central bank and "The Government shall not give instructions to NBH in the scope of its tasks defined in this Act".[15] In other words, the bank is independent of the government in monetary policy making although monetary policy has to stay within the limits of the central bank law.

With regard to the exchange rate, the central bank law states that "the order of determining and/or influencing the exchange rates is approved by the government in agreement with the NBH".[16]

The bank has to support the implementation of the economic policy program of the government with all monetary policy means available and has to make its opinion clear about the government's plans and actions. On the one hand, it is independent of the government and thus can fulfil its tasks in a balanced way in the long run and, on the other, is obligated by law to co-operate with the government.

The main bodies of the bank are the General Meeting, the Central Banking Council, the Board of Directors and the Supervisory Commission. The Central Banking Council, the policy board of the bank, makes decisions about the annual policy guidelines and the modifications of the policy instruments of the central bank, inclusive of exchange policy measures. The Council consists of the President of the bank, no more than five of its vice-presidents and the same number of other members as vice-presidents. A government representative is invited to all the meetings of the Central Banking Council in an advisory capacity.

The Council is appointed by the President of the Hungarian Republic on the proposal of the Prime Minister. The term of the President of the bank is six years (renewable); for the other council members, it is three years (renewable). The President of the bank is responsible for the execution of the decisions of the Council.

The Board of Directors supports the bank President in carrying out his tasks. The Board has a mere advisory function. The Supervisory Commission is the supervising organ of the bank. The Commission is obliged to inform Members of Parliament and the Minister of Finance who respectively elect and appoint it. The law does not say exactly about what the Commission has to inform the Minister and Parliament.

The General Meeting has numerous tasks, such as establishment and modification of the statutes and election and recall of the elected members of the Board of Directors. The shares of the bank are held by the State, which is represented by the Minister of Finance although the latter cannot exert much influence on the monetary policy of the bank through the General Meeting since it has no decisive voice in the monetary policy of the bank.

[14] Act LX on the National Bank of Hungary, art. 6.
[15] Ibidem, art. 45.
[16] Ibidem, art. 12(2).

The bank can finance the government through the central budget with a maximum of three percent of expected income of the central budget in that year. Other government bodies have to solve their deficit in the capital market or via the central budget. The bank has to justify the credit relations with public finances to Parliament.

A.5. Luxembourg

Luxembourg has had several monetary regimes since the French Revolution. First, the Dutch monetary system and, during the Belgian Revolution, the Belgian regime. Then the German *Zollverein* was in force until the end of the First World War. In 1922, the monetary union with Belgium (the Belgian-Luxembourg Monetary Union) was instituted.

The central bank, the Luxembourg Monetary Institute, was established in 1983. In 1994, a law was adopted to give the institute a greater degree of independence, as required in the Treaty of Maastricht.

According to article 2 of the law of 22 October 1993 "relative à l'Institut Monétaire Luxembourgeois", the bank has as its main task price stability and the government has no right of instruction. Article 5(2) of the central bank law of 1993 states very explicitly that the Luxembourg Monetary Institute cannot receive monetary policy instructions; "Dans l'exercice des pouvoirs et dans l'accomplissement des missions et des devoirs qui leur ont été conférés dans le domaine monétaire, ni l'Institut, ni un membre quelconque de ses organes de décision ne peuvent solliciter ni accepter des instructions ou organes de la Communauté européenne, des gouvernements des Etats membres ou de tout autre organisme".

The bank is in charge of exchange rate management, however the government has final authority over exchange rate policy. Luxembourg is still a member of the Belgian-Luxembourg Economic Union which means that exchange rate parity with Belgium is important, i.e. Belgium can exert indirect influence through its monetary policy on that of Luxembourg. However, because of the Union, both countries must have compatible monetary policies. Other tasks of the bank are management of the official reserves and stimulation of a well functioning payments system.

To achieve price stability, the bank can operate on financial markets or give advances against collateral. Article 24(1) states that it can no longer give credit to the government. It also exerts supervision in the financial sector.

The main bodies of the bank are the Board and the Council. The Board is the policy board and prepares measures and takes decisions in the context of the price stability objective. The members of the Board are the Director General and two to four Directors. They are all appointed by the Grand Duke on the proposal of the government. The term for the board members is six years, renewable. Dismissal from office is only possible in case of proven incompetence and no longer being able to fulfil the condition of "personal honour". The Council has no policy making powers but can give advice on monetary policy matters. Its three to five are members appointed by the government for four years, renewable. The Council is presided by the Director General of the bank.

Because of the Belgian-Luxembourg Economic Union, the bank can only issue a limited amount of money per year. For historical reasons *La Banque Internationale à Luxembourg* can also issue money, since 1967 however with a limit of 50 million Luxembourg francs a year.

A.6. New Zealand

At the beginning of this century, the New Zealand economy was based on the sterling standard; Australian and New Zealand pounds were linked to the British currency. Abolition of this parity caused problems for New Zealand, as the Australian pound devaluated more than the New Zealand pound. This resulted in the New Zealand demand for its own currency, which resulted in the creation of the central bank of New Zealand, the Reserve Bank.

The current central bank law, the Reserve Bank of New Zealand Act 1989, replaced the Reserve Bank Act of 1964. The act of 1989 was a result of the reaction to the weak economic performances in New Zealand during the period 1970-1980. The country suffered from an expanding government debt, yearly inflation of more than ten percent and an average annual economic growth of 1.4 percent. This strengthened the belief that economic policy had to change. As a consequence, long-term price stability was given more emphasis in monetary policy.

"The primary function of the Bank is to formulate and implement monetary policy directed to the economic objective of achieving and maintaining stability in the general level of prices".[17] In the formulation and the execution of monetary policy, the bank has to take account of the efficiency and soundness of the financial system. It has also to "consult with, and give advice to, the Government and such persons or organisations as the Bank considers can assist to achieve and maintain the economic objective of monetary policy".[18] The rationale for this is that only efficient monetary instruments should be used and that monetary and financial stability are closely linked, because radical changes in monetary policy can seriously damage the stability of the financial system. The obligation to co-operate with other parties prevents the bank from operating in a vacuum.

It is free to formulate monetary policy in order to achieve price stability. By choosing price stability and an independent central bank, the government showed that priority was given to reducing inflation and stimulating economic growth.

---

[17] Reserve Bank of New Zealand Act 1989, art. 8.
[18] Ibidem, art. 10.

However, monetary policy has to be clearly adjusted to price stability and "The Minister [of Finance] shall, before appointing, or reappointing, any person as Governor, fix, in agreement with that person, policy targets for the carrying out by the Bank of its primary function during that person's term of office, or next term of office, as Governor".[19] Those policy targets formulate limits for inflation for part of or for the entire term of the Governor.[20]

Also, the government has the right "from time to time, by order in Council, on the advice of the Minister, to direct the Bank to formulate and implement monetary policy for any economic objective, other than the economic objective specified in Section 8 of this Act, for such a period not exceeding 12 months as shall be specified in the order".[21] This is a right of instruction of the government; it can demand that the bank adjust monetary policy to the economic policy preferred by the government. It should be noted that this procedure is complicated, as it requires an order in Council, must be made publicly known and has to be laid before the House of Representatives.

The bank can act independently on the foreign exchange rate market, but the government has the final right of say in the exchange rate policy.

The management of the bank consists of the Governor and the Board of Directors. The Governor is appointed by the Minister of Finance on the proposal of the Board of Directors for a period of five years, renewable. He is the Chief Executive of the bank and must see to it that it fulfils its statutory tasks. Besides the Governor, there are one or two Deputy Governors. One is the Deputy Chief Executive of the bank and both are nominated by the Board for five years on the proposal of the Governor. The Governor decides the functions of the Deputy Governors. The Board of Directors has seven to ten members: the Governor and the Deputy Governor(s) of the bank and four to seven non-executive directors, appointed by the Minister of Finance for five years.

The Board supervises the bank and the Governor and ensures that price stability objectives are respected. "The Board may give advice to the Governor on any matter relating to the performance of the Bank's functions and the exercise of its powers",[22] i.e. the Governor alone is responsible for the monetary policy and achieving the Policy Targets Agreement: he is the policy board of the bank.

The bank does not give credit to the government because monetary financing is contrary to the price stability objective, although it is not legally forbidden.

A.7. Norway

Norges Bank, the central bank of Norway, was created in 1816. The bank functioned under the central bank law of 1892 until 1985, when a new one was adopted: the Act of 24 May 1985 relating to Norges Bank and the Monetary System.

---

[19] Ibidem, art. 9(1).

[20] The Governor of the Reserve Bank of New Zealand and the Minister of Finance agreed to a Policy Targets Agreement for 1993 of an inflation rate between zero and two percent.

[21] Reserve Bank of New Zealand Act 1989, art. 12(1).

[22] Ibidem, art. 52-63.

"Norges Bank is the country's central bank. The Bank shall be an executive and advisory body for monetary, credit and foreign exchange policy. It shall issue banknotes and coins, promote an efficient payments system domestically as well as vis-à-vis other countries, and monitor developments in the monetary, credit and foreign exchange markets.

The Bank may implement any measures customarily or ordinarily taken by a central bank. To further its objectives the Bank may engage in all types of banking business and banking services".[23] That is, price stability is obviously not its main objective.

"Norges Bank shall conduct its operations in accordance with the political and economic guidelines drawn up by the government authorities and with the country's international commitments".[24] In other words, the government determines monetary policy and bank has to follow that policy; it is not independent. The government has also an explicit right to give the bank instructions: "The King in council may pass resolutions regarding the activities of the Bank. Such resolutions may take the form of general rules or instructions in individual cases".[25] This right of instruction, however, should be seen as an ultimate means in case of a conflict between the government and the bank.

The bank has to put every important decision before the Minister of Finance. It also has to inform the public about the monetary, credit and foreign exchange situation. The external value of the Norwegian currency, the krone, and modifications thereof, are determined by the government. The bank is responsible for exchange rate management.

The principal bodies of the bank are the Executive Board and the Supervisory Council. The Governor and the Deputy-Governor of bank are chairman and deputy-chairman of the Board. They are appointed full-time for six years (renewable). The other five members are nominated part-time for four years with a maximum term of 12 years. The Board is the executive and advisory authority of the bank: it is in charge of its activities and administers its funds.

The Supervisory Council has 15 members, elected by Parliament for a term of four years. All members have a maximum term of 12 years. The Chairman and the Deputy-chairman are elected among the Supervisors, also by Parliament, for two years. The Council sees to it that the bank's activities are properly executed.

The bank can give the government seasonal and other short-term credit, with specific limits to be stipulated by Parliament. Under special circumstances there is also the possibility of long-term credit, whose limits are stipulated by Parliament.

---

[23] Act of 24 May 1985 relating to Norges Bank and the Monetary System, art. 1.
[24] Ibidem, art. 2.
[25] Ibidem, art. 2-3.

A.8. Poland

The National Bank of Poland, *Narodowy Bank Polski* (NBP), was created in 1948 when the Polish financial system was disrupted after the Second World War.[26] After 1950, when the last commercial banks were closed, the Polish financial system closely resembled the Soviet system. Until 1989, the NBP was the only bank in Poland. At the beginning of that year, however, it again became a real central bank as the division between central bank and commercial bank was re-established. The NBP was divided and retained only the traditional central bank objectives. Together with the re-establishment of the central-commercial bank division, the new statute for the Polish central bank came into force. Despite several adjustments to this statute, the Act on Narodowy Bank Polski is still the central bank law of Poland.

Article 1 proclaims the NBP as the central bank of the country with tasks such as issue of money, central clearing and credit institution as well as central banking institution for foreign exchange control.

The main objectives of the bank are "issuing legal tender of the Republic of Poland, granting refinancing credits to other banks, accepting deposits, carrying out monetary settlements, organizing operations in foreign currencies in accordance with provisions of the Foreign Exchange Control Law, performing banking services for the state budget and other activities as provided in the present act".[27] This last task signifies the supervision of the financial sector. The primary objective of the bank is aimed especially at strengthening the Polish currency. External stability rather than price stability has priority.[28]

The bank co-operates in the forming and execution of the economic policy of the government, within its range of possibilities and according to acts and resolutions of the Parliament. This means that the Parliament has influence on the bank through economic policy. "Within the range of its activities the National Bank of Poland initiates and forms monetary policy including also foreign exchange policy, according to the recommendations of the Sejm".[29] That is, the Parliament also has a direct influence on the bank's monetary policy.

The NBP has a President, Deputy Presidents and a Board of Management. The President, appointed by Parliament on the proposal of the President of the Republic for a term of six years, is in charge of the management of the bank.

Co-operation between the bank, Parliament and government is stipulated by law as the President of NBP takes part in meetings of Parliament and the Council of Ministers. The Deputy Presidents are appointed by the President of the Republic on the proposal of the President of NBP.

---

[26] The history of the central bank in Poland goes back further than 1948. The first bank fulfilling this function in Poland – the Bank of Poland – was established in 1924.

[27] Act on Narodowy Bank Polski, 1989, art. 6.1.

[28] It should, however, be mentioned that the real strength of domestic currency *vis-à-vis* other currencies depends mainly on controlling the level of inflation. So, price stability plays an important role in NBP policy, although it is not an explicit policy goal.

[29] Act on Narodowy Bank Polski, 1989, art. 6.2.1 and 6.2.2.

Members of the Board of Management are the President and Deputy Presidents of NBP and other members, directly nominated by the President of the bank. Neither the government nor Parliament have a representative on the Board of Management. The exact number of Deputy Presidents is not given in the central bank law; neither is the number of other members of the Board of Management.

The Board is the highest policy authority of the bank and "considers main issues within the scope of activities of the NBP and adopts resolutions necessary to perform tasks of the NBP, regarding in particular:

1) [...],

2) functioning of credit and monetary systems,

3) monetary policy,

[...],

7) interest rate policy,

[...].[30]

The NBP can finance the government by buying bills of exchange issued by State Treasury. On a yearly basis, this amount cannot exceed two percent of the forecast government expenses.

A.9. Portugal

The *Banco de Portugal* "is the central bank of the Portuguese Republic and in such capacity it shall ensure the internal monetary equilibrium and the external solvency of the currency".[31] Thus, it has to pursue price and exchange rate stability.

"As central bank, it shall be particularly incumbent on the Bank, taking into account the Government's guidelines, to:

a) Cooperate in the formulation of and execute the monetary and exchange rate policy;

b) Manage the foreign assets of the country or any other assets entrusted to it;

c) Act as intermediary in the international monetary relations of the State;

d) Provide for stability of the domestic financial system, performing for the purpose the function of lender of last resort".[32]

---

[30] Ibidem, art. 49.

[31] Organic Law of the Banco de Portugal, Approved by Decree-Law No. 337/90 of October 1990, art. 3.

[32] Organic Law of the Banco de Portugal, Approved by Decree-Law No. 337/90 of October 1990, art. 18.

The bank also advises the government on monetary, financial and exchange rate matters, supervises the financial sector and issues banknotes.

As noted above, it has no independent monetary policy authority but is alone responsible for the execution of monetary and exchange rate policy. Also, in execution of these policies, it "may carry out any operations justified by virtue of its capacity as central bank, namely the following:

a) To rediscount and discount for a period not exceeding one year, drafts, certificates of indebtness, invoice statements, warrants and other similar credit instruments, under the condition laid down by the Board of Directors;

b) To buy and sell securities issued by the Portuguese State;

c) To grant loans to credit and quasi-banking institutions for a period not exceeding one year".[33]

The main bodies of the bank are the Governor, the Board of Directors, the Board of Auditors and the Advisory Board.

The Governor has to represent the bank, act on its behalf with foreign or international institutions and to supervise the Board of Directors. Like the members of the latter, he is appointed by the council of ministers on proposal of the Minister of Finance for a renewable term of five years. He has the power to suspend decisions of the Board of Directors or by executive committees which he judges contrary to the law, the country or the central bank. However, such a suspension has to be approved by the Council of Ministers within 15 days, otherwise the suspension ceases to exist.

The Board of Directors consists of the Governor of the bank, one or two Deputy Governors of the bank and three to five Directors. The Board of Directors is responsible for all actions needed to achieve the objectives of the bank that are not within the competence of other bodies of the bank. It therefore follows that the Board is responsible for the price stability objective. The Board of Directors can delegate powers to executive committees. In practice, there are regular meetings between the Board and the Minister of Finance; however, the members of the Board cannot receive monetary policy instructions.

The Board of Auditors has four members: three are appointed by the Minister of Finance and one by the employees of the bank. The main task of the Board of Auditors is financial supervision of the bank.

The Advisory Board gives its opinion on the annual statement of the bank and on matters laid before the advisors by the Board of Directors.

"The State may resort to an account, free of charge, opened with the Bank whose debit balance shall not exceed 10 percent of the current revenue collected in the previous year".[34] Monetary financing is possible because "the Bank shall not grant credit to the State nor any other public-law juridical person except

---

[33] Ibidem, art. 35.
[34] Ibidem, art. 26.1.

through the underwriting of treasury bills under terms agreed between the Finance Ministry and the Bank with due observance of legal ceilings.[35]

Because of the Treaty of Maastricht, it should be noted that the central bank law of Portugal has to be modified to fulfil the conditions for an economic and monetary union in Europe. In order to meet these requirements, the bank has to become independent of the government.

A.10. Spain

The predecessor of the current Spanish central bank was the Bank of San Carlos, established in 1782. This merged with the Bank of Isabel II in 1847 and became the New Spanish Bank of San Fernando. With the first bank law in Spain, 1856, its name was changed to *Banco de España*. The Bank of Spain was nationalised in 1962 and became the central bank of Spain.

In 1980 a new statute for the bank was adopted; its tasks were redefined and its independence was strengthened. The present statute for the Bank of Spain was passed by the Parliament in October 1993 and adjusted the former central bank law to the Treaty of Maastricht.

The law of February 1, 1993, which increases the independence of the bank, is taken from the Statute for the European Central Bank and the Treaty of Maastricht. Parts of the 1980 law are used, especially regarding the governing bodies of the bank. The major changes have occurred in the field of monetary policy and financing government debt.

Article 2 of the law gives the bank control over monetary policy; it is responsible for formulating and executing monetary policy with price stability as its main objective. Monetary policy, however, has to support government economic policy if that policy is focused on stable prices and has no inflationary character.

According to article 6, exchange rate policy remains the government's concern, but the government has to consult with the bank on exchange rate matters, with a view to avoiding any potential conflict between exchange rate policy and the objective of price stability.

Other tasks of the bank are supervision of financial institutions, promoting stability of the financial system and issuing currency.

The main bodies are the Governing Council, the Executive Commission, the Governor and the Deputy Governor.

The Governor is appointed by the King on the proposal of the Prime Minister for one six-year term. The Deputy is appointed for the same term, but by the government on the proposal of the Governor of the bank.

---

[35] Ibidem, art. 27.1.

The Governing Council consists of the Governor, the Deputy Governor, six members, the General Director of Treasury and Finance, the Deputy Chairman of the National Stockmarket Commission, all the General Directors of the bank and the General Secretary of the bank. The six members are appointed by the government on the proposal of the Minister of Finance, in liaison with the Governor of the bank, for a term of eight years. The General Director of Treasury and Finance and the Deputy Chairman of the National Stockmarket Commission have no voting right concerning monetary policy making. The General Directors and the General Secretary of the bank have no voting right at all.

Guidelines and execution of monetary policy are fixed by the Governing Council. The Minister of Finance may by exception attend the meetings of the Council in an advisory capacity. Daily management is in the hands of the Executive Commission, whose members are the Governor and the Deputy Governor of the bank and two others, who are among the six members of the Governing Council and are appointed by it on the proposal of the Governor. The General Secretary is a member with no voting right. The General Directors of the bank may attend the meetings of the Commission in an advisory capacity.

The government has no right of instruction, in accordance with the main motive of the new statute, increasing the bank's independence. Also, the bank can no longer give the government credit. Monetary financing is forbidden in the new law of 1993, in accordance with the Treaty of Maastricht.

A.11. Czech Republic

The history of the Czech financial system is identical to the Slovak financial history, as these two Republics formed a single state until 1993.

The banking system in Czechoslovakia originated in 1918 when the Austro-Hungarian banks in Czech territory came under the control of the new Czechoslovakian State. At that time, the central bank was part of the Ministry of Finance. In 1926 those tasks were transferred to the National Bank of Czechoslovakia. After the Second World War, the Czechoslovakian financial system was replaced by the communist system and the State Bank of Czechoslovakia was created in 1950. This central bank was also the only commercial bank in the country, apart from two pre-war banks.

With the fall of the Berlin Wall in 1989, democracy was restored in Czechoslovakia and economic changes made. The division between central and commercial banking (embodied in law 130/1989 on the State Bank of Czechoslovakia) was replaced by the Act No. 22/1992 Collection of Laws on the State Bank of Czechoslovakia because the former could not adjust to the fast changing economic environment.

On November 25, 1992, the Federal Parliament of Czechoslovakia decided to dissolve the Czechoslovakian Republic. On January 1, 1993, the *Czech National Bank* was created as the first central bank of the Czech Republic. The new central bank law, the Act on the Czech National Bank of December 17, 1992 is very similar to its predecessor, Act 22/1992.

The Czech National Bank has a primary objective "to ensure the stability of the Czech national currency (the Crown). For this purpose the Czech National Bank shall [...] set monetary policy [...]".[36]

"In providing for its primary objective the Czech National Bank shall be independent of any instructions given by the Government".[37] That is, it has a strong independent position. Concerning exchange rate policy, "The Czech National Bank shall [...] proclaim the exchange rate of the Czech currency vis-à-vis foreign currencies".[38] Thus it is also responsible for exchange rate management. In other words, it is responsible for the internal and external value of the Czech currency.

Co-operation between the bank and government is stipulated by law: a government representative is allowed to attend the meetings of the bank Board in an advisory capacity, and the bank gives the government advice in the monetary and banking field.

The bank is governed by the Board. "The Bank Board shall set monetary policy and the instruments for the implementation of these policies, and shall decide on the measures to be taken in the sphere of monetary policy".[39] The Board consists of the Governor, two Deputy Governors and four other senior officers of the bank. All members are appointed by the President of the Czech Republic for a period of six years. The central bank law clearly stipulates the motives for dismissal of the Board members, in order to protect the independent position of the bank.

The bank can give credit to the government to help bridge temporary budget deficits, but the total amount of credit may not exceed five per cent of the previous year's State revenues.

[36] Act on the Czech National Bank, 17 December 1992, art. 5.
[37] Ibidem, art. 9(1).
[38] Ibidem, art. 35.
[39] Ibidem, art. 2.

REFERENCES

ALESINA, A. (1988), "Macroeconomics and politics", *NBER Macroeconomic Annual 1988*, Cambridge, pp. 13-52.

ALESINA, A. (1989), "Politics and business cycles in industrial democracies", *Economic Policy*, no. 8, April, pp. 55-98.

ALESINA, A. and SUMMERS, L. (1993), "Central bank independence and macroeconomic performance: some comparative evidence", *Journal of Money, Credit and Banking*, vol. 25, pp. 151-162.

BADE, R. and PARKIN, M. (1988), "Central bank laws and monetary policy", *Department of Economics, University of Western Ontario*, Canada, October.

CUKIERMAN, A. (1992), *Central Bank Strategy, Credibility and Independence: Theory and Evidence*, The MIT Press, Cambridge, Massachusetts.

DE HAAN, J. and STURM, J.E. (1992), "The case for central bank independence", in *Banca Nazionale del Lavoro Quarterly Review*, no. 182, September, pp. 305-327.

EIJFFINGER, S. and SCHALING, E. (1992), "Central bank independence: criteria and indices", *Department of Economics Research Memorandum*, Tilburg University, March, pp. 34-37.

EIJFFINGER, S. and SCHALING, E. (1993), "Central bank independence in twelve industrial countries", in *Banca Nazionale del Lavoro Quarterly Review*, no. 184, March, pp. 64-68.

EIJFFINGER, S. and SCHALING, E. (1995), "Central bank independence: theory and evidence", *European Journal of Political Economy*, forthcoming.

GRILLI, V., MASCIANDARO, D. and TABELLINI, G. (1991), "Political and monetary institutions and public financial policies in industrial countries", *Economic Policy*, Fall, pp. 366-375.

INTERNATIONAL MONETARY FUND (1993), *IMF International Financial Statistics Yearbook*, Washington, D.C.

UNGERER, H. (1990), "The EMS, 1979-1990, policies-evolution-outlook", *Konjunkturpolitik*, Bd. 36, Heft 6, pp. 329-362.

Part III
Empirical Evidence on Central Bank Independence

[13]

The Case for Central Bank Independence *

1. Introduction

An important issue in the process towards a European Monetary Union is the position of the European System of Central Banks (ESCB). At its meeting in Maastricht in December 1991, the European Council decided that the primary objective of the ESCB shall be to maintain price stability. The ESCB shall have a relatively independent position, similar to the Deutsche Bundesbank. Many economists have argued that the institutional set-up of a central bank may influence economic outcomes.[1] On the basis of a review of existing research and some new evidence, the case for an independent ESCB is discussed in this paper. In our empirical work, three different measures of central bank independence are used to examine whether the consequences of central bank independence are dependent upon the choice of the independence measure.

The paper is organized as follows. In the next section the relationship between the level of inflation and central bank independence is discussed, while in the third section the issue of inflation variability is examined. The fourth section reviews the impact that central bank independence may have on the level and financing of government budget deficits. The fifth section explores the relationship between central bank independence and economic growth. The final section provides some concluding comments.

---

* The authors would like to thank Willem Buiter, Sylvester Eijffinger, Lex Hoogduin, Ad van Riet and Elmer Sterken for their comments on a previous version of this paper.

[1] See, for example, BADE and PARKIN (1988), ALESINA (1989) and GRILLI *et al.* (1991).

BNL Quarterly Review, no. 182, September 1992.

2. Central Bank Independence and the Level of Inflation

It is widely believed that countries with an independent central bank have lower inflation than countries with a central bank which comes under direct control of the government (Parkin, 1987; Alesina and Summers, 1991). Why would central bank independence yield lower inflation? According to the older public choice view there exist strong political pressures on the monetary authorities to behave in accordance with the government's preferences. As Buchanan and Wagner put it:

> "A monetary decision maker is in a position only one stage removed from that of the directly elected politician. He will normally have been appointed to office by a politician subject to electoral testing, and he may even serve at the pleasure of the latter. It is scarcely to be expected that persons who are chosen as monetary decision makers will be the sort that are likely to take policy stances sharply contrary to those desired by their political associates, especially since these stances would also run counter to strong public opinion and media pressures... 'Easy money' is also 'easy' for the monetary manager.." (1977, pp. 117-18).

Monetary tightening aggravates the budgetary position of government: the reduction in tax income brought by a temporary slow-down of economic activity, possibly lower receipts from the inflation tax and the short-run increase in the interest burden on the public debt worsen the deficit. So "easy money" may be preferred by the government. Indeed, there exists some evidence that even the relatively independent Federal Reserve sometimes caters to the desires of the President and/or the Congress.[2] This evidence is either based on close inspection of the contacts between the polity and the central bank (see, *e.g.*, Havrilesky, 1988; Akhtar and Howe, 1991) or exists by testing whether monetary policy turns expansive before elections take place as predicted by Nordhaus's (1975) political

---

[2] It is generally assumed that Congress exercises little or no systematic control of the Federal Reserve. However, Grier (1991) provides evidence that changes in the leadership of Congress committees dealing with monetary policy are significantly correlated with monetary base growth. Kane (1980) views Congress and the Federal Reserve as having an implicit bargain: the Federal Reserve accepts blame for a bad economy in return for a grant of independence. However, when monetary policy causes too much electoral pain to Congress, the Federal Reserve must reverse course. For a critique on both views see Beck (1988).

business cycle theory (see, for example, Allen, 1986).[3] The impact of elections on U.S. monetary policy has been investigated quite extensively. The results are mixed (De Haan and Zelhorst, 1991). It is, of course, clear that the more independent a central bank is, the less it is under the spell of political influences.

A similar line of reasoning, as in Buchanan and Wagner (1977), is present in the literature originating with Barro and Gordon (1983), in which the traditional case for monetary policy rules is strengthened, based on the view that governments have an inherent tendency to misuse instruments at their disposal. Discretionary policy makers face an incentive to inflate the economy to achieve short-run reductions in unemployment. In Barro and Gordon's new-classical framework, repeated use of this instrument will raise inflationary expectations, causing higher inflation without eventually affecting the unemployment level. A policy rule is, therefore, clearly superior. An important institutional mechanism to enforce policy rules could be provided by independent agencies, like the central bank, which are not subject to each government's discretion. An independent central bank would, in this analysis, lead to lower inflation rates.[4] Neumann (1991) argues that the provision of a constitutional status of independence to the central bank is an effective device for government to commit itself to price stability over an infinite time horizon.

A third argument to explain why central bank independence may affect inflation has been put forward by Sargent and Wallace (1981). They distinguish between fiscal and monetary authorities. If fiscal policy is dominant – *i.e.* if the monetary authorities cannot influence the size of the government's budget deficit – money supply becomes endogenous. If the public are no longer able or willing to absorb additional government debt, the monetary authorities will be forced to finance the deficit by money creation. If, however, monetary policy is dominant, the fiscal authorities will be forced to reduce the deficit (or repudiate part of the debt).

---

[3] Recent work by Cukierman and Meltzer (1988) and Rogoff and Sibert (1988) shows that Nordhaus's (1975) insights, which were based on a model with a non-vertical long run Phillips curve, survive even when voters are not myopic as long as they have imperfect information.

[4] Toma (1982) argues, however, that the central bank tries to maximize its discretionary budgets, which causes excessive money growth. Since the central bank officials cannot directly pocket these earnings, they consume them in the form of high salaries, lavish offices, travel budgets or excessive number of employees. Boyes *et al.* (1988) report further evidence for this point of view.

The preceding analysis suggests that central bank independence may affect inflation across countries. In the upper part of Table 1 some simple regressions of the level of inflation in 18 OECD countries and central bank independence are shown.[5] Our first measure of central bank independence is based upon the measure used by Grilli *et al.* (1991 – see the Appendix for further details). In the period 1961-69 the coefficient of the independence dummy is not significantly different from zero. Given the fixed exchange rate regime, this is hardly surprising. It is quite clear that central bank independence exerts a negative influence on the level of inflation in the other periods.[6] The lower part of Table 1 shows the estimation results using Alesina's (1989) and Eijffinger and Schaling's (1992) measures for central bank independence. The number of observations is reduced to 14 and 11 OECD countries, respectively. As shown in the Appendix, the correlation between the various independence measures is low, indicating that different aspects of central bank independence are taken into account. The Alesina and Eijffinger-Schaling measures yield similar outcomes as the modified Grilli measure.

The results reported in Table 1 are in accordance with the conclusions of existing research.[7] Two objections may, however, be made against this type of analysis. First, inflation is not directly controlled by the monetary authorities and, second, factors other than central bank independence may be responsible for cross-country inflation differences. In response to the first criticism, we have replaced the inflation rate in our regressions by excess money growth, which is defined as the growth rate of the monetary base minus the growth rate of real GDP. The results are very similar to those reported in Table 1 and are, therefore, not shown. In response to the second criticism, we have re-estimated the model for excess money growth for the 1980s and have added three other explanatory variables: the number of government changes (freq), the number of government changes after which economic policy was changed signifi-

[5] Inflation is measured as the increase of the GDP deflator and is taken from the IMF's *International Financial Statistics Yearbook* 1990.

[6] When a dummy variable is added to differentiate between EMS countries and non-EMS countries it appears that the coefficient of this dummy is negative, but not significantly different from zero. The coefficient of the independence dummy hardly changes (–1.19).

[7] See Bade and Parkin (1988), Alesina (1989), Grilli *et al.* (1991) and Alesina and Summers (1991).

TABLE 1

CENTRAL BANK INDEPENDENCE AND THE LEVEL OF INFLATION

Explanatory variables:	1961-1969	1970-1978	1979-1987	1961-1987
Intercept	4.85	14.79	16.68	12.11
	(0.83)	(1.41)	(2.56)	(1.17)
Independence dummy	-0.11	-0.73	-1.22	-0.69
	(0.11)	(0.19)*	(0.35)*	(0.16)*
adj. R^2	-0.00	0.43	0.39	0.53
SE	1.32	2.25	4.07	1.87
Intercept	4.82	14.34	12.87	10.75
	(0.91)	(1.41)	(1.87)	(0.88)
Alesina dummy	-0.26	-2.28	-2.62	-1.78
	(0.39)	(0.47)*	(0.78)*	(0.37)*
adj. R^2	-0.04	0.64	0.44	0.63
SE	1.43	1.73	2.73	1.38
Intercept	3.30	12.17	10.58	8.68
	(0.62)	(1.60)	(1.88)	(1.21)
ES dummy	0.19	-1.20	-1.57	-0.86
	(0.20)	(0.51)*	(0.60)*	(0.36)*
adj. R^2	-0.01	0.31	0.37	0.32
SE	0.88	2.27	2.67	1.59

Notes: Standard errors are in parentheses. An asterisk indicates that the coefficient is significantly different from zero at the 95% confidence level. See the Appendix for details on the independence dummies.

cantly (sign), and the government budget deficit expressed as a fraction of GDP (def).[8] As explained by Grilli *et al.* (1991), the first two variables reflect political stability and polarization which the authors found to be important in explaining cross-country inflation differences. The results are reported in Table 2. It is clear that the coefficient of the Grilli-central bank independence dummy remains significantly different from zero, confirming our previous results.

[8] The data on freq and sign are taken from Grilli *et al.* (1991); data for government deficit are from the OECD's *Economic Outlook*, June 1991. Data for the monetary base are taken from the IFS (line 14).

TABLE 2

CENTRAL BANK INDEPENDENCE AND EXCESS MONEY GROWTH, 1980-1989

Explanatory variables:				
Intercept	0.18	0.17	0.14	0.14
	(0.04)	(0.05)	(0.04)	(0.06)
Independence dummy	–0.013	–0.012	–0.010	–0.010
	(0.005)*	(0.006)*	(0.005)*	(0.006)
Freq		0.0009		
		(0.005)		
Sign			0.014	
			(0.011)	
Def				–0.42
				(0.47)
adj. R^2	0.24	0.19	0.28	0.25
SE	0.06	0.06	0.06	0.06

3. Central Bank Independence and Inflation Variability

The preceding analysis suggests that central bank independence may reduce pre-election manipulation of monetary policy. If true, central bank independence may also result in more stable money growth and, therefore, less inflation variability. There is a related argument as to why an independent central bank may result in less inflation variability. Politicians not only strive to remain in office as long as possible, they are also partisan and wish to deliver benefits to their constituencies (Hibbs, 1987). There are indications that the pattern of unemployment and inflation tends to be systematically related to the political orientation of governments. Whereas right-wing governments generally give a high priority to lower inflation, left-wing governments are generally more concerned about unemployment. Existing evidence provides support for the view that the redistributional consequences of inflation provide an incentive for the left to be expansionary and for the right to be inflation-fighting (Alesina, 1989).[9] This implies that if there were a

[9] In the traditional partisan model there is an exploitable trade-off between inflation and unemployment. Recently a "rational partisan theory" has been put forward (see, for example, ALESINA and SACHS, 1988) which implies that differences between policies adopted by left- and right-wing governments are transitory and should occur immediately after the change of government.

regular change of government the inflation variability would be high, especially if the monetary authorities were dominated by elected politicians. However, a relatively independent central bank will not change its policy after a new government has been elected. So central bank independence may reduce inflation variability (Alesina, 1988).

Another reason why central bank independence may affect inflation variability has been put forward by Milton Friedman (1977) to explain why there exists a positive correlation between rates of inflation and variability of inflation across countries and across time for a given country.[10] In Friedman's analysis, a government may temporarily pursue a set of policy goals (output, employment) that leads to a high inflation rate, which induces strong political pressure to reduce it. The relationship between the level and the variability of inflation has been extensively investigated. Chowdhury (1991) has re-examined this issue for a sample of 66 countries for the 1955-85 period. His results indicate the presence of a significant positive relationship between the inflation rate and its variability. Figure 1 shows the scatter diagram for the level of inflation and its standard deviation for the 18 countries in our sample. Figure 1 clearly suggests the presence of a positive correlation between inflation and its variability for the periods after the demise of the Bretton-Woods system, but not for the period 1961-1969.

If inflation is low due to the independence of the monetary authorities, one would also expect that central bank independence yields a lower level of inflation variability. Using the Grilli-independence measure this is indeed the case for the entire sample period (upper part of Table 3). With one exception, this conclusion also holds for the sub periods. Similar results are reached when the Alesina and the Eijffinger-Schaling dummies are used (lower part of Table 3).[11] The differences that do occur are not due to differences in sample size. When we re-estimated the equation applying the Grilli-dummy for the Alesina and Eijffinger-Schaling groups of countries, similar results were reached. Our outcomes are in contrast to

[10] The discussion of the relationship between the level of inflation and its variability received an important impulse from Okun (1971) who conducted a cross-country study of 17 industrial economies for the period 1961-68. His results indicated that countries with high average inflation have more widely fluctuating inflation rates.

[11] We have also used the average absolute change of inflation as measure of inflation variability, but this does not change our outcome, which is in accordance with the findings of Chowdhury (1991).

the findings of Bade and Parkin (1988), who found no evidence for reduced inflation variability, but accord with the conclusions of Alesina and Summers (1991).

FIGURE 1

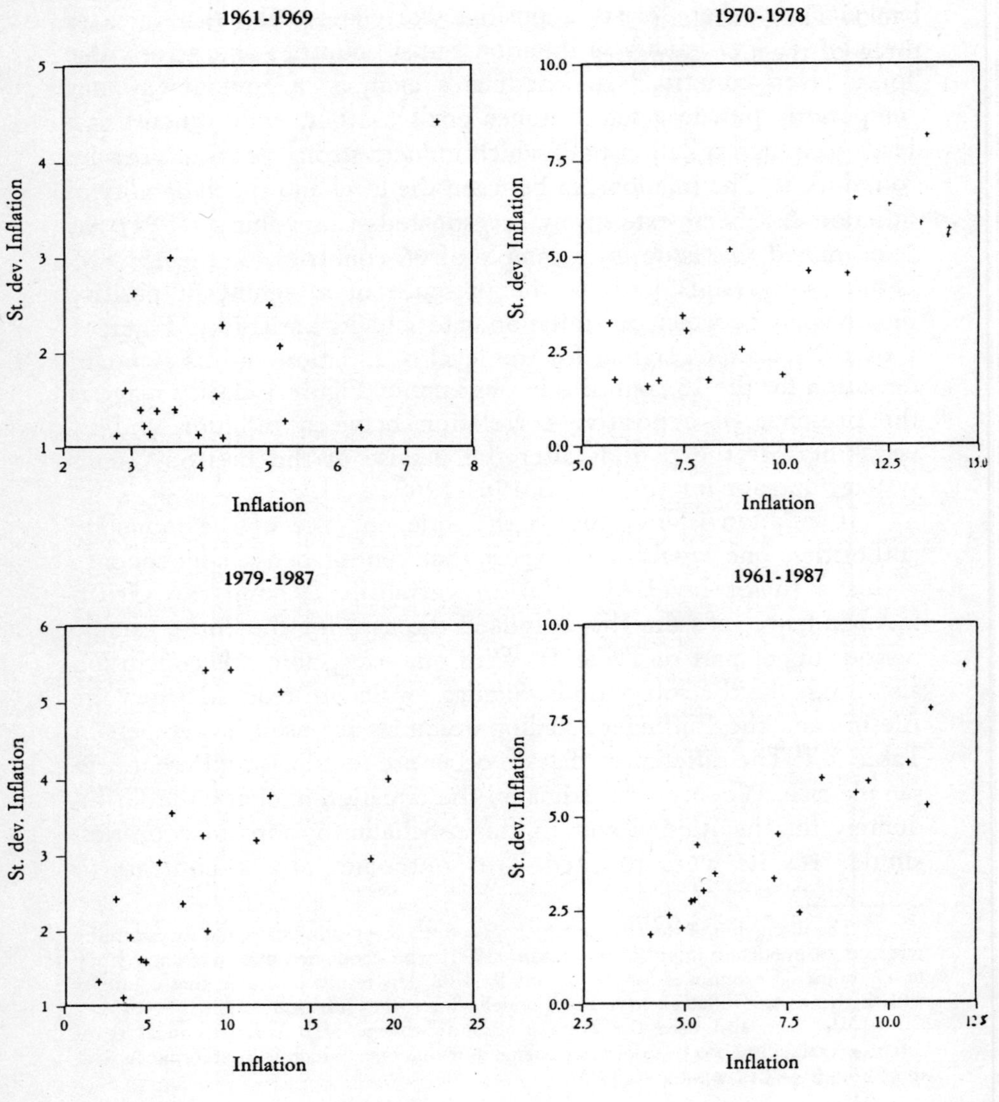

4. Central Bank Independence and Government Budget Deficits

An important test case for the independence of the central bank is whether they accommodate government budget deficits. Burdekin and Wohar (1990) have examined for eight countries whether deficit accommodation is more prevalent in countries with dependent central banks. They conclude that deficit accommodation occurs in at least three of the five countries with dependent central banks, while the most independent central banks (in Germany, Switzerland and the U.S.) do not accommodate deficits. These results accord with the pattern of deficit accommodation reported by Demopoulos *et al.* (1987) and Burdekin and Laney (1988), but are in contrast to the conclusions of other studies such as Giannaros and Kolluri (1985), Protopapadakis and Siegel (1987) and Barnhart and Darrat (1988) who found no evidence for a link between budget deficits and money growth, even in countries with a relatively dependent central bank.[12]

We have examined whether central bank credit to government, measured as the growth of the central bank's net claims on central government scaled by GDP, is influenced by central bank independence. Net claims are defined as central bank claims less government deposits with the central bank. The results are reported in Table 4. When the modified Grilli measure of central bank independence is used, it follows that relatively independent central banks provide less credit to government to finance budget deficits. However, when the Alesina and the Eijffinger-Schaling dummies are used, there is no support for this point of view (lower part of Table 4). These divergent outcomes are caused by differences in sample size. When we re-estimated the equations using the Grilli-independence measure for the Alesina and Eijffinger-Schaling groups of countries, respectively, it turned out that the coefficient of the Grilli-independence measure was insignificant in all regressions (not shown).

Central bank independence may also affect the size of the government budget deficit (Tabellini, 1986). A credible commitment not to inflate away the debt and not to provide monetary financing of

[12] DE HAAN and ZELHORST (1990) report that even in developing countries there is only limited evidence for a clear link between budget deficits and money growth.

TABLE 3

CENTRAL BANK INDEPENDENCE AND INFLATION VARIABILITY

Explanatory variables:	1961-1969	1970-1978	1979-1987	1961-1987
Intercept	2.77	7.15	4.15	7.58
	(0.51)	(1.02)	(0.82)	(1.00)
Independence dummy	–0.15	–0.46	–0.18	–0.49
	(0.07)*	(014)*	(0.11)	(014)*
adj. R^2	0.18	0.37	0.08	0.40
SE	0.81	1.63	1.31	1.61
Intercept	2.80	5.32	4.13	5.98
	(0.53)	(0.96)	(0.85)	(0.69)
Alesina dummy	–0.51	–0.80	–0.59	-1.03
	(0.22)*	(0.40)*	(0.35)	(0.29)*
adj. R^2	0.25	0.18	0.12	0.47
SE	0.83	1.50	1.24	1.08
Intercept	1.42	5.21	4.32	5.46
	(0.30)	(1.06)	(0.92)	(0.84)
ES dummy	–0.01	–0.61	–0.56	–0.66
	(0.10)	(0.34)	(0.29)	(0.27)*
adj. R2	–0.11	0.18	0.20	0.33
SE	0.43	1.50	1.31	1.19

Notes: Standard errors are in parentheses. An asterisk indicates that the coefficient is significantly different from zero at the 95% confidence level.

the deficit may strengthen the government's incentive to balance its budget.[13] Grilli *et al.* (1991) found no evidence for this point of view. Leone (1991) concludes that the experience of countries with chronic fiscal deficits seems to indicate that the establishment of limits on central bank lending to the government has not been sufficient to guarantee fiscal discipline. However, Parkin (1987) concludes that the

[13] The so-called "divorce" of July 1981 which freed the Italian central bank from the obligation to purchase all unsold public debt was partly motivated by the desire to moderate fiscal policy (TABELLINI 1987).

TABLE 4

CENTRAL BANK INDEPENDENCE AND CENTRAL BANK FINANCING OF GOVERNMENT BUDGET DEFICITS

Explanatory variables:	1961-1969	1970-1978	1979-1987	1961-1987
Intercept	0.0055	0.0186	0.0232	0.0150
	(0.004)	(0.006)	(0.007)	(0.004)
Independence dummy	−0.0002	−0.0018	−0.0023	−0.0013
	(0.0005)	(0.0008)*	(0.0010)*	(0.0006)*
adj. R^2	−0.05	0.18	0.23	0.17
SE	0.007	0.010	0.011	0.007
Intercept	0.0060	0.0124	0.0079	0.0099
	(0.005)	(0.005)	(0.004)	(0.003)
Alesina dummy	−0.0009	−0.0037	−0.0020	−0.0024
	(0.0020)	(0.0022)	(0.0015)	(0.0014)
adj. R^2	−0.07	0.12	0.06	0.15
SE	0.007	0.008	0.005	0.005
Intercept	0.0083	0.0096	0.0043	0.0068
	(0.006)	(0.007)	(0.003)	(0.004)
ES dummy	−0.0011	−0.0019	−0.0007	−0.0008
	(0.0018)	(0.0022)	(0.0010)	(0.0014)
adj. R^2	−0.07	−0.03	−0.05	−0.07
SE	0.008	0.010	0.004	0.006

Notes: Standard errors are in parentheses. An asterisk indicates that the coefficient is significantly different from zero at the 95% confidence level.

two countries in his sample that have the most independent central bank (Germany and Switzerland) have deficit processes with little uncertainty and steady state values that are very close to zero. Masciandaro and Tabellini (1988) examine five countries (Australia, Canada, Japan, New Zealand, and the United States) and find that New Zealand which had (until recently) the least independent central bank also had the highest average of deficits.

Table 5 shows the outcomes of regressions of the government budget surplus scaled by GDP and the dummies for central bank independence. It is quite clear that central bank independence matters for the level of government budget deficits. During the period 1979-1989 most countries had rapidly growing budget deficits, but in countries with an independent central bank deficits increased less. As the middle part of Table 5 shows, it makes a difference when the Alesina dummy is used: in the period 1979-87, for instance, the coefficient of the independence dummy is no longer significantly

TABLE 5

CENTRAL BANK INDEPENDENCE AND GOVERNMENT BUDGET DEFICITS

Explanatory variables:	1961-1969	1970-1978	1979-1987	1961-1987
Intercept	–0.03	–0.05	–0.12	–0.07
	(0.01)	(0.02)	(0.02)	(0.02)
Independence dummy	0.002	0.003	0.008	0.005
	(0.001)	(0.002)	(0.003)*	(0.002)*
adj. R^2	0.06	0.07	0.30	0.31
SE	0.015	0.026	0.034	0.023
Intercept	–0.03	–0.05	–0.08	–0.06
	(0.01)	(0.01)	(0.03)	(0.01)
Alesina dummy	0.007	0.010	0.014	0.013
	(0.003)	(0.006)	(0.011)	(0.005)*
adj. R^2	0.35	0.12	0.06	0.35
SE	0.009	0.022	0.036	0.018
Intercept	–0.02	–0.04	–0.06	–0.04
	(0.01)	(0.02)	(0.03)	(0.02)
ES dummy	0.003	0.006	0.007	0.005
	(0.002)	(0.005)	(0.009)	(0.005)
adj. R^2	0.10	0.03	–0.05	–0.01
SE	0.009	0.023	0.040	0.023

Notes: Standard errors are in parentheses. An asterisk indicates that the coefficient is significantly different from zero at the 95% confidence level.

different from zero. This is not caused by the exclusion of some high deficit countries (Greece, Ireland, Portugal) in the Alesina sample. When we re-estimated the equation using the Grilli independence measure for the Alesina sample of countries, the results are almost exactly the same as for the sample of 18 countries. The coefficient of the independence dummy for the period 1979-87 is 0.007, significantly different from zero. In the regressions in which the Eijffinger-Schaling dummy is used (lower part of Table 5), the coefficient is always insignificantly different from zero. This is also not caused by differences in sample size.

5. Central Bank Independence and Economic Growth

With respect to the effect of central bank independence on economic growth, two opposing views have been put forward in the literature. Some authors have argued that the real interest rate depends upon money growth, *i.e.* they assume that the Fisher hypothesis does not hold due to the Mundell-Tobin effect. A low level of inflation which is caused by restrictive monetary policy results in high real interest rates, which may have detrimental effects on the level of investment, and hence on economic growth. There seems to be evidence in favour of the first part of the argument: countries with a low level of inflation have high *ex post* real interest rates (figure 2).

There are, however, also some arguments as to why central bank independence may promote economic growth. First, an independent central bank may be less prone to political pressures and therefore behave more predictably, which may enhance economic stability and economic growth. Second, many economists, especially those involved in central banking, believe that even moderate rates of inflation impose significant economic costs on society. Recently Grimes (1991) and Fischer (1991) have provided evidence supporting the view that inflation is harmful to economic growth. One channel by which this effect may operate is increased inflation uncertainty. As previously pointed out, there exists a strong link between the level and the variability of inflation. High variability may lead to high inflation uncertainty which, in turn, may affect economic growth. As shown, central bank independence reduces inflation variability. If this reduction in inflation variability also leads to lower inflation uncertainty it may have a positive effect on economic growth. The empirical evidence on the relationship between inflation variability

FIGURE 2

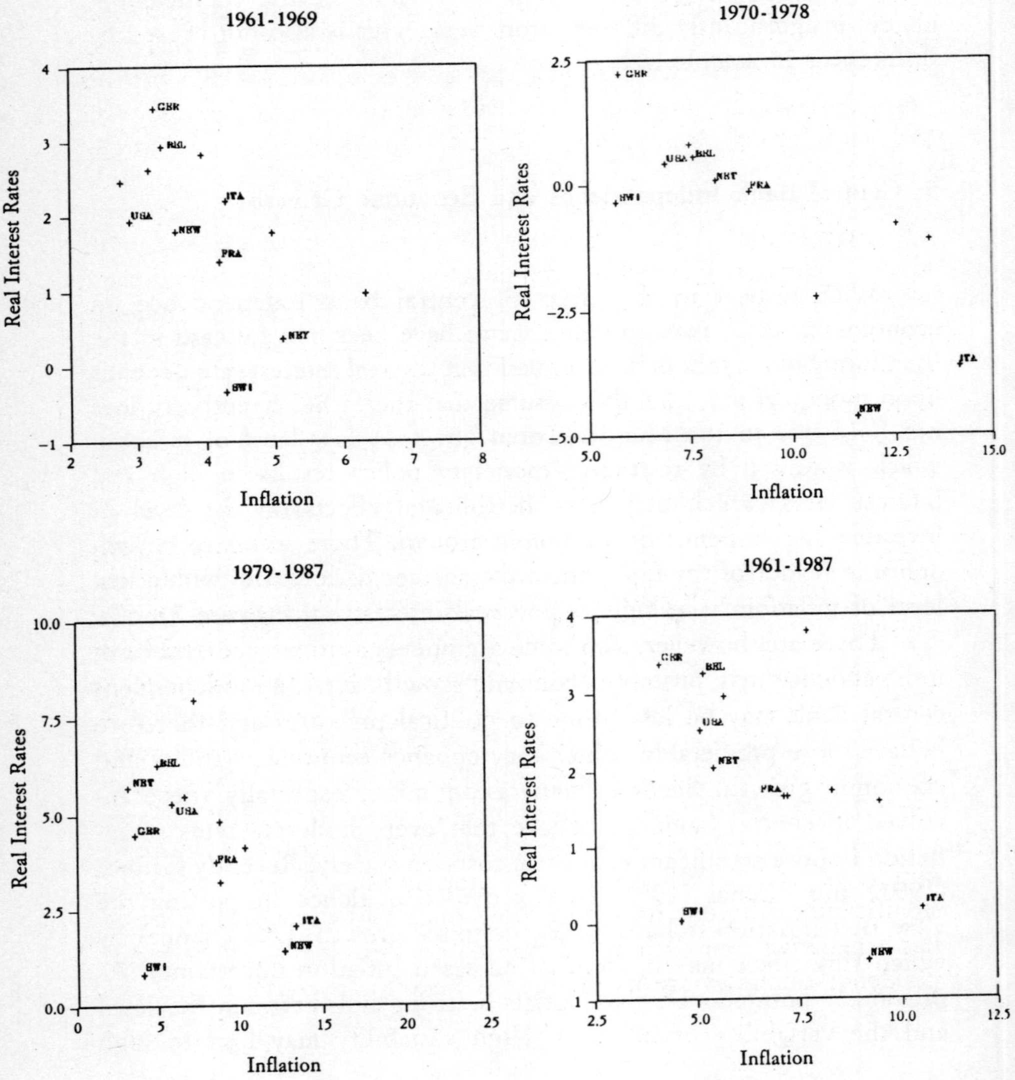

and inflation uncertainty on economic growth is, however, not very supportive for this point of view. Using annual data for 24 countries, Logue and Sweeney (1981) find no evidence for a significant negative impact of inflation variability on real growth. A similar conclusion is reached by Jansen (1989). Engle (1983) has found little evidence for a link between the relatively high rates of inflation experienced by the United States in the 1970s and inflation uncertainty. However, Cukierman and Wachtel (1979), for example, report a positive correlation between the rate of inflation and the dispersion on inflation forecasts gathered from the Michigan and Livingston inflation surveys. Recently Evans (1991) has published evidence which is consistent with the point of view that uncertainty about the long-term prospects for inflation is strongly linked to the actual rate of inflation.

Grilli *et al.* (1991) and Alesina and Summers (1991) conclude that central bank independence has no effect on economic growth. Although central bank independence seems to be associated with lower output growth, the estimated effect is generally insignificant. We reach a similar conclusion (Table 6). It is clear that, whatever measure of central bank independence is used, its coefficient is insignificantly different from zero. Given the widespread belief that a restrictive monetary policy may be harmful for economic growth, it is remarkable that central bank independence apparently has so few detrimental effects on real growth.

We have examined whether central bank independence has any influence on the variability of economic growth, measured by the standard deviation of GDP growth. It is likely that some kind of trade-off exists between the variability of inflation and the variability of output growth. Rogoff (1985) provides, for instance, a model in which independent central bankers engage in fewer stabilization policies at the expense of more cyclical variability in economic activity. Table 7 contains the estimation results, using the standard deviation of GNP growth as measure of output variability. There is no support for the view that central bank independence yields higher output variability. When the Grilli dummy is used, its coefficient is significantly different from zero only once and then the coefficient has a negative sign. When the Alesina and Eijffinger-Schaling independence dummies are used, there is also no support for increased

TABLE 6

CENTRAL BANK INDEPENDENCE AND ECONOMIC GROWTH

Explanatory variables:	1961-1969	1970-1978	1979-1987	1961-1987
Intercept	6.84	4.88	2.39	4.70
	(1.07)	(0.67)	(0.45)	(0.60)
Independence dummy	–0.20	–0.17	–0.02	–0.13
	(0.15)	(0.09)	(0.06)	(0.08)
adj. R^2	0.11	0.13	–0.06	0.08
SE	1.71	1.06	0.71	0.96
Intercept	5.46	3.96	2.33	3.94
	(1.24)	(0.65)	(0.52)	(0.70)
Alesina dummy	–0.02	–0.27	–0.01	–0.11
	(0.52)	(0.27)	(0.22)	(0.30)
adj. R^2	–0.08	–0.04	–0.08	–0.07
SE	1.94	1.02	0.76	1.10
Intercept	5.55	4.49	3.11	4.38
	(1.43)	(0.65)	(0.54)	(0.80)
ES dummy	–0.05	–0.36	–0.27	–0.23
	(0.46)	(0.21)	(0.17)	(0.26)
adj. R^2	–0.10	0.16	0.12	–0.02
SE	2.03	0.92	0.77	1.13

output variability (lower part of Table 7). This confirms results reported by Alesina and Summers (1991).

6. Concluding Comments

This analysis would suggest that central bank independence matters. An important issue for future research is to explain the behaviour of a relatively independent central bank, *i.e.* what does the objective function of such a central bank look like, and why? In the

TABLE 7

CENTRAL BANK INDEPENDENCE AND ECONOMIC GROWTH VARIABILITY

Explanatory variables:	1961-1969	1970-1978	1979-1987	1961-1987
Intercept	2.14	3.54	1.61	3.18
	(0.39)	(0.46)	(0.36)	(0.34)
Independence dummy	-0.01	-0.12	0.03	-0.08
	(0.05)	(0.06)*	(0.05)	(0.05)
adj. R^2	-0.06	0.15	-0.04	0.10
SE	0.62	0.73	0.58	0.55
Intercept	1.97	2.09	2.18	2.43
	(0.42)	(0.37)	(0.41)	(0.32)
Alesina dummy	0.01	0.21	-0.17	0.06
	(0.07)	(0.16)	(0.17)	(0.13)
adj. R^2	-0.08	0.04	0.002	-0.06
SE	0.66	0.60	0.59	0.50
Intercept	1.44	1.89	2.36	2.19
	(0.48)	(0.46)	(0.44)	(0.36)
ES dummy	0.17	0.22	-0.21	0.12
	(0.15)	(0.15)	(0.14)	(0.12)
adj. R^2	0.02	0.11	0.11	0.001
SE	0.68	0.66	0.62	0.51

Notes: Standard errors are in parentheses. An asterisk indicates that the coefficient is significantly different from zero at the 95% confidence level.

literature reviewed in this paper, it is generally assumed that a central bank which is less prone to political manipulation will follow less inflationary policies and behave more predictably. It should be pointed out, however, that the first part of this argument does not necessarily imply the second part.

Our analysis suggests that an independent central bank yields lower inflation rates without economic sacrifices such as lower output. Does this mean that a central bank should be as independent as possible? The answer depends, of course, on the costs and benefits of inflation. It is well known that the costs of inflation depend on the sources of the inflation, on whether it was anticipated and on the institutional structure of the economy (see Fischer and Modigliani, 1978, and Fischer, 1981). The benefits of inflation have generally been studied in a public finance context. Inflation implies proceeds for government due to the creation of high powered money ("seignorage") and/or reduction of the real value of its outstanding debt. Various authors have analyzed the optimal level of inflation. The less recent literature, of which Friedman (1971) is a well known example, only considers government revenue due to inflation. In more recent studies seignorage is treated like other taxes; optimal fiscal policy must minimize the social losses caused by various taxes under the restriction of the government budget constraint (Mankiw, 1987). Optimal fiscal policy considerations have been put forward by Dornbusch (1988) as an argument against European monetary integration (see also van der Ploeg, 1990). This view has been disputed by Gross (1990), who argues that the view that the loss of seignorage should be avoided rests on the assumption that outside the EMS these countries would choose the optimal amount of seignorage. As pointed out, however, there always exists a strong incentive for countries with a high level of public debt to use surprise inflation to reduce the real burden of servicing this debt. Furthermore, there is hardly any empirical support for the "optimal taxation" approach (see, for example Grilli *et al.,* 1991), so this argument against central bank independence does not seem to be well founded.

Groningen

JAKOB DE HAAN - JAN EGBERT STURM

APPENDIX

CENTRAL BANK INDEPENDENCE MEASURES

Country	Modified Grilli	Alesina	Eijffinger-Schaling
1. Australia	9	1	1
2. Austria	7	n.a.	n.a.
3. Belgium	5	2	3
4. Canada	9	2	1
5. Denmark	6	2	n.a.
6. France	5	2	2
7. Germany	12	4	5
8. Greece	4	n.a.	n.a.
9. Ireland	7	n.a.	n.a.
10. Italy	5	1/2	2
11. Japan	5	3	3
12. Netherlands	10	2	4
13. New Zealand	3	1	n.a.
14. Portugal	3	n.a.	n.a.
15. Spain	4	1	n.a.
16. Switzerland	10	4	5
17. United Kindom	6	2	2
18. United States	11	3	3

The modified Grilli measure is based on Table 12 and Table 13 of Grilli *et al.* (1991), measuring political independence (determined by: 1. the procedures for appointing board members; 2. the relationship between the governing board of the central bank and the government; and 3. formal responsibilities for monetary policy) and economic independence (determined by the influence of the government in deciding how much to borrow from the central bank and the nature of the monetary instruments under control of the central bank). The measure used in our empirical analysis consists of the total number of entries in both tables, except for the entries which are related to supervision of the banking system. Whether or not a central bank has any responsibility for bank supervision provides, in our view, no information as to its independence. Although it is, without doubt, true that the "lender of last resort" function of a central bank may conflict with its task of safeguarding the currency, transferring the task of banking supervision to another organization does not remove this potential conflict. Entries included are related to the appointment of the governing board, the relationship with government, constitution, and monetary financing of the government's budget deficit. A higher number of entries implies more independence. The Alesina independence measure is taken from Alesina (1989; 1988), while the measure of Eijffinger and Schaling is taken from

Eijffinger and Schaling (1992). The Alesina measure is based upon previous work by Bade and Parkin (1988), who distinguish between policy and financial independence. The degree of policy independence is determined using three criteria: (1) final responsibility for monetary policy; (2) the presence of a government official on the bank board; and (3) whether board appointments are made independent of government. Financial independence is also based upon three criteria: (1) the budgetary autonomy of the bank; (2) the determination of the board members' salaries; and (3) decision making on profit allocation. The Eijffinger-Schaling index is determined using three criteria: (1) responsibility for monetary policy; (2) the presence of a government official on the bank board; and (3) whether more than half of the board appointments are made independent of the government.

CORRELATION MATRIX OF THE VARIOUS INDEPENDENCE MEASURES

	Grilli	Alesina	Eijffinger-Schaling
Grilli	1.00		
Alesina	0.64	1.00	
Eijffinger-Schaling	0.47	0.82	1.00

J.D.H. - J.E.S.

REFERENCES

AKHTAR, M.A. and H. HOWE (1991), "The Political and Institutional Independence of U.S. Monetary Policy", in this *Review*, 178, 343-389.

ALESINA, A. (1988), "Macroeconomics and Politics", in: *NBER Macroeconomics Annual*, Cambridge: MIT Press.

ALESINA, A. (1989), "Politics and Business Cycles in Industrial Democracies", *Economic Policy*, 8, 57-98.

ALESINA, A. and J. SACHS (1988), "Political Parties and the Business Cycle in the United States", *Journal of Money, Credit and Banking*, 20, 63-82.

ALESINA, A. and L.H. SUMMERS (1991), "Central Bank Independence and Macroeconomic Performance: Some Comparative Evidence", Harvard University, mimeo.

ALLEN, S.D. (1986), "The Federal Reserve and the Electoral Cycle", *Journal of Money, Credit and Banking*, 18, 88-99.

BADE, R. and M. PARKIN (1988), "Central Bank Laws and Monetary Policy", University of Western Ontario, mimeo.

BARNHART, S.W. and A.F. DARRAT (1988), "Budget Deficits, Money Growth and Causality: Further OECD Evidence", *Journal of International Money and Finance*, 7, 231-242.

BARRO, R.J. and D. GORDON (1983), "Rules, Discretion, and Reputation in a Positive Model of Monetary Policy", *Journal of Monetary Economics*, 12, 101-121.

BECK, N. (1988), "Politics and Monetary Policy", in: T.D. Willett (ed.), *Political Business Cycles*, London: Duke University Press.

BOYES, W.J., W.S. MOUNTS and C. SOWELL (1988), "The Federal Reserve as a Bureaucracy: An Examination of Expense-Preference Behavior", *Journal of Money, Credit and Banking*, 20, 181-190.

BUCHANAN, J.M. and R.M. WAGNER (1977), *Democracy in Deficit*, Homewood.

BURDEKIN, R.C. and L.O. LANEY (1988), "Fiscal Policy Making and the Central Bank Institutional Constraint", *Kyklos*, 41, 647-662.

BURDEKIN, R.C. and M.E. WOHAR (1990), "Monetary Institutions, Budget Deficits and Inflation", *European Journal of Political Economy*, 6, 531-551.

CHOWDHURY, A.R. (1991), "The Relationship between the Inflation Rate and its Variability: The Issues Reconsidered", *Applied Economics*, 23, 993-1003.

CUKIERMAN, A. and A.H. MELTZER (1988), "A Positive Theory of Discretionary Policy, the Cost of a Democratic Government, and the Benefits of a Constitution", *Economic Inquiry*.

CUKIERMAN, A. and P. WACHTEL (1979), "Differential Inflationary Expectations and the Variability of the Rate of Inflation", *American Economic Review*, 69, 595-609.

DEMOPOULOS, C.D., G.M. KATSIMBRIS and S.M. MILLER (1987), "Monetary Policy and Central-Bank Financing of Government Budget Deficits", *European Economic Review*, 31, 1023-1050.

DORNBUSCH, R. (1988), "The European Monetary System, the Dollar and the Yen", in: F. Giavazzi, S. Micossi and M. Miller (eds.), *The European Monetary System*, Cambridge: Cambridge University Press.

EIJFFINGER, S. and SCHALING, E. (1992), "Central Bank Independence: Criteria and Indices", Tilburg University, *Research memorandum*, 548, forthcoming in *Suerf Papers*.

ENGLE, R.F. (1983), "Estimates of the Variance of U.S. Inflation Based upon the ARCH Model", *Journal of Money, Credit and Banking*, 15, 286-301.

EVANS, M. (1991), "Discovering the Link between Inflation Rates and Inflation Uncertainty", *Journal of Money, Credit and Banking*, 23, 169-184.

FISCHER, S. (1981), "Toward an Understanding of the Costs of Inflation II", in: *Carnegie Rochester Conference Series on Public Policy*, edited by K. Brunner and A.H. Meltzer, 15.

FISCHER, S. (1991), "Growth, Macroeconomics, and Development", *NBER Working Paper*, 3702.

FISCHER, S. and F. MODIGLIANI (1978), "Toward an Understanding of the Real Effects and Costs of Inflation", *Weltwirtschaftliches Archiv*, 114, 810-833.

FRIEDMAN, M. (1971), "Government Revenue from Inflation", *Journal of Political Economy*, 79, 846-856.

FRIEDMAN, M. (1977), "Nobel Lecture: Inflation and Unemployment", *Journal of Political Economy*, 85, 451-472.

GIANNAROS, D.S. and B.R. KOLLURI (1985), "Deficits Spending, Money, and Inflation: Some International Empirical Evidence", *Journal of Macroeconomics*, 7, 401-417.

GRIER, K.B., (1991) "Congressional Influence on U.S. Monetary Policy", *Journal of Monetary Economics*, 28, 201-220.

GRILLI, V., D. MASCIANDARO and G. TABELLINI (1991), "Political and Monetary Institutions and Public Financial Policies in the Industrial Countries", *Economic Policy*, 13, 341-392.

GRIMES, A. (1991), "The Effects of Inflation on Growth: Some International Evidence", *Weltwirtschaftliches Archiv*, 127, 631-644.

GROSS, D. (1990), "Seignorage and EMS discipline" in: P. de Grauwe and L. Papademos (eds.), *The European Monetary System in the 1990's*, London: Longman.

HAVRILESKY, T. (1988), "Monetary Policy Signaling from the Administration to the Federal Reserve", *Journal of Money, Credit and Banking*, 20, 83-101.

HAAN, J. DE and D. ZELHORST (1990), "The Impact of Government Deficits on Money Growth in Developing Countries", *Journal of International Money and Finance*, 9, 455-469.

HAAN, J. DE and D. ZELHORST (1991), "Positive Theories of Public Debt: Some Evidence for Germany", forthcoming in: H. Verbon and F. van Winden (eds.), *The Political Economy of Government Debt*, Amsterdam: North Holland.

HIBBS, D.A. (1987), *The American Political Economy*, Cambridge: Harvard University Press.

JANSEN, D.W. (1989), "Does Inflation Uncertainty Affect Output Growth? Further Evidence", *Federal Reserve Bank of St. Louis Review*, July/August, 43-54.

KANE, E. (1980), "Politics and Fed Policymaking: The More Things Change, the More They Remain the Same", *Journal of Monetary Economics*, 6, 199-212.

LEONE, A. (1991), "Effectiveness and Implications of Limits on Central Bank Credit to the Government", in: P. Downes and R. Vaez-Zadeh (eds.), *The Evolving Role of Central Banks*, Washington: IMF.

LOGUE, D.E. and R.J. SWEENEY (1981), "Inflation and Real Growth: Some Empirical Results", *Journal of Monetary, Credit and Banking*, 13, 497-501.

MASCIANDARO, D. and G. TABELLINI (1988), "Monetary Regimes and Fiscal Deficits – A Comparative Analysis", in: H.S. Cheng (ed.), *Monetary Policy in Pacific Basin Countries*, Dordrecht: Kluwer Academic Publishers.

MANKIW, N.G. (1987), "The Optimal Collection of Seignorage: Theory and Evidence", *NBER Working Paper*, 2270.

NEUMANN, M.J.M. (1991), "Precommitment by Central Bank Independence", *Open Economies Review*, 2, 95-112.

NORDHAUS, W. (1975), "The Political Business Cycle", *Review of Economic Studies*, 42, 169-190.

OKUN, A. (1971), "The Mirage of Steady Inflation", *Brookings Papers on Economic Activity*, 2, 485-498.

PARKIN, M. (1987), "Domestic Monetary Institutions and the Deficit", in: J.M. Buchanan, C.K. Rowley and R.D. Tollison (eds.), *Deficits*, Oxford: Basil Blackwell.

PLOEG, F. VAN DER (1990), "Budgetary Aspects of Economic and Monetary Integration in Europe", Center Tilburg University, mimeo.

Protopapadakis, A.A. and J.J. Siegel (1987), "Are Money Growth and Inflation Related to Government Deficits? Evidence from 10 Industrialized Economies", *Journal of International Money and Finance*, 6, 31-48.

Rogoff, K. (1985), "The Optimal Degree of Commitment to an Intermediate Monetary Target", *Quarterly Journal of Economics*, 110, 1169-1190.

Rogoff, K. and A. Sibert (1988), "Elections and Macroeconomic Policy Cycles", *Review of Economic Studies*, 55, 1-16.

Sargent, T.J. and N. Wallace (1981), "Some Unpleasant Monetarist Arithmetic", *Federal Reserve Bank of Minneapolis Quarterly Review*, 5, 1-17.

Tabellini, C. (1986), "Money, Debt and Deficits in a Dynamic Game", *Journal Economic Dynamics and Control*, 10, 427-442.

Tabellini, G. (1987), "Central Bank Reputation and the Monetization of Deficits: The 1981 Italian Monetary Reform", *Economic Inquiry*, 25, 185-200.

Toma, M. (1982), "Inflationary Bias of the Federal Reserve System: A Bureaucratic Perspective", *Journal of Monetary Economics*, 10, 163-190.

[14]

ALBERTO ALESINA
LAWRENCE H. SUMMERS

Central Bank Independence and Macroeconomic Performance: Some Comparative Evidence

THE DEGREE OF CENTRAL BANK INDEPENDENCE varies considerably across countries. Several authors including Bade and Parkin (1982), Alesina (1988, 1989), and Grilli, Masciandaro, and Tabellini (1991) found that more independent central banks are associated with lower levels of inflation. This note investigates whether one can find a correlation between central bank independence and the level and variability of real economic variables such as growth, unemployment, and real interest rates. Our conclusion is that while central bank independence promotes price stability, it has no measurable impact on real economic performance.

1. THEORY

As Rogoff (1985) notes, dynamic inconsistency theories of inflation of the type developed in Kydland and Prescott (1977) and Barro and Gordon (1983) make it plausible that more independent central banks will reduce the rate of inflation. Delegating monetary policy to an agent whose preferences are more inflation averse than are society's preferences serves as a commitment device that permits sustaining a lower rate of inflation than would otherwise be possible. Alesina and Grilli (1992) develop this argument by showing that the "median voter" would want to appoint a

The authors are indebted to Robert Barro for useful discussions, to two anonymous referees for comments and to Gerald Cohen and Jeffrey Mantz for research assistance. Alesina thanks the Sloan Foundation for financial support.

ALBERTO ALESINA *is the Paul Sack Associate Professor of political economy at Harvard University and a fellow of both the Center for Economic Policy Research and the National Bureau of Economic Research.* LAWRENCE H. SUMMERS *is professor of economics at Harvard University and an associate of the National Bureau of Economic Research.*

Journal of Money, Credit, and Banking, Vol. 25, No. 2 (May 1993)

central banker more inflation averse than himself. However, the "median voter" wants to be "time inconsistent" and recall the central banker, who, ex post, is being too conservative on the inflation front.

Insulating monetary policy from the political process avoids this problem and helps enforce the low inflation equilibrium. Without some degree of political independence, it would be impossible to appoint a central banker more inflation averse than a majority of the voters, which is a socially desirable goal.

What about the effect of central bank independence on real variables? Maintaining the presumption that monetary policy has real effects, plausible arguments point in varying directions. Central bank independence might improve real economic performance for several reasons. First, an independent central bank that is free from political pressure may behave more predictably, promoting economic stability and reducing risk premia in real interest rates. More specifically, an independent central bank may serve to insulate the economy from political business cycles either by preventing preelection manipulation of monetary policy as in the models of Nordhaus (1975), and Rogoff and Sibert (1988) or by reducing partisan shocks to policy following elections as in the models of Hibbs (1987) and Alesina (1988, 1989). For a more extensive theoretical and empirical discussion of the politics of monetary policy and of political business cycles see Willett (1988).[1]

Second, to the extent that high inflation has adverse effects on economic performance either by creating distortions, encouraging rent seeking activity, or by raising risk premia, one would expect central bank independence to improve economic performance. If, as is often suggested (for example, Romer and Romer (1989)) most U.S. recessions result from the Federal Reserve cracking down on inflation after it has been allowed to increase too much, one might expect that more consistently inflation-averse policy would be associated with less variable economic performance.

On the other hand, traditional arguments for monetary policies that are politically responsive stress that politically sensitive central bankers are likely to be more concerned than independent bankers with increasing output and reducing unemployment and real interest rates. If monetary policy can achieve these objectives one might expect independent central banks to achieve lower rates of inflation at the price of inferior real economic performance. Rogoff (1985) provides a formal model of this trade-off; in his model more inflation-averse central bankers engage in less discretionary stabilization economic policy and therefore tolerate more cyclical variability in economic activity.

The impact of central bank independence on economic performance is ultimately an empirical question. We therefore turn to the data.

2. MEASURING CENTRAL BANK INDEPENDENCE

The central difficulty in examining the question of central bank independence is measuring the independence of the central bank in different countries, a task at-

[1]This volume, in addition to political business cycles models, considers "bureaucratic" models of central banks, in which the latter are viewed as bureaucratic bodies whose goal is to maximize their influence.

tempted by several authors. Bade and Parkin (1982) construct a (1–4) scale of central bank independence for twelve countries based on the "political independence" of the central bank. Using the same criteria as Bade and Parkin, Alesina (1988) adds four more countries. Political independence is taken to depend on the institutional relationship between the central bank and the executive, the procedure to nominate and dismiss the head of the central bank, the role of government officials on the central bank board, and the frequency of contacts between the executive and the bank. We rely upon the amended version of the Bade and Parkin scale provided in Alesina (1988).

More recently Grilli, Masciandaro, and Tabellini (1991) construct a related measure of central bank independence that reflects both "political independence" and "economic independence." Political independence is defined essentially as in Bade and Parkin (1982), as the ability of the central bank to select its policy objectives without influence from the government. This measure is based on factors such as whether or not its governor and the board are appointed by the government, the length of their appointments, whether government representatives sit on the board of the bank, whether government approval for monetary policy decisions is required and whether the "price stability" objective is explicitly and prominently part of the central bank statute. "Economic independence" is defined as the ability to use instruments of monetary policy without restrictions. The most common constraint imposed upon the conduct of monetary policy is the extent to which the central bank is required to finance government deficit. This index of economic independence essentially measures how easy it is for the government to finance its deficits by direct access to credit from the central bank.[2]

Table 1 highlights the two indices and our averaging procedure: both indices are defined as *increasing* in the amount of *independence,* and are broadly consistent with each other.[3] In our empirical work which follows, we use the average of the two indices, which is reported in the last column of Table 1. Very similar results are obtained when either scale is used individually.[4]

It should be emphasized that the rankings summarized above reflect central banks' laws and constitutions. Such laws are subject to change, although quite infrequently. The rankings described above are relevant for the sample period studied here, 1955–88. Very recently, the degree of central bank independence has been increased in a few countries. These changes are, however, too recent to be relevant for our sample.[5]

[2]For more details on the construction of this index, the reader is referred to Grilli, Masciandaro, and Tabellini (1991).

[3]Broadly speaking, the difference between the two indices arises mostly from the fact that Grilli, Masciandaro, and Tabellini (1991) place more weight than Bade and Parkin (1982) on rules concerning monetary financing of government deficits.

[4]The index by Grilli, Masciandaro, and Tabellini is not available for the three Scandinavian countries (Finland, Norway, and Sweden). For two of these countries we relied on the Bade and Parkin index.

[5]This is the case, for instance, in Canada, Italy, and New Zealand. Changes in central bank laws might be endogenous, in the sense that governments may respond with institutional reforms to periods of high inflation. See Cukierman, Webb, and Neyapti (1991) for a discussion of this issue in a large sample of countries.

TABLE 1

INDEX OF CENTRAL BANK INDEPENDENCE

Country	BP[1]	GMT[2]	Conversion from GMT to BP[3]	Average GMT, BP[4]
Australia	1	9	3	2
Belgium	2	7	2	2
Canada	2	11	3	2.5
Denmark	2	8	3	2.5
France	2	7	2	2
Germany	4	13	4	4
Italy	1.5	5	2	1.75
Japan	3	6	2	2.5
Netherlands	2	10	3	2.5
Norway	2	NA	NA	2
New Zealand	1	3	1	1
Spain	1	5	2	1.5
Sweden	2	NA	NA	2
Switzerland	4	12	4	4
United Kingdom	2	6	2	2
United States	3	12	4	3.5

1. This is the index originally proposed by Bade and Parkin (1982) and extended by Alesina (1988).
2. Sum of the indexes of economic and political independence computed by Grilli, Masciandaro, and Tabellini (1991).
3. Conversion from the GMT scale to a (1) to (4) scale comparable with the BP scale. The conversion is as follows:

GMT index (i)	conversion
$i > 11$	4
$7 < i \leq 11$	3
$4 < i \leq 7$	2
$i \leq 4$	1

4. Average of columns (1) and (3).

3. CENTRAL BANK INDEPENDENCE AND MACROECONOMIC PERFORMANCE

Our empirical procedure is extremely simple. We plot various measures of economic performance covering the entire 1955–1988 period against measures of central bank independence. Using the data in the Appendix (Tables A1 and A2) we have verified that similar results obtain for the post–oil shock 1973–1988 period. Figure 1a verifies what previous work has highlighted—a near perfect negative correlation between inflation and central bank independence. Given the well-documented correlation between the level and variability of inflation, it is not surprising that Figure 1b reveals a strong negative relationship between inflation variability and central bank independence.

Figures 2a and 2b investigate the relationship between central bank independence and either the level or variability of economic growth. None emerges. Switzerland, which has an extremely independent central bank, shows much slower and variable growth than the average country in the sample, while Germany and Netherlands which also have relatively independent central banks have relatively good economic performance. On the other hand, countries with relatively dependent central banks such as Spain and New Zealand have relatively variable economic growth whereas France with a relatively dependent central bank has enjoyed steady growth.[6] Analo-

[6]These results are consistent with similar findings obtained independently by Grilli, Masciandaro, and Tabellini (1991), who use a different sample and methodology.

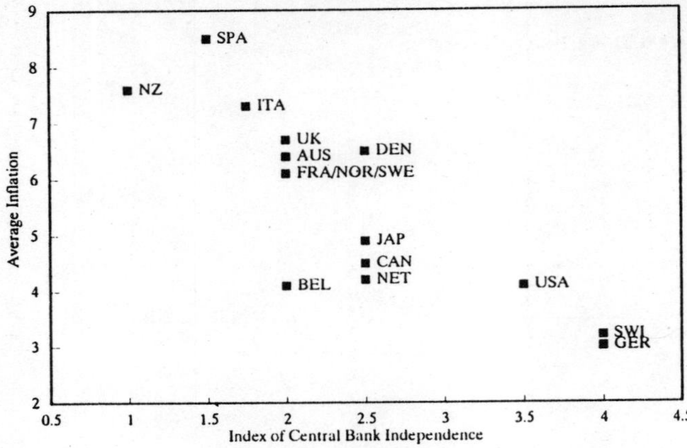

FIG. 1a. Average Inflation

gous results are obtained if one uses growth of GNP per capita, as shown in Figures 3a and 3b.

Figures 4a and 4b repeat the analysis for unemployment. Despite the fact noted by Summers and Wadwhani (1989) that the correlation between unemployment performance and real GNP growth performance is low, the unemployment measures also do not appear to be closely related to the measures of central bank independence.

Figures 5a and 5b examine the relationship between central bank independence and real interest rates. No clear relation can be found between independence and average ex post real interest rates. Nor does a comparison of central bank independence with the ex ante real interest rate measures (not shown) constructed by Barro

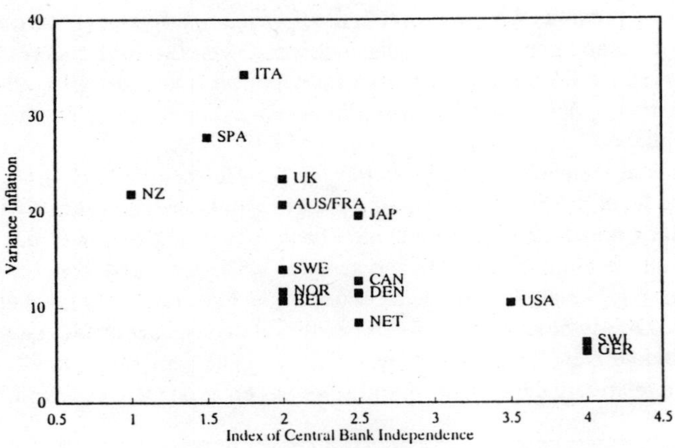

FIG. 1b. Variance Inflation

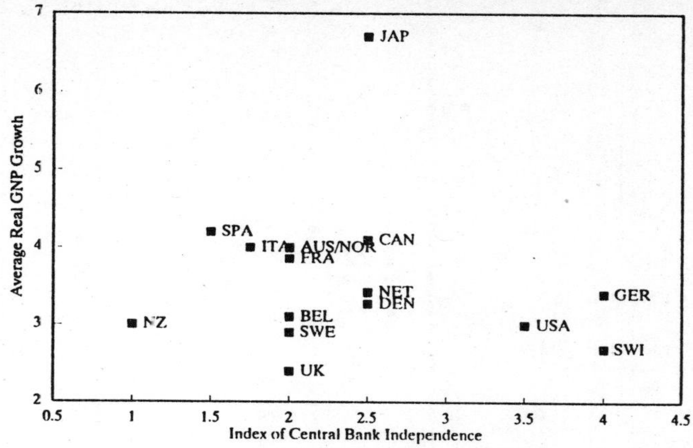

FIG. 2a. Average Real GNP Growth

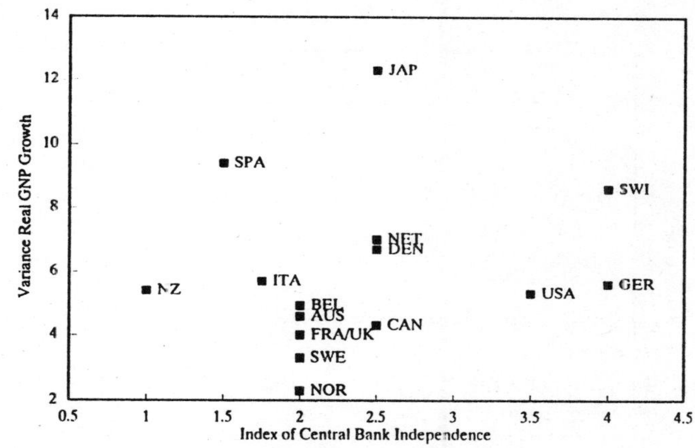

FIG. 2b. Variance Real GNP Growth

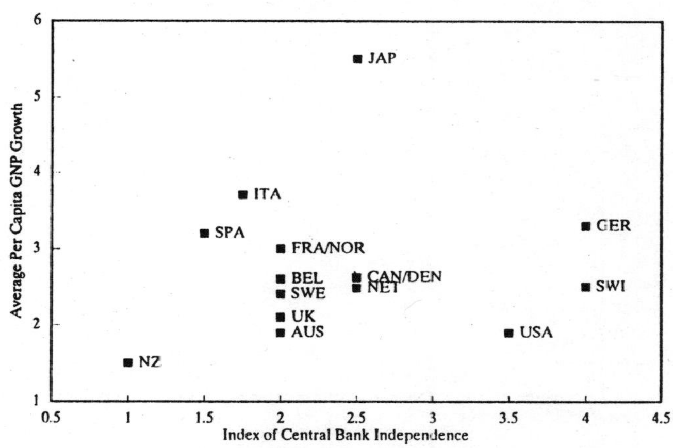

FIG. 3a. Average Per Capital GNP Growth

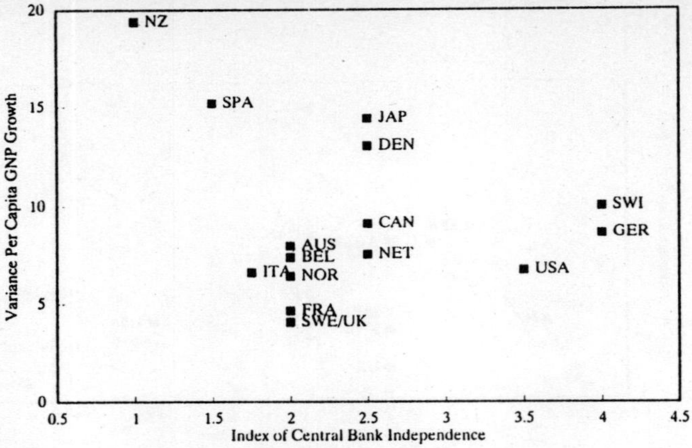

FIG. 3b. Variance Per Capital GNP Growth

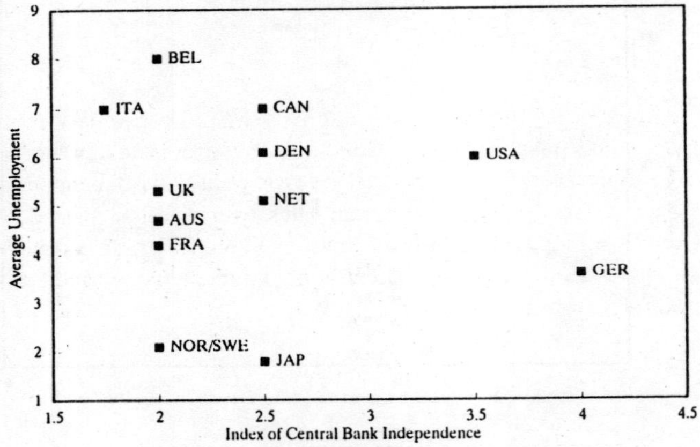

FIG. 4a. Average Unemployment

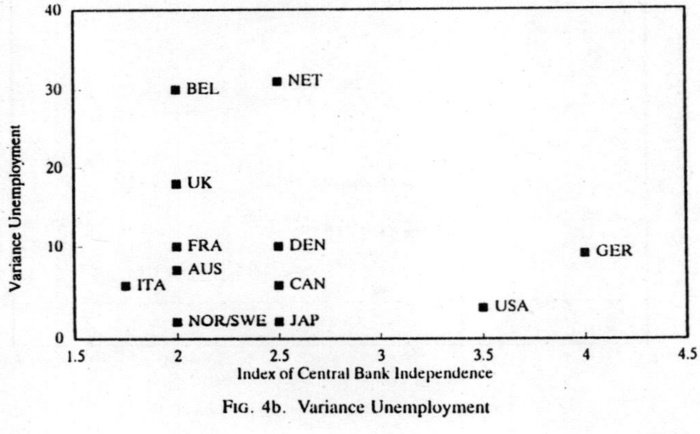

FIG. 4b. Variance Unemployment

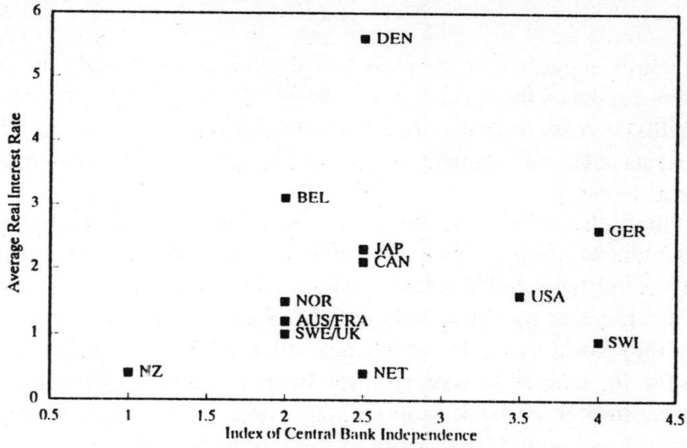

FIG. 5a. Average Real Interest Rate

and Sala-i-Martin (1990) reveal any pattern. While expansionary monetary policy may influence real rates in the short run, it does not appear that systematically expansionary monetary policy (at least of the type politically dependent central banks provide) operates to reduce average real rates over a longer period. On the other hand, as one would expect given our findings about inflation variability, there is a clear negative relationship between central bank independence and the variability of ex post real interest rates.

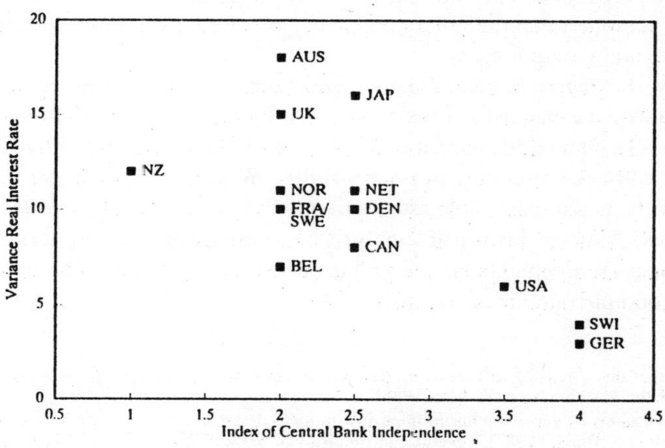

FIG. 5b. Variance Real Interest Rate

4. CONCLUSIONS

These results suggest that the monetary discipline associated with central bank independence reduces the level and variability of inflation but does not have either large benefits or costs in terms of real macroeconomic performance. This observation represents at least a fragment of evidence in support of theories emphasizing the neutrality of money.

Our findings also have implications for the ongoing debate over the optimal rules governing monetary policy. Most obviously they suggest the economic performance merits of central bank independence. More subtly, they raise questions about the benefits of rule-based monetary policies. Advocates of rule-based policies typically stress that they avoid dynamic consistency inflation. The findings here suggest that it is possible for nations to achieve these benefits without setting a monetary rule by insulating the central bank from political control. While it is possible that rule-based performance would be superior to discretionary performance on stabilization grounds, Summers (1988) notes a number of reasons why this is unlikely including unforeseen events and the possibility of an economy getting trapped in the neighborhood of a suboptimal equilibrium around which stabilization would be undesirable.[7]

The results here are not conclusive in the sense that we have looked at the data only in a very straightforward way; more detailed analysis of the relation between central bank independence and real performance is warranted. For example, it might be useful to use central bank independence as an instrument in studying the effects of intercountry differences in monetary policy, or to include additional control variables of the type considered in Summers and Wadwhani (1989) in assessing the impact of central bank independence on economic performance.

Furthermore, the degree of central bank independence is only one of several institutional factors, exchange rate arrangements, and exogenous shocks that influence economic performance in different countries.[8] Our results here do, however, create some presumption that the inflation benefits of central bank independence are likely to outweigh any output costs.

Finally, the degree of central bank independence may be an endogenous variable. For instance, the historical experience of a hyperinflation in Germany may have raised the German public aversion to inflation and its propensity to have an independent central bank committed to price stability. Within the sample period considered in this study, it is a reasonable assumption to hold central bank laws as constant and exogenous. A more "historical" analysis concerned with the long-term evolution of institutional arrangements should tackle issues related to the joint endogeneity between economic outcomes and institutions.

[7]For further discussion of various institutional rules and reforms with specific reference to the Federal Reserve see the last chapter in Willett (1988).

[8]For discussions of various other politico-institutional determinants of inflation in different countries see, for instance, Black (1982), several contributions in Willett (1988), Grilli, Masciandaro, and Tabellini (1991), Cukierman, Edwards, and Tabellini (1992).

APPENDIX: TABLE A1

CENTRAL BANK INDEPENDENCE AND ECONOMIC PERFORMANCE

Country	Average Index of Central Bank Independence	Average Inflation 1955–88	Variance Inflation 1955–88	Average Real GNP Growth 1955–87	Variance Real GNP Growth 1955–87	Average Per Capita Real GNP Growth 1955–87	Variance Per Capita Real GNP Growth 1955–87	Average Unemployment Rate 1958–88	Variance Unemployment Rate 1958–88	Average Real Interest 1957–88	Variance Real Interest 1957–88
Spain	1.5	8.5	27.8	4.2	9.4	3.2	15.2	n/a	n/a	n/a	n/a
New Zealand	1	7.6	21.9	3.0	5.4	1.5	19.4	n/a	n/a	0.4	12.0
Australia	2.0	6.4	20.8	4.0	4.6	1.9	7.9	4.7	7.0	1.1	18.0
Italy	1.75	7.3	34.3	4.0	5.7	3.7	6.6	7.0	5.0	n/a	n/a
United Kingdom	2	6.7	23.5	2.4	4.0	2.1	4.4	5.3	18.0	1.0	15.0
France	2	6.1	20.9	3.9	4.0	3.0	4.6	4.2	10.0	1.1	10.0
Denmark	2.5	6.5	11.5	3.3	6.7	2.6	13.0	6.1	10.0	5.6	10.0
Belgium	2	4.1	10.8	3.1	4.9	2.6	7.7	8.0	30.0	3.1	7.0
Norway	2	6.1	11.7	4.0	2.3	3.0	6.4	2.1	0.3	1.5	11.0
Sweden	2	6.1	14.0	2.9	3.3	2.4	4.3	2.1	0.3	1.0	10.0
Canada	2.5	4.5	12.8	4.1	4.3	2.6	9.1	7.0	5.0	2.1	8.0
Netherlands	2.5	4.2	8.4	3.4	7.0	2.5	7.5	5.1	31.0	0.4	11.0
Japan	2.5	4.9	19.6	6.7	12.3	5.5	14.4	1.8	0.3	2.3	16.0
United States	3.5	4.1	10.5	3.0	5.3	1.9	6.7	6.0	2.0	1.6	6.0
Germany	4	3.0	5.5	3.4	5.6	3.3	8.6	3.6	9.0	2.6	3.0
Switzerland	4	3.2	6.1	2.7	8.6	2.5	10.0	n/a	n/a	0.9	4.0

Sources: IMF, Summers and Heston, and OECD.

APPENDIX: TABLE A2

CENTRAL BANK INDEPENDENCE AND ECONOMIC PERFORMANCE IN THE POST-OIL SHOCK PERIOD

Country	Average Index of Central Bank Independence	Average Inflation 1973–88	Variance Inflation 1973–88	Average Real GNP Growth 1973–87	Variance Real GNP Growth 1973–87	Average Per Capita Real GNP Growth 1973–87	Variance Per Capita Real GNP Growth 1973–87	Average Unemployment Rate 1973–88	Variance Unemployment Rate 1973–88	Average Real Interest 1973–88	Variance Real Interest 1973–88
Spain	1.5	12.4	22.1	2.0	2.1	1.2	8.9	n/a	n/a	n/a	n/a
New Zealand	1	12.2	10.5	1.5	4.5	0.7	21.7	n/a	n/a	−.3	21.0
Australia	2.0	9.5	7.3	2.8	3.2	1.4	7.2	6.6	3.0	1.6	21.0
Italy	1.75	12.5	29.6	2.4	4.9	2.9	7.7	8.4	4.0	n/a	n/a
United Kingdom	2	6.7	23.5	1.6	4.1	2.0	7.8	8.8	15.0	0.9	27.0
France	2	8.2	12.6	2.1	1.3	1.5	4.1	7.0	6.0	2.1	10.0
Denmark	2.5	8.6	11.0	1.9	5.2	1.1	11.5	7.5	4.0	6.5	10.0
Belgium	2	6.0	11.9	1.7	3.8	1.5	10.1	12.8	20.0	3.6	12.0
Norway	2	8.2	5.6	3.9	3.3	3.0	6.3	2.2	0.3	2.4	14.0
Sweden	2	8.3	7.6	1.8	2.1	1.5	5.6	2.3	0.3	1.7	17.0
Canada	2.5	7.2	7.9	3.3	4.7	2.8	11.6	8.7	3.0	2.9	11.0
Netherlands	2.5	4.3	10.5	1.7	3.2	1.1	3.6	9.7	26.0	2.1	10.0
Japan	2.5	4.5	17.1	3.7	2.8	2.6	8.5	2.3	0.2	2.4	7.0
United States	3.5	6.4	11.1	2.4	6.5	1.6	9.8	7.2	1.0	2.1	11.0
Germany	4	3.4	4.0	1.8	3.3	1.8	6.9	6.2	6.0	3.0	3.0
Switzerland	4	3.1	4.3	1.0	8.1	1.4	11.0	n/a	n/a	1.6	3.0

Sources: See Table A1.

LITERATURE CITED

Alesina, Alberto. "Macroeconomics and Politics." In *NBER Macroeconomics Annual*, edited by Stanley Fischer, pp. 17–52. Cambridge, Mass.: MIT Press, 1988.

———. "Politics and Business Cycles in Industrial Democracies." *Economic Policy* 8 (Spring 1989), 58–98.

Alesina, Alberto, and Vittorio Grilli. "The European Central Bank: Reshaping Monetary Policy in Europe." In *Establishing a Central Bank: Issues in Europe and Lessons from the United States*, edited by Matthew Canzoneri, Vittorio Grilli, and Paul Masson, pp. 49–77. Cambridge: Cambridge University Press and CEPR, 1992.

Bade, Robert, and Michael Parkin. "Central Bank Laws and Monetary Policy." Unpublished, 1982.

Barro, Robert, and David Gordon. "Rules, Discretion, and Reputation in a Model of Monetary Policy." *Journal of Monetary Economics* 12 (July 1983), 101–22.

Barro, Robert, and Xavier Sala-i-Martin. "World Real Interest Rates." In *NBER Macroeconomics Annual*, edited by Olivier Blanchard and Stanley Fischer. Cambridge, Mass.: MIT Press, 1990.

Black, Stanley. "Strategic Aspects of the Political Assignment Problem in Open Economics." In *Political Economy of International and Domestic Monetary Reform*, edited by Raymond Lombra and Willard Witte, pp. 130–52. Iowa City: Iowa State University Press, 1982.

Cukierman, Alex, Sebastian Edwards, and Guido Tabellini. "Seignorage and Political Instability." *American Economic Review* 82 (June 1992), 537–55.

Cukierman, Alex, Steven Webb, and Bilin Neyapti. "The Measurement of Central Bank Independence and Its Effect on Policy Outcomes." Unpublished, 1991.

Grilli, Vittorio, Donato Masciandaro, and Guido Tabellini. "Political and Monetary Institutions and Public Finance Policies in the Industrial Countries." *Economic Policy* 13 (October 1991), 341–92.

Hibbs, Douglas. *The American Political Economy*. Cambridge, Mass.: Harvard University Press, 1987.

Kydland, Finn, and Edward Prescott. "Rules Rather than Discretion: The Inconsistency of Optimal Plans." *Journal of Political Economy* 85 (June 1977), 473–90.

Nordhaus, William. "The Political Business Cycle." *Review of Economic Studies* 42 (April 1975), 169–90.

Rogoff, Kenneth. "The Optimal Degree of Commitment to an Intermediate Monetary Target." *Quarterly Journal of Economic* 110 (November 1985), 1169–90.

Rogoff, Kenneth, and Anne Sibert. "Equilibrium Political Business Cycles." *Review of Economic Studies* 55 (January 1988), 1–16.

Romer, Christina, and David Romer. "Does Monetary Policy Matter? A Test in the Spirit of Friedman and Schwartz." In *NBER Macroeconomics Annual*, edited by Olivier Blanchard and Stanley Fischer, pp. 121–170. Cambridge, Mass.: MIT Press, 1989.

Summers, Lawrence. "Comment on Postwar Developments in Business Cycle Theory: A Moderately Classical Perspective." *Journal of Money, Credit, and Banking* 20 (August 1988), 472–76.

Summers, Lawrence, and Sushil Wadwhani. "The Determinants of the Cyclical Variability of Output." CLE Working Paper, 1989.

Willett, Thomas, ed. *Political Business Cycles*. Durham, N.C.: Duke University Press, 1988.

[15]

1 INTRODUCTION*

Recently, there has been worldwide interest in examining the scope for greater monetary policy autonomy for the central bank. At the EC-summit in Maastricht in December 1991 a Treaty on European Economic and Monetary Union (EMU) was agreed upon. According to this treaty, in the final stage of EMU - i.e. by 1997 or later - the European Central Bank is supposed to assume unlimited responsibility for monetary policy. Broadly speaking, according to Alesina and Grilli (1991), the accepted Statute guarantees a central bank as independent from national and European political institutions as the Bundesbank. Furthermore, in the Pacific Basin Countries the same tendency can be discerned. Since the end of 1989 governor Mieno strengthened the position of the Bank of Japan with respect to the Ministry of Finance, while New-Zealand enacted legislation in February 1990 that increased the independence of its Reserve Bank. Finally, in Central Europe, the Czech Republic, Poland and Hungary have been considering proposals concerning central bank independence.[1]

The theoretical rationale for central bank independence finds its origin in the ongoing 'Rules versus Discretion' debate. Authors like Barro and Gordon (1983a) and Rogoff (1985) argue that governments and central banks are tempted to impart an inflationary bias to the economy, thereby sacrificing long-term welfare to short-run political gains. The associated time-consistency problem can be overcome by legislative rules and by setting up politically independent central banks. Hence, one would expect countries with independent central banks to have a lower sustainable rate of inflation.

Unlike the well-developed theoretical literature,[2] there are only a few studies that compare actual monetary regimes between a large number of countries. The most comprehensive studies are Bade and Parkin (1988), Alesina (1988, 1989), Alesina and Summers (1991), Grilli, Masciandaro and Tabellini (1991) and Eijffinger and Schaling (1992, 1993). Focusing on more recent studies, it is striking that the conclusions of the latter are less clear-cut than the theoretical literature. For instance, contrary to Alesina and Summers, Bade and Parkin find no correlation between central bank independence and the variability of inflation. Next, unlike the prediction of the Rogoff (1985) model,[3] both Alesina and Summers and Grilli, Masciandaro and Tabellini find no association between central bank independence and (the variability of) real output growth.

In this paper on the basis of a single-stage Phillips-curve monetary policy game with extrinsic uncertainty - i.e. supply shocks - we derive several propositions concerning the

---

* The authors are grateful for helpful comments by Theo van de Klundert, Maarten van Rooij and an anonymous referee. Of course, the usual disclaimer applies. Schaling gratefully acknowledges financial support from the Netherlands Organization for Scientific Research (NWO).

1 For an interesting survey of central banking in emerging market-oriented economies see Federal Reserve Bank of Kansas City (1990).

2 For a survey of the 'state of the art' see Cukierman (1993).

3 This framework is summarized in Alesina and Grilli (1991).

relationship between central bank independence and (the variance of) inflation and output growth. These propositions are tested for twelve industrial countries (Australia, Belgium, Canada, France, Germany, Italy, Japan, the Netherlands, Sweden, Switzerland, the U.K. and the U.S.) for the post-Bretton-Woods period (1972-1991). In testing the game-theoretic model we use several indices of central bank independence based on the central bank laws of these countries.

The main conclusions of our paper can be summarized as follows. First of all, both our model and estimation results, give further support to the well-known inverse relationship between the degree of central bank independence and the level of inflation found by Alesina (1988, 1989). Secondly, contrary to Alesina and Summers (1991) and Grilli, Masciandaro and Tabellini (1991), we find no empirical evidence that the more independent the central bank is, the lower the variability of inflation. Thirdly, our estimation results reject clearly the proposition - implied by the Rogoff (1985) model - of a positive relation between independence and the variability of real output growth. In other words, inflation-averse central banks do not bear the costs of triggering recessions nor do politically sensitive central banks reap the benefits of avoiding recessions. Finally, no empirical relationship can be found between central bank independence and the level of real output growth in the long run. Hence, our empirical results support the proposition of Grilli, Masciandaro and Tabellini (1991) that having an independent central bank is like having a free lunch. There are benefits (lower inflation) but no apparent costs in terms of real output growth.

The plan of this paper is as follows. In section 2 we combine the Barro and Gordon (1983a) Phillips-curve monetary policy game with the Alogoskoufis (1993) model of wage and employment determination, to allow for persistence in the natural rate of output. In section 3 we use this model to analyse the theoretical relationships of central bank independence with the means and variances of inflation and real output growth. Finally, in section 4 we confront the propositions from the game-theoretic model with empirical evidence using the various indices of central bank independence.

2 A SIMPLE CLOSED ECONOMY MACROMODEL

2.1 The Model

The main purpose of sections 2 and 3 is to combine the Barro and Gordon (1983a) Phillips curve monetary policy game with the Alogoskoufis (1993) model of wage and employment determination, to allow for persistence in the natural rate of output. Next, following Cukierman (1993) chapter XVIII we use this model to analyse the effects of central bank independence on the mean and variance of inflation and real output growth.

We assume that there are two types of agents, wage-setters and the central bank. Wage-setters unilaterally choose the nominal wage every time period, and the central bank controls monetary policy to determine the inflation rate.

The timing of events is as follows. Wage-setters sign annual nominal contracts (Gray (1976), Fischer, (1977a)) at the beginning of each year, before monetary policy is chosen for that year.

Wage-setters know the domestic monetary regime, i.e. they know the weight of inflation stabilization relative to employment stabilization in the preferences of the central bank. They take this information into account in forming their expectations. Finally, employment is determined by competitive firms. We now move on to the supply side of the model.

2.2 Wage and Employment Determination

Consider the following supply block which is a closed-economy version of Alogoskoufis (1993). Capital will be assumed fixed, and output is given by a short-run production function of the following type

(2.1) $y_t = \beta \ell_t + \mu_t \qquad 0 < \beta < 1$

where lower-case letters refer to logarithmic deviations from steady state values[4]. Thus, y is the log of output, ℓ the log of employment, and μ a measure of productivity. β is the exponent of labour and is less than unity.

Having described the level of output, it remains to specify how productivity evolves over time. We use a stochastic trend specification discussed in Stock and Watson (1988). This specification says that over the long run productivity will grow at some average rate, labelled g. However, shocks to productivity, ν_t^{μ}, can cause productivity growth to deviate from its mean. Moreover, these shocks are persistent with respect to the level of productivity: once perturbed by an ν_t^{μ} shock, μ_t will show no tendency to return to its trendline. Hence, the supply shocks are assumed to have permanent effects on the economy's productive capacity.[5] The mathematical expression for the stochastic trend specification is a random walk with drift

(2.2) $\mu_t = g + \mu_{t-1} + \nu_t^{\mu}$

where g is the average (or expected) rate of growth of productivity (the drift of the μ-process), and ν^{μ} is a normally distributed productivity shock with zero mean and variance σ^2_{μ}.

Firms determine employment by equalizing the marginal product of labour to the real wage $w_t - p_t$. This yields the following employment function

(2.3) $\ell_t = \dfrac{-1}{1-\beta}(w_t - p_t - \mu_t)$

where w is the log of the nominal wage and p the log of the price level.

The nominal wage is set at the beginning of each period and remains fixed for one period. The objective of wage setters is to stabilize employment around a target employment level $l_i^s \equiv \bar{\ell}$.Denoting the log of the labour force by l^s, we assume $l_s^i < l^s$Thuss we employ the insider-outsider approach to the labour market (Blanchard and Summers (1986), Lindbeck and Snower (1986))[6]. Thus, wages in each period are set to minimize

---

4 For a variable $\hat{X}$ say, $x \equiv d\ell n\hat{X}$

5 We discuss the impact of demand shocks in section 3.

6 The advantages of this approach will become clear in section 3.2.

(2.4) $E_{t-1} (\ell_t - \bar{\ell})^2$

where E_{t-1} is the operator of rational expectations, conditional on information available at the end of period t - 1. The minimization of (2.4) is subject to the labour demand function (2.3).[7]

From the first-order conditions for a minimum of (2.4) subject to (2.3) the nominal wage is given by

(2.5) $w = E_{t-1} p_t + E_{t-1} \mu_t - (1 - \beta) \bar{\ell}$

Substituting (2.5) in the labour demand function (2.3), and the resulting equation in the production function, we get the following relation between employment, output and unanticipated shocks

(2.6) $\ell_t = \bar{\ell} + \frac{1}{1 - \beta} (p_t - E_{t-1} p_t + \nu_t^{\mu})$

(2.7) $y_t = \beta\bar{\ell} + \mu_t + \frac{\beta}{1 - \beta} (p_t - E_{t-1} p_t + \nu_t^{\mu})$

An unanticipated rise in prices $p_t - E_{t-1} p_t$ reduces the real wage, and causes firms to employ more labour. Thus, both aggregate employment and output exhibit a transitory deviation from their respective equilibrium or "natural" rates $\bar{\ell}$ and $\beta\bar{\ell} + \mu_t$[8].

On the other hand, an unanticipated shock to productivity increases the marginal product of labour, and given the real wage causes firms to employ more labour. Thus employment rises above $\bar{\ell}$, and output rises on account of both the higher employment (transitory effect) and the higher productivity (permanent effect).

Subtracting (2.6) from the labour force ℓ^s, using the approximation that the rate of unemployment $u \approx \ell^s - \ell$, and adding and subtracting $\frac{p_{t-1}}{1 - \beta}$, we get the following expression for the short-run determination of unemployment.

(2.8) $u_t = \tilde{u} - \frac{1}{1 - \beta} (\Delta p_t - E_{t-1}\Delta p_t + \nu_t^{\mu})$

where $\tilde{u} = \ell^s - \bar{\ell}$ and Δ is the first diference operator. $\tilde{u}$ can be thought of as the equilibrium of "natural" rate of unemployment in this model. Thus, (2.8) is the well known expectations augmented "Phillips curve". Unemployment deviates from its equilibrium rate only to the extent that there are unanticipated shocks to inflation or productivity. Anticipated shocks to inflation and productivity are refelected in wages (equation (2.5)) and do not affect unemployment. We

---

7 Alternatively, the loss-function could be assumed quadratic in both the deviations of employment and the real wage from certain target levels. For an analysis along these lines see Funke (1992).

8 Actual output and employment will equal their natural rates when all expectations are fulfilled. Hence, the natural rate of employment equals $\bar{l}$ and the natural rate of output is $\beta\bar{\ell} + \mu_t$.

can now incorporate the Phillips curve in a monetary policy game. This is the subject of the next section.

3 A STATIC GAME BETWEEN WAGE-SETTERS AND THE CENTRAL BANK

3.1 The Social Welfare versus the Political Approach to Central Bank Behaviour

In order to investigate optimal monetary policy - in which the inflation rate is treated as a directly controllable policy instrument[9] - consider a central bank that is concerned with both price stability and low unemployment. We assume a quadratic loss function, that penalizes both inflation and unemployment. More specificly we use

$$(3.1)\quad L_t = \frac{1}{2}(\Delta p_t - \Delta p^*)^2 + \frac{d_2}{2}(u_t - u^*)^2$$

where Δp^* and u^* are the inflation and unemployment targets of the central bank. The parameter d_2 measures the weight of unemployment stabilization relative to inflation stabilization in the preferences of the central bank.

The central bank chooses Δp and wage-setters "choose" $E_{t-1}\Delta p_t$. Normalizing Δp^* and u^* at zero yields

$$(3.2)\quad L_t = \frac{1}{2}(\Delta p_t)^2 + \frac{d_2}{2}(u_t)^2$$

According to Cukierman (1993), chapter III the recent literature on monetary policy games has given two competing interpretations to the loss function of the monetary policymaker in equation (3.1).

One part of the literature regards this function as a social welfare function and the central bank as a benevolent social planner (Kydland and Prescott (1977), Barro and Gordon (1983a, 1983b), Rogoff (1985) and Canzoneri (1985)).

The other part views the central bank as a mediator between different interest groups that try to push monetary policy in various directions. On this view, the loss function (3.1) reflects a distributionally motivated political compromise mediated through the central bank between the advocates of employment stimulation and the advocates of price stability (Weintraub (1978), Burns (1979), Kane (1980, 1982), Beck (1982), Wooley (1984), Hetzel (1985), Havrilesky (1987), Willet (1988) and Mayer (1990)). The coefficient d_2 then measures the relative political clout of the two groups (Cukierman and Meltzer (1986a), Cukierman (1986)).

The social welfare approach seems best suited to describe how a central bank *should* behave. However, (Cukierman (1993), chapter III) points out that it is a relatively weak paradigm for explaining the *actual* policies chosen by central banks. For as shown by Bade and Parkin (1988), Alesina (1988, 1989), Grilli, Masciandaro and Tabellini (1991) and Eijffinger and Schaling (1992) in most countries central banks are highly dependent on the government in general and

9 Depending on operating procedures the policymaker sets the money stock or the interest rate. However, it is simpler to think of the central bank to choose inflation directly. For a lucid exposition of monetary policy games with the money stock as policy instrument see Canzoneri and Henderson (1991).

the treasury or ministry of finance in particular. As a result, the policies implemented by central bankers are not independent from the general political proces in which distributional considerations are predominant. The impact of these considerations on the choice of policy varies with the degree of central bank independence. The greater the political independence given to the bank by law the smaller the impact of distributional and other political considerations on monetary policy.

More realisticly, we choose the political approach to central bank behaviour as the interpretation of equation (3.1). Hence we view the coefficient d_2 as a measure of the political dependence of the central bank. The lower d_2 the more independent the central bank[10]. That is, the degree of central bank independence equals d_2^{-1}

3.2 Time Consistent Inflation Policy

Following Alogoskoufis ((1993), p. 17) we start with a cooperative game, i.e. we assume that the natural rate of unemployment is efficient. In the context of the model of sub-section 2.1, this can be represented by the assumption that $\bar{l}$, the target employment level of wage-setters is equal to l^s, the effective labour force. In the latter case the central bank has no incentive to try and reduce unemployment below its equilibrium rate. As there is no conflict between the unemployment targets of wage setters and the central bank, the policy game can be seen as a cooperative one[11]. This state of affairs is summarized in the first column of table 1.

Table 1
Policy Games and Unemployment Targets

Central Bank	Wage-Setters	
	$\bar{l} = l^s$ $\tilde{u} = 0$	$\bar{l} < l^s$ $\tilde{u} > 0$
$u^* = 0$	$u^* = \tilde{u}$	$u^* < \tilde{u}$
Natural Rate	Efficient	Inefficient
Policy Game	Cooperative	Non-Cooperative

We now turn to the second column of table 1, i.e. the situation where the equilibrium unemployment rate is inefficiently high. In what follows we show that then the equilibrium inflation rate becomes proportional to the natural rate of unemployment. In this case discretionary monetary policy is no longer a Pareto-equilibrium, due to the time-inconsistency of optimal monetary policy.

---

10 An alternative approach is explicit modelling of the interaction of separate monetary and fiscal authorities. See e.g. Alesina and Tabellini (1987) and Cukierman (1993), chapter XVIII.

11 For a review of some important concepts of game theory see Blackburn and Christensen (1989).

Assuming that $\bar{l} < l^s$ i.e. that $\bar{u} > 0$ the central bank has incentives to systematically create inflation in order to reduce unemployment below its natural rate.

Substituting the Phillips curve (2.8) in the loss function (3.2) yields

$$(3.3)\quad L_t = \tfrac{1}{2}(\Delta p_t)^2 + \frac{d_2}{2}\left[\bar{u} - \frac{1}{1-\beta}\Delta p_t + \frac{1}{1-\beta}E_{t-1}\Delta p_t - \frac{1}{1-\beta}\nu_t^{\mu}\right]^2$$

From the first order conditions for a minimum of (3.3), i.e. $\dfrac{\partial L_t}{\partial \Delta p_t} = 0$, we obtain the central bank's reaction function to wage-setter's expectations

$$(3.4)\quad \Delta p_t = \frac{d_2(1-\beta)}{(1-\beta)^2 + d_2}\bar{u} + \frac{d_2}{(1-\beta)^2 + d_2}E_{t-1}\Delta p_t - \frac{d_2}{(1-\beta)^2 + d_2}\nu_t^{\mu}$$ [12]

Taking expectations conditional on information at t - 1 of (3.4) gives

$$(3.5)\quad E_{t-1}\,\Delta p_t = \frac{d_2}{1-\beta}\bar{u}$$

Equation (3.5) is the reaction function of wage-setters. Upon substituting (3.5) in (3.4) we get

$$(3.6)\quad \Delta p_t = \frac{d_2}{1-\beta}\bar{u} - \frac{d_2}{(1-\beta)^2 + d_2}\nu_t^{\mu}$$

Figure 1 shows the central bank's reaction function if $v_t^{\mu} = 0$, i.e. the average inflation rate as a function of the expected inflation rate.[13]

[INSERT FIGURE 1]

The only point at which expectations are rational is at point N, which represents the non-cooperative Nash equilibrium.

Denoting the average inflation rate by $\Delta\tilde{p}_t$, from (3.6) it follows that

$$(3.7)\quad \Delta\tilde{p}_t = \frac{d_2}{1-\beta}\bar{u}$$

Hence, at point N the inflation rate is above zero (the outcome in the cooperative case).

Subtracting (3.5) from (3.6) we obtain the following expression for unanticipated inflation

$$(3.8)\quad \Delta p_t - E_{t-}\,\Delta p_t = \frac{-d_2}{(1-\beta)^2 + d_2}\nu_t^{\mu}$$

12 Demand shocks can be included in the analysis by extending the model with an aggregate-demand curve. This would complicate the algebra without affecting our results.

13 This figure is based on a similar one in Blanchard and Fischer (1989), p. 597.

Upon substituting (3.8) in (2.8) we get

$$(3.9)\quad u = \bar{u} - \frac{1-\beta}{(1-\beta)^2 + d_2}\nu_t^{\mu}$$

Equations (3.7) and (3.9) highlight the time inconsistency of optimal monetary policy. The monetary policy strategy of the central bank, i.e. equation (3.4) is time-consistent in the sense that at each point in time the inflation rate selected is best, given the current situation. However, as can be seen from equations (3.7) and (3.9), the resulting policy is socially sub-optimal. It is sub-optimal since it results in an excessive level of inflation, i.e. it produces an inflationary bias with no gains in the form of systematic lower unemployment. This completes the description of the non-cooperative Nash equilibrium.

3.3 Results for Inflation and its Variance

Following Cukierman ((1993), chapter XVIII) in this section we investigate the effects of central bank independence on the mean and variance of inflation. Taking the first derivative of (3.7) with respect to d_2, we get

$$(3.10)\quad \frac{\partial \Delta \bar{p}_t}{\partial d_2} = \frac{\bar{u}}{1-\beta} > 0$$

From (3.10) we derive proposition (3.1).

PROPOSITION 3.1: The more independent the central bank (the lower d_2) the lower the average inflation rate.

Note that the greater $\frac{1}{1-\beta}$ (i.e., the greater the reduction in unemployment from unanticipated inflation in the expectations augmented Phillips curve (2.8)) and the larger the natural rate of unemployment the greater the inflation benefits of appointing independent central bankers.

We now consider inflation variability. Upon taking variances of (3.6) we get

$$(3.11)\quad \frac{\mathrm{Var}\ \Delta p_t}{\sigma_\mu^2} = \left[\frac{d_2}{(1-\beta)^2 + d_2}\right]^2$$

From (3.11) it follows that

$$\lim_{d_2 \to \infty} \left[\frac{d_2}{(1-\beta)^2 + d_2}\right]^2 = 1$$

That is, if the degree of central bank independence d_2^{-1} equals zero no stabilization of inflation is achieved. In this case, in fact Var $\Delta p_t = \sigma^2_\mu$, i.e. the variance of the productivity shock is completely transmitted to inflation.

Taking the first derivative of (3.11) with respect to d_2, we get

$$\frac{\partial(\text{Var } \Delta p_t/\sigma_\mu^2)}{\partial d_2} = \frac{2d_2(1 - \beta)^2}{[(1 - \beta)^2 + d_2]^3} > 0 \tag{3.12}$$

From (3.12) we derive propostion 2:

PROPOSITION 3.2: The more independent the central bank (the lower d_2) the lower the variance of the inflation rate.

By again differentiating (3.12) with respect to d_2, we find that

$$\frac{\partial^2(\text{Var}\Delta p_t/\sigma_\mu^2)}{\partial d_2^2} = \frac{2(1 - \beta)^2[(1 - \beta)^2 - 2d_2]}{[(1 - \beta)^2 + d_2]^4} \tag{3.13}$$

By setting $[(1 - \beta)^2 - 2d_2]$ equal to zero we find a point of inflection at $d_2 = \frac{(1 - \beta)^2}{2}$[14]. Using (3.12) and (3.13) we obtain Figure 2.

[INSERT FIGURE 2]

From Figure 2 we derive propostion 3.3.

PROPOSITION 3.3: If a highly independent central bank loses some of its independence at first this will strongly increase inflation variability. In this respect loss of independence matters less for weaker institutions.

---

14 Following Blanchard and Fisher (1989, p. 598) $\xi \equiv \frac{[1/(1 - \beta)]^2}{1/d_2}$ is, loosely speaking a measure of the utility gain from unexpected inflation: $\frac{1}{1 - \beta}$ gives the decrease in unemployment (see equation (2.8)), and $1/d_2$ the utility loss from higher inflation. Hence, at the point of inflection this utility gain equals 1/2.

10

This completes the description of the results on the mean and variance of inflation.

3.4 Results for Output and its Variance

In this sub section, we examine the effects of central bank independence on the mean and variance of real output (growth).

Adding and subtracting $\frac{\beta}{1 - \beta} p_{t-1}$ from (2.7) yields

$$y_t = \beta \bar{l} + \mu_t + \frac{\beta}{1 - \beta}(\Delta p_t - E_{t-1} \Delta p_t + \nu^{\mu}_t) \tag{3.14}$$

If we employ $\bar{y}_t$ as short-hand for $\beta\bar{\ell} + \mu_t$ we get

$$y_t - \bar{y}_t = \frac{\beta}{1 - \beta}(\Delta p_t - E_{t-1}\Delta p_t + \nu^{\mu}_t) \tag{3.15}$$

Equation (3.15) is the famous Lucas surprise supply function which says that unanticipatied inflation and/or productivity shocks cause transitory deviations of output from its equilibrium (mean) level $\bar{y}$.

Upon sustituting (3.8) in (3.15) we get

$$y_t - \bar{y} = \frac{\beta(1 - \beta)}{(1 - \beta)^2 + d_2} \nu^{\mu}_t \tag{3.16}$$

From (3.16) it follows that the mean level of output is independent from d_2, i.e. independent from the prevailing monetary regime. Of course, this result is just a corrollary of the natural rate property of the Alogoskoufis (1993) supply block[15].

Taking variances of (3.16) yields

$$\frac{\mathrm{Var}(y_t - \bar{y})}{\sigma^2_{\mu}} = \left[\frac{\beta(1 - \beta)}{(1 - \beta)^2 + d_2}\right]^2 \tag{3.17}$$

From (3.17) it follows that

$$\lim_{d_2 \to \infty} \left[\frac{\beta(1 - \beta)}{(1 - \beta)^2 + d_2}\right]^2 = 0 \tag{3.18}$$

That is, if the degree of central bank independence d_2^{-1} equals zero perfect stabilization of output is achieved. In this case, in fact Var $(y_t - \bar{y}_t) = 0$.

Taking the first derivative of (3.17) with respect to d_2 we get

[15] For instance, introducing multiperiod wage contracts (Fischer (1977b)), would imply policy non-neutrality. In the latter case the degree of central bank independence would show an inverse relation with the level of output.

$$\frac{\partial[\mathrm{Var}(y_t - \tilde{y}_t)/\sigma_\mu^2]}{\partial d_2} = \frac{-2\beta^2(1-\beta)^2}{[(1-\beta)^2 + d_2]^3} < 0 \qquad (3.19)$$

From (3.19) we derive proposition 3.4.

PROPOSITION 3.4: The more independent the central bank (the lower d_2) the higher the variance of output around its mean or natural level $\tilde{y}$.

Note that if $\tilde{y}_t = 0$ (e.g. Alesina and Grilli (1991)) proposition 3.4 is a statement about the actual variance of output. This is not the case in the present analysis. Actually the persistence of productivity shocks is inherited by the natural rate of output (c.f. Cukierman (1993), chapter XV).

We have

$$\tilde{y}_t = \beta\bar{\ell} + \mu_t \qquad (3.20)$$

Hence

$$\tilde{y}_{t-1} = \beta\bar{\ell} + \mu_{t-1} \qquad (3.21)$$

Upon substituting (2.2) in (3.20) we get

$$\tilde{y}_t = \beta\bar{\ell} + \mu_{t-1} + g + \nu_t^\mu \qquad (3.22)$$

Combining (3.22) with (3.21) yields

$$\tilde{y}_t = \tilde{y}_{t-1} + g + \nu_t^\mu \qquad (3.23)$$

Therefore in the present analysis the natural rate of output follows a random walk with drift. It is around this "walking" natural rate that output is being stabilized.

Again differentiating (3.19) with respect to d_2 we find that

$$\frac{\partial^2[\mathrm{Var}(y_t - \tilde{y}_t)/\sigma_\mu^2]}{\partial d_2^2} = \frac{6\beta^2(1-\beta)^2}{[(1-\beta)^2 + d_2]^4} > 0 \qquad (3.24)$$

Using (3.19) and (3.24) we obtain Figure 3.

[INSERT FIGURE 3]

This completes the description of the results on the mean and variance of output.

Now we move from levels to growth rates, i.e. we now examine the effects of central bank independence on the growth rate of output and its variance. Taking first differences of (3.16) we get

$$(3.25) \qquad \Delta y_t - \Delta \bar{y}_t = \frac{\beta(1 - \beta)}{(1 - \beta)^2 + d_2} \Delta \nu_t^{\mu}$$

From (3.23) we derive proposition 3.5.

PROPOSITION 3.5: The mean or average rate of growth of output $(\Delta \bar{y}_t)$ is independent from the prevailing monetary regime (d_2).

Taking variances of (3.25) we get

$$(3.26) \qquad \frac{\mathrm{Var}(\Delta y_t - \Delta \bar{y}_t)}{\sigma^2_{\Delta\mu}} = \left[\frac{\beta(1 - \beta)}{(1 - \beta)^2 + d_2}\right]^2$$

where ${\sigma_{\Delta\mu}}^2 \equiv \mathrm{Var}\ \Delta{\nu_t}^{\mu} = \sigma^2_{\mu} + \sigma^2_{\mu_{t-1}}$. Since (3.26) is simular to (3.17) the same discussion applies. Hence

PROPOSITION 3.6: The more dependent the central bank (the higher d_2) the lower the variance of the growth rate of output around its mean or average rate of growth.

Finally, we summarize the main propositions from this section in table 2

[INSERT TABLE 2]

In order to confront these propositions with some cross-country evidence we can now move on to empirical testing. This the subject of the next section.

4 EMPIRICAL EVIDENCE ON CENTRAL BANK INDEPENDENCE

4.1 Central Bank Independence and the Level of Inflation

According to Alesina (1988, 1989) and Alesina and Summers (1991) countries with an independent central bank will have a lower rate of inflation than countries with a dependent central bank. As stated in section 1, this well-known inverse relationship between central bank independence and the level of inflation is particularly sensitive to the numerical values of the various indices of central bank independence.

Furthermore, the negative correlation between central bank independence and inflation does not necessarily imply a causal relation from central bank independence to inflation or the other way around. The correlation could be explained by a third factor, e.g. the culture and tradition of monetary stability in a country, leading both to an independent central bank and a low rate of inflation.[16] As an example could be taken Germany, for which country one could argue that the hyperinflation in the 1920s caused such a culture and tradition of monetary stability.[17]

However, in our opinion the degree of central bank independence is the ultimate cause of the level of inflation. For central bank independence is the ability and willingness to conduct an autonomous monetary policy directed at price stability as the single policy goal. If not seriously hampered by other elements of economic policy, such as wage increases, budget deficits and government debt, it will eventually lead to low sustainable inflation.

Therefore, our regression analysis (OLS method) assumes the various indices of central bank independence to be the explanatory variables of the average inflation (CPI) on an annual base in the twelve countries considered (Australia, Belgium, Canada, France, Germany, Italy, Japan, the Netherlands, Switserland, the UK, the US and Sweden):

$$\text{(4.1)}\quad \text{average inflation} = a_0 + \overset{(-)}{a_{1*}} \text{ central bank independence} + \epsilon_t$$

We investigated empirically the policy independence index of Bade and Parkin (BP), the index of Alesina (AL)[18], the broad index of political independence of Grilli, Masciandaro and Tabellini (GMT) and a new index of policy independence, which we call the Eijffinger - Schaling (ES) index.[19] The ES-index of central bank independence is compared with previous indices (BP, AL, and GMT) in Eijffinger and Schaling (1993). This cross-section analysis of the empirical relation between these indices of central bank independence and the level of inflation should be interpreted carefully because of the limited degrees of freedom.

The relationship between the varions indices and average annual inflation is analysed for the whole post-Bretton-Woods period of twenty years (1972-1991). During the fixed exchange rate system of Bretton-Woods countries were fully committed to an exchange rate target and had no room to conduct and autonomous domestic monetary policy. Thus, before 1972 the empirical relation between central bank independence and inflation was much less straightforward than after 1972.[20]

Furthermore, the post-Bretton-Woods period is divided in two sub-periods of ten years each

---

16 According to the Commission of the European Communities (1990) p. 98 the causal relation implied by their regression analysis runs from inflation to central bank independence. This is certainly incorrect.

17 See Bresciani-Turroni (1953).

18 In Eijffinger and Schaling (1993) we show that the Alesina (1988, 1989) synthetic indicator of central bank independence is internally inconsistent and does not qualify as an index.

19 In the case of the GMT index, there is no ranking for Sweden and so the sample is only made up of eleven countries.

20 Regression analysis by De Haan and Sturm (1992), pp.308-309 empirically supports this view.

14

(1972-1981 and 1982-1991 respectively) in order to distinguish between the EMS countries (Belgium, France, Germany, Italy, the Netherlands and partly the UK) and non-EMS countries (Australia, Canada, Japan, Switserland, the US and Sweden). Before 1982 the EMS countries participated - some like France, Italy and the UK only partly - in the snake arrangement and - except the UK - in the initial orientation phase of the EMS (1979-1982) which was characterized by frequent and large realisments of central rates. After 1982 a period of consolidation (1982-1987) can be discerned within the EMS. According to Ungever (1990), this period was marked by "... a widespread consensus to follow stability-oriented policies, an increasing convergence in the development of costs, prices and monetary aggregates, and by long periods without realignments of central rates" (p. 338).[21]

Consequently, during the second sub-period (1982-1991) the negative correlation between central bank independence and inflation is expected to be less clear cut than during the first sub-period (1972-1981) because of the consolidation in the EMS countries towards exchange rate stability. From 1982 the domestic monetary policy in these countries - besides Germany as the anchor country - could have become increasingly endogenous by focussing on the exchange rate target.

[21] Ungerer (1990) makes a distinction between three phases of development of the EMS: the first phase (1979-1982) as a period of initial orientation, the second phase (1982-1987) as a period of consolidation and the third phase (1987-present) as a period of re-examination, in the light of uneasiness about the "asymmetry" of the system.

15

Table 3 Average annual inflation and the various indices of central bank independence.

Explanatory variables	1972-1991	1972-1981	1982-1991
Constant	11.546	15.025	8.068
	(6.931)	(6.579)	(5.534)
Bade-Parkin (BP)	-1.850	-2.252	-1.449
	(-2.850)**	(-2.531)*	(-2.550)*
Adj. R^2	0.393	0.329	0.333
RMSE	1.939	2.658	1.697
Constant	11.778	15.358	8.199
	(8.205)	(7.686)	(6.302)
Alesina (AL)	-1.981	-2.432	-1.529
	(-3.501)**	(-3.088)**	(-2.982)**
Adj. R^2	0.506	0.437	0.418
RMSE	1.750	2.435	1.586
Constant	8.822	12.481	5.162
	(5.686)	(6.315)	(4.013)
Grilli et.al. (GMT)	-0.395	-0.846	-0.243
(Political)	(-1.380)	(-1.683)	(-0.743)
Adj. R^2	0.083	0.155	-0.047
RMSE	2.456	3.129	2.036
Constant	11.014	14.383	7.645
	(9.998)	(9.144)	(7.604)
Eijffinger-Schaling	-1.433	-1.746	-1.119
(ES)	(-3.955)**	(-3.376)**	(-3.386)**
Adj. R^2	0.571	0.486	0.488
RMSE	1.630	2.327	1.488

Notes: t-values are in parentheses. One asterisk indicates that the coefficient is significantly different from zero at a 95% confidence level and two asterisks indicate that the coefficient is significant at a 99% confidence level.

Table 3 shows the estimation result of equation (4.1), which explains average annual inflation by the four indices of central bank independence for the whole period (1972-1991) and for both sub-periods (1972-1981 and 1982-1991) respectively. Except for the GMT index of political independence, the inverse relationship between inflation and central bank independence is very clear, although the Alesina and ES index proved to be more significant (higher t-value) than the BP index.[22] In case of the latter three indices, central bank independence is less significant (lower t-value) during both sub-periods than during the whole post-Bretton-Woods period.

Besides the GMT index, the various indices have approximately the same significance in both the first and second sub-period, while that in the second sub-period was expected to be lower than in the first as a consequence of the six EMS countries within the sample of twelve. These outcomes could be the result of the practice that most EMS countries used fully the bilateral band of ± 2¼% and, for Italy and since October 1990 the UK, the band of ±6%. Only the Netherlands and, from 1986, also France had an explicit exchange rate target for their currency vis-à-vis the Deutsche Mark.

What may be conluded from the cross-section analysis of these twelve countries regarding the relationship between central bank independence and the level of inflation and the quality of the four indices of central bank independence in particular?

Firstly, the negative relation between central bank independence and inflation proved to be very significant for all indices, except for the GMT index of political independence.[23] Clearly, the more independent a central bank is, the lower rate of inflation in the long run.

[INSERT FIGURES 4 AND 5]

Figure 4 shows that the BP index of policy independence has a significant, negative relation to average annual inflation despite some positive outliers (Italy and the UK) and some negative (Belgium and the Netherlands). The ranking by Bade and Parkin of the latter two countries is evidently too low. Furthermore, from figure 5 it can be seen that the Alesina 'index' has a more significant, negative relation to inflation, merely by the ad hoc adjusted ranking of Italy.

[INSERT FIGURES 6 AND 7]

However, figure 6 shows that the GMT index bears no clear (negative) relation to inflation in most of the eleven countries considered. This could be explained by the broadness of the GMT index comprising many features (see Eijfffinger and Schaling (1992)). This index, thereby, waters down the essential features of policy independence, i.e. (i) the procedures for appointing the central bank board, (ii) the relationship between, the central bank and government concerning the formulation of monetary policy, and (iii) the policy goals of the central bank regarding monetary policy making.

Finally, figure 7 shows that the ES index has an even more significant, negative relation to

---

22 De Haan and Sturm (1992) find different empirical results for a modified GMT index, measuring both political and economic independence "... except for the entries which are related to supervision of the banking system. Whether or not a central bank has any responsibility for bank supervision provides, in our view, no information as to its independence" (p. 323).

23 This is a consequence of the 'broadness' of the GMT-index. Because GMT use eight criteria in determining the degree of political independence, the essential characteristics of central bank independence are watered down. See Eijffinger and Schaling (1992), pp. 11-12.

inflation, although the positive outliers (Italy and the UK) remain. This could, perhaps, be explained by the half-fledged position of these countries with respect to the EMS. Nevertheless, the negative outliers (Belgium and the Netherlands) of the BP and Alesina index disappeared by the more consistent ranking of both countries according to their central bank laws within the context of monetary policy making.

Consequently, empirical evidence on the various indices of central bank independence supports Proposition 3.1 (see sub section 3.3) that the more independent the central bank - the lower d_2 - is, the lower the average inflation rate.

Of course, one should be well aware of the more or less subjective character of the research on central bank independence, which combines both legal-institutional and political-economic criteria and features in constructing indices.

4.2 Central Bank Independence and the Variability of Inflation

The variability of inflation reflects the degree of monetary and inflationary uncertainty in the economy.

Inflationary uncertainty implies that investers are not sure about the expected (ex ante) future level of inflation and, hence, about expected (ex ante) real interest rates. Therefore, they are less willing to take risks and to invest in either long-term financial assets or physical capital goods. As a consequence lenders demand a higher risk premium on their funds.[24] Thus, higher inflationary uncertainty - measured by the variability of realized inflation - will lead to higher expected real interest rates and to lower levels of investment and output growth.

What is the empirical relationship between central bank independence and the variability of inflation?

First of all, the variability of inflation is positively correlated with the level of inflation and, thereby, with the independence of central banks. Chowdhury (1991) investigated empirically the relation between the level and variability of inflation in 66 countries for the period from 1955 to 1985. He concluded that there is a significant, positive correlation between the level and the variability of inflation during this period. De Haan and Sturm (1992) also examined this relation in 18 industrial countries for the period from 1961 to 1987. They found a clear, positive correlation between both variables for the post-Bretton-Woods sub-periods 1970-1978 and 1979-1987, but not for the sub-period 1961-1969. Consequently, if a high degree of central bank independence results in a low level of inflation, this should also lead to a low variability of inflation. Nevertheless, the negative correlation between independence and inflation variability does not necessarily imply a causal relation from the first to the latter, but could be explained by a third factor. However, our regression analysis assumes the various indices of central bank independence (BP, AL, GMT and ES) to be the explanatory variables of the variance of monthly inflation (CPI) on an annual base in the twelve countries of our sample:

---

24 **Empirical research with respect to the influence of monetary and inflationary uncertainty on real interest rates in the United States is conducted by Mascaro and Meltzer (1983). They conclude that monetary uncertainty - measured by the variability of money growth - resulted in a risk premium for both the money and capital market interest rate in the period from October 1979.**

18

$$\text{(4.2) variance inflation} = b_0 + b_{1*} \overset{(-)}{\text{central bank independence}} + \eta_t$$

Again, the relationship between the various indices and the variance of monthly inflation is examined for the complete post-Bretton-Woods period of twenty years (1972-1991) and its two sub-periods of ten years (1972-1981 and 1982-1991). During the second sub-period the negative correlation between central bank independence and inflation variability is also expected to be less clear cut than during the first sub-period by the consolidation of EMS countries to exchange rate stability.

Table 4 *Variance monthly inflation and the various indices of central bank independence.*

Explanatory variables	1972-1991	1972-1981	1982-1991
Constant	0.326	0.289	0.214
	(1.343)	(0.749)	(2.453)
Bade-Parkin (BP)	-0.007	0.034	-0.023
	(-0.070)	(0.225)	(-0.680)
Adj. R^2	-0.100	-0.095	-0.051
RMSE	0.283	0.449	0.102
Constant	0.330	0.298	0.206
	(1.422)	(0.809)	(2.458)
Alesina (AL)	-0.008	0.030	-0.020
	(-0.090)	(0.209)	(-0.607)
Adj. R^2	-0.099	-0.095	-0.061
RMSE	0.283	0.449	0.102
Constant	0.577	0.771	0.217
	(3.741)	(3.004)	(5.928)
Grilli et.al. (GMT)	-0.080	-0.118	-0.023
(Political)	(-2.044)*	(-1.802)	(-2.480)*
Adj. R^2	0.241	0.184	0.340
RMSE	0.244	0.406	0.058
Constant	0.391	0.421	0.218
	(2.068)	(1.385)	(3.239)
Eijffinger-Schaling	-0.029	-0.018	-0.022
(ES)	(-0.472)	(-0.183)	(-0.976)
Adj. R^2	-0.076	-0.096	-0.004
RMSE	0.280	0.449	0.099

Notes: t-values are in parentheses. One asterisk indicates that the coefficient is significantly different from zero at a 95% confidence level and two asterisks indicate that the coefficient is significant at a 99% confidence level.

Table 4 shows the outcomes of equation (4.2) explaining the variance of monthly inflation by the four independence indices. The inverse relationship between inflation variability and central bank independence is only significant for the GMT index, in particular for the second sub-period (!), but not for the other indices.[25] Generally, the latter indices do not support, except for the GMT index, Proposition 3.2 that the more independent the central bank - the lower d_2 - is, the lower the variance of the inflation rate.

4.3 Central Bank Independence and the Level of Output Growth

Given the inverse relationship between central bank independence and the level of inflation - see sub-section 4.1 - one could argue that the expected (ex ante) level of inflation influences expected (ex ante) real interest rates and, thereby, the level of output growth according to the Mundell-Tobin effect. A rise in expected inflation will lead - by Mundell (1963) - to substitution of liquid assets by long-term financial assets and - according to Tobin (1965) - to substitution of liquid assets by physical capital goods, lowering the marginal efficiency of capital, and will result in a decrease of expected real interest rates. Thus, more independent central banks will mitigate inflationary expectations inducing higher expected real interest rates and lower levels of investment and output growth.[26]

However, Proposition 3.5 (in sub-section 3.4) states that the mean or average rate of growth of output is independent from the prevailing monetary regime (d_2). Therefore, our regression analysis assumes the four indices of central bank independence (BP, AL, GMT and ES) to be the explanatory variables of average output growth (volume of GDP) on an annual base, without postulating an expected sign for these variables:

(4.3) average output growth $= c_0 + c_{1*}$ central bank independence $+ \vartheta_t$

Again, we examined the relationship between the various indices and level of real output growth for the post-Bretton-Woods period (1972-1990) and its two sub-periods (1972-1981 and 1982-1990).

---

25 Our estimation results for the BP index are according with Bade and Pankin (1988). However, they contradict the findings of Alesina and Summers (1991) who averaged the Alesina index and the GMT index of political and economic independence.

26 Nevertheless, in theory it could be argued that a higher degree of central bank independence results in lower inflationary uncertainty leading to a decrease of expected real interest rates and, thereby, to an increase of investment and output growth. Empirical evidence in sub-section 4.2 rejects the first link of this transmission mechanism.

20

Table 5 Average annual output growth and the various indices of central bank independence.

Explanatory variables	1972-1990	1972-1981	1982-1990
Constant	3.039	3.459	2.575
	(4.563)	(4.191)	(4.428)
Bade-Parkin (BP)	-0.164	-0.366	0.061
	(-0.630)	(-1.139)	(0.269)
Adj. R^2	-0.058	0.026	-0.092
RMSE	0.775	0.960	0.677
Constant	3.064	3.153	2.567
	(4.843)	(4.532)	(4.627)
Alesina (AL)	-0.177	-0.396	0.065
	(-0.710)	(-1.295)	(0.299)
Adj. R^2	-0.047	0.058	-0.090
RMSE	0.771	0.945	0.676
Constant	3.153	3.113	3.202
	(6.653)	(4.900)	(8.046)
Grilli et.al. (GMT)	-0.129	-0.137	-0.122
(Political)	(-1.073)	(-0.848)	(-1.203)
Adj. R^2	0.015	-0.029	0.043
RMSE	0.750	1.006	0.630
Constant	3.268	3.627	2.870
	(6.708)	(6.221)	(6.293)
Eijffinger-Schaling	-0.227	-0.383	-0.054
(ES)	(-1.419)	(-1.999)*	(-0.359)
Adj. R^2	0.084	0.214	-0.086
RMSE	0.721	0.863	0.675

Notes: t-values are in parentheses. One asterisk indicates that the coefficient is significantly different from zero at a 95% confidence level and two asterisks indicate that the coefficient is significant at a 99% confidence level.

Table 5 shows the estimation results of equation (4.3). The relationship between real output growth and central bank independence proves to be insignificant, except for the ES index in the first sub-period. The BP and AL index also have higher t-values for the first sub-period than for the second.[27] These outcomes could be explained by relatively more restrictive monetary policies by independent central banks during the late 1970s - the high-days of monetary targeting - which resulted in a lower level of economic growth.

In general, empirical evidence on the various indices does support Proposition 3.5 stating that there is no relation between central bank independence and average real output growth. In other words, although a high degree of central bank independence is associated with a low level of inflation in the long run, it has no large costs or benefits in terms of real economic growth. Thus, in countries with an independent central bank no trade off can be found between inflation on the one hand and economic growth and unemployment on the other hand in the long term.

4.4 Central Bank Independence and the Variability of Output Growth

What is the relationship between the degree of central bank independence and the variability of real output growth? According to Rogoff (1985) independent central banks purchase a lower level of inflation at the price of a higher variability of real economic growth. By relying more on rules rather than discretion in policy making they tolerate more cyclical variability of economic growth. Consequently, Rogoff's conclusion corresponds very well with our Proposition 3.6 (see sub-section 3.4) stating that the more dependent the central bank - the higher d_2 - is, the lower the variance of the growth rate of output around its mean or average rate of growth.

Again, our regression analysis assumes the various independence indices (BP, AL, GMT and ES) to be the explanatory variables of the variance of monthly output growth (volume of GDP) on an annual base, postulating a positive sign for these variables:

$$(4.4)\ \text{variance output growth} = d_0 + \overset{(+)}{d_{1*}}\ \text{central bank independence} + \kappa_t$$

The empirical relationship between the four indices and the variability of real output growth is investigated also for the four independence indices. The coefficient for the BP and AL index do not have the expected, positive sign in any sample period. Besides, none of the coefficients appears to be significantly different from zero. The t-values prove to be the highest for the GMT index.[28] These estimation results imply, of course, that a higher degree of central bank independence does not lead to more variability of real economic growth, rejecting Proposition 3.6 quite clearly.

Therefore, having an independent central bank does not result in more variable inflation (see

---

27 These estimation results for the AL and ES index correspond with De Haan and Sturm (1992). They are also in accordance with Alesina and Summers (1991) and De Long and Summers (1992) for their "single overall index" based on an average of the Alesina and GMT political and economic independence index. It should be noticed that De Long and Summers (1992) find, however, a positive relationship between central bank independence and economic growth, controlling for initial GDP per worker levels (see in this respect their chart 6 on p. 16).

28 Our empirical evidence for the AL and ES index is in accordance with that of De Haan and Sturm (1992). Alesina and Summers (1991) and De Long and Summers (1992) also find for their averaged Alesina-GMT index no support with respect to the relation between independence and the variability of output growth. The same holds for its relationship regarding the average and variance of unemployment rates.

sub-section 4.2) nor in more variable economic growth in the short term. So, inflation-averse central banks do not trigger off recessions nor do politically sensitive central banks avoid recessions.

Table 6 *Variance monthly output growth and the various indices of central bank independence.*

Explanatory variables	1972-1990	1972-1981	1982-1990
Constant	1.812	2.898	0.981
	(2.901)	(2.037)	(2.620)
Bade-Parkin (BP)	-0.232	-0.419	-0.114
	(-0.954)	(-0.756)	(-0.781)
Adj. R^2	-0.008	-0.041	-0.037
RMSE	0.727	1.656	0.436
Constant	1.731	2.777	0.897
	(2.877)	(2.036)	(2.473)
Alesina (AL)	-0.202	-0.376	-0.080
	(-0.852)	(-0.699)	(-0.563)
Adj. R^2	-0.026	-0.049	-0.066
RMSE	0.733	1.662	0.442
Constant	0.784	0.889	0.406
	(1.748)	(0.837)	(1.633)
Grilli et.al. (GMT)	0.114	0.265	0.070
(Political)	(0.996)	(0.981)	(1.110)
Adj. R^2	-0.001	-0.004	0.023
RMSE	0.710	1.681	0.394
Constant	1.203	1.375	0.840
	(2.345)	(1.209)	(2.803)
Eijffinger-Schaling	0.018	0.185	-0.049
(ES)	(0.104)	(0.496)	(-0.497)
Adj. R^2	-0.099	-0.074	-0.074
RMSE	0.759	1.682	0.443

Notes: t-values are in parentheses. One asterisk indicates that the coefficient is significantly different from zero at a 95% confidence level and two asterisks indicate that the coefficient is significant at a 99% confidence level.

4.5 Conclusion

The main conclusions of this theoretical and empirical analysis of central bank independence with respect to the level and variability of inflation and economic growth are the following.

First of all, both our model and estimation results, give further support to the well-known inverse relationship between the degree of central bank independence and the level of inflation found by Alesina (1988, 1989). However, it should be emphasized that these results are particularly sensitive to the numerical values of indices. For example, the GMT index shows no clear inverse relation to inflation, whereas the ES index proves to have a very significant, negative relation.

Secondly, contrary to Alesina and Summers (1991) we find no empirical evidence - except for the GMT index - supporting our proposition that the more independent the central bank is, the lower the variability of inflation.

Thirdly, according to our proposition that the level of economic growth does not depend on the prevailing monetary regime, no relationship can be found between central bank independence and the level of real output growth in the long run. Our interpretation of this outcome is that the attainment and maintenance of low inflation by an independent central bank is not accompanied by large costs or benefits in terms of sustainable economic growth. The absence of a long-run trade off between inflation and growth implies that the establishment of central bank independence in countries, which did not use to have this, is a free lunch.

Fourthly and finally, our estimation results reject clearly the proposition of a positive relation between independence and the variability of real output growth. An independent central bank does not lead to more variable economic growth in the short run. In other words, inflation-averse central banks do not bear the costs of triggering recessions nor do politically sensitive central banks reap the benefits of the avoiding recessions.

REFERENCES

Alesina, A.:"Macroeconomics and Politics", NBER Macroeconomic Annual 1988, Cambridge 1988.

Alesina, A.:"Politics and Business Cycles in Industrial Democracies", Economic Policy, No 8, 1989, pp. 55-98.

Alesina, A. and V. Grilli: "The European Central Bank: Reshaping Monetary Politics in Europe", Paper prepared for the CEPR - Georgetown University - IMF Conference "The Creation of a Central Bank", April 1991.

Alesina, A. and L. Summers: "Central Bank Independence and Macroeconomic Performance: some Comparative Evidence", Working Paper Harvard University, 1991.

Alesina, A. and G. Tabellini:"Rules and Discretion with Non-Coordinated Monetary and Fiscal Policies", Economic Inquiry , 25, 1987, pp. 619-630.

Alogoskoufis, S.: "On Inflation, Unemployment and the Optimal Exchange Rate Regime", in F. van der Ploeg (ed.), Handbook of International Macroeconomics, Oxford 1993, forthcoming.

Bade, Robin and Michael Parkin,:"Central Bank Laws and Monetary Policy", Working Paper Department of Economics University of Western Ontario, October 1988.

Barro, R. and D. Gordon:"Rules, Discretion and Reputation in a Model of Monetary Policy", Journal of Monetary Economics, 12, 1983a, pp. 101-122.

Barro, R. and D. Gordon:"A Positive Theory of Monetary Policy in a Natural Rate Model", Journal of Political Economy , 91, 1983b, pp. 589-610.

Beck, N.:"Presidential Influence on the Federal Reserve in the 1970s", American Journal of Political Science, 1982, pp. 415-445.

24

Blackburn, K. and M. Christensen:"Monetary Policy and Policy Credibility: Theories and Evidence", Journal of Economic Literature, XXVII, 1989, pp. 1-45.
Blanchard, O. and S. Fischer:"Lectures on Macroeconomics", Cambridge 1989.
Blanchard, O. and L. Summers:"Hysteresis and the European Unemployment Problem" in S. Fischer (ed) NBER Macroeconomics Annual, Cambridge 1986.
Bresciani-Turoni, C.:"The Economics of Hyperinflation", London 1953
Burns, A.:"The Anguish of Central Banking", Per Jacobsson Foundation, Belgrade, 1979.
Canzoneri, M.:"Monetary Policy Games and the Role of Private Information", American Economic Review, 75, 1985, pp. 1056-1070.
Canzoneri, A. and D. Henderson:"Monetary Policy in Interdependent Economies A Game-Theoretic Approach", Cambridge 1991.
Chowdhury, A.R.: "The Relationship between the Inflation Rate and its Variability: The Issues Reconsidered", Applied Economics, 23, 1991, pp. 993-1003.
Commission of the European Communities: "One Market, One Money - An Evaluation of the Potential Benefits and Costs of Forming an Economic and Monetary Union", European Economy, No. 44, October 1990.
Cukierman, A.:"Central Bank Behavior and Credibility: Some Recent Theoretical Developments", Federal Reserve Bank of St. Louis Review, 68, 1986, pp. 5-17.
Cukierman, A.: "Central Bank Strategy, Credibility and Independence: Theory and Evidence", to be published by the MIT Press in Spring 1993.
Cukierman, A. and A. Meltzer:"A Theory of Ambiguity, Credibility and Inflation Under Discretion and Asymmetric Information", Econometrica, 54, 1986a, pp. 1099-1128.
Eijffinger, S. and E. Schaling:"Central Bank Independence: Searching for the Philosopher's Stone", Discussion Paper CentER for Economic Research, Nr. 9251, December 1992.
Eijffinger, S. and E. Schaling: "Central Bank Independence in Twelve Industrial Countries", Banca Nazionale del Lavoro Quarterly Review, No. 184, March 1993, pp. 1-41.
Fischer, S.:"Wage Indexation and Macroeconomic Stability", Carnegie Rochester Conference Series on Public Policy, 5, 1977a, pp. 107-147.
Fischer, S.:"Long-Term Contracts, Rational Expectations, and the Optimal Money Supply Rule", Journal of Political Economy, 85, 1977b, pp. 191-205.
Funke, N.:"Wage Formation and Monetary Policy Rules", Kiel Working Paper,No. 514, June 1992.
Gray, J.:"Wage Indexation: A Macroeconomic Approach", Journal of Monetary Economics, 2, 1976, pp. 221-235.
Grilli, V., D. Masciandaro, and G. Tabellini:"Political and Monetary Institutions and Public Financial Policies in the Industrial Countries", Economic Policy, 1991.
Haan, J. de and J.E. Sturm: "The Case for Central Bank Independence", Banca Nazionale del Lavoro Quarterly Review, No. 182, September 1992, pp. 305-327.
Havrilesky, T.:"A Partisanship Theory of Fiscal and Monetary Regimes", Journal of Money, Credit and Banking, 19, 1987, pp. 308-325.
Hetzel, R.:"The Formulation of Monetary Policy", Manuscript, Federal Reserve Bank of Richmond, August 1985.
Kane, E.:"Politics and Fed Policymaking: The More Things Change The More They Stay the Same", Journal of Monetary Economics, 1980, pp. 199-212.

25

Kane, E.:"External Pressure and the Operation of the Fed", in R. Lombra and W. Witte (eds) "Political Economy of International and Domestic Monetary Relations", Iowa, 1982, pp. 211-232.

Kydland, F. and E. Prescott:"Rules Rather Than Discretion: The Inconsistency of Optimal Plans", Journal of Political Economy, 85, 1977, pp. 473-492.

Lindbeck, A. and D. Shower:"Wage Setting, Unemployment and Insider-Outsider Relations", American Economic Review, Papers and Proceedings, 76, 1986, pp. 235-239.

De Long, J.B. and L.H. Summers: "Macroeconomic Policy and Long-Run Growth", Economic Review Federal Reserve Bank of Kansas City, 77, 1992, pp. 5-29.

Mascaro, A. and A.H. Meltzer: "Long- and Short-Term Interest Rates in a Risky World", Journal of Monetary Economics, 12, 1983, pp. 485-518.

Mayer, T.: (ed) "The Political Economy of American Monetary Policy", Cambridge, 1990.

Mundell, R.A.: "Inflation and Real Interest", Journal of Political Economy, 71, 1963, pp. 280-283.

Rogoff, K.:"The Optimal Degree of Commitment to an Intermediate Monetary Target", Quarterly Journal of Economics, 100, 1985, pp. 1169-1190.

Ungerer, H.: "The EMS, 1979-1990, Policies-Evolution-Outlook", Konjunkturpolitik, 36, Heft 6, pp. 329-362.

Stock, J. and M. Watson: "Variable Trends in Economic Time Series", Journal of Economic Perspectives, 2, 1988, pp. 147-174.

Tobin, J.: "Money and Economic Growth", Econometrica, 33, 1965, pp. 671-684.

Weintraub, R.:"Congressional Supervision of Monetary Policy", Journal of Monetary Economics, 1978, pp. 341-362.

Willet, T. (ed):"Political Business Cycles - The Political Economy of Money, Inflation and Unemployment", Durham, 1988.

Wooley, J.:"Monetary Politics - The Federal Reserve and the Politics of Monetary Policy", Cambridge, 1984.

Figure 1
Actual and Expected Inflation with an Inefficient Natural Rate

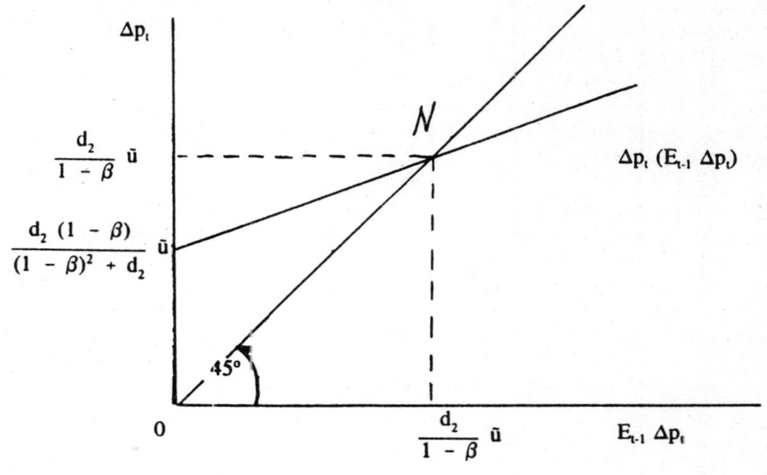

Figure 2 Central Bank Independence and the Variance of Inflation

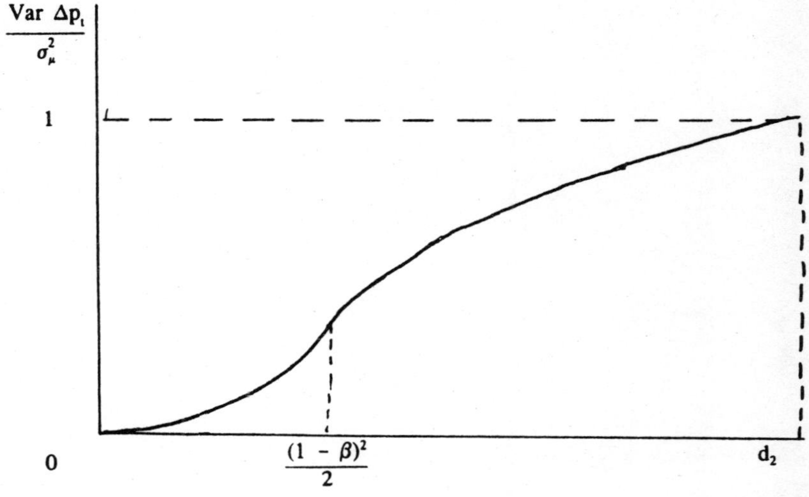

Figure 3 Central Bank Independence and the Variance of Output

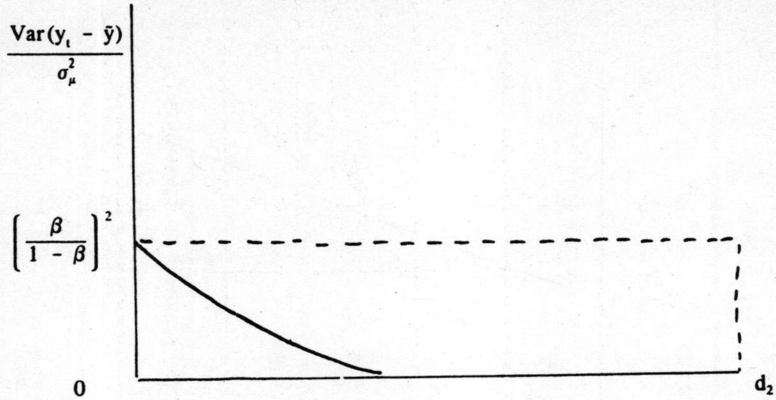

*Table 2 Central Bank Independence, Growth and Inflation**

Inflation		Growth	
Mean	Variance	Mean	Variance
$\frac{\partial \Delta \bar{p}_t}{\partial d_2} > 0$	$\frac{\partial \left[\frac{\operatorname{Var} \Delta p_t}{\sigma^2 \mu} \right]}{\partial d_2} > 0$	$\frac{\partial \Delta \bar{y}_t}{\partial d_2} = 0$	$\frac{\partial \left[\frac{\operatorname{Var}(\Delta y_t - \Delta \bar{y}_t)}{\sigma^2 \Delta \mu} \right]}{\partial d_2} < 0$
PROPOSITION 3.1	**PROPOSITION 3.2**	**PROPOSITION 3.5**	**PROPOSITION 3.6**

* Note degree of central bank independence $\equiv 1/d_2$.

Figure 4. The Bade-Parkin index and the level of inflation.

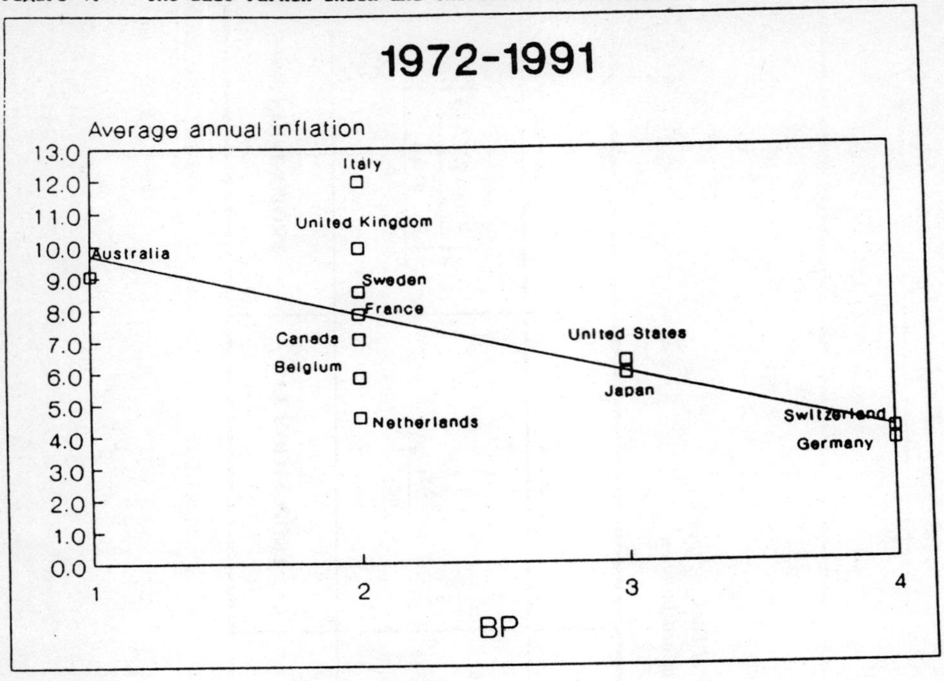

Root MSE	1.93880	R-square	0.4482
Dep Mean	7.07434	Adj R-sq	0.3930

Average inflation = 11.546 - 1.850 * BP
(6.931) (-2.850)

Figure 5. The Alesina index and the level of inflation.

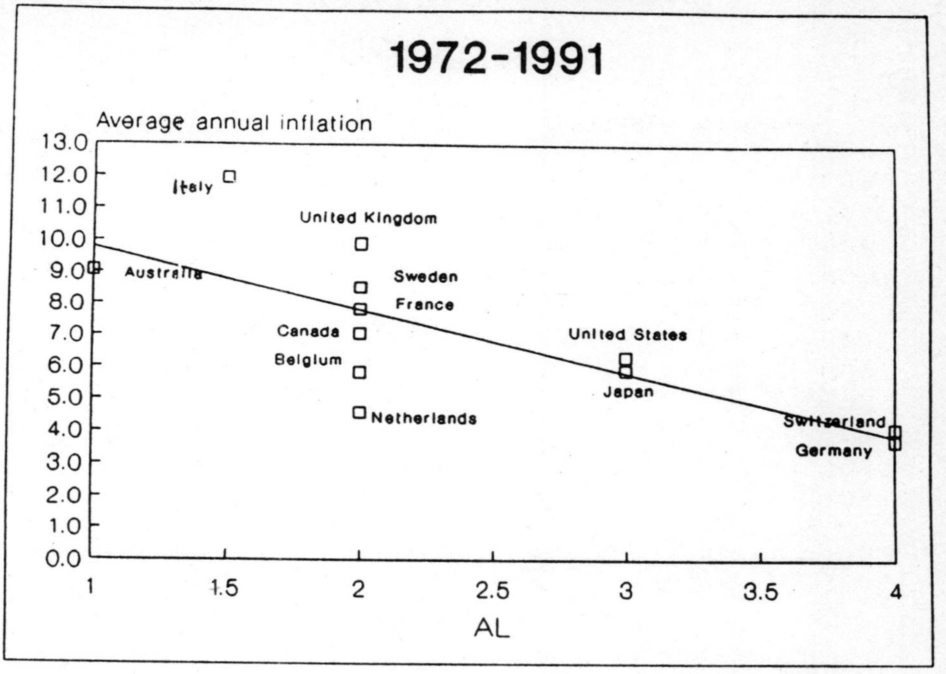

Root MSE	1.74958	R-square	0.5507
Dep Mean	7.07434	Adj R-sq	0.5057

Average inflation = 11.778 − 1.981 * AL
(8.205) (−3.501)

Figure 6. The Grilli-Masciandaro-Tabellini index and the level of inflation.

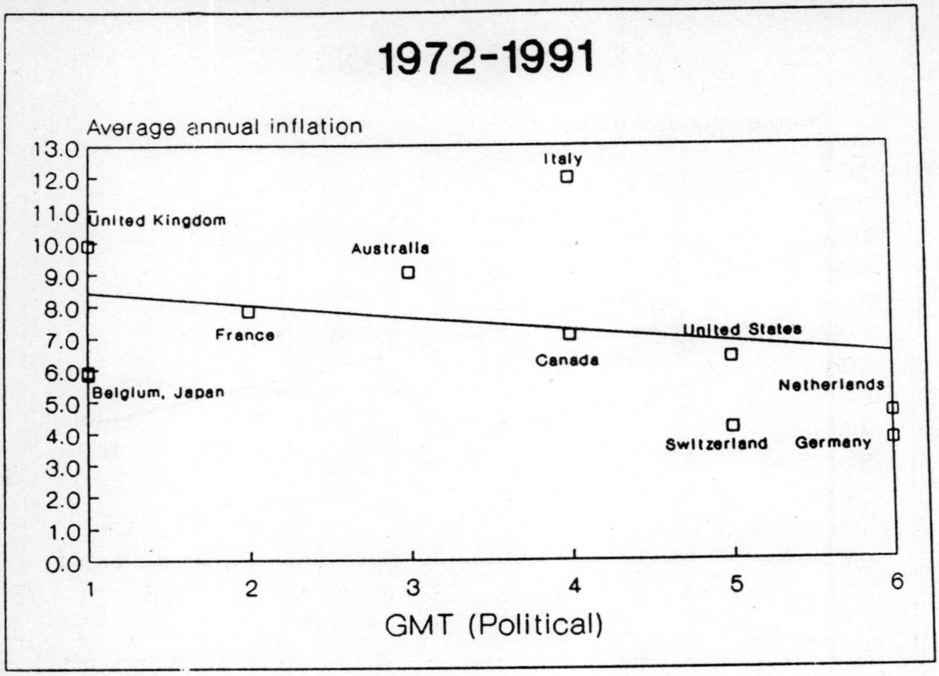

Root MSE	2.45595	R-square	0.1746
Dep Mean	6.94071	Adj R-sq	0.0828

Average inflation = 8.822 - 0.395 * GMT(Political)
(5.686) (-1.380)

Figure 7. The Eijffinger-Schaling index and the level of inflation.

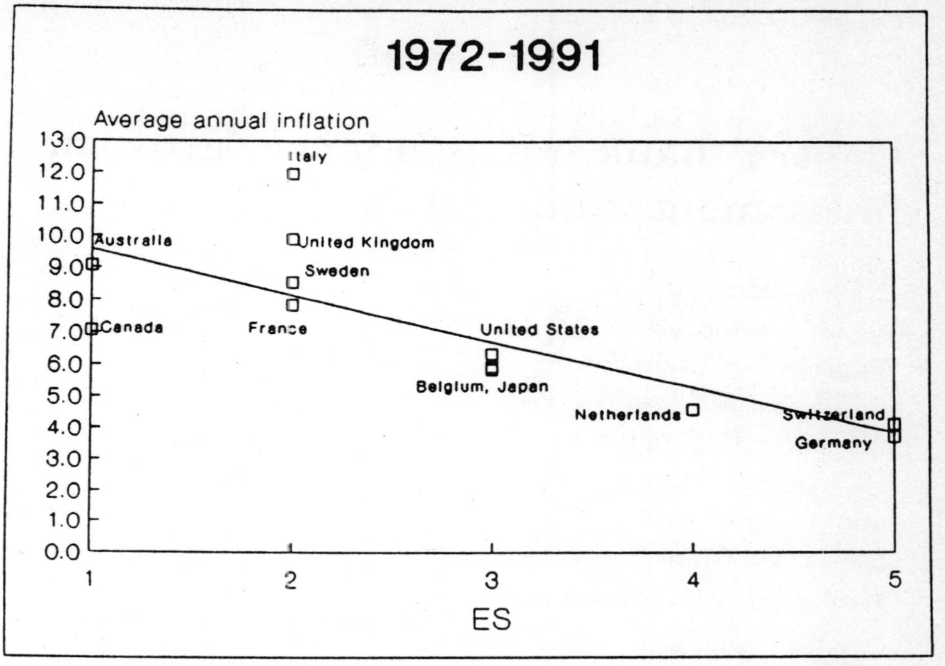

Root MSE	1.62994	R-square	0.6100
Dep Mean	7.07434	Adj R-sq	0.5710

$$\text{Average inflation} = \underset{(9.998)}{11.014} - \underset{(-3.955)}{1.433} * ES$$

[16]

Carnegie-Rochester Conference Series on Public Policy 39 (1993) 95-140
North-Holland

Central bank independence, growth, investment, and real rates*

Alex Cukierman†
Tel-Aviv University, Tel-Aviv 69978, Israel
Pantelis Kalaitzidakis
Columbia University, New York, New York 10027
Lawrence H. Summers
The World Bank, Washington, D.C. 20433
and
Steven B. Webb
The World Bank, Washington, D.C. 20433

Abstract

This paper uses new measures of central bank independence (CBI) for a sample of up to seventy countries in order to investigate the effect of CBI on growth, private investment, productivity growth, and the variability (over time) of growth, controlling for other variables. The proxies for independence are an aggregate index of legal independence based on sixteen specific features of the central banks' charters and the average turnover rate of central bank governors. The paper also addresses the issue of simultaneity between growth and inflation by using an index of political vulnerability of the central bank. This index is the fraction of political transitions which are followed, within a short period of time, by a replacement of the governor of the central bank.

A main finding of the paper is that CBI has a positive effect on growth in LDCs (less-developed countries) and no effect within industrial countries.

The paper also presents evidence on the relation between CBI and the distribution of interest rates.

*We are indebted to Matthew Canzoneri, William Easterly, Alan Gelb, and Allan Meltzer for useful comments and to participants at the Conference for a lively discussion.

†*Correspondence to:* Alex Cukierman, Department of Economics, Tel-Aviv University, Ramat-Aviv, Tel-Aviv 69978, Israel.

Elsevier Science Publishers B.V.

1. Introduction

It is generally believed that a high degree of central bank independence (CBI) reduces the inflationary bias of policy and enhances the credibility of stable monetary policies. To the extent that higher and less-stable inflation rates cause inefficient resource allocation and discourage investment, we would therefore expect more CBI to lead to higher growth on average. But, by reducing the scope for policies to maintain full employment and to encourage investment directly, more independence of the central bank (CB) may reduce the average performance of the economy and the long-run rate of growth.[1] Thus it is ambiguous a priori which way central bank independence will affect real growth.

Recent evidence supports the view that there is a clear-cut negative relation between CBI and the level and variability of inflation (Grilli, Masciandaro, and Tabellini (1991), Cukierman, Webb, and Neyapti (1992), Cukierman (1992, Chapter 20) and Alesina and Summers (1993). The evidence with respect to the relation between growth and CBI is not as clear. Grilli, et al. and Alesina and Summers find no relation between growth and CBI in industrial economies. Delong and Summers (1992), however, find, after controlling for initial GDP, a positive relation between growth and CBI in a sample of 15 industrialized economies.

Obtaining wider and more solid evidence on the relationship between growth and CBI is interesting for several reasons. First, it may shed some light on whether reduced discretion is good or bad for growth. Second, it should make it possible to determine whether the negative effect of inflation on growth found in recent studies like Fischer (1991) is due to unstable macroeconomic policies or to a reverse causality in which negative real shocks, by reducing real output growth, push the price level up.

Measuring CBI is not easy. Existing studies were therefore limited to industrial economies and to proxies of legal independence. Those proxies are poor indicators of actual independence in less-developed countries (LDCs). This paper utilizes new broadly-based and unified measures of CBI for a sample of about sixty countries. Those include aggregate indices of legal independence and the <u>actual</u> turnover of CB governors. Details appear in Cukierman, Webb, and Neyapti (1992) and in Chapter 19 of Cukierman (1992).

Recent literature (Barro, 1991, is a representative example) has identified a number of variables like initial GDP and education that partially account for the cross-sectional variability in rates of growth during the last three decades. After controling for some of those variables and other time-related

[1] Those who advocate such policies must believe that nominal contracts and/or informational asymmetries produce sufficiently long-lasting effects of money on the economy.

variables, like changes in terms of trade, this paper investigates the effect of CBI on growth. Both cross-sectional and pooled cross-section time series (across decades) regressions are tried.

The experiments reported here show no evidence of a relationship between growth and CBI within industrial countries but that growth is positively related to CBI in most LDCs. Differences in CBI also help account for differences in growth residuals between the two groups of countries. This evidence takes the form of a ceteris paribus significant negative relationship between growth and two measures of actual CB dependence. One measure is the frequency of turnover of CB governors and the other is the fraction of political transitions that is followed within a short period of time by a replacement of the CB governor. The first measure was found to be a good proxy for inflation in LDCs (Cukierman, Webb, and Neyapti (1992) and Chapter 20 of Cukierman (1992)). The second measure is a proxy for the political vulnerability of the CB. Both measures have a significant negative impact on growth within LDCs as well as in the entire sample of countries.

These proxies for CB dependence are also used to shed more light on the issue of potential reverse causality in growth equations in which inflation is used as a proxy for unstable monetary policy as an explanatory variable. This is done by using turnover, or the index of CB (political) vulnerability, or both as instruments for inflation. Controlling for other determinants of growth, the impact of inflation on growth is still negative, but less significant than in the ordinary least squares regressions. The paper also looks at the relation between private investment, productivity growth, and the intra-country variability of growth on one hand and CBI on the other. New evidence on interest rates and CBI is also presented. Both nominal and real rates are less variable the higher is CBI, and ex post real deposit rates are, in many cases, higher on average in countries with more independent central banks.

To make the paper self-contained, Section 2 discusses the construction of the indices of CBI used in the rest of the paper. Section 3 develops a benchmark growth equation and uses it to investigate the effect of CBI on growth. The issue of potential simultaneity between growth, inflation, and Central Bank governors' turnover is investigated empirically in Section 4. Evidence on private investment, productivity growth, and CBI is presented in Section 5. The relation between the intra-country variability of growth and of growth residuals on one hand and CBI on the other is taken up in Section 6. Section 7 presents new evidence on interest rates and CBI. The last section concludes.

2. Measures of central bank independence (CBI) – an overview

Central bank independence depends on many attributes which are not easily quantifiable. As a consequence, existing evidence on the relationship between growth and CBI relies only on legal independence and is restricted to the industrial countries (Grilli, Masciandaro, and Tabellini (1991) and Alesina and Summers (1993)). There often are serious gaps though, between legal independence and actual independence. These gaps are particularly notable in LDCs. Additional indicators of CBI are therefore needed.

For the most part the paper utilizes two proxies for CBI. The first is an aggregate index of legal independence based on sixteen characteristics of central bank charters. The second is the actual turnover of central bank governors. To deal with potential simultaneity problems, we also use an index of political vulnerability of the central bank. These indices are available for a sample of up to seventy countries, including all the industrial countries and up to fifty LDCs. We do not claim that these proxies capture all the dimensions of CBI, but they are the most comprehensive systematic measures currently available and probably the only ones that provide information on actual as well as on legal independence. This is particularly important for LDCs, where actual and legal independence differ substantially.

a. Legal independence[2]

Besides being an essential component of actual independence, legal independence is of independent interest for several reasons. First, it suggests the degree of independence that legislators meant to confer on the central bank (CB). Second, most existing attempts at the systematic characterization of CBI rely solely on legal aspects of independence. Availability of an index of legal independence is therefore needed to establish comparability with previous studies.

The specific features of legal independence, used to construct the aggregate index of legal independence, are constructed in the following manner: A code of independence is assigned to each central bank for each characteristic based on a limited number of narrow but relatively precise legal characteristics. Only the written information from the charters is used. Additional information on how the law is applied in practice is deliberately left out because it is reflected by separate indices.

The coded legal characteristics of "variables" can be divided into four groups: (1) variables concerning the appointment, dismissal, and term of office of the chief executive officer (CEO) of the bank (usually the governor); (2) variables concerning the resolution of conflicts between the executive branch

[2]This and the following subsection draw on Chapter 19 of Cukierman (1992).

and the CB and the degree of participation of the CB in the formulation of monetary policy and in the budgetary process; (3) final objectives of the CB as stated in its charter; and (4) legal restrictions on the ability of the public sector to borrow from the CB. Such restrictions take the form of various limitations on the volume, maturity, rates, and width of direct advances and of securitized lending from the CB to the public sector.

In coding various central banks by the degree of independence within each group of characteristics, the following criteria are used: central banks in which the legal term of office of the CEO is longer and in which the executive branch has little legal authority in the appointment or dismissal of the governor are classified as more independent on the CEO dimension. By the same logic, central banks with wider authority to formulate monetary policy and to resist the executive branch in cases of conflict are classified as more independent on the policy formulation dimension.

Central banks in which the only or main objective of policy (as specified in the charter) is price stability are classified as being more independent in this dimension than central banks with a number of objectives in addition to price stability. These banks are in turn classified as being more independent than banks with a large number of objectives or banks in whose charter price stability is not mentioned as an objective at all. This classification of the "objectives" variable is designed to capture the legal mandate of the bank to single-mindedly pursue the objective of price stability. (One of the few central banks in which such an unequivocal legal mandate exists is the Bundesbank.) It does not therefore reflect (as the previous two groups of variables) the general level of independence from government. It indicates, instead, the legal mandate of the CB to elevate the target of price stability above other objectives. In Rogoff's (1985) terminology, it measures how strong is the "conservative bias" of the CB as embodied in the law.

Similarly we classify banks in which the limitations on lending from the CB to the public sector are stricter as more independent to pursue the objective of price stability. These limitations encompass a number of more detailed variables such as separate limitations on advances and securitized lending and restrictions on maturities and on interest rates. Generally, the stricter the limitation, the higher is the independence coding given to the bank on that dimension. The comparability of various types of limitations is complicated because different countries specify limitations in terms of different reference variables. A few countries specify limitations in absolue cash amounts, and others use a percentage of CB liabilities. The most prevalent type of limitation is formulated as a percentage of revenues, and in a minority of cases as a percentage of government expenditures. The "bite" of these limitations obviously depends on the magnitudes of the reference variables. Other things the same, however, absolute cash limits are more binding than limits in terms of government revenues. The most accommodative limits are those specified in terms of government expenditures. These considerations are embodied in a "type of limit" variable and also influence the coding of the severity of limitations on loans to government via advances and securitized lending.

Limitations on lending are also classified as stricter, the nearer the rates paid by government to market rates and the shorter the maturities of the loans from the CB to the public sector. They are also stricter, the narrower the circle of institutions that are allowed to borrow from the CB and the smaller the discretion of the executive branch in deciding to whom the CB will lend and how much. In addition, central bank laws that prohibit the CB from buying government securities on the primary market are considered, ceteris paribus, stricter than laws that do not contain such a prohibition.

Altogether, sixteen different legal variables are coded using a scale ranging between 0 (smallest level of independence) to 1 (highest level of independence). The number of independence levels generally varies across legal variables depending on the fineness of data on alternative legal characteristics. Using a two-step procedure, the sixteen legal variables are aggregated into a single overall measure of legal independence. This overall index is basically a weighted average of the sixteen legal variables. It varies during the eighties, between a maximum of 0.69 (for Germany) and a minimum of 0.10 (for Poland). The median level of legal independence is about the same in developed countries and in LDCs. Further details on the coding of the legal variables appear in Table 19.1 of Cukierman (1992) or in Table 1 of Cukierman, Webb, and Neyapti (1992).

b. The turnover rate of Central Bank Governors as a proxy of actual independence

As most practitioners in the area of monetary policymaking are well aware, the legal status of a central bank is only one of several elements that determines its actual independence. Although there are important variations in the degree of completeness of different CB laws, many are highly incomplete and leave a lot of room for interpretation. As a result, factors such as tradition or the personalities of the governor and other high officials of the bank at least partially shape the actual level of CB independence. Even when the law is quite explicit, it may not be operational if there is a tradition or an understanding within government that things should be done in a different way. A striking example is Argentina, in which the legal term of office of the governor is four years. But there is also an informal tradition that the governor of the CB offers his resignation to the executive whenever there is a change of government or even of the finance minister. Argentinian governors invariably adhered to this tradition. As a consequence, the average actual term of office of the governor in Argentina during the 1980s was about ten months. Obviously the actual degree of independence of the Argentinian CB is substantially lower than the one implied by measures of legal independence including, in particular, the four-year legal term of office.

There are no obvious indicators of actual, as opposed to legal, CB independence. This is not because the matter is not important, but because it is hard to find systematic indicators of actual independence when it diverges from legal independence. The extreme case of Argentina, though, suggests that at least above some threshold the turnover rate of central bank governors is a proxy of (lack of) actual independence. The average yearly turnover rate between 1950 and 1989 ranges from a minimum of 0.03 (average tenure of 33 years) in Iceland to a maximum of 0.93 (average tenure of about thirteen months) in Argentina. Turnover rates in LDCs tend to spread into a range that has not been experienced in the developed countries (DC). The highest turnover among the DC is 0.2 (average tenure of five years) for Spain and Japan. More than half of the LDCs have turnover rates exceeding this.

Low turnover does not necessarily imply a high level of CB independence – a relatively subservient governor may stay in office longer precisely because he does not stand up to the executive branch. This may be true for countries with exceptionally low turnover rates such as Iceland, Denmark, Britain, and the United States. In such countries turnover is probably unrelated to independence. On the other hand, it is very likely that above some critical turnover rate CB independence is lower the higher the turnover rate of CB governors. One reason is that for sufficiently high turnover rates the tenure of the CB governor is shorter than that of the executive branch. This makes the governor more susceptible to influence by the executive branch and discourages him or her from trying to implement longer-term policies the lower the expected tenure. Since in most countries the electoral cycle is at least four years, it is likely that the threshold turnover is somewhere between 0.2 and 0.25 (average tenure of four to five years). In addition, for very short terms of office such as three years or less (turnover rates of 0.33 or larger), it is generally more difficult to implement long-term policies for any electoral cycle.

The benefits of price stability accrue after a while whereas the employment and high-interest costs of stabilization occur upfront. Similarly, a positive inflationary surprise produces immediate benefits, but the full costs of this policy (in terms of lower credibility and higher inflation) appear later. Central bank governors with shorter horizons in office are therefore more likely to succumb to inflationary temptations. Hence, there should be a positive association, at least above some threshold, between inflation and turnover. The evidence supports this implication for LDCs; for industrial economies the turnover rates are all below the threshold (Cukierman, Webb, and Neyapti (1992) and Chapter 20 of Cukierman (1992)). This result is consistent with the view that turnover is a reasonable proxy for CBI within LDCs but not necessarily in the group of industrial economies. By contrast legal independence appears to be a reasonable proxy for actual independence in developed economies but not in LDCs.

c. A measure of the political vulnerability of the central bank

A central bank whose chief executive officer is frequently replaced following political transitions is likely to be more dependent on the political authorities than a central bank in which the governor outlives most political changes. This notion is captured by using an index of political vulnerability of the central bank developed in Cukierman and Webb (1993). The index is defined as the fraction of times that a political transition is followed within 6 months by a replacement of the central bank governor. The index ranges between a minimum of zero for a number of countries (including the United States, Canada, and Austria) and a maximum of 1.375 (for Argentina). It is generally lower in developed economies than in LDCs. Within LDCs, it is higher in countries that alternate between democratic and authoritarian regimes. The vulnerability index is used in Section 4 in order to resolve potential problems of simultaneity between growth on one hand and inflation and political instability on the other. Section 4 also contains additional details on the construction of the vulnerability index and on a decomposition of turnover into political and nonpolitical components.

3. Growth and central bank independence

a. Introduction and background

Existing evidence on the relationship between growth and CBI is consistent with the view that growth is independent of CBI (Grilli, Masciandaro, and Tabellini (1991) and Alesina and Summers (1993)). This evidence is nevertheless, restricted to the industrial countries and it does not attempt to control for other important determinants of growth.[3] This paper extends the existing literature along three dimensions. First, it controls for other determinants of growth. Second, it enlarges the sample to sixty countries, including LDCs as well as industrial countries. Finally, it utilizes the new measures of CBI described in the previous section. Those measures are uniformly available for industrial and developing economies. An important finding of previous work that utilizes those measures is that legal independence performs relatively well in explaining inflation differentials among industrial

[3]A recent exception is Delong and Summers (1992) who control for initial GDP for a subset of the industrial countries.

countries, while the turnover rate of central bank governors performs better in explaining those differentials among the LDCs (Cukierman, Webb, and Neyapti (1992) and Chapter 20 of Cukierman (1992)). We therefore presume that legal independence is a better proxy for independence in industrial countries and the turnover rate of Central Bank Governors is a better proxy for LDCs. But we experiment with both proxies for all countries as well. The different meaning of legal independence in industrial and in developing countries is discussed in Chapter 23 of Cukierman (1992). Figure 1 presents a plot of the average per capita rate of growth between 1960 and 1988, from Summers and Heston (1991), against the average turnover rate of Central Bank Governors between 1960 and 1989. The data points are spread all over the plane, corroborating (in a wider sample) the findings of previous work, which found no relation between growth and CBI. A regression of per capita growth on turnover confirms the lack of a relationship. Similar results obtain with the aggregate legal measure of CBI.

b. Controlling for other determinants of differences in growth

Recent literature has identified a number of structural determinants of growth, like initial GDP and initial enrollment ratios for primary and for secondary education (Barro, 1991). In addition, changes in terms of trade, particularly in LDCs, are important for export-led growth. After experimenting with various specifications of growth equations, we finally settled on a benchmark equation in which per capita growth is regressed on initial GDP, initial primary and secondary education enrollment ratios, and a measure of change in terms of trade. The first three regressors are from the Barro-Wolf (1989) data set. The terms of trade are measured as the ratio of export unit values to import unit values from the International Financial Statistics for all the countries for which both of those measures are available. For the remaining countries (up to 15) a similar measure developed in The World Bank is used.[4] This benchmark regression is run initially on a cross-section of up to 55 countries during the period between 1960 and 1989. Adding either legal CBI or the turnover of Central Bank Governors during the same period does not produce significant coefficients for these proxies of CBI, as can be seen from the first two columns of Table 1.

Cross-section regressions over 30-year periods are likely to be missing the effect of time-dependent shocks on the time profile of growth within each

[4]Further details appear on p. 280 of the World Development Report (1991). We also experimented with other terms of trade measures but settled on this one because it is significant in the largest number of cases. Since most of the LDCs in the sample are small open economies, their terms of trade may be taken as exogenous. This assumption is more problematic for large developed economies like the U.S. and Japan.

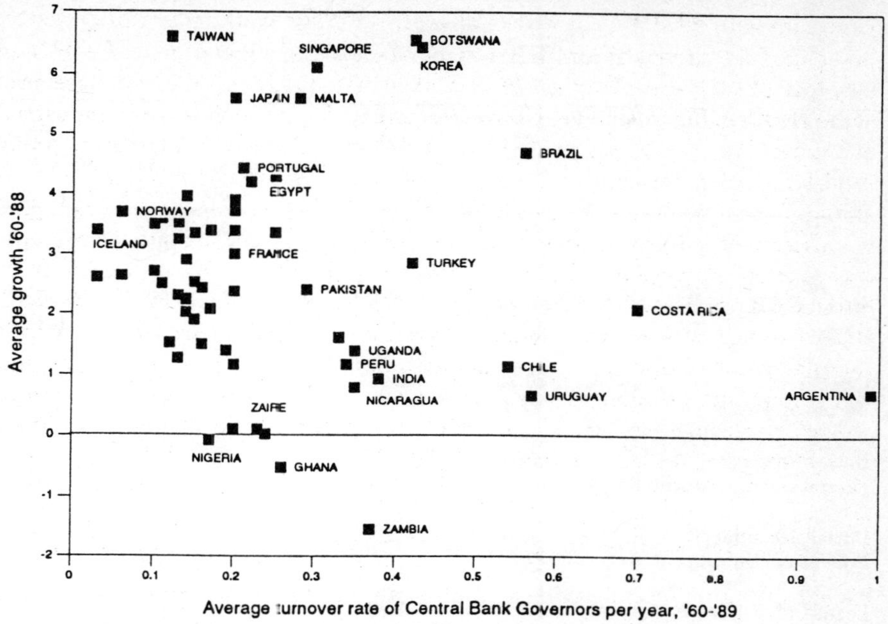

Figure 1

Growth and governors' turnover

Table 1:
Growth and CBI - Cross-Section and Panel

DEPENDENT VARIABLE: Per Capita Growth Rate	(1)	(2)	(3)	(4)	(5)
	Cross-Section		*Pooled Cross-Section Time Series (Panel)*		
Constant	1.37*	2.01*	0.28	0.62	0.94
	(1.8)	(2.3)	(0.3)	(0.6)	(1.0)
Initial GDP	-0.0005**	-0.0003*	-0.0002**	-0.0002*	-0.0002**
	(-3.6)	(-2.1)	(-2.2)	(-2.0)	(-2.6)
Change in Terms of Trade	20.26*	21.44*	28.33**	30.65**	30.01**
	(2.1)	(2.1)	(4.76)	(4.71)	(5.1)
Initial Primary Education Enrollment Ratio	2.25*	2.19*	0.73	0.95	1.12
	(2.4)	(2.1)	(0.7)	(0.9)	(1.2)
Initial Secondary Education Enrollment Ratio	3.60*	1.49	2.69*	2.55*	2.32*
	(2.3)*	(1.0)	(2.1)	(1.9)	(1.8)
Legal Independence		-1.92		-1.48	
		(-1.0)		(-0.9)	
Central Bank Governors Turnover Rate	-0.20				-2.17*
	(-0.1)				(-2.1)
Dummy for the '60s			2.41**	2.30**	1.91**
			(4.3)	(4.0)	(3.4)
Dummy for the '70s			1.77**	1.80**	1.56**
			(3.4)	(3.4)	(3.1)
$\bar{R}^2$	0.29	0.20	0.22	0.21	0.25
$P(\rho)$			0.05	0.12	0.07
No. of Observations	52	52	146	139	141

t-statistics are in parentheses under the coefficients.
$P(\rho)$ is the significance level of a first-order autoregressive coefficient from a regression of the residuals of each country in each decade on the residuals of the same country in the previous decade.
* significant at the 0.05 level.
** significant at the 0.01 level.

country.[5] In particular it is likely that over such a long period, terms of trade of individual countries move in offsetting directions, obscuring some of the potential effect of terms of trade on growth. To account for such effects we run a pooled cross-section, time-series regression in which the observations for each country are broken down by decades (1960–69, 1970–79, 1980–89). Rates of change are now decade averages and initial GDP and enrollment ratios for primary and for secondary education are now taken at the beginning of each decade. To account for other possible time-specific variations across the broad subperiods, decade dummies are included as well. Such a regression that does not include measures of CBI as regressors is shown in the third column of Table 1 (we refer to it as the benchmark panel regression). It is notable that the decade dummies are highly significant and that, in line with our prior, the rate of change in the terms of trade is substantially more significant than it was in the cross-section regressions. This supports the view that the panel benchmark is a more relevant point of departure.

We then add decade-specific proxies for CBI within each country as regressors. The results are summarized for aggregate legal CBI and for Central Bank Governors turnover in the fourth and fifth columns of Table 1. It is apparent that the first variable is insignificant. But the turnover of Central Bank Governors has a significant negative impact on per capita income growth. The coefficient of turnover implies that a 0.1 increase in turnover (one more per decade) reduces the average rate of growth, other things the same, by about 0.2 percent per year. To illustrate the orders of magnitude involved, consider Chile with an average yearly turnover of 0.54 and Indonesia with a turnover of about 0.22 over the 60–89 period. Taken literally, this implies that about 0.7 percentage points of the difference in average yearly growth rates between these two countries is attributable to the difference in turnover.

One should not interpret this to imply that a reduction of 0.1 in turnover without any other change will raise average yearly growth by 0.2 percent, but it is usually the case that a lower turnover of Central Bank Governors is associated with a more stable macroeconomic policy environment. When this, and other related factors, change in conjunction with the lower turnover, it seems reasonable to expect an increase in the average rate of growth of the order of magnitude implied by the regression results. A parable may sharpen the argument. Measuring turnover is analogous to taking the temperature of a sick patient. A high temperature is a signal that something is wrong. This does not mean that a reduction of temperature by means of aspirin without taking care of the root cause is going to cure the patient. However, after treatment of the root cause, a reduction in temperature is usually taken as

[5] Easterly, Kremer, Prichett, and Summers (1992) show that growth rates are highly unstable over time.

a signal of recovery. Similarly the reduction of turnover at the central bank without doing anything else is tantamount to the treatment of a symptom only. However, when the central bank is given more authority to pursue stable policies, this is normally accompanied by a reduction in turnover. In such cases, turnover is a good proxy for the quality of policymaking institutions.

In summary, although the experiments described in this subsection do not show any effect of legal independence on growth, the lack of actual independence as proxied by turnover does have a significant negative effect on growth when one controls for both cross-sectional and decade-specific factors.

c. The effect of outlier countries

Figure 2 presents a plot of the residuals from the benchmark cross-sectional regression (not shown in Table 1) against the turnover of Central Bank Governors. It is apparent from the figure that Botswana, Brazil, Korea, and Argentina are outliers. But there is a difference between the first three countries and Argentina. Botswana, Korea, and Brazil managed to maintain exceptionally high growth residuals in spite of sizeable turnover rates of Central Bank Governors. Argentina, by contrast, sticks out in that it has the highest turnover of Central Bank Governors and one of the lowest growth residuals.

In order to determine whether outliers are responsible for the existence or the absence of a relationship between growth and CBI, the panel regressions from Table 1 have been rerun without the outliers. The first two columns of Table 2 summarize the results with turnover as a proxy for dependence. Column 1 excludes all four outliers and column 2 only Botswana, Brazil, and Korea. The third column also excludes these three countries but replaces turnover with legal independence. The first two columns show that, independently of whether Argentina is included or excluded, lack of central bank independence as proxied by turnover has a highly significant negative impact on growth. Although significance is reduced somewhat (to 0.0018 and a t-statistic of -3.2) by the exclusion of Argentina, turnover is now still more significant than in the panel regression including the outliers (column 5 of Table 1). The exclusion of outliers also dramatically reduces the significance of cross-decades correlation in the residuals. The third column of the table reconfirms that legal independence is unrelated to growth.

Analysis of the correlation across decades between growth residuals and turnover within the four outlier economies reveals a definite negative correlation in Brazil, a mild negative correlation in Argentina and Korea, and no relation in Botswana.[6]

Equation (2) in Table 2 was reestimated with the addition of alternate measures of political instability, including the Barro-Wolf (1989) assassina-

[6]Observations on Botswana are available for only two of the three decades.

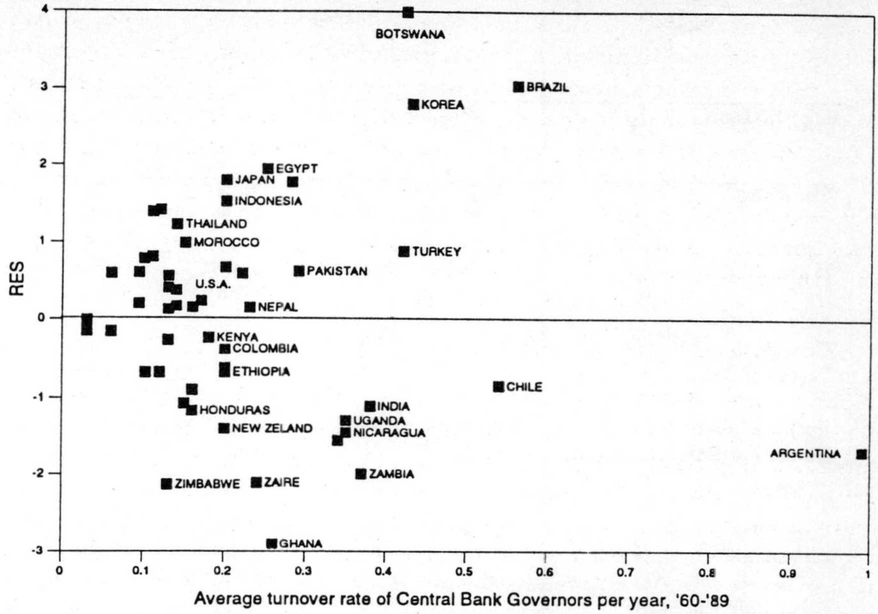

Figure 2

Cross-sectional growth residuals and governors turnover*

* RES are the residuals from a regression of per capita growth on initial values of GDP per capita, primary and secondary enrollment ratios, and the average change in terms of trade.

Table 2:
Growth and CBI Excluding Outliers

DEPENDENT VARIABLE: Per Capita Growth Rate	(1)[a] Pooled	(2)[b] Cross-Section	(3)[b] Time Series	(4)[b] Cross-Section
Constant	1.50 (1.6)	1.08 (1.3)	0.24 (0.2)	1.34* (2.3)
Initial GDP	-0.0002* (-2.3)	-0.0002* (-2.2)	-0.0001 (-1.5)	-0.0005** (-4.1)
Change in Terms of Trade	27.53** (4.9)	28.15** (5.1)	29.12** (4.6)	14.84 (1.9)
Initial Primary Education Enrollment Ratio	0.86 (0.9)	0.99 (1.1)	0.78 (0.7)	2.56** (3.4)
Initial Secondary Education Enrollment Ratio	2.09 (1.6)	2.11 (1.7)	2.40 (1.8)	3.23* (2.7)
Legal Independence			-0.81 (-0.5)	
Central Bank Governors Turnover Rate	-4.74** (-3.2)	-3.51** (-3.3)		-2.52* (-2.2)
Dummy for the '60s	1.82** (3.4)	1.92** (3.6)	2.35** (4.1)	
Dummy for the '70s	1.33** (2.7)	1.39** (2.9)	1.62** (3.1)	
$\bar{R}^2$	0.29	0.29	0.21	0.46
$P(\rho)$	0.54	0.52	0.52	
No. of Observations	130	133	131	49

t-statistics are in parentheses under the coefficients.
$P(\rho)$ is the significance level of a first-order autoregressive coefficient from a regression of the residuals of each country in each decade on the residuals of the same country in the previous decade.
* significant at the 0.05 level.
** significant at the 0.01 level.
[a] excluding Argentina, Botswana, Brazil, Korea
[b] excluding Botswana, Brazil, Korea

tions and revolutions and coups variables (not shown). In most cases the political instability variables were insignificant, and the sign of Central Bank Governors turnover remained significantly negative.

Thus, turnover of Central Bank Governors is negatively associated with growth for most of the countries in the sample. But for some high growers, like Botswana, Korea, and Brazil, other factors, not accounted for by our regressions, were sufficiently potent to overcome the negative effect of high turnover.[7] For example, it is likely that the discovery of diamonds in Botswana explains part of its high growth residual. One of the advantages of cross-country studies such as this one is that they focus the attention on special cases which can then be scrutinized more carefully, but we leave this more country-specific task for future work.

d. Growth and CBI within industrial countries and within LDCs

To examine the possibility that the relationship between growth and CBI differs between industrial and less-developed countries, we reestimate the basic regression from Table 2 separately for each group. The first two columns of Table 3 refer to industrial countries, with legal independence and Central Bank Governors turnover used alternately as proxies for CBI. Neither legal independence, nor Central Bank Governors turnover rates help to explain the variations in growth within the group of industrial countries. Since legal independence within those countries is also a reasonable measure of actual independence (Cukierman, Webb, and Neyapti (1992) and Chapters 20, 21 of Cukierman, 1992), this supports previous studies that found growth to be unrelated to CB independence in industrial countries. Grilli, Masciandaro, Tabellini (1991) and Alesina and Summers (1993) find no relation between growth and legal independence within most of the industrial countries, without controlling for other determinants of growth. Hence, our findings validate theirs, even after controlling for other factors that affect growth.

The third column of Table 3 presents the basic panel regression (excluding Botswana, Brazil, and Korea) for LDCs only, with turnover as the proxy for independence. In this group, turnover is negatively and significantly associated with growth. The terms-of-trade variable is extremely significant in LDCs, but insignificant in the regressions for industrial countries. In addition, the primary and secondary education enrollment ratios are insignificant within the subgroups. Initial GDP remains significant and negative, but only for the industrial countries. The significant level, $P(\rho)$, of the first-order coefficient of correlation between residuals of different decades raises the suspicion that there are additional country-specific effects within industrial countries

[7]But the tendency of within country residuals to be negatively related to turnover in some of those countries suggests that lack of CBI did not help growth in those countries.

Table 3:
Growth and CBI Within Industrial and LDCs - Panel

DEPENDENT VARIABLE: Per Capita Growth Rate	(1)	(2)	(3)
	Industrial		*LDCs*[a]
Constant	4.10	4.10	1.00
	(1.7)	(1.7)	(0.8)
Initial GDP	-0.0003**	-0.0003**	-0.0002
	(-2.8)	(-3.2)	(-0.9)
Change in Terms of Trade	-3.72	-3.92	30.45**
	(-0.3)	(-0.4)	(4.4)
Initial Primary Education Enrollment Ratio	0.07	0.15	1.13
	(0.0)	(0.1)	(0.9)
Initial Secondary Education Enrollment Ratio	0.87	0.89	1.85
	(0.7)	(0.7)	(0.8)
Legal Independence	-0.21		
	(-0.17)		
Central Bank Governors Turnover Rate		-0.80	-3.58**
		(-0.4)	(-2.7)
Dummy for the '60s	1.00	0.93	1.86*
	(1.3)	(1.2)	(2.1)
Dummy for the '70s	-0.12	-0.14	1.58*
	(0.8)	(-0.2)	(2.1)
$\bar{R}^2$	0.40	0.40	0.26
$P(\rho)$	0.01	0.01	0.77
No. of Observations	48	48	85

t-statistics are in parentheses under the coefficients.
$P(\rho)$ is the significance level of a first-order autoregressive coefficient from a regression of the residuals of each country in each decade on the residuals of the same country in the previous decade.
* significant at the 0.05 level.
** significant at the 0.01 level.
[a] excluding Brazil, Botswana, and Korea.

but not in LDCs.

Taken at face value, the results of this subsection support the view that growth is independent of CBI in industrial countries but that it is positively associated with it in LDCs. However, when both groups are examined together (Subsection c) turnover is even more significantly negative than within LDCs alone. This suggests that, controlling for other variables, turnover may also capture differences in growth between the two groups of countries. This conjecture is also supported by previous work which shows that CBI is substantially higher in developed than in developing countries and that the variability of independence within the second group is much higher.[8] The conjunction of these findings is consistent with the hypothesis that low independence retards growth in all countries but that this effect is not detected within industrial countries because of the smaller variability of CBI and the smaller number of countries in that group. Another possibility is that dependence has a detectable effect on growth only above a sufficiently high threshold.[9]

Perhaps, part of the negative association between growth and turnover is due to reverse causality–low growth leads to political instability which raises Central Bank Governors turnover. This issue is taken up in the next section.

4. Simultaneity between growth, inflation and Central Bank Governors turnover

a. The problem

The commonly held view of policy-oriented economists — that unstable macroeconomic policies retard growth — evolved from the experience of high-inflation Latin American economies, and is kept alive by recent developments in some Eastern European economies and the former Soviet Union. This view has been tested by adding inflation or its variability as regressors to growth equations. When this is done, inflation and its variability are found to have a significant negative impact on growth. See for example equation (7) in Fischer (1991) and the literature quoted therein. One problem with this way of testing for the effect of unstable macroeconomic policies is that inflation itself is an endogenous variable. It is affected by monetary policy but is

[8] Table 21.1 in Cukierman (1992) suggests that the overall level of independence is uniformly higher in industrial countries than in LDCs. The effective range of this index in the eighties is from 0.44 (minimum independence) to 0.04 (maximum independence). All the industrial countries in the sample have an overall index of independence below 0.1 and all the LDCs above it. The variability in the index is also substantially larger within the group of LDCs than within the group of industrial countries. The standard deviation of the index is 0.078 in the first group and only 0.022 in the second.

[9] It is possible that the insignificant effect of turnover within industrial countries may also be due to its weaker link with actual independence in that group of countries.

also influenced by other nonpolicy variables. In particular, a negative supply shock will lower the rate of growth and, given policy, raise the measured rate of inflation. Hence, the negative coefficient of inflation in the growth equation may be at least partly due to reverse causality – from growth to inflation.

A similar but perhaps more roundabout simultaneity problem may arise when Central Bank Governors turnover is used as a regressor in growth equations as is the case in the previous section. At least part of Central Bank Governors turnover is due to political instability. There is evidence that low growth increases political instability and that political instability reduces growth (Alesina, Ozler, Roubini, and Swagel (1991)). Hence, to the extent that part of Central Bank Governors turnover is related to political instability, its negative coefficient could be reflecting the negative effect of growth on political instability, and through it on turnover, rather than the effect of low independence on growth.

This section proposes and implements an empirical procedure that overcomes both simultaneity problems. The procedure and its logic are described in Subsection b. It is applied to our growth equations in Subsection c and to growth equations with inflation as a regressor in Subsection d.

b. A resolution of the simultaneity problem

To overcome possible reverse causality from growth to Central Bank Governors turnover via political instability we need measures of CBI that are independent of political instability. Such measures are developed in Cukierman and Webb (1993). They are based on a decomposition of Central Bank Governors turnover into a political component and a nonpolitical component. Any Central Bank Governors change that occurs within 6 months of a change in regime, a coup, a change of party, or a change in head of government is identified as a politically-induced change. Any change in Central Bank Governors that is not preceded within 6 months by one of the political transitions above is identified as being nonpolitical.

The nonpolitical component of Central Bank Governors turnover represents, by construction, that part of turnover that is orthogonal to political instability. A second measure of CBI that is independent from political instability may be obtained by decomposing the political component of Central Bank Governors turnover as follows:

$$TORP = VP$$

where $TORP$ is the politically induced component of Central Bank Governors turnover, V is the average number of politically-induced Central Bank Governors changes per political transition, and P is the average number of political transitions per unit of time. This decomposition states that the political component of Central Bank Governors turnover is due to two quite different components. One is the frequency, P, of political transitions. The other – V – is an index of the vulnerability of the governor of the central bank in the face of political changes. The lower V, the higher the institutional independence of the central bank. V is therefore a measure of CBI. Furthermore, it is much less likely to be correlated with political instability than $TORP$, since the effect of political instability on $TORP$ is captured, given V, through the variable P.

The nonpolitical turnover rate and the index of vulnerability provide additional measures of CBI that are largely independent of the degree of political instability. Since they are also positively correlated with turnover they may, alternatively, be used as instrumental variables for total turnover. Another advantage of V is that it is more likely than turnover to be proxying for CBI in low as well as in high ranges of the index. This extends its range of applicability to industrial economies, in addition to LDCs. The nonpolitical component of Central Bank Governors turnover and the index of vulnerability can also be used as instruments for inflation in Fischer (1991)-type growth equations, in which inflation is used as a proxy for unstable macroeconomic policies. Both instruments are correlated with inflation (Cukierman and Webb, 1993), but they derive from largely exogenous institutional characteristics of the central bank. They are, therefore, less likely to be subject to reverse causality than inflation.

c. Reestimation of growth equations using nonpolitical turnover and the index of CB vulnerability instead of turnover

This subsection focuses on the following question: How much of the significant negative impact of Central Bank Governors turnover on growth (found in Section 3) is due to reverse causality from growth to turnover. To answer this question we focus on the equations in which turnover had a significantly negative impact, like the second and the fourth columns of Table 2. Nonpolitical turnover and the index of CB vulnerability are unavailable for a number of observations. In order to separate differences in results due to instrumentation or to different measures of CBI from differences that are due to differing sample coverage, we estimate all equations using the same unified sample. Also, we reestimate some of the equations from Section 3 to establish sample comparability.

Table 4 reports results for the panel regressions. The first column just reproduces the second equation from Table 2, using the smaller sample. Except that the relative significance of primary and of secondary education enrollment ratios is reversed, the two equations essentially tell a similar story. In particular, Central Bank Governors turnover has a significant negative impact on growth in both. The second column presents an instrumental variables estimation of the same equation. The instruments are nonpolitical turnover, the index of central bank vulnerability, and all the remaining regressors except turnover. The effect of turnover, instrumented, on growth is still significant and negative; the level of significance only changes from 0.001 to 0.016. The effects of the other variables remain very similar. The third column shows a reestimation of the same equation with nonpolitical turnover and the index of CB vulnerability, instead of turnover. Nonpolitical turnover is insignificant but vulnerability has a significant negative impact on growth. The effects of the remaining variables are virtually unchanged. The fourth column is a reestimation of the third without the insignificant effect of nonpolitical turnover.[10] The four regressions in Table 4 were also reestimated for a unified sample composed of LDCs only (not shown). The qualitative results were similar to those shown in Table 4 for the whole sample.

Table 5 repeats some of the experiments in Table 4 for cross-sectional regressions. The first column reproduces the fourth regression from Table 2 for the unified sample. The second is an instrumental variables estimation of the first using nonpolitical turnover, CB vulnerability, and all remaining regressors except turnover as instruments. The third replaces turnover with CB vulnerability. In all equations a lower index of CBI is associated with less growth. Turnover has a significant negative impact on growth in the ordinary least squares as well as in the instrumental variables equations. The index of CB vulnerability also has a significant negative impact on growth.

The next two columns of Table 5 repeat the experiments in the second and in the third columns of the table only for LDCs. This severely reduces the number of observations (from 43 to 27). Both instrumented turnover and CB vulnerability are still negative. The first variable is significant, but the second only marginally so.

The main conclusion from this subsection is that the finding of Section 2 – that a low degree of CBI has a negative impact on growth – is robust to instrumental variables reestimation and to the introduction of alternate measures of CBI.

d. Instrumental variables estimation of growth equations with inflation as a regressor

Table 6 presents a sequence of panel experiments taking as a benchmark the second equation of Table 2 with inflation replacing turnover as a regressor. The first equation is the benchmark. It is meant to represent the family of growth equations in which (as in Fischer (1991) and in the literature quoted

[10]The cross-decades first-order coefficients of correlation between residuals are insignificant for all the regressions in Table 4.

Table 4:
Reestimation of Growth Equations with Instrumental Variables and with Alternative Measures of CBI[a]
(Panel with a unified sample)

	(1)	(2)[b]	(3)	(4)
Constant	1.18	1.15	0.72	0.39
	(1.4)	(1.3)	(0.8)	(0.5)
Initial GDP	-0.0002**	-0.0002**	-0.0002**	-0.0002**
	(-2.9)	(-2.9)	(-2.9)	(-2.8)
Change in Terms of Trade	28.05**	28.12**	30.19**	30.51**
	(5.1)	(5.1)	(5.3)	(5.4)
Initial Primary Education Enrollment Ratio	2.16*	2.15*	2.54*	2.57*
	(2.3)	(2.3)	(2.6)	(2.6)
Initial Secondary Education Enrollment Ratio	1.29	1.30	1.32	1.28
	(1.0)	(1.1)	(1.0)	(1.0)
Central Bank Governors Turnover Rate	-3.42**	-3.29*		
	(-3.3)	(-2.5)		
Nonpolitical turnover of Central Bank Governors			-2.39	
			(-0.7)	
Political Vulnerability of Central Bank			-1.41*	-1.49*
			(-2.2)	(-2.3)
Dummy for the '60s	1.26*	1.27*	1.32*	1.35*
	(2.4)	(2.4)	(2.4)	(2.5)
Dummy for the '70s	1.06*	1.06*	1.13*	1.15*
	(2.2)	(2.2)	(2.3)	(2.4)
$\bar{R}^2$	0.31	0.31	0.27	0.27
No. of Observations	119	119	119	119

[a] Excluding Botswana, Brazil, and Korea.
[b] Instrumental variables estimation. The Central Bank Governors turnover rate is instrumented with nonpolitical turnover, the political vulnerability of the CB, and all the remaining regressors.
t-statistics are in parentheses under the coefficients.
*designates significance at the 0.05 level.
**designates significance at the 0.01 level.

Table 5:
Reestimation of Cross-Sectional Growth Equations with Instrumental Variables and with Alternative Measures of CBI
(Unified Sample)[a]

	All Countries			LDCs	
	(1)	(2)[b]	(3)	(4)	(5)
Constant	1.58** (2.9)	1.74** (3.1)	1.18* (2.4)	1.55* (2.3)	1.12 (1.8)
Initial GDP	-0.0005** (-4.5)	-0.0005** (-4.5)	-0.0005** (-4.6)	-0.0008** (-2.5)	-0.0008* (-2.4)
Change in Terms of Trade	13.17 (1.6)	11.89 (1.4)	16.84 (2.1)	8.37 (0.9)	11.78 (1.3)
Initial Primary Education Enrollment Ratio	2.81** (3.9)	2.88** (4.0)	3.10** (4.2)	3.12** (2.9)	3.22** (2.9)
Initial Secondary Education Enrollment Ratio	2.33 (2.0)	2.18 (1.9)	2.18 (1.9)	4.41 (1.5)	4.39 (1.5)
Central Bank Governors Turnover Rate	-2.55* (-2.4)	-3.35** (-2.7)		-2.84 (-1.9)	
Political Vulnerability of Central Bank			-1.37* (-2.4)		-1.17 (-1.6)
$\bar{R}^2$	0.47	0.46	0.47	0.44	0.44
No. of Observations	43	43	43	27	27

[a] Excluding Botswana, Brazil, and Korea.
[b] Instrumental variables estimation. The Central Bank Governors turnover rate is instrumented with nonpolitical turnover, the index of CB vulnerability, and the remaining regressors.
t-statistics are in parentheses under the coefficients.
*designates significance at the 0.05 level.
**designates significance at the 0.01 level.

Table 6:
Instrumental Variables Estimation of Growth Equations with Inflation as a Regressor (Panel)[a]

	OLS	Instrumental Variables Estimation[b]		
	(1)	(2)	(3)	(4)
Constant	0.69 (0.9)	1.21 (0.6)	1.45 (1.2)	1.46 (1.6)
Initial GDP	-0.0002* (-2.3)	-0.0002 (-1.3)	-0.0002* (-2.3)	-0.0002* (-2.5)
Change in Terms of Trade	30.14** (5.6)	30.99** (3.6)	32.12** (5.0)	29.80** (4.8)
Initial Primary Education Enrollment Ratio	1.21 (1.3)	1.53 (0.6)	1.90 (1.6)	2.47* (2.3)
Initial Secondary Education Enrollment Ratio	2.00 (1.6)	1.65 (0.8)	1.46 (1.0)	0.62 (0.4)
Inflation	-1.87** (-3.9)	-3.26 (-0.5)	-5.45 (-1.3)	-4.57* (-2.5)
Dummy for the '60s	1.58** (3.0)	1.12 (0.4)	0.73 (0.8)	0.62 (0.9)
Dummy for the '70s	1.35** (2.9)	1.03 (0.7)	1.1 (1.8)	1.03 (1.9)
$\bar{R}^2$	0.36	0.29	0.01	0.07
No. of Observations	133	128	124	117

[a] Excluding Botswana, Brazil, and Korea.
[b] All regressors excluding inflation are used as instruments for inflation in equations (2)–(4). In addition, legal independence is used as an instrument in regression (2), nonpolitical turnover in regression (3), and CB vulnerability in regression (4).
t-statistics are in parentheses under the coefficients.
*designates significance at the 0.05 level.
**designates significance at the 0.01 level.

therein) inflation is used as a measure of unstable or "undesirable" macroeconomic policies. As in many equations of this type, inflation has a highly significant negative coefficient. But, as argued at the beginning of this section, this may be due to reverse causality running from growth to measured inflation. To explore this possibility the benchmark growth equation is reestimated, using legal independence and all the remaining regressors except inflation as instruments. The result appears in the second column of Table 6. The third column is similar in all respects to the second except that nonpolitical turnover is used as an instrument instead of legal independence. In the last column the index of CB vulnerability replaces nonpolitical turnover and everything else remains as in the third column.

With legal independence as the instrumental variable, inflation completely loses significance. This is at least partly because legal independence is a poor proxy for actual independence, particularly in LDCs. When nonpolitical turnover is used as an instrument, inflation again becomes less significant, although not as dramatically. But when the index of CB vulnerability is used as an instrument, the coefficient of inflation remains significantly negative.[11] The last index seems the best on a priori grounds, since it is likely to be a good proxy for CB independence in most countries. The significant correlation between residuals across adjacent decades, however, points to the existence of country specific effects.

To sum up: when inflation is instrumented with the best instruments, in terms of explaining inflation, it appears still to have a clear negative effect on growth, although not as strong as in the ordinary least squares estimates. We did not exhaustively conduct massive tests for robustness along the lines of Levine and Renelt (1992). Future work could usefully apply their robustness procedures to the measures of CBI used in this paper. We also did not control for the potential effect of exchange rate commitments on growth. It is likely that such commitments, to the extent that they are credible, are more important in countries with relatively low CBI.

5. Some evidence on private investment, productivity growth, and CBI

a. Private investment and CBI

The results in Section 3 show a positive association between growth and CBI. One of the possible channels through which it arises is that macroeconomic instability, which is caused by or reflected through low CBI, deters private investment. To examine this hypothesis, this section regresses pri-

[11] But it is not as significant as in the benchmark ordinary least squares regression. There is also a substantial deterioration in the goodness of fit in comparison to this benchmark.

vate investment on CBI and other variables that are likely to be important for investment. The range of experiments performed is dictated largely by the availability of data. We first tried to regress the share of private investment from the Barro-Wolf (1989) data set on initial GDP, primary and secondary education initial enrollment ratios, the change in terms of trade, Central Bank Governors turnover, and legal CBI, in cross-section for the period 1970–85. In some cases, the Barro-Wolf measures of assassinations and of revolutions and coups were added too. The number of countries was about 50. None of the variables had significant coefficients, including the measures of CBI.

We also experimented with data on private investment as a share of GDP for developing countries between 1970 and 1990. These data were recently compiled by the IFC (Pfeffermann and Madarassy, 1992). Regressions similar to these described above were tried with decade (seventies and eighties) panel data with a decade dummy for the seventies. Availability of data limited the sample to 30 countries.[12] Legal independence was always insignificant but the turnover of Central Bank Governors had a significant negative effect on private investment in a number of cases. Results using turnover as the index of CBI are summarized in Table 7. The first column is the basic benchmark regression. The Barro-Wolf assassination, revolution, and coups variables are added in the second column. The third and fourth columns reproduce the first two without Brazil and Korea. In the benchmark regression, three variables are significant: secondary education, the dummy for the seventies, and CB turnover, with a negative sign. The addition of assassinations and revolution and coups variables reduces the significance of turnover. When Brazil and Korea are excluded, the significance of turnover rises, and it remains significant even in the presence of the Barro-Wolf measures of political instability.

Additional separate regressions (not shown) for the seventies and the eighties reveal a significant negative effect of turnover on investment during the seventies but not the eighties.

b. Productivity growth and CBI

Another channel through which CBI could affect growth is productivity growth. To examine this possibility we regressed the Solow residuals for a group of (up to) 38 developing countries plus Spain in pooled cross-section time series regressions using the same variables that were used to account

[12]The countries are: Argentina, Brazil, Chile, Costa Rica, Ethiopia, Ghana, India, Indonesia, Kenya, Korea, Malaysia, Mexico, Morocco, Nepal, Nigeria, Pakistan, Peru, Philippines, Singapore, Tanzania, Thailand, Turkey, Uruguay, Venezuela and Zimbabwe. Data for Indonesia, Morocco, Nigeria, and Peru are available only during the eighties.

Table 7:
Private Investment, Productivity Growth and CBI in LDCs

	Dependent Variable: Private Investment (% of GDP)				Dependent Variable: (Solow Residuals)	
	(1)	(2)	(3)[a]	(4)[a]	(5)[b]	(6)[b]
Constant	5.23 (1.8)	4.34 (1.3)	5.67* (2.1)	7.17* (2.29)	-0.01 (-1.2)	-0.00 (-0.6)
Initial GDP	0.0008 (0.9)	0.0006 (0.6)	0.0008 (0.9)	0.001 (1.2)	-0.0000 (-0.2)	-0.0000 (-1.0)
Change in Terms of Trade	-4.65 (-0.2)	-3.08 (-0.1)	-16.88 (-0.9)	-23.19 (-1.1)	0.07 (1.3)	0.07 (1.4)
Initial Primary Education Enrollment Ratio	2.36 (0.6)	3.35 (0.8)	3.99 (0.3)	2.50 (0.7)	0.001 (0.1)	0.000 (0.0)
Initial Secondary Education Enrollment Ratio	12.30* (2.4)	12.52* (2.3)	6.09 (0.9)	4.83 (0.7)	0.03* (2.1)	0.03* (2.4)
Central Bank Governors Turnover Rate	-9.22* (-2.5)	-7.27 (-1.5)	-10.15** (-2.9)	-14.20** (-2.9)	-0.01 (-1.5)	-0.01 (-0.6)
Assassinations		-1.27 (-0.6)		2.11 (1.0)		0.00 (0.5)
Revolutions and Coups		0.41 (0.1)		0.10 (0.0)		-0.03* (-2.2)
Dummy for the '60s					0.01 (1.7)	0.01 (1.6)
Dummy for the '70s	2.99 (1.9)	3.28 (1.9)	2.15 (1.3)	1.58 (0.9)	0.01 (1.8)	0.01 (1.9)
$\bar{R}^2$	0.33	0.29	0.34	0.32	0.08	0.12
No. of Observations	34	34	30	30	77	77

[a] Excluding Botswana, Brazil, and Korea.
[b] Excluding Japan.
t-statistics are in parentheses under the coefficients.
*designates significance at the 0.05 level.
**designates significance at the 0.01 level.

for the behavior of investment.[13] As with the growth equations, the observations for each country are broken down into three decades (1960–69, 1970–79, 1980–89). Legal CBI is found to have no effect, and turnover has a marginally significant negative effect on productivity growth (see column five of Table 7). But when the Barro-Wolf political instability variables are added, turnover becomes insignificant (the last column of Table 7), and the effect of revolutions and coups is significantly negative. In other words, any negative effect that Central Bank Governors turnover might have had on productivity growth disappears once proxies for political instability are used along with it.

c. The share of investment in equipment and CBI

Delong and Summers (1991) have shown that countries with higher shares (in GDP) of equipment investment grow faster. A possible channel through which CBI affects growth is via an effect on equipment investment. To examine this possibility, we estimated a cross-sectional equation in which the average share of equipment investment between 1960 and 1985 was regressed on initial GDP, initial primary and secondary education enrollment ratios, average labor-force growth between 1960 and 1985, the initial GDP per worker gap, and Central Bank Governors turnover between 1960 and 1989. We also experimented with a version of the same equation adding a measure of the average change in the terms of trade.[14] Most variables were insignificant. But the coefficient of turnover was negative and significant at the 0.016 level in the first case and at the 0.066 level in the second.

d. Replacing turnover by CB vulnerability in investment equations

The four investment equations in Table 7 were reestimated using the index of CB vulnerability instead of turnover as a measure of CBI. Results (not shown) are similar to those in Table 7. The index of vulnerability has a significant negative impact on growth in all equations except in the counterpart of equation (2) in Table 7. This equation includes Brazil and Botswana in the sample as well as the assassination and revolution variables.

[13] As is well-known, the Solow residuals are the residuals from a logarithmic regression of output on labor and capital inputs. They were kindly supplied by Stan Fischer. The countries in the sample are those in the previous footnote plus Egypt, Greece, Hungary, Israel, Malta, Nicaragua, Panama, Portugal, Spain, Taiwan, Uganda, Yugoslavia, Zaire, and Zambia, minus Nepal, Singapore, and Uruguay. Not all decade-by-decade observations are available for all the 38 countries.

[14] In both cases Botswana, Brazil, and Korea were excluded.

e. Conclusions

The evidence yields some support for the view that, when CBI is sufficiently low, the lack of CBI retards private investment and reduces the share of equipment investment in GDP. There is also a weaker negative effect of CB dependence on productivity growth, but this effect appears to be proxying for the effect of political instability on productivity.

6. The intra-country variability of growth, CBI, and the level of development

Recent evidence (Easterly, Kremer, Prichett, and Summers (1992)) suggests that there are substantial variations over time in the rate of growth within a given country. This section presents preliminary evidence on possible links between the magnitude of these variations and the independence of the central bank.

Countries with more dependent central banks normally conduct more activist monetary policies in order to affect aggregate demand. It is an open issue, though, whether such activism actually dampens or increases the amplitude of business cycles. Political authorities are more likely than the central bank to pursue a variety of objectives besides dampening of the cycle. For instance, they might produce a political cycle (for a recent empirical survey see Alesina, Cohen and Roubini (1992)). Even when they aim to dampen the cycle, politicians may exacerbate it, along the lines of Friedman's long and variable lags argument (see also Meltzer (1987)). Hence, there are conflicting theoretical predictions about the relationship between a country's growth-rate variability and the independence of its central bank.[15] The type of relationship, if any, between the variability of growth and the level of CBI is an empirical matter, to which we now turn.

First, we calculate the variability over time in the per capita rate of growth for each country and then regress the resulting variances on legal independence and on turnover across countries. The time period is from 1960 to 1988. The same experiment is repeated for industrial countries and for LDCs separately. Legal independence is insignificant in all the experiments. For the entire sample of countries the turnover of Central Bank Governors has a significant positive effect on the variance of growth. The estimated relation is:

$$\begin{aligned} Var(G_i) &= \underset{(1.9)}{0.001} + \underset{(2.2)}{0.005} TOR_i \\ \bar{R}^2 = 0.06, DW &= 1.94, \text{ number of countries} = 63 \end{aligned}$$

[15] But theory <u>does</u> imply that, other things the same, policy is more activist the more dependent is the CB (Cukierman (1992) p. 355).

Here $Var(G_i)$ denotes the variance of the growth rate in country i and TOR_i denotes the turnover of Central Bank Governors within that country. t-statistics are in parenthesis under the coefficients. The relationship vanishes when reestimated separately within industrial countries and within LDCs. This suggests that turnover is proxying for some basic institutional differences (that matter for growth) between the two groups of countries but not within each group.

We saw in Section 3 that growth is affected by changes in a country's terms of trade. This is particularly true for LDCs in which fluctuations in terms of trade have a sizeable effect on growth. In order to make sure that this effect is not confounded with the effect of CBI on the variance of growth, we repeat the above regression with the standard deviation of growth residuals (after elimination of the variability that is due to a change in terms of trade) instead of the variance of growth. The standard deviations of growth residuals are calculated in the following manner. Regressions of yearly growth rates on yearly changes in terms of trade are estimated for each country separately. The net (of variations in terms of trade) variability of growth is proxied by the standard deviations of growth residuals from those country regressions. These standard deviations are then regressed (in cross-section) on turnover. The resulting equation is:

$$\begin{aligned} SD(RG_i) &= 0.032 + 0.050TOR: \\ & \quad\;\, (5.8) \qquad (2.5) \\ R^2 = 0.09, DW &= 1.56, \text{number of countries} = 54 \end{aligned}$$

Here $SD(RG_i)$ is the standard deviation of growth residuals from the first-stage regression in country i. Again, the central bank's legal independence is insignificant. When the above regression is repeated separately for industrial countries and for LDCs, turnover becomes insignificant as was the case when $Var(G_i)$ was the dependent variable.

The results support the view that, even after controlling for differences in the impact of terms of trade shocks, there is a negative relation between the variability of growth and CBI as proxied by Central Bank Governors turnover. But this relation seems to be capturing mostly differences between industrial countries and LDCs rather than differences between countries within each group. Stated somewhat loosely, the association between the variability of growth and Central Bank Governors turnover reflects that the average value of both variables is substantially lower in developed economies than in LDCs. When one controls for initial GDP, this variable has a significantly negative impact on the variability of growth (and of its residuals) and turnover becomes insignificant. We conclude that the general level of development has a stronger (negative) association with the variability of growth than CBI.

7. Interest rates and CBI

This section examines whether there are systematic relationships between the distribution of ex post real rates and CBI. Due to data limitations we experiment only with returns paid to savers. Most of the rates are real short-term deposit rates, whose maturity varies across countries. They were originally compiled by Gelb (1989) and extended in Easterly, Rodriguez and Schmidt-Hebbel (1992). The basic data are from the International Financial Statistics and from internal World Bank sources. The nominal interest rate is the average deposit (or passive) rate in the banking system for maturities which vary between 30 days and 18 months. The ex post real rate is obtained by adjusting the nominal rate by the actual rate of inflation over the appropriate maturity. Some of those rates are regulated to various extents. Hence, their relation with CBI also reflects differences in policy across central banks with different levels of autonomy.

The only existing attempt to uncover possible associations between real rates and CBI is in Alesina and Summers (1993). Using the Alesina (1988) legal measures of CBI for a sample of 18 countries, they find that: (1) there is no (cross-country) association between the level of ex post real rates and CBI; (2) the (intra-country) variability of real rates is inversely related to CBI. They attribute this finding to the negative association between the variability of inflation and CBI.[16]

a. The variability of interest rates and CBI

Table 8 presents regressions of the yearly standard deviation of the ex post real rate on legal independence and on Central Bank Governors turnover for all countries in the sample as well as for the subgroups of industrial and developing countries.[17] The first column of the table reveals a very strong positive association between real rates variability and turnover in the entire sample of countries (about 40). Although it has the expected negative effect on the variability of real rates, legal independence is not significant. The same regression is repeated separately for industrial countries and for LDCs in the second and third columns of the table. Results for LDCs are similar to the results for the combined sample. But the relative significance of legal independence and of turnover is reversed within the group of industrial countries. Legal independence has a negative and significant impact on the variability of real rates but turnover is insignificant within industrial countries.

---

[16]This association is quite strong. It obtains in the Alesina-Summers sample as well as in wider samples that also include LDCs (Chapter 22 of Cukierman (1992)).

[17]The regressions cover the period between 1965 and 1989. But the data span is shorter than that for some countries.

Table 8:
The Variability of Real Rates and CBI - Cross-Section

DEPENDENT VARIABLE: Standard Deviation of the Ex Post Real Deposit Rate

	(1) All Countries	(2) Industrial	(3) LDCs	(4) Industrial	(5) LDCs
Constant	**3.16**	**-3.92****	**9.49**	**4.23****	**2.60**
	(1.0)	**(4.4)**	**(1.5)**	**(8.2)**	**(0.9)**
Legal Independence	**-7.88**	**-3.97***	**-20.18**	**-4.13****	
	(-1.0)	**(-2.8)**	**(-1.2)**	**(-3.1)**	
Central Bank Governors Turnover Rate	**31.00****	**1.90**	**27.92****		**27.27****
	(5.55)	**(0.4)**	**(3.39)**		**(3.4)**
$\bar{R}^2$	**0.44**	**0.32**	**0.32**	**0.36**	**0.31**
No. of Observations	**39**	**16**	**23**	**16**	**24**

t Statistics are in parentheses under the coefficients.
*** significant at the 0.05 level.**
**** significant at the 0.01 level.**

Those findings support the conclusion of Alesina and Summers that real-rate variability is higher when CBI is lower. They also support the conclusion that the appropriate measure of CBI is legal independence for industrial countries and Central Bank Governors turnover for LDCs (Cukierman, Webb, and Neyapti (1992) and Chapter 20 of Cukierman (1992)). The last two columns of Table 8 repeat the subgroup regressions only with the appropriate measures of CBI for each group – legal independence for industrial and turnover for developing countries.

To examine the relation of CBI and the variability of nominal rates, we used three different nominal rates (all from the International Financial Statistics): the discount rate, the deposit rate, and the bond rate. The sample period and the number of countries vary across the different rates. The discount rate data cover the period from 1970 to 1989. The data for the remaining two rates range from 1978 to 1989. The number of countries is 54 for the discount rate, 57 for the deposit rate, and 33 for the bond rate. Table 9 presents regressions of the standard deviation of each of those nominal rates on legal independence and on Central Bank Governors turnover. The indices of CBI are adjusted in each case to cover roughly the same periods as the different nominal rates.

Table 9:
The Variability of Nominal Rates and CBI - Cross-Section

DEPENDENT VARIABLE: Standard Deviation of Designated Nominal Rate	(1) Discount Rate	(2) Deposit Rate	(3) Bond Rate
Constant	225.7	12.2	1.75
	(0.5)	(0.0)	(1.3)
Legal Independence	-1593.7	-1518.0	0.13
	(-1.5)	(-1.2)	(0.0)
Central Bank Governors	2419.7*	3004.5**	2.71
Turnover Rate	(2.5)	(3.8)	(0.7)
$\bar{R}^2$	0.11	0.20	-0.05
No. of Observations	54	57	33

t Statistics are in parentheses under the coefficients.
* significant at the 0.05 level.
** significant at the 0.01 level.

For the discount rate and the deposit rate, which are short-term instruments, turnover is found to have a positive and significant effect on nominal rate variability. Legal independence has the expected negative sign but is not significant. This is not surprising, since the sample includes both industrial and developing countries. No association is found between the longer-term bond rate and either index of CBI.

These findings suggest that the level of independence affects the variability of short-term nominal rates but not that of long-term rates. They also suggest that the relationship between CBI and the variability of real rates, detected above, is due not only to the effect of CBI on inflation variance but also to its association with the variability of nominal rates. A full empirical investigation of the channels through which CBI affects short-term real-rate variability would also have to consider its possible effect on the covariance between nominal rates and inflation. This is left for future work.

b. The level of real rates and CBI

Table 10 reports the average ex post real deposit rates and their standard deviations for the countries in the sample. The countries within each subgroup (industrial and developing) are arranged by the size of their standard deviations. Several facts are noteworthy. First, average real rates are negative in many countries. Second, the average level of real deposit rates in LDCs is substantially lower than in industrial countries (-3.2 percent versus 0.2 percent). Third, a comparison of the means and the variances in Table 10 suggests a negative correlation between them across countries. Simple regressions confirm that this relationship is significant for the whole sample of countries as well as within subgroups.

Figures 3 and 4 present plots of real rates on legal independence within industrial economies. Figure 3 covers the period from '65 to '89 and Figure 4 only the eighties. In both cases a clear positive relation emerges between the average real rate and legal independence. A regression of average real deposit rates between '65 and '89 on legal independence within industrial countries confirms this positive relationship at the 0.1 level of significance (first column of Table 11). Ireland appears to be an outlier. When it is excluded from the sample, the level of significance increases to 0.03 and the coefficient on legal independence increases, too (second column of Table 11).

To examine the relation between the real rate and CBI in LDCs, turnover is used to proxy CBI. The third column of Table 11 reports the corresponding regression. As in the case of industrial countries, there is a positive and significant association between the real rate and CBI in LDCs (recall that turnover is a measure of central bank dependence). But when Argentina, which is an outlier, is excluded the relation becomes insignificant.

In summary, there is a positive relation between the average return to savers and CBI in industrial economies and, depending on whether Argentina

Table 10:
Real Ex Post Deposit Rates - Mean Levels and Within Country Variabilities (Percentages)

Country	Mean	Standard Deviation	Country	Mean	Standard Deviation
Industrial					
Austria	0.4	1.2			
Germany	2.2	1.2			
Netherlands	1.6	1.5			
Denmark	2.4	1.6			
Finland	1.5	1.9			
Canada	3.1	2.5			
Belgium	-0.1	2.6			
Spain	0.4	2.8			
Sweden	0.7	2.8			
France	-1.8	3.2			
Italy	-0.8	3.3			
Japan	-1.7	3.7			
Norway	-0.0	4.6			
UK	-1.8	4.0			
Ireland	-2.7	3.8			
Australia	0.3	4.0			
Average	0.2				
LDCs			LDCs (cont.)		
Honduras	4.5	2.0	Zambia	-7.5	8.8
Malaysia	3.1	3.9	Mexico	-3.3	9.3
Morocco	-0.3	4.1	Venezuela	-1.3	9.3
Zimbabwe	-4.1	4.8	Peru	-10.9	9.5
Greece	-2.3	5.4	Turkey	-8.0	11.5
Colombia	0.1	5.5	Indonesia	5.1	12.9
Kenya	-2.2	5.7	Zaire	-15.1	16.6
Thailand	3.0	5.8	Ghana	-15.7	17.3
Pakistan	-1.6	6.0	Argentina	-18.6	19.0
Korea	4.7	6.2	Chile	-5.2	25.1
India	-0.7	6.9	Brazil	7.3	44.9
Nigeria	-6.3	8.1			
Philippines	-0.7	8.7			
			Average	-3.2	

Source: Calculated from Tables 4A and 4B (Statistical Appendix) in Easterly, Rodriguez, and Schmidt-Hebbel (1992).

Table 11:
Real Rate Levels and CBI - Cross-Section

Dependent Variable: Mean ex post real deposit rate	Industrial	Industrial (excl. Ireland)	LDCs
Constant	-1.26	-1.31	0.84
	(-1.3)	(-1.7)	(0.3)
Legal Independence	4.27	5.07**	
	(1.7)	(2.4)	
Central Bank Governors Turnover Rate			-13.48*
			(-2.0)
$\bar{R}^2$	0.12	0.26	0.11
No. of Observations	16	15	24

t statistics are in parentheses under the coefficients.
* significant at the 0.07 level
** significant at the 0.03 level.

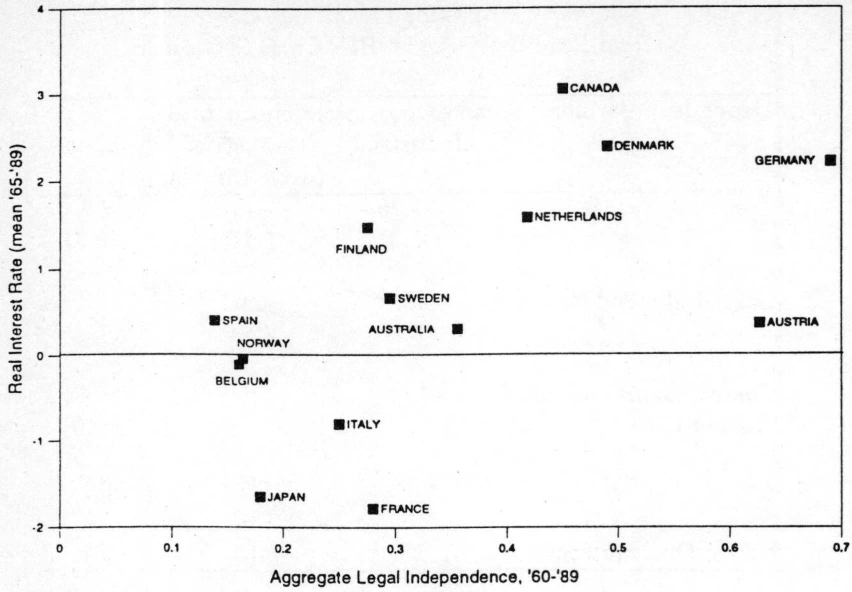

Figure 3

Average real ex post deposit rates and legal independence - industrial countries '60-'89

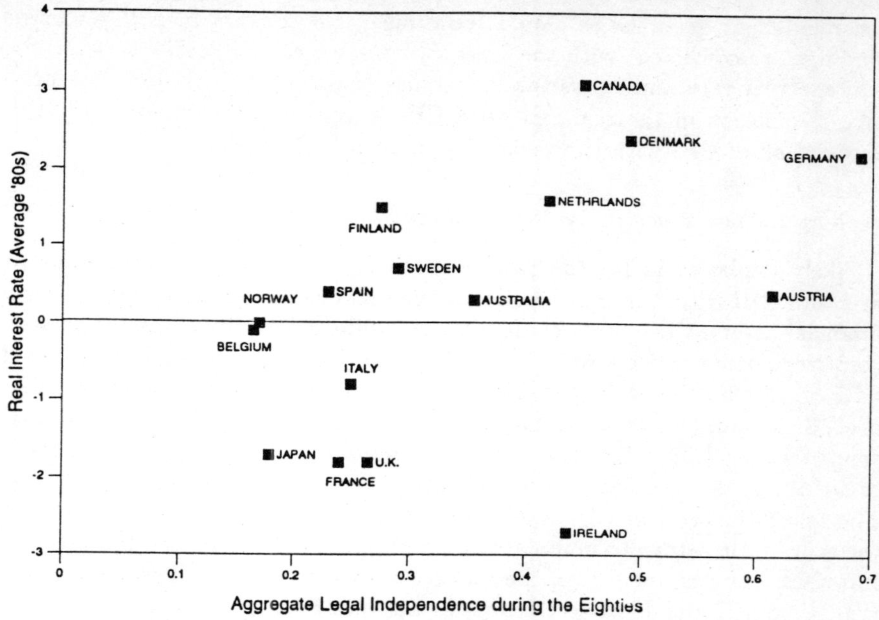

Figure 4

Average real ex post deposit rates and legal independence during the Eighties in Industrial Countries

is included or excluded, a similar relation or no relation in LDCs. These findings are consistent with the view that the negative relation between the average real rate and its variability across countries results from the positive association of the real rate with CBI in conjunction with the negative association of CBI with the variability of the real rate.

c. Why is there a positive relation between the average real rate and CBI?

A likely explanation for the positive association between the real deposit rate and CBI is that in most countries the real return to savers in short-term financial assets is below its competitive equilibrium level because of government regulation and periodic inflationary surprises. The lower the degree of CBI, the farther below its equilibrium value is the real return to savers. Figure 5 illustrates this idea graphically. Except for a small number of industrial countries, short-term financial savings in most countries can be represented as being on the portion of the supply-of-savings curve below equilibrium. The lower the level of CBI, the higher the interference of government with the short-term return to nominal savings through regulation and inflationary surprises. As a consequence, the realized return to savers is lower the lower CBI. Points H and L along the supply curve in Figure 5 illustrate this idea graphically. This view is consistent with the McKinnon and Shaw notion of financial repression (McKinnon (1973)). They developed this argument mostly for LDCs. Our finding that real returns to savers are substantially lower in LDCs is consistent with this view (see Figure 5). But our findings also point to some financial repression within industrial countries, as well as to the conclusion that, within this group, the level of financial repression goes down as CBI rises.

The relatively weak relationship between the real return to savers and CBI within LDCs may be explained as the consequence of two offsetting effects. A rise in CBI is associated with a reduced divergence between deposit rates and their equilibrium levels. This tends to push real rates up. On the other hand, by reducing real-rate variability, an increase in CBI may reduce risk premia and this tends to reduce real rates.[18] The second effect is probably more important in explaining differences in rates within LDCs because of the higher spread in variabilities within this group. (The standard deviation across countries of the real-rate variability within countries is about ten times larger among LDCs than among industrial countries.)

The type of financial repression associated with low CBI depresses the real level of savings and reduces the allocative efficiency of financial markets.

[18]This argument implicitly assumes that risk premia on real deposit rates rise on balance with the variability of these rates. This is the case only under some circumstances, since borrowers are willing to pay less when variability is higher and this tends to reduce real deposit rates.

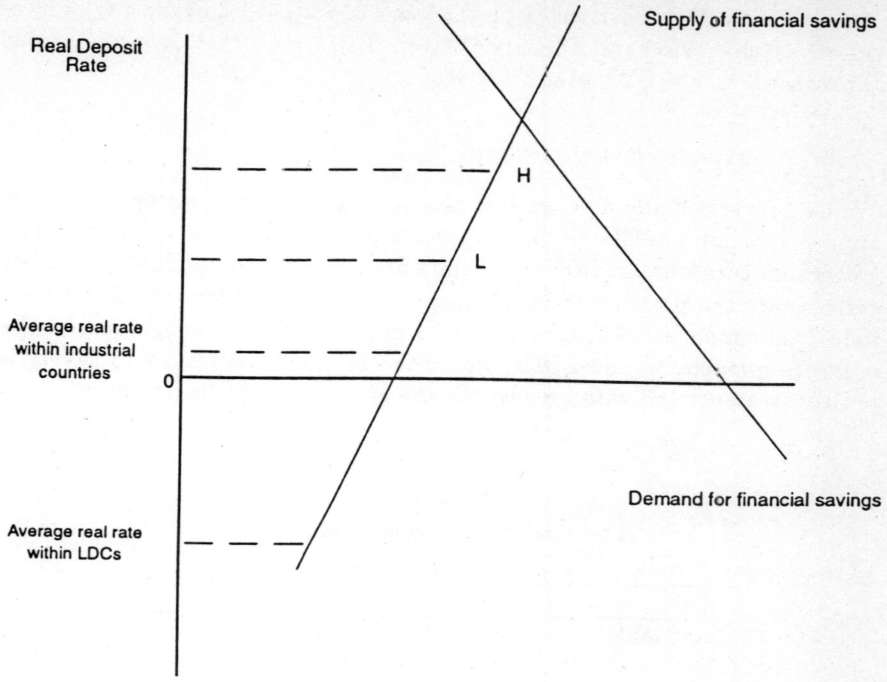

Figure 5

Central bank independence and real rates.

Recent evidence is consistent with the view that financial repression reduces growth (Gelb (1989) and Easterly (1991)). This may be yet another channel through which low CBI retards growth.

d. An intriguing empirical regularity

We also regressed the average real rate in each country on growth and the appropriate index of CBI (legal independence for industrial and Central Bank Governors turnover for LDCs). Results are summarized in Table 12. They corroborate the positive effect of independence on real deposit rates within industrial countries, even controlling for growth, which is insignificant. The opposite happens within LDCs, where the ex post real return to saving is positively associated with growth but the effect of CBI is insignificant.

Table 12:
The Real Rate, Growth, and CBI

	Industrial	LDCs
Constant	-0.13 (-0.1)	-6.98 (-3.2)
Legal Independence	4.41* (1.9)	
Central Bank Governors Turnover Rate		-0.97 (-0.2)
Per Capita Growth Rate	-0.30 (-0.6)	2.32** (4.7)
$\bar{R}^2$	0.23	0.50
No. of Observations	15	25

t statistics are in parentheses under the coefficients.
* significant at the 0.09 level
** significant at the 0.0001 level.

What is the meaning of the results for LDCs? One possibility is that governments of nations that grow faster tolerate more competitive returns to short-term financial assets. But causality may also be running in the opposite direction. Countries that tolerate more liberal financial markets grow faster. Clearly the issue deserves further work.

8. Concluding remarks

The empirical results of this paper in conjunction with earlier work support the view that higher CBI is associated with less inflation and more growth in LDCs, but only with less inflation in industrial economies. This difference in findings between the two groups of countries is consistent with the view that dependence on political authorities is bad for growth only when the level of dependence is sufficiently high. All industrial countries have more CBI than most LDCs.

What are the channels through which more CBI stimulates growth? This paper does not pretend to provide a full answer to this question, but the evidence in Section 5 suggests that, other things the same, private investment is lower the lower is independence, as proxied by turnover or by CB vulnerability. The results concerning the level of deposit rates and CBI also provide a possible channel. In economies with more dependent central banks, governments interfere more heavily in the capital market. This involvement reduces the allocative efficiency of the capital market and may reduce growth. The empirical work of Gelb (1989) and Easterly (1991) provides further support for this view.

Wider capital markets are also conducive to higher growth. King and Levine (1993) present evidence that the initial level of a country's financial development is one of the most reliable predictors of its subsequent rate of growth. To the extent that CBI and financial development are positively related, this provides another channel through which CBI and growth interact. But this should not be construed to imply that causality runs only from CBI to financial development – to growth. Deep capital markets and an elastic supply of funds to government may cause both higher growth and higher CBI. Thus, broad capital markets may well be enhancing growth directly as well as indirectly – by leading political authorities to delegate more authority to the central bank.[19]

The result that, ceteris paribus, growth is positively associated with CBI in LDCs seems reasonably robust. We have experimented with alternative measures of terms of trade and also repeated the regressions with and without outliers. To examine the possibility that our measures of CBI reflect the effect of political instability on growth rather than that of CBI, we added several measures of political instability in addition to the proxies for CBI. To disentangle more sharply the two effects, we also experimented with an

[19]A precise analysis of the last causal link appears in Cukierman (1993) and a broad discussion in Chapter 23 of Cukierman (1992).

index of the political vulnerability of the central bank. This index excludes, by construction, the direct effect of political instability on Central Bank Governors turnover and is therefore more likely to reflect CBI net of political instability. It is still possible that central bank vulnerability and political instability are positively correlated across countries. This actually turns out to be the case for regime instability. Even in that case the correlation between the two is small (Cukierman and Webb (1993)). We are therefore fairly confident that the effects of CBI on growth found here reflect more than just the effect of political instability.

References

Alesina, A., (1988). Macroeconomics and Politics. Fischer, S. (ed.), *NBER Macroeconomics Annual*, the MIT Press, Cambridge, MA.

Alesina, A. and Summers, L.H., (1993). Central Bank Independence and Macroeconomic Performance: Some Comparative Evidence. *Journal of Money Credit and Banking*, **25**: 157–62, May.

Alesina, A., Cohen, G.D., and Roubini, N., (1992). Macroeconomic Policy and Elections in OECD Democracies. Cukierman, A., Hercowitz, Z., and Leiderman, L. (Eds.), *Political Economy, Growth and Business Cycles*, the MIT Press, Cambridge, Massachusetts.

Alesina, A., Ozler, S., Roubini, N., and Swagel, P., (1991). Political Instability and Economic Growth. Paper presented at the NBER Conference on Political Economics, November 15–16, 1991.

Barro, R.J., (1991). Economic Growth in a Cross Section of Countries. *Quarterly Journal of Economics*, **106**: 407–443, May.

Barro, R.J. and Wolf, C.H., (1989). Data Appendix for Economic Growth in a Cross Section of Countries. Unpublished, Harvard University.

Cukierman, A., (1992). *Central Bank Strategy, Credibility, and Independence: Theory and Evidence*, the MIT Press, Cambridge, Massachusetts.

Cukierman, A., (1993). Commitment through Delegation, Political Influence and Central Bank Independence. Paper prepared for the conference, "A Framework for Monetary Stability," De Nederlandsche Bank, Amsterdam, October.

Cukierman, A., Webb, S.B., and Neyapti, B., (1992). Measuring the Independence of Central Banks and its Effect on Policy Outcomes. *The World Bank Economic Review*, **6**: 353–98, The World Bank, Washington D.C., September.

Cukierman, A., and Webb, S.B., (1993). Political Influence on the Central Bank – International Evidence. Manuscript, Tel-Aviv University, May.

Delong, B.J. and Summers, L.H., (1991). Equipment Investment and Economic Growth. *The Quarterly Journal of Economics*, **106**: 445–502, May.

Delong, B.J. and Summers, L.H., (1992). Macroeconomic Policy and Long-Run Growth. Manuscript, Harvard University, August.

Easterly, W., (1991). How Much Do Distortions Affect Growth? Manuscript, The World Bank, Washington, D.C., November.

Easterly, W., Kremer, M., Prichett, L., and Summers, L.H., (1992). Good Policy or Good Luck? Country Growth Performance and Temporary Shocks. Manuscript, The World Bank, Washington, D.C., March.

Easterly, W., Rodriguez, C.A., and Schmidt-Hebbel, K., (Eds.), (1992). *Public Sector Deficits and Macroeconomic Performance*, Manuscript, The World Bank, April. To be published by Oxford University Press in August 1994.

Fischer, S., (1991). Growth, Macroeconomics and Development. *NBER Macroeconomics Annual*, 329–79.

Gelb, A.H., (1989). Financial Policies, Growth, and Efficiency. PRE Working Paper 202, Country Economics Department, The World Bank, Washington, D.C., June.

Grilli, V., Masciandaro, D., and Tabellini, G., (1991). Political and Monetary Institutions and Public Financial Policies in the Industrial Countries. *Economic Policy*, **13**: 341–92.

King, G.R. and Levine, R., (1993). Finance, Entrepeneurship, and Growth. Paper presented at the February 8, 9, 1992 World Bank Conference on: How do National Policies Affect Long-Run Growth?

Levine, R. and Renelt, D., (1992). A Sensitivity Analysis of Cross-Country Growth Regressions. *American Economic Review*, **82**: 942–63, September.

McKinnon, R.I., (1973). *Money and Capital in Economic Development*, The Brookings Institution, Washington, D.C.

Meltzer, A.H., (1987). Limits of Short-Run Stabilization Policy. *Economic Inquiry*, **25**: 1–14, January.

Pfeffermann, G.P. and Madarassy, A., (1992). Trends in Private Investment in Developing Countries, Discussion Paper No. 14, International Finance Corporation, The World Bank, Washington, D.C.

Rogoff, K., (1985). The Optimal Degree of Commitment to an Intermediate Monetary Target. *Quarterly Journal of Economics*, **100**: 1169–1190, November.

Summers, R. and Heston, A., (1991). The Penn World Table (Mark 5): An Expanded Set of International Comparisons, 1950–1988. *Quarterly Journal of Economics*, **106**: 327–68, May.

World Development Report, (1991). The World Bank, Washington, D.C.

[17]

How Independent Should a Central Bank Be?

*Guy Debelle and Stanley Fischer**

The case for an independent central bank is increasingly accepted. The central banks of Chile, France, Mexico, New Zealand, and Venezuela have all had their independence enhanced; the Maastricht treaty requires national central banks participating in the European System of Central Banks to meet a prescribed standard of independence; and a lively discussion is under way in Britain of the desirability of making the Bank of England, now explicitly subservient to the Treasury, independent.[1]

This new orthodoxy is based on three foundations: the success of the Bundesbank and the German economy over the past 40 years; the theoretical academic literature on the inflationary bias of discretionary policymaking; and the empirical academic literature on central bank independence.[2] Every orthodoxy, even an incipient one, deserves to be questioned;[3] and there is indeed reason to be careful about the lessons

---

*At the time this paper was presented, Debelle was a Ph.D. student in the Department of Economics at the Massachusetts Institute of Technology, where Fischer was Professor of Economics. Debelle joined the Research Department of the Reserve Bank of Australia in September 1994; Fischer is on leave from MIT at the International Monetary Fund. The authors thank Rudiger Dornbusch and Peter Klibanoff for useful suggestions. This paper has also benefited from comments by participants at the Center for Economic Policy Research (Stanford)–Federal Reserve Bank of San Francisco conference in March 1994, and the Macroeconomics seminars at MIT and Harvard.

[1] See, for instance, Roll Committee (1993) and Vibert (1993).

[2] The analytic literature starts from Kydland and Prescott (1977); most recently, see Persson and Tabellini (1993) and Walsh (1993). The academic literature on central bank independence is comprehensively summarized in Cukierman (1992); see also Cukierman and others (1993).

[3] Hall (1994) questions the new conventional wisdom by focusing on the Bundesbank, arguing that its success is due more to the nature of wage bargaining in the German economy than to its independence.

drawn from recent work. In particular, the literature does not establish that more independence is necessarily better than less.

We examine each of the three legs of the current argument for central bank independence. First, while the Bundesbank has achieved an enviable record of producing price stability, it has done so in 1993–94, as in the early 1980s, at a high price in terms of forgone output. It is not self-evident that the Bundesbank's trade-off between inflation and output should be emulated in other countries. Indeed, it is puzzling that a central bank that supposedly commands massive credibility has, since 1980, presided over two big recessions in order to maintain low inflation.

Second, the academic literature on dynamic inconsistency does not point directly to an independent central bank as the solution to the inflationary bias of discretionary policy; rather, dynamic inconsistency was advanced originally as an argument for a monetary rule rather than discretion, and a monetary rule does not need an independent central bank. The more relevant game-theoretic argument derives from the work of Rogoff (1985) and suggests the appointment of conservative central bankers as a solution to the inflationary bias problem.[4] But the Rogoff approach also implies that a central bank can be too independent to be socially optimal.[5] Recently this literature has been taken in a new direction by Walsh (1993) and Persson and Tabellini (1993) to examine incentive contracts for central bankers, along the lines of the contract of the Governor of the Reserve Bank of New Zealand (Dawe 1990).

The empirical literature on central bank independence shows a significant negative correlation between average inflation over 10-year periods and a measure of independence (constructed from legal provisions) among developed countries. However, the coefficient on this measure is positive, although not significant, in a regression that also includes less developed countries (Cukierman 1992, p. 420). The negative correlation among industrialized countries may reflect merely the common influence of a national aversion to inflation that affects both inflation and central bank independence: As shown below, countries with less aversion to inflation will tend to have less independent central banks.[6,7] Cukierman and colleagues (1993), attempting to deal with reverse causation, show that growth and central bank independence

[4] Lohmann (1992) extends the Rogoff rule to allow the conservative central banker to be overruled by the government, at a cost; this produces a non-linear rule in which the central bank responds proportionately more strongly to large than to small disturbances.

[5] Freedman (1993) presents an interesting perspective on the increased interest in central bank independence, emphasizing the growing recognition of the need for a clear mandate for the central bank, and for central bank accountability.

[6] See Debelle (1994).

[7] Here the independence of the central bank is measured by the weight placed on inflation relative to that placed on output in the bank's loss function.

remain significantly positively correlated even when an instrumental variables procedure is used.

In discussing central bank independence, it is useful to draw a distinction between *goal independence* and *instrument independence*.[8] A central bank has goal independence when it is free to set the final goals of monetary policy. Thus, a central bank with goal independence could, for instance, decide that price stability was less important than output stability and act accordingly. Goal independence is related to the Grilli, Masciandaro, and Tabellini (1991) concept of political independence; however, by political independence they mean the central bank's ability to pursue the goal of low inflation free of political interference.[9] According to these authors, the German and Dutch central banks have the most political independence. A bank that has instrument independence is free to choose the means by which it seeks to achieve its goals.[10] The Reserve Bank of New Zealand, whose goals are precisely described in a contract with the government, has no goal independence; however, it has instrument independence since it chooses the method by which it tries to achieve the pre-assigned goals.[11] A central bank whose task was specified as attaining a given growth rate of the money stock would have neither goal nor instrument independence.[12]

In this paper we first review empirical evidence on the relationship between central bank independence and economic performance, in that context discussing the performance of the Bundesbank. Next a model developed by Debelle (1994) shows how to determine the optimal objective function for a central bank. We then discuss lessons of recent work on optimal incentive contracts for central banks and relate them to the distinction between goal and instrument independence for the central bank.

We will argue that industrialized countries face a real trade-off between the length and depth of recessions and the variability of inflation, and that the trade-off is not best left to a central bank that is isolated from political pressures. Rather, central banks need to be given a clear mandate and clear incentives to perform, and they must be *accountable* for their actions. Comparing the Federal Reserve and the

---

[8] The distinction is related to that drawn by Grilli, Masciandaro, and Tabellini (1991) between *political* and *economic* independence.

[9] Although these authors state in their text that this is their criterion, all but one of the eight variables they include in their measure of political independence relate to freedom from government intervention in central bank decisions.

[10] The definition here differs slightly from that of Grilli and his colleagues, who define economic independence by the extent of government access to central bank credit, by whether the central bank sets the discount rate, and by whether it supervises banks.

[11] Grilli, Masciandaro, and Tabellini (1991) would describe the Reserve Bank of New Zealand as having complete political independence.

[12] A little ambiguity exists here, since technical decisions still have to be made in deciding how best to hit a given money supply target.

Bundesbank, we will argue that while the Bundesbank has successfully defined a clearer mandate for itself, the Fed comes closer to meeting the accountability criterion—and that each could benefit from moving in the direction of the other.

Empirical Evidence on Central Bank Independence

Although both the Barro and Gordon (1983) and the Rogoff (1985) articles are usually cited in any discussion of the case for central bank independence, they have different implications. Barro and Gordon argue that the inflationary bias of the discretionary equilibrium in their model is a case for a monetary rule. In their initial non-stochastic equilibrium, the optimal rule would fix the money stock or money growth rate. Once uncertainty is introduced and the level of output is affected by shocks, the case becomes one for a feedback rule, in which monetary policy responds optimally to shocks. This would be a rule without discretion, and an independent central bank would not be needed, just a technical institute to implement the rule.

Rogoff's solution to the need for flexibility in monetary policy to respond to shocks is to install a conservative central banker with the discretion to respond to shocks and the conservatism to keep the mean rate of inflation low. Because the central banker is conservative, the response to shocks is also conservative; the optimal central banker is chosen by trading off the reduction in mean inflation secured by conservatism against the less than optimal trade-off between inflation and output variability produced by that same conservatism. It is not optimal in the Rogoff model to appoint a central banker whose only concern is low and stable inflation.

Interpreted in terms of goal and instrument independence, the Rogoff central bank can be thought of as having no goal independence—its goals are those of the appointed central banker—and full instrument independence.[13] It is important to note that the Rogoff model implies that if countries have central banks with differing degrees of conservatism, but are hit by similar shocks, then a trade-off should be observed between the variability of output and that of inflation, across countries.

The Rogoff approach is the basis for the definition of central bank independence as the relative weight on inflation in the central bank's loss function: The more single-mindedly the law specifies that a central bank seek to preserve the value of the currency, the more independent

[13] Alternatively, one could say that instrument independence is not explicitly discussed in the Rogoff central bank model.

Figure 1

Inflation and Central Bank Independence[a]

Industrialized Countries

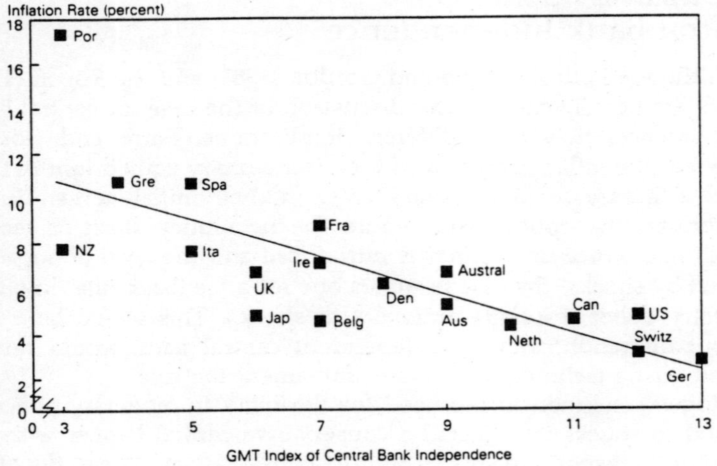

[a] As measured according to an index developed in Grilli, Masciandaro, and Tabellini (1991), here labeled GMT Index.

it is taken to be. This is the definition used in constructing most indices of central bank independence. It almost makes the basic empirical result of the independence literature, that central bank independence and inflation performance are negatively related (Figure 1), a tautology.[14] However, it is not a tautology, since the legal provisions on which most measures of central bank independence are based do not necessarily translate into effective action.[15]

The most striking result of the empirical work is that central bank independence appears to have *no* adverse consequences. Grilli, Masciandaro, and Tabellini (1991) show that the improved inflation performance associated with increased central bank independence for indus-

[14] In Figure 1 the inflation rate is plotted against the GMT (Grilli, Masciandaro, and Tabellini) index of central bank independence. Cukierman (1992), Chapter 19, compares the different indices.

[15] As noted above, the basic result does not apply when the sample is extended to include developing countries (Cukierman 1992).

Figure 2

Variance in Inflation and in Output Growth

Industrialized Countries, 1960 to 1992

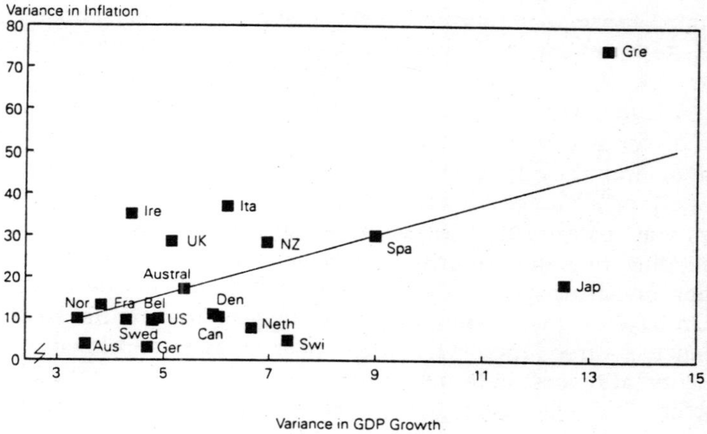

trialized countries does not come at a cost in terms of forgone growth. Similarly, for a cross-section of countries including less developed countries (LDCs), Cukierman and others (1993) find that while legal independence is negatively related to growth, the coefficient is not significant; an alternative (inverse) measure of central bank independence, the frequency of turnover of the central bank governor, is negatively related to growth (and positively related to inflation). Thus, improved inflation performance does not seem to come at a cost in terms of lower growth.

Figure 2 shows the relationship between the variability of inflation and the variability of GDP growth over the 1960–92 period, for the countries for which Grilli, Masciandaro, and Tabellini constructed measures of central bank independence (the GMT index). The association between these measures of variability is positive and significant, though the statistical significance disappears if Greece is excluded from the sample.[16]

---

[16] Alesina and Summers (1993) and Eijffinger and Schaling (1993) examine the relationship between alternative measures of central bank independence and inflation and output growth variability. Eijffinger and Schaling find that inflation variability is significantly negatively related only to the GMT index (in two out of three decades), and that

The standard loss function in this literature penalizes deviations of the *level* of output from its target level, rather than the variability of output growth. Using measures of output deviations from linear and quadratic trends (of log output), we still find a positive but insignificant correlation between output and inflation variability.

These results could reflect either reverse causation from inflation aversion to central bank independence or, closely related, the presence of a third factor that produces both economic stability and independence. As noted above, Cukierman and others (1993) have investigated the reverse causation issue econometrically. Havrilesky and Granato (1993) include both measures of the extent of corporatism[17] and the index of central bank independence in a regression for the rate of inflation, and they find that none of the measures of corporatism, separately or all together, enter significantly. By contrast, Hall (1994) argues that centralized collective bargaining at the industry level (with IG Metall setting the pattern) is at least as much responsible for low inflation in Germany as is the independence of the Bundesbank.

On balance, the existing evidence suggests that central bank independence is a free lunch:[18] It brings lower inflation and lower inflation variability, at no cost in terms of lower output growth or greater output variability. We will investigate the relationship between legal independence and inflation in more detail below.

Nonetheless, an important anomaly remains. Recall the implication of the Rogoff model that a negative relationship would be expected between the variability of output and of inflation if countries were being hit by the same shocks, and if the central banks were efficient but differed in their relative tastes for inflation and output variability. At least three factors could account for the positive relationship that in fact obtains (Figure 2). If the variance of shocks differs systematically by country, then we would expect to find a positive relationship, with countries that are hit by bigger shocks[19] having greater variability of both inflation and GDP growth. Or, if some central banks are more efficient than others, they would do better at stabilizing on both dimensions. Or, if more independent central banks are also more credible on inflation,

output growth variability is not significantly related to any of the measures of independence. Alesina and Summers find that inflation and inflation variability are negatively related to central bank independence, but that growth and the variability of growth are unaffected by it.

[17] They include three measures of the power of organized labor, two measures of the leftward leaning of the government, and two measures of the size of the public sector.

[18] This phrase was first used in the present context by Grilli, Masciandaro, and Tabellini (1991). See also Eijffinger and Schaling (1993) and Debelle (1994).

[19] These shocks could be self-inflicted: for instance, greater variability of government spending.

they may obtain a "credibility bonus" that makes the economy respond more rapidly to monetary policy changes.[20]

We are inclined to believe that the positive relationship between output and inflation variability shown in Figure 2 reflects both differences in the magnitude of shocks affecting different economies and differences in the efficiency with which policymakers respond to those shocks.[21] Countries with independent central banks are likely to be countries with more disciplined governments and thus are likely to suffer smaller self-inflicted shocks. Their central banks are likely to have better research staffs and abler and more experienced decision-makers. We suspect that the credibility bonus explanation would receive general support, but we are more skeptical and will return to the issue below.

The evidence reviewed here leaves little doubt that, on average, economic performance is better in countries with more independent central banks. But we will advance the view that, for the most sophisticated central banks, a trade-off remains between price level and output stability, and that a central bank can be too independent. We pursue the argument in a comparison of the Bundesbank and the Fed.

The Bundesbank and the Fed

Every central bank confronted with an inflationary shock has to decide how rapidly to try to reduce inflation; the more drastic the attempted correction, the larger will be the decline in output. To illustrate, by 1991 the Bundesbank knew that it faced rising inflation. It could at that point have tightened money and raised short-term interest rates to, say, 15 percent. Such a decision would have prevented some of the subsequent inflation, at a cost in terms of forgone output. Instead, it chose to fight the inflation more gradually. In the fall of 1993, it faced another decision, of whether to cut interest rates more rapidly, tending to increase output but at the cost of a slower decline in the inflation rate. It chose not to cut interest rates rapidly, thereby slowing the recovery from the recession.[22]

To return to the credibility bonus: It is widely agreed that the Bundesbank commands great credibility, as a result of both its indepen-

[20] Kenneth Rogoff has pointed out that the relationship would also be positive if countries differ only in the wedge between the natural rate of unemployment and the socially optimal rate.

[21] Taylor (1982) argues that the trade-off between output and inflation variability can differ across countries due to "taste" or structural differences, but that a trade-off does exist.

[22] We take it for granted here that a short-run trade-off exists between output and inflation, and that every central bank believes that too.

Table 1
Estimates of the Sacrifice Ratio

Country	Disinflation Period	Length (Quarters)	Output Loss of GDP (%)	Initial Rate of Inflation (%)	Change in Inflation Rate (Percentage Points)	Sacrifice Ratio
United States	1969:IV–1971:IV	8	6.29	5.67	2.14	2.94
United States	1974:I–1976:IV	11	9.56	9.70	4.00	2.39
United States	1980:I–1984:III	15	16.20	12.10	8.83	1.83
United States	1989:IV–1993:I	13	6.05	5.02	2.03	2.98
Germany	1965:IV–1967:III	7	6.22	3.67	2.43	2.56
Germany	1973:I–1977:III	18	11.20	6.92	4.23	2.64
Germany	1981:I–1986:III	26	21.20	5.86	5.95	3.56
Germany	1992:II–			3.96		

Source: Output losses and periods of disinflation are taken from Ball (1993) with the inclusion of corrections from a later version of that paper, and the authors' calculations.

dence and its consistent anti-inflationary behavior. This credibility should have enabled it to deal with inflationary shocks at less output cost than less credible central banks, such as the Federal Reserve. Nonetheless, since 1980 it has had to produce two major recessions to keep inflation low. From 1980 to 1983, the German economy was in recession as the Bundesbank fought the consequences of the second oil shock. From 1992 to the present, mid 1994, the German economy has been in recession as it fights the consequences of unification.

In Table 1 we present estimates of the output costs (as a percentage of GDP) of recessions in Germany and the United States since the first oil shock in 1973. Surprisingly, the output cost of German recessions is higher than that of U.S. recessions. Indeed, the sacrifice ratio in Germany is generally larger than that for the United States for all recent recessions.

In Figure 3 we plot output losses in recessions since 1962 against the GMT Index measure of central bank independence.[23] The overall relationship is positive; it is also statistically significant. This implies that the output loss suffered during recessions has on average been larger, the greater the independence of the central bank.

Using an expectational Phillips curve

$$y_t = y^* + \beta(\pi_t - \pi_t^e) + \varepsilon_t \qquad (1)$$

[23] This relationship was discovered independently by Adam Posen (1993). The output loss measures are taken from Ball (1993) with the inclusion of corrections from a later version of that paper.

Figure 3

Output Loss and Central Bank Independence[a]

Industrialized Countries

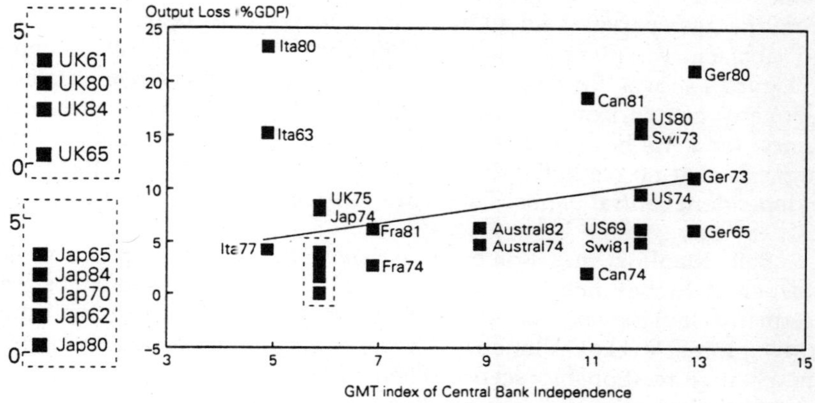

[a] As measured according to an index developed in Grilli, Masciandaro, and Tabellini (1991), here labeled GMT Index.

where y^* is the full employment level of output, π is the inflation rate, π_t^e is the expected inflation rate, and ε_t is a supply shock, the cumulative output loss during any disinflation is

$$L = \sum_{t_0}^{T} [\beta(\pi_t - \pi_t^e) + \varepsilon_t] \tag{2}$$

where t_0 is the starting point and T is the end of the disinflation. The more credible the central bank, the larger is β, for reasons demonstrated in Lucas (1973). Thus, comparing output losses in two countries, one factor, β, would tend to make the loss larger in the country with the more credible central bank: The Phillips curve in that country would be flatter. If the sum of unanticipated disinflation and the supply shocks were the same in the two countries, then the output loss would be higher in the country with the more credible central bank.

However, there is no reason whatsoever to expect the amount of unanticipated disinflation to be the same: When the more credible central bank announces that it will reduce inflation, the expected inflation rate should fall, and output should not. Thus, it is a puzzle for those who believe that the Bundesbank should have a credibility bonus that Germany has had to go through recessions at least as severe as those in the United States in order to secure reasonable price stability, particularly given Hall's (1994) argument that the pattern of wage bargaining in Germany is more conducive to low inflation.

Indeed, this evidence gives the clear impression that the Bundesbank's credibility is far greater in the asset markets—at least judging from the newspapers[24]—than in the labor markets. At present we have no satisfactory explanation for this difference, but as the positive slope in Figure 3 shows, the phenomenon extends beyond the United States–Germany comparison: Countries with greater central bank independence tend to have greater output losses during recessions. This suggests that no credibility bonus exists in the labor markets for more independent central banks: They have to prove their toughness repeatedly, by being tough.

Ball, Mankiw, and Romer (1988) show that the Phillips curve is steeper at higher rates of inflation; thus, the higher output cost in Germany (say) may be caused by the fact that it started disinflating from a lower initial level of inflation. However, controlling for initial inflation, the positive relationship seen in Figure 2 still remains. An alternative explanation for the relationship in Figure 2 is that different labor market features may affect the slope of the Phillips curve and hence the amount of unemployment and output loss necessary to achieve a given disinflation. Accordingly, we have run regressions that include a number of variables to capture labor market institutions, including the degree of wage flexibility, the degree of labor market unity, and the replacement ratio.[25] Only the replacement ratio entered significantly, but central bank independence remained significant in all cases.

In Table 2 we present the mean inflation rates and growth rates, as well as the variability of inflation and growth[26] for the United States and Germany for the period 1960 to 1992. Inflation in Germany was lower than that in the United States over the period, and growth rates were the same. The United States has more stable output and less stable inflation. No doubt the United States could have had more stable inflation, if its central bank had been more devoted to fighting inflation. Should it have had such a central bank? While the empirical results on central bank independence appear to say yes, since greater independence comes with lower inflation and no evident costs, the comparison with German

[24] That is to say, it is generally believed by asset market participants that the Bundesbank is a tough inflation fighter.

[25] The labor market variables are from Havrilesky and Granato (1993) and from Layard, Nickell, and Jackman (1991).

[26] Similar results hold for the variability of output around linear or quadratic trends.

Table 2
Inflation and Growth Rates and Variability

Quarterly data, Estimated over 1960 to 1992/3	United States	Germany
Average inflation	1.19	.84
Variance inflation	.69	.43
Average real growth	.73	.73
Variance real growth	.88	1.42
Sum squared residuals of log output against:		
Annual data		
linear trend	.049	.080
quadratic	.023	.029
Quarterly data		
linear	.208	.347
quadratic	.101	.128

performance suggests that a trade-off exists and that we should investigate further the question of how independent (in the sense of anti-inflationary) the central bank should be.

How Inflation-Averse Should the Central Bank Be?

In this section we present a model, from Debelle (1994),[27] in which to consider the optimal degree of inflation aversion of the central bank. The model includes a central bank that sets the inflation rate and a fiscal authority that sets (distortionary) taxes and government spending and receives seigniorage from the central bank. Output is produced by labor, whose nominal wage is predetermined; firms maximize after-tax profits and can hire the amount of labor they demand at the predetermined nominal wage.[28]

Society's loss function, or the loss function of the social planner, is given by:[29]

$$V_S = \frac{1}{2}\,[s_\pi \pi_t^2 + s_x(x_t - x^*)^2]. \tag{3}$$

[27] The model draws on Alesina and Tabellini (1987).

[28] The single-period version of the model is presented here; the model is extended in Debelle (1994) to two periods, which allows the government to issue debt.

[29] In Debelle (1994) the social loss function also includes government spending, as in the fiscal loss function below (equation 5). No significant results appear to depend on the inclusion of g, which is omitted here for easier computation.

This loss function may be interpreted as reflecting the preferences of the society or those of the government. It differs from the loss function of the fiscal authority (equation (5) below), which includes also the level of government spending.

The social planner desires to have inflation as close to zero as possible and to minimize the deviation of output (x) from its target level x^*. We set the inflation target at zero, recognizing that measurement error and perhaps downward nominal price rigidities imply a slightly higher rate, say around 2 percent.[30] The target x^* is the one that would be chosen if non-distortionary taxes were available; s_π and s_x are weights on the inflation and output objectives.

The monetary authority is also assumed to be concerned only about the levels of inflation and output:

$$V_M = \frac{1}{2}[\pi_t^2 + \mu(x_t - x^*)^2]. \tag{4}$$

The parameter μ denotes the relative weight the central bank places on output relative to inflation. It is generally interpreted as the inverse of the extent of central bank independence, and will be used in that sense unless otherwise noted. However, measures of central bank independence in the empirical literature incorporate financial linkages between the central bank and the government, as well as μ, and the framework of this paper will allow us to distinguish these concepts. The (standard) loss function (4) is consistent with most central bank charters, although these generally also include responsibilities for the financial system.

The fiscal authority's loss function

$$V_F = \frac{1}{2}[\delta_\pi \pi_t^2 + \delta_x(x_t - x^*)^2 + \delta_g(g_t - g^*)^2] \tag{5}$$

includes government spending as well as inflation and output. We assume that $\delta_x/\delta_\pi > \mu$, that is, that the fiscal authority puts relatively more weight on output relative to inflation than does the central bank.

Distortionary taxes are levied on production and are the only tax available to the government. An increase in taxation reduces output (which in equilibrium is always below its target level). Output is produced by labor, L, and is subject to a white noise productivity shock, a_t.

$$X_t = L^\gamma e^{a_t/2}. \tag{6}$$

[30] Very little in this paper depends on the optimal inflation rate, though of course the evaluation of central bank independence, which assumes lower inflation is better, does.

Workers set the nominal wage, w (in logs), to achieve a target real wage w^*,[31] so that

$$w = w^* + p^e. \tag{7}$$

The representative firm's profit function is given by:

$$PL^{\gamma}e^{a_t/2}(1 - \tau) - wL. \tag{8}$$

Solving for the firm's labor demand, and assuming it can hire the labor it demands at the given nominal wage, gives (the log of) output supply:[32]

$$x_t = \alpha(\pi_t - \pi_t^e - \tau_t - w^* + \log\gamma) + \frac{a_t}{2(1-\gamma)} \tag{9}$$

where $\alpha = \gamma/(1 - \gamma)$ and, for simplicity, we set $\gamma = 0.5$.[33]

The government budget constraint is given by[34]

$$g = \tau + \pi \tag{10}$$

where g and τ are expressed as a ratio to output. Although seigniorage is a non-linear function of inflation, it has been linearized here for simplicity; obviously, we assume that the economy is on the correct side of the Laffer curve.

Nash Equilibrium

The monetary authority chooses π_t and the government τ_t, taking expectations and each other's actions as given, after the workers have chosen the wage. Expectations are formed rationally. The reaction functions of the two authorities are as follows:

Monetary:

$$\pi = \frac{\mu}{1+\mu}(\pi^e + \tau + C - g^* - a), \tag{11}$$

[31] The target wage w^* may be explained by efficiency wage theories or an insider/outsider model. See the discussion in Alesina and Tabellini (1987), footnote 5, p. 621.

[32] Note that although the disturbance has been introduced in the supply function (6), it could as well have been incorporated directly as a demand shock in equation (9).

[33] Note from equation (10) that the problem of time inconsistency of optimal policy would disappear if the government had access to non-distortionary taxes, in this model as in Fischer (1980).

[34] As in Alesina and Tabellini (1987), the following assumptions are made. Money demand is given by $M_t = P_t + \bar{X}$ where $\bar{X}$ is independent of τ. Thus $\pi_t = m_t - m_{t-1}$. The government financing constraint is $G_t = \tau_t P_t X_t + M_t - M_{t-1}$ which when divided by nominal income gives $g_t = \tau + (M_t - M_{t-1})/M_t \bar{X}/X_t$ and hence approximates to equation (10).

Fiscal:

$$\tau = g^* + \frac{\delta_x - \delta_g}{\delta_x + \delta_g}\pi - \frac{\delta_x}{\delta_x + \delta_g}(\pi^e + C - g^* - a) \tag{12}$$

where $C \equiv (g^* + w^* - \log \gamma + x^*)$ is constant and independent of the policy weights.

These equations imply:

$$\pi_t = \frac{\mu\delta_g}{\delta_x + \delta_g + \mu\delta_g}C - \frac{\mu\delta_g}{\delta_x + \delta_g + 2\mu\delta_g}a_t, \tag{13}$$

$$x_t = x^* - \frac{\delta_g}{\delta_x + \delta_g + \mu\delta_g}C + \frac{\delta_g}{\delta_x + \delta_g + 2\mu\delta_g}a_t, \tag{14}$$

$$g_t = g^* - \frac{\delta_x}{\delta_x + \delta_g + \mu\delta_g}C + \frac{\delta_x}{\delta_x + \delta_g + 2\mu\delta_g}a_t, \tag{15}$$

$$\tau_t = g^* - \frac{\mu\delta_g + \delta_x}{\delta_x + \delta_g + \mu\delta_g}C + \frac{\mu\delta_g + \delta_x}{\delta_x + \delta_g + 2\mu\delta_g}a_t. \tag{16}$$

The key result is that, in contrast to the existing literature, inflation and output depend not only on the central bank's weight on output, but also on the fiscal authority's weights. They also depend on the parameters x^*, g^*, and w^*, which reflect the institutional and political structure of the economy.

The average level of inflation:

$$\bar{\pi} = \frac{\mu\delta_g}{\delta_x + \delta_g + \mu\delta_g}C \tag{17}$$

depends positively on the central bank's weight on output, μ. This is the standard time inconsistency problem: The more weight the central bank places on output, the greater the incentive to create surprise inflation. Since this is perceived by the workers, in equilibrium, higher inflation occurs but no gain in output. When the central bank's weight on output is zero ($\mu = 0$), then equilibrium inflation is zero.

Inflation depends positively on the spending target g^*, as an increase in the spending target requires more seigniorage financing. Inflation also depends positively on output and wages, as a higher output (employment) target cr a higher real wage target increases the monetary authority's desire to inflate. Inflation depends negatively on

Table 3
Effects of Parameter Changes on the Economy

	↑ μ	↑ δ_x	↑ δ_g	↑ x^*	↑ g^*
Inflation	↑	↓	↑	↑	↑
Output deviation $\lvert x - x^*\rvert$	↓	↓	↑	↑	↑
Govt. spending deviation $\lvert g - g^*\rvert$	↓	↑	↓	↑	↑

μ: monetary weight on output
δ_x: fiscal weight on output
δ_g: fiscal weight on government spending
x^*: output target
g^*: government spending target

the ratio of the fiscal authority's weights (δ_x/δ_g). An increased weight on the government spending target means that taxes are increased, thus reducing output and increasing the incentive of the monetary authority to inflate. An increased weight on output means that the fiscal authority reduces taxes to increase output, thus moving output closer to its target and reducing the incentive to inflate.

The average levels of output and government spending fall short of their respective targets, reflecting the trade-off the fiscal authority faces between spending and output. The difference between realized and targeted output is decreasing in μ, and decreasing in δ_x/δ_g. An increase in μ means that the central bank places more weight on the output objective, thus inflating the economy more and decreasing the level of distortionary taxes, while the opposite applies to the government spending gap. Table 3 summarizes these influences of the parameters on the economy.

The variance of inflation:

$$\sigma_\pi^2 = \left[\frac{\mu}{\delta_x/\delta_g + 1 + 2\mu}\right]^2 \sigma_a^2 \tag{18}$$

depends *positively* on μ and negatively on δ_x/δ_g.

The variance of output:

$$\sigma_x^2 = \left[\frac{1}{(\delta_x/\delta_g) + 1 + 2\mu}\right]^2 \sigma_a^2 \tag{19}$$

depends *negatively* on μ and δ_x/δ_g.

The increase in the variance of output when central bank independence is increased reflects the trade-off between flexibility and commitment highlighted by Rogoff (1985) and Lohmann (1992) and discussed at the beginning of this paper. When central bank independence is increased to reduce the time consistency problem, the willingness to respond to shocks is decreased.

Inflation and taxation may be positively or negatively correlated. They respond in opposite directions to the productivity shock, but in the same direction to changes in the parameters (g^*, w^*). Optimal tax theory implies that inflation should be positively correlated with the level of other distortionary taxes, as each tax should be set such that the marginal distortion is the same. However, that assumes that the taxes are set by one authority. Here, the inflation tax is set by the monetary authority, which has different objectives from the fiscal authority. It prefers less seigniorage, whereas the fiscal authority always wants a higher level of seigniorage for a given level of government spending. Empirical examination shows no definitive relationship between inflation and taxation.[35]

The general presumption in the literature is that the decline in inflation as a result of increasing central bank independence must always decrease the value of the loss function (except in terms of the loss of flexibility discussed above). However, this relies on the specification of the loss function solely in terms of the central bank's objectives. Here, although the inflation rate is clearly zero when the central bank is fully independent, society is not necessarily better off in this case. The expected loss in each period is:

$$E[V_S] = E\left[\pi^2\left(s_\pi + \frac{s_x}{\mu^2}\right)\right] \tag{20}$$

$$= [\mathrm{Var}(\pi) + (E[\pi])^2]\left(s_\pi + \frac{s_x}{\mu^2}\right). \tag{21}$$

The first term is increasing in μ; however, the second term is decreasing in μ, because while more central bank independence reduces the level and variance of inflation, it also decreases output.[36]

---

[35] See Grilli, Masciandaro, and Tabellini (1991), who found no systematic relationship across countries between the changes in the tax rate (expressed as the ratio of tax revenue to GDP) and changes in seigniorage (defined as the change in the money base relative to GDP).

[36] This conclusion may be overstated if further negative effects of inflation exist that are not captured in this simple model. For instance, inflation may have a negative effect on productivity (Selody 1990; Fischer 1993).

Optimal Aversion to Inflation by the Central Bank

Rogoff (1985) solved for the optimal degree of inflation aversion of the conservative central banker. His results were extended by Lohmann (1992), who shows that social welfare can be increased, at a cost, if the government retains the ability to override the conservative central banker. In equilibrium, the government does not overrule the central bank, but the threat of overruling ensures that the central bank follows a non-linear rule in which it responds more vigorously to large shocks than it otherwise would.

Implicitly, the social loss function in these articles is assumed to be that of the (original) central banker; it fails to be optimized only because of dynamic inconsistency. In our calculation of the optimal μ, we minimize (21) with respect to μ, thereby minimizing the social loss function (3).

While we do not obtain an explicit solution for μ (although it can be determined easily numerically), we can demonstrate the intuitive results that the optimal degree of central bank independence

- increases with society's aversion to inflation, and
- decreases with society's weight on output.

Thus, not surprisingly, the extent of central bank independence (defined as the central bank's aversion to inflation) may be determined by the country's underlying aversion to inflation. It remains true that for a given degree of inflation aversion, a country that institutes an independent central bank—with optimally chosen μ—will do better than one that simply endows the central bank with society's social welfare function. In this sense, the proposition that central bank independence enhances economic performance remains valid despite the endogeneity of central bank independence.

Stackelberg Equilibria

Although central bank independence is usually identified with μ in theoretical applications, empirical measures of it are closer to a more conventional sense of independence. By including provisions such as the term of central bank board members, and who chooses the governor, they come closer to measuring the central bank's ability to make decisions that are independent of those of the government.

The analytic model developed above does allow for independent decision-making by the central bank. It is conventional to examine the properties of only the Nash equilibrium, in which each actor takes the actions of the other as given. An alternative sense of the independence of the central bank relates to its need to accommodate the actions of the fiscal authority. To the extent that the central bank can fix its actions independent of the particular policy choice of the fiscal authority, it may be said to be more independent. We examine the effects of independence in this sense by considering alternative Stackelberg equilibria.

Assume first that the fiscal authority moves first. The fiscal authority can be thought of as having the superior commitment technology in this case.[27] This yields the following inflation rate:

$$\pi_F = \frac{\delta_g \mu(1 + 2\mu)}{\delta_\pi \mu^2 + \delta_x + \delta_g(1 + \mu)(1 + 2\mu)} C - \frac{\delta_g \mu(1 + 2\mu)}{\delta_\pi \mu^2 + \delta_x + \delta_g(1 + \mu)(1 + 2\mu) + \delta_g(1 + 2\mu)\mu} a_t. \tag{22}$$

The Stackelberg equilibrium in which the fiscal authority leads has to be interpreted with care. In the equilibrium that underlies equation (22), the fiscal authority sets the level of government spending, but the monetary authority still gets to determine the inflation rate before the level of taxes is set. However, in choosing g, the fiscal authority takes into account the reaction of the monetary authority to the fiscal authority's choice of g. This equilibrium may be a more appropriate description of fiscal-monetary interactions in practice than the Nash equilibrium.

The fiscal authority may be the leader in another, more direct sense: It can set both τ and g and force the monetary authority to print whatever amount of money is needed to finance the deficit. This "fiscal domination" equilibrium, an equilibrium not unknown in the real world, is examined at the end of this section.

Alternatively, if the monetary authority is the leader, choosing π first and leaving the fiscal authority to specify g or τ, the inflation rate is:

$$\pi_M = \frac{2\mu \delta_g^2}{(\delta_x + \delta_g)^2 + 2\mu \delta_g^2} C - \frac{2\mu \delta_g^2}{(\delta_x + \delta_g)^2 + 4\mu \delta_g^2} a_t. \tag{23}$$

A solution like (23) is more likely to obtain if the central bank has set a money or inflation target path, from which it will deviate only under well-defined conditions.

First we examine the inflation rates under these assumptions. We would expect the inflation rate to be higher when the fiscal authority leads than in the Nash equilibrium, and to be lower than in the Nash equilibrium when the monetary authority leads. We can show

$$\pi_F > \pi_N \Leftrightarrow 2\delta_x > \delta_\pi \mu. \tag{24}$$

[27] This interpretation was suggested by David Laibson.

Since the fiscal authority is likely to place more weight on output relative to inflation (δ_x/δ_π) than the monetary authority (μ), we expect $\pi_F > \pi_N$.

Comparing the inflation rate when the monetary authority is the leader with the Nash inflation rate:

$$\pi_M < \pi_N \Leftrightarrow \delta_x > \delta_g. \tag{25}$$

Inflation is lower when the central bank leads if $\delta_x > \delta_g$, a condition that is likely to obtain.

Society's loss functions under the two different scenarios are given by:

Monetary:

$$E[V_S] = [\mathrm{Var}(\pi_M) + (E[\pi_M])^2]\left(s_\pi + \frac{s_x}{\mu^2}\left(\frac{\delta_x + \delta_g}{2}\right)^2\right), \tag{26}$$

Fiscal:

$$E[V_S] = [\mathrm{Var}(\pi_F) + (E[\pi_F])^2]\left(s_\pi + \frac{s_x}{\mu^2}\right). \tag{27}$$

Next, we could ask whether it is better, from the viewpoint of society, for the central bank to be a Stackelberg leader. Comparing the expected value of the social loss function when the central bank is a Stackelberg leader with its value at the Nash equilibrium, the loss function is smaller (that is, society is better off) when the central bank leads if condition (25) above holds and if $\delta_g < 1$ and $\delta_g + \delta_x < 2$.[28] Thus, provided the fiscal authority weights output losses at the margin more heavily than increases in government spending and does not place a very high weight on output and government spending, it is better from a social viewpoint for the central bank to lead.

We can interpret this result as stating that it is better for the central bank to precommit to an inflation path than to move simultaneously with the fiscal authority, provided that the fiscal authority will not impose excessively distortionary taxes in order to finance desired government spending. This is not a ringing endorsement for monetary precommitment: Monetary precommitment can be expensive if the fiscal authority is not responsible.

[28] This is a sufficient condition for society to be better off when the central bank is a Stackelberg leader. Note that the normalization in the loss functions is that the weight on inflation in the central bank's loss function is one. Further, it is assumed through the budget constraint (10) that one unit of g can be financed with one unit of inflation.

Society is always better off in the Nash equilibrium than if the fiscal authority leads, provided condition (24) holds, that is, provided the central bank is more inflation-averse than the fiscal authority.[39] Thus, independence of the central bank, in the sense that it is not required to finance a predetermined deficit, is desirable in this model.[40]

If the central bank is exceptionally weak, the fiscal authority may be able to force it to finance a pre-specified deficit. In this *fiscal domination* equilibrium, the fiscal authority in effect sets g, τ, and π, and the central bank is a cipher. If this happens, it appears likely that the inflation rate is higher than in the Nash equilibrium, and social welfare is lower.[41] This means that the Stackelberg equilibrium, in which the monetary authority leads, is preferable to fiscal domination—another argument for central bank independence, appropriately defined.

Summary of Findings

In the models in this section, as in Rogoff (1985), conservative central bankers underreact to output shocks. In addition, we have shown that:

- The optimal degree of conservatism of the central bank depends on the society's aversion to inflation and output fluctuations;
- Society will be better off if the central bank precommits to an inflation rate, provided the fiscal authority is reasonably well behaved;
- If the central bank is more inflation-averse than the fiscal authority, society will be worse off if the fiscal authority is able to determine the size of the deficit that must be financed by the central bank.

Optimal Incentive Contracts

Nothing in the above analysis points to the desirability of a central bank having unlimited independence. As in Rogoff's (1985) model, it is not optimal for the central bank to be monomaniacal about inflation; it should also react to output fluctuations.

But it is possible to do better than the "optimal" central bank of the preceding section. First, as previously noted, Lohmann (1992) shows in the context of the Rogoff model how a non-linear reaction function,

[39] This is a sufficient condition.

[40] Debt financing is not possible in this single-period version of the model. Debelle (1994) examines the effects of debt financing in a two-period set-up.

[41] That is, this result holds for all but unusual parameter values.

enforced by the threat of government overruling of the central bank, can improve economic performance.

More radically, Walsh (1993) and Persson and Tabellini (1993) have shown that a contract between the government and the central banker, in which the central banker's remuneration is tied linearly to the negative of the inflation rate, can attain the first best equilibrium. They model the relationship between the central bank and the government in a principal-agent framework.

The conservative central banker reduces the inflationary bias of monetary policy that results from dynamic inconsistency, but at the cost of responding too conservatively to output disturbances. As Walsh shows, in the standard central bank loss function, the inflationary bias is the *same* in each state of nature. Accordingly, appointing a central banker who has the same loss function as society (equation 3), and penalizing the central banker by an amount proportional to the inflation rate, enables society to obtain the first best solution.[42]

It should be emphasized that while, in this contract solution, the government directly rewards the central banker purely on the basis of the behavior of the inflation rate, the central bank is also concerned about the stability of output. Monetary policy accordingly responds actively to output disturbances.

If the central banker is not motivated by a combination of a penalty[43] and society's loss function, then the government can attempt to motivate through rewards or penalties based on the behavior of both output and inflation.[44] Once again, it is possible to attain the first best solution.

This analysis again assumes that the loss function of the central bank is that of society. If it were not, but was still known at the time of the contract negotiation, the transfer would include an extra term reflecting the difference between society's and the central bank's loss functions. However, if the loss function of the central bank was not known, the central bank might have an incentive to create *less* than the socially desirable rate of inflation, because its payment is linear in the inflation rate.

The principal agent framework developed by Walsh and by Persson and Tabellini allows one to examine the issue of accountability. The central bank is accountable to the government (and hence the public) to

[42] This result is obtained by Walsh (1993) and also by Persson and Tabellini (1993). Walsh shows that the first best can also be obtained by penalizing the central bank by an amount proportional to the money stock—which is stochastically related to the inflation rate.

[43] Of course, it is only the marginal penalty that matters; the central banker has to be sufficiently well paid to want to take the job despite the risk of having to pay penalties.

[44] To obtain the first best outcome in this case, it is necessary to condition the central banker's penalty on the desired level of output. Walsh suggests this is difficult and that the first best solution may on this account be unattainable. It is not obvious why there should be any problem announcing a target unemployment rate, such as 5.5 percent.

achieve its inflation target. If it does not, then it is fined (which may in reality, take the form of dismissal). This issue is taken up in the next section.

The Central Bank Mandate and Accountability

The theories we have examined in this paper all imply that the central bank should have a clear mandate, whether in the form of a utility or loss function that specifies what it is to maximize, or in the form of a specific contract that penalizes inflation. In general, the contract instructs the central bank to minimize the social loss function plus the penalty for excess inflation. These theories are not equipped to deal with a fuzzy mandate or loss function, and it is difficult from the perspective of such theories to see the benefits of allowing the bank discretion as to its goals. That is, these theories all imply that central banks *should not* have goal independence.

The Reserve Bank of New Zealand has a clearly stated mandate to produce a particular path for or rate of inflation, one that is negotiated with the government. The agreement with the government allows for the inflation rate to be affected by supply shocks. The Federal Reserve has a vague mandate; that is, it has considerable goal independence. The Bundesbank is required both to maintain the value of the currency and to support the economic program of the government, provided that does not conflict with the goal of monetary stability. All three of these central banks have instrument independence.

The model in which the fiscal authority is a Stackelberg leader points to the importance of not leaving the fiscal authority with the power to fix the amount of deficit that must be financed by the printing of money. This type of central bank independence—freedom from having to finance the government—is likely to enhance economic performance.

The literature discussed in the previous section highlights the notion of *accountability*, emphasized by John Crow, former Governor of the Bank of Canada, and by the Roll Committee (1993). The central bank can be held accountable either in having to justify its behavior, or in having to pay a penalty for bad outcomes (or be rewarded for good outcomes). Accountability mechanisms differ. The Fed is accountable to the Congress, and to public opinion. The Bank of England is accountable to the Treasury. The Governor of the Reserve Bank of New Zealand is accountable to the government for meeting his contract. The Bundesbank has very little accountability: It does not have to account for its behavior to the legislature, though it could be argued that it is accountable to public opinion.

In an attempt to see which features of central bank structures account for superior inflation performance, we use the Grilli, Masciandaro, and Tabellini (1991) data and a series developed by Cukierman, Webb, and Neypati (1992). Recall that Grilli and his colleagues create an index of political independence: an equally weighted sum of zero or one dummies for different aspects of, first, the appointment procedures of the governor and board members and, second, the extent of commitment to a target of monetary stability. Their index of economic independence includes zero or one dummies for the extent to which the central bank is required to finance the government, its freedom to set interest rates, and whether it supervises banks.

We have created three indexes from these measures. The first is the presence of a statutory requirement that the central bank pursue monetary stability among its goals; this is called *INFOBJ*. The variable *INFOBJ* is a measure, albeit an imprecise one, of the *lack* of goal independence of the central bank. The second is the Grilli, Masciandaro, and Tabellini (GMT) measure of political independence, but excluding *INFOBJ*. This variable, *POL7*, includes the legal provisions relating to appointments and the central bank's relationship with the government. The third is the GMT measure of economic independence, minus the bank supervision criterion. This variable, *EC6*, consists of those measures relating to the central bank's right not to finance the government and its right to set the discount rate. It is a measure of instrument independence.

Cukierman, Webb, and Neypati examined the objectives of central banks laid out in their charters and ranked them on a scale from 0 to 1, depending on whether price stability was mentioned and whether other potentially conflicting objectives were included. We called this index *CUK*.

We ran regressions of the inflation rate against these four variables for 17 industrialized countries in the Grilli, Masciandaro, and Tabellini sample. Table 4 shows that the two variables most closely tied to inflation performance are INFOBJ and EC6. The variables grouped into POL7, which relate to appointment procedures, are not significantly related to inflation. However, while the (0, 1) objective variable INFOBJ was significant, the more disaggregated variable *CUK* was not.

Table 4 implies that inflation performance is likely to be better if the central bank has a mandate for monetary stability, that is, no goal independence, and if it has instrument independence. From this perspective, the Fed needs a less vague mandate.

. . . .

We conclude by discussing accountability and output–inflation trade-offs. We do not, at this stage, have any quantitative measures of the accountability of the central bank. To a very limited extent, the

Table 4
Inflation and the GMT Index

Variable	(1)	(2)	(3)	(4)	(5)
INFOBJ	−1.76	−2.28	−4.27		
	(1.72)	(1.61)	(1.30)		
POL7	−.41				
	(.45)				
EC6	−1.02	−1.02		−1.53	
	(.55)	(.55)		(.42)	
CUK					−.68
					(1.75)
$\bar{R}^2$	.44	.44	.37	.42	−.06

Standard errors in parentheses.

significance of *INFOBJ* in the equations in Table 4 provides some support for the notion that accountability matters; the extent is limited because inclusion of an objective in the charter does not mean the central bank is actually held accountable for achieving that objective.

Nonetheless, we suggest that accountability must be an important mechanism to improve central bank performance, for two reasons: First, all institutions need to be held accountable for their actions, or their performance suffers. Second, the cult of central bank independence, the appointment of independent central bankers, and the emphasis on inflation in the incentive contracts seen so far, appear to lead to an excessive concentration on inflation prevention and insufficient acknowledgment of the short-run trade-offs between inflation and output. Without accountability to elected representatives, such as the Congress, central banks run a very good chance of becoming too conservative. That is the argument for greater Bundesbank accountability.

This view runs into the obstacle that the trade-offs between inflation and output, and between inflation and output variability, implied by most of the models in this paper, do not show up in practice. We have run regressions similar to those in Table 4, with the growth rate of output and inflation and output variability as dependent variables, and have found no evidence of a trade-off. However, both theory and the comparison between the Bundesbank and the Fed in Table 1 suggest that a trade-off does exist for countries with first-rate central banks. And if the trade-off exists, then the most independent central bank is not likely to be the socially optimal central bank.

References

Alesina, Alberto. 1988. "Macroeconomics and Politics." *NBER Macroeconomics Annual 1988*, pp. 13–52. Cambridge, MA: The MIT Press.

Alesina, Alberto and Lawrence Summers. 1993. "Central Bank Independence and Macroeconomic Performance." *Journal of Money, Credit and Banking*, vol. 25, pp. 151–62.

Alesina, Alberto and Guido Tabellini. 1987. "Rules and Discretion with Non-Coordinated Monetary and Fiscal Policies." *Economic Inquiry*, vol. 25, pp. 619–30.

Bade, Robin and Michael Parkin. 1988. "Central Bank Laws and Monetary Policy." Department of Economics, University of Western Ontario (October).

Ball, Laurence. 1993. "What Determines the Sacrifice Ratio?" NBER Working Paper No. 4306.

Ball, Laurence, N. Gregory Mankiw, and David Romer. 1988. "The New Keynesian Economics and the Output-Inflation Trade-off." *Brookings Papers on Economic Activity*, vol. 19, no. 1, pp. 1–65.

Barro, Robert and David Gordon. 1983. "A Positive Theory of Monetary Policy in a Natural Rate Model." *Journal of Political Economy*, vol. 91, no. 4 (August), pp. 589–610.

Cukierman, Alex. 1992. *Central Bank Strategy, Credibility and Independence: Theory and Evidence*. Cambridge, MA: The MIT Press.

Cukierman, Alex, Pantelis Kalaitzidakis, Lawrence Summers, and Steven Webb. 1993. "Central Bank Independence, Growth Investment, and Real Rates." *Carnegie-Rochester Conference Series on Public Policy*, vol. 39 (December), pp. 95–104.

Cukierman, Alex, Steven Webb, and Bilin Neypati. 1992. "Measuring the Independence of Central Banks and Its Effect on Policy Outcomes." *World Bank Economic Review*, vol. 6, no. 1, pp. 353–98.

Dawe, S. 1990. "Reserve Bank of New Zealand Act 1989." *Reserve Bank Bulletin*, vol. 53, no. 1, pp. 29–36.

Debelle, Guy. 1994. "Central Bank Independence: A Free Lunch?" Mimeo, MIT (February).

Eijffinger, Sylvester and Eric Schaling. 1993. "Central Bank Independence: Theory and Evidence." Tilburg University, The Netherlands (February).

Fischer, Stanley. 1980. "Dynamic Inconsistency, Co-operation, and the Benevolent Dissembling Government." *Journal of Economic Dynamics and Control*, vol. 2, pp. 93–107.

———. 1993. "The Role of Macroeconomic Factors in Growth." *Journal of Monetary Economics*, vol. 32, no. 3 (December), pp. 485–512.

Freedman, Charles. 1993. "Designing Institutions for Monetary Stability: A Comment." *Carnegie-Rochester Conference Series on Public Policy*, vol. 39 (December), pp. 85–94.

Grilli, Vittorio, Donato Masciandaro, and Guido Tabellini. 1991. "Political and Monetary Institutions and Public Financial Policies in the Industrial Countries." *Economic Policy*, vol. 13 (October), pp. 341–92.

Hall, Peter A. 1994. "Central Bank Independence and Coordinated Wage Bargaining: Their Interaction in Germany and Europe." Forthcoming, *German Politics and Society*.

Havrilesky, Thomas and James Granato. 1993. "Determinants of Inflationary Performance: Corporatist Structures vs Central Bank Autonomy." *Public Choice*, vol. 76, pp. 249–61.

Kydland, Finn and Edward Prescott. 1977. "Rules Rather than Discretion: The Inconsistency of Optimal Plans." *Journal of Political Economy*, vol. 85, no. 3 (June), pp. 473–92.

Layard, Richard, Stephen Nickell, and Richard Jackman. 1991. *Unemployment: Macroeconomic Performance and the Labor Market*. Oxford: Oxford University Press.

Lohmann, Susanne. 1992. "Optimal Commitment in Monetary Policy: Credibility versus Flexibility." *The American Economic Review*, vol. 82, no. 1 (March), pp. 273–86.

Lucas, Robert E. 1973. "Some International Evidence on Output-Inflation Tradeoffs." *The American Economic Review*, vol. 63, no. 3 (June), pp. 326–34.

Persson, Torsten and Guido Tabellini. 1993. "Designing Institutions for Monetary Stability." *Carnegie-Rochester Conference Series on Public Policy*, vol. 39 (December), pp. 53–84.

Posen, Adam. 1993. "Central Bank Independence Does Not Cause Low Inflation: The Politics Behind the Institutional Fix." Mimeo, Harvard University, December.

Rogoff, Kenneth. 1985. "The Optimal Degree of Commitment to a Monetary Target." *Quarterly Journal of Economics*, vol. 100, no. 4 (November), pp. 1169–90.

Roll Committee. 1993. *Independent and Accountable: A New Mandate for the Bank of England.* Report of an independent panel chaired by Eric Roll. London: The Centre for Economic Policy Research, October.

Selody, Jack. 1990. "The Goal of Price Stability: A Review of the Issues." Bank of Canada Technical Report No. 54.

Taylor, John B. 1982. "Policy Choice and Economic Structure." Group of Thirty Occasional Paper no. 9.

Vibert, Frank. 1993. "The Independence of the Bank of England and the Maastricht Treaty." London: European Policy Forum, May.

Walsh, Carl. 1993. "Optimal Contracts for Independent Central Bankers: Private Information, Performance Measures and Reappointment." Federal Reserve Bank of San Francisco, Working Paper 93-02, May. Forthcoming as "Optimal Contracts for Central Bankers," *The American Economic Review.*

[18]

The Statistical Association between Central Bank Independence and Inflation *

THOMAS F. CARGILL

I. Introduction

Interest in the relationship between central banking institutions and inflation performance has increased during the past decade. While the institutional structure of central banks has always been an important topic, the recent interest is heighten by several factors. Monetary policy is now recognized as the primary instrument of policy and in this regard, many economists and central bankers accept the premise that central banks are capable of setting the long run inflation rate but incapable of achieving meaningful improvements in real performance. The real and financial disruptions of the inflation of the 1970s and early 1980s followed by high costs of required disinflation policies underlined the importance of long run price stability for economic growth. And finally, the financial liberalization process now offers a unique opportunity to restructure central banking institutions in a large number of countries.

As a result, economists have re-opened the agenda of how to structure a central bank to ensure price stability. Many believe central banks that are independent of other government institutions are more likely to generate lower average inflation rates than less independent central banks. There is a growing body of statistical studies attempting to document this view. Most of the studies build off of a methodology developed by Bade and Parkin (1982) in an unpub-

---

□ University of Nevada, Department of Economics, Reno (USA).

* Appreciation is expressed to Scott Shonkwiler, Kambiz Raffiee and Carl Walsh for assistance on the paper; however, all errors remain with the author.

BNL Quarterly Review, no. 193, June 1995.

lished, but frequently cited paper. The approach consists of investigating the relationship between the selected measure of central bank independence and inflation performance by either scatter diagrams or more formal regression models.

Important contributors to this literature include Alesina 1988; Burdekin and Willett 1991; Cukierman 1991; Cukierman, Webb and Neyapti 1993; Eijffinger and Schaling 1993 and 1995; and Grilli, Masciandaro and Tabellini 1991. Cukierman, Webb and Neyapti (CWN) offer the most ambitious indexation effort in terms of the number of central banks (72 developed and developing countries) and length of the time period considered (1950-1989).

These studies report a significant and negative statistical association between the constructed indexes and inflation performance when the index values are positively related to the degree of the central bank's formal independence from government. The confidence in these results is high among researchers; for example, Alesina and Summers (1993, p. 154) write that their own work "[...] verifies what previous work has highlighted – a near perfect negative correlation between inflation and central independence".

This literature is unusual in at least two regards. First, the most frequently cited paper on the subject remains unpublished; second, despite the obvious methodological, econometric and data problems the studies continue to emphasise the importance and general applicability of the results for central bank structure.

The claimed statistical association has influenced policy debate in at least three areas. First, proposals for a formally independent European Central Bank (Burdekin, Wihlborg and Willett 1992) reflect confidence in the statistical results. Second, the results were used in the debate over efforts by the House Banking Committee and the Clinton administration to reduce Federal Reserve formal independence (Berry 1993). Third, the statistical association is often mentioned as an argument for formally separating the central bank from government in developing countries that are in the process of restructuring their financial institutions and markets.

This influence is unfortunate for at least two reasons. First, focusing on formal rules defining the degree of central bank independence is not a productive approach to ensuring long run price stability. The inflation record of the Federal Reserve should be reason enough to reject the notion that formally independent central banks are less likely to be influenced by political institutions and more likely to generate better inflation performance (Mayer 1990). A more productive approach (Walsh 1992) lies along optimal contracts between the central bank and government to reward central banks for price stability and penalize them for inflation or deflation.

Second, the statistical association is not nearly as robust as alleged by the studies. In addition, the studies fail to account with a major contradiction offered by the inflation records of the Bank of Japan and the Federal Reserve, two of the most important central banks in the world.

This paper focuses on the second issue. The paper summarizes the comparative research on the Bank of Japan and the Federal Reserve contradicting the statistical association between formal independence and inflation performance as well as to point out a difficulty to rationalize ranking of the Bank of Japan and the Federal Reserve presented in the Bade and Parkin study. Second, simple regression estimates are used to illustrate the sensitivity of the statistical association to reasonable changes in specification and time periods. The negative correlation between inflation performance and measures of central bank independence weakens or disappears with changes in model specification and countries included in the regression.

A review of the comparative inflation records of the Bank of Japan and the Federal Reserve combined with the sensitivity of the statistical association to reasonable changes in specification suggests more caution is required than has been exhibited in the literature regarding the relationship between formal central bank independence and policy outcomes.

II. The Bank of Japan and the Federal Reserve

The Bank of Japan and the Federal Reserve are among the most important central banks in the world. Their differing institutional structure and differing policy outcomes suggests they deserve close comparative study for implications about the institutional structure of a central bank and policy outcomes.

First, comparison of inflation rates during the past twenty years shows the Bank of Japan with a better inflation record than the

Federal Reserve despite being a more formally dependent central bank. Average GDP Deflator inflation rates (International Monetary Fund 1992) for Japan and the United States are as follows:

Periods	Japan	United States
1962-75	7.2%	4.6%
1976-91	2.8%	5.6%

Considering that the average Japanese inflation rate in the first period is influenced by high inflation in the early 1970s and the fact that Japan grew in real terms at annual rates close to 10% in the 1960s suggests inflation performance in Japan in this subperiod is not nearly as negative as the averages indicate. In any event, the inflation rate during the past two decades in Japan has clearly been lower than in the United States.

The differing inflation performance cannot be explained by technical considerations but is more broadly the outcome of structural, political, and social characteristics of the Japanese economy (Cargill and Hutchison 1990). Japan's superior inflation record is often noted in the above studies, but is dismissed in one of three ways: the contradiction is not discussed in any detail in the majority of studies; a short but difficult to accept rationalization is offered;[1] or Japan is regarded as a special case (Parry 1992).

Second, the evolution of central banking in Japan and the United States during the past three decades illustrates the crudeness of the indexes. Consider the CWN ranking for the Federal Reserve and the Bank of Japan, though the same point can be made for many of the constructed indexes. CWN calculate the Bank of Japan and the Federal Reserve index at 0.18 and 0.48, respectively over the period from 1950 to 1989. The Federal Reserve index ignores the impact of the 1975 Concurrent Resolution 133 and the Humphrey-Hawkins Act of 1978 on the formal independence of the Federal Reserve as

[1] Cukierman, Webb and Neyapti (1993, p. 372) attribute the anti-inflation attitude and performance of the Bank of Japan to the Ministry of Finance. In this way Japan's inflation performance in the past two decades is no longer a contradiction to the maintained hypothesis that independent central banks generate superior price stabilization records. This argument, however, renders the maintained hypothesis difficult to test, but more important, the formal relationship between the Bank of Japan and the Ministry of Finance is only one of many factors that account for Japan's price stability and it is incorrect to argue that the Bank of Japan is a mere extension of the Ministry of Finance. These issues have been discussed in Cargill and Hutchison (1990), Henning (1994) and Suzuki (1987).

well as ignoring efforts of Governor Burns in 1976 and 1977 to ingratiate himself to the Carter administration and the fact President Reagan had the unprecedented opportunity to appoint all members to the Board of Governors by the time he left office in 1988. A time invariant index for the Bank of Japan is equally less defensible. The Bank of Japan has become more "independent" since the early 1970s (Cargill 1989; Henning 1994). After the inflation rate reached 30% in 1973, the Bank of Japan embarked on a long-range program of price stability from which they have not deviated. In fact the Bank of Japan is often regarded as a model central bank in terms of price stability (Hutchison and Judd 1989).[2]

The basic problem with indexes is they ultimately rely on a researcher's interpretation of central bank laws and as such, immediately expose the ranking to two problems. First, reliance on laws can be misleading even if all researchers agree on the same transfer function from laws to numerical index. The relative indexes assigned to the Bank of Japan and the Federal Reserve, being based on formal rules of organization and operation, fail to reflect the substantive differences in independence actually reflected in policy outcomes. Second, reliance on laws to construct indexes for many countries almost insures important historical, institutional, and structural changes occurring in a given country will be overlooked in the effort to construct a simple ranking. This leads one to regard the index as constant during periods of time for which events suggest the degree of central bank independence is changing.

Third, Bade and Parkin rank the Bank of Japan and the Federal Reserve as equally independent,[3] that is, both central banks are independent. This ranking is difficult to accept in light of the formal

---

[2] Even if these types of changes could be consistently incorporated into the independence index, they would result in only marginal index changes and in no event would alter the overall ranking of the Federal Reserve and the Bank of Japan. While the Federal Reserve has lost some formal independence in the past two decades and the Bank of Japan has gained some informal independence, the two central banks would remain at opposite ends of the spectrum of independence. Thus even with a more finely defined index that was lowered and raised slightly for the Federal Reserve and the Bank of Japan, respectively, the contradiction to the traditional view would remain. In addition, on close examination the Federal Reserve resorted to inflationary monetary policy in the second half of the 1960s before the 1975 Concurrent Resolution and the Bank of Japan initiated restrictive monetary policy in 1973 well before it gained some informal independence in the second half of the 1970s.

[3] The Bade and Parkin rankings are reproduced in Alesina and Summers (1993) and Eijffinger and Schaling (1993).

relationship each central bank has with its respective government and in light of the many studies that assign a significantly lower independence ranking to the Bank of Japan.[4] In fact, the Bank of Japan is generally regarded as one of the more formally dependent central banks. Formal dependence is a common feature of central banks in the Pacific Basin. The equal ranking is maintained without comment in two recent studies using the Bade and Parkin rankings (Alesina and Summers 1993; Havrilesky and Granato 1993). Those who persist using the Bade and Parkin rankings, at a minimum, need to rationalize the equal ranking or change the ranking.

III. Statistical association is less than robust

The CWN index is the most impressive effort to rank central bank independence in terms of the degree of differentiation between countries (21 industrial and 51 developing countries), extent of information used to calculate each country's index value, and period of time covered. Thus the CWN data are employed to illustrate that the statistical association is not robust as alleged in the published literature.

Annual inflation rates and the CWN indexes for 20 industrialized countries[5] from the period starting 1962 and ending 1991 are averaged over four time partitions:

(a) 1962-66, 1967-71, 1972-76, 1977-81, 1982-86 and 1987-91

(b) 1962-71, 1972-81 and 1982-91

(c) 1962-66, 1967-71, 1972-75, 1976-79, 1980-83, 1984-87 and 1988-91

(d) 1962-71, 1972-79 and 1980-91.

---

[4] Burdekin and Willett (1991), Cargill (1989), Cukierman, Webb and Neyapti (1991), Eijffinger and Schaling (1993), Henning (1994), and Grilli, Masciandaro and Tabellini (1991) all rank the Bank of Japan as having significantly less independence than the Federal Reserve.

[5] The CWN index for Luxembourg covers only the period from 1980 to 1989 and is thus removed from the sample in order to have a continuous set of data for all industrialized countries over the 1962-1991 period.

The analysis is confined to the industrialized countries ranked by CWN for three reasons: CWN find no statistical association between central bank independence and low inflation for the developing countries; other studies of central bank independence focus on only the industrialized countries; and reliability of any independence index is likely to be greater for developed than for developing countries.

The four time partitions are used to determine the sensitivity of the results to changes in time periods. The first and second time partitions represent five- and ten-year periods, respectively. The third and fourth time partitions incorporate the same end and start years of the periods employed by CWN and vary in length from four- to seven-year periods.

The relationship between inflation and central bank independence is estimated for four specifications:

(a) Inflation = f(Time Dummies, Index) with no adjustment to error term.

(b) Inflation = f(Time Dummies, Country Dummies, Index) with no adjustment to error term.

(c) Inflation = f(Time Dummies, Lagged Inflation, Index) with no adjustment to error term.

(d) Inflation = f(Index) with error term adjustment for heteroskedasticity and serial correlation via a method outlined in Kmenta (1986, pp. 622-625).

Table 1 reports the results for specification (a). This specification regresses the inflation rate on the appropriate time dummies and the index of independence for each country. Regression estimates are reported for all 20 countries and two-country partitions: (1) the 10 most independent central bank countries (Germany, Switzerland, Austria, Denmark, and the United States, Canada, Ireland, Netherlands, Australia, and Iceland); and (2), the 10 least independent central bank countries (Sweden, Finland, United Kingdom, Italy, and New Zealand, France, Spain, Japan and Norway).

The index coefficient is negative and significant at least at the .10 level for the 20 countries combined for each of the four time partitions. The statistical association, however, breaks down once the regression is estimated separately for the most and least independent

TABLE 1

Inflation = f(Time Dummies and Index)

Averaged Time Periods: 1962-66, 1967-71, 1972-76, 1977-81, 1982-86 and 1987-91.

	20 Countries		10 Countries		10 Countries	
Regressor	Coef.	T-Value	Coef.	T-Value	Coef.	T-Value
Constant	7.69	4.29*	21.86	4.55*	4.45	2.93*
PD1	−0.06	−0.03	−0.12	−0.38	−0.28	−0.21
PD2	1.26	0.68	1.09	0.34	1.16	0.89
PD3	6.93	3.75*	6.86	2.14*	6.84	5.26*
PD4	6.60	3.57*	6.19	1.93**	6.90	5.31*
PD5	3.37	1.82**	4.12	1.29	2.61	2.01*
Index	−7.79	−2.30*	−34.72	−4.04*	1.92	0.36
R^2	0.20		0.25		0.49	

Averaged Time Periods: 1962-71, 1972-81 and 1982-91

	20 Countries		10 Countries		10 Countries	
Regressor	Coef.	T-Value	Coef.	T-Value	Coef.	T-Value
Constant	9.38	4.62*	23.90	3.96*	5.93	3.56*
PD1	−1.08	−0.63	−1.58	−0.52	−0.86	−0.80
PD2	5.08	2.94*	4.46	1.48	5.56	5.13*
Index	−7.80	−1.73**	−34.67	−3.03*	1.64	0.26
R^2	0.20		0.27		0.57	

Averaged Time Periods: 1962-66, 1967-71, 1972-75, 1976-79, 1980-83, 1984-87 and 1988-91

	20 Countries		10 Countries		10 Countries	
Regressor	Coef.	T-Value	Coef.	T-Value	Coef.	T-Value
Constant	7.81	4.24*	22.56	4.67*	4.57	2.89*
PD1	−0.02	−0.01	−0.08	−0.02	−0.26	−0.19
PD2	1.31	0.67	1.13	0.33	1.19	0.87
PD3	6.86	3.50*	7.00	2.04*	6.56	4.80*
PD4	6.19	3.15*	5.41	1.58	6.79	4.98*
PD5	6.96	3.55*	8.02	2.34*	5.90	4.32*
PD6	1.30	0.66	1.29	0.38	1.30	0.95
Index	−8.20	−2.46*	−36.26	−4.28*	1.78	0.33
R^2	0.20		0.26		0.46	

* : Significant at the .05 level.
**: Significant at the .10 level.

TABLE 1 - *(contnd.)*

Constant Averaged Time Periods: 1962-71, 1972-79 and 1980-91

	20 Countries		10 Countries		10 Countries	
Regressor	Coef.	T-Value	Coef.	T-Value	Coef.	T-Value
Constant	10.53	5.23*	25.16	4.21*	7.38	4.51*
PD1	−2.11	−1.23	−2.57	−0.86	−1.92	−1.77
PD2	3.77	2.20*	3.11	1.04	4.25	3.92*
Index	−8.14	−1.83**	−35.24	− 3.1*	0.01	0
R^2	0.18		0.27		0.52	

* : significant at the .05 level
**: significant at the .10 level

central banks. The index coefficient is negative and significant at the .05 level for all four of the time partitions for the 10 most independent central banks; however, the index coefficient is insignificant and positive for the 10 lesser independent central banks. Thus, for the 10 less independent central banks there is no meaningful correlation between inflation performance and the index of central bank independence.

Table 2 reports the results for specification (b). In this case the inflation rate is regressed against time dummies, country dummies, and the independence index. Table 2 reports the results for only one time partition since the results are the same for other time partitions. The index coefficient is negative but insignificant at conventional levels of statistical confidence.

Table 3 reports the results for specification (c). The inflation rate is regressed on the lagged inflation rate and the independence index. The specification is estimated for the time partition permitting the largest number of time periods within a cross section. This regression models the inflation process as an adaptive process. The index coefficient is negative but not statistically significant at conventional levels of significance. Lagged dependent variable regressions estimated for other time partitions also yield an insignificant index coefficient.

TABLE 2

Inflation = f(Time Dummies, Country Dummies, and Index)
Averaged Time Periods: 1962-71, 1972-79 and 1980-91.

	20 Countries	
Regressor	Coef.	T-Value
Constant	5.53	1.87**
PD1	−2.11	−2.22*
PD2	3.81	3.94*
D1	1.61	0.21
D2	1.48	0.24
D3	2.02	0.30
D4	4.06	0.77
D5	1.71	0.34
D6	2.07	0.44
D7	5.48	1.20
D8	1.53	0.35
D9	3.37	0.92
D10	23.02	6.63
D11	2.91	0.96
D12	3.85	1.31
D13	4.36	1.32
D14	5.95	2.17*
D15	4.37	1.63
D16	2.51	0.85
D17	5.96	2.40*
D18	0.14	0.06
D19	2.63	1.07
Index	−5.23	−0.38
R^2	0.75	

Notes: See Table 1.

TABLE 3

Inflation = f(Time Dummies, Lagged Inflation and Index)
Averaged Time Periods: 1962-66, 1967-71, 1972-75, 1976-79, 1980-83, 1984-87 and 1988-91

	20 Countries	
Regressor	Coef.	T-Value
Constant	3.60	2.59*
Inf(t−1)	0.71	10.88*
Index	−3.11	−1.04
R^2	0.52	

Notes: See Table 1.

Table 4 reports the results for specification (d). This specification is the same as (a) without time dummies estimated by a GLS procedure.[6] The index coefficient is consistently negative and significant at the .05 level for all 20 countries; however, the index coefficient is insignificant for both the 10 most independent central bank countries and the 10 least independent countries.

Overall, these results suggest that the statistical association between inflation performance and central bank independence is not nearly so robust as alleged in the literature.

IV. Concluding comments

The claimed statistical association between formal measures of central bank independence and inflation is contradicted by the inflation records of two of the most important central banks in the world. The Bank of Japan, a formally dependent central bank, has generated a superior inflation record to the Federal Reserve, a formally independent central bank. Aside from this problem, the statistical association is not robust and subject to variation depending on countries included in the regression and regression specification. In one specification there is a statistical association for the 10 most independent central banks; however, the association is marginal or disappears when one adds country dummy variables, adjusts the residual process for serial correlation and heteroskedasticity, or models the inflation process as a lagged dependent variable regression. Using different time partitions appears to have little impact on the results.

In summary, the comparative performance of the Bank of Japan and the Federal Reserve and the lack of statistical robustness suggests that the claimed statistical association between low inflation and formal central bank independence should not be given the importance it has been afforded in discussions of how to structure a price stabilizing central bank.

---

[6] The estimation technique estimates a value of ρ for all cross sections since there is insufficient information to permit a separate ρ estimate for each central bank. This model is referred to as a Cross-sectionally Heteroskedastic and Time-wise Autoregressive Model and is described in Kmenta (1986). The estimates are obtained from the SHAZAM program (White, Wong, Whistler and Haun 1990).

TABLE 4

Inflation=f(Index), GLS Estimates

Averaged Time Periods: 1962-66, 1967-71, 1972-76, 1977-81, 1982-86 and 1987-91

	20 Countries		10 Countries		10 Countries	
Regressor	Coef.	T-Value	Coef.	T-Value	Coef.	T-Value
Constant	8.51	5.25*	10.01	2.64*	8.97	3.88
Index	−7.36	−2.48*	−9.72	−1.51	−7.75	−0.86
R^2	0.05		0.04		0.01	

Averaged Time Periods: 1962-71, 1972-81 and 1982-91

	20 Countries		10 Countries		10 Countries	
Regressor	Coef.	T-Value	Coef.	T-Value	Coef.	T-Value
Constant	9.03	6.45*	10.38	2.96*	8.46	4.12*
Index	−7.77	−3.13*	−9.89	−1.64	−1.83	−0.23
R^2	0.14		0.09		0	

Averaged Time Periods: 1962-66, 1967-71, 1972-75, 1976-79, 1980-83, 1984-87 and 1988-91

	20 Countries		10 Countries		10 Countries	
Regressor	Coef.	T-Value	Coef.	T-Value	Coef.	T-Value
Constant	8.49	−2.36*	8.7	2.39*	9.81	4.34*
Index	−7.29	5.43*	−7.3	−1.17	−11.34	−1.29
R^2	0.04		0.02		0.02	

Averaged Time Periods: 1962-71, 1972-79 and 1980-91.

	20 Countries		10 Countries		10 Countries	
Regressor	Coef.	T-Value	Coef.	T-Value	Coef.	T-Value
Constant	9.08	6.86*	10.33	2.64*	9.05	7.55*
Index	−7.81	−3.38*	−9.64	−1.45	−4.09	−0.54
R^2	0.16		0.07		0.01	

Notes: See Table 1.

REFERENCES

ALESINA, ALBERTO (1998), "Macroeconomics and politics", in Stanley Fischer ed., *NBER Macroeconomics Annual*, The MIT Press, Cambridge, Mass.

ALESINA, ALBERTO and LAWRENCE SUMMERS (1993), "Central bank independence and macroeconomic performance: some comparative evidence", *Journal of Money, Credit and Banking*, 25, May, pp. 151-162.

BADE, ROBERT and MICHAEL PARKIN (1982), "Central bank laws and monetary policy", unpublished.

BERRY, JOHN M. (1993), "More independence means lower inflation, studies show", *Washington Post*, February 17.

BURDEKIN, C.K. RICHARD and THOMAS D. WILLETT (1991), "Central bank reform: the Federal Reserve in international perspective", *Public Budgeting and Financial Management*, 3, pp. 619-649.

BURDEKIN, C.K. RICHARD, CLAS WIHLBORG and THOMAS D. WILLETT (1992), "A monetary constitution case for an independent European central bank", *The World Economy*, 15, March, pp. 231-249.

CARGILL, THOMAS F. (1989), *Central Bank Independence and Regulatory Responsibilities: The Bank of Japan and the Federal Reserve*, Salomon Brothers Center for the Study of Financial Institutions, New York University.

CARGILL, THOMAS F. (1993), "The Bank of Japan: a dependent but price stabilizing central bank", *Public Budgeting and Financial Management*, 5, pp. 131-139.

CARGILL, THOMAS F. and MICHAEL M. HUTCHISON (1990), "Monetary policy and political economy: the Federal Reserve and the Bank of Japan", in Thomas Mayer ed., *The Political Economy of American Monetary Policy*, Cambridge University Press, New York.

CARGILL, THOMAS F. and SHOICHI ROYAMA (1988), *The Transition of Finance in Japan and the United States: A Comparative Perspective*, Hoover Institution Press, Stanford.

CUKIERMAN, ALEX (1991), *Central Bank Strategy, Credibility and Independence*, The MIT Press, Cambridge, Mass.

CUKIERMAN, ALEX, STEVEN B. WEBB and BILIN NEYAPTI (1993), "Measuring the independence of central banks and its effect on policy outcomes", *World Bank Economic Review*, 6, pp. 353-398.

EIJFFINGER, SYLVESTER and ERIC SCHALING (1993), "Central bank independence in twelve industrial countries", *Banca Nazionale del Lavoro Quarterly Review*, no. 184, March, pp. 49-89.

EIJFFINGER, SYLVESTER and ERIC SCHALING (1995), "Central bank independence in another eleven countries", *Banca Nazionale del Lavoro Quarterly Review*, no. 192, March, pp. 39-83

GRILLI, VITTORIO, DONATO MASCIANDARO and GUIDO TABELLINI (1991), "Political and monetary institutions and public finance policies in the industrial countries", *Economy Policy*, 13, October, pp. 341-392.

HAVRILESKY, THOMAS and JAMES GRANATO (1993), "Determinants of inflation performance: corporatist structures vs. central bank autonomy", *Public Choice,* 76, pp. 249-261.

HENNING, RANDALL C. (1994), *Currencies and Politics in the United States, Germany, and Japan,* Institute for International Economics, Washington.

HUTCHISON, MICHAEL M. and JOHN P. JUDD (1989), "What makes a central bank credible?", *Weekly Letter,* Federal Reserve Bank of San Francisco, July 14.

INTERNATIONAL MONETARY FUND (1992), *International Financial Statistics: 1992 Yearbook,* International Monetary Fund, Washington.

KMENTA, JAN (1986), *Elements of Econometrics,* Macmillan Publishing Company, New York.

MAYER, THOMAS (1990), *The Political Economy of American Monetary Policy,* Cambridge University Press, New York.

PARRY, ROBERT T. (1992), "Low inflation and central bank independence", *Weekly Letter,* Federal Reserve Bank of San Francisco, July 17.

SUZUKI, YOSHIO ed. (1987), *The Japanese Financial System,* Clarendon Press, Oxford.

WHITE, KENNETH J., S. DONNA WONG, DIANA WHISTLER and SHIRLEY A. HAUN (1990), *SHAZAM: Econometrics Computer Program – Version 6.2,* McGraw-Hill Book Company, New York.

WALSH, CARL E. (1995), "Optimal contracts for central bankers", *American Economic Review,* 85, March, pp. 150-161.

Part IV
Determinants of Central Bank Independence

[19]

Why Central Bank Independence Does Not Cause Low Inflation: There Is No Institutional Fix For Politics

ADAM S. POSEN

Few institutional recommendations by economists have gained such rapid and wide acceptance as has that of granting central banks independence from short-term political control. In France, the new RPR/UDF government of 1993 made the freeing of the Bank of France a centerpiece of its economic program; scatterplots depicting a clear relationship between central bank independence and low rates of inflation have in recent years moved from academic journals to recurring status on the pages of *The Economist* and the *Financial Times*; from London to Kiev, national governments are urged to reconsider their control over monetary policy. And why should they not, since by all appearances granting central bank independence offers increased price stability at no cost, and perhaps a bonus, in real macroeconomic performance?[1]

Perhaps because the causal linkage between central bank independence and low inflation is illusory. In this paper, close examination of the postwar record in the advanced industrial democracies[2] reveals that none of the mechanisms that would explain central bank independence's[3] counter-inflationary effect hold. With the falsification of these claims, it is difficult to continue to believe that independence is a significant cause of low inflation, despite the association of the two. The basis for the apparent association between central bank structure and inflation rates must therefore be found elsewhere.

The elsewhere, it will be demonstrated, is politics. Institutions in democratic societies, however independently designed and constituted, are subject to ongoing pressure through threats of alteration to their powers. Central Banks are no exception, although the published analyses of central bank independence ignore this reality. When the ongoing market in institutions is not overlooked with regard to monetary policy, it becomes clear that the central bank's (henceforth CB) existence, capacities, and deflationary will are endogenous to the political effectiveness of opposition to inflation in the society. For reasons of interest, expertise, organization, and influence, successful opposition is only likely to arise out of the financial sector.

While this relationship between effective financial opposition to inflation and CB disinflationary policies happens to produce the oft observed association between CB independence and low inflation (because there is a correspondence between effective financial opposition to inflation and the founding of independent CBs[4]), the relative power of this interest coalition, and not the institutional structure of policy-making, explains the portion of cross-national inflation differences normally ascribed to the independence of CBs. Recognizing this reality allows a new appraisal of the proposed movements towards CB independence in various industrial democracies, as well as the effect on inflation of some until now seemingly unrelated policies.

I. Autonomy is Not Power, Nor is it Reputation Reality

The institutional fix of an independent CB is supposed to offer protection from inflation through three mechanisms—increasing the credibility of commitments to price stability, assuring a higher priority on inflation fighting in the net preference of the public sector, and putting up barriers to the monetization of government expenditure. These linkages have never been directly examined empirically, possibly because of the existence of an elegant theory based on dynamic inconsistency, inflationary surprises, and optimal degree of commitments,[5] or possibly because the clear correlation between measures of CB independence and rates of inflation appeared to make such examination superfluous. Yet, none of these imputed links manifest themselves in the industrial democracies.

A. Credibility

In the usual discussions of these theories, the establishment of an independent CB with strong anti-inflationary preferences is seen as a way for the state to bind its hands against the temptation of inflationary surprises.[6] As commitment increases credibility, the standard theory predicts that there would be smaller divergences between the CB's policies and people's expectations and, therefore, fewer costs and delays in adjusting to monetary policy shifts. This hypothesis can be dismissed almost out of hand both within and across countries. The United States, Germany, and Switzerland, by common assent possessors of three of the world's most independent CB's, all suffered from significant and protracted downturns in their economies whenever sharply anti-inflationary monetary policies were pursued between 1960 and the present. Meanwhile, the only examples of countries successfully combining inflation slowdowns with restrictive policy and limited real costs were all in countries below the median in measures of CB independence.[7]

Within countries, the arguments for the importance of credibility imply that independent CBs would accumulate a reputation for a counter-inflationary stance, as the public's expectations converge over time to the CB's true preferences and capabilities. Thus, we would also expect that for a given level of institutional independence, older CBs should offer more inflationary protection than younger ones, *ceteris paribus*. This effect also fails to show up in the record.

Consider the comparative performance of the US Federal Reserve Board and the German Bundesbank, as depicted in Figure 1.[8] Although

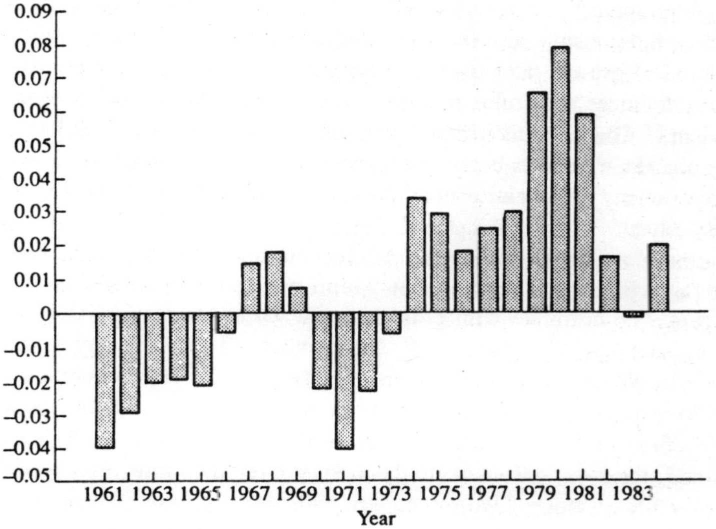

Fig. 1 Inflation Differential 1961–84

the Bundesbank is decades younger than the Federal Reserve, and it was explicitly modelled on its American counterpart, the trend over this period is towards increasingly larger surpluses of US inflation over the German levels, rather than of convergence to comparable levels of credibility.

Of course, there are many factors other than CB independence that contribute to a nation's inflation rate. Since the US and Germany both have multi-year wage contracts without indexing and reserve currency status, however, and on practically every other count the US would seem to have the upper hand in avoiding inflation (less openness to world trade, less dependence on foreign oil, weaker and smaller unions, no true left-wing party control of the executive . . .), and the US still has the higher inflation rate, it can certainly be concluded, at a minimum, that the public gaining experience with an independent CB has little effect on the rate of inflation.[9]

B. Anti-Inflationary Preferences

According to Rogoff's (1985) model and later extensions of it, where CBs are more independent, the conservative (that is long-horizoned and focussed on price-stability) preferences of CBers would be better reflected in monetary policy, as well as in the overall policy stance of the government.[10] Neverthelesss, there is no statistically significant negative relationship between independence of CBs[11] and the standard deviation of growth rates over the long-run, as one would expect were CB preferences to influence policy in the direction of lowered activism.[12] The explicit inclusion of price stability as 'the' goal in a CB's charter, a perhaps better indicator of preference, cannot be shown to explain any cross-national differences in inflation or growth variability either.[13]

Furthermore, while the evidence for political business cycles or monetary cycles is mixed, neither within nor across studies does CB independence correlate with cross-national variations in the extent of the phenomenon.[14] Even simply the number of years in any given decade in which a left-wing government held power has a significant predictive power for inflation across countries, holding CB independence constant.[15] In addition, as non-academic observers have long assumed, there is reason to doubt a truly overwhelming priority on price stability among CB preferences, even for the most independent CBs. Although it is impossible to measure CB preferences directly, assessment of the documentary record by Bernanke and Mishkin

(1992) makes clear that even the Deutsche Bundesbank and the US Federal Reserve show frequent concern for exchange rates, and occasionally for growth rates.[16]

C. Seignorage

Since seignorage is far more an issue for developing countries than for countries with largely legitimate and functioning tax collection systems, the empirical relevance of this factor to a discussion of inflation in the industrialized democracies is questionable. Yet, ratings of the statutory limits upon, or at least freedom from the requirement of, granting of credits to the government and financing of government deficits make up the lion's share of the measures of CB independence that have been used to demonstrate the anti-inflationary result of increasing CB autonomy.[17] Nevertheless, no significant relationship can be found between seignorage and the independence of CBs as measured along these legal lines in the sample of 17 industrial democracies considered in this paper.[18] This result conforms with prior work which sought in vain such relationships.[19]

D. Effect without a cause?

For purposes of this discussion of CB independence and inflation, it does not matter why the importance of credibility has proven to be unsupported by the historical data. The lack of visible credibility effects may be attributed to extensive long-term contracting or other market rigidities in the nations involved,[20] or to the possibility that what is taken by observers to be credible (e.g. a Volcker or Thatcher disinflationary policy) actually is not so in the minds of the public, or even to as yet undiscovered problems with the current state of theory. Similarly, explanations of why CB ability to resist politicized macroeconomic policy and seignorage has no apparent effect on economic outcomes are unimportant.

What does matter is that empirically, practically, for purposes of policy, differences in CB autonomy and reputation are *not* the sources of inflation differences among the advanced industrial countries on the order of magnitude of those usually ascribed to them. Therefore, while CB independence has a clear correlation with low rates of inflation, all the published arguments used to trace a causal link between these two are not borne out by economic reality. Accordingly, a new explanation must be found for the CB independence-inflation relationship that does not rely on such factors.

II. Nothing Contentious is ever Settled in Democracies

An empirically supported explanation of the association between CB independence and low inflation can only be arrived at through a proper understanding of politics. Although many economists consider the integration of institutional factors—such as CB independence—into their models to be already giving this devil his due, they are actually approaching democratic polities with a partial equilibrium mindset. The 'new political economy', which attempts to explain choices in the market for policy on the basis of institutional incentives, ignores the ongoing market in the power and prospects of the institutions themselves—and therefore ignores that democratic politics is by nature an ongoing process, interacting with, not settled by, institutions.

This omission is just as devastating to the explanatory power of models of macroeconomic policy-making in democracies as leaving out the foreign country's markets would be in models of international trade. Situations that arise, for example, where policymakers are unconstrained legally, and nevertheless forego strong actions only become explicable when the effects of this other political market is included; if policymakers are assumed to assess whether exercise of their freedom against any given moment's constellation of interests in a society could be institutional suicide, such hesitation is comprehensible.

As a result, it can be generally predicted that a public institution's actions must always have the support of a politically powerful interest coalition—as a form of (independent) life insurance;[21] when either the coalition's interest diminishes or its political effectiveness wanes,[22] so does the value of the insurance against institutional change for any given policy. The will of the institution to pursue policies that are unpopular with the opposing coalition's policies would decrease accordingly. Therefore, the changing relative strength of *interests* in society, not the institution's structure, is the source of policy decisions—and this strength is a function of the oft overlooked and always changing political background.

A. What A Model of Interests Means for Monetary Policy

Restating this general framework in the context of monetary policy begins with three observations: the existence and independence of CB institutions are subject to democratic control; inflation has significant redistributive effects; financial intermediaries as a group are harmed by inflation. Thus, while CB decision-makers form their policies in part in response to statutory constraints, they also simultaneously respond to the risks that anti-inflationary policies could lead to alterations in the autonomy and powers of the CB itself.[23] And financial intermediaries reduce this risk through political activities in order to gain from lowering the inflation level.

Recognizing that CB independence and policies are endogenous to the effectiveness of financial sector opposition to inflation (henceforth FOI) resolves the problems in current understanding raised above.[24] Most importantly, since CB independence is always at risk from proponents of inflation, and that risk both determines the policies pursued *and* is determined by the political strength of opposition to inflation, *there is no reason to expect that CB credibility or revealed policy preferences will have a fixed relationship with statutory independence*; instead, they will vary with developments in the ongoing political struggle over inflation.

This implies as well that *CB independence and low rates of inflation should occur together, without a causal link between them*, because they both are reflections of effective FOI. In this model, because inflation represents the occasional triumph of particular social interests in the political struggle, and not government pursuit of revenue and re-election, no relationship between CB independence and seignorage or political monetary cycles is expected; disinflation should remain costly because it is impossible to forecast the outcome of domestic politics, and thus monetary policy, over the long term.

B. Assessing Financial Opposition to Inflation

In order to test the 'interests not institutions' approach to cross-national inflation differences beyond its fit with the stylized facts, a reproducible measure of the interest and effectiveness of financial representives in opposing inflation is required. That, in turn, rests on an understanding of what makes this interest group have a stake in fighting inflation, and what enables it to do so.

The reasons why financial intermediaries are opposed to inflation are familiar enough not to require extended discussion. Fundamentally, intermediaries such as banks are nominal net creditors due to their leveraging of deposits into loans and to the non-marketable nature of their assets. As their emphasis on customer relations and longer-term lending increases, so does the stickiness of their nominal asset values.[25] What applies to financial *intermediaries*, does not necessarily apply to the financial *sector* as a whole. The financial sector's opposition to inflation to a first approximation should reflect the share of lending in its total activities because actively traded securities are not subject to the same extent of loss from inflation as intermediated assets.

This fact leads to the first indicator of the strength of financial interest in price stability: *Financial sectors having universal banking are expected to have stronger anti-inflationary sentiment than those without.* Not only do financial systems with universal banking tend to have markedly more of a lending than a securities orientation in total,[26] they avoid having a meaningful number of member firms who do not engage in classical bank lending at all; everyone is aware of the costs of inflation.[27] In addition, universal bank systems simply have an easier path to unity of political voice as they already face unified regulations and markets.

A second measure of financial interest in opposing inflation concerns the regulatory relationship between the financial sector and the CB. In brief, *the less regulatory power of the CB over the financial sector, the more strength of opposition to inflation by the sector is to be expected.* As with regard to universal banking, the issue is unity of purpose. Where the monetary authority restricts the allocation of credit or lending rates, or when it has supervisory responsibilities for banks, financial firms may come in conflict with the CB. They may seek to limit the CB's powers; they may lobby for a general credit easing to circumvent specific regulatory limits, despite the inflationary effect. When the CB does not have these responsibilities, the financial sector has no distraction from its support of the CB's commitment to price stability.

Turning to the question of effectiveness, the ability of the financial sector to influence the government's willingness to fight inflation (or, at least, to tolerate anti-inflationary monetary policy by the CB) is largely dependent upon the polity's willingness to defer to expertise. Rather than mustering votes directly, the financial sector gains access to elected officials by being their main outside source of information and advice about monetary policy.[28] And so it is reasonable to expect that polities with developed and stable avenues of interest aggregation will offer the prominence of financial expert opinion a more secure place in the policy process. This suggests two national political factors which should influence the effectiveness of FOI: party fractionalization and federalism.

Where a country's party system is more fractionalized, financial expert opinion is expected to be less influential. This is not a question of government instability caused by party fractionalization, which can be directly accounted for (and is, in this paper's statistical investigations). Rather, fractionalization is seen to be a source of increased logrolling and diminished government decisiveness. Where logrolling is frequent, issues such as monetary policy are more likely to be tied to and bargained off against other issues, and thus diminish the financial sector's influence (which is specialized). Where decisiveness declines, every government process or institution is seen as less legitimate and more realistically subject to change, and so the financial sector cannot offer the CB as much insurance.

Concern about the effect of political cleavages upon the process and legitimacy of government decision-making brings the distinction between federal and unitary states to the fore. Federal systems of national government are based on the principle of assigning decisions to the appropriate decision-makers, and avoiding conflict by delegation. While this is usually motivated by ethnic or regional cleavages, it has the general effect of insulating what are assigned as purely national issues—such as monetary policy—from numerous other policies, and of placing a premium in federal level discussions on those groups—such as the financial sector—that can offer a unified front across regions. Therefore, *financial opposition to inflation is expected to be more effective in federal systems of government.*

As with CB independence, the measurement of qualitative political factors that contribute to effective FOI is best done without illusions of precision. Nonetheless, an assignment of the 17 sampled industrial democracies to categories of whether they are above or below the median score for interest (universal banking yes/no plus weighted measure of regulatory freedom from the CB[29]) and effectiveness (federal political system yes/no minus measure of party fractionalization[30]) offers initial support for the hypothesized relationships between effective FOI, as measured, as inflation and CB independence, as can be seen in Table 1.

Table 1 Levels of Interest and Effectiveness of Financial Sector Opposition to Inflation (Group Average Inflation and CB Independence 1950–89)

	Low Interest	High Interest
High Effectiveness	Australia Canada U.Kingdom U.States New Zealand *(π = 5.184 Ind = 0.370)*	Germany Switzerland *(π = 3.299 Ind = 0.650)*
Low Effectiveness	Italy France Japan Spain *(π = 6.138 Ind = 0.208)*	Austria Belgium Denmark Greece Ireland Netherlands *(π = 5.563 Ind = 0.437)*

C. Inflation, CB Independence, and the Evidence of Politics

There is clear statistical evidence in support of drawing a causal link (rather than a mere association) between more effective FOI on the one side and higher CB independence and lower inflation rates on the other. The measure for effective FOI developed in the preceding section (combining the measures of interest and of effectiveness) proves to be a significant predictor of CB independence; furthermore, it continues to predict inflation significantly, although CB independence does not, when both factors are accounted for (detailed regression results are given in the Statistical Appendix). The commonly presumed direct tie between levels of CB independence and of inflation is cut by the economic record.

The results necessary to distinguish between the *interests* and the *institutional* models of inflation, however, merit more extended discussion. While the historical record that support from financial interests is crucial to the granting of independence to CB's[31] conforms with both models, they can be distinguished with respect to CB independence through two other predictions:

First, if the widely-held 'Ulysses and the Sirens of Seignorage' conception of monetary policy were correct, the founding of independent CB's would only occur where the right-leaning government thinks itself in danger of losing office to the left; government instability or turnover would be at least as important a predictor of CB independence as effective FOI. On the other hand, the interests model advanced in this paper denies the importance of government instability to CB independence altogether (since the purpose of CB independence is not to bind the hands of the government but to fight off inflationary advances championed by other interests).

Second, from the institutional perspecitve, the effective FOI would only be influential at the time of the CB's statutory design and cease to be a factor in CB independence (or inflation) thereafter. The interests model predicts that variance over time in the strength and effectiveness of FOI will have continual influence on the extent of CB independence (which does vary measurably over time).

Since neither the enumerated frequency of changes in government nor of the subset of changes classifiable as significant[32] has any predictive power for CB independence, while effective FOI has a significant positive effect on CB independence consistently over the entire time period[33] (see Appendix, Table 3), the evidence comes down clearly on the side of the interests theory.

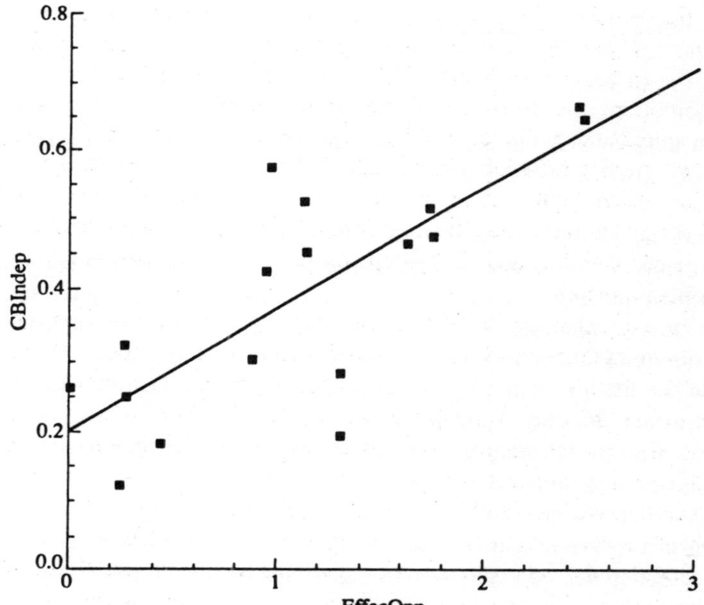

Fig. 2 Central Bank Independence and Financial Opposition to Inflation (Annual Averages 1950–89)

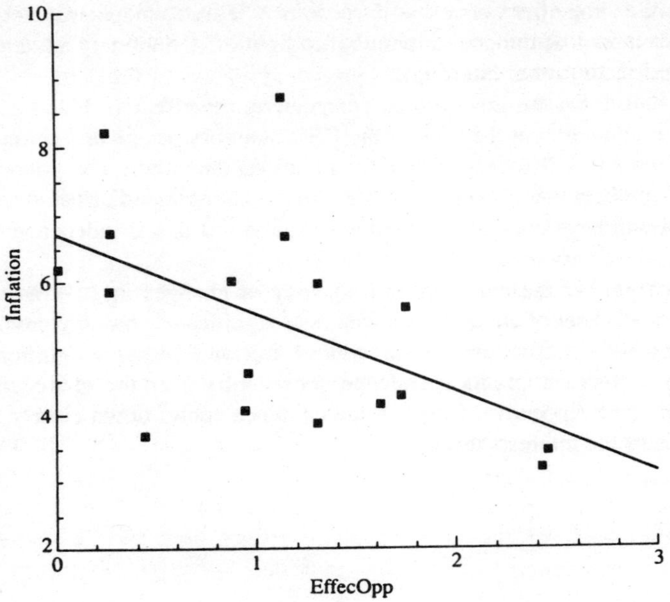

Fig. 3 Inflation and Financial Opposition to Inflation (Annual Averages 1950–89)

The statistical results with regard to inflation provide a similarly strong confirmation of this paper's 'institutions settle nothing' interpretation rather than one espousing a causal link between CB independence and lower rates of inflation. Most convincingly, there is the direct evidence that effective FOI (as here measured) has a significant negative correlation with inflation, while CB independence, holding the influence of FOI constant, does not[34] (see Appendix, Table 2).

Furthermore, the independent explanatory power of effective FOI, not captured by either CB independence or government instability, cannot be reconciled with the 'New Political Economy' approach, emphasizing governments and institutions as sources of inflation—just as the persistence of costly disinflations and highly variable growth rates *irrespective of CB independence levels,* and thus the absence of effects linking CB independence to inflation, also cannot. Only by recognizing that in democratic societies the struggle over inflation, as over any redistributive issue, is unending do these results become comprehensible. The effectiveness of FOI is a predictor of cross-national differences in inflation rates because CB's, like all democratically controlled institutions, can only pursue the policies that the give and take of politics allows.

III. Implications: Monetary Policy when Interests Delimit Institutions

Providing evidence of even policy economists' impatience with the nature of democratic politics is not terribly difficult, and drawing out the distorting effect on their models of this impatience is only a little more so. Yet, if practical men are the slaves of some contemporary group of economists (taking the liberty of updating Keynes to the current pace of opinion turnover), 'it is ideas, not vested interests, which are dangerous for good or evil'.[35] Recognition of the crucial role in price stability of the financial sector's desire and power to fight inflation—and of the concomitant overestimation of CB independence's importance to that fight—indicates where both threats of and safety from inflation really may be found.

The fundamental argument of this paper, that there is no institutional 'fix' for the redistributive struggle over monetary policy, implies that CBs designed with similar degrees of statutory independence will offer significantly differing degrees of protection from inflation over time as the political situation alters. It is not a coincidence, for example, that the threats to Federal Reserve independence mounted by Senator Paul Sarbanes and Representative Henry Gonzales, among others, have noticeably increased in the last few years along with the relative political and economic weakness of the American financial sector—irrespective of the contemporaneous extremely loose monetary policy. And the impact of these threats is being felt in today's continued Fed ease in the face of inflationary pressures.

The interests analysis therefore implies that heretofore seemingly unrelated changes in the organization of financial markets or political debate will have serious spillover effects upon inflation rates—and these should be taken into account in policy decisions. Since the worldwide trends of deregulation towards universal banking and of disintermediation by financial firms put pressure in opposing directions on the interest of the financial sector in opposing inflation, the macroeconomic effects of resolving this conflict must be considered. The tendency towards decentralization within European countries, and towards European federalism (with or without 'Subsidiarity') in general, should improve price stability by insulating financial opinion about monetary policy, and therefore perhaps allow some easing.

Ignoring the implications of the *interests* analysis of monetary policy not only leaves the policymaker unaware of these inflationary spillovers, it also leads to a false hope. When CB independence is solely imposed from above as an institutional solution, without a politically powerful anti-inflationary interest in the society to support it, it cannot be expected to afford the same low inflation level of those statutorily identical CBs that have such support. An independent Bank of France will only provide significant protection from inflation if the French financial sector is not only privatized and deregulated, but somehow gains a voice in the French technocratic state's decision-making (something no interest group has had significant success doing in the Fifth Republic); an independent Bank of England cannot bring about noticeably lower inflation so long as the British financial system is securities based, specialized, and CB regulated, and thus not strongly anti-inflationary.

Interestingly, from this paper's standpoint, the anti-inflationary effect of the proposed European Central Bank should be quite large. Financial supervision does not come under its responsiblities, so the financial sector should have minimal occasion for direct conflict with it. Moreover, the overwhelming majority of European national financial interest groups support it explicitly in hopes of opposing domestic inflation. As a symbol of European unity, and enshrined in an unlikely to be re-opened international treaty, it has a security from attacks upon its structure and existence that no national CB is ever likely to have.[36] Finally, the supranational federalism of Europe should remove influence upon its decision-making from all but the best organized and recognized interests.

The predicted anti-inflationary success of the European Central Bank, however, like all the predictions of this paper, rests on the ECB's political context, not on the institutional features of the bank itself. Inflation and all other contentious policy questions of distribution must remain open political debates in democratic societies, not as a matter of ethics (although it is), but because that is the reality of politics. In the words of the Bundesbank Chief Economist, Otmar Issing, 'Every society has, in the end, the inflation rate that it earns, and, in essence, also wants'.[37] And interests determine public wants far more than even independent institutions do.

Comments

Raymond Barre: As in EC countries we have been discussing for some months the independence of the Central Bank according to the requirements of EMU and as we have just changed the statutes of the Banque de France in a controversial political climate, I have been intrigued and pleased by this non-conformist essay. I have already been careful in my governmental responsibilities in France about sheltering the Central Bank from the pressure of the Treasury and political circles and I have supported the bill giving independence to the Banque de France. But I was not inspired by the view that there was a causal link between CB independence and low inflation; by itself, the CB cannot assure stability because inflation results from many factors. But, I have observed that the Banque de France, during inflationary periods in France, has played a discrete, but essential role as an adviser to the general economic policy of the Government. As to other EC members, I learnt by experience that central banks which enjoy statutory independence adapt their monetary policy to the fundamental orientations of the government's domestic and international policy, even when they disagree with the government: it is the case in Germany, in spite of all the protestations of independence we can hear of. I have also measured the 'single pillar role' played by the Banca d'Italia in the complexities of the Italian economic evolution.

For such reasons, I tend to share the view expressed that the causal linkage between central bank independence and low inflation is illusory and that the apparent association between central bank structure and inflation must be found elsewhere, i.e. in politics. The author is right when he underlines that monetary policy is driven by political interests in the society and that central banks take strong anti-inflationary action only when there is a coalition of interests politically capable of protecting it. His analysis of effective financial opposition to inflation is original. I am not sure that financial intermediaries are always and everywhere opposed to inflation; or that financial opposition to inflation is expected to be more effective in federal systems of government. As to the freedom of manœuvre of a CB fighting against inflation; it is the greater when the collective conscience of the population has been deeply impressed by historical experiences (hyperinflation in Germany); and the CB can act more efficiently when the economy is open to international flows of trade and capital and when the monetary authorities have a view on the exchange rate.

The author is confident in the anti-inflationary effect of the proposed European Central Bank. He remarks, rightly in my view, that success will rest on the ECB's political context, not on the institutional features of the Bank itself. What will be important will be the collective monetary discipline to which EC member States agree to submit themselves. There is also, in the independence of the ECB, a psychological factor which is essential to the German population.

This paper contains many ideas and points of view which are debatable, but stimulating. It is moreover refreshing by its non-conformism in the present conformist mood of economic thinking.

Lord Roll: This is a well-argued and clearly written essay on a subject of considerable importance and great current interest. It is also a controversial topic, and the author deserves further credit for not having shirked the task of stating his own position without equivocation. He may not be right in stating that the idea of central bank independence as an important anti-inflationary device 'has gained rapid and wide acceptance' since there are many—economists and finance ministry officials—who would side with the author in disputing the idea. But it is certainly a fashionable one.

The main thrust of the author's thesis is that monetary policy (the instrument which central bank independence is to make more effective) is driven by political interests; and that the anti-inflationary stance of these interests will determine the effectiveness of counter-inflationary policies including the actions of the central bank. There is much truth in this point, and the author brings both analytical and empirical support to it; and when he argues that there is no 'institutional fix' that will remove the 'redistributive struggle' that monetary policy represents, he makes a point that more mechanistic theories tend to overlook. It is this emphasis on the political aspects that also leads him—perhaps surprisingly—to the view that a European Central Bank, as envisaged in the Maastricht Treaty, could be free from the limitations on the effectiveness of the policies of national central banks which he has highlighted.

He does perhaps overstate his case and may not convince everybody that something may not be gained by a suitably organised independent central bank. His contribution to this important debate is, however, of very great value.

Bruce MacLaury: Adam Posen's provocative argument that the interest-group context in which a central bank operates is more important in predicting its likely success in fighting inflation than its formal legislative independence is surely correct. In particular, he effectively challenges the currently fashionable oversimplification that changing a central bank's charter to enhance its independence will assure an improved inflation record.

Independent central banks are anomalous institutions in democratic societies. Their mandate—to preserve the value of the currency in order to facilitate stable economic growth—requires a degree of insulation from short-term political pressures, or inflation-tolerant interest groups, as Posen might put it. Yet as public institutions, they cannot and should not be immune from ultimate public accountability. The genius of institutional arrangements, as with the courts and other quasi-independent public agencies, lies in finding the optimal degree of insulation from the popular will, usually manifested through interest group pressures.

Personally, while I think Posen's analysis is an important corrective to a single-minded focus on institutional arrangements and their causal consequences, I think he risks throwing out the baby with the bath water: institutional frameworks do matter, in much the same way that 'burden of proof' matters in legal proceedings. An institutional framework is a statement of public aspiration: not a guarantee of success, but not meaningless either. In practice, interest groups are strengthened if they can cite principle and rally to the cause of an institution that embodies that principle, in this case, an independent central bank.

I also question Posen's exclusive identification of universal banks as the paramount source of political backing for currency stability. They can be important, to be sure, but so can be organized retirees (grey panthers), or even institutional bond holders if aroused.

So it's a matter of emphasis. This well written, strongly argued, and imaginatively analyzed essay deserves its prize. It attacks an excessive focus on rules with a healthy dose of political reality. It draws some interesting and often persuasive policy inferences, e.g. regarding the likely inflation consequences of a European Central Bank. Most important, it provokes thought and counter-argument—the basis, in the end, of better policymaking.

Professor Barre, former Prime Minister of France and former Vice President of the European Commission, is a member of the Awards Committee. He is Deputé du Rhône to the Assemblée Nationale.

Lord Roll of Ipsden is President of S.G.Warburg Group plc and a member of the Awards Committee. He is a former senior official of H.M. Treasury and author of the classic work 'A History of Economic Thought' now in its 5th edition.

Bruce MacLaury is President of the Brookings Institution in Washington D.C., and a member of the Board of American Express Bank Ltd.. He is a member of the Awards Committee and Editorial Adviser to the *Review*. He has also been a senior official at the US Treasury Department and President of the Federal Reserve Bank of Minneapolis.

References

Alesina, A. (1988). Macroeconomics and Politics. In S. Fischer, ed., *NBER Macroeconomics Annual 1988*. MIT Press, Cambridge (US).

Alesina, A. (1989). Politics and Business Cycles in Industrial Democracies. *Economic Policy*, April.

Alesina, A. and V. Grilli (1991). The European Central Bank: Reshaping Monetary Politics in Europe. Centre for Economic Policy Research Discussion Paper Number 563.

Alesina, A. and L. Summers (1990). Central Bank Independence and Macroceconomic Performance: Some Comparative Evidence. Harvard University, Mimeo.

Barro, R. and D. Gordon (1983). Rules, Discretion and Reputation in a Model of Monetary Policy. *Journal of Monetary Economics*, 12: 101–122.

Bernanke, B. and F. Mishkin (1992). Central Bank Behaviour and The Strategy of Monetary Policy: Observations from Six Industrialized Countries. In *NBER Macroeconomics Annual 1992*, ed. O.J. Blanchard and S. Fischer. University of Chicago Press, Chicago.

Cukierman, Alex (1992). *Central Bank Strategy, Credibility, and Independence: Theory and Evidence*. MIT Press, Cambridge (US).

DeLong, J. and L. Summers (1992). Macroeconomic policy and long-run growth. Federal Reserve Bank of Kansas City, 16th Annual Economics Symposium in Jackson Hole, August 27 to 29.

Epstein, G. and J. Schor (1986). The Political Economy of Central Banking. Harvard Institute for Economic Research, Discussion Paper No. 1281, November.

Epstein, G. and J. Schor (1989). The Divorce of the Banca d'Italia and the Italian Treasury: A Case Study of Central Bank Independence. In *State, Market, and Social Regulation: New Perspectives on Italy*, ed. P. Lange and

M. Regini. Cambridge University Press, Cambridge (UK).

Epstein, G. and J. Schor (1990). Corporate Profitability as a Determinant of Restrictive Monetary Policy: Estimates for the Postwar United States. In T. Mayer, ed., pp. 51–63.

Feldstein, M. (1992). The Risk of Financial Crisis: Introduction. In *The Risk of Financial Crisis*, ed. M. Feldstein. University of Chicago Press, Chicago.

Gerschenkron, A. (1962). *Economic Backwardness in Historical Perspective*. Harvard University Press, Cambridge (US).

Goodman, J. (1991). The Politics of Central Bank Independence. *Comparative Politics*, April 1991.

Gordon, R. J. (1982). Why Stopping Inflation May Be Costly. In *Inflation: Causes and Effects*, ed. R.E. Hall. University of Chicago, Chicago.

Greider, W. (1987). *Secrets of the Temple: How the Federal Reserve Runs the Country*. Simon and Schuster, New York.

Grilli, V., D. Masciandaro, and G. Tabellini (1991). Political and Monetary Institutions and Public Financial Policies in the Industrial Countries. *Economic Policy*, October.

Havrilevsky, T. M. (1990). Distributive Conflict and Monetary Policy. *Contemporary Policy Issues*, 8:50–61.

Hodgman, D. R. and R.W. Resek (1983). Determinants of Monetary Policy in France, the Federal Republic of Germany, Italy and the United Kingdom: A Comparative Analysis. In D.R. Hodgman, ed., *The Political Economy of Monetary Policy: National and International Aspects*. Federal Reserve Bank of Boston.

Issing, O. (1992). Unabhaengigkeit der Notenbank und Geldwertstabilitaet. Jahresfeier der Akademie der Wissenschaften und der Literatur, Mainz, November 6.

Kydland, F. E., and E. C. Prescott (1977). Rules Rather Than Discretion: The Inconsistency of Optimal Plans. *Journal of Political Economy*, 85:473–492.

Lewis-Beck, M. S. (1988). *Economics and Elections: The Major Western Democracies*. University of Michigan Press, Ann Arbor.

Marsh, D. (1992). *The Bundesbank: The Bank That Rules Europe*. Heinemann, London.

Mayer, T., ed. (1990) *The Political Economy of Monetary Policy*. Cambridge University Press, 1990.

Rogoff, K. (1985). The Optimal Degree of Committment to an Intermediate Monetary Target. *Quarterly Journal of Economics*, November.

Statistical Appendix

Table 2 Inflation and Effective Financial Opposition to Inflation

Dependent Variable (equation number)	Inflation (I)	Inflation (II)
Sample (n = size)	40 Year Avg. (n = 17)	Avg. by decade (n = 68)
Explanatory Variables		
Intercept	5.02025**	7.29784**
	(1.18834)	(1.18978)
Effective FOI	–1.34691*	–1.36464**
	(0.69514)	(0.63096)
Significant Gov. Change	0.36240	0.58739*
	(0.40053)	(0.30432)
Frequency of Gov. Change	0.15748	0.10501
	(0.13563)	(0.11314)
Fixed Exchange Rate		–2.45057**
		(0.68816)
Central Bank Independence	1.37793	0.62993
	(3.18322)	(3.09680)
Adjusted R2	0.31627	0.50274
Standard Error	0.18771	0.44451

Standard errors are given in parentheses. A * (**) denotes significance at the 5% (1%) level. Equation II (Inflation Decade Averages) estimated by least squares weighted by decade (1950s = 1, 1960s = 2, etc.) to account for different inflation levels across decades for all countries. Equation I estimated by ordinary least squares.

Variable Definitions:

Dependent Variables: *Inflation* = Annual average change in CPI; *Central Bank Independence* = Central bank independence coded from legal aspects (Cukierman's (1992) LVAU).

Explanatory Variable: *Effective FOI* = Effective financial opposition to inflation. Constructed as Cbvsrg + Univbk + Federl – Fractn; *Cbvsrg*

Table 3 Central Bank Independence and Effective Financial Opposition to Inflation

Dependent Variable	Central Bank Independence (III)	Central Bank Independence (IV)
Sample (n = size)	40 Year Avg. (n = 17)	Avg. by Decade (n = 68)
Explanatory Variables		
Intercept	0.19529** (0.08824)	0.21142** (0.03246)
Effective FOI	0.16392** (0.04002)	0.15555** (0.01808)
Significant Gov. Change	–0.02334 (0.03429)	0.01407 (0.01079)
Frequency of Gov. Change	–0.00373 (0.01177)	–0.00274 (0.00423)
Adjusted R2	0.46855	0.51719
Standard Error	0.11999	0.11202

Standard errors are given in parentheses. A * (**) denotes significance at the 5% (1%) level. Equations III and IV estimated by ordinary least squares.

= Index of central bank regulatory role vis-à-vis the financial sector (constructed as described in note 29); *Univbk* = 1 if commercial banks are allowed to deal in at least two of securities, insurance, and/or equity stakes in corporations; *Federl* = 1 if nation has a federal political structure; *Fractn* = Party fractionalization in national politics (Defined as the probability that two legislators chosen at random belong to different parties. Average of 1960–64 and 1965–76 values. From Grilli, et al (1991) Table 3.1).

Control Variables: *Significant Gov. Change* = Number of significant changes in government composition per decade (From Grilli, et al (1991) Table B1); *Frequency of Gov. Change* = Number of changes in government composition per decade (From Grilli, et al (1991) Table B1); *Fixed Exchange Rate* = 1 if country belonged to a fixed exchange rate mechanism during that decade.

Notes

1 As argued in Alesina and Summers (1990) and DeLong and Summers (1992).

2 Here the industrialized democracies are represented by a sample of 17, chosen for ease of comparison to previous work and availability of data: Australia, Austria, Belgium, Canada, Denmark, France, Germany, Greece, Ireland, Italy, Japan, Netherlands, New Zealand, Spain, Switzerland, United Kingdom, and United States.

3 A thorough summary and distillation of the literature is given in Cukierman (1992).

4 See section II or the historical discussions of Goodman (1990) and Epstein and Schor (1986, 1989).

5 See Kydland and Prescott (1977); Barro and Gordon (1983); Rogoff (1985).

6 Grilli, et al (1991, p. 367) state, 'In practice, however, the main virtue of having an independent central bank is that it can provide credibility'.

7 See Gordon's (1982) comparative study of the costs of disinflation for discussion of the period 1960–80. The examples he gives are: France in 1963–66, Italy in 1963–68, Japan in 1976-80, and to some degree the United Kingdom in 1975–78. 'There are no other examples of such successful low-cost episodes of stopping inflation in other countries'. (p. 39) My research covering the period 1980 to the present has added no new disinflationary successes for credibility to this list, but turned up a number of further failures (including the second Volcker deflation in the US and the current post-reunification recession in Germany).

8 The 1961-84 period was chosen to begin with the Bundesbank's initial published data on inflation and end with the end of Reagan's first term (so as to give the US the most benefit of the doubt about anti-inflationary credibility). Data is from US Federal Reserve and Deutsche Bundesbank.

9 As always, there remains the cultural argument for German low inflation, i.e. the experience of two hyperinflations imbued German citizens with a great concern for price stability. Beyond the problems of explaining how this gets transmitted across generations except through the design of institutions such as the Bundesbank, and where this is expressed since German workers neither forego wage increases nor punish elected officials any more strongly for inflation than American or other European voters do (Lewis-Beck 1988), referring to culture simply shifts the burden of explanation for low inflation to the society surrounding the CB, which is in keeping with the explanation offered in the next section.

10 'Having a credible monetary policy may matter not only for the price and wage decisions of the private sector, but also for the budgetary decisions of the public sector'. Grilli, et al (1991, p. 365) Of course, the only reason to have an independent central bank is to appoint conservative CBer's who will make commitments to disinflation; loose money is always credible with or without a

CB, assuming that there is an inflationary bias to policy due to the short-run growth trade-off of surprise price rises (Barro and Gordon 1983).

11 Cukierman's (1992) measure *LVAU* (legal variables aggregate unweighted) is used throughout as the measure of central bank independence. The results presented in this paper, however, were also tested using Bade and Parkin's (1980) four point scale and Cukierman's *LVAW*, and proved to be robust across specifications of CB independence measures, except where noted. All these measures code known legal aspects of CB's.

12 An OLS regression of average standard deviation of growth by country by decade on normal measures of CB independence, with and without controls for between period time trends, membership in the EMS, as well as three different measures of government instability (elections per decade, government changes per decade, significant rulership changes per decade) and party fractionalization always results in a small and insignificant, albeit negative, coefficient on independence, irrespective of time-period considered.

13 CB objectives, as measured by the coding of what goals they have written into their charter (from the Bundesbank's sole commitment to price stability to the Swiss CB's listed multiple goals *not* including price stability) never are a statistically significant predictor of inflation rates or average standard deviations of growth rates, with whatever controls.

14 This conclusion was derived from analysis of the research results assembled by Lewis-Beck (1988, ch. 9). See also Alesina (1989) and Havrilevsky (1991).

15 A weighted by period LS regression of average inflation rate by decade for 1950–89 on both central bank independence and partisanship yields a large, positive, significant at the 1% level effect on inflation.

16 The journalistic histories (Marsh (1992) and Greider (1988)) of these two institutions, which are normally at the top of the independence charts, support this picture. The reaction function for Germany in Hodgman and Resek (1982) is additional evidence that the Bundesbank responded to considerations of industrial capacity utilization and exchange rates as well as of inflation. Moreover, the data from a questionnaire directed at 'qualified observers' meant to capture the aspects of 'actual' independence beyond the statutory definitions, codes the Bank of Italy, the Bank of England, and the Bundesbank as all giving the same priority (first) to price stability, despite ranking at the very top (Germany), in the middle (United Kingdom), and near the bottom (Italy) in legal CB independence. (Cukierman, 1992, p. 414).

17 Both Cukierman (1992) and Grilli, et al (1991) code multiple aspects of the rules regarding CB financing of government debt in their measures.

18 A regression of average annual seignorage on different measures of CB independence for 1950–89, whether on a decade by decade basis or pooling all 68 observations, even with controls for between period time-trends or the oil-shocks or membership in the EMS, never yields a significant negative coefficient.

19 See, for example, Grilli, et al (1991).

20 Although, over the course of decades, these should melt away if credibility leads to price stability.

21 Obviously, some institutions will be more subject to risk of change than others in democracies, with constitutionally grounded bodies being most secure. Nevertheless, even the United States Supreme Court has been known to temper its decisions at times for the sake of safety, whether in Marbury v. Madison (1803) securing its powers of judicial review at the cost of allowing Madison to dismiss the Federalists' appointments to the federal bench, or in Webster v. Planned Parenthood (1992) holding off from overturning Roe v. Wade's precedent for the sake of maintaining the Court's legitimacy (made explicit in the majority opinion).

22 As it may for exogenous reasons such as leadership changes, technological advances, demographic shifts, or national political movements. See II.A. for a discussion of this in the financial context.

23 Just as a politician must pursue re-election as a goal in order to achieve any other goals he might have, central bankers must pursue the autonomy to set monetary policy in order to achieve goals such as price stability over the long horizon.

24 Although some at first glance may find this view of CB independence and policy as largely determined by the power of a social interest group disturbing (or even reminiscent of conspiratorial theories of international finance), this model simply recognizes rational CB behavior in the face of an uncertain political environment. The CB's goals, insofar as they are price and financial stability, are by no means subverted, and to whatever extent the CB's motivations were the public interest in these goals, so they remain. Accepting this vision merely brings two always present realities into sharper view: first, that in a democratic society, the legal freedom to act and the power to act are not equivalent; second, that the choice of inflation rate is a choice about distribution.

25 Thus, Epstein and Schor (1990) have documented significant negative effects of both unanticipated and actual inflation upon US bank profits for 1961–85. Furthermore, as Feldstein (1992) details, inflation distorts and imperils the investment climate of financial intermediaries and their customers, increasing the risk of financial crisis.

26 In fact, attempts to use measures of national financial systems' relative emphasis on debt rather than equity confronted significant multicollinearity with a dummy of universal banking. Gerschenkron (1962) offers a plausible historical explanation for the undeniable coincidence of universal banking and debt financing.

27 Of course, even pure brokerage firms will tend to have some dislike for inflation due to its effects on the investment climate and the stability of the financial sector as a whole.

28 Even in countries where the banks do not own, and nominate governors to, part of the CB (like the US), or hold formalized regular meetings between

the financial sector association representatives and the CB decision-makers (like Germany), the financial sector's monitoring of the CB's actions and top personnel plays the most prominant role in the government's evaluation of CB policy—through public statements, personal interaction, provision of information, the employment of former CB officials, and the supply of nominees for CB governors. In contrast, potential supporters of looser money (such as labor or farmers) are unlikely to be seen to have similar claims to expertise in this area. Compounding this perception, the anti-austerity forces are likely, given their greater numbers and diversity, to be less coherent than the financial sector.

29 Constructed as (0.25) * (Regpow + Relend + Recred), where: Regpow = Banking supervision not entrusted to central bank (2), not entrusted to central bank alone (1), or solely central bank's responsibility (0); Relend = Central bank restrictions on private sector lending rates in place for >5 years in decade (0) or <=5 years (1); Recred = Central bank restrictions on private sector credit quantities/uses coded as Relend.

30 Defined as the probability that two legislators chosen at random belong to different parties.

31 Goodman (1990) discusses the necessity of such a financial coalition to the founding of the independent Bundesbank as successor to the Bank der Deutschen Laender in Germany, and the role the absence of such effective interests played in the setting up of the Bank of Italy and the Bank of France after the war. Similarly, Epstein and Schor (1985, 1989) trace the strengthening over time of the US Federal Reserve vis-à-vis the Treasury and the 'divorce' of the Bank of Italy in 1981 to the actions of financial interests.

32 Relying on the *World Handbook of Political and Economic Indicators'* definitions and data.

33 This result holds up when number of elections is substituted for either of the two displayed indicators of government turnover, or when any of these three is used alone as a variable, in regressions on measures of CB independence.

34 This result stands up irrespective of controls for membership in the EMS or in any fixed exchange rate system, for government instability, and for between decade changes in the level of inflation across countries.

35 John Maynard Keynes, *The General Theory of Employment, Interest and Money* (1936).

36 That is, until European unity were to be taken for granted; if EC rule were to become largely unquestionable, its perceived fragility to alteration of one of its building blocks would decrease, and the European CB might lose some of its supplementary protection from risk. But that is a very long term concern.

37 Issing (1992). Author's translation of 'Jede Gesellschaft hat letzlich die Inflationsrate, die sie verdient und im Grunde auch will'.

[20]

Commitment through Delegation, Political Influence and Central Bank Independence

ALEX CUKIERMAN*
Tel Aviv University and CentER

1. Introduction

Politicians in office often delegate authority over some areas of policy to partly independent institutions within the public sector. This paper takes the view that delegation is used as a partial commitment device. By specifying the objectives of an institution more or less tightly and by giving it broader or narrower powers, politicians determine the extent of commitment to a policy rule. The wider the set of contingencies over which the rule is binding, the stronger the commitment. This set is wider and an institution more independent the more politically costly it is, for the political principals, to override the decisions of the institution. Hence a public institution with broader power in a particular area of policy corresponds to a stronger commitment to given restrictions on policy in this area.

A main objective of this paper is to identify economic and political factors that induce politicians to delegate more or less authority to semi-independent public institutions. Although some of the ideas in the paper probably have wider applicability they are illustrated by means of delegation in the area of monetary policy. More delegation of authority in this area usually means that the central bank has a stronger mandate, as well as a sufficient degree of independence from government, to conduct monetary policy so as to achieve price stability.

Besides price stability monetary policy can be directed at achieving other objectives such as a high level of economic activity and stabilization policy. In addition, inflationary finance can be used to reduce the real value of existing government debt. The temptation to use monetary policy to achieve such objectives is stronger the more depressed is the economy and the larger the size of the public debt. It is well-known that these temptations lead to equilibria in which those objectives are not achieved (or only partially achieved), and in which the rate of inflation is suboptimally high[1]. Politicians in office can precommit monetary policy by delegating some or all of the authority to

* I have benefited from the comments of Eddie Dekel and Matthias Raith.

J.A.H. de Beaufort Wijnholds, S.C.W. Eijffinger and L.H. Hoogduin (eds.), A Framework for Monetary Stability, pp. 55–74.

conduct monetary policy to the central bank (CB) and by directing it through law or convention to give high priority to price stability. Recent evidence reveals that there are substantial cross-country variations in the degree of CB independence[2]. The main objective of this paper is to develop a conceptual framework that makes it possible to formulate hypotheses that can account for at least some of this variation in CB independence.

Politicians in office obviously do not have to delegate authority. When they decide to do that it is because such delegation serves their purposes. More independence to the CB entails both a benefit and a cost. The benefit is that by reducing inflationary expectations a higher level of CB independence reduces interest charges on new government debt and moderates wage increases. This moderation ultimately makes it possible to stimulate the economy with lower inflation. The cost involves a loss in flexibility for the party in office. This foregone flexibility could have been useful since its presence would have made it possible to engage in stabilization policy and to tax away some of the national debt via inflation. There is consequently a tradeoff between the credibility of low inflation and flexibility[3]. In extreme situations government can override the decisions of the CB, but such a course of action entails a political cost for the party (or parties) in office.

The above considerations are complicated further when the different parties competing for office disagree about the structure of government expenditures. In the presence of such disagreements the party currently in office may grant some independence to the CB also in order to restrict the ability of the opposition (if and when it accedes to office) to spend on public goods which are in low priority for the incumbent party[4]. When it decides how much independence to grant to the CB, the party in office weigh these various elements, taking into consideration the likelihood that it will not be re-elected.

The paper presents a precise analysis of the effect of these different factors on the tendency to delegate authority to the CB within a framework in which government is uncertain about the future state of the economy as well as about how long it will survive in office. The analysis suggests that the delegation of authority to the CB is used as a device to reduce interest charges on new government debt. The higher the importance attached by government to this objective, the larger the level of independence accorded to the CB.

The analysis also reveals that CB independence is higher the larger the average, employment motivated inflationary bias, the larger political polarization and political instability[5] and (under reasonable conditions) the larger the amount of funds that government plans to borrow on the capital market.

After having delegated some authority to the CB, the executive or legislative branches of government can redirect monetary policy either by overriding the bank openly or by exerting more subtle political pressure on it[6]. Sections 2 and 3 focus on the first channel and section 4 on the second one. The extent of political pressure is usually private information and the public learns about it gradually, but optimally. The main lesson from the analysis of this case is that, while in office, CB governors with lower survival probabilities display less resistance to expansionary political pressures than governors with higher survival probabilities. Recent evidence supports this implication[7].

Section 2 presents a model of delegation of authority and characterizes its equilibrium level. Comparative static results are presented and interpreted in section 3. Section 4 illustrates the effect of instability at the CB on the response of the latter to informal political pressures. This is followed by concluding remarks.

2. A MODEL OF ENDOGENOUS DELEGATION

a. An intuitive overview

This section illustrates some of the ideas in the paper by means of a precise model. There are two parties that randomly alternate in office. Both parties like a high level of employment and dislike inflation. Due to the existence of nominal wage contracts the party in office can affect employment by creating unanticipated inflation. Natural employment is affected by real economic shocks but is always below desired employment[8]. Because of the fluctuations in the natural level of employment, the value of unanticipated inflation to policymakers varies depending on the realization of these shocks. In periods of low natural employment, monetary surprises are more valuable than in periods with high levels of natural employment. Although they value high employment and price stability to the same extent, the two parties have different preferences with respect to the *composition* of government expenditures[9].

The government in office also wants to issue a fixed amount of bonds in order to finance the current budget deficit. All bonds are discount bonds. Hence the interest charge is paid up front. Other things the same, policymakers like to keep financing costs as low as possible. These costs depend in turn on what the public believes about the rate of inflation that will occur until the bonds are redeemed. If the public believes that inflation will be high, the nominal rate it demands is high and the finance charge is large. If the public believes that inflation will be low, the nominal rate that needs to be paid in order to place the bonds is low and the discount is small. Hence, other things the same, incumbent policymakers prefer lower inflationary expectations since they are associated with lower costs of financing the national debt.

But once bonds have been issued, nominal wage contracts concluded and real shocks to employment have realized the government in office is tempted to inflate. This temptation arises for two reasons. One is that once it is held by the public at a fixed nominal rate the real value of debt can be inflated away, thus alleviating the fiscal burden. The other is that given fixed nominal wage contracts the divergence between actual and desired employment can be reduced by unanticipated inflation. Since the public is aware of these temptations it requires a nominal interest that would compensate it for the average value of expected inflation. Obviously this raises the cost of financing the government debt. As is well known, government can reduce these costs by credibly committing its policy to a zero or low inflation at the outset[10].

I focus here on partial commitment through the delegation of authority to the CB. In the presence of delegation the bank is directed to focus first on the maintenance of price stability. But the political authorities can override its decisions at a cost. The larger the level of independence granted to the bank at the outset the larger the (political) cost of overriding its decisions and the stronger the commitment to price stability. But, given the level of independence, the price stability objective is abandoned if the realization of shocks is extreme enough to make the option to renege on it sufficiently attractive[11]. The stronger the commitment the lower inflationary expectations and the smaller is the discount on government bonds. This is a benefit for government objectives. But a stronger commitment also entails costs since it reduces government's ability to stabilize employment and to utilize the inflation levy on government debt. The level of CB independence is determined by weighing those opposing considerations optimally *before* nominal contracts are concluded and *before* the realization of shocks to natural employment.

To capture these elements I consider the following six-stage sequence of events. In the first stage the incumbent government decides how much authority to delegate to the CB. In the second stage it floats a fixed amount of discount bonds whose discount is determined by the real rate required by the public and by its inflationary expectation. Elections take place in the third stage and either the incumbent or the challenging party is voted into office and remains there until the end of the game. Nominal wage contracts are concluded in the fourth stage and shocks to the natural level of employment realize in the fifth stage. In the sixth and final stage the party in office decides whether or not to exert pressure on the CB to inflate and if it does – at what rate. Immediately after that bonds are redeemed. (A schematic representation of the sequence of events appears in Figure 1).

The benefit of a more independent CB is that higher independence reduces inflationary expectations. A cost of higher CB independence is that it restricts the ability of politicians to inflate the debt away making it more difficult to spend on the type of public good that they like. But, from the perspective of the incumbent party in stage 1, this cost differs depending on whether it is re-elected or not. If not re-elected, the incumbent party does not value the ability to inflate the debt away as much as it values this ability when it is reelected. The reason is that in the second case, this ability enables it to spend more on the public goods it likes, whereas in the first case this enables the other party to spend more on public goods which the incumbent party does not particularly care about. In different words, the incumbent party prefers a stronger level of commitment and therefore a more independent CB when it is certain of not being re-elected than when it is certain of being elected.

b. The formal structure

Viewed from the perspective of the first period, the incumbent party's objective is to maximize

$$as(1 - n) + \beta \underset{x}{E}[x(\pi - \pi^e) + \lambda Bs\pi + (1 - \lambda)bs\pi - \frac{d}{2}\pi^2 - \lambda c(x)], \quad (1)$$

$$B > b \geq 0, 1 \geq \beta, \lambda \geq 0, x > 0$$

where

$$c(x) = \begin{pmatrix} 0 - \text{if the political authorities respect the CB authority in stage 6} \\ c - \text{if the political authorities override the CB decisions in stage 6} \end{pmatrix}.$$

s is the (exogenous) amount of bonds that the incumbent government desires to sell (in stage 2), n is the nominal rate of interest necessary to induce the public to buy this quantity of bonds. Since government debt takes the form of discount bonds the government actually raises funds of size $s(1 - n)$ when it places an amount with a face value of s on the market. The parameter a measures how much the incumbent government values the ability to raise funds and n is the nominal rate of interest.

The remaining costs and benefits all materialize in the last period. They are therefore discounted by the political discount factor of the incumbent – β. π and π^e are actual and expected inflation respectively. The difference $\pi - \pi^e$ measures the amount of period 6's inflation which was not anticipated by individuals when nominal contracts that are based on π^e were concluded. It is well-known that unanticipated inflation has positive effects on employment and output[12]. The stochastic parameter x measures how valuable are the effects of stimulatory inflationary surprises to the incumbent government. It can be thought of as an index of the natural level of employment. The lower natural employment, the more valuable are positive surprises and the larger, therefore, x[13]. The important feature of x is that it is not known with certainty prior to its realization in the fifth stage. Thus, from the perspective of the first stage, in which the level of CBI is chosen, x is a stochastic variable. This is the reason for the appearance of the expected value operator, E, in equation (1).

λ is the probability that the incumbent party is re-elected, πs measures the inflation-induced reduction in the real value of the debt. The terms $Bs\pi$ and

$bs\pi$ respectively measure the benefit to period one's incumbent of this reduction when he remains and when he does not remain in office. The constraint $B > b$ reflects the view that the reduction in the real value of debt is more valuable to either party when it is in office. This presumption originates from the notion that when it is not in office, either party prefers a more independent CB since such a bank makes it more difficult for the other party to spend on a public good that is not desired by the first party. The term $(d/2)\pi^2$ measures the costs of inflation and d is a positive parameter which determines how seriously these costs are taken by either party.

Finally c is the political cost incurred by policymakers if they decide to override the commitment of the CB to price stability in period 6. The size of this (fixed) cost is larger the higher the degree of independence that was conferred on the bank in the first period. This cost is multiplied by λ (the probability of remaining in office) since the political blame for overriding the CB is directed only at the party in office at the time.

The following figure summarizes the sequence of events and moves.

1	2	3	4	5	6
CB independence is chosen by incumbent party	An amount s of bonds is sold to public	Elections take place	Nominal wage contracts (based on π^e) are concluded	x realizes	Incumbent party decides whether to override the CB. If it does it also picks inflation, π

Figure 1 Sequence of events and timing of moves

The figure is largely self-explanatory, but the following additional facts are worth noting:

1. The extent of delegation of authority as embodied in c, is chosen before the results of the elections, and the state of the economy as proxied by x are known. As a consequence, in choosing CB independence, the incumbent government has to weigh the benefits of commitment against the loss in flexibility associated with more independence to the CB.
2. Although they are influenced by events from all stages, the components of the objective function in equation (1) (or payoffs) are located in only two of the six stages. The component $as(1 - n)$ is located in stage 2 and all the other components in stage 6. Correspondingly β should be thought of as the discount factor between stage 2 and stage 6.
3. The incumbent government makes decisions in stages 1 and 6. The public makes decisions in stages 3 and 4, and nature moves in stage 5.
4. Government bonds are redeemed in stage 6 *after* the realization of inflation.

c. When does government override the CB?

I now turn to the derivation of equilibrium strategies. It is natural and convenient to start from the last period and to go backwards. In the last stage, uncertainty about the election result and the state of the economy (x) has been resolved and CB independence (c) and government debt (s) are taken as given. Hence the incumbent's party problem is given by

$$\underset{\pi}{\text{Max}}\ x(\pi - \pi^e) + Bs\pi - \frac{d}{2}\pi^2 \equiv \underset{\pi}{\text{Max}}\ V(\pi,x) \tag{2}$$

if it decides to override the authority of the CB. In the other case the CB is free to focus on price stability and $\pi = 0$. The solution to the problem in equation (2) is

$$\pi_D(x) = \frac{1}{d}(x + Bs) \tag{3}$$

where the index D that is attached to π stands for "discretionary" since when it overrides the CB, government acts in a discretionary manner.

When does government override the CB? To answer this question we calculate the value of government's objectives when π_D is chosen by using (3) in (2). This yields

$$V(\pi_D,x) = -x\pi^e + \frac{1}{2d}(x + Bs)^2 . \tag{4}$$

Government decides to override the CB and to inflate at rate π_D if and only if[14]

$$V(\pi_D,x) - V(0,x) > c \tag{5}$$

where, from (2), $V(0,x) = -x\pi^e$. Using this and (4) in (5) and rearranging, government overrides the CB if and only if

$$x > \sqrt{2dc} - Bs \equiv x_c . \tag{6}$$

Equation (6) states that, given x_c, government overrides the CB when the level of employment is sufficiently depressed – x is sufficiently high. But the larger CB independence (the larger c), the larger the value of x above which government overrides the CB. I assume $x_c > 0$ since otherwise there is no commitment at all and the problem becomes trivial.

d. Equilibrium expectations and wage contracts

Nominal wage contracts are agreed upon in stage 4 and are in effect until the end of the game. The level of the contract wage is higher the higher are inflationary expectations π^e. For simplicity and without loss of generality we proxy the contract nominal wage by π^e. In stage 4 individuals do not know x with certainty. But since they understand government's decision rule contingent on x they can use it to calculate the (statistical) expected value of inflation. This expected value is

$$\pi^e \equiv \underset{x}{E}\,[\pi\, x_c\,] = \int_0^{x_c} 0 \cdot dF(x) + \int_{x_c}^{\infty} \pi_D(x)dF(x) = \tag{7}$$

$$= \frac{1}{d}\{\int_{x_c}^{\infty} xdF(x) + Bs\int_{x_c}^{\infty} dF(x)\,\}$$

where F(x) is the distribution function of x.

Since, from equation (6), x_c is an increasing function of CB independence, equation (7) implies that inflationary expectations are lower the higher is CB independence.

e. Determination of the discount on government bonds

Let

$$s^d(r) = K + \alpha r, \quad \alpha > 0 \tag{8}$$

be the demand for government bonds in period 2 where r is the ex-ante real rate of interest. Since government insists on selling a quantity s of (in terms of face value) bonds, the real rate of interest is determined from

$$r = \frac{1}{\alpha}(s - K)\,. \tag{9}$$

When elected, both parties use the same decision rule in period 6. As a consequence, inflationary expectations are the same before and after elections. To obtain the real rate in equation (9), individuals have to be compensated for the expected rate of inflation π^e. Hence, the nominal rate, n, is

$$n = r + \pi^e = \frac{1}{\alpha}(s - K) + \pi^e\,. \tag{10}$$

Since bonds are of the discount type, a higher nominal rate implies that government raises less funds for the budget given the size of s.

f. Determination of CB independence

CB independence (c) is chosen by the party in office in period 1 before it knows whether it will be re-elected and before it knows what will be the state of the economy (x) after the elections. A higher level of CB independence reduces π^e. Such a reduction is beneficial for two reasons as can be seen from equations (1) and (10). First, it reduces the discount on government bonds. Second, a lower

π^e implies lower nominal wages and therefore, given x and π, a higher level of economic activity in period 6. But a higher level of CB independence also has costs since in some states of nature it prevents government from conducting anticyclical monetary policy and in the remaining states a political cost has to be paid for engaging in such policy. In addition, a higher level of CB independence reduces the scope for inflating away the national debt. Thus, by delegating more authority to the CB, government gains credibility, but loses flexibility. The level of CB independence is determined by optimally trading off these two elements in period 1.

Formally the government in office in period 1 chooses c so as to maximize the objective function in equation (1) subject to the relations given in equations (3), (6), (7) and (10). Substituting equations (7) and (10) into equation (1), rearranging, and dropping terms which do not depend on c the government's problem in period 1 can be expressed as

$$\underset{c}{\text{Max}}\, J(\cdot) \equiv \underset{c}{\text{Max}}\, \frac{as + \beta Ex}{d} \left[\int_{x_c}^{\infty} x dF(x) + Bs \int_{x_c}^{\infty} dF(x) \right] \tag{11}$$

$$+ \beta \int_{x_c}^{\infty} \left[\frac{1}{d} (x + Bs) \{ \frac{x}{2} + [(1 - \lambda)b + (\lambda - \frac{1}{2})B]s\} - \lambda c(x) \right] dF(x)$$

where x_c is given in equation (6). After some rearrangement, the first-order condition for an internal maximization of this problem is

$$J_c(\cdot) = [as + \beta \{ Ex + (1 - \lambda) [(B - b)s - \sqrt{\tfrac{dc}{2}}\,] \}]\, f(x_c) \tag{12}$$

$$- \beta\lambda \int_{x_c}^{\infty} dF(x) = 0$$

where f(x) is the probability density of x. Equation (12) determines the level of CB independence, c, as a function of various parameters. The second-order condition for an internal maximum is

$$J_{cc}(\cdot) = \sqrt{\frac{d}{2c}} \{ [as + \beta\{Ex + (1 - \lambda) [(B - b)s - \sqrt{\tfrac{dc}{2}}\,]\}] f'(x_c) \tag{13}$$

$$+ \frac{\beta}{2} (3\lambda - 1) f(x_c) \} < 0$$

where $f'(\cdot)$ is the derivative of $f(\cdot)$ with respect to x. Jointly sufficient, but not necessary conditions for the fulfillment of the second-order condition are $(B - b)s > \sqrt{dc/2}$, $f'(x_c) < 0$ and $\lambda < 1/3$. The second condition states that the probability density is decreasing at the critical value x_c and the third requires that the probability of re-election is smaller than 1/3. When $\lambda \geq 1/3$, the second-order condition implies that if $(B - b)s > \sqrt{dc/2}$, then $f'(x_c)$ must be negative.

3. Political and Economic Determinants of the Level of Central Bank Independence

This section uses the results of the previous section in order to characterize the political and economic factors that induce political authorities to delegate more authority to the CB. The results are derived by performing comparative static experiments with respect to various parameters on the first-order condition in equation (12). Derivations appear in the appendix. The section summarizes the main results in a series of propositions and discusses the intuition that underlies them. In all the propositions "other factors" that are not mentioned explicitly are held fixed.

PROPOSITION 1: The CB is granted more independence (c is larger) the larger Ex and "a".

The intuition underlying the proposition can be understood by noting from equation (3), that the average inflationary bias in the absence of any form of commitment by political authorities is

$$E\pi_D(x) = \frac{1}{d}(Ex + Bs) .$$

Hence, given s, the average inflationary bias is larger the larger Ex and the benefits of a partial commitment are therefore larger. As a consequence c is larger the larger is Ex as stated in the first part of the proposition.

A larger "a" means that the importance attached by political authorities to the reduction of the discount on government debt is larger. With a higher level of CB independence, expectations are lower, the nominal rate is lower and the discount on new government debt therefore lower. Hence the larger the importance attributed to decreasing the discount on bonds the larger the level of CB independence. I turn next to political factors.

LEMMA 2: The CB is granted more independence the smaller is b.

The meaning of the lemma can be understood by recalling that the term B – b measures the difference in the value of the option to inflate the debt away between a state in which a party is in office and a state in which it is not in office. The more polarized are the parties with respect to the structure of public expenditures, the larger the (positive) difference B – b. Hence a smaller b means that the level of polarization is larger. The lemma implies therefore

PROPOSITION 2: The CB is granted more independence the larger the degree of polarization about the structure of government expenditures.

The intuition is that the party in office likes a stronger constraint on the other party's ability to spend the larger the disagreement about the structure of public spending. This is achieved by imposing a stronger limit on the other party's ability to inflate the debt away through a higher level of CB independence.

PROPOSITION 3: The higher the level of political instability (the lower λ) the larger the level of independence that is granted to the CB provided political polarization is sufficiently large.

The precise meaning of "sufficiently large" is elaborated in the appendix. In any case the condition is only sufficient and not necessary. There are many other configurations of parameters, some of which are discussed in the appendix, for which proposition 3 holds. The intuition underlying the proposition is similar to the intuition underlying proposition 2. Given the level of polarization the party in office prefers a more independent CB the smaller are its re-election prospects. The party in office in period 1 obviously likes to have more flexibility for itself than for the other party. The smaller its chances of re-election the larger the benefits of CB independence in terms of restricting the other party's ability to spend in comparison to the cost of being similarly constrained. In addition the smaller the chances of re-election the smaller the likelihood that the incumbent party will incur the political blame for overriding the CB if future circumstances make such a course of action optimal.

The effect of the amount of bonds that government wishes to sell on CB independence is generally ambiguous. But there is a presumption that this effect is positive. Alternative sufficient conditions for a positive effect are summarized in the following proposition.

PROPOSITION 4: If either of the following conditions holds:
(i) $\lambda \geq 1/3$ and β is relatively small, or
(ii) λ is near to either 0 or 1
(iii) $f(x_c)$ is very small,
then CB independence is higher the larger is the amount of funds s, that government wishes to borrow from the public.

A larger s triggers two opposing effects on the tendency to delegate authority to the CB. On the one hand the reduction in the up-front discount on government bonds induced by higher independence is more valuable when government needs to raise more funds. But, by the same token, the value of ultimately retaining the option to inflate the debt away is also more valuable when s is larger. This tends to reduce the attractiveness of CB independence and operates, therefore, in the opposite direction. The proposition presents conditions under which the first effect dominates.

The effect of the parameter d on CB independence is unambiguous. Proposition 5 summarizes the result.

PROPOSITION 5: The CB is granted less independence the larger the relative concern of political authoritities for price stability (the higher d).

The intuition underlying proposition 5 follows. When d is high, the discretionary rate of inflation is lower for any given values of x and of s (see equation (3)) even in the absence of a commitment. As a result the benefits of any commitment level are smaller. This induces the executive and legislative branches of government to delegate less authority to the CB. An illustration of such a case is the U.K. In comparison to other central banks within industrial countries, the Bank of England is relatively dependent. But there is concurrently an anti-inflationary stance within the British civil service. Proposition 5 suggests that the conjunction of those facts may not be accidental.

4. INSTABILITY AT THE CENTRAL BANK AND INFLATION

Recent evidence shows that (within the group of less developed countries (LDC's)) there is a positive association between the turnover rate of central bank governors and average inflation across countries[15]. This section briefly describes a conceptual framework in which the policy chosen by the CB governor is influenced by the probability of his removal even when he remains in office and the CB is not formally overridden.

To this point the analysis has presumed that, if not officially overridden, the CB always sticks to a zero inflation policy. But governments often manage to influence CB policy through more subtle channels and pressures[16]. This section uses a framework in which the timing and extent of these pressures is the private information of the governor to show that the higher the probability that the governor will be removed from office, the higher inflation even when the governor remains in office.

The formal model is an extension of the model of a policymaker with an (extended) information advantage as presented in chapter 10 of Cukierman (1992). As long as he is in office the governor possesses an objective function with a *changing* but persistent relative emphasis on the creation of surprises versus price stability. In the present context this shifting weight can be thought of as originating in changes in the extent of political pressures on the CB. The public never gets to observe these pressures directly but can draw noisy inferences about their current and future state from past inflation rates. These inferences are noisy because the CB does not have perfect control over the rate of inflation.

Let s be the probability of survival of the governor in office in period t given that he has remained in office until period t – 1[17]. In states of nature in which he is not in office the governor does not care about either price stability or surprise creation[18]. The relevant part of the governor's objective function is

$$E_0\left\{[\pi_0 - \pi_0^e]x_0 - \frac{\pi_0^2}{2} + \sum_{i=1}^{\infty} (s\beta)^i\left[[\pi_i - \pi_i^e]x_i - \frac{\pi_i^2}{2}\right]\right\} \tag{14}$$

$$+ \sum_{i=1}^{\infty} s^{i-1}(1 - s)K$$

where $x_i = A + p_i$, $p_i = \rho p_{i-1} + v_i$, $A > 0$ and $0 < \rho < 1$. v_i is a normal variate with zero mean and variance σ_v^2. Here π_i is actual inflation in period i and π_i^e the rate of inflation expected for that period at the beginning of the period. β is the discount factor and x_i is a stochastic variable whose realizations are restricted to the positive orthant[19]. It reflects the potency of political pressures on the CB. The larger x_i the stronger are the pressures of the political establishment on the governor to expand the money supply. x_i is private information. Its positive serial correlation reflects the presumption that when pressures are above their mean level they tend to remain above it for some time. K is the *constant* level of utility experienced by the governor when not in office. s^i is the probability that the governor survives in office until the end of period i and $s^{i-1}(1 - s)$ is the probability that he terminates at the beginning of that period after having survived until the end of the previous period. Equilibrium is of the Nash variety; taking the (rational) process of expectation formation by the public as given, the governor plans rates of monetary expansion and inflation so as to maximize the objective function in equation (14); taking the behavioral rule of the governor as given, the public forms expectations so as to minimize the mean (square) forecast error.

Application of the results in chapter 10 of Cukierman (1992) to this case reveals that equilibrium inflation is given by

$$\pi_i = \frac{1 - s\beta\rho}{1 - s\beta\lambda}A + \frac{1 - s\beta\rho^2}{1 - s\beta\rho\lambda}p_i + \psi_i \tag{15}$$

where ψ_i is a normal variate with zero mean and variance σ_ψ^2. ψ_i characterizes the (lack of) precision of monetary policy in controlling inflation. λ is a known function of ρ, σ_v^2 and σ_ψ^2 and satisfies the following inequality

$$\lambda \leq \rho\ . \tag{16}$$

Note that since s, β, ρ and λ are all smaller than one, the coefficients of A and of p_i are positive. How does an increase in the governor's survival probability affect equilibrium inflation? The following proposition provides an answer to this question.

PROPOSITION 6: For any given realization of the political pressure shock (p_i) and of the control error (ψ_i) the rate of inflation is higher the lower is the survival probability, s, of the central bank governor.

PROOF: In part 2 of the Appendix.

Proposition 6 provides precise underpinning for the intuitively plausible notion that a governor with a low probability of survival in office will inflate at a higher rate than a governor with a higher probability of survival. The reason is that part of the cost of *currently* more expansionary monetary policy takes the form of higher *future* inflationary expectations. A governor who is less sure of being in office in the future is obviously less sensitive to this cost. He therefore inflates at a higher rate.

Two facts are worth noting. First, due to the dynamic nature of his optimization problem, the governor's policy while in office is influenced by what he perceives to be his future survival probability. Second, a lower survival probability raises the CB inflationary response to any given level of political pressure.

For LDC's proposition 6 is supported by evidence presented in chapter 20 of Cukierman (1992) and in Cukierman and Webb (1993).

5. Concluding Remarks

Preliminary empirical evidence suggests that legal CB independence is larger when party instability is larger and lower when regime instability is higher[20]. The first type of instability is usually relevant for constitutional democracies while the second is characteristic of non-democratic regimes in which changes in government occur through coups or other non-constitutional means. Part of this evidence is consistent with the implications of this paper. In particular the implication that a higher level of political instability is conducive to more independence for the CB is supported by the finding that legal CB independence is higher when party political instability is larger. The reason is that party instability occurs mainly in democratic countries and that in such countries legal independence is an important determinant of actual CB independence[21]. Hence in such countries legal independence is a reasonable proxy for the *actual* level of independence that political authorities *meant* to confer on the CB. This observation, in conjunction with the positive empirical relationship found between legal independence and party political instability are consistent with proposition 3.

Since the framework of the paper is appropriate mostly for constitutional regimes, the observed negative relationship between regime instability and legal independence is not directly explainable by it. It is possible, however, that it arises because in non-democratic regimes the structure of the regime makes it unlikely that a serious commitment can be upheld by constitutional means.

This reduces the effect of legal CB independence on expectations and with it the tendency of the regime to use legal CB as a commitment device. This effect is stronger the more unstable the regime since it is widely known that a new regime does not necessarily respect the institutions erected by the previous one. Those remarks should be viewed as conjectures to be tested in future work.

Some of the lessons to be learned from this paper are that:

1. A certain degree of CB independence is granted in order to reduce interest charges on government debt.
2. In many cases the tendency to delegate authority to the CB is stronger the larger the national debt. The 1986 "divorce" between the Italian CB and the Italian Treasury can be understood in these terms[22].
3. When capital markets are wide (α in equation (8) is small) it is likely that government will try to raise more funds through the capital market. In conjunction with the second conclusion this implies that, other things the same, governments of countries with wider capital markets will delegate more authority to the CB. This conclusion is supported by the observation that some of the most independent central banks are found in countries with well developed capital markets. Germany and the U.S. are examples.

But, on the other hand, proposition 5 suggests that if there is a strong preference for price stability within the executive branch of government, the tendency to delegate authority to the CB is likely to be lower. An example is the U.K. in which the traditional anti-inflation stance of the British civil service reduces the need for a highly independent CB.

The paper suggests that the need to rely on CB independence is greater the stronger is the inflationary bias under discretion. Furthermore this statement is independent of whether this bias arises because of employment considerations or because of a strong desire to reduce the real value of government debt. More generally, any factor that increases the tendency to inflate under discretion, such as a higher degree of polarization, also raises the tendency to delegate authority to the CB.

In order to influence monetary policy after having delegated some authority to the CB, political authorities do not always have to override the Bank openly. Instead they can exert more subtle political pressure (Havrilesky, 1992). The paper shows that CB governors who are less likely to survive in office find it more difficult to resist inflationary pressures. This conclusion is particularly relevant for LDC's.

What are the insights from the discussion of commitment through delegation in the area of monetary policy to other areas of policy? This is a largely open question. My feeling is that, at least for democracies with a certain minimal level of concensus, higher levels of political instability are likely to lead to more delegation of authority to semi-independent public institutions.

70

Appendix

1. *Proof of the propositions in section 3*

By the implicit function theorem

$$\frac{dc}{dD} = -\frac{1}{J_{cc}}\frac{\partial J_c}{\partial D} \tag{A1}$$

where D is a dummy parameter. Since J_{cc} is negative by the second-order condition in equation (13) the signs of dc/dD and of $\partial J_c/\partial D$ are identical. It is therefore enough to find the sign of the second term in order to determine that of the first one.

PROPOSITION 1: From equation (12)

$$\frac{\partial J_c(\cdot)}{\partial Ex} = \beta f(x_c); \quad \frac{\partial J_c(\cdot)}{\partial a} = sf(x_c). \tag{A2}$$

The proof is completed by noting that both expressions are positive and by letting D = Ex, a.

LEMMA 2: From equation (12)

$$\frac{\partial J_c(\cdot)}{\partial b} = -\beta(1-\lambda)sf(x_c)\ . \tag{A3}$$

The proof is completed by letting D = b and by noting that (A3) is negative.

PROPOSITION 3: From equation (12)

$$\frac{\partial J_c(\cdot)}{\partial \lambda} = -\beta[f(x_c)\{(B-b)s - \sqrt{\frac{dc}{2}}\} + \int_{x_c}^{\infty} dF(x)]\ . \tag{A4}$$

This expression is negative if

$$B - b \geq \frac{1}{s}\sqrt{\frac{dc}{2}} \tag{A5}$$

or, equivalently, if the level of political polarization is sufficiently high. Letting D = λ it follows that if (A5) is satisfied

$$\frac{dc}{d\lambda} < 0\ . \tag{A6}$$

For a given level of polarization the result in (A6) is more likely to obtain the higher s and the lower d.

PROPOSITION 4: From equation (12)

$$\frac{\partial J_c(\cdot)}{\partial s} = \beta(1-\lambda)(B-b)f(x_c) - [Hf'(x_c) + \beta\lambda f(x_c)]B \tag{A7}$$

where H is the coefficient of $f(x_c)$ in equation (12). This equation implies that H is positive. Note that H is also the coefficient of $f'(x_c)$ in equation (13). When $\lambda \geq 1/3$ the second-order condition in equation (13) implies that $Hf'(x_c) < 0$. Hence, if in addition β is sufficiently small the expression in (A7) is positive. This establishes part (i).

The second-order condition is equivalent to the condition

$$Hf'(x_c) + \beta\lambda f(x_c) - \frac{1}{2}\beta(1-\lambda)f(x_c) < 0\,. \tag{A8}$$

When $\lambda \to 1$ this condition reduces to

$$Hf'(x_c) + \beta f(x_c) < 0$$

which implies that the expression in (A7) is positive. When $\lambda \to 0$ the first-order condition in equation (12) implies that

$$c = \frac{2}{d}\left[[\frac{1}{\beta} + B - b]s + Ex\right]^2$$

from which it follows that c is an increasing function of s. This establishes part (ii).

If $f(x_c)$ is very small the second-order condition implies again $Hf'(x_c) < 0$. Since $f(x_c)$ is small, this implies that the expression in (17) is positive which establishes part (iii).

PROPOSITION 5: From equation (12)

$$\frac{\partial J_c(\cdot)}{\partial d} = \frac{1}{2}[-\beta(1-\lambda)f(x_c)\sqrt{\frac{c}{2d}} + \{Hf'(x_c) + \beta\lambda f(x_c)\}\sqrt{\frac{2c}{d}}]$$
$$= \left[Hf'(x_c) + \beta\lambda f(x_c) - \frac{1}{2}\beta(1-\lambda)f(x_c)\right]\sqrt{\frac{c}{2d}}\,. \tag{A9}$$

The modified form of the second-order condition in (A8) implies that the expression in (A9) is negative. Hence, higher values of d are associated with lower levels of central bank independence.

72

2. *Proof of proposition 6*

Totally differentiating equation (15) with respect to s and rearranging

$$\frac{d\pi_i}{ds} = -K[(1 - s\beta\lambda\rho)^2 A + (1 - s\beta\lambda)^2 \rho p_i] \qquad (A10)$$

where

$$K \equiv \frac{\beta(\rho - \lambda)}{(1 - s\beta\lambda)^2 (1 - s\beta\lambda\rho)^2}. \qquad (A11)$$

Since $\rho - \lambda > 0$, K is positive. Since $A \geq p_i$ and $(1 - s\beta\lambda\rho)^2 > (1 - s\beta\lambda)^2\rho$ it follows that the expression in square brackets on the right-hand side of (A10) is positive. Hence

$$\frac{d\pi_i}{ds} < 0$$

which establishes proposition 6.

NOTES

1. See, for example, chapters 3 and 4 of Cukierman (1992).
2. Evidence for developed economies appears in Grilli, Masciandaro and Tabellini (1991) and for both developed and less developed economies in chapters 19 and 21 of Cukierman (1992) or in Cukierman, Webb and Neyapti (1992). The evidence in the first reference is based on CB charters and in the last two on CB charters as well as on the rate of turnover of CB governors.
3. Recent discussions of this tradeoff in the context of the employment motive for monetary expansion appear in Lohmann (1992) and in Cukierman, Kiguel and Liviatan (1992).
4. Alesina and Tabellini (1990) and Tabellini and Alesina (1990) have shown that such a conflict induces the incumbent to use public debt as a device for restricting the ability of the opposition to spend. In their framework the debt cannot be inflated away. Implicitly they assume therefore a fully independent CB. Here the degree of independence of the CB and therefore the extent to which government debt is inflated away are determined endogenously for a given level of debt. Hence this paper and theirs complement each other.
5. For reasons that are elaborated in the conclusion these results are restricted to democratic regimes.
6. Recent evidence on this kind of political pressure in the U.S. appears in Havrilesky (1992).
7. Details appear in chapter 20 of Cukierman (1992) and in Cukierman, Webb and Neyapti (1992).
8. Natural employment is the level of employment that prevails in the economy in the absence of monetary surprises. The assumption that it is below desired employment reflects the view that due to union power or minimum wage legislation the natural real wage is above its market clearing level. This point of view is developed explicitly in chapter 3, section 3.6 of Cukierman (1992).
9. Alesina and Tabellini (1990) and Tabellini and Alesina (1990) investigate the consequence of this conflict for the level of government debt. Cukierman, Edwards and Tabellini (1992) analyze its consequences for the efficiency of the tax system.

10. See chapter 6, section 6.4 of Persson and Tabellini (1990) or chapter 4, section 4.4 of Cukierman (1992).
11. A similar conception of CB independence appears in Lohmann (1992).
12. A precise mechanism that produces this relation is discussed in chapter 3, section 3.6 of Cukierman (1992). It is based on the interaction of nominal wage contracts with a natural real wage that is higher than that which would clear the market.
13. The positivity of x reflects the presumption that due to market power in the labor market, there always is an inflationary bias. Details appear in chapter 3 of Cukierman (1992). Variations in x may also reflect changes in the relative strength of price stability and of pro stimulation advocates within a given party.
14. I assume that when indifferent government respects the independence of the CB.
15. See chapter 20 of Cukierman (1992) or Cukierman, Webb and Neyapti (1992).
16. A recent documentation of some of these channels for the U.S. Fed appears in Havrilesky (1992).
17. I assume for simplicity that this probability is constant and independent from events in other periods.
18. This somewhat extreme assumption is used for simplicity. The main result would go through even if he cared but less than in periods in which he is in office.
19. More precisely the probability that p_i is negative and exceeds A in absolute value is negligible. Details appear in appendix A to chapter 9 of Cukierman (1992).
20. Details appear in chapter 23 of Cukierman (1992).
21. Evidence and a discussion appear in Cukierman, Webb and Neyapti (1992) and in chapters 20 and 23 of Cukierman (1992).
22. For details see Epstein and Schor (1986).

References

Alesina, Alberto and Guido Tabellini (1990), "A Political Theory of Fiscal Deficits and Government Debt in a Democracy", *Review of Economic Studies*, 57, 403–414, (June).

Barro, Robert and David Gordon (1983), "A Positive Theory of Monetary Policy in a Natural Rate Model", *Journal of Political Economy*, 91, 589–610, (August).

Cukierman, Alex (1992), *Central Bank Strategy, Credibility and Independence; Theory and Evidence*, MIT Press, Cambridge, MA.

Cukierman, Alex, Sebastian Edwards and Guido Tabellini (1992), "Seigniorage and Political Instability", *American Economic Review*, 82, 537–555, (June).

Cukierman, Alex, Miguel Kiguel and Nissan Liviatan (1992), "To Commit or Not to Commit to an Exchange Rate Rule: Is Dollarization the Answer?" *Revista de Analisis Economico*, 7,73–90, (June).

Cukierman, Alex, Steven Webb and Bilin Neyapti (1992), "Measuring the Independence of Central Banks and its Effect on Policy Outcomes", *World Bank Economic Review*, 6, 353–398, (September).

Cukierman, Alex and Steven Webb (1993), "Political Influence on the Central Bank – International Evidence" manuscript, (May).

Epstein, Gerald and Juliet Schor (1986), "The Divorce of the Banca d'Italia and the Italian Treasury: A Case Study of Central Bank Independence", *Harvard Institute of Economic Research Discussion Papers*, No.1269, (September).

Grilli, Vittorio, Donato Masciandaro and Guido Tabellini (1991), "Political and Monetary Institutions and Public Financial Policies in the Industrialized Countries", *Economic Policy*, 13, 341–392.

74

Havrilesky, Thomas (1992), *The Pressures on American Monetary Policy*, Kluwer Academic Publishers, Norwell, MA.

Lohmann, Susanne (1992), "Optimal Commitment in Monetary Policy: Credibility versus Flexibility" *American Economic Review*, 82, 273–286, (March).

Persson, Torsten and Guido Tabellini (1990), *Macroeconomic Policy, Credibility and Politics*, Harwood Academic Publishers, London, Paris and New York.

Tabellini, Guido and Alberto Alesina (1990), "Voting on the Budget Deficit", *American Economic Review*, 80, 37–49, (March).

[21]

Public Choice **85**: 335–351, 1995.

Variation in central bank independence across countries: Some provisional empirical evidence

JAKOB DE HAAN

GERT JAN VAN 'T HAG*

Department of Economics, University of Groningen, P.O. Box 800, 9700 AV Groningen, the Netherlands

Accepted 5 September 1994

Abstract. In this paper seven hypotheses to explain variation in central bank independence across countries are tested. The predictions based upon the theory that delegation of authority by politicians to the central bank is used as a commitment device are not supported: central bank independence is not higher the larger the employment motivated inflationary bias, the higher political instability or the larger the government debt. Central bank independence is positively related to historical inflation experience and negatively with political instability. We do only find limited support for the view that countries with a universal banking system and countries whose central banks do not regulate financial institutions have more independent central banks.

1. Introduction

It is often argued that a high level of central bank independence coupled with some explicit mandate for the bank to aim for price stability are important institutional devices for the assurance of price stability. Still, impressionistic observation suggests that legal central bank independence may be neither necessary nor sufficient for low inflation. While Japan, for instance, has a relatively dependent central bank, it has also an average inflation rate which belongs to the lowest within the OECD area. Similarly, according to Cukierman's (1992) ranking, Greece has a relatively independent central bank and quite a high level of inflation. These observations are, however, not inconsistent with the view that, other things the same, a higher degree of independence is conducive to lower inflation (Cukierman, 1992). Indeed, many authors have found empirical support for this view.[1]

Arguing that central bank independence is important, implies another ques-

* The authors would like to thank various participants at the Meeting of the European Public Choice Society in Valencia (April 1994) and the referee for their comments on a previous version of the paper.

tion: what explains existing variation in central bank independence across countries? Recently Cukierman (1992, 1994) and Posen (1993a) have formulated various hypotheses that can account for at least some of the variation in central bank independence. Central in the analysis of Cukierman (1992) is the view that delegation of authority by politicians is used as a (partial) commitment device.[2] The more independent the central bank, the stronger the commitment of policymakers. As argued by Lohmann (1992), more central bank independence entails both benefits and costs. The benefits consist of lower interest rates and moderate wage increases due to lower inflationary expectations, whereas the costs involve a loss of flexibility for government. The foregone flexibility could be useful to lower unemployment or to inflate part of the national debt away. Central in the analysis of Posen (1993a) is the view that political interests in society drive monetary policy, because central banks will take strong anti-inflationary action only when there is a coalition of interests politically capable of protecting it. In industrialized societies that role, so the argument goes, is played by the financial sector. Posen (1993a) argues that this financial sector opposition against inflation is the true source of the correlation between central bank autonomy and inflation.

This paper aims at testing some of these hypotheses, using data for as large a group of industrialized countries as possible. The paper is organized as follows. In the following section the hypotheses and the intuition behind them are briefly introduced. Section 3 discusses the various measures of central bank independence and the other data that we use in our analysis. Since we aim for as large a sample of OECD countries as possible, we employ the measures of central bank independence as suggested by Grilli, Masciandaro and Tabellini (1991) and Cukierman (1992) and variants thereof. Although various authors have suggested alternative measures, they relate generally to a small group of countries and are, therefore, not very suited for our purpose.[3] Section 4 presents our results and the final section summarizes the paper.

2. Determinants of central bank independence

The explanation of differences in central bank independence across countries has received scant attention in the literature. Cukierman (1994) has recently formulated a number of hypotheses. In this section we will present these and some other hypotheses put forward to explain cross-country differences in central bank independence.

Cukierman's (1994) hypotheses are all derived from a similar framework as that of Lohmann (1992). By delegating monetary powers to an independent central bank, government may be able to improve the credibility of monetary policy. Lack of credibility is due to the time-consistency problem of monetary policy. By granting independence to a conservative central banker who places a higher weight on inflation stabilization than the policymaker, credibility may be increased, which eliminates (or at least reduces) the inflationary bias. However, policy makers do not retain flexibility to employ monetary instruments to stabilize employment or to reduce the real value of existing debt. The need to use monetary policy for these purposes is stronger the more depressed is the economy and the larger the size of the public debt. Consequently, there is a tradeoff between the credibility of low inflation and the loss of flexibility. On the basis of this framework the following hypothesis can be derived:

(1) Central bank independence is higher the larger the average employment motivated inflationary bias.

Unanticipated inflation has positive effects on output and employment in case of nominal wage rigidity. The lower natural employment, the more valuable are inflationary surprises for government. As the public is well aware of this, the credibility effects of granting the central bank an independent status will exceed the costs due to the implied loss of flexibility.[4] We refer to Cukierman (1994) for a formal deduction of this hypothesis.

Along similar lines the next hypothesis can be derived:

(2) The larger the amount the government plans to borrow on the capital market – i.e., the higher the stock of government debt – the more independent the central bank will be.

A high level of government debt implies that reduced credibility may increase the interest burden substantially, exceeding the benefits of a one-time reduction in the real value of government debt from an unexpected inflationary shock. The benefits of reducing the inflationary bias are in that case higher than the costs due to the loss of flexibility (see Cukierman, 1994, for further details).[5]

In the discussion so far, we have assumed that there is no disagreement among various policymakers. The above considerations are somewhat complicated when different political parties competing for office disagree about the structure of government expenditures. In that case, by granting some independence to the central bank the political party in power may restrict the ability of the opposition to spend on public goods that it favours when it comes in office. So the incumbent party has also to take into account this consideration, in combination, of course, with the likelihood that it will remain in power. In this framework, Cukierman (1994) derives the following hypothesis:

(3) The higher the level of political instability, the more independence that is granted to the central bank.

The political party in office prefers a more independent central bank the smaller its reelection prospects, since the larger are the benefits of central bank independence in terms of restricting the other party's ability to spend like it prefers. Note that political instability in this case refers to a change of the political parties which are in office. One may, however, argue in favour of another relationship between central bank independence and political instability. If inflation surprises are valuable in the short run – either because of the employment gains or the reduction in the real value of government debt –, and if the chances for a politician to be thrown out of office are high, it may be worthwhile to be in a position that monetary policy of the central bank can be overrun. The short-run benefits of this policy may exceed the long-run costs of a higher inflation rate. Given the limited time horizon of politicians they will prefer to have the option to use inflation surprises, which is impossible, or at least more difficult, if the central bank is very independent. In other words, a high degree of political instability may result in less central bank independence. Note that political instability in this case refers to the time horizon of politicians.[6]

The following hypotheses have also been suggested in the literature:

(4) A high rate of inflation is likely to result, at least after a while, in a lower level of central bank independence.

Cukierman (1992) argues that high inflation encourages processes that make it easier for the executive to influence monetary policy. Sufficiently high and sustained inflation leads to the evolution of automatic or semi-automatic accommodative mechanisms, like indexation of contracts in the labour and capital markets. The evolution of indexation gives rise to monetary conventions that encourage the central bank to accommodate inflation. Cukierman (1992) presents the outcomes of bivariate Granger causality tests in which the turnover rate of the central bank's governor is used as a proxy for actual as opposed to legal central bank independence. The evidence supports the view that there is a two-way Granger causality between inflation and central bank independence. Lagged turnover affects current inflation, and a higher lagged inflation is associated with a current higher turnover of central bank governors. This view is strongly at odds with the following hypothesis, which has been put forward by various authors.

(5) Experiences with periods of high levels of inflation cause popular support for anti-inflationary monetary policy and an independent central bank.

It is often argued, notably by German authors, that the *Bundesbank* is quite independent and can follow its staunch anti-inflation policies, since that is what the German people wanted, given their experience with the hyperinflations of the past (Bofinger, 1992). Recently, Debelle (1993) has developed a model in which he shows that the more weight society places on inflation, the more independent a central bank it will desire. Thus the observed differences in central banks across countries may be the result of optimal decisions of societies with different objective functions. As Issing (1993: 18) states: "it is no coincidence that it is the Germans, with their experience of two hyperinflations in the 20th century, who have opted for an independent central bank which is committed to price stability."

Finally, it has been argued that if there seems to be a link between central bank independence and low inflation, it is because countries whose financial sector is most opposed to inflation are also the most eager for their central banks to be independent. Countries' differing tolerance of inflation may partly reflect the sorts of financial systems they have. Countries with a universal banking system are likely to oppose inflation more strongly, since lending tends to be more significant in such systems, and so the financial sector will be more aware of the costs of inflation (Posen, 1993a). So, our sixth hypothesis is:

(6) Countries with a universal banking system will have more independent central banks.

In a similar vein, Posen (1993a) has argued that the less regulatory powers the central bank has over the financial sector, the more strength of opposition to inflation is to be expected. This leads to the following hypothesis:

(7) Countries whose central banks do not regulate financial institutions are keener against inflation, and have, therefore, more independent central banks.

The last hypothesis is related to the debate whether central banks should be entrusted with supervising powers. As pointed out by De Beaufort Wijnholds and Hoogduin (1994) various arguments have been put forward in support of both views. The most important argument in favour of separating the monetary policy and prudential supervision functions is based on the fear that the central bank's anti-inflationary stance would be undermined by a large injection of liquidity, aimed at keeping one or more important financial institutions from going under. Another argument for keeping prudential supervision out of the central bank, is the experience that bank failure or rescue operations can be messy and thereby damaging to the central bank's reputation and thus affect its autonomy. The most important argument in favour of combining the functions is that the coordination of monetary policy and prudential supervision will be strengthened. Furthermore, central banks generally act as lenders of last resort, even if they are not responsible for prudential supervision. Apart from the provision of immediate liquidity, the central bank is often the pivot in organizing rescue operations for troubled banks. In contrast to Posen (1993a), De Beaufort Wijnholds and Hoogduin (1994) conclude that it appears possible to maintain central bank autonomy if the central bank is also entrusted with supervision responsibilities.

3. The data

It is quite difficult to measure the degree of legal independence of various central banks, let alone the degree of actual independence. As pointed out by Cukierman (1992) actual, as opposed to formal independence not only depends on legislation, but also on a myriad of other factors like informal arrangements with government, the quality of the personnel of the bank, and the personalities of key individuals in the bank. Obviously these other factors are impossible to quantify and most existing research has therefore focused on legal independence. As we will show, however, the ranking of the degree of central bank independence of the same country shows a remarkable divergence in various studies. Ranking of central bank statutes by their degree of legal independence involves subjective judgment. We therefore use many different proxies to characterize independence, since each proxy is a noisy indicator that captures a somewhat different aspect of central bank independence.

Table 1 summarizes various of these measures. The first column shows Cukierman's (1992) proxies of legal independence, for the period 1980–89 (LVAU). These are based upon: (1) variables concerning the appointment, dismissal and terms of office of the chief executive officer of the bank; (2) variables concerning the resolution of conflicts between the executive branch and the central bank; (3) the final objectives of the central bank as stated in its charter; and (4) legal restrictions on the ability of the public sector to borrow from the central bank. Altogether sixteen different legal variables are coded, which were subsequently aggregated by Cukierman into eight variables, using a certain weighing scheme. The unweighed index of these variables yields LVAU. This measure ranges from zero (dependent) to one (independent). As an alternative, the second column of Table 1 reports the total score of the aforementioned sixteen legal variables discerned by Cukierman (1992). This variable is called SUMLV. The measure of central bank independence reported in column (3) is based upon Grilli, Masciandaro and Tabellini (1991). GMTT is the sum of their economic and political independence measures. The first is based on variables related to monetary financing of the deficit and the nature of the monetary instruments under the control of the central bank, while the second denotes political independence and is constructed on the basis of (1) the

Table 1. Various measures of central bank independence

Country	(1) LVAU	(2) SUMLV	(3) GMTT
1. Australia	0.31 (11)	5.85 (10)	9 (6)
2. Austria	0.58 (3)	9.19 (2)	9 (6)
3. Belgium	0.19 (19)	3.36 (17)	7 (9)
4. Canada	0.46 (7)	7.81 (4)	11 (4)
5. Denmark	0.47 (6)	5.18 (11)	8 (8)
6. Finland	0.27 (4)	2.27 (20)	NA
7. France	0.28 (13)	4.35 (13)	7 (9)
8. Germany	0.66 (2)	10.01 (1)	13 (1)
9. Greece	0.51 (4)	8.32 (3)	4 (16)
10. Iceland	0.36 (10)	5.92 (9)	NA
11. Ireland	0.39 (9)	5.96 (8)	7 (9)
12. Italy	0.22 (17)	3.53 (16)	5 (14)
13. Japan	0.16 (20)	3.33 (18)	6 (12)
14. Netherlands	0.42 (8)	5.92 (8)	10 (5)
15. New Zealand	0.27 (14)	4.23 (14)	3 (17)
16. Norway	0.14 (21)	3.78 (15)	NA
17. Portugal	NA	NA	3 (17)
18. Spain	0.21 (18)	2.84 (19)	5 (14)
19. Sweden	0.27 (14)	4.62 (12)	NA
20. Switzerland	0.68 (1)	7.25 (5)	12 (2)
21. U.K.	0.31 (11)	6.28 (6)	6 (12)
22. U.S.	0.51 (4)	6.26 (7)	12 (2)

Note. LVAU denotes Cukierman's (1992) legal independence measure, ranging from 0 (dependent) to 1 (independent). SUMLV is the sum of the scores regarding 16 legal variables as discerned by Cukierman (1992). A higher entry indicates a higher degree of independence. GMTT is the sum of the economic and political independence measures of Grilli et al. (1991). A higher entry indicates more independence. The ranking of the various countries is shown in parentheses.

procedure for appointing the members of the central bank governing bodies; (2) the relationship between these bodies and the government; and (3) the formal responsibilities of the central bank. A higher score for GMTT indicates a higher degree of independence.

A first thing to note is that, although both the measures of Cukierman (1992) and Grilli et al. (1991) are based on a similar approach they yield sometimes rather different outcomes. Whereas the Netherlands, for instance, is at position eight according to LVAU, it is fifth when GMTT is used. Another example of widely diverging outcomes is Greece. This is confirmed by the partial correlation coefficients of the various measures which are shown in Table 2.[7]

All other data and their sources are described in the Appendix. Note that the sample period of the dependent and the explanatory variables generally all refer to the 1980s.

Table 2. Correlation of various central bank independence measures

	LVAU	SUMLV	GMTT
LVAU	1.00	0.88	0.70
SUMLV		1.00	0.59
GMTT			1.00

4. Estimation results

The hypotheses outlined in Section 2 will be tested in a very simple way in this section. By running cross-section regressions we try to detect whether a significant correlation exists between our central bank independence measures and various explanatory variables as suggested in the literature. Absence of a significant relationship implies that the hypothesis concerned is rejected. Note, however, that in case of a significant relationship the results may also be interpreted as support for the reverse causation hypothesis. This problem may occur in testing the first and second hypothesis.[8]

Basically two groups of hypotheses can be discerned. First, the hypotheses following from the work of Cukierman (1992, 1994), and second, the hypotheses suggested by Posen (1993a). Given the limited number of observations, and consequently, the limited degrees of freedom, we have first estimated bivariate OLS regressions to test the hypotheses of Cukierman. Next, we report the estimates of a regression in which the Cukierman hypotheses are tested jointly. The hypotheses of Posen (1993a) will also be tested jointly.

We start our investigation by examining the relationship between central bank independence and the employment motivated inflationary bias (hypotheses 1). A problem arises as how to measure the inflationary bias. We have used two proxies:

- the equilibrium unemployment rate for the 1980s as estimated for 19 OECD countries by Layard, Nickell and Jackman (1991);
- the difference between the actual unemployment rate and the equilibrium unemployment rate. See the data appendix for further details.

Table 3 reports the outcomes of some simple OLS regressions in which three measures of central bank independence (LVAU, SUMLV and GMTT) are the dependent variables. Since both proxies yield the same outcome, we only report the regressions in which the equilibrium unemployment rate during the 1980s acts as explanatory variable.[9] It follows from Table 3 that the coefficient of the employment motivated inflationary bias proxy is never significantly different from zero.

Table 3. Testing hypothesis 1

Dependent variable	Constant	Equilibrium unemployment	R^2 (adj)	Number observat.	SEE
LVAU	0.40 (0.08)	−0.01 (0.01)	−0.04	19	0.17
SUMLV	5.95 (0.98)	−0.09 (0.14)	−0.03	19	2.13
GMTT	9.58 (1.55)	−0.22 (0.21)	0.01	16	2.88

Standard errors are in parentheses.

Table 4. Testing hypothesis 2

Dependent variable	Constant	Government debt ratio	R^2 (adj)	Number observat.	SEE
LVAU	0.48 (0.08)	−0.002 (0.002)	0.06	21	0.15
SUMLV	6.48 (1.10)	−0.02 (0.02)	−0.01	21	2.09
GMTT	9.84 (1.84)	−0.04 (0.03)	0.04	18	3.04

Standard errors are in parentheses.

Table 4 reports the test outcomes of the second hypothesis, which proclaims that the higher the level of government debt the more independent the central bank will be. The ratio of government gross debt to GDP is used as the explanatory variable. It follows that in none of the regressions the coefficient of the government debt ratio differs significantly from zero, which is not in accordance with Cukierman's (1994) model.

Tabels 5A and 5B report the outcomes of simple OLS regressions, using two measures of political instability, which have been used in the literature to proxy political instability:

- CHANGE, which traces the frequency of government changes during the 1980s.[10] Under the definition of this variable a government change occurs after each election and if a change takes place with respect to the parties participating in the governing coalition. This variable intends to measure the chance for a politician of being thrown out of office and therefore all elections are included, even if the government is reelected. The source of this variable is Keesing's Historic Archives (see the Data appendix for further details).
- SIGNIFICANT, which traces the frequency of significant government changes, i.e., when another party (or coalition) comes into power (see also Grilli et al., 1991). The source for this variable is Bank's Handbook of the World, various issues.

Two interesting conclusions can be drawn from Tables 5A and 5B. First,

Table 5A. Testing hypothesis 3

Dependent variable	Constant	Political instability measure: SIGNIFICANT	R^2 (adj)	Number observat.	SEE
LVAU	0.44 (0.06)	−0.03 (0.02)	0.05	21	0.16
SUMLV	6.26 (0.78)	−0.30 (0.27)	0.01	21	2.07
GMTT	9.64 (1.09)	−0.76 (0.38)*	0.23	18	2.73

Standard errors are in parentheses.
 * Significant at the 10 percent level.
 ** Significant at the 5 percent level.

Table 5B. Testing hypothesis 3

Dependent variable	Constant	Political instability measure: CHANGE	R^2 (adj)	Number observat.	SEE
LVAU	0.56 (0.08)	−0.04 (0.02)**	0.24	21	0.14
SUMLV	7.91 (1.05)	−0.50 (0.21)**	0.20	21	1.87
GMTT	11.35 (1.58)	−0.71 (0.30)**	0.29	18	2.61

See notes under Table 5A.

in contrast to Cukierman's (1994) hypothesis, there appears a negative relationship between central bank independence and political instability, i.e., the more politically unstable a country is, the less independent its central bank is. Second, the coefficient of our proxy for political instability CHANGE is generally significantly different from zero.[11] Finally, we have experimented with the variable FREQUENCY of Grilli et al. (1991), which resembles our variable CHANGE, except that only actual government changes are included and not elections as such. This gave similar results (not shown).

Next, we have tested hypotheses (4) and (5). Table 6 presents the outcomes of simple regressions in which the average level of inflation between 1900 and 1940 is the explanatory variable.[12] It follows that apparently the inflation experience is positively correlated with central bank independence, which is in accordance with hypothesis 5.

We have also estimated a model in which the equilibrium unemployment rate, the government debt ratio, CHANGE and the average level of inflation between 1900 and 1940 are all included as explanatory variables. The results are shown in Table 7. As follows from this table, the outcomes are basically in accordance with the previously reported results. Whereas the coefficients of

Table 6. Testing hypotheses 4 and 5

Dependent variable	Constant	$P_{1900-40}$	R^2 (adj)	Number observat.	SEE
LVAU	0.30 (0.04)	0.58 (0.21)**	0.43	16	0.13
SUMLV	4.94 (0.50)	8.07 (2.89)**	0.31	16	1.79
GMTT	7.91 (0.76)	6.91 (3.81)*	0.22	13	2.31

See notes under Table 5A.

Table 7. A joint test of hypotheses 1 to 5

Dependent variable	Constant	Equilibrium unemployment rate	Government debt ratio	CHANGE	$P_{1900-40}$	R^2 (adj)	Number observat.	SEE
LVAU	0.35	0.02	0.000	−0.033	0.47	0.42	16	0.13
	(0.12)	(0.01)	(0.002)	(0.016)*	(0.22)**			
SUMLV	6.94	0.07	0.02	−0.65	7.77	0.62	16	1.33
	(1.16)	(0.16)	(0.02)	(0.20)**	(2.20)**			
GMTT	12.17	−0.03	−0.02	−0.53	4.98	0.36	13	2.09
	(2.17)	(0.31)	(0.04)	(0.34)	(3.62)			

See notes under Table 5A.

the equilibrium unemployment rate and the government debt ratio are never significantly different from zero, the coefficients of the proxies for political instability and the inflation experience of countries generally remain significant, except for the measure of Grilli et al. (1991), which is due to the limited number of observations. Our results for the model in which CHANGES is replaced by SIGNIFICANT also does not change our previous conclusions (not shown).

As the next step in our analysis, we have tested the hypotheses of Posen (1993a) that financial sector opposition to inflation determines monetary policy and central bank independence. This author provides information both on the existence of a universal banking system and on the involvement of the central in prudential supervision (see Posen, 1993b). On the basis of this information we have constructed two variables. The variable UB is one in case of a universal banking system, and zero otherwise.[13] The variable central bank oversight (CBO) is 0 in case of high oversight; 1 in case of medium oversight and it is 2 in case of low oversight.[14] Since this information is also included in the construction of the central bank independence measure GMTT, the independent variable in row three of Table 8 is the adjusted GMTT measure. It follows from Table 8 that the coefficient of both variables is only significantly different from zero in case LVAU is the independent variable. This conclusion also holds in case CBO and UB are used individually (see Table A1 in the

Table 8. Testing hypotheses 6 and 7

Dependent variable	Constant	Central bank oversight (CBO)	Universal banking (UB)	R^2 (adj)	Number observat.	SEE
LVAU	0.43 (0.06)	−0.10 (0.04)**	0.16 (0.06)**	0.36	17	0.13
SUMLV	6.15 (0.91)	−0.78 (0.63)	1.32 (1.03)	0.05	17	2.08
GMTT (adj)	7.57 (1.15)	−1.17 (0.80)	1.48 (1.30)	0.07	17	2.63

See notes under Table 5A.

Appendix). This result is in sharp contrast to the outcomes reported by Posen (1993a), who argued that his results were not sensitive with respect to the choice of the central bank independence measure.[15] We conclude that there is, at best, only mixed support for Posen's (1993a) hypotheses.[16]

Finally, we have estimated a model in which all suggested explanatory variables are included. Despite the very low degrees of freedom left, basically the same conclusions are reached (see Table A2 in the Appendix).

5. Concluding comments

In this paper seven hypotheses that can account for at least some of the variation in central bank independence across countries are tested, using simple OLS regressions. Three hypotheses follow from the theory of Cukierman (1993), which predicts that central bank independence will be higher the larger the employment motivated inflationary bias, the higher political instability and the larger the government debt. However, our findings are not in accordance with this theory. If anything, central bank independence is negatively related to political instability. We also do not find support for Cukierman's (1992) hypothesis that a high rate of inflation is likely to result, at least after a while, in a lower level of central bank independence. On the contrary, we conclude the higher the level of inflation between 1900–1940, the more independent the central bank. Finally, we do only find limited support for Posen's (1993a) view that countries with a universal banking system and countries whose central banks do not regulate financial institutions have more independent central banks.

Finally, our results cast some new light on the literature in which a negative relationship between central bank independence and inflation is reported. This finding is often used as argument to grant an independent status to central banks (see, e.g., De Haan and Sturm, 1992; Alesina and Summers, 1993). However, it may be that the observed negative relationship between inflation and central bank independence is simply a reflection of the underlying preferences of the economy in question and of its political structure. Those economies with a strong anti-inflation preference and a high degree of political stability are likely to have instituted an independent central bank. This implies that making a central bank more independent, a process currently underway in many countries, may not be enough to reduce the inflationary bias in high inflation countries.

Notes

1. See De Haan and Sturm (1992) for a review of the debate on the economic consequences of central bank independence.
2. See also Neumann (1991) for this approach to central bank independence.
3. For alternative measures see, e.g., Eijffinger and Schaling (1993), Bade and Parkin (1988) and Alesina (1988).
4. Note, however, that it may be argued that the causality runs in the other direction. Central bank independence may reduce equilibrium unemployment, because it renders monetary policy more credible.
5. Again reverse causation may occur. Central bank independence may reduce the debt ratio, because debt financing is less likely to be accommodated by monetary policy. Alternatively it may be argued that central bank independence may increase the debt ratio, because it renders monetary financing of government expenditure more difficult. De Haan and Sturm (1992) find some evidence that relatively independent central banks provide less credit to government to finance budget deficits.
6. In some recent studies the impact of political instability on inflation are examined. See, e.g., Edwards and Tabellini (1991) and Cukierman, Edwards and Tabellini (1992).
7. The Kendall correlation coefficients (R_k) of these measures are:

   R_k (LVAU,SUMLV) = 0.71; R_k (LVAU,GMTT) = 0.52 and R_k (SUMLV,GMTT) = 0.43.

8. An alternative testing strategy is to test whether changes over time in central bank independence can be explained on the basis of the various hypotheses outlined in Section 2. Although it would be very interesting to follow this approach, it is as yet not possible, given the rather *limited variation over time* in central bank independence in OECD-countries. In Appendix A of Cukierman (1992) the codings for his legal variables for four sample periods are presented. There is hardly any change over time. If an increasing number of central banks get a more independent status, like those of New Zealand and France, it may become possible to follow this alternative testing strategy.
9. To examine whether outliers influenced our testing results, we reestimated the equations including a dummy for the observation with the highest residual. Generally, the conclusions do not change.
10. See De Haan and Sturm (1994) who have used this variable in their analysis of government debt growth in the European Communities. Grilli, Masciandaro and Tabellini (1991) have also used a similar variable in their analysis.
11. In the third row of Table 5B a dummy is added for New Zealand, which appeared an important outlier. If this dummy is not include the coefficient for CHANGE is: −0.57 (0.33).
12. We have also performed regressions in which the after World War II inflation up to 1980 was the independent variable. However, here identification problems arise since the variation in central bank independence between 1950–80 and 1980–89 is very limited, so one easily comes up with the negative correlation between inflation and central bank independence reported in the literature.

13. Belgium, Denmark, Germany, Greece, Ireland, the Netherlands and Switzerland have a universal banking system, while Australia, Austria, Canada, France, Italy, Japan, New Zealand, Spain, the UK and the USA don't.
14. Using the information as provided by Grilli et al. as to whether the central bank is responsible for banking supervision, we have also constructed a variable SUPER which is two if the central bank is not entrusted with banking supervision, which is one if supervision is not entrusted to the central bank alone and which is zero otherwise. This yielded generally the same results (not shown).
15. Posen (1993a: 63) has also employed LVAU in his regressions, but notes that his results "prove to be robust across specifications of CB independence measures".
16. Similar results show up in case of bivariate regressions (not shown).

References

Alesina, A. (1988). Macroeconomic and politics. *NBER Macroeconomic Annual 1988*. Cambridge: Cambridge University Press.

Alesina, A. and Summers, L.H. (1993). Central bank independence and macroeconomic performance: Some comparative evidence. *Journal of Money, Credit, and Banking* 25: 151–162.

Bade, R. and Parkin, M. (1988). Central bank laws and monetary policy. Unpublished. University of Western Ontario.

Bofinger, P. (1992). Discussion. In M.B. Canzoneri, V. Grilli and P.R. Masson (Eds.), *Establishing a central bank: Issues in Europe and lessons from the US*, 77–80. Cambridge: Cambridge University Press.

Cukierman, A. (1992). *Central bank strategy, credibility, and independence*. Cambridge: MIT Press.

Cukierman, A. (1994). Commitment through delegation, political influence and central bank independence. In J.O. de Beaufort Wijnholds, S.C.W. Eijffinger and L.H. Hoogduin (Eds.), *A framework for monetary stability*. Dordrecht: Kluwer Academic Publishers.

Cukierman, A., Edwards, S. and Tabellini, G. (1992). Seigniorage and political instability. *American Economic Review* 82: 537–555.

Debelle, G. (1993). Central bank independence: A free lunch? Mimeo. Department of Economics, MIT. October.

Edwards, S. and Tabellini, G. (1991). Explaining fiscal policies and inflation in developing countries. *Journal of International Money and Finance* 10: 516–540.

Eijffinger, S. and Schaling, E. (1993). Central bank independence in twelve industrial countries. *Banca Nazionale del Lavoro Quarterly Review* 184: 1–41.

De Beaufort Wijnholds, J.O. and Hoogduin, L.H. (1994). Central bank autonomy: Policy issues. In J.O de Beaufort Wijnholds, S.C.W. Eijffinger and L. Hoogduin (Eds.), *A framework for monetary stability*. Dordrecht: Kluwer Academic Publishers.

De Haan, J. and Sturm, J.E. (1992). The case for central bank independence. *Banca Nazionale del Lavoro Quarterly Review* 182: 305–327.

De Haan, J. and Sturm, J.E. (1994). Political and institutional determinants of fiscal, policy in the European Community. *Public Choice* 80: 157–172.

Grilli, V., Masciandaro, D. and Tabellini, G. (1991). Political and monetary institutions and public financial policies in the industrial countries. *Economic Policy* 13: 341–392.

Issing, O. (1993). Central bank independence and monetary stability. *Occasional paper* 89. Institute of Economic Affairs.

Layard, R., Nickel, S. and Jackman, R. (1991). *Unemployment, macroeconomic performance and the labour market*. Oxford: Oxford University Press.

Lohmann, S. (1992). Optimal commitment in monetary policy: Credibility versus flexibility. *American Economic Review* 82: 273–286.

Maddison, A. (1991). *Dynamic forces of capitalist development*. Oxford: Oxford University Press.

Neumann, M.J.M. (1991). Precommitment by central bank independence. *Open Economies Review* 2: 95–112.

Posen, A.S. (1993a). Why central bank independence does not cause low inflation: There is no institutional fix for politics. In R. O'Brien (Ed.), *Finance and the international economy 7*. Oxford: Oxford University Press.

Posen, A.S. (1993b). Central banks and politics. *Amex Bank Review* 20(9): 5.

Data appendix

EU = Equilibrium unemployment for 1980s from Layard, Nickel and Jackman (1991: 436).

AU = Actual unemployment rate from: from the same source.

Debt = Government debt as a percentage of GDP, 1980–89 (except for: Switzerland (80–84), New Zealand (80–88) and Iceland (80–88)). Source: *OECD Economic Outlook*, and IMF, *Government Finance Statistics Yearbook* 1987 and 1991.

Change = Measure of political instability (1980–89). Source: *Keesing's Historic Archives*.

Significant = Measure of political instability (1980–89). Source: *Bank's Handbook of the World*, various issues.

$P_{1900-40}$ = Inflation over the period 1900–1940. Source: Maddison (1991).

Country	EU	AU	Debt ratio	Significant	Changes	$P_{1900-40}$
1. Australia	6.10	7.67	23.8	1	4	1.7
2. Austria	2.95	3.14	42.4	2	3	21.6
3. Belgium	7.04	11.07	101.3	4	8	6.1
4. Canada	8.14	9.48	51.1	2	3	1.5
5. Denmark	7.30	8.56	51.5	1	5	2.5
6. Finland	4.65	5.01	16.6	3	4	6.6
7. France	7.81	8.98	39.8	4	6	5.7
8. Germany	4.04	6.07	38.2	1	4	65.0
9. Greece	na	na	37.5	3	5	na
10. Iceland	na	na	26.1	5	5	na
11. Ireland	13.09	14.12	95.8	5	5	na
12. Italy	5.42	6.87	67.0	6	10	4.9
13. Japan	2.14	2.51	60.9	1	8	3.6
14. Netherlands	7.27	9.89	55.9	3	5	1.1
15. New Zealand	3.91	4.18	59.9	1	3	na
16. Norway	2.50	2.51	43.8	3	5	2.3
17. Portugal	na	na	50.8	4	6	na
18. Spain	14.95	17.74	29.2	1	4	na
19. Sweden	2.36	2.21	58.6	2	4	2.0
20. Switzerland	1.44	1.87	13.1	0	2	1.5
21. U.K.	7.92	10.32	54.1	0	2	1.9
22. U.S.	6.36	7.38	41.3	1	3	1.2

Appendix

Table A1. Testing CBO and UB individually

Dependent variable	Constant	Universal banking (UB)	R^2 (adj)	Number observat.	SEE
LVAU	0.33 (0.05)	−0.14 (0.07)*	−0.14	17	0.15
SUMLV	5.37 (0.67)	−1.21 (1.04)	−0.02	17	2.12
GMTT (adj)	6.40 (0.87)	−1.31 (1.35)	−0.00	17	2.73

Dependent variable	Constant	Central bank oversight (CBO)	R^2 (adj)	Number observat.	SEE
LVAU	0.48 (0.06)	−0.09 (0.05)*	−0.15	17	0.15
SUMLV	6.61 (0.85)	−0.71 (0.64)	0.01	17	2.12
GMTT (adj)	8.10 (1.07)	−1.09 (0.80)	0.05	17	2.65

Table A2. Table 7 excluding Scandinavian countries for which Posen does not provide data (n = 13) as to enable comparison with extended table also including CBO and UB

Dependent variable	Constant	Equilibrium unemployment rate	Government debt ratio	Change	$P_{1900-40}$	R^2 (adj)	Number observat.	SEE
LVAU	0.71	−0.01	−0.00	−0.04**	0.33	0.61	13	0.11
	(0.11)	(0.02)	(0.00)	(0.02)	(0.19)			
SUMLV	8.66	−0.06	−0.00	−0.61	6.55	0.83	13	0.87
	(0.91)	(0.13)	(0.02)	(0.14)**	(1.51)**			
GMTT	12.17	−0.04	−0.02	−0.53	4.98	0.36	13	2.09
	(2.17)	(0.31)	(0.04)	(0.34)	(3.61)			
GMTT (adj)	10.51	0.06	−0.03	−0.41	5.03	0.30	13	2.14
	(2.22)	(0.32)	(0.04)	(0.35)	(3.70)			

Table 7 excluding Scandinavian countries and including CBO and UB as explanatory variables

Dependent variable	Constant	Equilibrium unemployment rate	Government debt ratio	Change	$P_{1900-40}$	CBO	UB	R^2 (adj)	Number observat.	SEE
LVAU	0.65	−0.00	−0.00	−0.02	0.29	−0.07	0.11	0.76	13	0.09
	(0.09)	(0.01)	(0.00)	(0.02)	(0.16)	(0.04)	(0.05)*			
SUMLV	8.71	−0.06	−0.00	−0.60	6.77	−0.06	−0.23	0.78	13	1.00
	(1.06)	(0.16)	(0.02)	(0.20)**	(1.80)**	(0.46)	(0.61)			
GMTT (adj)	10.38	0.02	−0.03	−0.53	3.72	1.26	0.63	0.23	13	2.25
	(2.40)	(0.36)	(0.05)	(0.46)	(4.07)	(1.37)	(1.04)			

Correlationmatrix

	Equilibrium unemploy-ment	Government debt ratio	Change	$P_{1900-40}$	Universal banking (UB)	Central bank oversight (CBO)
Equilibrium unemployment	1.00	0.35	0.01	−0.31	−0.10	0.18
Government debt ratio		1.00	0.66	−0.12	0.11	0.22
Change			1.00	−0.09	−0.02	0.53
$P_{1900-40}$				1.00	0.29	−0.01
Universal banking (UB)					1.00	−0.05
Central bank oversight (CBO)						1.00

[22]

THE WORLD BANK ECONOMIC REVIEW VOL. 9, NO. 3 397–423

Political Influence on the Central Bank: International Evidence

Alex Cukierman and Steven B. Webb

Political influence on the central bank is measured here by looking at the probability that a central bank governor will be replaced shortly after a political change of government. The governor changes about half the time within six months of a nonconstitutional or other radical change of government—a military coup or a restoration of democracy. The governor is much less likely to change within six months following a routine change in the head of government—about one-fourth of the time in developing countries and one-tenth in industrial countries. These indicators vary across countries and correlate statistically with inflation and its variability and with real growth and real interest rates. Differences in the vulnerability of the central bank to political instability, in political instability itself, and in central bank turnover in nonpolitical periods seem to be a major part of the explanation for why developing countries have, on average, higher and more variable inflation than industrial countries do.

Economists and policymakers generally feel that the degree of autonomy of the central bank from political authorities is an important determinant of policy choices and of economic performance. Empirical verification of these presumptions has been difficult, however, because the autonomy of the central bank is not easily quantified. Most previous studies have used legal indexes from central bank charters to quantify the autonomy of the central bank (Parkin 1986; Grilli, Masciandaro, and Tabellini 1991; Alesina and Summers 1993). These measures help account for cross-country inflation differentials within industrial economies but not within developing economies. Low inflation is not associated with the legal independence of central banks in developing countries because of the small degree of association between actual and legal independence among those countries. In industrial countries, the frequency with which a central bank governor is replaced within three months of the time designated by law is more than ten times higher than in other periods. In developing countries it is only 2.2 times higher.

Alex Cukierman is with the Department of Economics at Tel-Aviv University and with the Center for Economic Research at Tilburg University, the Netherlands, and Steven B. Webb is with the Latin America and the Caribbean Country Department III at the World Bank. The authors acknowledge important research assistance by Charles Guo, Pantelis Kalaitzidakis, Bilin Neyapti, Pedro Rodriguez, and Kenneth Xu and assistance by Stephan Haggard and Yasuhito Asami in reviewing the political data in detail. The authors are thankful for the useful comments of several individuals and groups, including Thomas Havrilesky, Suzanne Lohmann, and Sylvia Maxfield. Research for this article was funded by World Bank research grant RPO 677-77.

Hence, more behavioral indexes of independence are called upon. Cukierman, Webb, and Neyapti (1992) and Cukierman (1992) made an initial step in this direction by using the actual average term in office of the governor as a proxy for central bank independence in developing countries. They found a significant negative association between this proxy and inflation across developing countries. The use of this proxy is based on the presumption that below some threshold a shorter term in office of the chief executive officer (to whom we refer as "governor," although the actual title may be president or chairman) of the bank is associated with lower central bank independence. It should be noted, in this context, that actual terms in office in developing countries are substantially lower than in industrial countries. Cukierman (1994) shows theoretically how the expected length of tenure of the central bank governor relates inversely to inflation because of the governor's effective rate of time preference. This article presses the inquiry further by taking account of how turnover of the governor relates to political events.

Although considerable evidence now establishes the negative association between inflation and central bank autonomy, the reduction of political influence on the central bank is not the only institutional device for assuring price stability. Regardless of whether a country has a dependent central bank, the country may still enjoy price stability if it consistently pegs its currency to that of a country with stable prices. Examples include Argentina in recent years, Belgium, the Netherlands, and some francophone African countries. An even stronger commitment to maintain a fixed exchange rate is to use a foreign currency for legal tender, as in Panama. But it should be emphasized that central bank autonomy and various degrees of commitment to a fixed exchange rate are complementary institutional arrangements and are not mutually exclusive. This article focuses on the documentation and the effects of the varying degrees of political influence on the central bank. We and others have investigated the effects of exchange rate commitments elsewhere. Empirical investigations of the effect of exchange rate pegs on inflation appear in Cukierman, Rodriguez, and Webb (forthcoming) and in Anayadike-Danes (1995). Cukierman, Kiguel, and Liviatan (1992) offers a general discussion of dollarization.

A variety of research—theory, case studies, and statistical analysis—shows that political instability worsens macroeconomic policy and outcomes (Edwards and Tabellini 1991; Haggard, Kaufman, and Webb 1992; Haggard and Webb 1994). The effects are strongest on inflation, but other variables such as growth and the real interest rate are also affected. Some macroeconomic deterioration results from the direct effects of political change on policy, particularly fiscal policy. Some also come from the effect on institutions, such as the central bank, and on their ability and incentive to follow policies for the long-run benefit of the economy. So the research agenda includes the question of the relative importance of different channels through which political instability influences economic outcomes, as well as the underlying questions of whether and how political instability affects institutions such as the central bank.

It seems likely that different kinds of political instability would have quite different effects. If political changes reflected changes in basic attitudes toward economic policy or if they were traumatic and irreversible for the politicians involved, then the instability would motivate politicians to control the central bank tightly and keep it at their disposal to help them stay in power. If, however, the political changes were alternations in power of two or three parties that shared a consensus on many basic tenets of economic policy, then the parties might agree to grant the central bank considerable autonomy to pursue price stability, so that the aspect of economic policy on which they agreed would not suffer from the political contests over other issues. These questions motivated the research for this article, although the article does not answer all of them.

This article presents new behavioral indexes of political influence on the central bank. The indexes focus on the propensity of the governor of the bank to lose office following a political transition. The data base and the indexes derived from it were designed to address four specific questions derived from the broader questions in the previous paragraphs.

First, is turnover at the central bank significantly different shortly after political transitions than in other periods? To answer this question, we compare the frequency with which governors are changed in periods shortly after a political transition with that in other periods. We refer to these other periods as "nonpolitical," although recognizing that even then some turnover may result from political influence. Nevertheless, in the presence of heavy political influence we should expect central bank governors to be changed with significantly higher frequency in periods immediately after political transitions, which we call "political periods," than in the nonpolitical periods. The tests presented in the article suggest that this is indeed the case for the entire sample of sixty-seven economies, for the subgroup of developing economies, and, surprisingly, for the industrial economies as well. Given this result, the frequency with which central bank governors are changed in political periods can serve as an index of the extent of political influence over the central bank and thus lead to more refined indicators of central bank autonomy.

Second, for how long does a political transition, after its occurrence, increase the probability of a change of the central bank governor? To answer this question we examine a number of two- or three-month successive intervals following political transitions and calculate the frequency of changes at the central bank within each interval. The frequency of changes is high on average immediately after a political transition and usually decreases as more months go by. The cutoff between political and nonpolitical periods is obtained by considering the last interval within which the frequency of changes at the central bank is significantly higher than the average frequency at the ten-month-or-more lag. The demarcation line between political and nonpolitical periods is then defined as the upper bound of this critical interval. With this procedure, periods within six months of the latest political transition are defined as political in the overall sample, and any period beyond that is nonpolitical.

Third, is the political vulnerability of the central bank systematically related to the level of economic development and the type of political regime? We calculate a measure of the political vulnerability of the central bank and examine its relation with a country's level of development and the nature of its regime (whether it is always democratic, always authoritarian, or mixed). Vulnerability of the central bank is defined as the fraction of political transitions that are followed, within the subsequent political periods, by a replacement of the governor of the bank.

Frequent removal from office of the bank's governor following political transitions probably reflects gross political influence, because the governor's term in office is not shielded by law or custom from political changes. This type of influence has been common in developing economies, such as Botswana, China, Costa Rica, and Indonesia, and has been particularly high in countries that switch between democratic and authoritarian regimes, such as Brazil, Chile, India, the Republic of Korea, Nicaragua, Peru, and Uruguay. In Argentina before the 1990s, even though the law specified a four-year term, the governor was always replaced when the government changed. Among industrial economies gross political influence on the central bank is rare—Sweden appears to be an exception—but more subtle and mild influences are common. For instance, in the United States, the index of central bank vulnerability is zero, implying the absence of gross political influence. But, as documented in Havrilesky (1992), there are several other, milder, channels of political influence on the Federal Reserve.

Fourth, is the political vulnerability of the central bank systematically related to measures of economic performance such as inflation, growth, and interest rates? Cross-sectional and panel-data regressions provide evidence on this question.

The article is organized as follows. Section I presents the data set and discusses the conventions used to organize it. The procedure for distinguishing between political and nonpolitical changes of central bank governors is developed and applied in section II to the entire sample as well as to broad subgroups of countries. Section III discusses indexes of central bank political vulnerability for broad subgroups of countries and investigates the effect of different types of political transitions on central bank vulnerability. The effects of vulnerability and of nonpolitical turnover on inflation, growth, and real rates are briefly examined in section IV. Section V estimates empirically how much of the strong cross-sectional association between inflation and its variance is due to their common association with central bank vulnerability and nonpolitical turnover. Section VI follows with concluding remarks.

I. The Data

To assess and quantify the degree of political influence on the central bank, we have put together a multicountry data set on political and central bank instability. Political instability is measured by counting political transitions of various types. Instability at the central bank is measured with data on the frequency and timing of replacement of central bank governors. The research focuses on variables that were available for a large number of countries on a uniform basis.

The sample consists of sixty-seven economies with matched data on political and central bank instability. The economies are listed in table A-1. The sample includes all the major industrial and developing economies, but excludes most Eastern European economies. The data cover 1950–89, where possible, but start later for economies that achieved political independence or established a central bank after 1950. The data are divided into two subperiods: 1950–71, corresponding to the Bretton Woods era, and 1972–89. In each subperiod as well as in the total period, an economy is included only if data are available for at least ten years because data for shorter periods would often be unrepresentative.

Political Transitions

Instability of the executive branch of government seems most relevant for central bank autonomy. Consequently, we selected four types of political change as indicators of political instability: change of the head of government, change of the party in government, change of the fundamental rules of government as embodied in switches from authoritarian to democratic regimes or vice versa, and irregular changes of government from one authoritarian ruler to another. These types of changes form a hierarchy, so that each political event is coded as a level of instability: a change of the head of government without a change of party (low instability); a nonviolent change of party without a change of type of government (medium instability); an irregular change of authoritarian government without a change of form of government—a coup—(type 2 authoritarian); or a change of the form of government between democratic and authoritarian—a coup against a democratic government or a restoration of democracy—(high instability).[1]

Our previous research indicated that the autonomy of the central bank differed markedly between industrial and developing countries (Cukierman, Webb, and Neyapti 1992). Here we examine whether this distinction is also important for the effects of political instability on the central bank. Within each economic group, countries are divided into subgroups with democratic regimes for the whole period, with authoritarian regimes throughout, and with regimes that alternate between democratic and authoritarian. We classified as democratic only the countries and periods in which the head of government was chosen as a result of competitive elections. All others were classified as authoritarian, covering a variety of systems in which the government did not face serious pressure from electoral politics. The classifications thus differ somewhat from what one would

1. Data come from and were checked against several sources. The most comprehensive single source, and usually the initial one, is *The Europa World Yearbook*. Changes of only the economic team (not necessarily including the central bank) are also events that may be relevant for assessing central bank autonomy. To investigate the relevance of these events, we have begun collecting data on changes of the Minister of Finance or Treasury. These data are less readily available than information on changes of the head of government, and we do not yet have information on a broad enough sample to report the results.

code as the degree of political liberty, such as with Gastil's indexes. We chose to exclude from our data political events that challenged and perhaps threatened to change a government but did not do so—strikes, riots, attempted coups, and elections in which the previous government was reelected. To assess the implications for an institution such as the central bank, it seemed better to focus on institutionally well-defined events that actually changed the government to which the bank reported.

Changes at the Central Bank

The raw data on instability at the central bank consist of the actual dates of changes of the governors of the central banks in our sample of countries. The turnover of governors is only an imperfect indicator of actual central bank independence in developing countries (for more discussion of this proxy, see Cukierman, Webb, and Neyapti 1992; Cukierman 1992; and Cukierman and others 1993). Low turnover does not always imply a high level of central bank independence—relatively subservient governors may stay in office longer precisely because they do not stand up to the executive branch. This may be true for countries with exceptionally low turnover rates such as Denmark, Iceland, and the United Kingdom and for countries with stable authoritarian governments. In such countries, low turnover is probably unrelated to independence. Above some threshold turnover rate, however, higher turnover of the governor reflects lower central bank independence.

Sufficiently high turnover rates make the tenure of the central bank governor shorter than that of the executive branch and thus make the governor more susceptible to influence by the executive branch and more discouraged from trying to implement longer-term policies. Because the electoral cycle is at least four years in most countries, the threshold turnover rate is probably between 0.2 and 0.25 (implying a governor's tenure of four to five years). In addition, governors with very short terms of office, such as three years or less, generally have more difficulty in implementing long-term policies (for example, the maintenance of price stability) for any electoral cycle. One limitation of the turnover variable is that all the industrial countries have turnover rates at or below the threshold rate in the years we examine. Turnover rates in developing countries, however, span a range that goes well above the threshold point.

The measures of political influence on the central bank developed here consider the links between political instability and subsequent turnover at the central bank and hence appear to be relevant for both industrial and developing economies. They also make it possible to distinguish between the frequencies of changes at the central bank in political periods, as defined earlier, and in nonpolitical periods. A relatively high frequency of turnover in the political periods indicates substantial influence of political instability on the central bank. A relatively high level of turnover the rest of the time most likely indicates that the central bank is more dependent even in politically tranquil times.

II. Political Change and the Timing of Central Bank Turnover

To what extent does political instability translate into instability at the central bank? Are there systematic differences in central bank turnover between periods immediately following a political change and nonpolitical periods? If there are differences, how does their magnitude vary with country characteristics? To answer these questions, this section measures political instability by the frequency of political transitions, as defined in section I, and instability at the central bank by the turnover of the governors.

Before attempting to give precise answers to these questions, it is instructive to take a broad look at the data. Table 1 presents central bank turnover figures (measured as the number of changes of central bank governor per month) for various intervals following a political transition. Thus, the average frequency of changes of governor within one month following a political transition is 0.063 per month; within two to three months it is 0.026, and it is only 0.015 at ten months or more after a political transition.[2] These numbers correspond to governors' average terms of office of 1.3, 3.2, and 5.6 years, respectively.[3]

The numbers in table 1 can be interpreted as estimates of the probability per month of a change in central bank governor conditional on being within a time interval, i, that follows a political transition by i to $i+2$ (or by i to $i+3$) months.[4]

Table 1. *Frequency of Change of Central Bank Governor at Various Intervals by Economy Group, 1950–89*
(number of changes per month)

Economy group	Number of economies	*Interval (number of months since a political transition)* 0–1	2–3	4–6	7–9	10 or more
All	67	0.063	0.026	0.025	0.013	0.015
Industrial						
All 20	24	0.008	0.013	0.013	0.003	0.009
Democratic only	18	0.020	0.009	0.015	0.002	0.009
Mixed	2	0.060	0.000	0.000	0.024	0.013
Developing						
All	47	0.096	0.041	0.034	0.022	0.018
Democratic only	9	0.046	0.016	0.065	0.011	0.025
Authoritarian only	16	0.089	0.017	0.006	0.025	0.015
Mixed	22	0.105	0.053	0.038	0.023	0.019

Source: Authors' calculations.

2. When a change in central bank governor occurs within a short time after two or more previous political transitions, the central bank change is attributed only to the most recent political transition.

3. In other words, let x be a turnover number from table 1; then, the corresponding average term in office, in years, is given by $1/12x$.

4. This interpretation requires the probability of two or more changes within a subperiod to be negligible. Because the time intervals considered are only two or three months, this assumption is supported by the data.

Table 1 reveals that, for the entire sample of economies, this probability decreases monotonically with the number of months that have elapsed since the last political transition. It is almost three times larger in the zero-to-one-month interval than in the two-to-six-month intervals. For seven-month intervals and beyond, this probability drops further—to about 60 percent of its value in the two-to-six-month intervals.

Central bank changes within one month of a political transition are highly likely to result directly from the political change, but central bank changes more than nine months after a political transition are unlikely to be the result of a change in government and are more likely to be largely nonpolitical. The challenge is to find the average elapsed time across countries, presumably between one and nine months, at which to set the cutoff between political and nonpolitical periods. We take the probability of turnover long after a political change (ten months or more) as a background rate against which to compare months in the intermediate range. The political period would then be defined to include months at intervals (after a political change) for which the average rate of central bank turnover is significantly higher than the background rate.

The appendix describes the tests for differences between the probability of a change of central bank governor ten or more months after a political change and the probability in each of the intervals with shorter lags, using the normal approximation to the binomial distribution. It shows that for the whole sample the probability of a turnover at the central bank is significantly larger in the zero-to-one-month, two-to-three-month, and four-to-six-month intervals than in the ten-month-and-more interval. The average probability of a change of central bank governor during the seven-to-nine-month interval following a political change does not differ significantly from the probability in the ten-or-more lag period. Hence, the evidence in the appendix supports a choice of six months following a political transition as the cutoff between political and nonpolitical periods in the overall sample.

In summary, for the entire sample of economies, the evidence supports the view that instability at the central bank rises in periods following political transitions and that this increase is significant. The estimated probability of a change of governor at the central bank is more than two times larger in periods within six months after a political transition than in periods that are more removed from political change. Thus, political instability increases instability at the central bank and weakens its independence from political authorities.

The profile of estimated probabilities of a change at the central bank varies between industrial and developing economies and between economies with different political regimes. We distinguish three types of political regimes: stable democracies, stable authoritarian regimes, and mixed regimes (those alternating between democratic and authoritarian regimes). Most industrial economies are stable democracies, none are authoritarian-only for the period under investigation, and only two (Spain and France) are mixed regimes. Developing economies include all three political regimes—democratic only, authoritarian only, and mixed.

Table 1 also presents the estimated probability of a change of central bank governor at various intervals following a political transition for the different subgroups of economies. The probability of central bank turnover is higher in developing economies than in industrial countries at all intervals . The frequency declines monotonically for developing economies but has two peaks for industrial economies—one in the zero-to-one-month interval and a lower peak in the four-to-six-month interval. The tests reported in the appendix reveal that for developing economies the appropriate cutoff between political and nonpolitical periods is at six months as in the overall sample, and there is clear evidence of a link between political instability and instability at the central bank.

The average frequencies of central bank turnover within the three political subgroups of developing economies are summarized in the lower part of table 1. In the authoritarian and mixed subgroups, the two largest, the frequency in the zero-to-one-month interval is substantially higher than in the subsequent intervals. Statistical tests reveal that in all three cases the difference in frequencies between the zero-to-one-month interval and the ten-month-or-more interval is significant. Comparing the three subgroups, the average frequency of central bank instability in the zero-to-one-month and the two-to-three-month intervals is highest on average in the countries with mixed regimes, second highest in authoritarian-only countries, and lowest in democratic-only countries.

The evidence is less dramatic for industrial economies, but still supports the view that in those countries the average frequency of central bank changes in the zero-to-one-month interval after a political change is significantly higher than the background frequency in the ten-month-or-more interval. The frequencies in the two-to-three-month, four-to-six-month, and seven-to-nine-month intervals are not significantly different from the frequency for the ten-month-or-more lag. Thus, for industrial economies as a subgroup we locate the cutoff between political and nonpolitical periods after the zero-to-one-month interval. We present most of the results in the rest of the article for both the zero-to-one-month and zero-to-six-month cutoffs.

The tendency of mixed regimes to have higher frequencies of central bank changes than democracies in the zero-to-one-month interval also appears within the industrial countries, although this finding is based only on the experience of France and Spain. Also, as was the case for industrial democracies, there is a second peak in the four-to-six-month interval for democratic-only developing economies.

III. Political Vulnerability of Central Banks

Computing the frequency of central bank turnover in intervals at various lags from political changes was important for assessing the size and duration of the effect of political changes on the propensity for central bank turnover. For a summary measure of political influence, however, we compute an index of the political vulnerability of the central bank, defined for each country as the fraction of political transitions that are followed promptly by a replacement of the central bank governor:

$$V(i) \equiv \frac{\text{Number of replacements of the central bank governor within } i \text{ months following a political transition}}{\text{Number of political transitions}}, \quad i = 1, 6.$$

Table 2 reports average values of the index of central bank political vulnerability for industrial and developing economies as well as for democratic, authoritarian, and mixed regimes within each group. The overall average value of vulnerability is 0.24. That is, almost a quarter of all political transitions are followed by a replacement of the central bank governor within six months. As with the frequency of turnover, the vulnerability varies widely across country groups and subgroups. Political vulnerability is more than three times larger in developing economies than in industrial ones. A similar picture (not shown) emerges when the sample is broken into two subperiods (1950–71 and 1972–89). Central banks of developing economies with mixed regimes are the most vulnerable on average.

Table A-1 in the appendix presents the vulnerability of central banks to all types of political transitions for individual economies by subgroups. For economies with a small number of political transitions in a subperiod, the vulnerability ratios are highly sensitive to the effect of a truly nonpolitical central bank

Table 2. *Political Vulnerability of Central Banks by Economy Group, 1950–89*

Economy group	Vulnerability[a] Within six months	Vulnerability[a] Within one month	Frequency of political change (per year)
All	0.24	0.12	0.27
Industrial	0.10	0.05	0.32
Developing	0.35	0.18	0.24
Industrial			
Democratic only	0.10	0.04	0.32
Mixed	0.12	0.12	0.33
Developing			
Authoritarian only	0.22	0.17	0.14
Democratic only	0.30	0.09	0.18
Mixed	0.39	0.20	0.30

a. Average share of political transitions followed by a replacement of the central bank governor within the noted period.

Source: Authors' calculations.

change accidentally happening after a political change.[5] Although vulnerability numbers for individual economies in such cases should be viewed cautiously, they are still useful for the overall statistical analysis. Within each subgroup, central banks are arranged in descending order of their political vulnerability in 1972–89. By this measure, Sweden has the most politically vulnerable central bank among industrial democracies in that subperiod. Among democratic-only developing economies, the central bank of Botswana is the most vulnerable. Among developing economies with mixed regimes, the Argentine central bank is the most vulnerable, with sometimes more than one change of governor in the first six months after a political change.[6]

The last column of table 2 reports the average frequency of political transitions per year for each country group. Industrial economies have political transitions more frequently than developing economies, because they have much more frequent democratic changes of government, with and without party changes. Within developing economies, the subgroup with mixed regimes has a frequency of political transitions that is about twice that of either democratic-only or authoritarian-only regimes. Authoritarian-only regimes have the lowest number of political changes of any type.

We now have four indicators of central bank autonomy: the two developed in Cukierman, Webb, and Neyapti (1992)—the index of legal autonomy and the (total) turnover rate of the governor—plus vulnerability and its complement, the frequency of nonpolitical turnover of the governor. Of course the latter two can be reaggregated into the total turnover rate by making appropriate adjustments of units and multiplying vulnerability by the frequency of political transitions in each country. How different are these four measures? Table 3 shows the matrix of correlation coefficients for the four measures and the frequency of political turnover. Most of the various indicators are not closely correlated to one another, although total turnover is closely correlated with its two derivatives. The frequency of political transitions, an indicator of vibrant democracy or of more-fundamental political instability, is not significantly correlated with the various central bank variables.

How is the political vulnerability of the central bank affected by the type of political instability in a country? To answer this question, we regressed the indexes of central bank vulnerability at lags of zero to one month and zero to six months on various types of political transitions, on a dummy for developing countries, and on a dummy for purely authoritarian regimes. Table 4 summarizes the results. With the vulnerability index for the lag of zero to six months,

5. This has been the case at least once in Jamaica and once in the Netherlands. In the Netherlands the decision to replace the governor in 1967 was made prior to the adjoining political transition, but was inplemented after it (de Haan 1995). Thus, vulnerability is a noisy measure of political influence whose quality rises with the number of political transitions in a country.

6. In the 1990s, Argentina has vastly increased its commitment to price stability by upgrading the autonomy of its central monetary institution and by endowing it with the authority to function as a currency board.

Table 3. *Correlation between Various Indicators of Central Bank Autonomy, 1950–89*

Indicator	*Index of legal central bank autonomy*	*Total central bank turnover*	*Vulnerability*	*Frequency of political change*
Total central bank turnover	–0.05			
Vulnerability (six months)	–0.11	0.78		
Frequency of political transitions	–0.05	0.06	–0.11	
Nonpolitical central bank turnover	–0.02	0.88	0.60	–0.21

Source: Authors' calculations.

the developing-country dummy has a significant positive impact on central bank vulnerability. But none of the indicators of political change had a statistically significant effect on vulnerability. Low- and medium-level changes clearly have no effect, which is consistent with the ambiguous theoretical priors. For high-level political change, the coefficient has a positive sign, as expected, but is not quite significant, although it was with some earlier versions of the sample.

The vulnerability of central banks to political influence depends on the type of political transition. Table 5 reports the indexes of political vulnerability by

Table 4. *The Impact of Political Change on Central Bank Vulnerability, 1950–89*

Explanatory variable	*Estimates* For lag of 0–1 month	*Estimates* For lag of 0–6 months
Constant	0.09	0.16**
	(1.61)	(2.16)
High-level political change	0.73	0.96
	(1.46)	(1.44)
Type-2 authoritarian transitions	–0.16	–0.47
	(–0.29)	(–0.65)
Medium-level political change	–0.15	–0.22
	(–0.92)	(–1.01)
Low-level political change	–0.09	–0.19
	(–0.52)	(–0.78)
Dummy for purely authoritarian regimes	0.04	–0.08
	(0.55)	(–0.79)
Dummy for developing countries	0.09	0.24***
	(1.48)	(2.96)
Number of observations	110	110
Adjusted R^2	0.059	0.143

** Significant at the 5 percent level

*** Significant at the 1 percent level.

Note: The estimated equation is a pooled cross–sectional time–series regression in which there are two observations for each country, one for 1950–71 (where available) and one for 1972–89. The dependent variable is central bank vulnerability. *t*-statistics are in parentheses.

Source: Authors' calculations.

type of political transition for different economy groupings. The fraction 0.61 at the intersection of the mixed developing-economy row with the "high-level" column means that 61 percent of high-level political transitions in developing economies are followed within six months by a replacement of the central bank governor. The other numbers in the table are defined in a similar manner. There is generally little difference between the vulnerability to medium-level and to low-level political transitions within each country group. The vulnerability to medium- and low-level political transitions is more than twice as high in developing economies as it is in industrial ones. Furthermore, this difference seems to be due to a difference in the level of development, rather than to differences in regimes, because in democratic developing economies vulnerability to medium- and low-level political transitions is more than twice as large as that of industrial democracies. The vulnerability to these types of political transitions in mixed-regime developing economies is of the same order of magnitude as the vulnerability in democratic developing economies.

The highest level of central bank vulnerability occurs in the face of high-level political transitions, which are all in developing economies (with mixed regimes, by definition). For developing economies as a whole, central bank vulnerability to type-2 authoritarian transitions (0.46) is larger than vulnerability to medium- and low-level transitions by a factor of almost two. The 0.46 figure, however, masks quite different tendencies in authoritarian-only regimes, which have an average vulnerability of 0.20, and in mixed regimes, where type-2 authoritarian transitions lead to an average vulnerability of 0.55.

Table 5. *Central Bank Vulnerability (within Six Months) by Type of Political Transition and Economy Group*

Economy group	*Type of political transition*			
	High level[a]	*Type-2 authoritarian*[b]	*Medium level*[c]	*Low level*[d]
All	0.58	0.46	0.15	0.19
Industrial	0.00	n.a.	0.11	0.08
Developing	0.61	0.46	0.24	0.26
Industrial				
Democratic	n.a.	n.a.	0.11	0.08
Mixed	0.00	n.a.	0.12	0.17
Developing				
Authoritarian only	n.a.	0.20	n.a.	0.23
Democratic only	n.a.	n.a.	0.24	0.25
Mixed	0.61	0.55	0.24	0.28

n.a. Not applicable, because there were no political transitions of that type for that category of country.

a. Change of regime, from democratic to authoritarian or vice versa.

b. Replacement of one authoritarian regime by another one.

c. Change of party without a change in regime.

d. Change of head of government without a change in regime or party.

Source: Authors' calculations.

Table 6. *Estimates for Central Bank Vulnerability and Inflation, 1950–89*

	Estimation with six-month vulnerability index		*Estimation with one-month vulnerability index*	
Explanatory variable	*Dependent variable is transformed inflation, D*	*Dependent variable is standard deviation of D*	*Dependent variable is transformed inflation, D*	*Dependent variable is standard deviation of D*
Constant	0.046*	0.019	0.054**	0.020
	(1.73)	(1.28)	(2.16)	(1.53)
Vulnerability	—	—	0.164***	0.106***
(lag 0–1 months)			(3.95)	(4.79)
Vulnerability	0.092***	0.070***	—	—
(lag 0–6 months)	(2.89)	(4.02)		
Nonpolitical turnover	—	—	0.158**	0.108***
(lag over 1 month)			(2.12)	(2.73)
Nonpolitical turnover	0.239***	0.108**	—	—
(lag over 6 months)	(2.60)	(2.14)		
High-level	0.312	0.237**	0.208	0.193*
political change	(1.50)	(2.08)	(1.04)	(1.83)
Type-2 authoritarian	0.308	0.190	0.268	0.167
transitions	(1.38)	(1.56)	(1.24)	(1.45)
Medium-level	0.044	0.010	0.029	0.003
political change	(0.65)	(0.27)	(0.44)	(0.09)
Low-level	0.126*	0.041	0.109	0.028
political change	(1.72)	(1.02)	(1.53)	(0.74)
Dummy	0.030	0.023	0.016	0.017
authoritarian only	(0.98)	(1.37)	(0.52)	(1.08)
Dummy first period	−0.087***	−0.021**	−0.083***	−0.019*
(1950–1971)	(−4.53)	(−2.02)	(−4.44)	(−1.95)
Dummy	−0.007	−0.005	0.006	−0.001
developing countries	(−0.26)	(−0.32)	(0.22)	(−0.10)
Number of observations	110	110	110	110
Adjusted R^2	0.34	0.34	0.37	0.41

—Not available.
* Significant at 10 percent level.
** Significant at 5 percent level.
*** Significant at 1 percent level.
Note: t-statistics are in parentheses.
Source: Authors' calculations.

IV. Effects of Central Bank Vulnerability on the Economy

Besides being of independent interest, measures of central bank autonomy are useful for testing the effect of this autonomy, or its absence, on the economy. Such a project is largely beyond the scope of this article. Nevertheless, this section and the next briefly report evidence on the relation between some of our measures and the performance of the economy as reflected by inflation, real growth, and real interest rates.

Each of these variables is regressed in a pooled cross-sectional time series on central bank vulnerability, on nonpolitical turnover, and on other control variables. Nonpolitical turnover is measured as the average number of nonpolitical changes of central bank governor (more than one month or more than six months after the latest political transition) per year.

Inflation

Previous work has shown a significant positive relationship between inflation or the rate of depreciation in the real value of money (*D*) and the (total) turnover of central bank governors for developing economies (Cukierman, Webb, and Neyapti 1992: tab. 7; Cukierman 1992: tab. 20.2).[7] Table 6 here extends the effort by relating *D* and its standard deviation to the index of vulnerability, nonpolitical turnover, various types of political instability, and three dummies: one for the Bretton Woods era, one for having only authoritarian regimes in the period, and one for being a developing country. This formulation makes it possible to evaluate the relative importance of lack of central bank autonomy and of political instability for the creation of inflation. Table 6 shows results with the zero-to-one-month and zero-to-six-month measures of vulnerability, and the results are very similar for the two different measures. The regressions in table 6 back the view that the first channel is more important.

The political vulnerability of the central bank as well as nonpolitical turnover at the bank have a positive and significant impact on inflation (*D*) and its variability. Political instability, particularly of the high-level sort, contributes to increased inflation variability. Low-level political instability has a marginally significant effect in raising the level of inflation. Medium-level political instability—alternation between parties (in a democracy)—has essentially zero effect on inflation, probably because frequent transitions of this sort require fundamental consensus on policy issues. Also, worldwide inflation is lower during the Bretton Woods period, even after allowing for the effect of other variables. This is consistent with the view that fixed exchange rates have a stronger disciplinary effect on policy than flexible rates do. But the higher worldwide inflation after 1972 may also be the result of the larger shocks that affected the world economy in the post–Bretton Woods period. The insignificant authoritarian-only dummy means that having an authoritarian rather than a democratic

7. $D = \pi/(1 + \pi)$, where π is the annual inflation rate.

regime throughout does not help to explain differences in average inflation, once the central bank and political variables are taken into account. A dummy is not needed for mixed-regime countries, because the variable for high-level political changes is nonzero only in mixed-regime countries.

The most important result in table 6 is the insignificance of the dummy variable for developing economies. Inflation is significantly higher on average in developing economies, and this could not have been accounted for by just looking at the overall frequency of turnover at the central bank (Cukierman, Webb, and Neyapti 1992). Once turnover is disaggregated into its constituent parts, however, and account is taken of the different types of political instability, the distinction between developing and industrial economies no longer contributes to explaining differences in inflation outcomes. In other words, the differences in vulnerability of the central bank to political instability, in central bank turnover in nonpolitical periods, and in political instability can fully account for the developing economies having higher average inflation than industrial economies.

Growth

Recent empirical literature on growth has identified several variables, such as initial gross domestic product (GDP) and education, that are significantly related to real growth (see Barro 1991, for example). Does the degree of anti-inflation commitment by the monetary authorities, for which our indexes of central bank autonomy are a proxy, have any significant impact on growth after controlling for these variables? Table 7 answers this question by presenting growth equations that take account of initial GDP, initial primary and secondary education enrollment ratios, a decade-by-decade change in terms of trade, and our indexes of central bank autonomy. With a full sample of countries, nonpolitical turnover of central bank governors has a marginally significant positive sign, contrary to priors. Brazil, Korea, and Botswana are outliers, however, because they achieved high growth despite high rates of central bank turnover and high vulnerability. With those countries excluded, the six-month vulnerability indicator has a significantly negative sign.[8] This finding supports the view that, other things being equal, higher political dependence of the central bank tends to retard growth in most countries. It is possible that political vulnerability of the central bank is a proxy for general economic and political instability, both of which deter growth, possibly by slowing down investment and innovation. There is some evidence that in developing countries, higher central bank vulnerability is associated with lower levels of investment (Cukierman and others 1993). Sorting out the channels through which political vulnerability of the central bank affects growth clearly deserves further work.

8. Botswana could legitimately be discarded from the sample, because its growth was primarily due to the discovery of diamonds, not to good macroeconomic policy. Brazil and Korea seem to be simply countries where lack of central bank autonomy was not a hindrance to growth, at least not in the period covered here. Further justification for the exclusion of these countries appears in Cukierman and others (1993).

Table 7. *The Impact of Central Bank Vulnerability and Nonpolitical Turnover on Economic Growth, 1960–88*

	Estimate	
Explanatory variable	*Full sample*	*Sample minus three*[a]
Constant	–0.15	0.73
	(–0.15)	(0.77)
Initial GDP	–0.22**	–0.25***
	(–2.46)	(–2.83)
Change in terms of trade	28.9***	28.1***
	(4.87)	(5.01)
Initial primary education enrollment ratio	2.03**	2.53***
	(1.98)	(2.55)
Initial secondary education enrollment ratio	1.59	1.34
	(1.22)	(1.04)
Nonpolitical turnover of central bank governors	5.80*	–2.39
	(1.80)	(–0.66)
Political vulnerability of central bank	–0.78	–1.51**
	(–1.15)	(–2.30)
Dummy for the 1960s	1.69***	1.42***
	(3.01)	(2.61)
Dummy for the 1970s	1.39***	1.11**
	(2.74)	(2.26)
Number of observations	129	120
Adjusted R^2	0.23	0.26

* Significant at the 10 percent level.
** Significant at the 5 percent level.
*** Significant at the 1 percent level.

Note: The sample consists of, at most, three observations (one for each decade) for each country. The estimated equation is a pooled cross-sectional time-series regression. The dependent variable is real per capita GDP growth. Central bank vulnerability is characterized in terms of changes in central bank governors that occur within six months of a political transition. *t*-statistics are in parentheses.

a. Botswana, Brazil, and the Republic of Korea are excluded.

Source: Authors' calculations.

Real Interest Rates on Deposits

Previous evidence (Alesina and Summers 1993; Cukierman and others 1993) suggests there is a negative relation between the variability of ex post real interest rates and central bank independence. In our work, we have used as proxies for central bank independence the bank's legal independence for industrial economies and the bank's turnover of governors for developing economies. We now reexamine the relation between central bank independence and real interest rates by using central bank vulnerability and nonpolitical turnover as proxies for a lack of central bank independence. The second column of table 8 presents the effect on the variability of real rates. It appears that both central bank vulnerability and nonpolitical turnover significantly increase the variability of ex post real deposit rates. This further supports and amplifies the conclusion that the variability of ex post real deposit rates is lower in countries with more independent central banks. Although it has the expected negative sign, the coefficient on legal independence is not significant.

Table 8. *The Impact of Alternative Measures of Central Bank Autonomy on the Ex Post Real Deposit Rate*

	Estimate	
Explanatory variable	*Dependent variable is real ex post deposit rate, R*	*Dependent variable is standard deviation of R*
Constant	1.98	1.04
	(0.64)	(0.3)
Vulnerability	−5.56*	8.68**
(lag 0–6 months)	(−1.89)	(2.1)
Nonpolitical turnover	−1.98	36.24***
(lag more than 6 months)	(−0.15)	(3.0)
Legal independence	−3.26	−5.60
of central bank	(−0.48)	(−0.7)
Number of observations	34	34
Adjusted R^2	0.05	0.52

* Significant at the 10 percent level.
** Significant at the 5 percent level.
*** Significant at the 1 percent level.
Note: t-statistics are in parentheses.
Source: Authors' calculations based on data from Easterly, Rodriguez, and Schmidt-Hebbel (1992), Cukierman, Webb, and Neyapti (1992), and Cukierman (1992: ch. 19).

The first column in table 8 relates the average level of the ex post real deposit rate to measures of central bank independence. The higher the political vulnerability of the central bank, the lower the average real deposit rate, which corroborates a similar finding in Cukierman and others (1993). The effect of lowering the real deposit rate probably reflects the higher implicit taxation of financial savings in countries with more politically dependent central banks.

V. Central Bank Independence and the Mean and the Variability of Inflation

The strong cross-country association between the mean and the variability of inflation is a well-known empirical regularity. When legal independence and the total turnover of central bank governors are used as proxies for central bank independence, up to a quarter of this association is accounted for by their common association with central bank independence (Cukierman 1992: ch. 18, 22). For this article, the same experiment was repeated with central bank vulnerability and nonpolitical turnover as indexes of central bank autonomy. Legal independence was added as a regressor in industrial economies. To calculate the fraction of the correlation between the mean and the standard deviation of inflation that results from their common association with central bank independence, we proceeded as follows. First, the cross-sectional covariance between D (the rate of depreciation in the real value of money) and its standard deviation was calculated. Second, both D and its standard deviation were regressed on central bank vulnerability, nonpolitical turnover, and (for industrial economies) legal independence. The predicted values of D and of its standard deviation were also calculated. Third, the covariance between those predicted values was calculated and compared with the overall covariance between D and its standard deviation.

The experiment was done for the entire 1950–89 period and for the subperiods 1950–71 and 1972–89. The fractions of the covariability between D and its standard deviation that are the result of their mutual link to central bank independence are 0.30 for the whole period and 0.40 and 0.31 for the two subperiods. Thus, with the more refined measures of central bank autonomy presented in this article, about one-third of the association between inflation and its variability is attributable to their common association with central bank independence.

VI. Concluding Remarks

Stability and other characteristics of government institutions have always been recognized in economic history and in country studies as crucial determinants of macroeconomic stability. Recently this recognition has spread to theoretical work on macroeconomics and has been the focus of some cross-country statistical analysis (Fischer 1991; Edwards and Tabellini 1991; Cukierman, Edwards, and Tabellini 1992; Alesina and others 1995; Haggard, Kaufman, and Webb 1992). A survey appears in Alesina and Perotti (1994). As one would expect, political instability is positively related to inflation and negatively related to growth. There are various theories for how political instability causes macroeconomic instability, most of them not mutually exclusive. One contender is that political instability shortens time horizons of policymakers and that it decreases the ability of the political system to efficiently resolve disputes over real incomes.

This article has demonstrated that political instability causes instability at the central bank as well. But the spillover from political instability to instability at the central bank varies across country groups and types of political transitions. It is particularly large when the political regime changes from democratic to authoritarian or vice versa. This finding supports the view that when political change is deep enough to involve fundamental rules of the game and in other circumstances where political change would probably mean the party in power would not be back soon, if ever, then the expected effect of greater political instability would be shortened time horizons, as discussed above, and therefore less autonomy and stability for the central bank. Each new government would want to use the central bank to try to stay in power as long as possible and would have little concern for the associated detrimental longer-run effects. However, greater frequency of low- and medium-level political change, such as just changing the head of government or the party, does not on average lead to reduced central bank autonomy as proxied by its political vulnerability. Actually, in democratic governments in which the party changes frequently, the ruling party might typically lack the strength to impose its will unilaterally and might thus agree to a compromise that would endure changes of party. This was explicit in the setup of the reformed Chilean central bank in 1989 (Arriagada and Graham 1994). An analysis of the effect of political instability on central bank independence in countries with democratic and stable rules of the political process appears in Cukierman (1994).

An important issue for future work is the possibility of reverse causality between the performance of the economy and our measures of gross political influence on the central bank. The largely cross-sectional nature of the variables in this article precludes the use of Granger-Sims and other methods to test the exogeneity of our measures of political instability with respect to the performance of the economy. Hence, strictly speaking, it is possible that some of the significant relationships between these two groups of variables are due to causality running from the economy to political influence. This is probably less likely to be the case for real interest rates than for real growth. There is evidence that real growth is affected by political instability (Barro 1991; Alesina and others 1995) which may, in turn, cause instability at the central bank.

The measure of central bank vulnerability, however, is more likely to be exogenous with respect to the economy than other behavioral indexes of political influence on the central bank. Even if political instability responds to the performance of the economy, vulnerability—defined as the ratio between instability at the central bank and political instability—depends on slowly changing institutions and sociopolitical norms, and thus may be largely exogenous to the current economic performance.

Because the main contribution of this article is in the extraction of empirical regularities by matching two new data sets, our approach has been inductive rather than deductive. We deliberately avoided committing to and testing a particular model because we believe that at this early stage the broad regularities in the data can be uncovered more efficiently without positing a particular model. Our hope is that the regularities uncovered here will encourage the construction of more precise models and further empirical testing of hypotheses.

Table A-1. *Political Vulnerability of Central Banks for Individual Economies by Subgroup, 1950–71 and 1972–89*

	1950–71				1972–89			
	Vulnerability (within six months)	Number of political transitions	Number of central bank turnovers		Vulnerability (within six months)	Number of political transitions	Number of central bank turnovers	
Economy			Total	Nonpolitical[a]			Total	Nonpolitical[a]
Industrial, democratic								
Sweden	0.000	1	2	2	0.500	4	4	2
Ireland	0.000	5	3	3	0.286	7	3	1
Japan	0.200	5	4	3	0.222	9	4	2
Belgium	0.000	9	2	2	0.167	6	3	2
Switzerland	0.059	17	2	1	0.167	18	3	0
Finland	0.105	19	3	1	0.125	8	2	1
Italy	0.071	14	1	0	0.077	13	2	1
Australia	0.333	3	1	0	0.000	3	3	3
Austria	0.000	4	3	3	0.000	2	3	3
Canada	0.000	3	2	2	0.000	4	2	2
Denmark	0.143	7	2	1	0.000	4	0	0
Germany, Fed. Rep.	0.333	3	2	1	0.000	2	2	2
United Kingdom	0.000	6	2	2	0.000	3	2	2
Iceland	0.000	3	1	1	0.000	7	0	0
Netherlands	0.143	7	1	0	0.000	3	1	1
New Zealand	0.250	4	2	1	0.000	5	4	4
Norway	0.000	6	2	2	0.000	7	1	1
United States	0.000	4	2	2	0.000	4	3	3
Industrial, mixed								
France	0.056	18	2	1	0.500	2	4	3
Spain	n.a.	0	5	5	0.167	6	3	2
Developing, authoritarian								
Egypt	0.000	3	8	8	1.000	1	4	3
Mexico	0.250	4	2	1	0.667	3	4	2
China	—	—	—	—	0.500	2	4	3

(Table continues on the following page.)

Table A-1. *(continued)*

Economy	1950–71: *Vulnerability (within six months)*	1950–71: *Number of political transitions*	1950–71: *Number of central bank turnovers: Total*	1950–71: *Number of central bank turnovers: Nonpolitical*[a]	1972–89: *Vulnerability (within six months)*	1972–89: *Number of political transitions*	1972–89: *Number of central bank turnovers: Total*	1972–89: *Number of central bank turnovers: Nonpolitical*[a]
South Africa	0.000	4	2	2	0.500	2	3	2
Taiwan (China)	0.000	3	2	2	0.500	4	2	0
Ethiopia	n.a.	0	0	0	0.400	5	5	3
Hungary	—	—	—	—	0.333	3	2	1
Yugoslavia (former)	n.a.	0	5	5	0.100	10	4	3
Kenya	n.a.	0	2	2	0.000	1	2	2
Morocco	0.167	6	4	3	0.000	4	2	2
Romania	—	—	0	0	0.000	1	3	3
Tanzania	n.a.	0	1	1	0.000	1	2	2
Uganda	—	—	0	0	0.000	4	2	2
Indonesia	1.000	1	5	4	—	0	3	3
Qatar	—	—	0	0	—	0	0	0
Singapore	n.a.	0	1	1	n.a.	0	6	6
Zaire	0.000	1	2	2	—	0	4	4
Developing, democratic								
Botswana	—	—	—	—	1.000	1	6	5
Costa Rica	0.400	5	10	8	0.750	4	11	8
Malta	0.000	1	1	1	0.500	2	5	4
Jamaica	1.000	1	3	2	0.333	3	7	6
West Samoa	—	—	—	—	0.333	3	3	2
Barbados	—	—	—	—	0.000	4	2	2
Israel	0.000	3	2	2	0.000	6	3	3
Bahamas	—	—	—	—	n.a.	0	3	3
Developing, mixed								
Argentina	1.714	7	20	8	1.111	9	16	6
Brazil	0.500	8	9	5	1.000	5	11	6

Chile	0.750	4	6	3	1.000	1	12	11
India	0.000	2	6	6	0.667	6	7	3
Korea, Rep. of	n.a.	0	2	2	0.667	3	6	4
Peru	0.333	6	11	9	0.667	3	6	4
Uruguay	1.000	2	6	4	0.600	5	6	3
Colombia	0.167	6	5	4	0.500	4	3	1
Poland	0.000	1	0	0	0.500	6	6	3
Venezuela	0.167	6	5	4	0.500	4	7	5
Honduras	0.200	5	2	1	0.400	5	3	1
Portugal	0.000	1	4	4	0.385	13	7	2
Turkey	0.600	5	7	4	0.273	11	7	4
Greece	0.053	19	2	1	0.250	8	5	3
Ghana	0.000	4	2	2	0.200	5	4	3
Nigeria	0.000	2	2	2	0.200	5	3	2
Nepal	0.250	4	3	2	0.143	7	3	2
Panama	1.500	2	4	1	0.125	8	2	1
Thailand	0.250	4	4	3	0.111	9	3	2
Malaysia	0.000	3	0	0	0.000	2	2	2
Pakistan	0.167	6	4	3	0.000	3	5	5
Philippines	0.000	4	3	3	0.000	2	2	2

—Not available. Vulnerability is not available when data on either the number of political transitions or the number of central bank turnovers are not available.
n.a. Not applicable.
Note: Within each subgroup, central banks are arranged in descending order of vulnerability during the 1971–89 subperiod.
a. The nonpolitical turnover is defined as the number of changes in the governor of the central bank that occurred more than six months after a political transition.
Sources: Authors' calculations.

APPENDIX. TESTS FOR THE DETERMINATION OF THE CUTOFF BETWEEN POLITICAL AND NONPOLITICAL PERIODS

To test for possible differences between the probability of a change of central bank governor in the ten-month-or-more intervals and in each of the other intervals in table 1, we use the normal approximation to the binomial distribution. More specifically, let c_i be the number of changes of central bank governor in interval i following a political transition. As in table 1, i may assume the interval values (0–1), (2–3), (4–6), (7–9), and (10 or more). We denote each of these intervals by its lower bound. Thus i assumes the values 0, 2, 4, 7, and 10. Let n_i be the number of intervals of type i in the sample. This number is determined by the total number of political transitions in the sample. The frequency of central bank governor changes within interval i is given by

(A-1) $$f_i = c_i/n_i \text{ for } i = 0, 2, 4, 7, 10.$$

Let P_i be the true conditional probability of a change of central bank governor in interval i following a political transition. The null hypotheses to be tested are

(A-2) $$H_o\text{: } P_i = P_{10} \text{ for } i = 0, 2, 4, 7$$

against each of the alternative hypotheses that P_i is significantly larger than P_{10}. The specification of the alternative hypotheses accommodates the possibility that the probability of a turnover at the central bank is larger at shorter lags following a political transition. Under each of the null hypotheses the values

(A-3a) $$z_i \equiv \frac{f_i - f_{10}}{\sqrt{\bar{f}_i(1-\bar{f}_i)\left[\frac{1}{n_i}+\frac{1}{n_{10}}\right]}}, i = 0, 2, 4, 7$$

where

(A-3b) $$\bar{f}_i = \frac{c_i + c_{10}}{n_i + n_{10}}, i = 0,2,4,7$$

have approximately a standard normal distribution, provided both n_i and n_{10} are larger than 30.[9] (See, for example, Huntsberger, Croft, and Billingsley 1980: 302.) The null hypotheses should be accepted for small values of the z_i's and rejected for large positive z_i's. Table A-2 displays these statistics.

9. These conditions are always satisfied for the entire sample of economies and the two main subsamples. For $i = 0, 2$, the terms n_i and n_{10} are the numbers of two-month periods in the appropriate intervals. For $i = 4, 7$, they refer to the number of three-month periods. This variation in the length of the basic time unit is introduced to make its length identical to the number of months within each interval (two months for $i = 0, 2$ and three months for $i = 4, 7$). In either case, the value of n is sufficiently large to make the normal approximation to the binomial valid.

Table A-2. *Values of the Test Statistic Z_i for the Null H_0: $P_i = p_{10}$*

Economy group	*Interval (number of months)* 0–1	2–3	4–6	7–9
All economies	12.0	2.8	2.9	–0.6
Industrial	3.2	–0.2	1.1	–1.6
Developing	13.0	4.0	3.3	–0.7

Note: Sample size is sixty-seven economies.
Source: Authors' calculations.

Because a z_i of 1.96 implies that the null is rejected at the 0.05 level, we conclude that the probabilities of a turnover at the central bank are significantly larger for the 0–1, 2–3, and 4–6 intervals than for the 10-or-more intervals. However, there is no significant difference in the probability of a change of central bank governor between the seven-to-nine-month and the ten-or-more-month intervals. The evidence in table A-2 therefore supports the conclusion that for the whole sample the cutoff between political and nonpolitical periods occurs at a lag of six months following a political transition. Accordingly, we define periods of up to six months following a political transition as political and periods seven or more months after the latest political transition as nonpolitical. The respective frequencies are 0.037 and 0.015, respectively. The z statistic testing the significance of the difference between these two estimated probabilities is a huge 9.6.

A replication of these tests separately for each of the two economic categories of countries reveals that for developing countries the appropriate cutoff between political and nonpolitical periods is still at the upper end of the 4–6 interval. For developing economies the z statistic also very significantly rejects the null hypothesis that the frequency within the entire period of zero to six months is no different from the frequency in periods that are seven or more months after a political transition.

In the industrial economies, the probability of a change at the central bank in the 0–1 interval is significantly higher than in the 10-or-more interval. The frequencies in the two-to-three-month, four-to-six-month, and seven-to-nine-month intervals, however, are not significantly different from frequencies in the 10-or-more interval. Thus, for industrial economies we should locate the cutoff between political and nonpolitical periods after the 0–1 interval.

References

The word "processed" describes informally reproduced works that may not be commonly available through library systems.

Alesina, Alberto, Sule Ozler, Nouriel Roubini, and Phillip Swagel. 1995. "Political Instability and Economic Growth." Draft.

Alesina, Alberto, and Lawrence H. Summers. 1993. "Central Bank Independence and Macroeconomic Performance: Some Comparative Evidence." *Journal of Money, Credit and Banking* 25(May):151–62.

Alesina, Alberto, and Roberto Perotti. 1994. "The Political Economy of Growth: A Critical Survey of the Recent Literature." *The World Bank Economic Review* 8(3):351–71.

Anayadike-Danes, M. K. 1995. "Comment on 'Measuring the Independence of Central Banks and Its Effect on Policy Outcomes' by Cukierman, Webb, and Neyapti." *The World Bank Economic Review* 9(2):335–40.

Arriagada, H. G., and Carol Graham. 1994. "Chile: The Maintenance of Adjustment and Macroeconomic Stability during Democratic Transition." In Stephan Haggard and Steven B. Webb, eds., *Voting for Reform: Democracy, Political Liberalization and Economic Adjustment.* New York: Oxford University Press.

Barro, R. J. 1991. "Economic Growth in a Cross Section of Countries." *Quarterly Journal of Economics* 106(May):407–43.

Cukierman, Alex. 1992. *Central Bank Strategy, Credibility, and Independence: Theory and Evidence.* Cambridge, Mass.: MIT Press.

———. 1994. "Commitment through Delegation, Political Influence, and Central Bank Independence." In J. O. de Beaufort Wijnholds, S. C. W. Eijffinger, and L. H. Hoogduin, eds., *A Framework for Monetary Stability.* Boston: Kluwer Academic Publishers.

Cukierman, Alex, Sebastian Edwards, and Guido Tabellini. 1992. "Seigniorage and Political Instability." *American Economic Review* 82(June):537–55.

Cukierman Alex, Miguel Kiguel, and Nissan Liviatan. 1992. "How Much to Commit to an Exchange Rate Rule? Balancing Credibility and Flexibility." *Revista de Analisis Económico* 7(1, June):73–89.

Cukierman, Alex, Steven B. Webb, and Bilin Neyapti. 1992. "Measuring the Independence of Central Banks and Its Effect on Policy Outcomes." *The World Bank Economic Review* 6(3):353–98.

Cukierman, Alex, Pantelis Kalaitzidakis, Lawrence H. Summers, and Steven B. Webb. 1993. "Central Bank Independence, Growth, Investment, and Real Rates." *Carnegie-Rochester Conference Series on Public Policy* 29(Autumn):1–46.

Cukierman, Alex, Pedro Rodriguez, and Steven B. Webb. Forthcoming. "Central Bank Autonomy and Exchange Rate Regimes—Their Effects on Monetary Accommodation and Activism." In Harry Huizinga and Sylvester Eijffinger, eds., *Positive Political Economy: Theory and Evidence.*

de Haan, Jakob, 1995. Personal communication. University of Groningen, the Netherlands. August.

Easterly, William, C. A. Rodriguez, and Klaus Schmidt-Hebbel, eds. 1992. "Public Sector Deficits and Macroeconomic Performance." Draft.

Edwards, Sebastian, and Guido Tabellini. 1991. "Explaining Fiscal Policies and Inflation in Developing Countries." *Journal of International Money and Finance* 10 (March, Supp.):16–48.

The Europa World Yearbook. Various years. London: Europa Publications.

Fischer, Stanley. 1991. "Growth, Macroeconomics, and Development." In Olivier J. Blanchard and Stanley Fischer, eds., *NBER Macroeconomics Annual 1991.* Cambridge, Mass.: National Bureau of Economic Research.

Grilli, Vittorio, Donato Masciandaro, and Guido Tabellini. 1991. "Political and Monetary Institutions and Public Financial Policies in the Industrial Countries." *Economic Policy: A European Forum* 6(October):341–92.

Haggard, Stephan, Robert Kaufman, and Steven B. Webb. 1992. "Democracy, Dictatorship, and Inflation in Middle-Income Countries." World Bank, Country Economics Department, Washington, D.C. Processed.

Haggard, Stephan, and Steven B. Webb. 1994. *Voting for Reform: Democracy, Political Liberalization and Economic Adjustment*. New York: Oxford University Press.

Havrilesky, Thomas. 1992. *The Pressures on American Monetary Policy*. Norwell, Mass.: Kluwer Academic Publishers.

Huntsberger, D. V., D. J. Croft, and Patrick Billingsley. 1980. *Statistical Inference for Management and Economics*. 2d ed. Boston: Allyn and Bacon.

Parkin, Michael. 1986. "Domestic Monetary Institutions and Deficits." In J. M. Buchanan, C. K. Rowley, and Robert Tollison, eds., *Deficits*. New York: Basil Blackwell.

[23]

1. Introduction[1]

Recently, in many countries both political and monetary authorities have shown an increasing interest in the objective of monetary stability and the position of the central bank. As pointed out by Persson and Tabellini (1993) recent policy reform, as well as historical experience, suggests two different routes to price stability.

The first way is the *legislative* approach, namely to create by law a very independent central bank with an unequivocal mandate to focus on price stability. Interest in this approach is motivated by the success of the Deutsche Bundesbank in maintaining one of the lowest rates of inflation for several decades. Moreover, the accepted statute of the European Central Bank is strongly influenced by the law governing the Bundesbank. Moreover, France and Spain reformed their central bank laws that made the Banque de France and the Banco de Espana more independent of government. Furthermore, countries in Central and Eastern Europe, such as the Czech Republic, Hungary and Poland, increased the legal independence of their central banks. Finally, in Latin America there are also tendencies toward granting more independence to the central banks in countries like Argentina, Chile, Mexico and Venezuela. Academic contributions in this area are Rogoff (1985a), Neumann (1991) and Lohmann (1992).

The second way is the *targeting* or *contracting* approach, namely to let the political principal of the central bank impose an explicit inflation target for monetary policy, and make the central bank governor explicitly accountable for his success in meeting this target. Recently, New Zealand, Canada, and the United Kingdom have made some progress on this route. Along these lines New Zealand enacted legislation that increased the independence of its Reserve

---

1 The authors owe a debt of gratitude to Marco Hoeberichts for his empirical support. They are also grateful to Marno Verbeek for his valuable suggestions with respect to the latent variables method. Helpful comments by an anonymous referee, seminar participants at the Konstanz Seminar on Monetary Theory and Monetary Policy, the Bank of England and by delegates at the twenty-seventh Money, Macro and Finance Research Group Annual Conference are gratefully acknowledged. An earlier version was circulated as CentER Discussion Paper No. 9579. Karen Adams helped prepare the paper. Of course, the usual disclaimer applies.

Bank, whereas in the United Kingdom there is now a lively discussion of the desirability of making the Bank of England more independent.[2] Important theoretical work on this approach is done by Walsh (1995) and Persson and Tabellini (1993).

In this paper we build on the Rogoff (1985a) model and therefore restrict the analysis to the legislative approach. Empirical work on the legislative approach [Alesina (1988, 1989), Grilli, Masciandaro and Tabellini (1991), Cukierman (1992), Eijffinger and Schaling (1993a, 1993b, 1995), De Haan and Sturm (1992), Alesina and Summers (1993)] has focused on the quantification of independence using a number of legal attributes from central bank laws. These studies focus on the *positive* issue of the relation between monetary regimes and economic performance. Broadly speaking, the conclusion is that the more independent the central bank, the lower the inflation rate, while the rate of output growth is unaffected.

However, this literature does not explain the observed differences in central bank independence. For instance, no explanation is offered for the very high independence of the Bundesbank. It has often been pointed out that this independence may be explained by Germany's underlying aversion to inflation associated with its experience of hyper-inflation in the 1920s.[3]

This brings us to a key issue in the political economy of central banking: the relation between institutional design and individual and collective preferences. Here the question to be dealt with is the *normative* issue of how independent a central bank should be, ie the optimal degree of central bank independence.

An important study in this field is Cukierman (1994). Building on the seminal paper of Lohmann (1992), he wants to identify the economic and political factors that induce politicians to delegate more or less authority to the central bank. His theory predicts that central bank independence will be higher the larger the employment-motivated inflationary bias, the higher political instability and the larger the government debt.

---

2 For a recent discussion about the independence of the Bank of England and the associated inflation targeting framework see Centre for Economic Policy Research (1993).

3 See for instance Issing (1993).

These predictions were tested and, subsequently, rejected by De Haan and Van 't Hag (1994) using regression analysis (OLS method). In testing Cukierman's model, they employ measures of central bank independence that - in Rogoff's (1985a) terminology - reflect the strength of the 'conservative bias' of the central bank as embodied in the law. In Cukierman's model, following Lohmann (1992), central bank independence is defined as the *cost of overriding* the central bank, rather than as the degree of *conservativeness*. Cukierman's (1994) theory also generates propositions about *optimal* regimes, while the legal measures describe *actual* monetary regimes.

In this paper we try to overcome these pitfalls. Building on the Rogoff (1985a) model, we identify central bank independence as the degree of conservativeness rather than the political cost of overriding the central bank. We extend this model to the open economy case and allow for deviations from purchasing power parity. Using a graphical method, we develop a new way of determining the optimal degree of conservativeness. As in Lohmann (1992), this degree depends on the balance between *credibility* and *flexibility*. However, unlike Rogoff and Lohmann, we are able to express the upper and lower bounds of the interval containing the optimal degree of conservativeness in terms of the structural parameters of the model.

Furthermore, we derive several propositions concerning the relation between economic and political factors and the optimal degree of central bank independence. We show that optimal central bank independence is higher, the higher the natural rate of unemployment, the greater the benefits of unanticipated inflation (the slope of the Phillips curve), the less inflation-averse society, the smaller the variance of productivity shocks, the smaller real exchange rate variability and the smaller the openness of the economy. These propositions are tested for nineteen industrial countries (Australia, Austria, Belgium, Canada, Denmark, Finland, France, Germany, Ireland, Italy, Japan, New Zealand, the Netherlands, Norway, Spain, Sweden, Switzerland, the United Kingdom and the United States) for the Bretton-Woods period and after (1960-93). In testing the model we employ a *latent variables* method (LISREL) in order to distinguish between actual and optimal monetary regimes.

The paper is organised into four remaining sections, followed by three appendices. In section II we present the theoretical model. Section III contains the derivation of the optimal degree of central bank independence. In section

IV we test the model with the latent variables method. Our conclusions are given in section V.

2. A simple macromodel

The main purpose of this section is to combine the Alogoskoufis (1994) model of wage and employment determination with an open economy variant of the Rogoff (1985a) model. We assume that there are two types of agents, *wage-setters (the union)* and the *central bank*. Wage-setters unilaterally choose the nominal wage every period, and the central bank controls monetary policy.

The sequence of events is as follows. In the first stage wage-setters sign each period nominal wage contracts [Gray (1976), Fischer (1977a)]. Wage-setters know the domestic monetary regime. They take this information into account in forming their expectations. In the second stage stochastic shocks to productivity and the real exchange rate realise. These shocks are random and cannot be observed at the time wage contracts are signed. In the third stage the central bank observes the values of the shocks and - contingent on the chosen regime - reacts to the shocks accordingly. In the fourth and final stage employment is determined by competitive firms. This timing of events is summarised in Figure 2.1.

Figure 2.1. The sequence of events

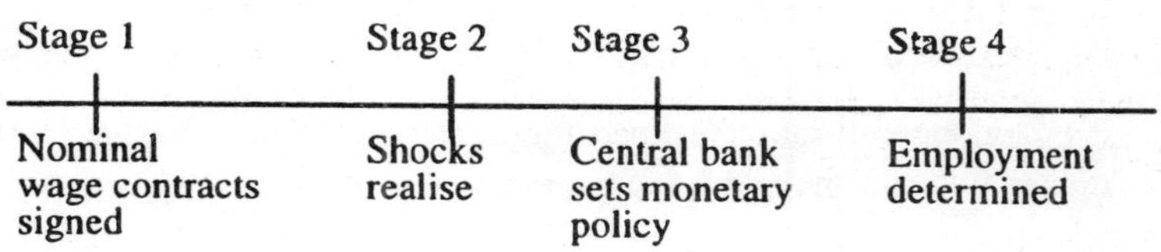

We now move to the supply side of the model.

II.1.Aggregate supply

Consider the following supply block. Capital will be assumed fixed, and output is given by a short-run Cobb-Douglas production function

$$y_t = \beta l_t + v_t \qquad 0 < \beta < 1 \qquad \textbf{(2.1)}$$

where lower-case letters refer to logarithmic deviations from steady state values. Thus, y is the log of output, l the log of employment, and v a measure of productivity. β is the exponent of labour and is less than unity.

Having described the level of output, it remains to be specified how productivity evolves over time. For simplicity we assume that shocks to productivity are normally distributed with zero mean and finite variance

$$v_t \sim N(0, \sigma^2_v) \tag{2.2}$$

Firms determine employment by equalising the marginal product of labour to the real wage $w_t - p_t$. This yields the following employment function

$$\ell_t = -\frac{1}{1-\beta}(w_t - p_t - v_t) \tag{2.3}$$

where w is the log of the nominal wage and p the log of the price level.

The nominal wage is set at the beginning of each period and remains fixed for one period. The objective of wage-setters is to stabilise the real consumer wage around a target level. Thus, wages in each period are set to minimise

$$W_t = E_{t-1}\left[\frac{1}{2}(w_t - p_{c_t} - \tau)^2\right] \tag{2.4}$$

where E_{t-1} is the operator of rational expectations, conditional on information at the end of period $t - 1$. τ is the real wage target of the union.[4]

The consumer price index p_c is defined as

$$p_{c_t} = (1-\mu)p_t + \mu(p_t^* + e_t) \tag{2.5}$$

4 Alternatively, the loss function (2.4) could be assumed quadratic in both the deviations of employment and the real wage from certain target levels. For an analysis along these lines see Schaling (1995), Chapter 7.

where μ is the share of imports in GDP, e is the nominal exchange rate (defined as the domestic currency price of foreign exchange) and p^* is the foreign price level. Equation **(2.5)** can be rewritten as

$$p_{c_t} = p_t + \mu q_t \qquad \textbf{(2.6)}$$

where q is the real exchange rate $p^* + e - p$. Having redefined the CPI in terms of the producer's price level (p) and the real exchange rate, it remains to specify how the *nominal* exchange rate is determined.

Here we are concerned with the factors that ultimately determine the degree of central bank independence, that is, with the longer-term behaviour of the exchange rate. As pointed out by Mussa (1991, page 14), long-term relationships between movements in nominal exchange rates and the ratio of national price levels support the empirical relevance of purchasing power parity.[5] Therefore, we assume the nominal exchange rate to be governed by

$$\Delta e_t = \Delta p_t - \Delta p^*_t + w_t \qquad w_t \sim N(0, \sigma^2_w) \qquad \textbf{(2.7)}$$

where Δ is the first-difference operator and w is a shock to the first difference of the real exchange rate with zero mean and finite variance σ^2_w. We assume this shock is uncorrelated with the supply shock, ie $E_{t-1}v_t w_t = 0$.[6] From the first-order conditions for a minimum of **(2.4)**, the CPI-indexed nominal wage is given by

$$w_t = E_{t-1} p_{c_t} + \tau^7 \qquad \textbf{(2.8)}$$

---

5 It is well known that this theory has, generally, provided a poor explanation of shorter-term movements of exchange rates. See eg Dornbush (1976, 1988).

6 In future work this assumption will be relaxed. Then the shocks to the real exchange rate will result from the difference between domestic and foreign shocks to productivity.

7 For a similar specification see Rogoff (1985b, page 212). Note that the nature of the employment contract is such that the union agrees to supply whatever amount of labour is determined by firms in period t, provided firms pay the negotiated wage.

Taking account of **(2.6)** - **(2.7)** and of the fact that shocks to the real exchange rate cannot be observed at the time wage contracts are signed, we get

$$w_t = E_{t-1}p_t + \tau \quad \textbf{(2.9)}$$

Substituting **(2.9)** in the labour demand function **(2.3)**, yields the following relation between employment and unanticipated shocks

$$\ell_t = \ell^* + \frac{1}{1-\beta}(p_t - E_{t-1}p_t + v_t) \quad \textbf{(2.10)}$$

where $\ell^* \equiv \frac{-\tau}{1-\beta}$. An unanticipated rise in prices $p_t - E_{t-1}p_t$ reduces the real wage, and causes firms to employ more labour. Thus, aggregate employment exhibits a transitory deviation from its equilibrium or 'natural' rate l^*.[8]

Subtracting **(2.10)** from the labour force l^s, using the approximation that the rate of unemployment $u \approx l^s - l$, we get the following expression for the short-run determination of unemployment

$$u_t = \tilde{u} - \frac{1}{1-\beta}(p_t - E_{t-1}p_t + v_t) \quad \textbf{(2.11)}$$

where $\tilde{u} = l^s - l^*$. $\tilde{u}$ can be thought of as the *equilibrium* or *'natural'* rate of unemployment in this model. Thus, **(2.11)** is the well-known expectations augmented Phillips curve. Unemployment deviates from its equilibrium rate only to the extent that there are unanticipated shocks to inflation or productivity. Anticipated shocks to inflation, productivity and the real exchange rate are reflected in wages [equation (2.8)] and do not affect unemployment. We can now incorporate the Phillips curve into a monetary policy game. This is the subject of the next section.

---

8 Actual employment equals its natural rate when all expectations are fulfilled. Hence, the natural rate of employment equals l^*.

II.2. Time-Consistent Equilibrium under a 'Conservative' Central Banker

As stated by Rogoff (1985a, page 1,180), the adoption of central bank independence may be viewed as an institutional response to the time-consistency problem.

Suppose, for example, that through a system of rewards and punishments the central bank's incentives are altered so that it places some direct weight on achieving a low rate of growth for a nominal variable such as the price level, nominal GNP, or the money supply. Rogoff demonstrates that society can make itself better off by selecting an agent to head the central bank who is known to place a greater weight on inflation stabilisation (relative to unemployment stabilisation) than is embodied in the social loss function L_t. The social loss function L depends on deviations of unemployment and CPI inflation from their *optimal* (socially desired) levels

$$L_t = \frac{1}{2}(\Delta p_t - \Delta p^{\tau}) + \frac{\chi}{2}(u_t - u^{\tau})^2 \qquad \textbf{(2.12)}$$

where $0 < \chi < \infty$ and Δp^{τ} and u^{τ} are society's CPI inflation and unemployment targets. The parameter χ is the relative weight of unemployment stabilisation relative to inflation stabilisation in the preferences of society. Normalising $\Delta p^{\tau} u^{\tau}$, p_{t-1} and q_{t-1} at zero and using **(2.6)** we get[9]

$$L_t = \frac{1}{2} p_{c_t}^2 + \frac{\chi}{2} u_t^2 \qquad \textbf{(2.13)}$$

Rogoff shows that, in choosing among potential candidates, it is never optimal to choose an individual who is known to care 'too little' about unemployment.

9 Price-level targeting and inflation-rate targeting are equivalent here, since $p_{c_{t-1}}$ is known at the time the central bank commits itself to achieving a target for Δp_{c_t}. Once monetary control errors are taken into account it becomes important to make the distinction between a *zero inflation target* and a *target of price stability*. See Fischer (1994, pages 281-85).

Suppose, for example that in period t - 1 society selects an agent to head the central bank in period t. The reputation of this individual is such that it is known that, if he is appointed to head the central bank, he will minimise the following loss function

$$I_t = \frac{(1+\varepsilon)}{2} p_{c_t}^2 + \frac{\chi}{2} u_t^2 \qquad 0 < \varepsilon < \infty \tag{2.14}$$

When ε is strictly greater than zero, then this agent places a greater relative weight on CPI inflation stabilisation then society does. Hence, following Eijffinger and Schaling (1993b, page 5) we view the coefficient ε as a measure of the *political independence* of the central bank. The higher ε the more independent the central bank. Note that, if $\varepsilon = 0$, equation **(2.14)** reduces to the social loss function **(2.13)**.

Thus, stochastic equilibrium is derived under the assumption that the monetary authorities attempt to minimise loss function I, given by equation **(2.14)** above. Substituting the definition of the CPI [equation **(2.6)**] and the Phillips curve **(2.11)** in the loss function **(2.14)** yields

$$I_t = \frac{1+\varepsilon}{2}[p_t + \mu q_t]^2 + \frac{\chi}{2}[\tilde{u} - \frac{1}{1-\beta}p_t + \frac{1}{1-\beta}E_{t-1}p_t - \frac{1}{1-\beta}v_t]^2 \tag{2.15}$$

From the first-order conditions for a minimum of **(2.15)**, ie $\partial I_t/\partial p_t = 0$, taking account of **(2.7)**, and again using the normalisation $q_{t-1} = 0$, we obtain the central bank's reaction function to the union's inflationary expectations

$$p_t^I = \frac{(1-\beta)\chi}{(1+\varepsilon)(1-\beta)^2+\chi}\tilde{u} + \frac{\chi}{(1+\varepsilon)(1-\beta)^2 + \chi} E_{t-1}p_t^I - \frac{1}{(1+\varepsilon)(1-\beta)^2+\chi}$$

$$[\chi v_t + \mu(1+\varepsilon)(1-\beta)^2 w_t] \tag{2.16}$$

where superscript I stands for independent central bank regime. Taking expectations conditional on information at t-1 of **(2.16)** gives

$$E_{t-1}p_t^I = \frac{\chi}{(1-\beta)(1+\varepsilon)}\tilde{u} \qquad (2.17)$$

Equation **(2.17)** is the reaction function of the union. The resulting GDP price level is

$$p_t^I = \frac{\chi}{(1-\beta)(1+\varepsilon)}\tilde{u} - \frac{1}{(1+\varepsilon)(1-\beta)^2 + \chi}[\chi v_t + \mu(1+\varepsilon)(1-\beta)^2 w_t] \qquad (2.18)$$

while the unemployment rate is given by

$$u_t^I = \tilde{u} - \frac{(1+\varepsilon)(1-\beta)}{(1+\varepsilon)(1-\beta)^2 + \chi}[v_t - \mu w_t] \qquad (2.19)$$

Note that a real depreciation *increases* unemployment (it acts like an adverse productivity shock). The reason for this is simple. Shocks that tend to cause real depreciations of the domestic currency are stabilised by the central bank [equation **(2.16)**], because of their potentially adverse effects on CPI inflation.

The associated monetary tightening causes - given the level of nominal wages - a rise in real labour costs (reducing the producer's wage), thus driving down labour demand. Given the supply of labour, unemployment then increases.

3. Optimal commitment in monetary policy: credibility versus flexibility

III.1. Social Welfare under Central Bank Independence

We are now able to evaluate central bank independence from the perspective of society. To facilitate exposition in later sections, following Rogoff (1985a, pages 1,175-76), we shall first develop a notation for evaluating the expected value of society's loss function under any arbitrary monetary policy regime 'A', $E_{t-1}L_t^A$:

$$E_{t-1}L_t^A = \frac{1}{2}[\chi\ \tilde{u}^2] + \Pi^A + \Gamma^A \quad (3.1)$$ [10]

where $\Pi^A \equiv 1/2\ (\tilde{p}_{c_t}^A)^2$, $\tilde{p}_{c_t}^A$ is the mean CPI in period *t*, and

$$\Gamma^A \equiv \frac{1}{2}\ E_{t-1}\ \{\chi\ [\frac{v_t}{1-\beta} + (p_t^A - E_{t-1}p_t^A)/(1-\beta)]^2 + (p_{c_t}^A - E_{t-1}p_{c_t}^A)^2\}$$

Again, the first component of $E_{t-1}\ L_t^A$, $1/2[\chi\ \tilde{u}^2]$ is non-stochastic and invariant across monetary regimes. It represents the *deadweight loss* due to the labour market distortion ($\tilde{u} > 0$). This loss cannot be reduced through monetary policy in a time-consistent rational expectations equilibrium. The second term, Π^A, depends on the mean inflation rate. This term is also non-stochastic but does depend on the *choice* of monetary policy regime.

The final term, Γ^A, represents the *stabilisation component* of the loss function. It measures how successfully the central bank offsets disturbances to stabilise unemployment and CPI inflation around their mean values.

By substituting the results relevant for the central bank [**(2.18)** and **(2.19)**] into society's loss function **(2.12)** and taking expectations, we obtain the *I* regime counterpart of expression **(3.1)**. Abstracting from the (common) deadweight loss, one gets

$$\Pi^I + \Gamma^I = \frac{\chi^2}{2[(1+\varepsilon)(1-\beta)]^2}\tilde{u}^2 + \frac{\chi[(1+\varepsilon)^2(1-\beta)^2+\chi]}{2[(1+\varepsilon)\ (1-\beta)^2+\chi]^2}\sigma_v^2$$

$$+\frac{\chi\mu^2[\chi+(1+\varepsilon)^2(1-\beta)^2]}{2[(1+\varepsilon)(1-\beta)^2+\chi]^2}\sigma_w^2 \quad (3.2)$$

10 We derive equation **(3.1)** in Appendix A.

III.2. The Rogoff Theorem

Rogoff (1985a) showed that it is optimal for society (the principal) to select an agent to head the central bank that places a large, but finite weight on inflation. In this section we generalise this result for an *open* economy. The *optimal degree* of central bank independence ε^* is defined as that value of *e* that minimises the expected value of the loss function of society $E_{t-1} L_t^I$.

To solve for the value of *e* that minimises $E_{t-1} L_t^I$, differentiate (3.2) with respect to ε

$$\frac{\partial E_{t-1} L_t^I}{\partial \varepsilon} = \frac{\partial \Pi^I}{\partial \varepsilon} + \frac{\partial \Gamma^I}{\partial \varepsilon} \tag{3.3}$$

$$\frac{\partial \Gamma^I}{\partial \varepsilon} = \frac{\chi^2 (1-\beta)^2 \varepsilon \, [\sigma_v^2 + \mu^2 \sigma_w^2]}{[(1+\varepsilon)(1-\beta)^2 + \chi]^3} \tag{3.4}$$

$$\frac{\partial \Pi^I}{\partial \varepsilon} = \frac{-\chi^2 \tilde{u}^2}{(1+\varepsilon)^3 (1-\beta)^2} \tag{3.5}$$

We are now ready to prove:

Proposition 3.1: With a *positive* natural rate of unemployment, in an open economy the optimal degree of central bank independence lies between *zero* and *infinity* (For $\tilde{u} > 0, \; 0 < \varepsilon^* < \infty$).

Proof: Note that $\varepsilon > -1$ by assumption. Thus, by inspection of (3.5), $\partial \Pi^I / \partial e$ is strictly negative. Note also, by inspection of (3.4), that $\partial \Gamma^I / \partial \varepsilon$ is strictly negative for

$$\frac{-[\chi + (1-\beta)^2]}{(1-\beta)^2} < \varepsilon < 0, \text{ zero when } \varepsilon = 0 \text{ and positive for } \varepsilon > 0.$$

Therefore, $\partial E_{t-1} L_t^1/\partial\varepsilon$ is strictly negative for $\varepsilon \leq 0$. $\partial E_{t-1} L_t^1/\partial\varepsilon$ must change from negative to positive at some sufficiently large value of *e*, since as *e* approaches positive infinity, $\partial\Gamma^1/\partial\varepsilon$ converges to zero at rate ε^{-2}, whereas $\partial\Pi^1/\partial\varepsilon$ converges to zero at rate ε^{-3}. Consequently, $\varepsilon^* < \infty$.[11]

The intuition behind this result is the following. From **(3.5)** it can be seen that increasing the central bank's commitment to inflation stabilisation decreases the credibility component of the social loss function. On the other hand, from **(3.4)** it follows that having a more independent central bank increases the stabilisation component of the loss function.

Hence, optimal commitment in monetary policy involves trading off the *credibility* gains associated with lower average inflation versus loss of *flexibility* due to a distorted response to productivity and real exchange rate shocks.

III.3. The Ultimate Determinants of Central Bank Independence

Proposition **(3.1)** is Rogoff's theorem. Rogoff is unable to write down a closed-form solution for ε^*. He is also unable to derive propositions concerning the comparative static properties of this equilibrium. The following section can be seen as an *extension* of the Rogoff theorem.

Using a graphical method, we develop an alternative way of determining the optimal degree of central bank independence. Next, we show how this result is conditioned on the natural rate of unemployment ($\tilde{u}$), society's preferences for unemployment stabilisation (χ), the variance of productivity shocks (σ_v^2), the slope of the Phillips curve ($(1-\beta)^{-1}$), the variance of shocks to the real exchange rate (σ_w^2) and the degree of openness (μ).

---

11 As pointed out by Rogoff (1985a, page 1,178), it is extremely difficult to write down a closed-form solution for ε^*.

By setting (3.3) equal to zero we obtain the first-order condition for a minimum of $E_{t-1} L'_t$

$$0 = \frac{\partial \Pi^{\mathrm{I}}}{\partial \varepsilon} + \frac{\partial \Gamma^{\mathrm{I}}}{\partial \varepsilon} \tag{3.6}$$

Substituting (3.4) and (3.5) into (3.6), yields

$$\frac{-\chi^2 \tilde{u}^2}{(1-\beta)^2 (1+\varepsilon)^3} + \frac{\chi^2 (1-\beta)^2 \varepsilon [\sigma_v^2 + \mu^2 \sigma_w^2]}{[(1+\varepsilon)(1-\beta)^2 + \chi]^3} = 0 \tag{3.7}$$

Equation (3.7) determines ε^* as an implicit function of χ, $\tilde{u}$, σ_v^2, β, σ_w^2 and μ. A solution for ε^* always exists and is unique.

To show this we adapt a graphical method used by Cukierman (1992, pages 170-72) in the context of a dynamic game.

Rewrite (3.7) as

$$\varepsilon = \frac{[(1+\varepsilon)(1-\beta)^2 + \chi]^3 \tilde{u}^2}{[\sigma_v^2 + \mu^2 \sigma_w^2](1-\beta)^4 (1+\varepsilon)^3} \equiv F(\varepsilon) \tag{3.8}$$

The function $F(\varepsilon)$ on the right-hand side of equation (3.8) is monotonically decreasing in ε that[12]

$$F(0) = \frac{[(1-\beta)^2 + \chi]^3 \tilde{u}^2}{[\sigma_v^2 + \mu^2 \sigma_w^2](1-\beta)^4}, \quad \lim_{\varepsilon \to \infty} F(\varepsilon) = \frac{(1-\beta)^2 \tilde{u}^2}{[\sigma_v^2 + \mu^2 \sigma_w^2]} \quad \text{and}$$

---

12 These statements are demonstrated in Appendix B to this paper.

$$\frac{(1-\beta)^2\tilde{u}^2}{[\sigma_v^2+\mu^2\sigma_w^2]} < F(\varepsilon) < \frac{[(1-\beta)^2+\chi]^3\tilde{u}^2}{[\sigma_v^2+\mu^2\sigma_w^2](1-\beta)^4}$$

We are now ready to prove:

Proposition 3.2: $\frac{(1-\beta)^2\tilde{u}^2}{[\sigma_v^2+\mu^2\sigma_w^2]} < \varepsilon^* < \frac{[(1-\beta)^2+\chi]^3\tilde{u}^2}{[\sigma_v^2+\mu^2\sigma_w^2](1-\beta)^4}$

Proof: The left-hand side of (3.8) is a 45-degree straight line through the origin. Since

$F(0) = \frac{[(1-\beta)^2+\chi]^3\tilde{u}^2}{[\sigma_v^2+\mu^2\sigma_w^2](1-\beta)^4}$ and $\frac{\partial F}{\partial \varepsilon} < 0$, these two functions must intersect at one and only one point. Moreover, since

$\frac{(1-\beta)^2\tilde{u}^2}{[\sigma_v^2+\mu^2\sigma_w^2]} < F(\varepsilon) < \frac{[(1-\beta)^2+\chi]^3\tilde{u}^2}{[\sigma_v^2+\mu^2\sigma_w^2](1-\beta)^4}$, the intersection occurs at a value of ε that is bounded between $\frac{(1-\beta)^2\tilde{u}^2}{[\sigma_v^2+\mu^2\sigma_w^2]}$ and

$\frac{[(1-\beta)^2+\chi]^3\tilde{u}^2}{[\sigma_v^2+\mu^2\sigma_w^2](1-\beta)^4}$.

Figure 3.1 illustrates the argument graphically. Clearly, a solution for ε exists and is unique.

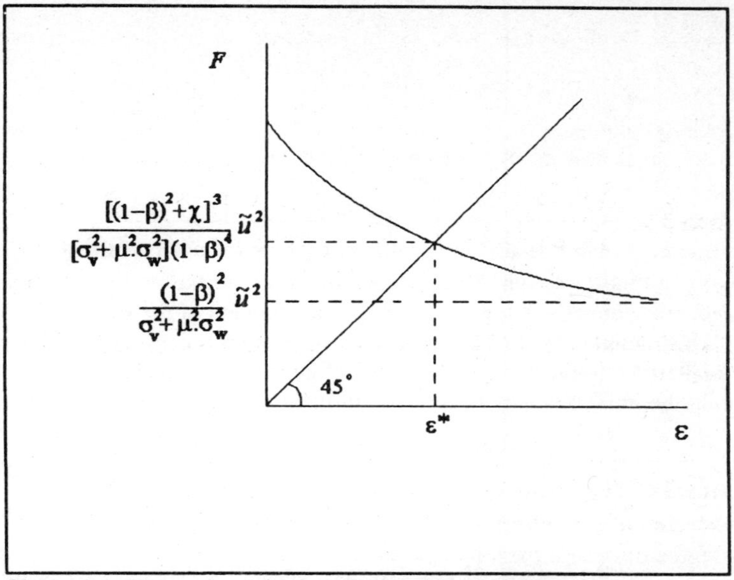

Figure 3.1. The optimal degree of central bank independence

We are now ready to investigate the factors affecting the optimal degree of central bank independence. Hence, we identify *economic* and *political* factors that induce politicians to delegate more or less authority to this institution. We show that the delegation of authority to the central bank depends on the natural rate of unemployment, society's preferences for unemployment stabilisation, the variance of productivity shocks, the slope of the Phillips curve, the degree of openness of the economy and the variance of shocks to the real exchange rate. The results are derived by performing comparative static experiments with respect to various parameters on Figure 3.1. Derivations appear in Appendix B. We summarise the main results in six propositions.

Proposition 3.3: The higher the *natural rate of unemployment* (the higher $\tilde{u}$), the higher the optimal degree of central bank independence.

Proof: Appendix B shows that $\frac{\partial F}{\partial \tilde{u}} > 0$, implying that when goes up, the curve $F(\varepsilon)$

in Figure 3.1 shifts upward. As a consequence, the equilibrium value of ε increases.

The intuition behind this result is the following. A higher natural rate of unemployment implies a higher time-consistent rate of inflation [see equation **(2.18)**] and, consequently, a higher credibility component of the social loss function. This means that society's credibility problem is increased. Hence, with an unaltered relative weight placed on inflation versus unemployment stabilisation the monetary authorities' commitment to fight inflation is now too low.

Proposition 3.4: The higher *society's preferences for unemployment stabilisation relative to inflation stabilisation* (the higher χ), the higher the optimal degree of central bank independence.

Proof: Appendix B shows that $\frac{\partial F}{\partial \chi} > 0$, implying that when χ goes up, the curve $F(\varepsilon)$

in Figure 3.1 shifts upward. Thus, the equilibrium value of ε increases.

The underlying intuition is that, if society becomes more concerned with unemployment and more lax about inflation, the time-consistent inflation rate goes up [see equation **(2.18)**]. Therefore, society's credibility problem becomes more pressing. With an unchanged relative weight placed on inflation stabilisation, the balance between credibility and flexibility needs to be adjusted in favour of increased commitment of fighting inflation.

Proposition 3.5: The higher the *variance of productivity shocks* (the higher σ_v^2), the lower the optimal degree of central bank independence.

Proof: Appendix B shows that $\frac{\partial F}{\partial \sigma_v^2} < 0$, implying that when σ_v^2 goes up, the curve $F(\varepsilon)$ in Figure 3.1 shifts downward. Therefore, the equilibrium value of ε decreases.

This result may be explained as follows. If the variance of productivity shocks increases, ceteris paribus, the economy becomes more unstable. Thus, the need for active stabilisation policy increases (the Γ^l component of the social loss function goes up).

With an unaltered relative weight placed on inflation stabilisation the balance between credibility and flexibility needs to be shifted towards more monetary accommodation.

Proposition 3.6: If society is relatively unconcerned with inflation $\left(\chi > \frac{(1+\varepsilon)(1-\beta)^2}{2} \right)$, the greater the ***benefits of unanticipated inflation*** (the higher $(1-\beta)^{-1}$), the higher the optimal degree of central bank independence.

Proof: Appendix B shows that, if $\chi > \frac{(1+\varepsilon)(1-\beta)^2}{2}$, $\frac{\partial F}{\partial (1-\beta)^{-1}} > 0$, implying that when $(1-\beta)^{-1}$ goes up, the curve $F(\varepsilon)$ shifts upward. Consequently, the equilibrium value of ε increases.

The intuition behind this proposition is that, if the benefits of unanticipated inflation rise [see equation **(2.11)**], it becomes more tempting to inflate the economy. Therefore, society's credibility problem gains in importance. With the same emphasis on inflation stabilisation, the balance between credibility and flexibility needs to be shifted towards increased commitment to price stability.

Proposition 3.7: If the economy is more open to international trade (the higher μ), the *lower* the optimal degree of central bank independence.

Proof: Appendix B shows that $\frac{\partial F}{\partial \mu} < 0$, implying that when m goes up, the curve $F(\varepsilon)$ in Figure 3.1 shifts downward. Therefore, the equilibrium value of ε decreases. The underlying argument is the following. If the economy becomes more open, domestic inflation and unemployment become more vulnerable to shocks to the real exchange rate. This means that if m goes up, *ex ante* variability of both inflation and unemployment increase [see equations (**2.18**) and (**2.19**)]. Note that this implication is consistent with empirical evidence found by Romer (1993, page 884) that openness accounts for a substantial fraction of the variation in inflation among countries. As a consequence the need for active stabilisation policy by the central bank increases. Thus, the balance between credibility and flexibility needs to be shifted towards more monetary accommodation.

Proposition 3.8: The higher real exchange rate variability (the higher σ_w^2), the *lower* the optimal degree of central bank independence.

Proof: Appendix B shows that $\frac{\partial F}{\partial \sigma_w^2} < 0$, implying that when σ_w^2 goes up, the curve

$F(\varepsilon)$ in Figure 3.1 shifts downward. Therefore, the equilibrium value of *e* decreases.

The intuition is similar to that behind the previous proposition. If *ex ante* real exchange rate variability rises, both domestic inflation and unemployment will become more volatile [see equations (**2.18**) and (**2.19**)] Thus, the need for active stabilisation policy increases (the Γ^d component of the social loss function goes up). So, the balance between credibility and flexibility must be shifted towards less commitment.

Table 3.1. The ultimate determinants of central bank independence

Economic and political factors					
$\bar{u}$	χ	σ_v^2	$(1-\beta)^{-1}$	μ	σ_w^2
Natural rate of unemployment	Society's preferences for unemployment stabilisation	Variance of productivity shocks	Gains from unanticipated inflation (slope of Phillips curve)	Degree of openness	Variance of shocks to the real exchange rate
$\frac{\partial \varepsilon^*}{\partial \bar{u}} > 0$	$\frac{\partial \varepsilon^*}{\partial \chi} > 0$	$\frac{\partial \varepsilon^*}{\partial \sigma_v^2} > 0$	$\frac{\partial \varepsilon^*}{\partial (1-\beta)^{-1}} > 0$	$\frac{\partial \varepsilon^*}{\partial \mu} > 0$	$\frac{\partial \varepsilon^*}{\partial \sigma_w^2} > 0$

In order to confront these propositions with some cross-country evidence, we can now move on to the empirical evidence. This is the subject of the next section.

4. Empirical evidence

In this section, the ultimate determinants of central bank independence discussed before are empirically investigated. We will use, for that purpose, the *latent variables* method (LISREL) to make a distinction between the *optimal* and *actual (legal)* degree of central bank independence. The reasons for this distinction are two-fold. First, the propositions derived in the former section are related to the optimal degree of central bank independence and *not* to the actual (legal) degree. These propositions formulate the relationship between the optimal degree and four *economic* and *political* factors in a country:

- the natural rate of unemployment (positive relation);[13]
- society's preferences for unemployment stabilisation relative to inflation stabilisation (positive relation);
- the variance of productivity shocks (negative relation);
- the slope of the Phillips curve (conditional positive relation);

[13] In addition Lockwood *et al* (1994) show how the optimal degree of conservativeness (ODOC) increases with unemployment persistence. Levine and Pearlman (1995) show how the ODOC increases with both nominal and real wage rigidity.

- the degree of openness (negative relation); and
- the variance of shocks to the real exchange rate (negative relation).

These determinants, reflecting the economic and political structure of a country, explain theoretically the optimal degree of central bank independence in that country.

Second, there is also an identification and measurement problem. Whereas the determinants of central bank independence will change *frequently* during the sample period (ie the period 1960-93), the actual degree - approximated by the legal indices of central bank independence - will hardly change in the same period. The stickiness of actual (legal) central bank independence results from the fact that central bank laws are *very occasionally* adjusted in practice, especially in the industrial countries during the post-war period.[14] Moreover, it could be questioned whether the legal indices of central bank independence are a good measure of actual central bank independence (see also: Eijffinger and De Haan, 1995).

IV.1.The data

As proxies for the ultimate determinants of central bank independence, we have chosen the following economic and political variables (see for a detailed account of these variables: Appendix C). For the natural rate of unemployment, the *non-accelerating inflation rate of unemployment* (NAIRU) is taken from Layard, Nickell and Jackman (1991). They estimated the NAIRU for nineteen industrial countries in the period 1960-88. The proxy for society's preferences for unemployment stabilisation relative to inflation stabilisation is the number of years that a *left-wing (socialist) party* has been in government as a share of the *total* number of years (WLEFT). For, a left-wing government has a higher preference for unemployment stabilisation and, thereby, the optimal degree of central bank independence increases under a left-wing government. The variance of productivity shocks is proxied by the *variance of output growth* (GDP) on an annual basis (VPROD). We compute the slope of the Phillips

14 Very recently, some countries within the European Union - eg France and Spain - have made their central banks more independent from government because this is required by the Maastricht Treaty on Economic and Monetary Union. These changes of central bank laws are, however, too infrequent to be applicable for our empirical analysis of the determinants in the industrial countries.

curve, using labour's income share in GDP.[15] Because data for labour's income share are not available for all countries in our sample, we have taken the ratio between the *compensation of employees* paid by resident producers to resident households and GDP (SLOPE).

The degree of openness is measured by the ratio between the *imports of goods and services* and GDP (OPEN). The proxy for the variance of shocks to the real exchange rate is the variance of the ratio between the *CPI inflation minus GDP deflator* and the degree of openness (VREER).

Therefore, the *optimal* degree of central bank independence (OPCBI_M) is explained by the following variables, taken in deviation from their mean (M)

$$\text{OPCBI\_M} = a_1 \times \overset{(+)}{[\text{NAIRU\_M}]} + a_2 \times \overset{(+)}{[\text{WLEFT\_M}]} + a_3 \times \overset{(-)}{[\text{VPROD\_M}]} +$$

$$a_4 \times \overset{(+)}{[\text{SLOPE\_M}]} + a_5 \times \overset{(-)}{[\text{OPEN\_M}]} + a_6 \times \overset{(-)}{[\text{VREER\_M}]} \qquad \textbf{(4.1)}$$

The expected signs are denoted above the explanatory variables. The optimal degree of central bank independence is assumed to be a *latent* variable in our empirical model. Next to the *observed* explanatory variables measured in deviation from their mean (NAIRU_M, WLEFT_M, VPROD_M, SLOPE_M, OPEN_M and VREER_M), we need the actual (legal) degree of central bank independence as an *observed* variable. The actual degree of central bank independence is approximated by the legal degree, according to the four main indices of central bank independence in the literature.

The index of Alesina (AL) is a narrow measure of independence and based on Alesina (1988, 1989). The total index of political and economic independence of Grilli, Masciandaro and Tabellini (GMT) is a broad measure based on Grilli, Masciandaro and Tabellini (1991). The index of policy independence of Eijffinger and Schaling (ES) is, however, a narrow measure based on Eijffinger and Schaling (1993a, 1995) and extended by Eijffinger and Van Keulen (1994). These three legal indices have been normalised so that their values

15 Since we use a Cobb-Douglas production function [equation **(2.1)**], the production elasticity of labour, β, equals labour's income share in GDP.

range, theoretically, from zero to one (AL_N, GMT_N and ES_N). The unweighted legal index of Cukierman (LVAU) is a very broad measure of independence and derived from Cukierman (1992). The Cukierman index is already normalised on its theoretical scale. Thus, the optimal degree of central bank independence is also normalised (OPCBI_NM) to have the same unit of measurement as the legal indices.[16]

For our cross-country analysis, a set of nineteen industrial (OECD) countries is taken which are ranked - with some exceptions - by the above-mentioned indices. The sample period that we have chosen covers more than thirty years, namely the period 1960-93 (for NAIRU and VREER: 1960-88 and 1960-89, respectively). The argument to choose such a long period is that it contains many political and business cycles and, thus, comprises changes of the political and economic structure affecting the optimal degree of central bank independence.

IV.2. The latent variables method

According to Bentler (1982), the essential characteristic of a *latent variable* is revealed by the fact that the system of linear structural equations in which the latent variable appears cannot be manipulated so as to express this variable as a function of *measured* variables only.[17]

Aigner, Hsiao, Kapteyn and Wansbeek (1984) state that, since 1970, there has been a resurgence of interest in econometrics in the topic of models involving latent variables. 'That interest in such models had to be restimulated at all may seem surprising', in the opinion of Aigner *et al*, 'since there can be no doubt that economic quantities frequently are measured with error and, moreover, that many applications depend on the use of observable proxies for otherwise unobservable conceptual variables' (page 1,323).

16 As a consequence of the latent variables method (LISREL), these observed indices of central bank independence are also measured in deviation from their means: AL_NM, GMT_NM, ES_NM and LVAU_M. If all variables have an expected value zero, than their covariance equals $E[x\ y]$.

17 For this definition of a latent variable, see: Bentler (1982). A clear overview of the latest variable method is given by Aigner, D (*et al*) (1984).

Estimation of a simultaneous equations model with latent variables can be done by means of a computer program for the analysis of covariance structures, such a LISREL (Linear Structural Relations). The idea behind LISREL is to compare a sample covariance matrix with the parametric structure imposed on it by the hypothesised model. Under normality, LISREL delivers *Full Information Maximum Likelihood* (FIML) estimates of the model parameters. Because of its general availability, LISREL is the most important tool for handling latent variables.

The specification of the latent variables model to be analysed by LISREL is as follows.[18] Let η be the latent *dependent* variable, ie the latent optimal degree of central bank independence, and ξ be the latent *explanatory* variables, in our case the six ultimate determinants of central bank independence, satisfying a system of linear structural relations

$$\eta = B \cdot \xi + \zeta, \tag{4.2}$$

with B being the coefficient matrix and ζ the disturbances. It is assumed that η, ξ and ζ have *zero* expectations, and that ξ and ζ are *uncorrelated*. Instead of the latent vectors η and ξ, the vectors ψ and ξ are *observed*, such that

$$y = \Lambda_y \cdot \eta + \gamma \tag{4.3}$$

and

$$x = \Lambda_x \cdot \xi + \delta, \tag{4.4}$$

with Λ_y and Λ_x the coefficient matrices, and γ and δ the vectors of measurement errors, *uncorrelated* with η, ξ, ζ and each other, but possibly correlated among themselves. The observed vectors y and x are measured as deviations form their

---

18 In order to avoid overlapping symbols between sections II and III (theoretical model) and section IV (latent variables model), our notation differs from that of the LISREL manual. Having one latent dependent variable, we use B and γ, respectively, instead of the symbols Γ and ε for the LISREL manual. Compare also Aigner *et al* (1984, pages 1,370-71) in this respect.

means, thus, having *zero* expectations and a covariance equal to $E[x\ y]$. This implies, of course, that γ and δ have also zero expectations.

Therefore, y is a vector of *observed* legal indices of central bank independence (AL, GMT, ES and LVAU), normalised and measured in deviation from their means,

$$y = \begin{bmatrix} AL\_NM \\ GMT\_NM \\ ES\_NM \\ LVAU\_M \end{bmatrix} \qquad \textbf{(4.5)}$$

and x is a vector of *observed* explanatory variables, being the non-accelerating inflation rate of unemployment (NAIRU), the percentage of years of a left-wing government (WLEFT), the variance of output growth (VPROD), the compensation of employees as share of GDP (SLOPE), the degree of openness (OPEN) and the variance of shocks to the real exchange rate (VREER), measured in deviation from their means

$$x = \begin{bmatrix} NAIRU\_M \\ WLEFT\_M \\ VPROD\_M \\ SLOPE\_M \\ OPEN\_M \\ VREER\_M \end{bmatrix} \qquad \textbf{(4.6)}$$

So, equations **(4.3)** and **(4.4)** become, respectively

$$\begin{bmatrix} AL\_NM \\ GMT\_NM \\ ES\_NM \\ LVAU\_M \end{bmatrix} = \begin{bmatrix} \lambda_{y1} \\ \lambda_{y2} \\ \lambda_{y3} \\ \lambda_{y4} \end{bmatrix} . \eta + \begin{bmatrix} \gamma_1 \\ \gamma_2 \\ \gamma_3 \\ \gamma_4 \end{bmatrix} \qquad \textbf{(4.3')}$$

and

$$\begin{bmatrix} NAIRU\_M \\ WLEFT\_M \\ VPROD\_M \\ SLOPE\_M \\ OPEN\_M \\ VREER\_M \end{bmatrix} = \begin{bmatrix} \lambda_{x1} & & & & & \\ & \lambda_{x2} & & & & \\ & & \lambda_{x3} & & & \\ & & & \lambda_{x4} & & \\ & & & & \lambda_{x5} & \\ & & & & & \lambda_{x6} \end{bmatrix} . \begin{bmatrix} \xi_1 \\ \xi_2 \\ \xi_3 \\ \xi_4 \\ \xi_5 \\ \xi_6 \end{bmatrix} + \begin{bmatrix} \delta_1 \\ \delta_2 \\ \delta_3 \\ \delta_4 \\ \delta_5 \\ \delta_6 \end{bmatrix} \qquad \textbf{(4.4')}$$

Furthermore, Φ and Ψ are defined as the covariance matrix of ξ and the variance of ζ, respectively, and Θ_γ and Θ_δ as the true variance-covariance matrices of γ and δ, respectively. Then it follows from the above assumptions that the variance-covariance matrix Σ of $[y', x']'$ is

$$\Sigma = \begin{bmatrix} \Lambda_y [B\Phi B' + \Psi] \Lambda_y' + \Theta_\gamma & \Lambda_y B\Phi\Lambda_x' \\ \Lambda_x \Phi B' \Lambda_y' & \Lambda_x \Phi \Lambda_x' + \Theta_\delta \end{bmatrix} \qquad \textbf{(4.7)}$$

Assuming that the latent explanatory variables (ξ) equal the observed (x), thus $\xi = x$, then $\Theta_\delta = 0$ and $\Lambda_x = I$, and equation **(4.7)** simplifies to[19]

$$\Sigma = \begin{bmatrix} \Lambda_y \left[B\Phi B' + \Psi \right] \Lambda_y' + \Theta_\gamma & \Lambda_y B\Phi \\ \Phi B' \Lambda_y' & \Phi \end{bmatrix} \tag{4.8}$$

The parameters occurring in Σ (Λ_y, B, Φ, Ψ, Θ_γ) are estimated on the basis of the matrix S of second sample moments of x and y. In order to identify all parameters, *additional* restrictions on the parameters have to be imposed. Given these restrictions and the structure that equation **(4.8)** imposes on the data, LISREL computes FIML estimates of the parameters when $[y', x']$ is normally distributed, ie when the following criterion is minimised

$$\ln|\Sigma| + \mathrm{tr}\,[S\Sigma^{-1}] \tag{4.9}$$

To be able to identify all parameters of the model, we have made the following two additional restrictions:

(i) $\lambda_{y1} = \lambda_{y2} = \lambda_{y3} = \lambda_{y4} = 1$, which implies that the latent optimal degree of central bank independence (η) has the *same* unit of measurement as the observed legal indices of central bank independence (y);[20] and

(ii) Θ_γ is diagonal, which implies that the correlation between the observed legal indices of central bank independence (y) is *only* caused by the latent optimal degree (η).[21]

19 So, we make only a distinction between the *latent* optimal degree of central bank independence (h) and the *observed* actual degree (y) measured by the legal indices of central bank independence. Thus, the optimal degree of central bank independence is derived from the covariances of the four legal indices.

20 This restriction is a consequence of the *normalization* of all observed legal indices and the latent optimal degree of central bank independence so that their values range, theoretically, from zero to one.

21 The measurement errors (g) in equation (4.3) are, thereby, uncorrelated.

IV.3. The empirical results

On the basis of the restrictions given in the former section, LISREL computes *Full Information Maximum Likelihood* estimates of the parameters of the model. Computation with LISREL renders two different kind of estimations. First, the relationship between the *optimal* degree of central bank independence (η, here renamed as OPCBI_NM) and the explanatory variables (NAIRU_M, WLEFT_M, VPROD_M, SLOPE_M, OPEN_M and VREER_M), reflecting the ultimate *determinants* of central bank independence, is estimated.[22] Second, by estimating this relationship and calculating the optimal degree of central bank independence for each country (OPCBI_NM), the comparison between the *optimal* degree and the *legal* indices of central bank independence (AL_NM, GMT_NM, ES_NM and LVAU_M) can be made. Such a comparison is only possible if both the optimal degree and the legal indices are *normalised* on their theoretical scale and measured in deviation from their means.[23]

Next to the differences of individual legal indices with the optimal degree, the *average difference* (AVDIF) may be calculated in the following way:

$$AVDIF = \frac{[AL\_NM] + [GMT\_NM] + [ES\_NM] + [LVAU\_M]}{4} - [OPCBI\_NM] \qquad \textbf{(4.10)}$$

This average difference is *positive*, if the average of legal indices exceeds the optimal degree, and *negative*, if the optimal degree exceeds the average of legal indices.

---

22 Because all variables are measured in deviation form their mean and have, thus, zero expectations, the constant is eliminated from the model.

23 Note that the legal index of Cukierman (LVAU) is already normalized on its theoretical scale, ie in theory its lowest value is 0 and its highest value 1.

A positive average difference indicates that the legal degree of central bank independence should be *decreased*, whereas a negative average difference that the legal degree should be *increased* in order to bring it closer to the optimal degree based on the ultimate determinants of central bank independence.

Table 4.1 shows the estimation results, with all restrictions imposed in the former section, for the sample period 1960-93 (for NAIRU and VREER, the sample period 1960-88 and 1960-89, respectively).

From Table 4.1, it can be seen that all explanatory variables of the optimal degree, except NAIRU, have the expected sign. Only one explanatory variable (SLOPE) is significant at a 5% significance level. The other explanatory variables have relatively low *t*-values.

Nevertheless, we have calculated the optimal degree on the basis of the ultimate determinants for each country and the average difference between these variables. Positive average differences - of 0.20 or higher - are found for Germany and Switzerland, implying that the legal degree of central bank independence exceeds the optimal degree and that the legal degree should be decreased. Negative average differences - of 0.20 or lower - are observed for Australia, Norway, Sweden and the United Kingdom, meaning that the optimal degree exceeds the legal degree and that the legal degree should be increased.

For the other countries - Austria, Belgium, Canada, Denmark, Finland, France, Ireland, Italy, Japan, the Netherlands, New Zealand, Spain and the United States - the average differences are relatively small, indicating that there is no reason to adjust the central bank law in these countries from the perspective of the ultimate determinants. In some countries - notably France and Spain - the central bank has, recently, been made more independent from government which can be explained by another argument: a prerequisite for entering the third phase of Economic and Monetary Union in Europe is, among others, the independence of the *national* central banks of the participating countries.

Table 4.1: Table based on estimation with all restrictions

Sample period 1960 - 1993 for all variables (except for NAIRU and VREER)

OPCBI_NM = -0.016*NAIRU_M + 0.003*WLEFT_M - 0.012*VPROD_M + 0.374*SLOPE_M - 0.188*OPEN_M - 0.001 * VREER_M R^2=0.42 DF=23
(1.041) (0.019) (0.669) (1.858) (0.618) (0.359)

	NORMALISED INDICES				TRANSFORMED INDICES					DIFFERENCES (INDEX - OPCBI_NM)				
COUNTRY	AL_N	GMT_N	ES_N	LVAU	AL_NM	GMT_NM	ES_NM	LVAU_M	OPCBI_NM	AL_NM	GMT_NM	ES_NM	LVAU_M	AVDIF
AUSTRALIA	0.00	0.56	0.00	0.31	-0.38	0.07	-0.42	-0.05	0.029	-0.41	0.04	-0.45	-0.08	-0.22
AUSTRIA		0.56	0.50	0.58		0.07	0.08	0.22	0.038		0.04	0.04	0.18	0.09
BELGIUM	0.33	0.44	0.50	0.19	-0.05	-0.05	0.08	-0.17	-0.031	-0.02	-0.02	0.11	-0.14	-0.02
CANADA	0.33	0.69	0.00	0.46	-0.05	0.20	-0.42	0.10	0.012	-0.06	0.19	-0.43	0.09	-0.05
DENMARK	0.33	0.50	0.75	0.47	-0.05	0.01	0.33	0.11	-0.006	-0.04	0.02	0.34	0.12	0.11
FINLAND	0.33		0.50	0 27	-0.05		0.08	-0.09	0.016	-0.06		0.06	-0.10	-0.04
FRANCE	0.33	0.44	0.25	0.28	-0.05	-0.05	-0.17	-0.08	0.018	-0/.07	-0.07	-0.19	-0.10	-0.11
GERMANY	1.00	0.81	1.00	0.66	0.62	0.32	0.58	0.30	0.067	0.55	0.26	0.51	0.23	0.39
IRELAND		0.44		0.39		-0.05		0.03	-0.117		0.07		0.15	0.11
ITALY	0.17	0.31	0.25	0.22	-0.22	-0.18	-0.17	-0.14	-0.095	-0.12	-0.08	-0.08	-0.04	-0.08
JAPAN	0.67	0.38	0.50	0.16	0.28	-0.11	0.08	-0.20	-0.127	0.41	0.01	0.21	-0.07	0.14
NETHERLANDS	0.33	0.63	0.75	0.42	-0.05	0.14	0.33	0.06	0.015	-0.06	0.12	0.31	0.05	0.10
NEW ZEALAND	0.00	0.19	0.50	0.27	-0.38	-0.30	0.08	-0.09	-0.146	-0.24	-0.16	0.23	0.06	-0.33
NORWAY	0.33		0.25	0.14	-0.05		-0.17	-0.22	0.050	-0.10		-0.22	-0.27	-0.20
SPAIN	0.00	0.31	0.00	0.21	-0.38	-0.18	-0.42	-0.15	-0.208	-0.17	0.03	-0.21	0.06	-0.07
SWEDEN	0.33		0.25	0.27	-0.05		-0.17	-0.09	0.229	-0.28		-0.40	-0.32	-0.33
SWITZERLAND	1.00	0.75	1.00	0.68	0.62	0.26	0.58	0.32	0.128	0.49	0.13	0.45	0.19	0.32
UK	0.33	0.38	0.25	0.31	-0.05	-0.11	-0.17	-0.05	0.143	-0.19	-0.26	-0.31	-0.19	-0.24
US	0.67	0.75	0.50	0.51	0.28	0.26	0.08	0.15	0.118	0.17	0.14	-0.04	0.03	0.08

Notes: _N stands for normalised variables;
_M stands for deviation of variables from their means;
t-values in parentheses.

The relatively low *t*-values for the explanatory variables in Table 4.1 could, probably, be attributed to the many severe restrictions imposed on the model by LISREL and the two additional restrictions made by us ($\lambda_{y1} = \lambda_{y2} = \lambda_{y3} = \lambda_{y4} = 1$ and Θ_γ is diagonal) to identify all parameters of the model. Relaxing some of these restrictions might improve the *t*-values of the explanatory variables.[24]

Table 4.2 gives the empirical results, if we relax *cumulatively* five restrictions on the covariances, for the sample period

1960-93 (for NAIRU and VREER: 1960-88 and 1960-89, respectively). All other restrictions on the model remain imposed.

Testing structural models, a univariate Lagrange Multiplier test is carried out for most elements in the model matrices that are constrained to equal constants. When the test statistic, having a χ^2_1-distribution, has a value larger than 2.71 the restriction is rejected at a significance level of 10%. In the first regression, with all restrictions imposed, the constraint that the covariance of γ_2 and ξ_3 equals zero is rejected. This means that the disturbances of the GMT-index and the variance of productivity shocks (VPROD) are correlated. The test statistic has a value of 6.74, which is the highest of all restrictions. Therefore, we have lifted this restriction and tested the modified model.

24 See in this respect: Aigner, Hsiao, Kapteyn and Wansbeek (1984, page 1,371). The relaxing of restrictions could imply that, although the latent variables method is still used, the assumptions of LISREL are not valid anymore.

Table 4.2: Table based on estimation with cumulative relaxation of restrictions
Sample period 1960 - 1993 for all variables (except for NAIRU and VREER)

Lifted Restriction	Estimation Equation	R^2 and DF
no lifted restriction	OPCBI_NM = -0.016 * NAIRU_M+0.003 * WLEFT_M-0.012 * VPROD_M+0.0374 * SLOPE_M-0.188 * OPEN_M-0.001 * VREER_M (1.041) (0.019) (0.669) (1.858) (0.618) (0.359)	R^2=0.42 DF=23
γ_2,ξ_3	OPCBI_NM = -0.013 * NAIRU_M+0.024 * WLEFT_M+0.037 * VPROD_M+0.651 * SLOPE_M-0.392 * OPEN_M-0.003 * VREER_M (0.713) (0.135) (2.255) (3.091) (1.126) (2.628)	R^2=0.55 DF=22
γ_2,ξ_6	OPCBI_NM = -0.010 * NAIRU_M+0.108 * WLEFT_M+0.013 * VPROD_M+0.529 * SLOPE_M-0.078 * OPEN_M-0.000 * VREER_M (0.580) (0.657) (0.573) (2.366) (0.212) (0.140)	R^2=0.35 DF=21
γ_2,ξ_1	OPCBI_NM = -0.016 * NAIRU_M+0.003 * WLEFT_M+0.012 * VPROD_M+0.374 * SLOPE_M-0.188 * OPEN_M-0.001 * VREER_M (0.041) (0.019) (0.669) (1.858) (0.618) (0.359)	R^2=0.40 DF=20
γ_3,ξ_1	OPCBI_NM = -0.005 * NAIRU_M+0.124 * WLEFT_M+0.011 * VPROD_M+0.445 * SLOPE_M-0.033 * OPEN_M-0.000 * VREER_M (0.336) (0.816) (0.556) (2.151) (0.099) (0.201)	R^2=0.33 DF=19
γ_3,ξ_5	OPCBI_NM = -0.004 * NAIRU_M+0.121 * WLEFT_M+0.010 * VPROD_M+0.421 * SLOPE_M-0.069 * OPEN_M-0.001 * VREER_M (0.280) (0.849) (0.561) (2.164) (0.252) (0.332)	R^2=0.35 DF=18

Notes: _N stands for normalised variables;
_M stands for deviation of variables from their means;
t-values in parentheses.

Table 4.3 Average differences with cumulative relaxation of restrictions
Sample period 1960 - 1993 for all variables (except for NAIRU and VREER)

COUNTRY	no lifted restriction	γ_2,ξ_3	γ_2,ξ_6	γ_2,ξ_1	γ_3,ξ_1	γ_3,ξ_5
AUSTRALIA	-0.22	-0.17	-0.16	-0.16	-0.15	-0.16
AUSTRIA	0.09	0.14	0.14	0.12	0.12	0.12
BELGIUM	-0.02	.01	0.01	-0.01	-0.01	-0.01
CANADA	-0.05	-0.04	0.03	0.01	0.02	0.1
DENMARK	0.11	0.13	0.08	0.08	0.08	0.08
FINLAND	-0.04	-0.05	-0.05	-0.06	-0.06	-0.06
FRANCE	-0.11	0.00	0.02	0.00	0.02	0.00
GERMANY	0.39	0.43	0.45	0.45	0.46	0.45
IRELAND	0.11	0.13	0.10	0.06	0.06	0.05
ITALY	-0.08	-0.02	-0.03	-0.07	-0.06	-0.08
JAPAN	0.14	0.06	0.06	0.09	0.09	0.10
NETHERLANDS	0.10	0.08	0.13	0.12	0.12	0.12
NEW ZEALAND	-0.03	-0.12	-0.16	-0.13	-0.14	-0.13
NORWAY	-0.20	-0.04	-0.13	-0.14	-0.14	-0.14
SPAIN	-0.07	-0.20	-0.12	-0.16	-0.15	-0.17
SWEDEN	-0.33	-0.37	-0.33	-0.29	-0.30	-0.30
SWITZERLAND	0.32	0.12	0.21	0.25	0.23	0.24
UK	-0.24	-0.31	-0.22	-0.20	-0.20	-0.21
US	0.08	0.20	0.04	0.09	0.08	0.09

Now the restriction on the covariance of γ_2 and ξ_6 to be zero has the highest test statistic. So, this restriction has been lifted implying that the disturbances of the GMT-index and the variance of shocks to the real exchange rate (VREER) can be correlated. This process goes on until there is no restriction left with a test statistic higher than 2.71. The results of the subsequent estimations are summarised in Table 4.2. From this table, it is clear that the *t*-values of all explanatory variables, except NAIRU, improve considerably with the lifting of the restriction on the covariance of [γ_2, ξ_3] between the GMT-index and the variance of productivity shocks. The last variable becomes even significant at a 97,5% confidence level. All explanatory variables, except NAIRU and VPROD, have the expected sign. If we compare the coefficients of the explanatory variables in this table with those in Table 4.1, the estimated coefficients do not always seem robust.

Therefore, we have also calculated the optimal degree of central bank independence and the average difference with the legal indices (AVDIF) for each country. Table 4.3 shows the average differences in case of a cumulative relaxation of the five restrictions on the covariances. The positive average differences for Germany and Switzerland appear to be still in place. The negative average differences for Australia, Norway, Sweden and the United Kingdom also still remain. Relatively small average differences are found for countries, like Belgium, Canada, Finland, France, Italy, Japan and the United States. Apparently, these countries have central bank laws which correspond more or less with their optimal degree based on the ultimate determinants, in sofar as they are captured in our empirical model.

5. Conclusions

What may be concluded from the previous sections?

First, it is possible to derive propositions on the basis of our theoretical model which formulates the relationship between the optimal degree of central bank independence and six ultimate determinants in a country, namely the natural rate of employment, the society's preferences for unemployment stabilisation relative to inflation stabilisation, the variance of productivity shocks, the slope of the Phillips curve, the degree of openness and the variance of shocks to the real exchange rate. These determinants, reflecting the economic and political structure of a country, refer only indirectly to the actual (legal) degree of central bank independence.

Second, to distinguish between the optimal and actual (legal) degree of central bank independence the latent variables method (LISREL) appears to be very fruitful as an empirical model. Not only enables this method us to explain the optimal degree by proxies for the ultimate determinants (NAIRU, WLEFT, VPROD, SLOPE, OPEN and VREER), but also to compare the optimal degree with the legal indices of central bank independence (AL, GMT, ES and LVAU). The latent variables method, based on nineteen industrial countries, for the sample period 1960-93 (except for NAIRU and VREER) leads to estimations which support our theoretical model reasonably, if we relax cumulatively five restrictions on the covariances.

Third, the comparison between the optimal degree and the legal indices of central bank independence renders some interesting results. Some countries - like Germany and Switzerland - seem to have a suboptimally high degree of central bank independence, whereas other - such as Australia, Norway, Sweden and the United Kingdom - appear to have a suboptimally low degree. For countries such as Belgium, Canada, Finland, France, Italy, Japan and the

United States, it is fair to conclude that these countries have more or less an optimal degree of independence.

Finally, it should be mentioned that both our theoretical and empirical model can be extended with other economic and political determinants of central bank independence. One could, for example, extend the model with the degree of political instability and uncertainty in a country. These extensions constitute our research agenda for the future.

Appendix A. The derivation of the expected value of society's loss function under an arbitrary monetary policy regime

In this Appendix, following Rogoff (1985a, pages 1,175-76), we develop a notation for evaluating the expected value of society's loss function under any arbitrary monetary policy regime 'A', $E_{t-1} L_t^A$ (equation (3.1) of the text). Unemployment under regime A is given by

$$u_t^A = \tilde{u} - \frac{1}{1-\beta}(p_t^A - E_{t-1} p_t^A + \mu_t) \qquad \textbf{(A.1)}$$

Squaring and taking expectations yields

$$E_{t-1}(u_t^A)^2 = \tilde{u}^2 + E_{t-1}[\frac{\mu_t}{1-\beta} + \frac{1}{1-\beta}(p_t^A - E_{t-1} p_t^A)]^2 \qquad \textbf{(A.2)}$$

The CPI under regime *A* can be expanded as

$$p_{c_t}^A = \tilde{p}_{c_t}^A + (p_{c_t}^A - E_{t-1} p_{c_t}^A) \qquad \textbf{(A.3)}$$

where $\tilde{p}_{c_t}^A$ is the mean (expected) CPI in period *t*. Squaring and taking expectations, in turn, yields

$$E_{t-1}(p_{c_t}^A)^2 = (\tilde{p}_{c_t}^A)^2 + E_{t-1}(p_{c_t}^A - E_{t-1} p_{c_t}^A)^2 \qquad \textbf{(A.4)}$$

The expected value of society's loss function under regime *A* is

$$E_{t-1} L_t^A = \frac{1}{2} E_{t-1}(p_{c_t}^A)^2 + \frac{\chi}{2} E_{t-1}(u_t^A)^2 \qquad \textbf{(A.5)}$$

Substituting **(A.2)** and **(A.4)** into **(A.5)**, one obtains equation (3.1) of the text.

Appendix B. Derivation of the properties of the function *F(ε)* in the first order condition

(1) Demonstration that $\frac{\partial F}{\partial \varepsilon} < 0$.

The first derivative of *F* with respect to *e* is given by

$$\frac{\partial F}{\partial \varepsilon} = \frac{-3\tilde{u}^2 \chi[(1+\varepsilon)(1-\beta)^2+\chi]^2}{[\sigma_v^2 + \mu^2\sigma_w^2](1-\beta)^4(1+\varepsilon)^4} \tag{B.1}$$

which is negative.

(2) Demonstration that $\frac{\partial^2 F}{\partial \varepsilon^2} > 0$.

The second derivative of *F* with respect to *e* is given by

$$\frac{\partial^2 F}{\partial \varepsilon^2} = \frac{6\tilde{u}^2 \chi\Gamma[\Gamma-\chi]}{[\sigma_v^2 + \mu^2\sigma_w^2](1-\beta)^4(1+\varepsilon)^5} \tag{B.2}$$

where $\Gamma \equiv (1+\varepsilon)(1-\beta)^2 + 2\chi$, **(B.2)** is positive.

(3) Demonstration that $F(0) = \frac{[(1-\beta)^2+\chi]^3\tilde{u}^2}{[\sigma_v^2 + \mu^2\sigma_w^2](1-\beta)^4}$.

This can be shown by direct examination of the right-hand side of equation **(3.8)** at $\varepsilon = 0$.

(4) Demonstration that

$$\frac{(1-\beta)^2\tilde{u}^2}{[\sigma_v^2 + \mu^2\sigma_w^2]} < F(\varepsilon) < \frac{[(1-\beta)^2+\chi]^3\tilde{u}^2}{[\sigma_v^2 + \mu^2\sigma_w^2](1-\beta)^4}.$$

Since $F(0) = \dfrac{[(1-\beta)^2+\chi]^3\tilde{u}^2}{[\sigma_v^2 + \mu^2 \sigma_w^2](1-\beta)^4}$,

$\lim\limits_{\varepsilon\to\infty} = \dfrac{(1-\beta)^2\tilde{u}^2}{[\sigma_v^2 + \mu^2\sigma_w^2]}$ and $\dfrac{\partial F}{\partial \varepsilon} < 0$, $F(\varepsilon)$ must be bounded between

$\dfrac{(1-\beta)^2\tilde{u}^2}{[\sigma_v^2 + \mu^2\sigma_w^2]}$ and $F(0)$.

(5) Demonstration that $\dfrac{\partial F}{\partial \tilde{u}} > 0$.

The first derivative of *F* with respect to χ is given by

$$\frac{\partial F}{\partial \tilde{u}} = \frac{2[(1+\varepsilon)(1-\beta)^2+\chi]^3\tilde{u}}{[\sigma_v^2 + \mu^2\sigma_w^2](1-\beta)^4(1+\varepsilon)^3} \qquad \textbf{(B.3)}$$

(B.3) is positive.

(6) Demonstration that $\dfrac{\partial F}{\partial \chi} > 0$

The first derivative of *F* with respect to χ is given by

$$\frac{3[(1+\varepsilon)(1-\beta)^2 + \chi]^2\tilde{u}^2}{[\sigma_v^2 + \mu^2\sigma_w^2](1-\beta)^4(1+\varepsilon)^3} \qquad \textbf{(B.4)}$$

It can easily be checked that **(B.4)** is positive.

(7) Demonstration that $\dfrac{\partial F}{\partial \sigma_v^2} < 0$.

The first derivative of F with respect to σ_v^2 is given by

$$\frac{\partial F}{\partial \sigma_v^2} = \frac{-[(1+\varepsilon)(1-\beta)^2 + \chi]^3\tilde{u}^2}{[\sigma_v^2 + \mu^2\sigma_w^2](1-\beta)^4(1+\varepsilon)^3} \qquad \textbf{(B.5)}$$

(B.5) is negative.

(8) Demonstration that $\dfrac{\partial F}{\partial (1-\beta)^{-1}} > 0$.

The first derivative of F with respect to $(1-\beta)^{-1}$ is given by

$$\frac{\partial F}{\partial (1-\beta)^{-1}} = \frac{[2\chi-(1+\varepsilon)(1-\beta)^2][(1+\varepsilon)(1-\beta)^2+\chi]^2 2\tilde{u}^2}{[\sigma_v^2 + \mu^2\sigma_w^2](1-\beta)^3(1+\varepsilon)^3}. \qquad \textbf{(B.6)}$$

(B.6) is positive if $\chi > \dfrac{(1+\varepsilon)(1-\beta)^2}{2}$.

Appendix C. The data

NAIRU: R Layard, S Nickell and R Jackman, *Unemployment, Macroeconomic Performance and the Labour Market*, Oxford, Oxford University Press, 1991. Estimates for NAIRU 1960-88, Table 14, Chapter 9.

WLEFT: Winkler Prins Encyclopedie, 1990. A J Day (ed.), *Political Parties of the World*, London, Longman, 1988, (# years that a left-wing party has been in the government, either alone or in a coalition)/(total # years), 1960-93.

VPROD: OECD Main Economic Indicators. Growth rate of GDP in US$ in 1985 prices and exchange rates, 1960-93.

SLOPE: National Accounts of OECD Countries, 1960-77, 1977-89, 1978-92. 1/[1 - (Compensation of employees paid by resident producers/GDP)], in current prices. OECD, Paris, 1979, 1991, 1994.

OPEN: National Accounts of OECD Countries, 1960-77, 1977-89, 1978-92. (Imports of goods and services/GDP), in current prices. OECD Paris, 1979, 1991, 1994.

VREER: OECD National Accounts, Main Aggregates, Vol. I, 1960-89, Paris, 1991. Variance of [(CPI inflation-GDP deflator)/OPEN], CPI inflation and GDP deflator calculated from private final consumption expenditure price index and GDP price index, respectively.

References

Aigner, D J, Hsiao, C, Kapteyn, A and Wansbeek, I (1984), 'Latent Variable Models in Econometrics', Chapter 23 in Griliches, Z and Intriligator, M D (eds.), *Handbook of Econometrics,* Vol II, Amsterdam: Elsevier Science Publishers, pages 1,321-393.

Alesina, A (1988), 'Macroeconomics and Politics', in: Fischer, S (ed.), *NBER Macroeconomics Annual*, Cambridge: MIT Press, pages 13-61.

Alesina, A (1989), 'Politics and Business Cycles in Industrial Democracies', *Economic Policy*, 8, pages 55-98.

Alesina, A and Summers, L (1993), 'Central Bank Independence and Macroeconomic Performance: Some Comparative Evidence', *Journal of Money, Credit, and Banking,* 25, pages 151-62.

Alogoskoufis, S (1994), 'On Inflation, Unemployment and the Optimal Exchange Rate Regime', in: van der Ploeg, F (ed.), *Handbook of International Macroeconomics,* Oxford: Basil Blackwell, pages 192-223.

Bentler, P M (1982), 'Linear Systems with Multiple Levels and Types of Latent Variables', Chapter 5 in: Jöreskog, K G and Wold, H (eds.), *Systems Under Indirect Observations: Causality, Structure, Prediction,* Part I, Amsterdam: North-Holland Publishing Company, pages 101-30.

Centre for Economic Policy Research (1993), *'Independent and Accountable: A New Mandate for the Bank of England'*, A Report of an Independent Panel Chaired by Eric Roll, October.

Cukierman, A (1992), *'Central Bank Strategy, Credibility and Independence: Theory and Evidence'*, Cambridge, MIT Press.

Cukierman, A (1994), 'Commitment through Delegation, Political Influence and Central Bank Independence', in: de Beaufort Wijnholds, J, Eijffinger, S and Hoogduin, L (eds.), *A Framework for Monetary Stability,* Dordrecht/Boston/London: Kluwer Academic Publishers, pages 55-74.

Dornbusch, R (1976), 'Expectations and Exchange Rate Dynamics', *Journal of Political Economy*, 84, No. 6, December, pages 1,161-176.

Dornbusch, R (1988), 'Exchange Rates and Inflation', Cambridge, MIT Press, pages 265-92.

Eijffinger, S and Schaling, E (1993a), 'Central Bank Independence in Twelve Industrial Countries', *Banca Nazionale del Lavoro Quarterly Review*, No. 184, March, pages 1-41.

Eijffinger, S and Schaling, E (1993b), *'Central Bank Independence: Theory and Evidence'*, Discussion Paper, CentER for Economic Research, No. 9325, May.

Eijffinger, S and Schaling, E (1995), *'Central Bank Independence: Criteria and Indices'*, *Kredit und Kapital,* Heft 13, pages 105-218.

Eijffinger, S and Van Keulen, M (1994), *'Central Bank Independence in Another Eleven Countries'*, Discussion Paper, CentER for Economic Research, No. 9494, November. Forthcoming in: *Banca Nazionale del Lavoro Quarterly Review.*

Eijffinger, S and De Haan, J (1995), *'The Political Economy of Central Bank Independence'*, Working Paper, Tilburg/Groningen. Forthcoming in: *Princeton Special Papers in International Economics*, Princeton University, Princeton, New Jersey.

Fischer, S (1977a), 'Wage Indexation and Macroeconomic Stability', *Carnegie-Rochester Conference Series on Public Policy*, 5, pages 107-47.

Fischer, S (1994), *'Modern Central Banking'*, in Capie, F, Goodhart, C, Fisher, S and Schnadt, N: 'The Future of Central Banking', Cambridge University Press, pages 262-308.

Gray, J (1976), 'Wage Indexation: A Macroeconomic Approach', *Journal of Monetary Economics*, 2, pages 221-35.

Grilli, V, Masciandaro, D and Tabellini, G (1991), 'Political and Monetary Institutions and Public Financial Policies in the Industrial Countries', *Economic Policy*, 13, pages 341-92.

Haan, J De and Sturm, J (1992), 'The Case for Central Bank Independence', *Banca Nazionale del Lavoro Quarterly Review*, No. 182, September, pages 305-27.

Haan, J De and Van't Hag, G (1994), '*Variation in Central Bank Independence across Countries: Some Provisional Empirical Evidence*', Working Paper, University of Groningen. Forthcoming in: *Public Choice*.

Issing, O (1993), 'Central Bank Independence and Monetary Stability', Institute of Economic Affairs, *Occasional Paper*, No. 89.

Layard, R, Nickell, S and Jackman, R (1991), 'Unemployment, Macroeconomic Performance and the Labour Market', Oxford, Oxford University Press.

Levine, P and Pearlman, J (1995), 'Wage Rigidities, Conservative Bankers and Monetary Union', *SCIES Discussion Paper*, University of Surrey.

Lockwood, B, Miller, M and Zhang, L (1994), 'Delegating Monetary Policy when Unemployment Persists', *Discussion Paper*, University of Exeter.

Lohmann, S (1992), 'Optimal Commitment in Monetary Policy: Credibility versus Flexibility', *American Economic Review*, 82, March, pages 273-86.

Mussa, M (1991), 'Exchange Rates in Theory and in Reality', *Essays in International Finance*, No. 179, Princeton University.

Neumann, M (1991), 'Precommitment by Central Bank Independence', *Open Economies Review*, 2, pages 95-112.

Persson, T and Tabellini, G (1993), 'Designing Institutions for Monetary Stability', *Carnegie-Rochester Conference Series on Public Policy*, 39, pages 53-84.

Rogoff, K (1985a), 'The Optimal Degree of Commitment to an Intermediate Monetary Target', *Quarterly Journal of Economics*, 100, pages 1,169-190.

Rogoff, K (1985b), 'Can International Monetary Policy Coordination be Counterproductive?', *Journal of International Economics*, 18, pages 199-217.

Romer, D (1993), 'Openness and Inflation: Theory and Evidence', *Quarterly Journal of Economics*, CVIII, No. 4, November.

Schaling, E (1995), '*Institutions and Monetary Policy: Credibility, Flexibility and Central Bank Independence*', Edward Elgar, Aldershot.

Walsh, C (1995), '*Optimal Contracts for Central Bankers*' *American Economic Review*', No 1, March 1995, pages 150-67.

[illegible]

[illegible] *[illegible] of the [illegible]* [illegible]

[illegible] (19[illegible]) [illegible] *Journal of Geomagnetism* [illegible]

[illegible] (19[illegible]) [illegible]

[illegible] 1995, pages [illegible]

Name Index

The International Library of Critical Writings in Economics

1. Multinational Corporations
   Mark Casson
2. The Economics of Innovation
   Christopher Freeman
3. Entrepreneurship
   Mark Casson
4. International Investment
   Peter J. Buckley
5. Game Theory in Economics
   Ariel Rubinstein
6. The History of Economic Thought
   Mark Blaug
7. Monetary Theory
   Thomas Mayer
8. Joint Production of Commodities
   Neri Salvadori and Ian Steedman
9. Industrial Organization
   Oliver E. Williamson
10. Growth Theory (Volumes I, II and III)
    R. Becker and E. Burmeister
11. Microeconomics: Theoretical and Applied (Volumes I, II and III)
    Robert E. Kuenne
12. The Economics of Health (Volumes I and II)
    A.J. Culyer
13. Recent Developments in Macroeconomics (Volumes I, II and III)
    Edmund S. Phelps
14. Urban and Regional Economics
    Paul C. Cheshire and Alan W. Evans
15. Modern Public Finance (Volumes I and II)
    A.B. Atkinson
16. Exchange Rate Economics (Volumes I and II)
    Ronald MacDonald and Mark P. Taylor

17. The Economic Value of Education: Studies in the Economics of Education
Mark Blaug

18. Development Economics (Volumes I, II, III and IV)
Deepak Lal

19. The New Classical Macroeconomics (Volumes I, II and III)
Kevin D. Hoover

20. The Economics of the Environment
Wallace E. Oates

21. Post Keynesian Theory of Growth and Distribution
Carlo Panico and Neri Salvadori

22. Dynamic Labor Demand and Adjustment Costs
Giorgio Galeazzi and Daniel S. Hamermesh

23. The Philosophy and Methodology of Economics (Volumes I, II and III)
Bruce J. Caldwell

24. Public Choice Theory (Volumes I, II and III)
Charles K. Rowley

25. Evolutionary Economics
Ulrich Witt

26. Economics and Psychology
Shlomo Maital and Sharone L. Maital

27. Social Choice Theory (Volumes I, II and III)
Charles K. Rowley

28. Non-Linear Dynamics in Economic Theory
Marc Jarsulic

29. Recent Developments in Experimental Economics (Volumes I and II)
John D. Hey and Graham Loomes

30. Monopoly and Competition Policy (Volumes I and II)
F.M. Scherer

31. The Economics of Technical Change
Edwin Mansfield and Elizabeth Mansfield

32. The Economics of Exhaustible Resources
Geoffrey Heal

33. The Economics of Institutions
Geoffrey M. Hodgson

34. The Economics of Transport (Volumes I and II)
Herbert Mohring

35. Implicit Contract Theory
Sherwin Rosen

36. Foundations of Analytical Marxism (Volumes I and II)
John E. Roemer

37. The Economics of Product Differentiation (Volumes I and II)
Jacques-François Thisse and George Norman

38. Economic Growth in Theory and Practice: A Kaldorian Perspective
John E. King

39. Markets and Socialism
Alec Nove and Ian D. Thatcher

40. Recent Developments in the Economics of Education
Elchanan Cohn and Geraint Johnes

41. The Theory of Inflation
Michael Parkin

42. The Economics of Location (Volumes I, II and III)
Melvin L. Greenhut and George Norman

43. Financial Intermediaries
Mervyn K. Lewis

44. The Political Economy of Privatization and Deregulation
Elizabeth E. Bailey and Janet Rothenberg Pack

45. Gender and Economics
Jane Humphries

46. Macroeconomics and Imperfect Competition
Jean-Pascal Bénassy

47. Labor Economics (Volumes I, II, III and IV)
Orley C. Ashenfelter and Kevin F. Hallock

48. The Economics of Altruism
Stefano Zamagni

49. The Economic Analysis of Rent Seeking
Robert D. Tollison and Roger D. Congleton

50. Economics and Biology
Geoffrey M. Hodgson

51. The Economics of Ageing
John Creedy

52. Fiscal and Monetary Policy (Volumes I and II)
Thomas Mayer and Steven M. Sheffrin

53. The Economics of Information (Volumes I and II)
David K. Levine and Steven A. Lippman

54. Transaction Cost Economics (Volumes I and II)
Oliver E. Williamson and Scott E. Masten

55. Agricultural Economics
George H. Peters

56. International Debt (Volumes I and II)
Graham Bird and P. Nicholas Snowden

57. Economics and Discrimination (Volumes I and II)
William A. Darity, Jr

58. Business Cycle Theory
Finn E. Kydland

59. International Trade (Volumes I and II)
J. Peter Neary

60. The Money Supply in the Economic Process
Marco Musella and Carlo Panico

61. Small Firms and Economic Growth (Volumes I and II)
Zoltan J. Acs

62. Producer Cooperatives and Labor-Managed Systems (Volumes I and II)
David L. Prychitko and Jaroslav Vanek

63. Ethics and Economics (Volumes I and II)
Alan P. Hamlin

64. The Economics of the Family
Nancy Folbre

65. The Economics of Training (Volumes I and II)
Orley C. Ashenfelter and Robert J. LaLonde

66. Chaos Theory in Economics: Methods, Models and Evidence
W. Davis Dechert

67. General Equilibrium Theory (Volumes I, II and III)
Gérard Debreu

68. Economic Growth: Theory and Evidence (Volumes I and II)
Gene M. Grossman

69. Long Wave Theory
Christopher Freeman

70. The Economics of Communication and Information
Donald M. Lamberton

71. The Foundations of Public Finance (Volumes I and II)
Peter Jackson

72. The Theory of the Firm
Mark Casson

73. The Economics of Uncertainty (Volumes I and II)
John D. Hey

74. The Economics of Global Warming
Tom Tietenberg

75. The Development of Ecological Economics
Robert Costanza, Charles Perrings and Cutler Cleveland

76. Economic Growth in the Long Run: A History of Empirical Evidence (Volumes I, II and III)
Bart van Ark

77. The Economics of Productivity (Volumes I and II)
Edward N. Wolff

78. The Economics of Population: Key Modern Writings (Volumes I and II)
Julian L. Simon

79. Political Business Cycles
Bruno S. Frey

80. Cultural Economics: The Arts, the Heritage and the Media Industries (Volumes I and II)
Ruth Towse

81. Law and Economics (Volumes I, II and III)
Richard A. Posner and Francesco Parisi

82. Independent Central Banks and Economic Performance
Sylvester Eijffinger

Future titles will include:

Industrial Policy
David B. Audretsch

Mathematical Economics
Graciela Chichilnisky

Input-Output Analysis
Heinz Kurz, Erik Dietzenbacher and Christian Lager

Economic Demography
T. Paul Schultz

Market Process Theories
Peter Boettke and David Prychitko

Culture, Social Norms and Economic Behaviour
Mark Casson

The Economics of Local Finance and Fiscal Federalism
Wallace Oates

Price Theory and its Applications
F.M. Scherer and B. Saffran

The Economics of Housing
John M. Quigley

International Finance
Robert Z. Aliber

Welfare Economics
William J. Baumol and Janusz A. Ordover

The Economics of Inequality and Poverty
A.B. Atkinson

The Economics of Crime
Isaac Ehrlich

The Economics of Integration
Willem Molle

The Rhetoric of Economics
Deirdre McCloskey

Migration
Oded Stark

The Economics of Defence
Keith Hartley and Nicholas Hooper

Consumer Theory
Kelvin Lancaster

The Economics of Business Policy
John Kay

Microeconomic Theories of Imperfect Competition
Jacques Thisse and Jean Gabszewicz

The Economics of Increasing Returns
Geoffrey Heal

The Balance of Payments
Michael J. Artis

Cost-Benefit Analysis
Arnold Harberger and Glenn P. Jenkins

The Economics of Unemployment
P.N. Junankar

Gender in Economic and Social History
K.J. Humphries and J. Lewis

Privatization in Developing and Transitional Economies
Colin Kirkpatrick and Paul Cook

The Economics of Energy
Paul Stevens

The Economics of Intellectual Property
Ruth Towse

The Economics of Tourism
Clem Tisdell

The Economics of Organization and Bureaucracy
Peter Jackson

The Economics of Commodity Markets
David Greenaway and Wyn Morgan

Realism and Economics: Studies in Ontology
Tony Lawson

Women in the Labor Market
Marianne A. Ferber

New Developments in Game Theory
Eric S. Maskin

The International Economic Institutions of the Twentieth Century
David Greenaway

The Economics of Structural Change
Harald Hagemann, Michael Landesmann and Roberto Scazzieri